FRANCO
A BIOGRAPHICAL HISTORY

FRANCO

A BIOGRAPHICAL HISTORY

BRIAN CROZIER

LONDON

EYRE & SPOTTISWOODE

First published 1967
© 1967 Brian Crozier
Printed in Great Britain for
Eyre & Spottiswoode (Publishers) Ltd
11 New Fetter Lane, EC4
by Cox & Wyman Ltd,
Fakenham, Norfolk

for Lila,
my wife

Contents

Illustrations

Maps

© 1967 W. Bromage

Acknowledgments and thanks for permission to reproduce photographs are due to the Ministry of Information, Madrid, for *1a* to *3b*,
6a to *8a*, *9a*, *9b*, *10a* to *11b*, *12b*, *13a*, *14b*, *15c*, *19a* to *21b*, *23a* and
23b; to Radio Times Hulton Picture Library for *4* to *5b;* to The
Associated Press Ltd for *8b*, *10a*, *11c*, *12a*, *13b*, *14a*, *14c* to *15b*, *16a*
to *18*, *22a* and *24;* and to the Spanish Embassy, London, for *22b*.

Foreword

When the Spanish Civil War broke out, in July 1936, I was not quite eighteen. I knew little about politics and was not, at that time, particularly interested in public affairs. I had a number of Communist friends, whom I admired because they were hard-working and seemed to me to be well-informed. What they said about the breakdown of the capitalist system seemed to make sense; it was, at all events, consistent with our family experience of the Great Depression. John Maynard Keynes was just a name. I had little respect for the Baldwin government, or for the Conservatives in general, whom I held responsible for the plight of the unemployed. I was deeply impressed by Mr Churchill's warnings (in the London *Evening Standard*, I believe) about the new German menace on the horizon, and thought the Conservative Party complacent for ignoring them. I considered Hitler and the Nazis as an unmitigated evil; and I still do. I was still, at that time, doubtful about Mussolini, for had he not drained the Pontine Marshes and made the trains run on time? I had no time for Oswald Mosley's Blackshirts.

The Spanish events greatly stimulated my interest in politics and international affairs; and in this, of course, I was not alone. In due course, I joined Victor Gollancz's Left Book Club, which for two years or so served as my political tutor. During the whole of the Civil War, and for many years after, I accepted the simple verities of the left about what went on and what it was all about. It was indeed crystal-clear. The Spanish Republic was a democracy, like Britain and France, the two countries I knew best, and Australia, where I was born. It was under assault from international fascism. The so-called Nationalists were themselves fascists, led by a fascist general, named Franco.

From Arthur Koestler's *Spanish Testament*, I had learnt about Spanish Nationalist atrocities. This clinched it: the Spanish fascists really were akin to the Nazis who were helping them. There were, of course, atrocity stories about the Republican side. But these I automatically discounted, for the Republicans were democrats, like the British and French, and democrats didn't do such things. Equally, I bridled at the tendency of papers like the *Daily Mail* to refer to the

B

Republicans as 'Reds', which I took to be simply a smear typical of the Right. I knew, of course, that the Russians were helping the Republicans. This was vaguely disquieting because of those mysterious Russian purge trials. Still, the fact that the Russians were helping the democratic side fight off the fascists was a point in Russia's favour. I suffered for every Republican setback, was elated by Republican counter-offensives, and warmly supported that courageous statesman, Dr Negrín.

Then came Munich, the defeat of the Spanish Republic and the outbreak of the Second World War. In 1943, I found myself working as a sub-editor on Reuter's central desk. There were many Spaniards at Reuter's in those days, all of them Republican exiles. Their presence revived my interest in their country. I took up Spanish studies, and practised my monosyllables on them. Most of them were fine men, *simpáticos* and liberal. Knowing them confirmed the rightness of the moral support I had given to the Republic. After a while, I was regularly invited to their political lunches and teas, as 'a friend of Spain'. And indeed, I was and remain a friend of Spain. I kept my Spanish friendships during the World War. Then, one by one, my Spaniards left London, bound for various points of exile. I remember them all with the liveliest sympathy, and I hope they will not hold this book against me, should they, on their side, remember me.

I was not to know, when I read some of the more lurid descriptions of Nationalist atrocities in *Spanish Testament,* that Mr Koestler was at the time of writing it, a Comintern agent, or indeed anything but what he purported to be – a special correspondent of the London *News Chronicle*. During the four or five years I spent with that newspaper, nobody ever suggested to me that he had not been a *bona fide* correspondent. Indeed it was not till 1954, when Arthur Koestler published *The Invisible Writing*, that the truth about his Spanish assignment was revealed. Understandably, Mr Koestler let it be known that he intended *Spanish Testament* to remain out of print.

It is, of course, far from my purpose to blame Mr Koestler for the circumstances of his professional life at the time of the Spanish Civil War. I mention his case simply to show how easy it was, at that time, for the Communists to persuade ordinary people of good will in the West to accept their distortions and propaganda as the truth.

To doubt, as Descartes taught, is to begin to discover the truth. Once I had begun to doubt the 'truth' about Nationalist atrocities, I began to question my assumptions about the Spanish Republic. It was not, however, until the autumn of 1965, when I was commissioned to write this book, that I had a chance to study the Spanish problem afresh and in depth. True, I had gone to Spain ten years earlier, on the first of many assignments for the London *Economist*, and had discovered that the Franco régime – though not to my personal taste – was by no means as black as I had assumed it to be. And I had learnt a good deal about contemporary Spain from 1961 onwards in the interests of a weekly talk I gave for the Spanish Service of the BBC. But here was a chance to devote the bulk of my time to recent and current Spanish history.

It was a condition of my contracts with the British and American publishers of this book that I should obtain the co-operation of the Spanish authorities and such access to Spanish archives as would enable me to authenticate doubtful facts. It was agreed by all concerned, myself included, that without such co-operation and such access, Franco's biography would not be worth writing. With this end in view, I went to Madrid in November 1965. There was no question, however, of my attempting to gain the sympathies of the Spanish authorities by undertaking to write only the good things about the Spanish Chief of State. Indeed, both in the audience I then had with General Franco, and in my talks with high officials and with the Minister of Information and Tourism, Sr Fraga Iribarne, I emphasized that I had no intention of writing yet another sycophantic biography of the Caudillo, of which there had already been too many. I argued that whatever one's views about Franco, he was too important for sycophancy, and that his apologists had not done him justice. I also recalled that I was a man of democratic views and that I had been an ardent supporter of the Republic during the Civil War. And I pointed out that whatever I wrote, the mere fact of my undertaking to write a biography of Franco might be enough for me to be labelled a fascist by the Left.

After some understandable hesitation, my arguments were accepted, and after some months of preliminary work, I moved to Madrid with my family at the end of the summer of 1966.

This, then, is the genesis of this book. Although my conclusions are, on the whole, very favourable to Franco, I have not set out to please him or the disparate Movement he led. I have said unpleasant things about both, and indeed I have no instinctive sympathy with either. I am neither a Roman Catholic, nor a hunter or a fisherman; Franco is all three. He is a soldier; I have never served in the armed forces. The only things I can think of that we have in common is that we both hate Communism and have been known to pass the time with paint and canvas. Nevertheless, as I wrote this book and studied the evidence, my feelings for Franco changed from antipathy to grudging admiration.

It may be asked: How can I be sure of my facts? My answer is that every now and again, a fact does remain in doubt. I am a journalist by training, not a historian, but have used historical as well as journalistic techniques in writing this book. All the facts have been submitted to tests of considerable scepticism, as indeed is essential in a field in which so many facts and even dates are in dispute. Neither the Republican nor the Nationalist myth about Franco and about the Civil War stands up to scrutiny. If this book helps to destroy them, it will not have been written in vain. Whenever possible, the evidence of books and documents has been supplemented by private conversations, with both supporters and opponents of Franco. The result is, I believe, a close approximation to the truth. The interpretation of the facts and of Franco's role in history is, of course, entirely my own.

It only remains for me to explain the plan of the book. The first chapter is a 'profile' of Franco, and states the enigma that was to be resolved. It was written in Madrid, immediately after my first meeting with him. The second is a summary and interpretation of Spanish history from 1810 to 1892, the year of Franco's birth; for it is impossible to understand the Spanish Civil War without this backward glance. This chapter can, of course, be skipped at the outset, and read later. But it is an essential part of the book.

The biographical narrative, properly so called, begins with Part II and ends with Part VI. Part VII is a brief attempt to assess the importance of Franco in Spanish and world history.

London, Shoreham-by-Sea, Madrid   BRIAN CROZIER
September 1965–July 1967

Acknowledgments

It is never possible for a writer to thank everybody who, in one way or another, has contributed to the writing of a book. The longer the book, the truer this is. I therefore plead for the forgiveness of anyone who feels he or she should have been named, and thank all who, in one way or another, have helped me. These include some who would prefer not to be named, and others who helped me in the course of their duties. Among the latter were many Spanish officials, whose help was given with courtesy, patience and diligence. My special thanks are due to: Captain Sir Basil Liddell Hart, for kindly allowing me to consult his personal files; Sr D. Joaquín Arrarás and M. Claude Martin, who helped to elucidate the chronology of Franco's early career; and Sr D. Luis Bolín, for showing me some of his own material, and other services. My daughter Isobel Crozier made a major contribution in research, translating, indexing and proof-reading. Her younger sister Caroline bore stoically the upheaval of transplanting to an alien scene.

FRANCO
A BIOGRAPHICAL HISTORY

PART I

Man, Myth and History

1 *Man and Myth*

The eyes are large, opaque and quite expressionless. When they rise to fix the visitor, they look startlingly the same, with Franco in his seventies, as in the faded pictures of the meagre youth in uniform on his way to the Moroccan wars half a century earlier. The nose was, and remains, aquiline and sensitive; the mouth, with its scarcely perceptible moustache, small and – his enemies would say – disdainful, perhaps even a little cruel. The hands are small and well shaped, but he uses them very little. The voice is thin and now sounds old, though it was once capable of greater oratorical projection than his detractors allow. His lisp is more pronounced than it need be, even in Castilian Spanish.

As the cartoonists observed many years earlier, he is short and plump. He sits very upright in his chair and reads a visitor's type-written questions without glasses at a middle distance suitable for a man of fewer years. Before walking off, he squares his shoulders: his stride is firm and slightly solemn.

Solemnity and pomp are indeed the keynotes of Franco's 'court', as one is tempted to call it. One needs to visit the Spanish Head of State in audience at the Pardo Palace, close to Madrid, to realize, in fact, that there is probably nothing incongruous in Franco's mind in the paradox of this kingless monarchy. For Franco is, to all intents and purposes, the king *ad interim*. Full morning dress or uniform with medals is the required garb for audiences. The proper tone of voice, in the ornate waiting-room with its Goya tapestries and its garish carpet, woven for Ferdinand VII in 1825, is a hush near-whisper. The setting of this summer residence, with its rococo or Empire furnishings and elaborate ceremonial, is appropriately pre-Republican. Falling short of imperial grandeur, it is well chosen for an interim monarchy.

There are two Franco myths, neither of which is at all helpful to a biographer. The 'hero' myth is an inescapable part of the régime. It permeates the 'approved' biographies and the controlled press with a sticky syrup of sycophancy. According to the hero myth, Franco is the saviour of the western world, the defender of the faith and of Christian civilization, the crusader against atheist Bolshevism, brave, wise and far-seeing beyond compare, the man who gave Spain twenty-five years of peace and more – the *Paz Española* of the posters and leaflets of 1964.

The 'monster' myth is no less irrelevant. As the monster myth has it, Franco is the fascist general who murdered the Republic and with it Spanish democracy, who worked hand in glove with Hitler and Mussolini; the last surviving dictator, who has no business being where he is, having got there by drowning Spain in blood with the help of the major Fascist powers, and who sits like lead on the conscience of the western world.

Since these contradictory images cannot both be true, it seems unlikely that either, taken separately, can be regarded as a contribution to our knowledge of Franco. Unlikely, that is, except in a rather indirect sense. One may, for instance, deduce from the impotent and apoplectic fury his name provoked, and largely continues to provoke, among leftists and liberals (in both the American and the British senses of the second word) that Franco's capacity for arousing hatred was at least as great as his gift to inspire devotion; and one is entitled to ask why. Again, one can only suppose that he enjoys, and probably insists on, the adulation with which he is surrounded, and to mark this taste as an element in his complex character. Let us note in passing, however, that Franco is by no means alone among contemporary statesman in enjoying the hero cult. Stalin did, according to Khrushchev, who succeeded him and called it the 'cult of personality'. So does Mao Tse-tung of China, while the lyrical extravagances of the Ghanaian press in praise of the ex-Redeemer, Nkrumah, made the Spanish press look timid and reticent.

The man, then, must be separated from the myth, and the statesman from the man, just as his achievements need to be isolated from the emotional antipathies born of his association with fascism and the enemies of the western allies during the Second World War.

By any standards, Franco has had an extraordinary career, and the key to it lies far more in his character than in his mind. Not that he lacks intelligence, far from it. But it is a calculating intelligence, well laced with cunning, unusually well adapted to the winning of victories and the maintenance of power, and far less to the making of contributions to political theory. Unlike General de Gaulle, he has written little of enduring value. This did not, however, stop him from registering in February 1964 as a member of the General Society of Spanish Authors under the pen-name of Jaime de Andrade on the strength of two works: *Diary of a Battalion* (1922) and the screen-play for the film *Raza* (Race), shot in 1940.

His eloquence, though designed to touch patriotic or even xeno-phobic depths in the Spanish people, sounds hollow and pompous to the uncommitted stranger. Indeed his relative lack of oratorical powers makes him an exception among contemporary dictators; and so, too, has the increasing moderation of his régime, as the years have passed. Hitler grew more sanguinary as time went on, and so did Stalin. The fact that this has not been true of Franco seems to disap-point his detractors, who explain it away by pointing to his need to improve the 'image' of his régime in America, which provides aid, and in western Europe, which sends tourists. There may be something in this, but the fact itself remains and is part of Franco's biography, along with friendship with the Axis and reprisals after the Civil War.

Franco's character, then, merits close attention. It is a singular character, especially in a Spaniard. Different words can be found to describe it, according to one's standpoint. His enemies would call him a cold fish; his supporters call him cool. Many anecdotes, some of them apocryphal, are told to illustrate his coolness. Among the authentic ones, perhaps the most striking is one that can be inter-preted as showing coldness of heart as well as coolness of judgment. When the news of the death of his old friend General Mola in a plane crash was brought to Franco in June 1937, the bearer of the tidings exclaimed: 'A great loss, General!'

'Yes,' said Franco, 'as you say. A great loss, but not simply as far as the war goes. Here, we can replace him. In peace-time, on the other hand, I fear this may not be easy and that we may miss him.'[1]

With the coolness goes an extraordinary physical courage, which became legendary during Franco's Moroccan years, and which amounts to a complete indifference to danger, of the kind which made General de Gaulle walk erect through the streets of liberated Paris while bullets whistled from the rooftops. In de Gaulle, perhaps, this was an aspect of his Messianism. In Franco, the Messianism was complemented by fatalism. 'God,' he used to say, 'has given me life, and only God can take it away.'

God, indeed, almost did, one day in June 1916, when a Moroccan bullet went through his abdomen. Until then, in four years of incessant fighting, he had stayed unmarked, so that, in Moorish eyes, he had acquired an aura of invulnerability. Arrarás, his first biographer, recounts that on one occasion during those fighting years, a shot blew the cork of a Thermos flask out of his fingers as he was about to drink its contents of coffee. Unperturbed, says Arrarás, he drank his fill, then turned towards the enemy encampment, exclaiming:'Let's see if you can aim better next time!'[2]

True or false, this incident forms part of the hero myth. Indeed that combination of manliness and courage which the Spanish-speaking peoples call *hombría* is a legitimate part of Franco's character that made a hero of him in the eyes of many Spaniards long before he commanded the Nationalist troops during the Civil War. The enduring loyalty of the officers who served with him or under him in Morocco was a strong factor in his successful conduct of operations from 1936 on. His hero image, however, was built on more precocious foundations. Three times awarded the medal of Military Merit, he was promoted captain at twenty-two, major at twenty-three and colonel at thirty-two, to become – at thirty-three – the youngest general in Europe since Bonaparte, as indeed each promotion had made him the youngest of his rank in the Spanish Army.

As an officer, then, Franco was brave and lucky; but he was also efficient and cautious. Though always ready to lead his men in a battle charge, he was never foolhardy. He would study a situation before attacking and was infinitely reluctant to squander his resources, human or material. Bravery, efficiency, caution: it was a combination of qualities that made him a brilliant tactical commander and later an outstanding administrator as Director of the Military Academy at Saragossa. It has been said that he was less successful as a strategist during the Civil War. Von Thoma and other German officers who served at his side were exasperated at the deliberation of his methods, which they found old-fashioned and out of tune with their own *Blitzkrieg* mentality.[3] But his resources were smaller than theirs and he was less inclined than they might have been to regard his men as expendable. And in the end, he won.

He won, and he survived. His capacity for survival is indeed in itself a major achievement in a world hostile to everything he stood for as the last remaining 'fascist' dictator after the defeat of the Axis partners who had helped him to victory in the Civil War. No less astonishing was his success in keeping Spain out of the Second World War and denying Hitler the use of Spanish territory.

For these achievements, too, one must look for the key in Franco's complex character. With his native Galician caution went cunning and a faculty of ambiguity that made men of diverse opinions assume that he was on their side or resist any suggestion that he was not. He had been King Alfonso's favourite general; but he refused to join his brother general, Sanjurjo, in a plot against the Republic in 1932 and crushed the uprising of the Asturian miners against that same Republic two years later. Yet when the time came, he too rose against the Republic, and in the end buried it.

He was inevitably dubbed a fascist for accepting aid from the German and Italian dictators during the Civil War and for making Spain's version of a fascist party – the Falange – the core of his 'Movement'. But he was never particularly fascist, just as he had never been particularly monarchist or republican. Although he accepted help from Hitler, he gave refuge to thousands of Hitler's Jewish victims during the Second World War and revived citizenship rights for the Sephardic Jewish community of Salonika, to save it from Nazi persecution. Above all, Franco was a professional soldier, dedicated to the maintenance of discipline and order, with a minimal interest in constitutional forms and a paternalistic conception of his patriotic duty. Supporters of the 'monster' myth would call him an opportunist; to upholders of the 'hero' myth in its mildest form, he is simply a pragmatist.

Certainly, no modern dictator has been less 'ideological'. He used the Falange because it was willing to fight the Republic, but gaoled its leader, Hedilla, and gradually emasculated the party (while allowing it to retain patronage and other privileges) after the Second World War. He used the Carlists for the same reason, but sent their leader, Fal Conde, packing into exile and rewarded them by grooming the young Don Juan Carlos, son of the rival Pretender, Don Juan, for the Spanish Throne. By passing over Don Juan himself, he made sure that though Spain had been proclaimed a monarchy (in 1947), the throne should be without an incumbent during Franco's own lifetime or pleasure. Some of Franco's enemies hated others, and he did not discourage their hatred; his supporters were welcome so long as they kept their personal ambitions well hidden and concealed their criticisms.

His treatment of Hitler was masterly. Conceding nothing save public adulation for the Nazis, he countered German demands with interminable delays, pleas of material needs and other stratagems. In the end, all Hitler had to show for his aid to Spain was a portfolio of mining concessions. The meeting of the two dictators at Hendaya on the Spanish border in 1940 must have had elements of high comedy about it. Alone among the Führer's interlocutors, Franco got the better of him, to the point when the exasperated Hitler confided that he would sooner have three or four teeth extracted than go through that experience again.[4] In these war-time dealings and haggles with the Nazis, Franco was ably assisted by his brother-in-law and Foreign Minister, Serrano Súñer, whose subtlety, intelligence and agility more than compensated for Spain's weakness and exhaustion in the face of the victorious German military machine. But he, too, was removed when his presence became inconvenient; and since he had been the only politician willing to stand up to Franco, the Caudillo was at last surrounded entirely by yes-men.

Through all his years of military and political prowess, Franco never seems to have doubted that he was born to command, or that it was his patriotic duty to be successful. His detractors pay more attention to his passion for self-advancement, which is undeniable, than to his patriotism, which is equally patent. Here again, one's choice of words is crucial. If one disapproves of an ambitious man, one refers to his lust for power; if one approves, one praises his drive and the normality of his search for success. As for patriotism, it is a sentiment that embarrasses many people while it thrills others. To the former, Franco's speeches make fulsome reading; to the latter – in Spain, at any rate – they play on emotional chords, and indeed arouse xenophobic depths of passion which Franco tapped to his advantage during the post-war years of Spain's ostracism.

At any rate, in his search for success and power, Franco seems to have been singularly untroubled by the sensual temptations that plague lesser men. Here again, one faces a choice of emotive or merely informative words. Puritanism? Asceticism? Self-discipline? Deficiency of the sexual instinct? Adherence to Christian morality? The facts seem to be more important than the verbal cloak. And his enemies and supporters alike agree that he has never drunk to excess, nor smoked at all, nor gone with women. He is said to have told his subordinates in Morocco: 'I don't want women here, or drunken orgies, or Masses.'[5]

In view of his later reputation for piety, this desire to exclude religion, or at any rate, the intrusions of the Church into Army life, seems surprising. But this, too, is authenticated: during his early years, Franco avoided the Mass, as he avoided women and drink. Neither God nor the Devil, it seems, tempted him, and this freedom from spiritual or sensual distractions left him free to devote all his energies to mastering the profession of arms.

It is a harsh profession, not least in Spain, which has traditionally produced an infantry of outstanding toughness, and Franco became a strict disciplinarian, requiring of his men unquestioning obedience and exalted devotion to duty. But his discipline was enforced without distinction of rank. A story told to the London *Sunday Express* of 15 May 1938, by Diego Hidalgo, War Minister in one of the Republican cabinets, makes the point. A liberal and a kindly man, Hidalgo liked to round off a tour of garrisons with a pardon for military prisoners. One day, having learnt that an officer was under close arrest in a fortress under Franco's command he asked the general to grant a pardon. Franco replied that he would do so only if the Minister turned his request into an order. 'Why? What has the man done?' asked Hidalgo. 'The gravest thing an officer can do,' was Franco's reply: 'He slapped a private.' The Minister gave way and congratulated Franco.[6]

The general didn't reserve his discipline only for the officers and men under his command. He was always his own harshest disciplinarian. Gifted with a strong constitution, he taught himself endurance and resistance. His stubby legs could outwalk the legs of younger men when he himself had reached late middle age and the joys of the shoot had replaced the forced marches of earlier days. And his subordinates speak with mingled awe and amusement of the physical self-control that enables him to preside over a Cabinet meeting lasting many hours, or hold audiences from 9.30 a.m. till 3 p.m. without refreshment or apparent need to relieve himself. His Ministers are less hardy.

Perhaps the least pardonable trait of Franco's character is his own incapacity to forgive his enemies on the side of 'anti-Spain', though he was always remarkably indulgent towards friends who betrayed him. The Civil War had produced horrors on both sides, though probably nothing on the Nationalist side equalled the atrocities of the Red terror on the Republican. Hugh Thomas, scaling down the wilder charges of partisans on either side, still found that the Republicans had put 60,000 to death in the areas they controlled, while the Nationalists, as they advanced, summarily executed perhaps 10,000 fewer.[7] On the other hand, Gabriel Jackson, the American historian, quotes wildly different figures – so different that one almost wonders whether he is writing about the same events.[8] But in the end, the fighting was over and the victors were installed in the rubble of Madrid. Was this a time for revenge or for forgiveness? This was Spain, where only blood can wash away the stain of blood; and Franco chose revenge. For three years, the firing squads spoke, removing supporters of 'the other Spain' – many of them admittedly war criminals – from the land of the survivors. Tens of thousands of luckier ones stayed on in gaol. This, too, is part of the biography of General Franco, together with the milder fact that over the years massive amnesties reduced Spain's prison population to one of the lowest in Europe.

General Franco's private life was always exemplary. His former chief, General Sanjurjo, who would have been Commander-in-Chief of the Nationalist forces during the Civil War had he not died in a plane crash, was a philandering swashbuckler, as indeed was the former dictator of the 1920s, General Miguel Primo de Rivera. Had Sanjurjo lived through to victory, it is conceivable that the public tone of Spanish life would have developed a licentious tinge of which Franco would never have approved. Decorum, however, plays an important part in the lives of the Francos; neither the general nor his wife, Doña Carmen Polo de Franco, is amused by departures from Christian standards of behaviour.

Both attend Mass several times a week, and at public religious ceremonies, Franco appropriates the ancient kingly privilege of walking under a canopy. Fittingly, since Franco is an uncrowned monarch, he receives new ambassadors in the former Royal Palace, and they arrive in a gilt stage-coach with mounted guards.

Away from the Pardo or the Royal Palace, however, Franco sheds pomp to play with the youngest among his six grandchildren or shoot movies of them. Until his doctor advised against it in the 1950s, he played tennis regularly. But long after that, his favourite sports were hunting and fishing. In 1957 he was awarded the title of National Amateur Champion of tuna fishing with rod and reel, having caught a 712 lb specimen, the largest ever landed by rod in Spanish waters. He once told an American reporter he had shot 8,420 partridges in one year. Golf is another pastime, and two or three times a year he attends a bullfight, though *aficionados* complain that the bull rarely seems to attract his undivided attention.

He likes to paint for relaxation, seascapes being his favourite subject. One of his more successful works, however, is a self-portrait in the uniform of an admiral – an interesting piece of visual wish-fulfilment, for he had originally opted for a naval career. In matters of art, as in other things, he is a patient man. When he asked the late painter Elías Salaverría, who had been commissioned to paint his portrait, how many sittings would be needed, the answer was, 'Three of one hour each.' He then expressed a preference for one sitting of three hours, and posed immobile for 180 minutes while the artist sketched and painted.

Few things have ever been allowed to disturb the even rhythm of Franco's life. He works from 10 a.m. till mid-afternoon, then lunches frugally, allowing himself a single glass of wine, neither more nor less. Back at his desk at 5 or 6 p.m., he works till 10, when dinner is served. At midnight, he and Doña Carmen recite the Rosary together, then he reads himself to sleep. Twice a week, he grants audiences – military on Tuesdays, civil on Wednesdays. My own turn for this first audience came at nearly 3 p.m., after a crowded Wednesday morning during which three dozen dignitaries, home and foreign, had preceded me. He does not, as some statesmen do, receive visitors from behind his desk, and indeed it would be impracticable to do so, since his stature is small and the desk is permanently piled two feet deep with files. This image scarcely squares with the rest of his methodical personality, but he is said to

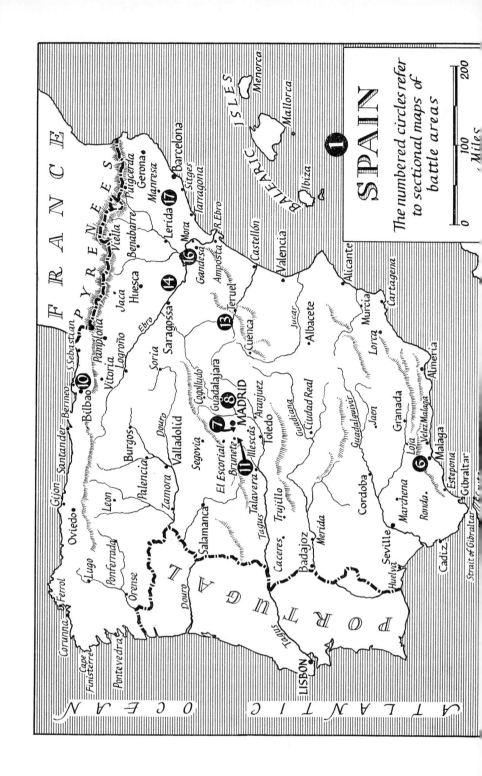

enjoy surprising his Ministers by fishing out a specific document unerringly from the right pile. This he has occasion to do every second Friday, when he presides over a Cabinet meeting that sometimes lasts until dawn on Saturday.

When Franco travels around Spain, he likes to use a vintage black Rolls-Royce, adorned with the national coat-of-arms; another large car, filled with red-bereted bodyguards, precedes him. Security is strict: the newspapers are not allowed to publish advance details of his movements and, in the towns, police are stationed every ten yards along the route.

This, then, is the cautious, patient, astute, well-ordered man who for more than twenty-five years has held Spain's destiny in his hands. Untroubled by personal doubts and deeply sceptical of the ability of his countrymen to rule themselves, he has given Spain tranquillity after a terrifying blood-letting, ended her isolation and moved her with characteristic deliberation into the twentieth century.

Beneath a towering Cross lies Franco's 'pyramid', that tremendous underground mausoleum and basilica, the Valley of the Fallen, in which, at last, the dead of the defeated side have achieved, albeit on sufferance, the posthumous right to be considered Spaniards. This gigantic monument is not, however, the only work that will give Franco's name a place in the history books. It is the purpose of this study to make a provisional assessment of that place as it may look as the passions of earlier decades subside.

2 *The Social and Historical Background*

With or without Franco, Spain would have had a civil war. But the desperate situation of 1936 was a long time in the making. The extremes of climate and of passions, of wealth and poverty, of philosophy and political advocacy that constitute Spain and the Spanish people contained the seeds of self-destruction. In 1892, when Franco was born, anarchist outrages were rife, and so were executions. The First Republic had been buried eighteen years earlier, and the ill-starred reign of Alfonso XIII began when Franco was twelve. When he was six, in 1898, the humiliating Spanish–

American War left Spain weak and diminished, and shook the already enfeebled foundations of the parliamentary rule instituted in 1876.

This, then, was Franco's background, as it was that of all Spaniards and of their vengeful and tragic civil war. Let us look more closely at this background.

From 1814, when the Monarchy was restored after the Peninsular War, Spain was in a condition of incipient – and often actual – civil conflict. It was in no sense a simple conflict. Any number of ways might be found to describe it, each true and each only part of the truth. At various times, it was a social conflict, between the poor and illiterate peasants and workers on one hand, and the forces of tradition – Army, Church and Crown – on the other. It was a constitutional conflict, between Republicans and Monarchists, and a regionalist one, between Catalan or Basque federalists and Castilian centralists. And then again, it was a war of ideas, with liberalism, Marxism and Anarchism competing for allegiance. Above all, perhaps, it was a conflict between authority and the concept of liberty.

The ragged army of fighting monks and peasant generals that had helped drive out Napoleon's invaders had no say in the deliberations of the elected Cortes of Cadiz which, in 1810, began to draft a new constitution. Fighting was consistent with illiteracy, but politics was not. That was the business of the elected lawyers and priests, landowners and Army officers. The constitution that emerged in 1812, however, still stands as a monument to shattered liberal and democratic hopes. True, the deputies swore duty to God and King, committing themselves to the defence of the Spanish realm, the Catholic religion and the throne of the absent king, Ferdinand VII. But these unexceptionable bows to tradition were subverted by dangerous ideas, such as the abolition of lordly privileges, the suppression of the Inquisition, popular sovereignty and universal suffrage. It was a heady brew, but the enjoyment it dispensed was short-lived.

Waiting in the wings, in the soft confinement of Valençay, Ferdinand had promised to respect the constitution promulgated in his name by the elected representatives of the sovereign people. But then, throughout his life, he was ever ready to make promises for the sake of expediency. No sooner was he safely back on Spanish soil than he denounced it. These lofty issues passed over the heads of the voiceless masses. To them, Ferdinand was the Desired One – *El Deseado* –

and he captured the people's imagination by cultivating the friend-ship of matadors.[1] His quarrel was not with the masses but with the liberals whose constitution seemed to threaten his divine right to reign. Vindictive, cowardly and treacherous, he vented his fury on them in a prolonged persecution that drove them to seek refuge where they could find it, for instance in the Masonic lodges whose secrecy was conducive to conspiracy.

The Army had helped Ferdinand back to his throne, but was angered by his incompetence and his intrigues. Nor was it immune to the liberal contagion. Most of the revolts that punctuated Ferdi-nand's reign originated in the Army, which sheltered many liberals from the king's spies and police, whatever the more reactionary generals might think of such untraditional behaviour. It was two rebellious officers who, in January 1820, proclaimed the restoration of the Constitution of 1812. Alarmed and ready to grovel, as always in sight of danger, the king declared himself willing to lead the way on 'the constitutional path'. By this time, he was in the hands of the revolutionaries. Freed in the wake of an invading French Army, he broke his word again, repudiating his liberal concessions and launch-ing a second persecution more brutal than the first. The orgy of repression lasted until his death in 1833.

Ferdinand's death brought fresh hopes to the liberals, but ushered in a further period of civil strife. The dead king's energetic fourth wife, María Cristina of Naples, took over as Regent and proclaimed a new constitution, the *Estatuto Real* or Royal Statute, in 1834. Less advanced than the Constitution of 1812, it split the liberals into those willing to accept it, who called themselves *Moderados*, and those who clamoured for 1812, known as the *Progresistas*.

Nothing was solved. Certainly Spain was not made safe for liberalism. Nor was the Monarchy inviolate. Under the prevailing Salic Law, Ferdinand's throne should have gone to his brother, Don Carlos. But María Cristina, having presented the king with two daughters, was anxious to see her first-born, Isabella, succeed him. She persuaded him, then, before his death, to set aside the Salic Law. Deprived of the throne, Don Carlos went to war.

Conflicting streams of protest and reaction converged in his bitter-ness. Legitimacy was only one of the Carlists' war aims: another was the restoration of the Inquisition, which Napoleon's brother Joseph and the liberals of Cadiz had abolished. To the Carlists, liberalism,

Protestantism and laxness were synonymous. Not unnaturally, the Church supported Don Carlos and the Jesuits were his militant army, just as the Freemasons were the liberals'. As for the people, their loyalties were divided. In 1834 and 1835, the mob burned down convents and churches in many Spanish towns, just as they did a century later, before and during the Spanish Civil War. But in the North, the peasants of the Basque provinces and Catalonia, of Navarre and Aragon, rose in support of the Carlists and the Church.

At first sight, this alliance of peasants and priests looks paradoxical, but special circumstances account for it. Ferdinand and other Bourbon kings had whittled down local rights and privileges in the name of a centralising policy which the relatively prosperous peasants of the North resented. The liberals, though against monarchic tyranny, were as centralist as the Bourbons. The northern peasants were afraid of further liberal encroachments, and the Church feared its lands might be seized and sold if the liberals triumphed. Hence the alliance of peasants and priests under the Carlist banner.

This first Carlist War lasted five years, from 1834 to 1839, completed the economic ruin of Spain started by the Napoleonic wars, and left the Army as the dominant political force in the country. The generals, as Wellington had found, were incompetent, but held the towns. The Carlist guerrillas, though often brilliantly led, held the mountains and parts of the countryside, but failed to take the towns. On both sides, as in the Civil War a century later, prisoners and hostages were killed on a large scale. Don Carlos himself, though English volunteers were fighting on his side, ordered the killing of all English prisoners from the other side – for a government-sponsored force of 10,000 men had been sent from England to defend the Spanish Regency. His orders were carried out.[2]

Ruthlessness did not save Don Carlos, however. In 1837, the Carlist General Maroto had four colleagues shot and sued for peace. The Convention of Vergara, on 31 August 1839, safeguarded the rights of the Basque and Navarrese peasants, but obliged Carlos to go into exile. The Carlist officers were taken into the Regency's Army.

The constitutional battle had gone on while the Carlist War was fought, and it went on after the War was won. The Regent, María Cristina, had little taste for representative government and would have ruled despotically, had she been strong enough. Already unpopular, she had further fallen in public approval when the secret of her marriage in 1833 to one Ferdinand Muñoz came out. A dashing young guardsman, his ambitions were progenitive rather than political: his consort and protector gave him a dukedom and bore him a large family, at first unbeknownst to the populace. The *Progresistas* were outraged by these goings-on and by the Regent's despotic trends, and rose in revolt in Andalusia in the south, Madrid in the centre, and Aragon and Catalonia in the north. On 12 August 1836, a curious incident forced María Cristina to concede the liberals' demands. The royal family was passing the summer at La Granja and a group of sergeants took advantage of its presence to burst into her room and call on her to restore the Constitution of 1812. She remonstrated but gave in and appointed a *Progresista* Ministry which, in turn, had the Cortes proclaim yet another constitution in 1837 on lines that compromised between 1812 and the Royal Statute of 1834.

And now, for the first time, Spain had a taste of military rule. One of the Regency's Army officers, General Espartero, had led his men to victory over the Carlists. Now, embracing the *Progresistas'* cause, he developed political ambitions of his own, forced María Cristina to leave the country and took over the Regency himself. A model for the long line of military dictators in the Hispanic countries, Espartero found jobs for the 'boys', that is, for the soldiers and *Progresistas* who supported his bid for power. His own 'progressism' was suspect. In October 1841, a year after the ex-Regent's departure, he suppressed a Cristinist uprising at Pamplona. And a year after that, when the industrialists of Catalonia protested against his free trade policy, he had Barcelona bombarded, with heavy loss of life.

This blood-letting displeased many of his followers and there were few to support him when, in May and June 1843, a group of hostile officers, led at first by a Catalan *Progresista*, General Prim, rose against him. In July, he embarked for England, and a short-lived coalition government pronounced 'national execration' upon the departing 'Duke of Victory', as he had been known in his time of glory.

The victorious junta, composed of *Moderados, Progresistas* and Republicans, was not, by its nature, durable. One thing they did agree on was that they had had enough of regents. They got over the problem by declaring Isabella, who was thirteen, to be of age. And she handed effective power to the most determined of the *Moderados*, General Narváez, whose dictatorship lasted seven years.

Before glancing at Isabella's unsatisfactory reign, it may be useful to examine some of the social consequences of the turbulent period I have been outlining. For the Church, in particular, it was a time of vicissitudes. The reactionary 'image' of the Spanish Church is of comparatively recent origin. In the sixteenth and seventeenth centuries, the identification of Church with people was as complete in Spain as it had been anywhere in Europe since the middle ages. Rich with the social experience of colonizing and proselytizing in the New World, the priests and monks were the defenders of the poor against the rich and powerful. A degeneration began in the middle of the seventeenth century, keeping pace with the decay of the overstretched Spanish empire.

And then, in 1700, the Bourbons came to Spain. The first of them, Philip V, a melancholy and irresolute youth, allowed able French advisers to run the country, and the financial and centralizing reforms they introduced clashed both with the Church as a body and with the regional sentiments and privileges of the northern provinces. Under Charles III, whose enlightened despotism began in 1759, the brooding clash between Church and State came to a head. The Jesuits were expelled in 1767 and the powers of the dreaded Inquisition were curbed, the last victim being a woman burnt in 1780 for carnal knowledge of the devil.

The Napoleonic invasion found the priests and monks fighting at the side of the peasant *guerilleros* who resisted the invaders. But this was the last time the unity of Church and people manifested itself on a national scale: the alliance of the priests and peasants in the first Carlist War being confined to the northern provinces. But the Cadiz liberals who drew up the 1812 Constitution were as centralist and anti-clerical as the Bourbons' advisers, and the breach between Church and State grew wider. Daring where the Bourbons had hesitated, they abolished the Inquisition. (That body had already been abolished by Joseph Bonaparte in 1808, but the act of a conqueror was less significant than that of free Spaniards.) This was the beginning of the end for the alliance of orthodoxy and authority, for though the Inquisition was twice again restored and abolished, it finally disappeared on 15 July 1834.

The liberals' clash with the Church, however, went deeper even than the abolition of its hated instrument might suggest. The Church was stripped, not merely of power over men's bodies and souls, but of its lands. The unwitting author of this social revolution was not a

Spaniard but an Englishman, for it was above all the influence of Adam Smith's ideas of competitive and acquisitive mercantilism that underlay the liberal assault on the Church. Two men especially carried Adam Smith's message to the Spaniards: Caspar Melchor de Jovellanos and Juan Álvarez y Mendizábal. Jovellanos is usually regarded as Spain's greatest economist, and his *Report on the Agrarian Law* (1787) was in effect an attempt to adapt Adam Smith's teachings to Spain's land problem. His influence was paramount within the Cadiz Cortes of 1810–14. The way to pay off the public debt, he had told the Cadiz liberals, was to sell off the common lands, and follow this up by selling off Church lands as well. During the first liberal phase, only the common lands were disposed of; it was Mendizábal who extended the policy to Church property.

Mendizábal, a Jewish financial wizard from Cadiz, had set up shop as a banker in London, with enormous success. Having financed a military campaign in Portugal, he returned to Spain as the man who claimed he could pay for the war against the Carlists. His recipe was to confiscate Church property and sell it on the open market. This, he thought, would not only pay for the war but create a new class of liberal, property-owning families whose stake in constitutional rule would contribute to national stability. The deed of confiscation and sale was accomplished under his decrees of 19 February and 8 March 1836.

The consequences of Mendizábal's decrees were less happy, in the long run, than he could have foreseen. One of them was that the redistribution of land completed the divorce of the Church from the people as well as from the State. Another was that the Church, now on the defensive, was driven to find alternative financial means of support. Not unnaturally, this drive for self-sufficiency was spearheaded by the Jesuits. Expelled in 1767, the Society of Jesus was allowed to return under Ferdinand VII, and though turned out again in 1835, 1854 and 1868, it found time in its intervals of legality to invest its funds most profitably and cultivate the patronage of the rich and powerful. The Church as a whole benefited from these efforts, so that – whether in favour or persecuted, it regained a position of power or influence, according to the party in power. But whereas it had once been identified with the people, it now became increasingly identified with absentee landlords and the idle rich.

While all this was going on, an upper middle class was rising to political power. Espartero, the 'Duke of Victory', had been the champion of the lower middle class people who had joined his banner. Narváez, the *Moderado* general who replaced him as dictator, was the man of the new capitalists and newly rich who had bought the Church lands – often for a song – in the buyers' market that followed the spoliation of religious property.

By the middle of the nineteenth century, then, the explosive elements of the Civil War of the late 1930s were all present: a politically inclined Army, a Church that had allied itself with the moneyed class, an anti-religious peasantry (the men, of course, not the women), and an anti-clerical body of liberals.

Let us return now to the unedifying whims and intrigues of the crowned and uncrowned rulers of Spain. Generous and impulsive by nature, Isabella II was also politically irresponsible and insatiably addicted to the pleasures of the bed and boudoir. Let us waste no time over the 'affair of the Spanish marriages', which revolved around Isabella and her sister Luisa Fernanda and shattered (not for the last time) the *entente* between England and France. Isabella was fobbed off with the dull and pious duke of Cadiz who, it is said, was impotent. This infirmity did not, however, stop Isabella from producing nine children, with the help of a succession of lovers. Her early taste ran to generals, but her strong man, General Narváez, took exception to her choice of the dashing General Serrano as current lover and banished him to Granada. Turning now for advice to Sor Patrocinio (who had become known as the Bleeding Nun because of the stigmata she was alleged to have developed during the Carlist War, and claimed to work miracles), she restored the convents and readmitted the Jesuits. While the Queen played off one courtier against the other, the government was alternately in the hands of the conservative *Moderados* and the liberal *Progresistas*. Insurrections and *pronunciamientos* punctuated the reign, while the scandals of the court discredited the monarchy. A son – fathered, it is said, by a Catalan colonel – came in 1857 and was destined, in 1875, to mount the throne as Alfonso XII. But the most scandalous of her choices, in the opinion of the remarkably outspoken press of the day, was Carlos Marfori, whom she made Minister of State. A cook's son, he had been an actor until he met his royal mistress.

This was in 1868 and it was the last straw. A *junta* of liberal generals, under her former favourite Serrano, now a marshal, issued a revolutionary manifesto, and launched an insurrection. Isabella fled to France and a provisional government under Serrano banned the Society of Jesus again, proclaimed universal suffrage and sanctioned a free press. After two years of provisional rule, disturbed by Carlist and republican uprisings, the revolutionaries tried hard to find a 'democratic king'. This, said General Prim, the Prime Minister, was like looking for an atheist in heaven. The man they did find, Prince Amadeo of Savoy, hardly qualified, but he misguidedly accepted. On 27 December, the day he landed in Cartagena, Prim was assassinated. Isolated and regarded on all sides as a foreign intruder, the unfortunate Amadeo I reigned for two years, then could stand it no longer and abdicated. The same day – 12 February 1873 – the First Spanish Republic was born, by the overwhelming wish of the Cortes.

Typically, the Carlists had abstained from the vote. Indeed they had already been up in arms for three years, under the exiled Don Carlos, grandson of the first. Personally, he was charming enough to persuade the traditionalists who saw him as their saviour to forget that he spoke Spanish with an Italian lilt. But he was no leader. And his followers fought with fanatical frightfulness, killing off prisoners, tarring and feathering women, hurling captives to their deaths from great heights and even destroying railway trains in their longing to return to a mythical past where all was order and religious peace.

The fragile First Republic was out of its depth, unable to contain the Carlists militarily or to govern effectively while the war went on. To add to its burdens, Barcelona and the southern cities of Malaga, Seville, Granada, Cadiz and Murcia declared themselves to be 'cantons' in the summer of 1873, started issuing their own money in the name of 'Federalism', and rose in arms when the central government challenged their right to do so. In September, a determined centralist, Emilio Castelar, came to power and set about restoring the State's authority, but he gave up the attempt on 2 January 1874; and a military junta issued the usual *pronunciamiento* and brought back Marshal Serrano at the head of a provisional government. The Republic's days, however, were numbered, and at the end of the year a group of generals rallied to Alfonso, who had come of age and declared himself in favour of a constitutional monarchy. The end of the Republic was also the beginning of the end of Carlism and in February 1876 peace returned when Don Carlos fled the country.

The Bourbons had come back in exceptionally favourable circumstances. Republicanism had been tried and found wanting. The Pope, who had misguidedly recognized Don Carlos as Carlos VII, king of Spain, was persuaded to recognize Alfonso instead. The inducement offered is itself important: the new régime's concessions to the Papacy were of the kind that even a Don Carlos might have approved. The ecclesiastical budget was increased; Protestant schools and churches were closed down, and civil marriages were abolished.

This religious orthodoxy, though politically expedient, was more apparent than real. With the Restoration came a desire to create constitutional forms that could be respected and then actually to respect them. A new Cortes had been elected in January 1876, and in July it approved a new constitution that compromised between previous ones in an attempt to avoid both the anarchy of republicanism and the absolutism of the Carlists. It was a successful attempt. In religion, despite the measures mentioned above, tolerance was promised to all. In politics, the king remained the effective ruler, since he had the power to choose his Ministers, and the Cortes was 'ministerial' in the sense that it took its orders from the Ministry. But there was a bicameral Parliament, and an interesting experiment in the two-party system now began, which gave Spain sixteen years of peace and freedom from *pronunciamientos* (with the solitary exception of an unsuccessful attempt by General Villacampo to restore the Republic in 1886).

This considerable achievement was largely the work of the ablest Spanish civilian statesman of the nineteenth century, Cánovas del Castillo. Cánovas was a sceptical intellectual, liberal by inclination but steeped in the realities of Spanish history. Though fascinated by English parliamentarianism, he had convinced himself through prolonged study of Spain's 'decadence' that his countrymen were incapable of making a similar system work, or indeed of governing themselves. Since it was, nevertheless, undesirable that the same men should cling to power indefinitely, and desirable that as many politicians as possible should see advantage in the service of the State, he concluded that alternations of power were necessary. But he was percipient enough to see that a two-party system could work only where the two parties were broadly in agreement about constitutional essentials (as is true, even today, of the two major parties in Britain and the United States). In Spain, therefore, certain conditions had to be fulfilled for a two-party system to work: agreement between two outwardly 'rival' political leaders to respect the conventional façade of parliamentary rule, and willingness of each to allow his party to be defeated at the polls at suitable intervals. Inevitably, this implied a very limited suffrage.

Although there was a strong dose of cynicism in this recipe for stability, Cánovas undoubtedly regarded it as a necessary period of tutelage in preparation for a truer form of parliamentary rule. He was lucky in finding, in Praxedes Sagasta, another politician who was willing to be the leader of the alternative party. And so the system of *turnismo* was born. The Minister of the Interior would determine the composition of each Cortes, by agreement with the provincial party chiefs, and the elections were managed by the traditional local political bosses, known as *caciques*. The whole system was protected – or better, guaranteed – by the king's right of dissolution and his willingness not to abuse it.

During Cánovas's lifetime (he was assassinated in 1897), the system, though cynical and based on a mere shell of parliamentary rule, worked extraordinarily well. Even the Carlists were won over, or some of them, for Cánovas coaxed the ex-Carlist leader Pidal into Parliament as leader of a party, the *Unión Nacional*. In education, too, he was willing to break new ground. Though the Catholics had been given the monopoly of *religious* education, the *non-religious*, too, were allowed their say. The outcome was the creation in 1876, the year of the new constitution, of the famous *Institución Libre de Enseñanza*, which went on to create a whole generation of anti-clerical leaders in Catholic Spain.

This very liberalism contained in itself the seeds of future civil strife. But there was more to it than that. Cánovas's rigged two-party system was doomed above all because of the invasion of Spain by foreign political ideas, which, for one reason or another, appealed to many Spaniards, and by the first surge of modern economic development which created the conditions in which these ideas were likely to flourish.

Among the ideas, the most potent were Anarchism and Marxism, in that order. If one studies a chronology of this period of Spanish and European history, one notices that 1868 was not only the year when Isabella II fell, but also the year when Fanelli, the personal emissary of that misguided revolutionary giant and father of violent anarchism, Bakunin, arrived in Apain. One sees also that 1872, when Don Carlos unwisely invaded Spain, was also the year when militant Marxism came to Spain with the Congress of the Regional Federation of the First Communist International at Cordoba; that two years later the International was declared illegal, only to be re-legalized in 1881; that the Spanish Socialist Party was founded in 1879 and trade unions were declared legal in 1881. These dates in the influx of ideas are at least as important as the doings of kings and parliaments.

Generous by nature, Gargantuan in size, and violent in political persuasion, Mikhail Bakunin brought to Spain a message that might have been specially designed for Spaniards of the dispossessed classes – destroy God and the State by violence. Atheism was essential, for religion assumed man to be evil, whereas he was good, good enough at least to run his own affairs without priests or politicians to tell him how to behave. Since the State stood in the way of man's liberty, it too must be destroyed – not by political action, since politics was itself an evil – but by violence. Once the State was destroyed, man could set about organizing his own affairs, in small groups, each of them manageable and viable.

Bakunin's doctrine, which he called Anarchism, appealed to funda-mental responses in the Spanish soul: its frugality and thirst for brotherhood, its distrust and resentment of authority, whether religious or secular, and its taste for violence as a protest against injustices and those responsible for them. Not least, it appealed to the Spaniard's love of his village or home town – the *patria chica* – and suspicion of central rule. For in this country of difficult communica-tions and striking differences of soil, climate and even language, regionalism – to the point of separatism – has always been a powerful force. Small wonder, then, that the Spanish Anarchists were among the most determined supporters of the Federal movement which proclaimed independent 'cantons' in southern Spain and Barcelona in 1873 during the short-lived First Republic.

Though the Anarchists were with the Federalists in wanting to break away from the centralized State, however, their social and political ideas were deeply at variance. The Anarchists were revolu-tionaries and wanted their still theoretical small groups to take over the fields and factories. In their eyes, the Federalists were just bourgeois politicians.

The Federal movement is nevertheless important in modern Spanish history. Like other self-respecting movements, it had its theoretician, a shy but upright little man called Pi y Margall. A Catalan (and therefore, almost by definition, a regionalist), a bank clerk and writer of sorts, he was deeply influenced, as Bakunin was, by the doctrines of the Frenchman, Proudhon. But whereas Bakunin had seized on Proudhon's anarchist socialism, Pi y Margall was more deeply attracted by his federative theories, as expressed in the Frenchman's *Du Principe Fédératif*, which Pi translated into Spanish. Ultimately, Pi's doctrines led, as Bakunin's did, to small group Anarchism. But whereas Bakunin's methods were revolutionary, Pi was a reformist. Much to Pi y Margall's surprise, a variegated crowd flocked to his federal banner until he found himself Prime Minister for a brief few weeks in the summer of 1873. Alas his federal theories were *too* contagious: it was at this point that Barcelona and the southern towns grew impatient with his gradualism, took the law into their own hands and proclaimed the cantons that brought about the collapse of the government, and with it, of the federal experiment.

Bakunin's followers shared Pi y Margall's opposition to centralism, and little more; with the Marxists they shared a brief common history and a belief in violence, but little else. Bakunin had joined Karl Marx's First International in 1869, but soon the Marxists and the Bakuninists were quarrelling over fundamentals. Marx wanted the workers to seize the power of the State for themselves; Bakunin wanted to destroy the State itself. The chasm was unbridgeable and Bakunin, expelled from Marx's International, founded an International of his own. By that time, his ideas, ably propagated by his personal emissary, the Italian Giuseppe Fanelli, in a torrential mixture of French and Italian, with much meridional mimicry and gesticulation, had gained many adherents in Spain. Bakunin's ideas, not Marx's, dominated the Spanish Regional Federation of the International that was set up at Barcelona in June 1870.

Shortly afterwards, the dissensions between Bakunin and Marx started coming into the open and the Spanish branch of the Federation split between Marxians, who were known as *Autoritarios*, and the Bakuninist *Anarquistas*. Alternatively, the Marxians called themselves 'communists' and the Bakuninists, 'collectivists'. Alarmed, Marx sent his son-in-law, Paul Lafargue (who had been educated in Cuba and spoke fluent Spanish), to Spain in December 1871 to organize his followers and fight Bakunin's. Lafargue was successful, but Anarchism persisted, and the Marx-Bakunin split spread throughout the Spanish intellectual Left and organized labour. Typically, it was in Madrid, where the *Autoritarios* were strong, that Marxian socialism took root, whereas Anarchism's strongholds were industrial Barcelona and the rural South. It was in Madrid that the *Autoritarios* founded the *Partido Democrático Socialista Obrero*, in May 1879; and though the Socialists went to Barcelona in 1888 to found their labour federation, the *Unión General de Trabajadores* (UGT), they soon had to move to Madrid because Anarchism was too strong in Catalan Barcelona. (It was not until 1910, however, that the great rival anarcho-syndicalists organization, the *Confederación Nacional del Trabajo*, or CNT, was founded.)

As in other countries, organized labour grew against a background of initially aggressive capitalism. Barcelona was becoming the Manchester of Spain, and on a similar foundation of cheap textiles and sweated labour. Heavy industries were springing up in the Basque areas and the growing financial power of the Bilbao banks stretched tentacles into Spain's authoritarian centre. Between Catalonia's self-made businessmen and the anarchist workers – their ranks swollen by waves of Andalusian migrants steeped in Messianic agrarian anarchism – it was war. The strike was a protest, its industrial purpose of little or no relevance, for the ultimate object of striking was to provoke the collapse of the existing order.

Dynamic industrialization, especially in Catalonia, not only brought violence but turned the creeping problem of regionalism into a festering sore. Culturally, as well as commercially and industrially, Barcelona felt itself to be the natural capital of Spain, for its great economic expansion coincided with an intense Catalan linguistic and literary renaissance. Resentment of Madrid's authority was further heightened by the central capital's *laissez-faire* policies reintroduced by Serrano's Liberals after they had overthrown Isabella II. Earlier – in 1842 – Espartero had bombarded Barcelona when the Catalan industrialists protested against his free trade policy. What the industrialists wanted was protection. Since Madrid insisted on opening the floodgates to foreign imports, the only remedy, it

1a Franco as a cadet at the Military Academy in Toledo (1907). With him *(seated)* is his brother Nicolás in Naval cadet's uniform.

1b Franco graduates as a second lieutenant (1910).

2*a* Major Franco in a forward position in Morocco (1922).

2*b* Major Franco with the former Rif rebel El Mizzian, whose son fought on the Nationalist side during the Spanish Civil War.

seemed to them, was to break with Madrid and claim autonomy for Catalonia.

While the Spanish State was thus being rent asunder, the rifts within the Spanish nation were growing deeper. The clash between the new proletariat and the new capitalists was only one aspect of Spain's social problem. Another was to be found in the countryside, where *caciquismo* was a synonym for brutality and injustice. The *caciques* controlled the villages, sometimes by the dozen, and at election times, the peasant who didn't vote the way the *cacique* told him would be beaten up. Nor was there any remedy in the courts, where patronage and the bribery or intimidation of witnesses made a mockery of justice.

Though Cánovas's *turnismo* gave Spain relative stability and peace, its success rested both on *caciquismo* and on universal corruption and tax evasion in high places. Cánovas himself, says Brenan, gave out more than twelve hundred titles and orders in five years, while his Home Minister, Romero Robledo, granted himself 282,000 pesetas for irrigating his own estates.[3] Since the dispossessed as well as the idle rich believed in violence as a solution to injustice or dissidence, the inherent causes of a civil war were always present. Moreover, since *turnismo* itself depended on *caciquismo*, no attempt was made to tackle landlordism and the allied problem, the great estates or *latifundios*. And the Church was identified, in the minds of the landless peasants and propertyless workers, with entrenched privilege and the repression of the poor.

It was not the least of Cánovas's achievements, on the other hand, to have neutralized the Army as a political factor. By building up the king as a focus of loyalty, he discouraged incipient makers of *pronunciamientos*; and by posting potentially dangerous officers to Cuba and other garrison duties abroad, he made assurance doubly sure. Alfonso XII, however, though willing to make *turnismo* work, was to let Cánovas down in other ways. Between his two marriages and during the second, to the Archduchess María-Cristina of Hapsburg-Lorraine, he led a life of indiscreet dissipation which, in the end, ruined his health and brought fresh discredit upon the Court. His son, who was to be Alfonso XIII, was born in May 1886, after his death, and the alternation of Conservatives and Liberals continued during María-Cristina's Regency (1885–1902).

In external affairs, the Regency rounded off a long period of

c

decline. Between 1816 and 1825, Spain had lost most of her New World colonies, and though she eventually won the Ten Years' War with Cuba (1868–78) her imperial sun was setting fast. With the sole exception of Africa, the Spanish Empire passed into history with the disastrous Spanish–American War of 1898.

Spain had virtually ceased to play a part in European power politics. The Madrid conference of 1880, however, gave Spain a voice – with France as the dominant partner – in 'protecting' Morocco. But this was to be a muted voice, for seven years later, by adhering to the Anglo–Italian Mediterranean Agreement, the Spaniards accepted limitations on their freedom to do what they liked in North Africa. It was a far cry from Philip II.

Internally, meanwhile, the peace of the Restoration was drawing to an end. In 1891, a band of Andalusian peasants marched into Jerez wielding sticks and scythes and shouting 'Death to the bourgeoisie'. And in 1892 the Anarchists of Barcelona embarked on a prolonged orgy of bomb throwing.

This was the year of Franco's birth.

PART II

War

1 *Early Days*

Galicia looks out to sea and a spine of mountains cuts it off from the Spanish hinterland. To other Spaniards, 'overseas' means Africa; to the Galician, or *Gallego*, it stands for America. Geography and a rainy climate have given the Galicians a temperament as far removed as may be from the energetic volubility of the Asturian or the grave austerity of the Castilian. The Galician is canny and suspicious, and shuns impulsive decisions. If he dreams of a uniform, it is a sailor's. By birth and in all these respects, Francisco Franco is a Galician.

He is, perhaps, quintessentially Galician in that he was born in the peaceful deep-water harbour of El Ferrol, now renamed in his honour El Ferrol del Caudillo, whose ocean-gazing impulse is heightened by inaccessibility on the landward side. On both sides of the family, Franco's grandfathers were naval administrators. His father, Nicolás Franco y Salgado Araújo, was a naval paymaster who twice went to the Philippines in a warship, sailing from El Ferrol. He married Pilar Baamonde* y Pardo in 1890, and she bore him five children: Nicolás, Francisco, Pilar, Ramón and Paz.

According to the military parish register of San Francisco, in El Ferrol,[1] Francisco Franco y Baamonde Salgado Pardo was born at 12.30 on the night of 3 to 4 December 1892, and was baptized on 17 December, with the names of Francisco, Paulino, Hermenegildo and Teódulo. His first schooling was at the College of the Sacred Heart, in El Ferrol, and inevitably – in a family of such antecedents – he went on to the Naval College, where he passed his *Bachillerato*, or Matriculation, in preparation for entry into the Naval Academy. As

---

* Both 'Franco' and 'Baamonde' (usually spelt 'Bahamonde') are said to be Jewish names.

luck had it, however, he never made the Academy, for the entrance
examinations to this institution were suspended before he could sit
for them, for reasons of economy during a period of financial
stringency for the Spanish State. His elder brother Nicolás had already
been admitted to the Academy and went on to have a naval career.
As for Francisco, he sat instead for the entrance examinations of the
Infantry Academy in Toledo, which he entered on 29 August 1907.
His military career – and doubtless his political one as well – was
therefore due to the accident of an administrative decision.

The Navy had ceased, in any case, to offer the alluring opportunities that had once stirred the youth of El Ferrol. Indeed the Navy of
imperial days had been virtually destroyed by the American fleet in
the Spanish–American War. In the naval *milieu* of the Franco's, this
traumatic experience must have dominated the table talk and the
playground chatter alike between Francisco's fifth and sixth birth-
days. *El desastre*, it was called, without the need for further clarification, and it marked a whole galaxy of writers, collectively known as
'the generation of '98' – men like Miguel de Unamuno, Azorín,
Ortega y Gasset and Pío Baroja – whose novels or speculations were
less concerned with the causes of a military defeat than with the
rottenness of the Spanish State and the state of the Spanish soul.
These liberal and intellectual voices of protest, much though they
added to the literary glories of Spain, could have aroused little
interest or approval in the little naval world of El Ferrol, concerned
with the ignominy of Spain's imperial sunset and the black but
splendid fate of Spanish courage.

For had not the gallant Admiral Cervera called out the antiquated
vessels of his Atlantic Fleet to give battle to the modern American
battleships off Cuba, knowing that this was a fight against hopeless
odds? Already in the Far East, Admiral Montojo's pitiful force, including the old wooden *Castilla* which had to be towed into battle,
had been utterly destroyed off Manila in April by Commodore
Dewey's Pacific Squadron. Now in July, Rear-Admiral Sampson's
fighting vessels annihilated Cervera's Atlantic Fleet and the Spanish
admiral was taken prisoner. Spain was broken. On 10 December
1898, just after Francisco Franco's sixth birthday, the Spaniards
signed the Treaty of Paris, withdrawing from Cuba and ceding
Puerto Rico, Guam and the Philippines to the United States. Nor
was the $20 million paid over by the Americans for the 'sovereignty'

of the Philippines an adequate measure of the affront to Spanish pride.

But the repercussions were material and international as well as psychological and regional. The Catalan industrialists had extensive interests in Cuba and benefited from the wall of tariffs erected around the island against other countries' trade. When Cubans of Spanish blood, including the Cuban deputies in Madrid, started agitating, first for administrative reforms, then for autonomy, the Catalans were the first to oppose them. But when Cuba won not merely autonomy but independence, the Catalans blamed its loss on the intransigence of the central government. Autonomy for Cuba had been unthinkable in their eyes when a similar status was being denied to Catalonia. But now that Cuba and the other colonies were independent, why shouldn't Catalonia, too, get its independence? Thus the *desastre* accentuated Spain's worst regional cleavage.

Indeed, it brought lasting international consequences as well. To some extent, it even had a bearing on the ostracism from which Franco Spain suffered forty years later, and in turn on Franco's defiance of democratic and liberal opinion. For Spain's Cuban policy offended both the anti-colonial sentiments and the nascent power of the United States as expressed in the fundamentally anti-Spanish Monroe Doctrine of 1823. Its execution, moreover, outraged the liberal emotions of the American public. To these causes of anti-Spanish feeling should be added the material one of appetite for the Cuban market and the jingoistic one of indignation over the *Verginius* incident.

The *Verginius* was a United States vessel which the Spaniards seized during the Ten Years War, shooting the fifty-seven Cuban rebels on board. A major Spanish–American crisis was narrowly averted when Castelar's Republican government handed back the *Verginius* and paid compensation. But all the pent-up anti-Spanish feelings of the Americans came bubbling up again when the Cubans rose a second time in 1895, reaching a crescendo when the ruthless General Weyler started repressing the islanders with cruel severity. By this time, public opinion in the United States was thoroughly aroused and a section of the American press was openly advocating intervention. In the meantime, the United States granted belligerent status to the Cuban rebels and began to supply them with arms.

Realizing the danger, Cánovas, who was in power, hurriedly

prepared legislation granting further autonomy to Cuba, but he was assassinated by an Italian fanatic on 9 August 1897, before his bill could be approved by the Cortes. His successor, Sagasta, recalled General Weyler, revived and improved on Cánovas's autonomous concessions and offered special trade terms for the United States in Cuba. But it was too late. Public opinion in America was looking out for a *casus belli*, and found it on 15 February 1898, when the US cruiser *Maine* exploded in Havana harbour, in mysterious circumstances and with great loss of American lives. Accident or sabotage? Whatever the cause of the explosion, Spain's disclaimers and appeals to the Pope fell on deaf ears, and President McKinley called for the evacuation of Cuba by the Spanish forces. The war was on.

The point to note, however, is that in American eyes, this was a righteous war against Spanish colonialism and militarism, whereas in Spanish eyes it was an act of naked aggression by an upstart federal Republic against Spain's traditional monarchy. On both sides, memories of 1898 added bitterness to the emotional clash of the 1930s and 1940s between 'fascist' Spain and American democracy. Nor was it surprising that Americans saw in General Franco a spiritual descendant of the 'infamous' General Weyler.

In Spain itself, the disaster affected different groups and classes in different ways. The liberal intellectuals of 'the generation of '98' were driven to meditate upon and expose the rottenness of the ruling classes; whereas the traditionalists, including the Army, blamed the defeat on the rottenness of the liberal politicians. The Anarchist workers joined the urban intellectuals in an upsurge of revulsion against militarism: 200,000 ordinary Spaniards, like themselves, had died of wounds or yellow fever and other tropical diseases in a cause that had ended in humiliation. They clamoured to know why. The officers, on the other hand, as the hard core of the Army, bitterly resented the attacks to which they were now subjected. Overstaffed and underpaid, ill-equipped and jealous of the politicians' right to the spoils of office which at one time were theirs for the picking, the officers regained their taste for politicking, if not, in the immediate period ahead, for the old-fashioned *pronunciamiento*.

Franco grew up in an atmosphere that naturally favoured the military view of the disaster of 1898 and supported the political proneness of the Army and its diagnosis of the country's ills. Even while he was attending the College of the Sacred Heart and the Naval

College at El Ferrol, the Army's resentments were reaching an explosive crisis over events in another port, the seething, bustling capital of Catalanism: Barcelona. The bomb outrages that had punctuated Francisco's birth had gone on. Unfortunately, General Weyler had now been made Captain-General of Catalonia, and his natural taste for bleak repression went with the intransigently centralist attitude of the predominantly Andalusian and Castilian officer corps. As the Anarchists went on throwing or laying bombs, Weyler ordered mass arrests of Anarchists and other anti-clericals, executing some and causing others to be tortured in the frightful Montjuich dungeons. The assassination of Cánovas was an Anarchist protest against repression and injustices.

The disaster of 1898 put a temporary end to all this violence, but in January 1902 it broke out again in Barcelona, where it took the form of widespread riots, culminating in a general strike in February. Weyler was still captain-general, and he resumed his tortures and executions. By this time, under the trans-Pyrenean influences of the Frenchman, Georges Sorel, Anarchism was transforming itself into Anarcho-Syndicalism, that is, trade-unionism on Anarchist lines, to the total exclusion of the bourgeois who had flirted with Anarchism for libertarian ends. Weyler's repression did not kill Anarchism, or Catalan separatism, it merely strengthened the Catalan Anarchists' bitterness and resentment of centralist, and indeed all, authority.

In 1909, two years after Franco had entered the Infantry Academy at Toledo, the Rif tribesmen of Morocco attacked Spanish railway workers, and the War Minister, General Arsenio Linares, proposed to call up the reserves and raise an expeditionary corps. Immediately, the workers of Barcelona came out in a general strike, and in the ensuing wave of protests against conscription, the rioters once again turned their passion against the clergy, setting fire to churches and convents here and there throughout Catalonia. Once again the fortress of Montjuich was crowded with the tortured bodies of innocent and guilty alike.

These then were the military talking points of Franco's infancy and youth, a period to which his official biographers have paid perhaps less attention than it merits, presumably because in some respects it falls short of the hero myth. It seems to have been a rather unhappy childhood. His father, who has become virtually an 'unperson' in official eyes, was a gay companion, a bibulous amorist with little taste for family life. He left home and Franco's mother, a 'widow' during her husband's lifetime, was much given to hours of solitary weeping. (She died at sixty-eight in 1934, while on her way to Rome on a Catholic pilgrimage. Her husband, licentious to the end, died in Madrid in 1942; he was eighty-eight and had been made a General of Marines on his retirement.[2]) Since Franco's conscious childhood was spent under his mother's care and within earshot of whispered admonitions about his absent father, it is likely that these were the roots of his later puritanism.

The sourest of Franco's biographers, Luis Ramírez, makes much of this explanation, and though he piles it on for denigratory purposes, there is probably something in it. Certainly the approved biographers give one nothing to go on; glossing over potential areas of unpleasantness to the extent of cutting out all references to the Franco ménage, leaving only the customary words of praise for the beauty and piety of the mother.

It is fair to suppose that Paquito – as he was called in affection – built up a smouldering resentment against his father and that his mother's deepening piety surrounded her with a frigid shell of reserve, so that Francisco – and the other three – were driven inward on their own resources. To the outward world, however, Franco's mother gave nothing away, and her pride and dignity were also among the formative influences in his character. At all events, he revered his mother as much as he was determined not to resemble his father, and – since he was destined for a naval career – to become the real sailor his father had failed to be.

In Paquito's case, this must have been a more traumatic experience than with his sister or brothers. By nature, he was excruciatingly shy. The eldest, Nicolás, in contrast, not only was named after his father, but took after him as well. A cheerful extrovert, easily satisfied with his own performance, content with borrowed ideas and standards, he seemed less affected by the oppressive atmosphere of the fatherless household than Paquito. As for Ramón, the daring aviator of later years and the first to fly across the south Atlantic, he too was an extrovert, but of a very different kind: imaginative, intelligent, a talker of natural brilliance, and not without an understandable vanity, he lived so intensely for the thrill of the moment that he too was less affected than Francisco by the gap in their lives.

A family picture of Francisco and Nicolás, both in naval cadets' uniform, illuminates the contrast in their characters. Nicolás is seated plump-cheeked, not at all dissatisfied with his own image. Francisco stands behind him, thinner, more inward-looking, more diffident, his huge opaque eyes filled with unsolved questions. Ramírez writes of his fits of melancholy or excessive seriousness, withdrawn, deeply conscious of a supposed inferiority, yet liable, if challenged, to display an almost aggressive obstinacy. Francisco and Ramón, being nearest in age, often scuffled together, and Ramón, though much the more pugnacious, was not always the winner, for the wily Paquito kept his temper better and made up in stratagems for what he lacked in aggressivity.

Pazita, the last-born, had died first – she was only five – and her elder sister, Pilar, shared as an equal in the masculine games of her three brothers.[3]

One evening, when Paquito was about seven, Pilar placed a red-hot needle on her brother's wrist. As the skin sizzled, she realized the enormity of her deed and burst into tears. Gritting his teeth, Paquito remained impassive, then said: 'How rude! You know how burnt skin smells.'[4] This precocious display of stoicism, though retailed by two of Franco's most sedulous myth-makers, may well have been true. At least, it is in character.

Shy and lonely though he was, Francisco seems to have had his share of the pranks and physical exertions of boyhood, playing bush *futbol*, purloining the gangplanks of the ferries for games of 'pirates', and falling with regrettable frequency into the cold waters of the harbour. But most of all, perhaps, he preferred the patient hours spent fishing with home-made rods.

His voice was a torment to him, especially when it was breaking. High, sweet and unmasculine, liable at puberty to reach a piccolo falsetto without warning, it became an object of ridicule and mimicry during his last months at the College of the Sacred Heart. And this, too, drove him inwards.

Another source of torment was his diminutive size and deceptively fragile build. At fifteen, tiny and baby-faced, he entered the Infantry Academy at Toledo, and one of the instructors, muttering something about giving the lad a weapon appropriate to his size, handed him a short-barrelled musketoon instead of the heavy regulation rifle. On his dignity, the young Franco drew himself up to his full height and said: 'Whatever the strongest man in my section can do, so can I.'[5]

This did not, however, save him from the taunts and ragging that are the lot, it seems, of the newcomer in military institutions. It was not, on the other hand, in Franco's nature to take these in his stride. Twice running, an older boy hid Francisco's books under a bed and had him reprimanded for not finding them. The second time, Franco grabbed a heavy candelabra and hurled it at his tormentor. In a flash, all was pandemonium. Someone put the lights out and books, pillows and fists started flying. Denounced as the culprit in the ruins of the dormitory, Franco was summoned before the College authorities. His explanation was typical of the man he became. 'Dignity,' he said, approximately in these words, 'cannot tolerate a joke like this, repeated once too often.' His punishment, however, was light. Other cadets confirmed his story. Moreover, Franco, furious though he was, refused to denounce the boy who had provoked him. This was held in his favour. So, too, was the fact that a future officer had taken steps to gain the respect of his brother officers.

It was a hard, clear life, full of the simple certainties of discipline, obedience and duty. With Franco, on that twenty-ninth day of August 1907 when he entered the Infantry Academy of Toledo, were 381 other new boys, including Juan Yagüe Blanco and others who later won fame in battle. As they stood to attention, responding to the clarion, they heard the Commandant, García Toledo, erect beside the unfurled flag of Spain, call out the words: 'Do you pledge your oath to God and promise yourself to the king?'

And Franco, with the others in unison, replied: 'We do.'

Soon they would learn the Academy's own anthem, singing out the words:

'You still have left your faithful infantry.
Which knows how to vanquish for it knows how to die.'

This was the school of one kind of Spain: traditionalist, Catholic and monarchist. A generation of Nationalist officers passed through its training grounds, toughening its collective body with drill and sharpening its mind with the study of the theory, art and history of war. Memories of France's crushing defeat at Sedan were still lively in the minds of the instructors and the model they held up for the cadets to admire, imitate, and if possible emulate, was Bismarck's victorious Prussian Army. Their own Army, they were taught, was the backbone of the nation, and its function and duty were to defend the monarchy and society itself against subversion.

This, then, was one kind of Spain, the Spain of duty and readiness to die for King and fatherland, defending the Cross against heretics. And at that precise moment in Spanish history the other Spain – the Spain of humanism, liberalism and tolerance – was forming its own generation of Spaniards, later to constitute the helpless moderates of the Second Republic and to be swamped by the left-wing extremists during the Civil War. For it was in 1907, the year Franco entered the Infantry Academy, that Castillejo, a disciple of the greatest Spanish humanist and educator of the nineteenth century, Don Francisco Giner, created the curiously named *Junta para Ampliación de Estudios*. A natural offshoot of Giner's famous *Institución Libre de Enseñanza*, 'the true nursery of contemporary Spain',[6] the *Junta* became a kind of non-confessional forcing ground for the natural genius of the intellectually gifted.

This, too, was Spain, but it was not the Spain Franco grew to know as his fatherland, to be defended unto death. While the ebullient Castillejo was fostering the spirit of free inquiry, the young Franco was studying the early battles of the protracted Moroccan war, and mastering the theory of military topography, soon displaying an expertise which impressed his instructors. And Morocco indeed was the inevitable next stage in his military life.

2 *Moroccan Days*

For the young Franco, Morocco was the road to glory and lightning promotion. He spent the best part of fifteen years there – between 1912 and 1927 – starting as a second liteutenant and ending as a general. And he was still only thirty-four when he returned to Spain for good.

Morocco had become a running sore on Spain's underbelly. Neither politically nor economically was there anything in the situation to fire the imagination. True, the prospect of pacifying Spain's former conquerors kindled a spark in Spanish breasts, but the poor and barren land was a prize which Britain's mercantile imperialism might have disdained. Besides, war as such was unpopular since the great disaster of 1898, and the Moroccan war was to be fought throughout with a paucity of means and a grudging political support that caused the Spanish efforts always to fall short of full success. Indeed its climax was another disaster – the defeat of General Silvestre's force at Anual on 21 July 1921, with the loss of 15,000 men. For the Spanish Army, however, at least in the early stages, Morocco offered a challenge and an opportunity to redeem the reputation of Spanish arms. Later, the interminable campaign took its toll of morale, and bitterness mingled with the undoubted heroism of the Spanish fighting men.

In the heyday of Western imperialism, before the First World War, it was normal for territories to be carved up between the powers that coveted them. This was to be the fate of the ancient but decaying Cherifian Kingdom. The French were pushing into Morocco from the East, but were content to leave a part of Western Morocco to the Spaniards; and the British, who had no wish to see the French installed south of Gibraltar, approved. Spain already had five garrison towns in Morocco, and the French agreed in 1904 that the Northern Mediterranean belt should be reserved to Spain as a zone of influence. The Spaniards, however, were in no hurry to move into 'their' part of Morocco until 1911, when the French occupied Fez and, psychologically at least, forced their hand. On 27 November 1912, a Franco–Spanish agreement defined the position of the Spanish zone in relation to the Protectorate which General Lyautey had established for France. By this time, albeit half-heartedly, Spain was in the Moroccan death-trap, under the hypocritical pretext of bringing the rebel tribes under the authority of the Sultan.

This was easier said than done. The defiant Kabyles of the Atlas and Rif mountains had always reserved the right to disobey their traditional ruler. Now they saw no reason for obeying the pacifying infidel. Climate and topography were their natural allies. It was a violent climate, changing from heat to cold with dramatic suddenness, especially in the northern zone, which was Spain's. Winter brought furious snowstorms, and summer, stupefying heat. When day changed to night, the thermometer would plummet twenty or thirty degrees. The men would emerge frozen from their tents, ears and throats wrapped tight against the penetrating cold, only to tear off scarves and sweaters when the first heat of the sun attacked them.

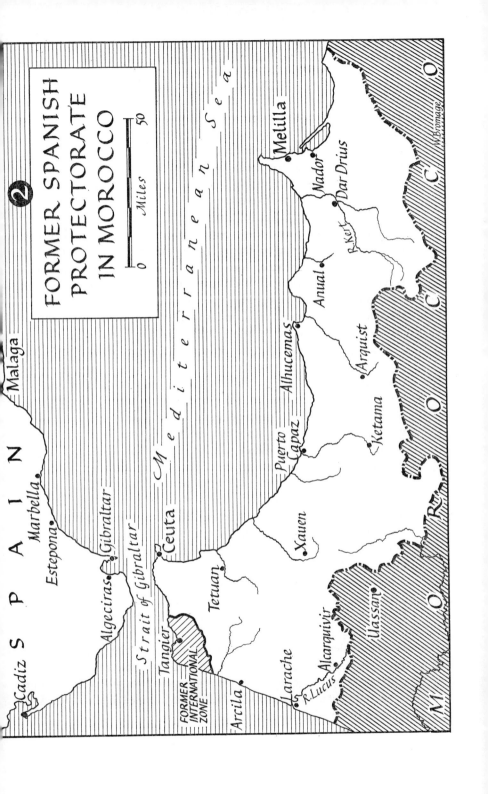

FORMER SPANISH
PROTECTORATE
IN MOROCCO

Miles

0   50

Cadiz

S   P   A   I   N

Malaga

Marbella

Estepona

Algeciras

Gibraltar

Strait of Gibraltar

Tangier

Ceuta

Tetuan

FORMER
INTERNATIONAL
ZONE

Arcila

Larache

R.Lucus

Alcarquivir

Uassan

Xauen

Mediterranean Sea

Puerto
Capaz

Alhucemas

Ketama

Melilla

Nador

Dar Drius

R.Kert

Anual

Arquist

M   O   R   O   C   C   O

R.

M.Bromage

To the man's-eye-view of the fighting soldier, the terrain was a chaos of ill-defined mountains, running in all directions and forbiddingly sheer. There was stony desert on the plain, yielding – especially in Gomara, Senahaya and Ketama – to forests, with soaring, majestic cedars at Yguermalen, 6,000 feet above sea level.[1] And the fighting went on at all levels, for the Berber tribesmen swooped down on the Spaniards from their mountain fortresses, and the pursuing Spaniards had to climb to give them chase.

Second Lieutenant Franco arrived in Morocco on 24 February 1912, after a grey and boring period of garrison duty in his native town. He had graduated from Toledo on 13 July 1910, but had evidently been considered too young, at seventeen, for immediate service overseas. Then his luck changed. His former chief, Colonel José Villalba Riquelme, who had been Director of the Toledo Academy, was appointed Commander of the 68th Regiment of Africa. Franco asked to serve under him and Riquelme assented.

Melilla, one of the Spanish *presidios* on the Moroccan coast – like Ceuta a Spanish city for centuries – was at that time a dirty, unkempt place on the margin of civilization. The prospect of war and the presence of soldiers had attracted a ragged swarm of peddlers and shoeblacks anxious to provide some of the goods and services of which the poverty-stricken shops were bereft. This was Franco's first sight of Africa, but he didn't stay long in Melilla. General Dámaso Berenguer, who was later to relieve the failing dictator, Primo de Rivera, of the Premiership, was organizing a 'Native Police' (*Policía Indígena*) in which Moorish recruits were to serve under Spanish officers. In time, this force, renamed *Regulares Indígenas*, was to become a shock assault corps of the Spanish Army in Morocco. Berenguer called for volunteers to lead it, and Franco was one of the first to put his name down.

Strategically, the Spanish position was precarious. Apart from Ceuta and Melilla, the Spaniards occupied Larache and Ksar-el-Kebir on the Atlantic, but the hinterland escaped their control. A towering figure, bearded and majestic in his flowing white robe, El Mizzian, ruled the Kert valley. His orders kept the Moors on the move, harassing Spaniards who ventured far from their bases. And with him went a legend of invulnerability, the aura of a chief immune to mortal hurts. 'Only a golden bullet can kill me!' he boasted. And his men believed and died for him.[2]

For the Spaniards, even more than for the Moors, it was a cruel little war. The Moors, on home ground, harassed the Spanish units, much as the Spanish *guerrilleros* had harassed the French during the Napoleonic invasion. Forced marches under the beating sun exhausted the foreigners, who lacked everything and were in hostile territory. Everything, in fact – water and food, wood and forage for the animals – had to be carried by pack mule.

Berenguer had spent months in Algeria, studying the organization of indigenous forces under French command. When he came to set up his own *Regulares*, Algerians were in the majority. The cavalry was under the command of Major Miguel Cabanellas, and Francisco Franco served in one of his companies. There was little confidence in the loyalty of the *Regulares* among the officers, who mounted a special Spanish guard at night to prevent a treacherous attack from within.

They needn't have worried, for when the time came the *Regulares* fought courageously. On 14 May 1912, the order came to attack the village of Haddu-Allal-u-Kaddur. As the *Regulares* advanced against tenacious firing, General Berenguer, who was watching their progress from a height through his field binoculars, turned to a subordinate and exclaimed: 'That section on the right seems to be making pretty good going!'

'That's Franquito's,' came the reply.

It was Franco's baptism of fire.

As the company reached the confines of the village, the Moors broke out to meet it and give battle, led by El Mizzian himself, erect on his nervous Arab horse. A Spanish corporal named Gonzálo Sauco took careful aim. When he fired, El Mizzian fell to the ground. The golden bullet had found its target. As though paralysed, the disbelieving Moors froze, then fled in dismay and panic.

Thereafter, the Spaniards and their *Regulares* advanced without meeting resistance, until they occupied forty square miles of territory. In July, Franco was promoted first lieutenant – the only promotion he owed to mere seniority. And his first Red Cross of Military Merit came his way.

The Melilla region being pacified, it was the turn of Ceuta in the West to give trouble. On 13 February 1913, General Alfau set out from Ceuta to Tetuan with a column of 2,500 men. Wherever they stopped, they met with friendliness and hospitality. Tetuan itself seemed an oasis of peace and luxury after the sordid coastal town they had left. It offered the glamour of its medina, a maze of narrow streets displaying damask cloths and bright-hued tissues and heavy with the scents of musk and sandalwood. It brought back, too, gratifying memories of earlier feats of arms, such as General O'Donnell's spectacular capture of the city in 1860.

But the peace and gratification were illusory and ephemeral. Soon the Moors were teasing the Spaniards from all sides, kidnapping and murdering any who ventured forth until, in desperation, General Alfau had the city encircled by parapets.

By June 1914, the situation had so deteriorated that an urgent call for reinforcements went out to Melilla. As the *Regulares* covered the hundred miles from Melilla to Ceuta, on foot, two of them dropped dead of sunstroke. Sleeping at Ceuta, the *Regulares* rose next morning to enter the fray, for by this time the Riffians had invested the road from Ceuta to Tetuan, rallying to the call of El Raisuni, lord of Beni Aros, who had proclaimed the Holy War and personally led his Kabyles in action.

In September, Lieutenant Franco commanded his men in the battle of Izarduy and captured heights that were fiercely defended by the Kabyles. It was his performance in this hard fought action that made General Berenguer decide that in Franco, Spain had the makings of a great military leader. One of his colleagues, Artillery Lieutenant Jorge Vigón, later described a typical evening spent under canvas. Captain Mola was there, and Yagüe. There was 'also a Lieutenant from El Ferrol, dark, always calm, never noisy, active and cordial, and who was being proposed for promotion to captain. His name was Francisco Franco.'[3] As they talked, they groused over their inadequate equipment, discussed the attacks the politicians and revolutionaries were making against the Army, the king's readiness to defend it, and the simple pleasures of leave, not least the chance to eat a decent meal and sleep between clean sheets.[4] This little group of officers stayed together and later became Franco's loyal companions and subordinates during the Civil War. The legend of his military prowess, already germinating in 1914, was indeed one of the great contributory factors in the absolute political power he came to wield in later years.

The war went on, confused to the point of incoherence, with El Raisuni sometimes in dissidence, sometimes collaborating with the

Spaniards against local rivals. On 15 January 1915, after the capture of Beni Hosmar, Franco was mentioned in a dispatch. Shortly afterwards, at the unprecedented age of twenty-two, he was promoted Captain. By rights, he should now have left the *Regulares* to serve in another regiment, but he dreaded the prospect of a transfer to garrison life in some sleepy town in Spain and fought against it with such effect that he was allowed to stay with his *Regulares*.

On 25 May, he was transferred to the Third Tabor Regiment as paymaster; but his bureaucratic duties did not disqualify him from combat. Soon after, he was awarded his third cross of Military Merit (the second had come a year earlier). He, too, like El Mizzian, was beginning to acquire a reputation for invulnerability. Early in 1916, after four years of ceaseless fighting, only seven of the forty-two officers in the *Regulares* of Melilla remained unwounded and Franco was one of them. His Moors, and doubtless the enemy Kabyles, talked in hushed tones of the 'baraka' that protected him against ill luck.

Then, on 28 June, Franco was seriously wounded while leading the assault against well-defended heights in the battle of Biutz. One of his men fell wounded and dropped his rifle. Franco stooped to pick it up and load it when an enemy bullet pierced his abdomen.

He was carried on a stretcher to the camp of Kudea-Federico where the doctors declared that he was in no state to be removed to the military hospital at Ceuta. What they feared was a perforation of the bowel, but as they discovered later, the bullet had avoided vital organs. His parents, hastily summoned to the military encampment, didn't know this and were relieved to find him still alive. Despite the risk of infection at the height of the Moroccan summer, he soon recovered and was sent to Spain to convalesce.

The communiqué of the battle of Biutz had this to say about Franco's part in it:

> Captain of Regulares Don Francisco Franco Bahamonde distinguished himself greatly by his unsurpassable valour, his gifts of leadership and the energy he displayed in a hard combat during which he was gravely wounded.*

* *Centinela*, p. 30. The word 'unsurpassable' (*insuperable* in the original) comes out incorrectly as *innegable* ('undeniable') in Montojo's Spanish translation of Martin's book (p. 31), presumably because of its resemblance to the French word *inégalable*, Martin's correct translation of *insuperable*.
(See Martin, French edition, p. 25.)

His first reward was the Cross of María Cristina and the Medal of 'Sufferings for the Fatherland'. For obscure reasons, which Galinsoga tentatively attributes to the heavy casualties in the unit under Franco's command, the exclusive Cross of San Fernando with Laurels, for which he had also been recommended, was refused him. But Franco was less interested in decorations than in promotion. His own reckoning was that, for experience and proved capacity for leadership, if not by seniority, he ought to be made a major. The High Command in Morocco, while recognizing his merits, hesitated to recommend a further promotion on account of his youth. To force the issue, Franco addressed a personal petition to King Alfonso XIII, accompanied by a detailed *curriculum vitae* that deeply impressed the king.* Belatedly, the High Commissioner, General Gómez Jordana, decided that even at twenty-three, Franco would carry the right measure of authority as a major, and endorsed his petition. So Franco, who was beginning to emerge as an ambitious officer as well as an able one, became the youngest major in the Spanish Army,† with retrospective effect from 29 June, the date of his battle wound.

A further period of intense fighting followed after Franco had recovered from his wound. Then, on 4 March 1917, he was transferred to the Prince's Regiment, at that time on garrison duty in Oviedo, capital of Asturias. His first stay in Morocco had lasted five years.

3 *Garrison Duty*

Franco took up his duties in Oviedo on 31 May 1917. It was a time of quietude, of nascent love and study. His reputation for precocious valour and competence had preceded him, and the *comandantín*, or 'little major', as he was called, soon became a local celebrity. Every

---

* See Appendix.

† Coles, on p. 117 of his biography, attributes Franco's preference to promotion over decorations to his desire to win the hand of his future bride, explaining that Franco was only a second lieutenant when he met her. In fact, however, he was already a major when they first met, so his petition to the king must be attributed to ambition, not love.

afternoon he left the hotel where he was lodged for a ride on horse-back, and a little crowd of admirers used to gather to see him off.

One admirer who was not to be found in the crowd of locals was a schoolgirl of fifteen, tall and gravely beautiful, with dark eyes and a pale face framed by cascading black tresses, and already with that touch of distinction and imperiousness that later befitted a First Lady. She was Señorita Carmen Polo y Martínez Valdés and Franco fell in love with her, immediately and irretrievably.

From the first, he faced a problem of communication: how to break through the barriers of Spanish social convention and convey his sentiments? During the next few months, he was to use a variety of ingenious devices. His favourite one was to dine at the restaurant which Carmen and her parents frequented and slip a letter into the pocket of her overcoat as it hung from its hook. After a modest in-terval, she began to reciprocate, and communication was established.[1]

The *comandantín* took to waiting for Señorita Carmen at the school gates and walking at least part of the way home with her. One day, screwing up a courage more at home on the battlefield than in the boudoir, he brought himself to ask her father for her hand. The request was greeted with a minimum of enthusiasm: she was too young and he wasn't old enough! Moreover, he was a soldier, risking his life daily – well, not just now in Oviedo, but liable to fight again and threaten any bride with early widowhood . . .

There was, indeed, more to it than this. Carmen came of a learned, aristocratic family, liberal and anti-military by disposition. Her father, Don Felipe Polo Flores, was a cultivated as well as a wealthy man, the son of Don Claudio Polo y Astudillo, a Professor of Literature and the author of works addressed to a rarefied minority. Her mother's family, Martínez Valdés, belonged to the ancient nobility of the Principality of Asturias. Don Felipe was an *abandonista* who saw little point in wasting lives and money in defence of Morocco. So that in addition to his youth and modesty of means, Francisco Franco suffered the defect, in Polo's eyes, of symbolizing a caste he disliked and a policy he reproved.[2]

Franco and Carmen settled down to a war of attrition on the parental front.

There was plenty for Franco to do while he waited. Nostalgic though he was for the hot, hostile sands of North Africa and its distant horizons, his African fighting days seemed to be over. The dazzling speed of the promotions that had come his way was brought home to him when, on arriving in Oviedo, he rediscovered two of the men who had been his contemporaries at El Ferrol and had travelled with him to Morocco. Now the two – his cousin Francisco Franco Salgado and Camilo Alonso Vega – were still junior officers and he had left them far behind. Was it not likely that he – Franco Bahamonde – would one day reach the highest rank in the Army?

To this end, which seemed to him plausible if not probable, Franco now set about conscientiously improving his education and widening his technical and theoretical grasp of military science. He devoured books that seemed likely to contribute to the educative needs of a higher officer in a country where there is no tradition of divorce between the armed forces and politics. History and sociology, politics and science, seasoned the inevitable diet of military works and periodicals. He was particularly fascinated by books on Napoleon,[3] and Coles records that years later – during the Civil War – he sent a special emissary into Republican territory to secure a copy of Machiavelli's *The Prince*, annotated by Napoleon.[4] Franco's interest in this partnership of Florentine and Corsican is wonderfully suggestive.

Among Franco's duties at Oviedo was that of lecturing to his brother officers. He had ready-made material in his Moroccan experience, but now that he was at home in northern Spain, this seemed to him curiously small in scale in comparison with the titantic battles of the 1914–18 War, in which Spain was mercifully neutral. Poring over reports from France, of the Marne and the Somme and Verdun, Franco extracted lessons based on the logistics of contemporary artillery duels. He had been a tactical leader, a winner of campaign medals. Now he began thinking in strategic terms.

Until 1917, Spain had had a fairly profitable neutrality. The belligerents started losing their markets, especially in Latin America, to Spain; and Spanish merchants grew prosperous on their sales of cereals abroad. The national debt, created by the disaster of 1898, began to dwindle and the gold reserve to soar. When the war broke out, the reserve had stood at £23 million; by the time it ended, Spain held £89 million of gold. Meanwhile iron and munitions were in demand and as Spanish supplies rose to meet it, industry grew, and with it industrial tensions, especially in Asturias and Catalonia.

Echoes of the first stage of the revolutionary upheaval in Russia fanned the flames of violence among the Anarchist and Socialist workers, to whom, by and large, the Great War and the Moroccan conflict alike were imperialist irrelevances. But there was fodder, too, for industrial indignation. By the end of 1916, Spain had lost 89,000 tons of shipping to the submarine war, and at the end of January 1917 Germany proclaimed an absolute blockade. Prices were soaring, and so were the profits of the black marketeers and speculators. Yet another showdown was on the way, another stage in the recurrent clash of irreconcilable forces.

This time, however, there were new and sinister features in the line-up of traditional antagonisms. Syndicalism of an unexpected kind now spread from the industrial workers to the Army. Discontent among the officers was widespread. One of the causes of it was what might be called the 'industrial' side of the question: salaries were fixed, and low. A young officer, especially, found it difficult to make ends meet if single, and impossible if married. This had been true even before the German submarines took their toll and gold started flowing in. Now it was worse: the officers were becoming the proletarians of the Spanish establishment.

Then there was the Moroccan war in which Spanish officers and men were dying in greater numbers than seemed necessary because the Army was starved of modern equipment and arms, while the parties rotated in Parliament, appointed and dismissed according to the king's whim.

Some time in 1916, probably (the date is uncertain, the event being clandestine), the officers started organizing secret *juntas de defensa*. In more than one sense, these *juntas* were officers' *sindicatos* or trade unions. On the 'industrial' side, they wanted to improve pay and conditions, just as the workers' trade unions occasionally did. They had grown tired of the favouritism the king's *casa militar* showed in selecting officers for promotion. They were dissatisfied with the way the medical corps was organized.

But there was a political side to the *juntas*, too, just as there was with the trade unions. For a long time now, the Army had kept out of politics. Now, the officers thought, the time had come when notice should be served that the age of *pronunciamientos* was not necessarily dead. The *juntas* wanted a government that would take its orders from them, and no nonsense about regional separation, in Catalonia or elsewhere. In June 1917, the Infantry's own *junta de defensa*, under Colonel Benito Márquez, published a manifesto, saying, 'We do not want power for ourselves, but we believe we have the right to insist that power should be in good hands.'[5]

Already the *juntas'* claim to dictate policy had provoked the fall of the Romanones government, and the June ultimatum was provoked by the order served by his successor, Manuel García Prieto, for the arrest of *junta* leaders. Now García Prieto fell, and *his* successor, Dato, gave in to the *juntas'* demands, dissolving, among other things, the Assembly which had been set up in Barcelona by the Renovation movement that was sweeping Spain that fateful summer.

The monarchy was sick, and the Renovation movement was yet another sign of it. Indeed the malaise of the monarchy itself merely reflected a deeper sickness inherent in Spain's archaic power structure, under which political power – at the king's pleasure – always seemed, in the last analysis, to be wielded by the great landowners of Castile and Andalusia. This displeased everybody else – the energetic industrialists of Barcelona, Bilbao and Oviedo and the men who worked in their factories, the Socialist Party and the Radicals under the Barcelona demagogue Lerroux, whose speeches called on the people to burn the churches and kill the priests. For once, the Left and the Right were united, as were the Conservatives and the Liberals, the separatists and the centralists – for Lerroux, though a Catalan, was a centralist, while the Conservative Barcelona business man Francisco de Asis Cambó, leader of the separatist *Lliga*, was also a leading light in the Renovation movement.

In July all members of the Cortes who supported Renovation – seventy-one of them, or rather less than ten per cent of both houses – met in Barcelona and declared that they now constituted an Assembly that would make preparations for a freely elected Constituent Cortes. The revolutionary intent of the Renovation movement was now unmistakable, though it would be wrong to think of it as monolithically anti-Monarchist. Cambó, for instance, had made it clear that what he was interested in was electoral reform, decent government and modernization. Whether such improvements took place under the monarchy or a Republic did not matter to him.

Faced with this situation, the *juntas de defensa* hesitated. The Leftish groups in the Renovation movement had been making overtures to the rank and file of the Army, with such success that the officers must have doubted whether they would be obeyed if it came to firing on revolutionary mobs.[6] Moreover, bitterly though the *juntas* opposed the separatists who now seemed to be abandoning their separatism in favour of Renovation, many of the reforms proposed by the movement were just the kind of thing the officers themselves had been agitating for. On the other hand, the *juntas* viewed with great distaste and apprehension the participation of the Socialists and Radicals in the Renovation movement.

In the end, this was to be the deciding factor. For now the Socialists and workers came out with revolutionary demands of their own.* Already, in May 1916, the Socialist-controlled *Unión General de Trabajadores* (UGT) had publicly demanded the abolition of industrial privileges and an end to 'unproductive expenditures, especially the criminal war in Morocco'[7] – demands that were, by implication, revolutionary in intent since they were not industrial but political. On 27 March, the UGT combined with the Anarchist CNT (*Confederación Nacional del Trabajo*) to issue a joint manifesto threatening a general strike if the workers' political demands were not granted. And in August the opportunity to do so came with the government's refusal to give in to the demands of the UGT railway workers who were then on strike. Thereupon the leaders of the UGT and CNT, meeting together on the night of 9 August, jointly called a General strike for the 13 August. It was left in no doubt that the aim of the strike was to provoke the downfall of the monarchy and establish a socialist democratic republic.

Declaring the strike illegal, the government called on the Army to suppress it. The *juntas*, now faced with a revolutionary workers, movement, no longer hesitated, as they had over the reformist Renovation movement. Orders to suppress the strike were issued.

The toughest challenge to authority was in Asturias, where, correspondingly, the Army's repression was most brutal. We must now turn to Franco's part in these events.

Franco himself had never joined the officers' *juntas*. Indeed the officers in service in Morocco viewed the *juntas* with deep distrust; and those who, like Franco, had been stationed at Dar Dríus when the *juntas* first came into the news, were the most hostile.[8] Though he

---

* Brenan, in his otherwise comprehensive outline of these events, unaccountably fails to point out the revolutionary nature of the workers' demands (pp. 64–5).

was not, therefore, politically involved in the clamour for a suppression of the strike, he could hardly have been oblivious of current events, even if he had not been called upon to play his part in the suppression. One of the leaders of the Renovation had been the prominent Oviedo industrialist, Melquíades Álvarez; and the demands of the movement, together with the partly parallel demands of the *juntas*, must have been common talk within the garrison. But now Oviedo became the militant centre of the general strike. Everywhere else in Spain – in Madrid and Vizcaya, in Barcelona, Valencia and Santander – the strikers had returned to work as soon as the troops had shown themselves. In and around Oviedo, however, the Asturian miners were defiant. The commander of the garrison, General Burguete, ordered the troops to fire on them. Major Franco set out in command of a company of the King's Regiment, a section of machine-gunners of the Prince's Regiment and a detachment of Civil Guards. When he and his colleagues had finished their work, the strike was broken. It had lasted three days and its repression had cost the lives of seventy strikers,* with several hundred wounded and some two thousand taken prisoner. Among these was the young Socialist leader Largo Caballero, later known as 'the Lenin of Spain' and one of Franco's most determined enemies during the Civil War.

Ramírez makes an attempt to represent Franco as a conscious tool of 'capitalism' for his part in the repression of the Asturian miners in 1917. He is more convincing when he complains that for Franco, this was just another job to do, and a matter of indifference to him whether he was fighting Spanish miners or Moroccan insurgents, both being rebels. Franco was in fact obeying orders and carrying out a set task with his customary efficiency.

There was, however, more to it than that. In this as in other respects, 1917 was a turning point in Franco's life. Two disconnected strands in his professional training came together in his conduct of operations. He had learned the art of war and military leadership and lately he had been studying the civil arts of government. Now, faced with revolutionary violence and disobedience, he became the instrument of order and authority in a civil conflict. Ramírez is guilty of ideological distortion, however, when he asserts that Franco could not have cared less for the rights or the needs of the

* Brenan's figure (p. 65); Ramirez (p. 73) puts it at one hundred, for all Spain.

miners. Indeed he seems to have devoted as much time as his duties permitted, at the time of the strike, informing himself on the strikers' claims and of their wages and conditions, on the trade union system in Asturias and on the more sordid side of the employers' behaviour.[9]

What is certain is that Franco took a fundamental decision at the time of the Oviedo crisis: no matter what happened, and wherever it lay within his power, he would never permit revolutionary disorder in Spain. Within a few weeks, the Bolshevik Revolution in Russia and the widespread violence that came in its train, confirmed him in his view and created what was to be a lifelong hatred of Communism.

After the collapse of the general strike, Franco returned to normal garrison life until 30 September 1918, when he went to Valdemoro, south of Madrid, to take part in an advanced shooting course for infantry officers organized by the Central Infantry School. It was there that Franco met a man who was to have a considerable influence on the next phase of his career: Lieutenant-Colonel José Millán Astray. Like Franco, Millán Astray was a Galician, but the physical contrast between the two men was striking. Franco was small, still slight, shy and taciturn. Millán was a taller, vigorous, voluble man. Aged about forty at the time, he had fought in the Philippines and in Morocco, where he had not met Franco, although he too had been with the *Regulares*. Millán Astray knew about Franco, however, and his reputation for bravery. The two men – with two others – had been picked to referee the shooting contests, and they became firm friends.*

Here, Millán Astray thought, was the man he was looking for to help him in a project that was taking shape in his mind. Spain, too, he had decided, must have its Foreign Legion, on the lines of the Legion already set up by the French. The Madrid bureaucrats seemed to have little enthusiasm for his idea, but here was a human asset that could become a strong selling point with the War Ministry: Franco. Millán Astray, of course, would command the Legion. But this calm

---

* Millán Astray himself, on pp. 9–10 of *Franco el Caudillo* (Salamanca, 1939), says he met Franco in 1919 while they were both on the shooting course and adds that Franco was twenty-seven and that he was forty. But his memory must have been at fault, for the shooting course took place in 1918, when Franco was twenty-five.

and methodical young man, with his exceptional service record, would ensure success.

'From the day I first had the luck of meeting Franco,' he wrote later, 'I perceived very clearly his extraordinary qualities and his aptitudes. As my constant thought in those days was the foundation of the Legion, I judged that I should need the help of extraordinary men and principally of a man who would be my lieutenant to complete everything I lacked to carry out the whole of my great enterprise. After making Franco's acquaintance, I thought only of Franco.'[10]

Millán Astray does not seem, however, to have mentioned his plans to Franco at this early stage, for not long after his return to Oviedo on 30 November, the young major was thinking along quite different lines, in terms of a career as a staff officer. At any rate, Franco asked for a special dispensation to enable him to enter the War College (*Escuela de Guerra*), where staff officers were being trained, although the regulations laid down that the course was limited to lieutenants and captains. When his application was refused on the ground that he was a major, he replied that it was not his fault that he had reached the rank of major so fast, and that in any case he ought to qualify on the ground of his youth. The argument, how-ever, failed to impress the commandant of the College.

Franco renewed acquaintance with Millán Astray in June 1920, in Madrid, where both men had gone to take the oath to the flag of the Prince of Asturias. Millán's main purpose, however, was to press the case for the creation of a Foreign Legion before the then War Minister, General Tovar. This time, Millán Astray told Franco about his project and communicated his enthusiasm to the little Galician. In time, he communicated it to the Ministry as well, with the warm support of General Berenguer, the High Commissioner in Morocco. In October 1919, Millán Astray was given permission to go to Sidi Bel Abbes in Algeria to study the organization of the French Foreign Legion. And on 28 April 1920, the War Minister – by this time, the incumbent was a civilian, Viscount de Eza – created the *Tercio Extranjero*, as it was to be called, and appointed Millán Astray as its commander.

Millán Astray had obtained the Ministry's permission to choose his own officers and he immediately asked Franco to be his assistant. Franco didn't hesitate: 'Yes,' he said, 'I'll be the Number Two.'

But months went by before the formal summons came. Back in Oviedo, Franco was making plans for his wedding, Señorita Carmen Polo having finally worn down her parents' resistance to the marriage. Then in September 1920, Millán Astray sent him a telegram telling him the time had come. He deferred his wedding – not, as it turned out, for the last time – and set off for Morocco.

Later, the Legionaries were to make a song of Franco's conflict between love and duty. To the marching tune of *La Madelon*, they sang the lines:

> *El commandante Franco*
> *es un gran militar*
> *que aplazó su boda ir a luchar.*

Roughly rendered, these lines mean that Major Franco was a great fighting man who put off his wedding to go to the wars.

4 *The Spanish Foreign Legion*

They were a motley crowd, a hundred or so of them, fair-haired foreigners in quest of adventure, Spanish Civil Guards dismissed for some peccadillo, ex-soldiers who could not stay away from a fight. Franco, whose appointment to the Legion was formally confirmed on 27 September 1920, was among them, and they crossed the strait from Algeciras on 10 October. As their ship, the *Fernández Silvestre*, drew near the *Presidio* of Ceuta on the Moroccan coast, a motor-boat appeared. In it, upright and waving his forage cap, was the lean, enthusiastic figure of Lieutenant-Colonel Millán Astray. Franco alighted, ahead of his Legionaries, and the two men embraced on the quayside.

'At last,' wrote Franco, 'we were together! The leader was there, and in the boat were the tools for the job.'

Franco's second stay in Morocco is better documented than the first, partly because he now had a more important part to play in the Moroccan war, but mainly because he himself left an account of his life as Commander of the First Battalion of the Legion – *Diario de* *una Bandera* (Diary of a Battalion*). Since this is Franco's only literary work of consequence, it is of special interest, and indeed it is important both as historical source material and for the light it throws on Franco's character and personality.

It is a soberly written account, with a soldierly lack of stylistic pretension, austere at times to the point of bareness, at others happily picturesque in description; yet, perhaps unexpectedly, neither without emotion nor even without humour.

Millán Astray belonged to the school that doesn't gloss over the probability of blood and toil or tears and sweat. Or of death. Under his leadership the Legionaries took to crying 'Long live death' as they charged. His technique was to line up his men and single one out for the question: 'Do you know why you're here?' Before the man had a chance to answer, the colonel would apostrophize the recruits in his stentorian voice:

> You're here to die! Yes, to die! Now that you've crossed the Strait, you've lost your mother, your sweetheart and your family. From today, the Legion is everything to you. Service comes before everything, in the honour you have taken on, which is to serve Spain and the Legion. There's still time left to consider whether you really are ready to make the sacrifice. When you've thought it over, you may tell your captain what your final decision is.[1]

As his chief thundered out his words of caution and glory, Franco looked into the eyes of his men and thought he saw a spark of emotion in some. All they had to do, as he put it, was to tell the doctor they had a sore throat, while there was still time. But not one of them did.

Among the hundred who had made the crossing that day from Algeciras were a German ex-officer, an Italian airman, two Frenchmen, four Portuguese and a Maltese. Of the hundred, about a score failed their medical, and Franco pictures them pleading to be allowed to fight, with tears streaming down their cheeks. One of the most distressed was a sickly-looking youth who wept as he pleaded: 'Please Sir, let me be a Legionary! I promise to be a good soldier! You must let me: it's a penance.'

As he blurted out the last sentence, Millán Astray's ears pricked up.

* Strictly, a *Bandera* was smaller than a battalion.

A penance? What kind of penance could bring a frail young man to the Foreign Legion? The youth explained. He had been a novice in a monastery, but had yielded to worldly temptations and walked out. Later, repentance gained the upper hand and he went back cap in hand to the Prior, who told him he must do penance by volunteering for the Legion. If, after four years as a Legionary, he still wanted to become a monk, he would be readmitted to the Order.

Millán Astray would have liked to help the poor youth, but it was patent that his frail physique was not made for marching and fighting in the burning desert. So the disconsolate novice was sent back into the world whose delights he had so briefly tasted.

The sound of limb were marched three kilometres from the central Plaza of Ceuta, where they were divided into units and given their first pay. This, says Franco, they soon spent in a final orgiastic fling in Ceuta before marching orders.

On 16 October, the three companies that constituted the First Bandera marched to Riffien under Franco's orders, where training was to begin. Life in the camp evidently had its funny sides. Franco used to watch the men line up for their pay in the early days, and a number of them, unable to remember the fictitious names they had given on enlisting, would surreptitiously consult a scribble on a piece of paper in their pockets before stretching out their right hands.

One day, he writes, an elderly Legionary, his white head held high but dragging his feet with weariness, his beard unkempt, crossed the street. As he passed an officer, he raised his arm in salute. The officer looked closely, then the two men embraced: the old man was the officer's father. On another occasion, Millán Astray, who was about to enter his quarters, found a tall, fair-bearded Legionary in the doorway, holding an impressive hake in his right hand. '*Mi Teniente-Coronel,*' he explained, 'I spent the night fishing and have brought you this fish.' This, he added, was why he was missing from camp the night before.

One of the first things that happened to the Battalion was a telephone call announcing the imminent visit of a British general, whom Franco does not name. Franco bustled his men to order and in marched the general to the strains of the British and Spanish national anthems, followed by *Tipperary*. Franco records that the general's visit was the highest honour his men had been given. Not only was the general satisfied, but he gave proof of it shortly before Franco wrote his book by praising the Spanish Foreign Legion in the British press. This precocious evidence of Franco's attachment to things British is not without significance.

Riffien was just a prologue. The tougher and more prolonged period of training took place at Uad Lau, where Franco's Legionaries arrived on 2 November 1920. They were there for six months, and for all that has been said about the harshness of Franco's discipline,* the Legionaries do not seem to have had too bad a time under his orders.

He seems indeed to have worked on the principle of keeping everybody busy rather than punishing those who might otherwise have been idle. Gambling, for instance, was prohibited, but gamblers were not punished. If a game was found to be in progress, the players were simply dispersed. Those who wanted to try their luck were encouraged to do so in the competitions of all sorts that were constantly being organized. Boxing, shooting and horse riding were the most popular. A Swiss recruit beat a Spaniard in the finals of the shooting contest, but the undisputed king of the ring among the Legionaries was a big and aggressive American Negro whose stated name was William Brown and whose fists won him respect and renown in surrounding villages. At first, the locals had taken him for a Moor, but – writes Franco – he soon proved his North American origin to them by his boxing prowess. His constant scrapes did nothing to improve his appearance and he was never seen other than ragged and dirty.

The day began with physical training in shirtsleeves followed by combat drills. After a rest came a brief period of theoretical instruction, in which equal emphasis was given to explanations of the character of the war in Morocco and to moral training aimed at building a Credo of the Legion. Much of the afternoon and evening went in shooting instruction and competitions for small prizes in silver money. At nightfall, the men used to crowd around the officers asking for drink vouchers. But there was so much drunkenness in the early days that severe limits had to be imposed on voucher issues. As for the officers, their administrative duties, neglected during the day's endeavours, kept them busy long after nightfall. 'Such,' writes

* E.g. Thomas, p. 121: 'He was known as a strict, even a cruel, disciplinarian.'

Franco, with the smug literalness that is one of his characteristics, 'is the virtuous and active life of the officers of the Legion.'

Sunday was the only day of rest, and its sleep was broken late in the morning by *Reveille*. The afternoon brought a greater variety of organized games than week-days did, with football and wrestling as well as boxing. Some of the officers, on the other hand, elected to mount their horses and organize fantastic chases of the innumerable wild dogs that crowded around the camp.

An ingenious Austrian, Werner, spent his spare time building a gigantic weather-vane, which in the end he hoisted on to the highest building in the camp. It was an officer in full uniform, with a sabre in his right hand. Every time the wind blew, the officer raised his sabre and saluted.

A Legionary named Gamoneda turned out to be Kuku, who had been a circus clown in Spain, and when duty allowed he would regale the others with his jokes and tricks.

Another Legionary, unnamed, used to offer five *duros* to anybody who could defeat him in a wrestling bout.

And so the days went by, slow and peaceful.

Distractions being few at Uad Lau, some Legionaries took evening walks towards the nearest beach, not to swim, since night was falling, but to make passes at the young Moorish girls who gathered to fetch water at the wells. As soon as a Moor appeared, the girls would pretend to flee like frightened birds, scared by the presence of Christians. But once their co-religionary was out of sight, they would come back to the well to laugh and chat in the eternal language of signs and dancing eyes. The more persistent Legionaries pressed on with their courtship and many a time, Franco records, 'the old olive trees of the sacred wood were mute witnesses of the Legion's gallantry.'

There were no fights. Those who looked like coming to blows were taken to their officer who gave them boxing gloves and instructed them to settle their differences, to a running accompaniment of derisive cries from their companions. The sting of hostility removed, the two usually took off their gloves, no longer to fight but to shake hands and part good friends. This, at all events, is Franco's possibly euphemistic account.

When Christmas came, the Germans were given permission to put up a tree, complete with coloured lights. The officers covered the branches with bottles of German beer and the Germans rewarded them with songs of their own country. The wine and the beer, and the good fellowship, flowed until daybreak.

Shortly after, 'an unfortunate event filled our camp with grief'. A Moorish Legionary had fired point blank at a police lieutenant, mortally wounding him. Two Legionaries had chased the Moor, dodging his shots until one stunned him with a blow on the head. 'Next day, the cowardly treason was punished and the Legionaries and Police marched in arms before the Moorish murderer's corpse. The camp lived a night of grief for the loss of Lieutenant Malagón, a first-rate soldier, kindly and fair.'

There is more in this strain. One day the incident worth recording is that of the Legionary who dives in to the river to save two Moorish girls being carried away by the current. Another, Franco introduces 'Dr' Colbert, a Corporal intern full of fantastic stories of his past splendour, who called himself 'Doctor' to facilitate his amorous conquests.

The long wait came to an end in April. General Berenguer, the High Commissioner, had decided to isolate that perennial rebel, El Raisuni, who was back in dissidence, by occupying the Gomara mountains, with the object of consolidating Spanish-held Xauen.

The thought of action had a tonic effect on Major Franco. But he was soon disillusioned by the elusiveness of the Rif guerrillas in the environs of Xauen, the Holy City. Such fighting as went on was entrusted to the *Regulares* and discontent spread among the Legionaries, who improvised a satirical song at their own expense:

> Who are those soldiers
>   with the pretty hats?
> Must be the Legion,
>   filling sacks with earth.

'Nobody is satisfied,' Franco told his Diary. 'A great disappointment can be seen on our chief's face. He counsels patience: the day of combat will come. But in our hearts we are all discouraged. What is happening to our Credo?'

About this time, the first signs of Franco's political dissatisfaction with the Metropolis can be discerned in the following passage:

3a Lieutenant-Colonel Franco leaves the Church of San Juan, Oviedo, with his bride, the former Senorita Carmen Polo y Martinez Valdés, on 16 October 1923.

3b Lieutenant-Colonel Franco on the beach at Axdir, Spanish Morocco.

Echoes from Spain are reaching our life in Xauen. The nation lives quite apart from the campaign in the Protectorate and views with indifference the action and sacrifice of the Army and of that selfless body of officers which day in day out pays its tribute of blood amidst the burning rocks.

What insensitivity!

His indignation was aroused when a copy of the Forces' review arrived, giving details of official plans for the creation of a purely colonial Army. This, he underlined, meant *sentencing those of Africa not to go back to Spain*, thus depriving the peninsular Army of its best practical school and guaranteeing freedom from duty in Morocco to home-based officers. In hot anger, he dashed off a protesting article and sent it to the review, but it never saw the light of day. This was in May 1921.

From now on, the tone of the Diary grows more sombre, the tributes to fallen companions more frequent – for the fighting grew fiercer later in the spring – and notes of bitterness creep into the narrative. But the major's eye for picturesque detail never deserts him. The Legionaries march through a village reserved for lunatics and cats, greeted by furtive looks and maniacal laughter from the first and indolent complacency from cats stretched across the door-ways, who, it seems, were the object of a certain religious respect from the natives . . . Or again, a Legionary finds a Moorish woman hiding in the hollow of a tree in a ravine and hauls her before Franco: 'We find ourselves with a one-eyed, ugly woman who gives the lie to the fair sex. "Take her to the General!" says our Lieutenant-Colonel, turning his head away fast. What an apparition to see before a battle!'

At 2 a.m., the stentorian voice of Millán Astray breaks the silence with an order to wake up Major Franco. There was no need. He steps out of his tent and asks what is happening.

'One of the battalions has to leave for Fondak as soon as possible,' says Millán Astray. 'As we don't know why and where it will have to go next, you will have to draw lots. It could just as easily mean action or having to garrison some post in the rear.'

The luck of the draw fell on Franco's First Battalion. There was no way of penetrating the mystery of this sudden order, which seemed in some uneasy way, to be connected with rumours of bad news from Melilla. Two days' march lay ahead. Half-way, the Legionaries

D

stopped at a wood to rest and bathe in the river. And at 11 p.m. on the second day, they reached the walls of Fondak in the teeth of a tearing gale. After a hasty meal, the exhausted marchers could not face putting up their tents and flopped down to sleep in the dry ditches on the roadside.

Hardly had they dropped off when the field telephone rang insistently. The Legionaries must be at Tetuan before dawn, said an officer's voice. 'Impossible,' said Franco, 'the men are exhausted; but we might make it by ten.'

At 3.30 a.m. *Reveille* is sounded and the soldiers have to be aroused one by one from their oblivious sleep. At 9.45, they are in the streets of the city.

A peasant comes up to them and shouts: 'There's been a disaster at Melilla and General Silvestre has committed suicide.' The indignant Legionaries chase the peasant away, and as he leaves he mutters that he's only repeating what they told him in the military casino at Ceuta.

The peasant was right and had brought advance tidings of one of the great disasters of modern military history. Or, looked at another way, a masterpiece of guerrilla warfare.

The story really begins in 1919 with a personal quarrel between General Manuel Fernández Silvestre, who was in command at Melilla, and the redoubtable Abd el Krim, at that time working in the Office of Native Affairs in the same town. Slighted by the Spanish General, Abd el Krim took to the mountains of his Beni Uriaghel tribe stretching inland from Alhucemas Bay on the Rif coast. There his brother joined him, and they took an oath of vengeance.

By the summer of 1921, two Spanish forces were preparing to reduce the Riffians. One, under General Dámaso Berenguer, was based on Tetuan. The other, at Melilla, consisted of some 20,000 men, under General Silvestre.

Indecision was Silvestre's undoing. He had planned to advance along the coast to the East, but a small reverse at Abarran halted him. He consulted Berenguer and decided to stop operations until the Moors in the West had been defeated. Relaxation, however, is fatal to the regular commander faced with a determined chieftain of irregulars. While Silvestre and his men eased their tensions in unmartial leisure, Abd el Krim, at the head of only a few hundred guerrillas, swooped down from the hills and surrounded the fort of

Igueriben. Once again, General Silvestre dithered. His first impulse was to relieve the defenders. General Navarro, based on Anual, had already tried this and failed. Frightful news of hardships at Igueriben was coming out. Water had run out and the defenders were reduced to drinking sweetened urine. Silvestre called for reinforcements, but without mentioning the danger which he must have known his forces faced. Rounding up every man he could get hold of, including clerks and other non-combatants, he decided to push forward and dislodge the besiegers of Igueriben. On reaching Anual, he launched his first attempt, which ran into heavy resistance. Panicking, he changed his mind and ordered his men back to Anual. At the same time and unaccountably, he authorized the defenders of Igueriben to attempt a sortie. The waiting Moors cut them down and Silvestre authorized them to surrender, but their commander, Major Benítez, decided to fight to the death. His last telegram read: 'The leaders and officers of Igueriben . . . die but do not surrender.' Only a handful of survivors reached Anual.

Now Silvestre telegraphed Melilla for reinforcements, belatedly stressing the urgency of his need. Already the Moors were moving in to cut his communications. Could the camp at Anual hold out? Several days would be needed before the reinforcements arrived. Desperate by now, Silvestre held a council of war on the night of 21 to 22 July, and decided on a general retreat. He might have been well advised to delay the order while he restored some discipline and martial spirit among the men under his command. But no sooner was the decision taken than the order to pull back along the coast was issued. The demoralized troops marched out in poor order and ran straight into Moorish fire. Suddenly, the *Indígenas* on the Spanish side turned on the Spaniards and added their fire to the bullets of Abd el Krim's guerrillas.

Soon Silvestre's force was fleeing in panic, pursued by the avenging Moors, whose blood lust had been aroused by tales of Spanish rape and other interference with their womenfolk. Some 15,000 Spaniards were hacked to pieces. No prisoners were taken. As for Silvestre, he had vanished, and it was later presumed that, overcome by the enormity of his failure, he had committed suicide.*

* But Viscount de Eza, the former War Minister, attributes the disaster to Silvestre's death in action, which left his men leaderless: *Mi Responsabilidad en el Desastre como Ministro de la Guerra* (1923), p. 511.

The Legionaries covered the last lap of the journey to Melilla by ship from Ceuta. As the ship drew near, a High Commission motor-boat drew alongside and an alighting official gave out the news in these words: 'The General Command, nothing left of it; the Army, defeated; the whole place wide open; the town demented and seized by panic.'

Indeed Abd el Krim's Moors were at the gates of the city, with nothing to stop them from putting its 50,000 inhabitants to the sword. Sated with blood and horror, however, they merely waited and watched.

The population greeted the Legionaries in a frenzy of joy and relief. The balconies were crowded with applauding citizens; weeping women kissed the passing soldiers. Cigars, fruit and refreshments were produced. In contrast, a cold greeting awaited the *Regulares* who reached Melilla a few hours later and were made to take the blame for the alleged treachery of Silvestre and his men.

Survivors were coming in, their pupils (says Franco) dilated with terror, recounting the horrors of the pursuit, with Moorish women following their men to finish off the wounded. Some of the returning Spaniards were naked or wore only their shirts, and wandered, out of their minds, unaware of their surroundings.

'Our hearts weep for the defeat,' wrote Franco in his Diary.

The disaster was another nail in the coffin of Spain's constitutional monarchy. Alfonso himself had given his blessing to Silvestre's plan. Within a few days, the fruit of twelve years' painfully slow penetration of eastern Morocco had been cast away. Another *desastre* had befallen Spain, of emotional dimensions to compare with 1898. Once again, Spanish pride had been humiliated, and the heroism of the ordinary Spanish fighting man sacrificed on the least glorious of altars – administrative ineptitude and political corruption. So, at any rate, it seemed to many Spaniards.

Opposition to the Moroccan war grew, especially on the Left, and Professor Besteiro, spokesman of the Socialists, expressed the general unease and indignation when he asked the Cortes: 'Is it conceivable that an army could reach the degree of slackness reached by the Spanish Army?' The government fell, and Antonio Maura, the Conservative leader, an able but despotic man who had been in power when the Moroccan war started, was called back to office. His first concern was to stop the rot in Morocco and regain the territory that had been lost. He ordered every available soldier to Morocco and over the next few months, 140,000 of them crossed the Strait. The barrel, however, was all too clearly being scraped. General Berenguer was appalled by the quality of the troops that were reaching him, and of their material.

It is a conglomeration of units (he wrote[2]), all deficient in material, in instruction and in numbers, for the battalions are around 450 men with their machine-gun companies and until all this is organized and well-prepared from all points of view, from the command to the marching soldiers, we have no guarantee that the troops will be able to fight effectively. It is a really extra-ordinary case, for the question is not simply to reinforce an army with new elements, but to create an army to fight tomorrow.

The Commander-in-Chief, General Sanjurjo, made the best of a bad job. There was enough equipment to supply 36,000 men at a reasonably high standard, and on 17 September, he gave the order for the counter-attack.

Franco's First Battalion of the Legion played an important part in the campaign, for at the outset Millán Astray was gravely wounded in the chest as he was pointing out an objective to his chosen lieu-tenant. Franco was appointed acting Commander of the Legion. He was twenty-eight. Much of his Diary from this point on consists of horrific rediscoveries of the disaster as the road to Anual was retraced, and of tributes to fallen comrades. Here and there, his eye alights on some moving scene:

A pretty young Moorish girl lies stretched out on the ground. An enormous red stain spreads from the heart over her white vestments; her forehead is still warm. Poor dead girl, victim of the war! The Legionaries look at her with loving respect . . .

His cousin, Franco Salgado, is wounded, and Lieutenant-Colonel Mola is carried off bleeding on a stretcher. His 'faithful and beloved' adjutant, Baron de Miseña, falls before his eyes, with a bullet through his forehead. Major Fontanes, Commander of the Second Battalion, is mortally wounded in the stomach. 'The Legion is fighting,' writes Franco, 'it has lost one of its best leaders and the soldiers are sad; their eyes do not weep because no tears are left in their sockets. They have seen so many officers and comrades fall!'

He himself seems to have a charmed life. The bullets whistle all around him, killing or wounding his companions and passing him by. Millán Astray records that he used to stand erect under fire, disdaining parapets or other forms of cover. His self-possession never deserted him, and another of his admirers, General Esteban Infantes, writes of the coolness with which he took decisions at the height of a battle.

One by one, former strongpoints were being recaptured: Nador and Tahuima, Sebt and Ulad Dau, Atlaten, Gurugú and Esponja, Zeluán and Monte Arruit, Uisán and Ras Medina, Dríus, Ambar and Tuguntz, and other place-names still – so many chapter headings in the second half of the *Diario de una Bandera*. At Nador, a scene of pillage and massacre awaited the Legionaries and a huge communal grave had to be dug to relieve the congested streets of piled up Spanish corpses. At Monte Arruit, an even more horrific picture greets them, of 'defiled and barbarously mutilated bodies', their heads crushed and beyond identification. This was all that was left of General Navarro and his men after they had formally surrendered to the Moors. A thirst for revenge grew among the Legionaries, and the assault of the Uisán heights gave them the chance to slake it.

The tribe of Beni Bou-Ifrur had been guilty of the worst atrocities and so long as it controlled Uisán, which dominated its territory, it could elude the advancing Legion. The massive heights, with their sheer rocks and precipitous ravines, challenged and frustrated the Legionaries at the same time. The thick walls of the fortress at the summit, now guarded by the Moors and within their easy reach, were impervious to the Bandera's artillery. By day, a direct assault would have invited certain failure. By night, the weather increased the hazards. By the time the Legion reached the foot of Uisán, winter had come and torrential rains soaked the Legionaries and turned the roads into quagmires.

While they waited for the weather to improve, Franco worked out a plan, which General Sanjurjo approved. Stealth was to be the formula. At 4 a.m. on 10 October the Legionaries set out on foot, leaving behind those of them who had colds and whose sneezes might betray their presence, together with potentially noisy mules and horses. Rifles were concealed under their capes, so that no shiny metal parts should show. Thirty men carried the machine-guns and ammunition.

The Legionaries climbed the escarpment 'like ghostly blacks', as silent as they were invisible. Drawing near the fortress, they could see the smoke from the Moorish guards' cigarettes. With a few yards still to cover, the Moors heard their cautious footsteps and ran, firing shots in the air to attract their companions from beyond the fortress. Throwing caution to the winds, the Legionaries accelerated their pace, beating the Riffians to the fort with twenty yards to spare. Dawn was breaking. The ensuing fight lasted all day, and at dusk, having lost three killed and five wounded, the Legion controlled the heights of the Beni Bou-Ifrur tribe. That night, the victorious column displayed a telegram of congratulations from the High Command.

With the Uisán heights under control, the First Battalion proceeded to encircle the Beni Bou-Ifrur villages, with a mission of systematic punishment. After the guns had fired on the villages, the Legionaries completed the work, the success of which Franco records with laconic ruthlessness, mentioning that on 2 December 1921, two columns penetrated deep into Beni Bou-Ifrur territory, 'and this tribe, which had so distinguished itself by its cruelties, has been destroyed'.

Punishment was not automatically Franco's reaction, however, when faced with evidence of Moorish atrocities. The vengeance exacted against the Beni Bou-Ifrur created a new climate of submissiveness, and as the Legionaries advanced, more and more Riffians came forward to surrender. In January 1922, they reached Dríus, where General Silvestre might have held his ground against Abd el Krim's avengers, had he kept his head. While the Chief of Police was discussing surrender terms with the local guerrillas, Franco came upon a blood-spattered wall in whose shadow lay the remains of massacred Spanish troops. 'A wave of indignation passes over us,' writes Franco. But this was no longer the time for vengeance, and he adds: 'The Legionaries must not enter the village. Let them not see all this infamy and ruin our policy!'

A period of quiet followed, which Franco put to use by training the newer recruits, whose performance left much to be desired, and

having wells dug.* As the calm interlude looked like being prolonged, he put in a request for home leave, his first since he had
returned to Morocco in October 1920. There was no chance of getting to Oviedo where his fiancée patiently awaited him, but his
mother, who had lived through anxious days, was relieved to see him,
and El Ferrol greeted him with the enthusiasm small towns reserve
for the local boy who makes good. Franco had only been home a
few days when an urgent telegram from General Sanjurjo brought
him back. The fighting had started again, and as soon as he reached
Dar Drius by plane, he was put in command of the vanguard of the
Legion.†

In the ensuing action, says Arrarás, Franco, observing through
his field glasses that a detachment of *Regulares* was beginning to
retreat in disorder, rode into the fight and whipped the men back into
action. He himself makes no mention of this incident, though he does
record that the Legionaries filled the gap left by fleeing soldiers who
had abandoned their tanks (he devotes nearly two pages to a technical discussion of the value of tanks in this kind of warfare; as he
dryly noted, they stopped when petrol ran out).

April brought the operations to a close. By then, the whole of the
territory lost to Abd el Krim as a result of the disaster of Anual had
been recovered.

The *Diario de una Bandera* ends at this point. Franco tidied it up a
little, wrote a penultimate chapter of reflections on the Anual disaster
and a final one in tribute to the 'heroic infantrymen', and published
his Diary in book form later in the year 1922.

Not long after, an obscure Austrian agitator, gaoled for his part in
the 'beer hall putsch' of November 1923, began to write his only
literary work, *Mein Kampf*. Since Franco's enemies have found it
convenient to lump him with Hitler, his helper in the Civil War, in a
general anathema on 'fascism', it is worth pointing out that the

---

* Galinsoga, *Centinela*, p. 61. Franco mentions the period of quiet but does
not say how it was filled. In general, he is reticent about his civil accomplish-
ments. Millán Astray records that Franco created a model farm and waterworks
which fed and watered the Legionaries at Dar Riffien (cf. Martin, p. 42).

† Arrarás, *Franco*, p. 79. The chronology of this period is confused, however.
Arrarás says operations were resumed on 18 March, while Galinsoga gives 29
March as the date (p. 70). Franco himself makes no mention of home leave, and
records fighting on 7, 8, 14, 17 and 18 March.

character that emerges from the pages of the *Diario* is strikingly different from that of the author of *Mein Kampf*. The Hitler of later years was already visible in *Mein Kampf*'s hysterical tones of paranoia and megalomania. Hate dominated his soul and his thirst for German *Lebensraum* pointed the way to the *Götterdämmerung* of the Berlin bunker. In military service, he had stuck at the rank of corporal, and his superiors had failed to detect in him any particular gift of leadership. He burst upon a humiliated people hungry for his visions of a Teutonic millennium.

There is nothing of all this in Franco's book, though he, too, wrote at a time of national humiliation. The dominant traits that emerge from his Diary are: professionalism, exaltation of the military virtues, loyalty and modesty, and an almost total lack of interest in politics. Each in turn deserves a few words.

Professionalism. Courage is not enough: the soldier must know *how* to fight. Discipline is important; so are tactics and weapons. More than once, the young major quotes the Moors' pitying reference to the Spanish officer in their pidgin Spanish: *Teniente Fulano no saber manera* (roughly, 'Lieutenant Smith don't know how'). The man who 'don't know how' is a dead man. Surprise is the instrument of victory, and stones, used for cover, ensure survival. He criticizes the Hotchkiss machine-gun and pleads for a light tank adapted to Moroccan fighting conditions.

The military virtues. The pages of the *Diario* are crowded with references to heroism and the glory of a soldier's death. Some of these make tedious reading for readers who are neither Spaniards nor soldiers. On one page, for instance, he praises the example of a soldier who spends his last moments on earth 'singing the glories' of his commanding general. On another, he records that the sight of marching Legionaries brought home to him 'the greatness of the race' – presumably of the Spanish race, which was that of the officers, many of the Legionaries, being, by definition, foreigners.

Franco's reiterated insistence on the primacy of character over everything else that makes a good soldier is, however, an important clue to the successes of his own career in later life. 'The most precious thing in this war,' he writes, 'is not the material but the men.' And when, towards the end of his book, he analyzes the cause of the disaster at Anual, he writes the following revealing passage:

In Morocco, at all times, political and military work have gone hand in hand, and it was not the absence of the former that led us, as some believe, to the disaster of July. There may have been errors or blunders in our police work, but it would not be right to find in these the causes of the disaster; let us examine our consciences, let us look at our lethargic virtues, and we shall find the crisis of ideals which converted into a rout what ought to have been a small reverse.

In Franco's eyes, then, the disaster was due above all to a failure of leadership. Later in the same chapter, he stresses the need for officers with a creed of ideals, which sustains itself without a 'fistful of pesetas'.

Loyalty and modesty. I have already quoted a number of tributes to fallen comrades. There were many more. Though he could be coldly, professionally ruthless, as in his summary account of the destruction of the Beni Bou-Ifrur tribe, he was deeply moved by the deaths of the men who served with him or under him. More often than not, emotion gains the upper hand, but occasionally stoicism takes over. 'In war,' he exclaims, 'the heart has to be sacrificed!'

Franco's modesty may seem surprising in one who had already clearly revealed his ambitions, at least in the military sense. But the fact is there: Franco hardly mentions himself in his book. He praises the courage and glory of his companions but says nothing of his own, even by implication. When describing the actions he led, he avoids the first person singular, and shelters behind impersonal reflexive Spanish verbs that preserve his anonymity. His own deeds of valour, which are inherent in his account and punctuated by his medals and promotions, have been recounted subsequently – often with sycophantic zeal – by his Spanish biographers.

Indifference to politics. I have quoted a passing reference to Franco's fear that the anger of the Legionaries might 'ruin our policy'. Elsewhere, as we have seen, he laments official plans for the creation of a colonial Army. And in one rather naïve phrase, after recording the savagery of Moorish women who kill off the wounded and remove their clothing, he comments that this was their way of 'paying back the benefits civilization had brought them'. This was the extent of his interest in politics, as revealed in the *Diario*. Nor was this particularly surprising, since it is a record of a soldier's life far from the political centres of Spain.

Anybody reading the *Diario de una Bandera* in the 1920s might have guessed that Franco would reach the top in his military career. Only a clairvoyant could have guessed that he would become Spain's Chief of State.

5 *Enter a Dictator*

There seemed no end to the Moroccan war, and while it dragged on the political crisis sparked off by the Anual disaster went from bad to worse. The civil power seemed incapable of deciding whether to give the Army the means of victory or pull out altogether from the Riffian hornets' nest. Public clamour for an inquiry into the causes of the disaster was gathering strength. Maura, who had sent 140,000 men to join the defeated forces in Morocco, would have liked to avoid any public examination of his predecessors' policies. On all sides the whisper that the king himself had egged Silvestre on to his doom was being heard. An inquiry, thought Maura, might do more than shake the parliamentary system: it might mean the overthrow of the monarchy.

In the end, however, the public pressure overcame Maura's resistance, and he appointed General Picasso to conduct an investigation. As the General went about his work, a trial of strength began between the Army and the politicians. The *juntas de defensa* were against the publication of any evidence that might put the blame for the disaster on the Army as such: the politicians, they said, were to blame for failing to give the Army the tools for the job. And to drive the point home, the *juntas* launched a campaign of charges and threats against the civilians. Maura retaliated by disbanding the *juntas de defensa* and formally replacing them by *juntas informativas*, responsible to the War Minister. The officers, however, were stronger than he was and they forced him out of office at the beginning of 1922.

Maura's successor, José Sánchez Guerra, despite his bellicose-sounding name, reversed Maura's policy of reinforcing the Moroccan-based Army. He ordered the repatriation of 20,000 troops, halted the Melilla zone operations and decided against the Army's scheme for a

landing in the Bay of Alhucemas, which Franco himself, in the con-
cluding pages of his *Diario*, had supported as the key to victory over
the Rif insurgents.

This return to parsimony further incensed the *juntas*. In the meantime, Picasso's report had been submitted to a committee of the
Cortes. It was an explosive document. Neither politically nor
materially had Silvestre's advance been properly prepared. Leading
officers, said the report, had left their units in the field for the
gambling tables of the Kursaal at Melilla. But part of the report was
being suppressed, including, it was said, a letter from Alfonso XIII
to Silvestre ordering him to push ahead and 'pay no attention to the
Minister of War, who is an imbecile'.[1]

It was against this troubled political background that Franco's
Bandera and the other units of the Spanish Army were reconquering
the ground lost by Silvestre. On 12 May 1922, the Spaniards entered
Tazarut, headquarters of El Raisuni, the intermittent fighter, who
had lately received considerable deliveries of arms from Abd el
Krim's brother.

Franco had been in the thick of the fighting throughout that
spring. On 14 June, a General Order revealed that Sanjurjo had proposed Franco's promotion to Lieutenant-Colonel for 'war-merit' and
cited him 'for his exceptional qualities (*condiciones*) of competence,
activity and valour in all the actions in which he has taken part with
his column, distinguishing himself notably and demonstrating that he
possesses qualities of leadership of a superior category'.

On the 30 June, General Berenguer, the Commissioner-General in
Morocco, awarded Franco the Military Medal in a statement recording that he had 'particularly distinguished himself at the head of two
Banderas, demonstrating that he possessed the most brilliant military
qualities . . . always in the first line, knowing how to inspire the
Banderas of the *Tercio* (Legion) with his intrepid spirit and lead them
according to the best principles of military technique'.

Major Franco was not decorated with his new medal until 12 January 1923, when the officers of the camp at Dar Drius gathered
around him in a great demonstration of enthusiasm for the little
Gallego.[2] Simultaneously came two signs that Franco's opposition
to the plan for a separate colonial Army had found an audience in
high quarters. The much-wounded Millán Astray, who, besides having his chest pierced, had lost an eye and an arm, was transferred to

the command of the Pavía Regiment, while Franco's own return to garrison duty in Oviedo was announced.

For Carmen Polo, this seemed like the end of the long wait. Her fiancé had not allowed his fighting life to interfere too much with the flow of letters, but he had never been a man of many words. In his laconic, almost telegraphic style, he wedged selected phrases of tenderness between concise descriptions of battles. Señorita Carmen was now twenty. Nearly five years had elapsed since her first meeting with the *comandantín*. Her patience was not, by any means, exhausted. But she was ready for marriage, and he, in his latest letters, had told her it was high time he settled down. For now he was thirty.

Before rejoining his regiment and his fiancée, Franco spent some days at El Ferrol on home leave. His mother, with Ramón and Francisco on the Moroccan front, had spent long and anxious times.* Together, mother and son knelt to offer prayers before the altar of the Virgin of Chamorro. And back in Morocco, while Franco was at El Ferrol, another Order of the Day cited him for distinguished action during the battle of Tizzi-Assa on 28 October 1922:

> Full of enthusiasm (the Order ran), he wields, employs and disposes with singular skill the forces under his orders; shows himself tireless in activating the fortification works, personally directing the installation of the forces that had to stay in these positions, and brilliantly protects the orderly withdrawal of the columns.

On 21 March, Francisco reached Oviedo and was reunited with his Carmen. It was a time of serene happiness and joyous expectancy. Nothing now seemed to stand in the way of their long delayed wedding.

Their plans were well advanced, with everything settled except the date of the ceremony when an unexpected event again shattered Senorita Carmen's hopes.

The blow fell on 8 June. Three days earlier, Lieutenant-Colonel Rafael Valenzuela, who had succeeded Millán Astray as Commander of the Legion, was killed in a battle to relieve a Spanish convoy attacked on its way to Tizzi-Assa. Who was to succeed him? To bring Millán Astray back in his condition seemed out of the question. Franco was the obvious choice, but he was 'too young' and a mere

* His biographers make no mention of his father's feelings.

major. These thoughts flashed across Franco's mind as he read the headlines recording Valenzuela's death.

Franco, nevertheless, it had to be, and on 7 June Alfonso XIII called a special Cabinet meeting to approve the promotion that Sanjurjo had recommended a year earlier. On 8 June, the *comandantín* learned that he had become the youngest lieutenant-colonel in the Spanish Army and that he was appointed Commander of the Legion.

Señorita Carmen was proud but heartbroken at the news. As in 1920, her wedding was postponed and anxious days of separation lay ahead.

A few days later, Madrid's leading politicians and scientists, intellectuals and artists, economists and military men attended a banquet in honour of the new Chief of the Spanish Foreign Legion. After dinner a fellow Galician rose with his glass aloft and made a morbid little speech which many of the guests found in bad taste. 'As a Galician,' he said, 'I request of the Government that if Franco finds a glorious death in Africa, his body should be buried beside the sepulchre of the Apostle Santiago, in Campostela, just as Valenzuela was buried in Saragossa, near the Virgin of Pilar.'[3]

Indignant murmurs greeted these pessimistic words, in which some of those present feared to find an evil omen. Franco alone sat impassive. His life, he was often to say in later years, was a gift of God, who would take it away in his own good time, no matter what a fellow Galician might say.

On 18 June 1923, Franco arrived at Ceuta to take over his new command. The following day, he issued a special 'Order of the Legion', the last paragraph of which is worth quoting, for there is little doubt that when every allowance has been made for the stylized pomp of such military prose, this passage precisely reflects Franco's concept of the Legion:

Keep forever pure the Legionary spirit, have blind confidence in your fortitude, keep faith in the Credo of the Legion, splendid legacy of your first Legionary chief, and preserve in your memories the example of the most glorious infantryman, of the finest Legionary, Lieutenant-Colonel Valenzuela, who with his cap and his thought aloft died for our beloved Legion.

Long live Spain! Long live the King! Long live the Legion! Your Lieutenant-Colonel. – Franco.

Within a few days, Franco was in action. The defenders of the besieged fortress of Tifaruín were nearing the end of their tether and had appealed for relief. The Air Force sent two men in a plane to fly over the fort with a message of comfort: 'Hold on,' it ran in effect, 'Franco is coming.' Shortly after the message had been delivered, Moorish fire hit the plane, which crashed in flames in a ravine. But before crashing Tifaruín's signalled reply had been picked up and transmitted. 'If Franco is coming,' it said, 'we shall resist. Long live Spain!'

Placing some of his men in an exposed position to draw the enemy's fire, Franco attacked the Moors in the rear. They fled in disorder and Tifaruín was relieved.

Carmen Polo's fiancé was biding his time. By the autumn a lull had set in in the Riffian fighting. Franco was granted a month's leave for matrimonial purposes.

The wedding took place in the Church of San Juan in Oviedo, on 16 October 1923. As Commander of the Legion, Franco was a 'Gentleman of the Chamber' of H.M. King Alfonso XIII who, as a mark of esteem, 'sponsored' the marriage and nominated the Military Governor of Oviedo, General Antonio Losada, to represent him at the ceremony.

The couple were together only for the month's leave he had been granted. Another separation then began, when he returned to his duties in Morocco.

From that point forward, ceremonial gestures of this kind represented the extent of the king's assertion of authority. On the night of 12 September 1923, a rip-roaring Andalusian aristocrat, General Miguel Primo de Rivera, marquess of Estella, disowned the king's government. From his Barcelona headquarters as Captain-General of Catalonia, he issued a *pronunciamiento* in traditional style, threatening the king's ministers with gaol and declaring it imperative to liberate the country from 'the professional politicians, the men who for one reason or another are responsible for the period of misfortune and corruption which began in 1898 and threatens to bring Spain to a tragic and dishonourable end.' The Royal Will itself, added the manifesto, had been caught and imprisoned in the meshes of 'the wide net of greedy politics'.

All over the country, garrisons responded to Primo de Rivera's call and declared themselves in revolt. The king, who was summering in his Palace of Miramar, in San Sebastian, hurried back to Madrid and summoned his prime minister, the marquess of Alhucemas. The marquess was in favour of strong royal action against the author of the *pronunciamiento* and his followers. But Alfonso rightly judged the situation to be hopeless and dismissed Alhucemas, handing power to Primo and the other generals. The dictatorship had begun.

It was the end of Cánovas's experimental parliamentary system and of the Constitution of 1876. It was also the real end of the monarchy, even though the king did not formally abdicate until 1931. Too long had Alfonso played at politics, making and breaking cabinets as the whim moved him: he had been on the throne for twenty-one years, and there had been thirty-three ministries. Nor had a solution been found to the endemic problems of separatism and terrorism in Catalonia, where some seven hundred political murders were recorded in the five years from January 1919.[4] The First Republic had been a farce; the restored monarchy had begun well but now was whimpering its way into the shadows.

The monarch's apparent personal responsibility for the Anual disaster made it impossible for him to deal with the crisis that centred around the inquiry into its causes. The Sánchez Guerra cabinet had been brought down by a stormy debate in the Cortes on the Picasso report, against an insistent Socialist clamour that responsible individuals should be punished.

The Picasso report being too explosive for publication, the Cortes appointed its own commission of inquiry. By September, the commission's own report was ready and it was arranged that it should be published on 15 September. No serious attempt had been made to keep its contents secret, and it was known to implicate both the king and certain politicians who had abetted him in his taste for arbitrary action. Although Primo de Rivera had no wish to save the politicians he felt bound to protect the king from the consequences of his own folly. He therefore challenged the government's authority almost on the eve of the date fixed for the publication of the second Anual report, and one of the first acts of the military directorate he set up was to seize the files of the commission of inquiry.

For all that, everybody liked Don Miguel Primo de Rivera. He was, as the Spaniards say, *simpático*, a huge man with Gargantuan appetites, both alimentary and sexual. His Andalusian flow of words never deserted him and he issued decrees when he felt like it, often enough when drunk. Sometimes, in the sober light of the morning after, he revoked his own work of the night before. Given to prodigious bouts of work and play, he would shut himself up with brother officers and facile women, when the cares of office seemed too heavy, disconnect the telephones and plunge himself into relaxing revelry. This, too, like courage in battle, is an aspect of *hombría* and the Spaniards loved him for it, especially during the first years of his rule when things were going his way.

Nor was the dictator in any meaningful sense a fascist, although King Alfonso compared him to Mussolini (king and dictator paid an official visit to Italy in November 1923, and expressed admiration for fascism, but that is the kind of remark that is inseparable from official visits). He was too good-natured for that and, for a general, pacifically inclined. Indeed his first thought was to put an end to the Moroccan war.

He had been relieved of his job as Military Governor of Cadiz as early as 1917 for advocating a gradual withdrawal from Morocco and an exchange of Ceuta for Gibraltar.[5] As soon as he came to power, he promised 'a rapid, dignified and sensible solution to the Moroccan question'.

This kind of remark made Primo de Rivera's brother officers uneasy, and among those who felt this way was Franco himself. In an article in the *Revista de Tropas Coloniales*, entitled 'Passivity and Inaction', he had complained of the inveterate habit successive governments had of reducing supplies or numbers as soon as the Spaniards had recovered lost ground. This, he argued, created a vicious circle, for as soon as Spanish pressure eased, the Moors regrouped and attacked. That way, victory was always just out of reach and the war never ended.

Certainly Abd el Krim, though he had lost the territory he had won by his victory over Silvestre, was nowhere near defeat. A born organizer, he had set up a Riffian State in the mountains and villages, with its own officials and the beginnings of a regular army. He was able not only to keep up the pressure on the Melilla front, but to extend his sway westward at the expense of the wily but ageing El Raisuni.

Franco himself was getting used to being called in to retrieve apparently impossible situations. One such was building up in July 1924. With Abd el Krim still active in the east, the tribes in the western zone were rising against the Spanish authorities. Communications between the scattered Spanish posts were becoming daily more difficult. One of the hardest pressed Spanish positions was at Koba Darsa, in the mountainous Uad Lau region. Four times, a supply convoy had tried to reach the defenders and each time had been forced back by Moorish crossfire. The Command at Tetuan was against a fifth attempt, which seemed doomed to failure. Were the defenders of Koba Darsa to be left to die? A voice volunteered: 'Why not call in Franco?'

At that time Franco was far away at García Uria, in the Gomara tribal area. Tetuan's urgent message reached him in the small hours. He mounted his horse and galloped to a prearranged spot, where a car awaited him.* At mid-morning, he was in the High Commission where he learned that Koba Darsa's will and ability to fight was nearing its end. Franco laid down his conditions: full powers to carry out his plans, and a boat to take him to Uad Lau, the roads being unsafe.

At 1 p.m. he was at Uad Lau, whose little group of officers looked glum and indecisive. 'We're going to save Koba Darsa,' exclaimed Franco.

As he pored over the maps, one of the officers observed gloomily: 'You can't get across the river.'

'There's no need to,' countered Franco.

'We attack at three,' he added presently.

The others looked astonished. It was nearly three already and the sun was beating down with the force of molten lead. Besides, they pointed out, this was siesta time.

'That's just it,' Franco rejoined. 'All the Moors will be asleep. We'll catch them by surprise.'

And so it proved. At 4.30, the enemy was in flight and the survivors of Koba Darsa fell into the arms of the relieving column.

As night fell, Franco got back to Uad Lau, where he asked for a glass of milk. He had forgotten to eat for twenty hours.

Brilliant though the Koba Darsa operation had been, it was a fleeting silver lining in heavy storm clouds. Fighting in concert, El

* Arraras's account (p. 97). Galinsoga, the most determined myth-maker, has him galloping all night (p. 87).

Raisuni's tribes and Abd el Krim's had set the whole Protectorate ablaze. The Moors were besieging Xauen and Tetuan and had cut the road to Tangiers.

About this time, General Primo de Rivera decided to cross the Strait and see for himself whether anything could be done to retrieve what seemed a desperate situation. Strategically, he still inclined to pessimism, though tactically, he himself launched limited operations as soon as he arrived at Tetuan, which relieved the besieged cities and restored communications with Xauen and Tangiers. A rapid reconnaissance of the whole territory, however, convinced him that a number of Spanish positions would have to be abandoned, and he stated his opinion publicly.

On 18 July, the dictator arrived at Melilla and brought with him a plan for a withdrawal from Beni Said and Tafersit, and declared on arrival: 'Spain cannot keep on maintaining her soldiers on cliffs which it is costly to supply.'

As he reached the Army camp at Ben Tieb, outside the city, he saw banners which proclaimed in large letters: 'The Legion never retreats.'

With his Banderas standing at attention, Lieutenant-Colonel Franco read out a speech of surprising harshness: 'This soil we tread,' he said, 'is Spanish earth, for it has been acquired at the highest price and paid with the dearest money: the Spanish blood that has been shed.

'When we ask to stay on, it is not for our comfort or convenience, for we well know that, to carry out any order to advance, we have to form the vanguard, and the road of conquest is irrigated by our blood and escorted by the dead we leave on our march.

'We reject the idea of retreating, because we are persuaded that Spain is in a position to dominate the zone under her and impose her authority in Morocco.'[6]

During the luncheon in honour of the dictator, Franco appears to have made a further speech in which he softened the impact of his earlier words, repeating his view that it would be wrong to abandon Morocco, but declaring, in the name of the Legion and of the *Regulares*, that neither blood nor effort would be spared to carry out His Excellency's orders.[7]

The genial Don Miguel was too good-natured to take issue with Franco in the presence of fellow-officers. He merely thanked the

Legion's Commander for giving him a chance to explain his Moroccan policy. Both in blood and in money, he observed, Morocco had become a burden that Spain was no longer able to bear.

He sat down in an embarrassed silence that was eloquent of the soldiers' disapproval. One officer, however, raised his voice to exclaim: 'Very bad, *mi general*!' The speaker was not Franco but a dashing young Major, José Varela, whose record of bravery compared with Franco's and who later fought at Franco's side in the Civil War.*

After lunch, General Primo de Rivera toured the camp, accompanied by Franco and other officers. He seems to have been looking for a painless way of rebuking Franco, and found it as the party passed before one of the Legion's barracks on whose wall some unknown hand had copied out one of the articles of the Legionary's Credo: 'The spirit of the Legion is one of blind and fierce combativeness before the enemy.'

Turning to Franco, the General remarked: 'This article ought to be reworded, to read: "The spirit of the Legion is of blind *obedience* and fierce combativeness before the enemy!"' His emphasis on 'obedience' was not lost on Franco who, however, was too convinced a believer in discipline to take up the argument.

There was yet another confrontation between the two men before the day was out. At nightfall, the dictator called Franco to his office, not to rebuke him but to exchange views with him. Don Miguel remarked that he was glad Franco had expressed his views with such clarity. Franco repeated that even if he disagreed with orders given, he would obey them. Franco urged the general, however, to consider the arguments against a policy of withdrawal. No diplomatic gains could be made, he said, against a background of retreat. The only way to bring the Moroccan war to a satisfactory conclusion was to strike a decisive blow at the enemy. And the only way to do this was to make a landing in Alhucemas Bay.

The dictator, too, had fought in Morocco. Though he could not ignore the viewpoint of officers like Franco and Varela, he no longer saw the problem from the standpoint of a serving officer but from that of a statesman under pressure from the public and the

---

* General F. Javier Marinas: *El General Varela*. Varela was twice awarded the Laureadas de San Fernando, Spain's highest medal for gallantry.

financiers alike to bring the costly and unpopular war to an end. Moreover, he himself had lanced the abscess of the Anual disaster crisis only just in time, when it was on the point of bursting. A landing on a scale large enough to be decisive seemed an unnecessarily perilous adventure, courting further disaster.

The two men parted company courteously, agreeing to disagree. General Primo did, however, give in to the extent of ordering more limited withdrawals than he had originally envisaged. And in time he became converted to the Alhucemas plan.

6 *The Alhucemas Landing*

As Franco had feared, the Moors were quick to respond to the news that a retreat had been ordered. Tribe after tribe fell upon the withdrawing Spaniards in what was soon a general uprising in the western zone of the Protectorate. On 12 August 1924, the Spanish newspapers carried an officially inspired report that the Moroccan news was 'unsatisfactory'. At Chentafa, a lieutenant burnt himself and other survivors to death rather than surrender after supplies had run out; at Dar Akobba, Lieutenant-Colonel Mola – the conspirator of 1936 – settled down to a protracted siege.

For Franco, who had carefully studied the history of French Morocco while he helped to make history on the Spanish side, the situation closely paralleled that of 1914, when Marshal Lyautey had resisted orders from Paris to pull back to the coast, knowing that to do so would spark off a generalized tribal insurrection.

Primo de Rivera, on the other hand, had to strike a compromise between political realities and military exigencies. Never a man to shirk the consequences of his own decisions, he announced on 5 September that he and several other members of his military directorate would transfer their headquarters from Madrid to Tetuan. Appointing himself High Commissioner and General Officer Commanding, he took over the supreme direction of Moroccan operations. His plan was simple: to hold on to what he called 'useful Morocco', that is the coastal fringe, comprising the roads from Tetuan to Tangiers and Larache, and from Ceuta to

Tetuan. All positions in the mountains of Yebala and Gomara were to be abandoned.

Tetuan itself was under potential threat when the dictator and his fellow officers arrived, for the Gorgues heights commanding the approaches to the city had been under siege for a week. Five columns, the leading one consisting of Legionaries under Franco, were sent to relieve the Gorgues defenders. Franco, who had scarcely finished protecting the evacuation of another strongpoint, set about scaling the heights. Whirling snow added to the hazards of precipitous drops, and the operation took two days and two nights. On 18 September, after a twenty-one day siege, the Gorgues heights were cleared of the enemy.

Almost immediately, the young lieutenant-colonel was entrusted with a far bigger operation: to lead General Castro Girona's troops in the relief and evacuation of Xauen. This was much the same operation as General Silvestre had tried to carry out and failed. As planned, the operation fell into three phases – to reach Xauen, to round up other garrisons in the region and regroup them in Xauen, and finally to evacuate some 10,000 men. It turned out to be one of the toughest assignments of the Moroccan war. Setting out on 23 September, Franco and his men immediately ran into murderous fire and harassing guerrilla actions. After ten days of incessant fighting, Franco's vanguard reached Xauen. It was 2 October and the city had withstood a month's siege.

After a few days' rest, Franco and his men set about the second phase of the plan, relieving the regional forts one by one. By the end of the month, all the survivors had been regrouped in Xauen.

The fate of Silvestre's Army weighed heavily on the memory of General Castro Girona, who confided that the responsibility of so many lives was 'a tremendous worry' to him.[1] Franco, however, remained curiously calm as the tension of the approaching evacuation mounted all around him. During the night of 15 November, the peninsular troops were successfully evacuated, leaving only Franco and the five Banderas of the Legion. Though tense, Castro Girona had remembered the lessons of Anual and there was no panic. Franco himself wanted to give the watching Moors the impression that the Legion was there to stay. While everything likely to be of value to the Riffians was quietly destroyed, he ordered his men to go about their routine as though nothing was afoot. A group of them, however, were given needles and thread with a load of straw and a bundle of Legionaries' uniforms. Their orders were to manufacture realistic-looking stuffed soldiers to 'guard' the parapets while the Banderas slipped away.

Before giving marching orders, Franco walked around the city, with words of comfort here and there, for instance to the Sephardic Jews who, in their archaic Castilian, were expressing their fear of Moorish violence. Most of them were abandoning their humble dwellings to seek refuge, if they got that far, with other Sephardic communities in Tetuan and Tangiers. In one of the narrowest streets he caught sight of an ancient Moor, 'perhaps a centenarian', with whom he had a long talk which he later recorded in a colourfully written article in the *Revista de Tropas Coloniales*. The old man, a cousin of El Raisuni, reproached Franco with disturbing the lives of the Moors, only to abandon them, and Franco countered with a lecture on the benefits of civilization which the Spaniards had brought, only to be spurned and betrayed by the natives.

'You don't understand,' exclaimed the old man. 'Don't blame the natives for everything that goes wrong. You look at the Moors, but all you can see is their robes. You don't know the inner reasons of our behaviour: you will never know them. When the Mujahiddin [fighters in the Holy War] come – that's the reason you can't understand: every good Moslem must help the Mujahiddin, always. There isn't a village that doesn't succour or shelter them, directly or indirectly, some with arms, others with gifts, the most timid ones with their silence. This is the Mujahiddin's right of asylum.'

This interview left Franco pensive.

Calm and methodical to the end, he gathered his officers and NCOs around him on the eve of the evacuation, and told them the retreat was going to be hard, with many killed or gravely wounded. He then gave them detailed orders for a settlement of all outstanding monetary accounts. Each captain was charged with collecting his men's money and recording the amount that would be owed to those who survived. Lieutenants were to take over from captains who were killed or incapacitated. 'We must,' said Franco, 'avoid confusions and errors that might cast doubts on the honesty of each and all of us.'[2]

This order, typical in all respects of Franco's cool approach to a crisis, was good psychology: instead of worrying about the retreat and the battles ahead, officers and men settled down to their arithmetic.

At midnight on 17 November, the Legionaries started filing out of Xauen, leaving the parapets to their straw defenders. Before dawn, they were running into Riffian fire. Smelling blood, the Moors tried to seize what they took to be a chance of repeating their spectacular victory of 1921. And for a while, they looked like succeeding. For two days, gales and torrential rains slowed down the retreating Spaniards, whose vehicles sank in the mud to their axles. At Souk el-Arba, the Spaniards were blocked for three weeks, but broke out on to the Tetuan road, with Franco covering the rear. Twenty-five days after leaving Xauen the first regiments reached Tetuan. Discipline had been preserved to the end, and the bulk of the 10,000 were saved.

'Nobody,' said Primo de Rivera to a foreign journalist, 'has fought harder or with greater perseverance and capacity in Morocco.' The more effusive Millán Astray ascribed the entire success of the retreat to the subject of the dictator's remark – Franco.

Once again, eulogious references to Franco filled the Orders of the Day; and on 7 February 1925, the king promoted him to full colonel, for 'battle merits', leaving him in command of the Legion. He was thirty-two and the youngest colonel in the Spanish Army. But since the king's order was retrospective to 21 January 1924, historically speaking Franco became a colonel at thirty-one.

Now the triumphant Abd el Krim was monarch of all he surveyed, and marked the fact by proclaiming himself Sultan of Morocco. Forty tribes acknowledged his authority, and 80,000 warriors obeyed his commands. His rival El Raisuni had become his captive towards the end of 1924. His ambitious eye roved southward toward Fez, which he envisaged as his capital.

Franco, though promoted for his part in the retreat from Xauen, had not reconciled himself to the Riffian victory which that retreat implied. Had he not written, in his *Diario de una Bandera*, two years earlier, that 'Alhucemas is the focus of the anti-Spanish rebellion, the road to Fez, the short cut to the Mediterranean'? To him, the key to victory was in Alhucemas Bay.

Gradually, in the months of relative quiet that followed the withdrawal of 1924, the dictator was allowing himself to be converted to this view. The senior generals who were his colleagues on the Military Directorate were pessimists, however, and Don Miguel vacillated. He was seeing a lot of Franco, whose impressive record of successes lent a weight to his opinions that his youth could not have supported.

'They tell me,' he told Franco one day, 'that this Alhucemas business could be our catastrophe . . . that it's almost impossible.'

'Given courage, it can't fail,' countered Franco. 'It's mathematically safe.'

'All the same, I'm being reminded of the English setback at the Dardanelles.'

'Those who say this don't want Spain to triumph, nor do they deserve the glory of Alhucemas, which is certain!' Franco exclaimed.

'Certain . . Certain . . .' murmured Primo de Rivera on a sceptical note.

Franco said firmly: 'The country, General, would not forgive you if you didn't put an end to the Moroccan problem, and the key to that problem is at Alhucemas. If you, General, don't do it, someone else will, because it is not only possible but necessary, and you will lose the success and the glory which await you there for the good of Spain.'[3]

Whether these slightly grandiloquent words were precisely those used by Franco in one of his talks with Primo de Rivera there is no doubt that they reflected his innermost conviction. Alone, they might not have outweighed the pessimistic counsels of the dictator's closest colleagues. But now a new turn of events convinced General Primo that the Alhucemas solution was inescapable.

The French, under Lyautey, had been pushing northward in their gradual conquest of the territory they claimed under their treaty of 1904 with the Spaniards. As they drew near the borders of the Spanish Protectorate, they ran into fierce resistance from Rif tribesmen, who appealed to Abd el Krim for help. Earlier, perhaps, than he had planned, the Lion of the Rif* – as he had been known since his massive victory of 1921 – threw his army, with its forty captured cannon commanded by a German deserter from the French Foreign

* General Sanjurjo was also called 'Lion of the Rif' by his enthusiastic followers.

Legion, into a drive that took the French utterly by surprise. By June, his forces were threatening Fez.

Alarmed, Paris sent Marshal Pétain, the victor of Verdun, to Morocco, to command the local forces. The reinforcements for which Lyautey had been vainly clamouring, were sent at last, and Lyautey, who had been doing two jobs at once, was able to devote all his time to administration, while Pétain did the fighting.

Until then, the French had looked on with smug amusement at the military difficulties encountered by the Spaniards. But their first taste of Abd el Krim's methods opened their eyes: to hold Fez and Marrakesh was one thing, to repulse the Riffian fury quite another. Content to watch the Spaniards while they alone were in trouble, the French now wanted concerted action. Overtures were made to the dictator who, on 28 July 1925, received Marshal Pétain in Tetuan. He listened while the marshal, still psychologically attuned to the massive scale of the Great War operations, outlined a grandiose plan for the conquest of the Atlas passes in preparation for an offensive against the vital centres of the Rif, Axdir and Targuist. Then Don Miguel produced the dusty folder in which the now disgraced General Berenguer had kept the contingency battle plans for a landing at Alhucemas Bay. Now, said Primo de Rivera, was the time to strike, since Abd el Krim's depleted forces were in no position to resist the landing.

Pétain accepted. It was agreed that the Spanish forces would undertake the landing, protected by a Franco-Spanish fleet. Each of the dictator's generals having turned down the honour of leading the Spanish troops, Primo de Rivera himself took on the job, staking his reputation and indeed his power on the wisdom of his judgment.

Logistically, it was a considerable operation. Some 18,000 men were to be landed, 9,000 each from Ceuta and Melilla, with Franco and his Legionaries to form the vanguard of the Ceuta column under General Saro. While the stockpiling of supplies went on at Ceuta and Melilla, the warships gathered, together with a heterogeneous collection of merchantmen and landing craft of the type the British had used at the Dardanelles.

After a diversionary naval fire to the east of the point chosen for the landing, Franco's assault troops went ashore – 'with dash and mastery', wrote General Goded[4] – on the night of 7 September and established a lodgment at low cost. Anxious days went by while heavy seas impeded the build-up of forces and the food supplies of those who had landed dwindled. By 20 September, however, 15,000 men had disembarked. Two days later, the main operation began, with orders given to scale the heights of Malmusi Alto and Morro Viejo.[5] Franco's assault troops led the way toward the first of these objectives. Reporting later on his success, General Saro wrote:

I make a special mention of Colonel Franco, who in his most brilliant action in this combat, confirmed once again the opinion which all, without exception, have of his competence, skill, courage, serenity and all the exceptional qualities that make him a leader worthy of all praise.

Again and again, in official accounts of the Alhucemas battles, we find the names of officers who were later to be Franco's companions in the Nationalist insurrection of 1936, men such as Muñoz Grandes, the Commander of the Blue Division in Russia, Goded who wrote the standard work on the Moroccan war, and Varela, wounded in the siege of Madrid. Franco himself was in the thick of the fighting from 17 September till 2 October, when his shock troops drove the last defenders away from Abd el Krim's stronghold on Mount Amekrán. Soon flames enveloped the Rif leader's eyrie; and the road to Axdir lay wide open.

Abd el Krim was in flight, but instead of pursuing him – as Goded, for instance, would have wished – the Spanish Army allowed him to get a further wind. It was not until 10 July 1927 that General Sanjurjo was able to proclaim that the whole of Spanish Morocco had been pacified.

Franco himself did not take part in the last phases of the pacification. But his reward had come, for a royal decree of 3 February 1926, promoted him to Brigadier-General. Simultaneously, he was awarded his second Military Medal, and made Commander of the French Legion of Honour. At thirty-three, he was the youngest general in Spain and all Europe. The Superior Committee of Generals, in recommending him for promotion, had used words which his Spanish biographers later seized upon as prophetic: 'He is a positive national asset, and surely the country and the Army will derive great benefit from the singular aptitude of Colonel Franco for higher posts.'

PART III

Peace

❈

I *The King's Favourite General*

By temperament, Franco was a fighting soldier. Garrison life bored him and administration held little appeal. Politics was a primarily civil activity, which at best made the wheels of the military machine run smoothly, and at worst impeded soldiers in their duty to the motherland. In those distant days of the 1920s, Franco placed this duty foremost in his code of behaviour but had not yet begun to identify himself with the nation. So long as the State was not funda-mentally threatened, politics were not his concern. And so long as the government of the day maintained its authority, it was his duty to obey its orders.

For ten years, from 1926 to 1936, General Franco served the State by obeying the orders of the government of the day. He obeyed the dictator and was loyal to the king. When the king abandoned his throne, Franco was loyal to the Republic as he had been loyal to the Monarchy. He obeyed the orders of successive Republican govern-ments, protesting only when such orders appeared to threaten the vital interests of the Army. And he defended the Republic against its enemies. For ten years he kept out of plots and conspiracies, even though his own brother or his companions-in-arms were involved. When the great conspiracy of 1936 gathered strength, he sat in initially as an observer rather than as a participant. Astonishing as it seems, in the light of his prolonged success as politician and states-man, General Franco became a political general by historical acci-dent.

Therein, indeed, lies the inner secret of Franco's hold on power, a process in which persuasion – normally an essential ingredient of political success, whether of parliamentary or demagogic rule – has played no part. When he was a fighting general, Franco obeyed the politicians' orders and expected his own military orders to be obeyed by his subordinates. When history made him a political general and Chief of State, his concept of the State and of duty remained unaltered. The only difference was that he had now become the State and all authority came from him. Obedience and discipline remained central to his view of the nation and its public manifestations.

When Franco returned to Spain in 1926, Primo de Rivera's dictatorship was still riding high. And yet, all-powerful though the dictator appeared to be, his rule never looked anything but provisional. Indeed he himself had always disclaimed any idea of permanence, and his own *pronunciamiento* had described his impending seizure of power as a 'brief parenthesis' between periods of constitutional legality. His trouble, and Spain's, was that the parenthesis had ceased to be brief, while the end was always just out of sight. He was strong, but vulnerable; indispensable for a while, but incapable of recognizing that the period of his usefulness might be drawing to a close.

No greater contrast could be imagined than that between his dictatorship and Franco's. In a crisis, Franco's way was to sit tight and say nothing. Primero de Rivera spoke and acted incessantly, taking the people into his confidence with a candour that was engaging at first but began to pall when his luck ran out, rushing from improvization to improvization, often brilliantly, but towards the end, desperately. A political tyro, innocent of academic training, he was original because unhampered by preconceptions. Franco was to display, in later years, a preference for inaction over wrong action. Primo would act first and think later; if his second thoughts cast doubts on the wisdom of his first choice, he would undo his own decrees or simply disregard a law which he himself had instituted.

His approach to government was simple and passionate. The trouble with politics was politicians, who were corrupt and inefficient. So the politicians must go. The press stuck up for constitutional rule – that is, in his eyes, for the politicians – so the press must be silenced. For every problem there was a solution, and it was not to be found in books. He would tackle every problem and solve it as best he could. If he made a mistake, he would say so, publicly and honestly, and do his best to correct it. A torrent of word and deed carried him forward, and an astonishing run of luck favoured his endeavours, though he himself attributed his successes to intuition and divine guidance. He could have added energy and hard work. Certainly, Primo de Rivera was a trier.

The dictator saw all issues with a soldierly directness and it rarely occurred to him that others might not share his approach or support his proposed solution. Himself a mighty eater, he exhorted Spaniards to eat only one large meal a day. Though an Andalusian aristocrat and an Army officer, he championed women's rights and aspired to relieve the poor of their poverty. Deeply touched by the plight of the poorest Madrileños, who had had to pawn their bedsheets, he used his first budget surplus to redeem them from the pawnbrokers. He gave the workers cheap housing and a health service, and persuaded Largo Caballero, the Socialist leader, to collaborate with him by the twin baits of social welfare and hostility towards the Anarchists.

Though Primo de Rivera admired Mussolini (who, of course, had been a Socialist before he founded modern fascism), his borrowings from Italy were slight. True, he replaced all political parties by an organization of his own, called the Patriotic Union (which, he said, was not a party, and which was united only in that its variegated members all stood to gain something from the dictatorship). But he was not interested in Mussolini's corporative State and fell short of being a true totalitarian. His motive was 'Nation, Church and King' and he always made it clear that the order in which these words appeared was significant: the Nation was more important than the Church, and the King came a bad third.

Though Primo de Rivera was Spain's first dictator of the twentieth century, and Franco her second, the line of descent from one to the other was indirect. The first dictator's son, José Antonio, prophet and martyr of the Falange, was a spiritual and ideological link of sorts. But for many years now, his name, though officially revered, has mainly served as a reminder of faded dreams and frustrated hopes. If anything, Franco is even less ideological a ruler than Primo de Rivera was.

Another difference between the two régimes is worth mentioning. Though Primo de Rivera's power was absolute while it lasted, it derived in the last resort from the king and the Army. That is another reason why the dictatorship was essentially provisional. In contrast, Franco came to be 'Caudillo by the Grace of God', and Chief of State. There being no higher authority than his, he became, in effect, life sovereign, so that his régime was provisional only in the sense that it was limited by his own mortality.

Franco's role under the dictatorship was marginal, but not unimportant in terms of his own career. Primo had appointed him Commander of the First Infantry Brigade of the First Division in Madrid. It undoubtedly irked him to become a 'courtier general' at a time when his former companions-in-arms were still chasing the Moors into the hills, but his new life offered compensations in terms of personal standing. His influence was negligible, but he was soon to be, for what this was still worth, the king's favourite general. For some time, indeed, Alfonso had favoured Franco with special marks of affection and esteem. On 1 March 1925, when Franco was still Colonel of the Legion, the king sent him a medal blessed by the Virgin of Pilar, with a note couched in the familiar 'tu':[1]

> Please wear this medal – so military and so Spanish – which will surely protect you.
> My congratulations and my thanks for your action. You know how much your very affectionate friend loves and appreciates you.
> Alfonso XIII

In October 1927 – three months after the official end of the Moroccan war – the king and queen invited Franco to accompany them to Morocco, where Alfonso presented a special flag to the Legion. This, too, was a sign of honour, to Franco as well as to the fighting men he had commanded. At Ceuta, in the midst of his old friends, he was a guest at a banquet in honour of his former chief, General Berenguer, the former High Commissioner in Morocco, who had been placed on the reserve, but in compensation had been given an earldom as Count of Xauen. The atmosphere was easy, relaxed and self-congratulatory. The humiliation and tragedy of Anual seemed far away now that Spanish victories had brought peace to Morocco.

There was little for Franco to do but see to the requirements of the Regiments of the King and of Leon, which composed his

5a Statesman of a vanished Spain:
Antonio Maura.

5b King and dictator,
September 1923.
Alfonso XIII and
General Primo de Rivera.

6 Alcalá Zamora's successor, President Azaña (*right*) with Miguel Maura, Minister of the Interior.

First Brigade, and inspect them on ceremonial occasions. Soon, however, he was to be given a bigger job, which was to test his powers of improvization and organization to the utmost, while still a far cry from the fields of action which by temperament he preferred.

With his generous, expansive nature, the dictator had not borne a grudge against Franco over their earlier differences of opinion. The young general's advocacy of a landing at Alhucemas had proved well-founded and he had played a role of distinctive courage in the operation. Now Primo de Rivera's thoughts turned again towards Franco in connection with a project which had been maturing at the back of his mind. One day in the early autumn of 1927, shortly after Franco's return from his Moroccan trip in the king's company, Don Miguel summoned Franco to his office and unburdened himself.[2]

'We need a united Army,' said Primo, in approximately those words.

Franco nodded, cautiously. This was common ground, but what was the Marquess of Estella getting at?

The dictator explained. The academic side of military training for officers was too regionalized, he argued. Regionalism was bad enough in Spain already, and there was no need for the Army to make things worse. What one now had was an Army of Catalan officers, and Basque or Castilian officers, instead of a solid, united corps of Spanish officers, ready to forget their provincial origins and their innate individualism. If the nation was to be united, then its Army, too, must be given the built-in unity that could only come from a centralized training scheme.

With all this, Franco could readily agree, and he could now see where the conversation was leading, since Primo de Rivera's Directorate had just created a General Military Academy at Saragossa. It was just like Primo de Rivera to launch his plan before thinking it through. The Military Academy existed on paper only. It had no staff, no equipment, no programme and – so far – no students. More fundamentally, it lacked a Director.

'We need a soldier with military prestige and administrative ability,' said Primo. 'You are the man for the job.'

Franco, who had been growing more silent and withdrawn as Don Miguel warmed to his exposition, expressed objections. The job, he declared, ought to go to someone like his former chief and creator of the Foreign Legion, Millán Astray. In all respects, this would be the ideal choice. Here was a natural leader of men who, in addition, had been a professor at the Toledo military academy. Moreover, he had lost an arm and an eye in combat and was therefore barred from further active service.

Primo de Rivera allowed Franco his say, then gently rejected his arguments. He had given the matter careful thought, he said, and Franco was the man he wanted.

At this point it became clear that the dictator's proposal was turning into an order. As was his wont, Franco bowed and accepted.

Two other important things happened to Franco in 1928. One is universally known and has brought him nothing but joy: the birth of his daughter Carmencita – now Marquesa de Villaverde and the mother of Franco's seven grandchildren. The other has not, to my knowledge, been told before, and brought him, not joy, but knowledge and a spur to action – the knowledge of an enemy, and the ambition to defeat him.

For it was in 1928 that Franco, whose experiences of 1917 had already alerted him to the danger of Bolshevism, first began a systematic study of communism. He started subscribing to a Swiss anticommunist publication, the *Bulletin de la EIA* – the journal of the *Entente Internationale Anti-communiste*, of Geneva, whose President was the late National Councillor Aubert.

It was Franco himself who mentioned the bulletin to me, saying that he had been a subscriber for many years and, through it, had had access to much material about the Comintern which few people were bothering to study. That way, he followed communist tactics in Spain throughout the life of the Second Republic. He was aware, for instance, that the Spanish Communists were under orders to foment strikes and violence, in order to provoke repressive measures by the authorities. This, he said, enabled Socialist deputies to make speeches in the Cortes calling for the banning of the *Guardia Civil* and for further cuts in the Army.

Until the Civil War began, Franco never missed an issue of the bulletin, and he was careful to notify the publishers of his changes of address when he was transferred to the Balearics and to the Canaries. Moreover, he persuaded certain other officers to subscribe to it. As a result, he claims, the events of 1936 did not come as a surprise to them, and they were ready to deal with the Communists.*

In some respects, the situation Franco faced at Saragossa reminded him of conditions in the Legion when he had first taken up his duties. Every amenity was lacking and everything had to be created from scratch. A start had been made on the building in an open space known as San Gregorio, but the War Ministry's credits amounted to a discouraging trickle. The key people, at this stage, were architects and builders, carpenters and plumbers. But Franco knew all about red tape, delays and disappointing deliveries. Furniture and equipment, from canteen stoves to filing cabinets, had to be planned for and ordered well in advance. And even while the building went on, prospective teachers and specialists had to be interviewed and appointed so that the finished structure should be more than a shell – a living centre of military doctrine. Seated at a sergeant's table in a bare room at the Carmen barracks at Saragossa, Franco received a constant stream of visitors, drew up budgets, wrote to the War Ministry for further funds and studied reports on foreign military academies, from Sandhurst and Saint-Cyr to West Point, for useful hints on organization.

One day, surveying the chaos of stone and mortar, lead pipes and wood-shavings that was to be the General Military Academy, he made a brief and confident announcement: 'The entrance competition will be held in June 1928 in the Grupo Escolar Joaquín Costa. The courses will begin in October.'

By relentless pressure on all who had a hand in the project, Franco managed to stick to his schedule. In the late summer of 1928, he made a quick trip to Germany, where he attended the exercises of the Berlin garrison and visited the Dresden military training centre.[3] Seven hundred and eighty-five candidates had sat for the Saragossa Academy's competitive entrance examination, but only two hundred

---

* General Franco's collection of files of the *Bulletin de la EIA* was lost, along with other possessions, when his Madrid house and its contents were sequestrated by the Republican authorities after the 1936 military uprising began. The *Entente Internationale Anticommuniste* itself, which had maintained close relations with the Antikomintern, destroyed its own files, for reasons of Swiss neutrality, on the outbreak of world war in 1939. Some of the details I give, which supplement Franco's own recollections, were obtained on my behalf by the Spanish Ambassador in Berne, Don Juan de Lojendio, Marques de Vellisca.

and fifteen of them had made the grade. On 2 October, back from Germany, Franco watched them enter the gates for the first time.

For three days, the cadets underwent intensive military training. Then on 5 October, they were paraded before Primo de Rivera in an impressive inaugural ceremony. Franco thought this an appropriate occasion to address the new boys – Spain's future Army officers – with a message of austerity and devotion to duty in the Spartan tradition of the Spanish Foreign Legion. Military life, he warned them, comprises hardships, work and sacrifices. 'Do not forget,' he said in conclusion, 'that he who suffers wins victories, and that to resist and vanquish every day is the school of victory.'

Though Franco's choice of words was hardly original or profound, his message was clear. To supplement it – and still in the tradition of the Legion and of Millán Astray's death and glory credo – he drafted Ten Commandments for the aspiring officer. Summarily paraphrased, they ran as follows:[4]

First Commandment:	Love your country and be faithful to your King.
Second Commandment:	Cultivate a great military spirit.
Third Commandment:	Be chivalrous in spirit.
Fourth Commandment:	Carry out your duties faithfully and precisely.
Fifth Commandment:	Never grumble and do not tolerate the grumbles of others.
Sixth Commandment:	See to it that you are loved by your inferiors and appreciated by your superiors.
Seventh Commandment:	Be ready to volunteer for any sacrifice by asking – and wishing – to be used on occasions when the risks and the fatigue are greatest.
Eighth Commandment:	Be a good comrade.
Ninth Commandment:	Develop a love of responsibility and decision.
Tenth Commandment:	Show courage and abnegation.

To some extent, these were conventional maxims. They were also singularly typical of General Franco, who had so often practised what he now preached, especially his Seventh Commandment. But perhaps, in the retrospect of history, the most typical of all, in its curiously prophetic flavour, was the Fifth. 'Thou shalt not grumble,' Franco had told his cadets, at a time when Primo de Rivera was giving much the same injunction to the Spanish people. Neither the dictator of the 1920s nor the Caudillo of Spain liked Spaniards to grumble. And each in his way was convinced he knew best what was good for them.

Traditional though Franco's moral training was, his methods were considered advanced in his day. He regarded the parrot-memorizing of military manuals as a counter-productive form of teaching, guaranteed to produce bored junior officers without initiative. Instead, he insisted on plenty of practical work, lectures with cinematic illustrations, and manœuvres in conditions that simulated those he and his Legionaries had had to overcome in the Moroccan mountains. In winter, snow was their element. In summer, he led them in assaults on the heights of Canfranc against the resistance of imaginary Riffians.

While Franco was making a going concern of the Military Academy, Primo de Rivera was running into trouble. His achievements were considerable and were generally recognized, but he was making more enemies every month. He had brought peace to Spain after the long blood-letting of Morocco. He had given the country a network of modern highways and built dams where water lay idle previously. He had given the railways new rolling stock and encouraged industry with the support of an expanding steel output. The workers seemed reasonably happy, and the peasants were encouraged by the mild beginning of land reform. A young, brilliant but erratic Finance Minister, Calvo Sotelo – whose murder in 1936 sparked off the Nationalist uprising – had made a partially successful attempt to tackle tax reform.

Trade, too, had soared in the early years of the dictatorship by something like 300 per cent. Indeed, it was the world boom of the 1920s, as much as anything Primo de Rivera did, that accounted for the striking success of his policy, which, in effect, substituted prosperity for politics. When the first ripples of the world depression began to hit the shores of Spain, prosperity started receding. Calvo Sotelo tried in vain to maintain the value of the peseta by buying Spanish currency in London. By this time great industrialists like Francisco de Asis Cambó, and outstanding economists, such as Flores de Lemús, had had enough of the dictator and his financial and economic policies. For some time, they had been complaining that Primo de Rivera was too fond of State corporations at the expense of private enterprise, and to the exclusive benefit of the workers. This was bad enough when the country's money was sound, but quite intolerable with a falling peseta.

Inevitably, the intellectuals became disenchanted with the régime much sooner than the financial and industrial Right. The philosopher Eduardo Ortega y Gasset had this in common with Primo de Rivera that he, too, had attacked the corrupt parliamentary régime the dictatorship had replaced. But he soon turned against the dictator for his censorship, his regimentation of the universities and his blind faith in clerical control of education. Another famous philosopher, Miguel de Unamuno, was deprived of his Chair of Greek at Salamanca when a letter in which he had attacked the dictatorship was published without his permission in Argentina.

More seriously, from the standpoint of Don Miguel's political survival, he alienated a section of the Army by abolishing the Artillery officers' system of promotion based on seniority only (a safeguard against nepotism). When an artillery barracks went on strike in 1926, he suspended the entire artillery officer corps without bothering to consult the king. This arbitrary act shocked infantry and cavalry men as well as their gunner colleagues, and set off a cry of indignation against the king, who had allowed it to happen without a murmur.

At the end of January 1929, the artillery officers at Ciudad Real went into revolt in support of a coup led in Valencia by the seventy-year-old ex-premier, Sánchez Guerra. The coup collapsed, not least because the garrison commander at Valencia, General Castro Girona, had a wife who, says Raymond Carr, 'could not resist the social prospects of a new command in Morocco, offered her husband by the government'.[5] Though Castro Girona was in sympathy with Sánchez Guerra, his wife won and he arrested the rebellious old civilian. In October, however, a tribunal of brigadier-generals found him Not Guilty of sedition – an insulting rebuff to the dictator.[6]

In March 1929, two months after the Valencia affair, Primo de Rivera, faced with a wave of agitation from students and professors, closed down Madrid and other universities. The dictator himself seems to have sensed that his lease of political life was running out, but he was reluctant to leave yet another constitutional void behind him, to be filled no one knew how. His solution was to appoint a National Advisory Assembly and call on it to draft a new constitution. Primo wanted work, not words, from his assemblymen, and limited all speeches to thirty minutes. The Assembly worked, all right, but its draft constitution pleased nobody, least of all the king, who found he had lost his dearest privilege – that of hiring and firing ministers – which he would now have to share with a fascist-type Council.

The king began to wonder how he could get rid of the dictator he had appointed without losing his throne in the process. Oblivious of the hostility he had aroused, Primo de Rivera lifted the censorship, only to reel back under the impact of the torrential criticism he had released. Tired and ailing, he now faced a rumble of rebellion among the southern garrisons. Harassed on all sides, he developed acute insomnia. For some time now, his intuitions had been growing rarer and less successful. But on 26 January 1930, he called on intuition once again to solve his problems. As he saw it, it was all a question of confidence, that is, of the Army's confidence in him. The Army had made him, and it was now up to the Army to support him or deny him. By-passing the king yet again, he wrote to all the Captains-General, offering to resign immediately if they no longer wanted him. Their replies were evasive, but clear enough: the Army no longer backed him. Two days later, he resigned and left the country, to die seven weeks later in Paris, a broken man.

General Franco took no part in any of the military conspiracies against the dictator, much less in the civilian ones. To all intents and purposes, his only interest was in perfecting the academic organization he had created. He had accepted his appointment as Director from Primo de Rivera, and he remained at his post after the dictator's fall. On 5 June 1930, Alfonso XIII visited the Saragossa Academy, accompanied by General Berenguer, to hand over a flag to the cadets and receive their oath of allegiance. He declared himself full of enthusiasm over their bearing, embraced Franco in their presence and announced that he would invite them to mount guard at the Royal Palace.[7] Later that year, he sent the Prince of Asturias to Saragossa to open the school year.

Shortly afterwards, Franco's work at Saragossa attracted praise from a man whose prestige then stood high, though it was to crumble nine years later in the path of the advancing German Panzers who had by-passed the allegedly impregnable Maginot Line he had built to stop them. André Maginot, at that time France's War Minister, dropped in at the Military Academy to present Franco with the Legion of Honour, conferred on him by the French Republic for his part in the Alhucemas landing which, it will be remembered, was part of a joint Franco-Spanish plan of campaign. Having been shown around the Academy, and listened to Franco's explanation of his training methods, Maginot reported on his return to Paris:

> It is not merely a model organization but, of its kind, the most modern centre in the world. Spain may be proud to have in its school for officers the last word in military technique and pedagogy. General Franco, although young, struck me as a mature leader and a director full of experience, clear-sightedness and the psychology of command.[8]

Maginot's parting words to Franco were an invitation to visit the French Ecole Supérieure de Guerre. At a time when the military prestige Marshal Foch had won for French arms in 1918 remained untarnished, Maginot's praise and his invitation to Franco constituted a compliment to which Franco was not insensible. In November, he went to Versailles, where he met General Pétain, attended a course of lectures and basked in the glow of Franco-Spanish friendship, so lately sealed on the Moroccan battlefields.

He returned to find the monarchy in its last protracted death throes. In vain had the king tried to dissociate himself from Primo de Rivera. Alfonso was blamed both for the frivolous succession of cabinets that led to the dictator's take-over, and for sanctioning the dictatorship. Now the crowd as well as the intellectuals sensed that wanting to get rid of Primo, he was merely trying to save his own skin. Significantly, the demonstrators who gathered in various Spanish towns the day Don Miguel fell shouted 'Down with the king'.

The king, on his side, could sense the hostility that was mounting against him. A bolder or less arrogant man might conceivably have saved the throne by turning to the politicians who had helped to turn Primo de Rivera out, even though their support for the monarchy was doubtful – men like Count Romanones, the former Foreign Minister, who had resigned in 1917 because of attacks on him by supporters of Germany; or Sánchez Guerra, the former Prime Minister who was riding the crest of popularity after his plot and acquittal. These men and others waited in the wings, hoping for a summons to the palace, which never came.

Alfonso, however, was not a Bourbon for nothing. Ignoring the politicians, he turned to old General Berenguer, who had become head of his Military Household and whose only qualification for dealing with a critical political situation of this kind was that he was known to have disapproved of the dictator's methods. Poor Berenguer was ill as well as old; in time, he took to a wheel-chair. Charged with the king's mission, he filled the cabinet with 'friends of the king or friends of friends of the King'.[9]

Berenguer's solution for the crisis of the régime was simple but unworkable, for confidence, not only in Alfonso XIII but in the monarchy itself, was already too deeply shaken for a backward look to the last century. What Berenguer wanted was a return to the 1876 constitution which had enabled Cánovas del Castillo to introduce carefully regulated alternations of party rule. But what had worked for the most gifted Spanish statesman of his day could hardly work for a tired old general in the incipient turmoil of 1930. He might, perhaps, have bulldozed a measure through a docile Cortes – had he been younger, more decisive and more energetic. But he was none of these things. He hesitated and delayed his summons to the Cortes, while anti-Alfonso sentiment gathered strength.

Sánchez Guerra struck the first blow with a speech of masterly ambiguity, in which he declared: 'I am not a Republican, but I recognize that Spain has a right to be a Republic.'[10] This was a signal for the politicians and generals to indulge in their favourite pastime in moments of dissatisfaction – conspiracy. Meeting in the shadows in Madrid and other cities, were a number of men who later played prominent roles in the great drama of the Republic and Civil War. Francisco Franco was not among them; but his brother Ramón was.

Among the plotting politicians one finds Niceto Alcalá Zamora, who was to become the first President of the Republic; Manuel Azaña, a liberal intellectual and pamphleteer, who was to be Prime Minister and to succeed Alcalá as President; Alejandro Lerroux, the

fiery orator of the Barcelona underworld, who took his Radical Party
into Alcalá's coalition government. These men, all of whom for
different reasons disapproved of the revolutionary Catalan separatism, conferred with revolutionary Catalan separatists in a San
Sebastian hotel in August 1930 and made a common cause with them,
in the interests of overthrowing the monarchy.[11] Together they set
up a Revolutionary Committee, under Alcalá Zamora's chairmanship, which later became the Second Republic's Provisional Government.

The soldiers, too, were conspiring. General Gonzálo Queipo de
Llano, an irrepressible character who had been placed on the reserve
by Primo de Rivera for remarking on the coincidence that the
dictator's UP stood for public urinal as well as for Patriotic Union,
was among the most enthusiastic plotters. His personal grievance
was that Berenguer refused to reinstate him, his political one that the
king's new saviour declined to disown the dictator's acts.[12] It is
intriguing, in the light of Queipo de Llano's later prowess as a
Nationalist general, to find him among the Republican conspirators;
but as we have seen, he had his reasons.

A still more spectacular military plotter was Major Ramón
Franco. At that time, if somebody had asked a Spaniard-in-the-street
if he had heard of Franco, the answer would have been: 'Yes, of
course, the airman.' General Francisco Franco's Moroccan exploits,
exceptional though they were, could hardly compete in publicity
value with Ramón's eye-catching flight across the South Atlantic in a
Dornier, the *Plus Ultra*, early in 1926. Acclaimed by delirious crowds
in Rio de Janeiro, Buenos Aires and Montevideo, he had been
decorated by Alfonso on his return and a monument was erected in
recognition of his piloting feat.[13] He soon quarrelled with both the
king and the dictator, however, when he was placed on the reserve
after he had failed to reach New York on another flight – having
been too impatient to wait for the plane that was being sent to him
and taking off in a machine of his own choice.

Ramón Franco's only asset, apart from his popularity, was the fact
that in Berenguer's eyes, he could do no wrong.[14] A shrewder man
than Berenguer was watching him, however, in General Emilio
Mola Vidal. This, too, was intriguing in the light of later history. In
1936, Mola was the arch-conspirator against the State. But in 1930,
far from conspiring, he was watching out for conspirators, having

accepted – reluctantly it is true – the direction of the Security Police from Berenguer.

In character, Ramón Franco was strikingly different from Francisco. Impetuous and foolhardy, he plotted in broad daylight, hopping from place to place to whip up feelings against the monarchy, meeting Catalan extremists and – the police thought – running arms for good measure. Reports on all these activities duly reached Mola, who grew worried. Not that he credited Ramón with the qualities necessary for success for, in his eyes, the airman 'lacked intelligence, prestige and other indispensable conditions'.[15] But he did think Major Franco capable of joining in any plot, whether Republican, syndicalist or communist, if it brought him into the limelight. Since his duty was to protect the State, he could not ignore Ramón's attitude. But he was reluctant to arrest Ramón who, like Francisco, had fought by Mola's side in Morocco.

Seeking a way out, he decided to take Francisco Franco into his confidence, and asked him to have a quiet talk with his brother and appeal to him to behave himself.[16] Sceptical, General Franco said he didn't think it would make any difference to Ramón's plans, but he was willing to try. On 10 October 1930, the Franco brothers dined together in Madrid, but nothing came of it, as Francisco had anticipated. A private talk between Mola and Major Franco also left the airman unabashed.

Shortly after, on receipt of fresh reports of Ramón's revolutionary activities, Mola ordered his arrest. Almost immediately, however, he escaped, hid in Madrid and pressed on with his plans for a *coup d'état* which was to bring in the Republic. Alas for the revolutionaries, things soon started going wrong. A dissatisfied Army officer who had served under General Franco in Morocco but had been passed over for promotion, Captain Galán, jumped the gun, by ordering the garrison of Jaca, in Aragon province, which he commanded, to take up arms against the king. He fancied his chances of bringing in all the Pyrenean garrisons, capturing Huesca and Saragossa and even provoking a general strike. But he had struck too soon.

From his desk at the Saragossa Military Academy, General Franco telephoned the regional commander to offer his cadets to put down the rebellion. Thus in 1930 as in Oviedo in 1917 at the time of the general strike, Franco's dominant concern was the restoration of law and order. It was a matter of indifference to him whether the rebels

were miners or Army officers. Nor did personal feelings play a part
in his thinking, for he was well aware that his brother Ramón was in
sympathy, and possibly in league, with the Jaca plotters. As it turned
out, however, Franco's cadets were not needed, for reinforcements
from Huesca quickly overwhelmed the rebellious garrison.

This ought to have been the signal for the Madrid plotters to
change their plans and bide a more suitable time. But neither Queipo
de Llano nor Ramón Franco was the kind of man to allow considerations of timing to influence them. On 16 December, four days
after Galán's ineffectual coup, they went into action in their turn.
Striking at dawn, Ramón and Queipo, at the head of a group of
officers, mainly of the Air Force, seized the aerodrome at Cuatro
Vientos and called the Army and the people to arms. It was a tragi-
comic affair. Ramón and Queipo had hailed a taxi in Madrid to drive
them to the aerodrome. On the way, Queipo gloomily noted that the
tramways were running. This, he thought, suggested a normality
that was hardly compatible with revolution. Against that, a few bar
pianists were playing the Marseillaise – revolutionary in intent,
though scarcely native-born.[17]

Not to be deterred, Ramón grabbed a military aircraft and flew
over the Royal Palace to demonstrate that he and his followers were
the masters of the capital. He had intended to drop a few bombs, but
the sight of women and children strolling or playing in the palace
gardens deterred him.[18] Rather sheepishly, he flew back to Cuatro
Vientos. At this point, discretion at last became the better part of
valour, and he and Queipo slipped over the Portuguese border,
taking refuge first in Lisbon, then in Paris.

There was nothing Berenguer and Alfonso could do about Ramón
Franco and Queipo de Llano. But the unfortunate Captain Galán and
his assistant, Lieutenant García Hernández, were in their power and
they decided to make an example of them. Both were tried by a
Military Tribunal, condemned to death and executed.

The executions were a grave error of judgment on the part of the
threatened monarch. They made martyrs for the Republicans and
caused thousands of wavering monarchists to change camp. Alfonso
emerged as a cruel monster; and Berenguer lost his last chance of
playing the conciliator and saving the monarchy. Republican sentiment was further fanned by a number of distinguished intellectuals,
including Ortega y Gasset and Dr Gregorio Marañón, who, in

February 1931, formed an anti-monarchist group called 'In the Service of the Republic'.[19] The king had never paid much attention to intellectuals. He was now to find that they had become a power in their own right.

Berenguer was getting nowhere and knew it. When he resigned at last, in February, the king turned to the acquitted rebel ex-premier, Sánchez Guerra and asked him to form a government. Once again, an element of comedy crept into the desperate situation. Alcalá Zamora and the whole of his San Sebastian Revolutionary Committee were in gaol, he himself having been arrested one Sunday as he was leaving Church. So it was to gaol that Sánchez Guerra went in search of ministers. To Alfonso's shock, however, the Revolutionary Committee *en masse* turned down Sánchez Guerra's approach.

Running short of candidates, the king now appealed to Melquíades Alvarez, a mild Republican who thought of republicanism as a lever with which to get the monarchy to do things that needed to be done, such as bringing democracy to Spain. Once again, he was disappointed, for Melquíades proposed the appointment of unacceptable people, including General Goded, one of the military conspirators who had forced the resignation of Primo de Rivera. At this stage, the king gave up his belated efforts to come to terms with the opposition and retreated into his shell, calling on a mild and ineffectual naval officer, Admiral Aznar, to form a Ministry. The resulting brew had a very familiar flavour. All the staunch monarchists were there, including Count Romanones and Juan de la Cierva, a Conservative lawyer who had been *cacique* of Murcia. General Berenguer took the War Ministry.

The end was even nearer than the shrewdest observers supposed. Everyone realized that elections could not long be delayed, but Romanones sought to take the sting out of them by starting off with municipal instead of general elections. This device might have worked six months or a year earlier, but the swing in public opinion was greater than had been guessed in an age that had not yet felt the impact of Dr Gallup's methods. The public, in fact, was quite as ready to express its opinion by means of local elections as by the national ones.

The voting took place on 12 April 1931, and on that day, General Franco, punctilious as usual about his duties, voted with the rest in the College of Arrabal in Saragossa. He was back in his study at the

Military Academy when the astonishing results started coming in. Nearly all the cities and large towns, from Madrid to Barcelona, from San Sebastian to Seville, had voted overwhelmingly in favour of the Republican parties. Romanones was thunderstruck. The king wondered what to do. True, the largest cities, in general, had voted against him, but the countryside still seemed solidly monarchist, and some of the more conservative provincial capitals, including Burgos and Cadiz, had remained loyal to the Crown. Could anything be saved from the wreckage?

From his academic fastness, Franco asked himself the same question. The answer – a clear negative – came to him in the form of a coded message from General Berenguer, addressed to all the military chiefs. Calling for serenity and patriotism on the part of the Army, the War Minister's message went on:

> Keep in close contact with all the garrisons in your region, recommending to everyone to have absolute confidence in the maintenance at all price of discipline and giving all assistance in keeping public order. This will be a guarantee that the destinies of the Nation shall follow, without suffering upheavals that would cause serious damage, on the logical course imposed by the supreme national will.

Relieved of its flowery ambiguity, Berenguer's message could only mean that it was the duty of the Army to support the Republic, since the people were voting against the Monarchy. If Berenguer – the king's first hope to preserve his throne – thought this, then surely the Monarchy was doomed.

On 14 April, Franco's old chief in the Legion, General Millán Astray, telephoned from Madrid to say that General Sanjurjo – a close friend of Primo de Rivera's who had opposed Berenguer's monarchical rescue operation – had let it be known that he could no longer guarantee the loyalty of the Civil Guard in the event of disorders.

This was the death blow, but Alfonso still hesitated, torn between the conflicting pieces of advice that were coming to him from his friends and ministers. There were the bellicose ones, especially La Cierva and General Cavalcanti, a former head of the king's Military Household whom Alfonso had allowed Primo de Rivera to send on a sinecure mission to the Balkans when he was proving troublesome.[20] These men urged the king to stand and fight. After all, they argued, the countryside was with him and so were some of the towns, while much of the Army remained loyal. If he stood his ground, he would win.

On the other side were milder and wiser men who pointed out that local republics had already been proclaimed in Seville and Barcelona, so that it was no longer a question of simply dispersing unruly mobs with a show of force: for the king to stand his ground would mean a civil war.

And now the king did perhaps the only noble and memorable thing in his self-centred reign of intrigue and folly: he decided to spare his country the horrors of a civil war. He accepted the advice of Count Romanones, who wrote urging him to leave the country. On hearing the results of the municipal elections, he had complained: 'We are out of fashion.'[21] Now, declaring 'I do not want a single drop of blood to be spilt for me', he had himself driven to Cartagena, where he boarded the cruiser *Príncipe Alfonso, en route* for Marseille and exile.[22] The royal family followed by road, crossing the border into France at Hendaya, where Queen Victoria and her children burst into long-repressed tears on leaving Spain.

When the moment of truth came, then, King Alfonso XIII showed a deeper awareness of the consequences of his actions than the indignant generals were to show in 1936 (or, alternatively, than the government of the Second Republic showed in deciding to resist their uprising). It is important to add, although it does not diminish the credit that must be allowed him, that he did not abdicate, but merely left the country. His parting manifesto, indeed, while admitting that he might have committed errors, added explicitly: 'I do not renounce any of my rights.'[23] It was thus open to him and his descendants to maintain that the Republic was an illegal interval in the country's history, and that Spain remained a kingdom.

It was left to Count Romanones, who had sped the king on his journey into exile, to speed the *de facto* demise of the monarchy, and indeed by the king's express order. His parting words to Romanones recalled that Alcalá Zamora had once been the Count's secretary. He urged the Count to see Alcalá with a view to arranging for the transition from one régime to another – and also, he added, 'to do the necessary with regard to my journey and my family's'.[24] The two

men – Romanones and Alcalá – met in the home of Dr Marañón, and
power now passed to the Revolutionary Committee, which became
the Provisional Government of the Second Republic.

At midnight on 14 April, General Fernández Heredia, commander
of the Saragossa military region, handed over his charge to the
Provisional Government's nominee, General Gómez Morato.[25]
On the next day, the king's favourite general summoned his cadets in
the Military Academy and declared:

> The Republic having been proclaimed and the high powers
> having been concentrated in the Provisional Government, the
> duty of all at this moment is to cooperate with discipline and solid
> virtues so that peace may reign and the nation be guided into
> normal juridical channels.
>
> At all times, discipline and the precise fulfilment of duty have
> reigned in this centre. Now these are more necessary than ever, and
> the Army, serene and united, must sacrifice all thought and all
> ideology for the good of the nation and for the tranquillity of
> the motherland.

For Franco, now as ever, discipline, duty and obedience came
first. Certainly they still came before 'thought and ideology'. His
guarded and stilted announcement amounted to an undertaking that
he would serve the Republican State as he had served the monarchical. But nobody who heard or read his words could say that he had
welcomed the Republic with enthusiasm.

As various earlier biographers have noted, Alejandro Lerroux, one
of the founders of the Second Republic, has left a fair and accurate
account of General Franco's state of mind in the critical days of the
fall of the Monarchy, in his idiosyncratic book of memoirs, *La
Pequeña Historia*.[26] Before Primo de Rivera had resigned, Lerroux
listened to a friend's enthusiastic praise and asked him what could be
expected of the young general.

'You may be sure,' said the friend, 'that he is not plotting. I know
him well. But when I get the chance, I shall sound him out to see
what he's thinking. I wouldn't dare do otherwise.'

Not long after, Lerroux's friend had a talk with Franco in Madrid
and went back to see the Radical leader. Franco, he said, 'realized the
difficult situation that faced the monarchy and the country. But one

could not count on him to plot, nor to take part in a military rebellion.'

'But a day could come,' Lerroux objected, 'when not only the Republic but the country itself called for him.'

'I told him that,' the friend interrupted, 'and he answered that if he saw "power lying helpless in the streets" and therefore felt that the motherland was in danger of falling into anarchy, there would be no need of conspiracy or previous commitments, for he would place his sword at the service of the cause of order, whoever might represent it.'

Five more years were to pass before these prophetic words came true.

2 The Second Republic

The vast and joyous crowd that choked the approaches to Madrid's popular nerve-centre – the Puerta del Sol – on 14 April 1931, was in a state of Republican euphoria. Its collective emotion and unreasoning conviction told it that the Second Republic was about to usher in the millennium Spain had been awaiting. The motor traffic consisted of two cars, inching forward in the inchoate human mass. They contained the saviours-apparent of the country: Niceto Alcalá Zamora and his friends. The sky above the capital was Spring-happy. The cheers and shouts that rang out were of civic joy. It seemed unthinkable that anything but happiness in the fulfilment of the general will lay ahead. And if it occurred to anyone to think otherwise, the thought remained unexpressed.

Alcalá Zamora and his friends, the founders of the Spanish Second Republic, were, on the whole, intelligent men and well-intentioned. They were, however, inexperienced; and it soon became apparent that they had little in common, save a general belief that the monarchy had had its day and that the Republic would succeed where the king and his men had failed. Since they were, one and all, players in the penultimate act of the great Spanish tragedy, of whose unfolding they were certainly unconscious that April morning in Madrid, they deserve to be introduced.

There was nothing revolutionary about the Provisional Government's Prime Minister, Alcalá Zamora. Indeed there was something reassuring about this portly, middle-class Andalusian from the Cordoba region, with his unquenchable and infinitely flowery oratory. (Henry Buckley recalls how he solved the problem of reporting his breakneck delivery verbatim: by simply copying out a previous speech and cabling it. Nobody knew the difference.[1]) He had made ministerial rank on two occasions but would have no truck with the dictatorship and conspired against it in its final stages. A lawyer by original vocation, he was a pious man, and during his election campaign for the Constituent Assembly, he promised a Republic which even people to the right of him could serve, a régime in which there would be a room for a Senate and in which the Church would be represented. 'I do not assume,' he exclaimed, 'the responsibility of a Kerensky to implant a convulsive and epileptic Republic.'[2] He was, as we have noted, a well-intentioned man.

A far more complex, and historically more fateful, figure was Alcalá's War Minister, who later became in turn Prime Minister and President: Manuel Azaña. This gifted man could well stand as the archetype of the literary intellectual in politics. Not for him the comforting bourgeois conventions of Alcalá Zamora. Though neither a Marxist nor an advocate of violence, Azaña was a revolutionary in intent, in the Spanish context, since he was determined to reduce both the Church and the Army to dimensions of his choosing. His was a secular Republican approach in the French tradition. Aged fifteen, he had told his tutor at the Augustine monastery school at El Escorial that he had decided to drop Catholic observance.[3] He passed his law exams and went to Paris where his natural anti-clericalism solidified.

This podgy, sallow man with the thick glasses and the heavy jowls made up in intellectual brilliance and splendid oratory what he lacked in physical appeal. The son of a wealthy soap manufacturer and landowner, he was born in Cervantes' home town, Alcalá de Henares. After an unsuccessful spell of farming after his father's death, he entered the civil service. His bent had always been literary, though he had little success as a writer. In 1913, when he was thirty-three, he found his world on being appointed secretary to the *Ateneo*, a famous Madrid club which had long been the natural habitat of politically inclined intellectuals (and which Primo de

Rivera, not surprisingly, was later to close down). He was the *Ateneo*'s secretary for seven years, and was elected president in 1930. Meanwhile, he had translated much of Dickens and written an autobiographical and anti-clerical study of the Augustine friars of El Escorial, whom he knew so well.

Azaña entered politics in 1927 when he founded the Party of Republican Action with a group of other intellectuals. He was mixed up in the Jaca conspiracy but was obscure enough to escape to France and return to Madrid unnoticed. Many knowing Spaniards laughed on learning that he had been appointed War Minister in the Provisional Government, for they wondered what on earth he might know about war. Few remembered that he had written a pamphlet on the organization of the French Army or were aware that he had well-defined ideas about the kind of Army Spain ought to have.

He was a vain man and liked to hear himself compared with Mirabeau. In the same vein, he once wrote that if he ever found himself in power, he would rather take Robespierre than Marcus Aurelius for a model. He would have felt at home in Paris in 1789, before being claimed – as no doubt he would have been – by the guillotine. His fundamental error was in supposing that the Spain of 1931 was ripe for the sweeping laicization wrought in France by the revolution, or if it were, that the job could be done peacefully. He too was a well-intentioned man, by his own, very special lights; and a personally incorruptible one (as Robespierre had been).

Two other members of the Provisional Government – Francisco Largo Caballero and Indalecio Prieto – should be mentioned together, for they represented divergent tendencies in the Socialist movement. In the critical days of the Second Republic, Largo Caballero was to preach violent revolution, and his contribution to the climate of political extremism was massive and unforgivable. Prieto, a more intelligent man and a more moderate one, was often forced into extremist attitudes by the need to compete with Largo. By 1936 he was trying, rather desperately, to arrest the descent into violence. And when the worst happened, he tried to prevent the embattled Republic from falling into the hands of the Communists, whose ally Largo had become.

Violence and association with the Communists were not the only issues on which the two men quarrelled. Prieto bitterly reproached Largo Caballero for collaborating with Primo de Rivera. Perforce, as Socialists, the two worked together; but they never really saw eye to eye. Both had had to make their way in life with little initial aid, but Largo Caballero went through a harder school, earning his first meagre pesetas as a bookbinder, aged seven. He rose to prominence rapidly in the UGT, which he joined in 1890, when he was twenty-one, was one of the organizers of the revolutionary general strike of August 1917, and in 1930 was appointed by the Socialist Party as its representative on Alcalá's Revolutionary Committee. Prieto, younger than Largo by fourteen years or so, lost his father when he was six. A native of Oviedo, he learned shorthand in that city's workers' centre and found a job on *La Voz de Vizcaya*. Later he joined the staff of *El Liberal*, in Bilbao, where powerful men took an interest in his career, to such effect that he became the paper's proprietor in 1932. Twenty years earlier, he had entered politics, becoming a deputy for Vizcaya. In 1917, he too played an important part in urging the workers to strike for revolutionary ends. The dictatorship turned him anti-monarchist and his articles and speeches against Alfonso XIII, before and after the monarch's departure, were of exceptional virulence.

Both Largo Caballero and Prieto were fiery orators, but Largo – who had a definite but unfortunate charisma – had the advantage of a handsome, elder statesman's appearance. Prieto, overlaid with fat, nevertheless riveted his audiences by his torrential and impassioned flow of words – which used to alarm Azaña, who thought that at any moment he would choke himself to death. When the test came, however, he emerged as a more moderate man than his Socialist rival. But in 1931, the middle class of Spain could not have guessed this of him, and his appointment as Finance Minister in the Provisional Government caused alarm and led to a flight of capital.[4] Prieto, indeed, had not been particularly keen on accepting the finance portfolio, for which his only qualification was his prowess as a self-made businessman. Nobody, on the other hand, could deny that Largo Caballero was at home as Minister of Labour.

In comparison with these four men, the other members of the Provisional Government were of less importance. Alejandro Lerroux was an ageing demagogue who had once incited the crowds to burn churches. He felt mildly slighted at having been offered the Foreign Affairs portfolio, but accepted it all the same. His days of popular glory, when, as Emperor of the Paralelo – Barcelona's red light and gambling den district – he went around in purple robes, with a bodyguard of young toughs, seemed far away.[5] He might well have reflected, twirling his impressive white moustache, that overthrowing a Monarchy was more fun than founding a Republic.

A protégé of Lerroux's, Diego Martínez Barrio, had a job created for him in the Provisional Government at Lerroux's behest, as Minister of Communications. Temperamentally, the two men were very different. Where Lerroux was expansive and ebullient, Martínez Barrio was pensive and withdrawn. The older man was a Freemason because he thought it was a useful thing to be; but the younger took Freemasonry very seriously and was Great Master of the Grand Orient of Spain. Indeed he had built a private Masonic temple in his own home. A self-educated man of acknowledged intelligence, Martínez Barrio had once worked as a lad in the Seville slaughterhouse.

Another Freemason in the government, with the title of First Assistant Great Master, was Marcelino Domingo, a former lay schoolteacher from Tortosa, who was now Education Minister. Mixed up in innumerable plots, he too, like Azaña, aspired to make a 'French' revolution in Spain. A better known name was that of Miguel Maura y Gamazo, who basked in the reflected glory of his monarchist father, Antonio Maura. A spectacular orator, whom Azaña considered devoid of ideas, Miguel Maura joined the government – in the important post of Minister of the Interior – for much the same reasons that had brought in Alcalá Zamora: as a guarantee of conservative stability in an administration that might otherwise have looked menacingly revolutionary. The Minister of Justice, Fernando de los Ríos y Urruti, was a Malagan of fifty-two who was Professor of Political Science at Madrid University when called to office. A product of the famous *Institución Libre de Enseñanza* and a nephew of its founder, Francisco Giner de los Ríos, Fernando had all the ideas – about the Church and the Army, for instance – that might have been expected to appeal to Azaña. The War Minister, however, found him pedantic and stubborn.[6]

A hard man to please, Azaña. He thought more highly, however, of the new Minister for the Navy, Casares Quiroga, a Galician from Corunna and a founder member of the Autonomous Republican Galician Organization (ORGA). 'The best man in the government,' was Azaña's self-effacing verdict.

The oddest man out in this first Republican team was surely Luis Nicolau d'Olwer, Minister of Economics, who represented the Catalan Action Party. At one time d'Olwer – who was born in Barcelona – had worked with Cambó, the *Lliga Regionalista*. But Cambó was too gradual for him and he helped to found *Acció Catala* to agitate for Catalan independence. An able man, he was of course at loggerheads with such anti-separatists as Lerroux and Álcalá Zamora. His presence in the Provisional Government was a sop to the Catalan leftists who had blessed the Revolutionary Committee. There was also a Minister of Development, Álvaro de Albornoz, another protégé of Lerroux's and quite the least distinguished member of the team, whom Lerroux himself wrote off as 'a sleepwalker and café politician'.[7]

The new team looked frail, and was. Politically, it responded to the needs and facts of the situation, since it represented the Left, the Right and the Centre. But the mixture, though logical, was in itself a guarantee of impermanence, even if the government had not been labelled 'Provisional'. This was not, *per se*, a valid reproach. In a situation of public calm, the provisional character of the government and its disunited composition would not greatly have mattered, for it would simply have yielded, in due course, to a more solidly anchored administration. But this was a situation, not of public calm, but of revolutionary euphoria, almost indeed of Messianic advent. Almost immediately, Alcalá Zamora and his mainly well-intentioned men were faced with disorderly challenges to their authority. These they regrettably failed to meet, at least in the initial stages, when action might have been decisive.

Almost immediately, too, it became apparent that under the powerful influence of Manuel Azaña, who dominated the cabinet, the government was determined to move much farther and faster down the path of radical change than its provisional character might have justified. And in so doing, it ran into its first mild clash with General Franco. On 18 April, only four days after the advent of the Republic, the General was surprised to see his portrait on page 1 of the monarchist *ABC*, with a caption describing him as the new High Commissioner in Morocco. From his office in the Saragossa Military Academy, he dictated a letter correcting what he rightly believed to be an error on the newspaper's part:

The Provisional Government which today directs the nation [he wrote] could not have thought of this, nor should I have accepted any non-obligatory post that might be interpreted by anybody as premature condescension [*complacencia*] on my part towards the régime recently installed, or as a consequence of having been in the least lukewarm or reserved in the accomplishment of my duties or in the loyalty which I owed and still felt towards those who until yesterday incarnated and represented the monarchical régime. On the other hand, I am firmly resolved to respect and defer to, as I have until today, the national sovereignty, and I am eager that this should express itself through adequate juridical channels.[8]

My translation of Franco's words does not, I believe, do violence either to the style or the spirit of the original. If one were asked to select a passage that best represented the writer's native Galician evasiveness, compounded by the man's own caution – in other words, the passage that best explained his infinite capacity for survival – this would be it. By this letter, the general declared his intention to serve the Republic, especially after it had acquired constitutional legitimacy, while recalling that he was and remained loyal to the king and the king's men. This was not, by any stretch of the imagination, rebellious talk. Nor was it, on the other hand, in the slightest degree enthusiastic, still less sycophantic, towards the new masters of Spain. Those who read Franco's letter in *ABC* – who must, one assumes, have included Alcalá Zamora and his Ministers – might even have sensed a faint and conditional threat of future displeasure should the Government exceed the very limited mandate conferred upon it by the municipal elections and the king's flight. Azaña and his colleagues, however, were hardly in the mood to heed veiled warnings from the king's favourite general.

They were strengthened in this view by an incident that occurred about the time Franco sent his letter to *ABC*. General Berenguer, Primo de Rivera's successor, had been arrested for having sanctioned the execution of the officers who had led the short-lived uprising at Jaca. Before appearing before a special military tribunal in Madrid, he was asked to pick a high officer to defend him, and proposed General Franco. Franco accepted but was forbidden to attend the military tribunal, which was to sit in Madrid, on the technical ground that he was disqualified by being a member of the Saragossa garrison, not the Madrid one.[9] This seemed to demonstrate two things: that he remained a staunch monarchist, and that the Republic was determined to keep him in his place.

Azaña and most of his colleagues had no time for residually monarchist generals. What they wanted, above all, was to identify themselves with the mood of the people, which they interpreted as Republican, radical and secular. For many anonymous Spaniards, however, the fall of the monarchy was a signal of release from burdensome paternalism and authority, whether of the Church, of the king or of the State. For them, the Republic meant permissiveness: *their* mood was of revolutionary anarchy. When the Republic was still only a few hours old, they overturned the statues of Philip III and Isabella II in Madrid. In Seville, trade unionists seized the arsenal, captured the central gaol – destroying its records – and set the prisoners free. In Bilbao, much the same thing happened. In Valencia, Republican supporters who marched to the Model Prison to let the prisoners know they would shortly be amnestied, found themselves threatened by pistols which the inmates had seized from their guards.[10]

There were worse things in store.

At the beginning of May, Cardinal Segura, Archbishop of Toledo and Primate of Spain, published a pastoral letter which praised the king for his defence of the Church and which, by implication, attacked the Provisional Government's religious policy as a potential assault on the Church's traditional rights. Perhaps, at this early stage of the Republic's existence, this was a misguided thing for the Archbishop to have done. At any rate, it irritated Azaña and his anti-clerical colleagues, and newspapers supporting the government immediately branded the pastoral letter as a provocation to the people.

This seems to have been the signal 'the people' were waiting for. In Madrid, an anti-monarchist crowd tried to set fire to the royalist *ABC*'s offices, and the Civil Guard opened fire, killing two. Later that night, a mob orator who had entered the Ministry of the Interior, harangued an angry crowd from a window, calling for the disarming of the Civil Guard, the expulsion of the religious orders and the dismissal of the Minister of the Interior, Miguel Maura.

Maura himself proposed to his hastily assembled colleagues that the Civil Guard should immediately be called out in strength to deal

with the developing wave of disorders which, he told them, he knew
from information received would turn into a general strike the
following day. He was overruled, and the police were ordered to use
persuasion only – no weapons – to bring the mob to its senses.[11]

In the early hours – it was now 11 May – the mob, seeing that the
Civil Guard though present was passive, sprinkled the Jesuit Church
of San Francisco de Borja with petrol and set it alight. Obeying
orders, the Civil Guard looked on; more surprisingly, so did the
Fire Brigade. Encouraged, the mob repeated its exploits in a lengthening list of churches, convents, monasteries and religious schools. It
was 1834 and 1835 all over again. To many Spaniards, the passage of
one hundred years had changed nothing. Freedom meant, primarily,
freedom to burn the churches. And what was the Republic if not the
advent of freedom?

Inspired by the Madrileño example, incendiary mobs sprang up in
Seville and Granada, Murcia and Valencia. In Cadiz, Algeciras and
Jerez, too, churches and convents were burnt down, before the
passive or approving eyes of the Republican authorities.

It is hard, today, to determine just how many church buildings
were burnt down in those two days, or who the arsonists were.
The figures vary enormously, and so do the labels of those blamed,
which range from monarchists and provocateurs to communists of
varying hues. Indignant Spanish Nationalists quote high figures and
blame the 'reds'.[12] Some recent writers, such as Gabriel Jackson, opt
for low figures and do not try to guess the identity of the guilty.[13]
Jackson is, I think, wrong to play down the importance of the
church-burnings, which he does largely on the ground that the main
Republican political parties, including the Socialists, all condemned
these outrages. This argument seems to me to miss the point, which
is that the Provisional Government, as a deliberate act of policy,
declined to restore public order in incidents involving the destruction of Church property.

When news of the first convent burning was brought to Azaña, he
exclaimed: 'All the convents of Spain are not worth the life of a
Republican!'[14] According to Miguel Maura, it was Azaña who was
most categorical in his opposition to calling out the Civil Guard.
Alcalá Zamora, though himself a pious man, feebly told foreign correspondents that there were so many convents in Spain that even the
French Army – at that time the largest in the world – would not have

been big enough to stop the mobsters. For two days, the Government did nothing. Then Maura's colleagues gave in and allowed him full powers to restore order; which he then did within a few hours.

It was the attitude of Azaña and his colleagues – except Maura and possibly Lerroux, whose evidence needs to be treated with caution – rather than the number of incidents or of the mobsters involved that made the burning of the convents a fateful event in the history of the Spanish Second Republic. Whatever one may say about low church attendances, and however much one may find to criticize in the Church, Spain remained a Catholic country, even though Azaña himself had declared that it no longer was one. In the eyes of the middle and upper classes, and of Spanish women of all classes, Azaña now stood as the man who would not lift a finger to prevent anti-religious outrages, who sat and watched while the House of God burned. In the eyes of the majority of Army officers, including Franco, the Government which Azaña dominated and which he was soon to lead had demonstrated its weakness and incompetence by the low priority it accorded to the maintenance of public order. Unfortunately, the subsequent actions of the Provisional Government and some of its successors confirmed all these fears. The fact that Azaña had shown himself supremely reluctant to shed the blood of fellow-Republicans stood him in good stead politically with his own followers; but it was an attitude that deepened the fundamental cleavage within the Spanish people.

After the burning of the convents, the Republic's rift with the Catholic world worsened dramatically. Cardinal Segura had left for Rome on 13 May, the day after the second round of outrages, declaring that his personal safety was no longer assured. On 20 May, the Government proclaimed religious freedom and banned the exhibiting of saintly images in schoolrooms on the hygienic pretext that the kissing of such images was unhealthy. On 30 May, the Vatican vetoed the proposed appointment of Luis Zulueta as the Republic's Ambassador, and on 3 June, the Spanish bishops collectively protested against the suppression of compulsory instruction and other violations, as they saw them, of the Church's rights under the 1851 Concordat between Madrid and Rome. Slipping across the border incognito on 13 May, Cardinal Segura was escorted to Irun and took refuge in Bayonne, resigning his see; he was later interned beyond the Loire at the request of the Spanish authorities. The following day,

Catholics from various northern districts gathered in the bullring at Pamplona to protest against the archbishop's departure.

Having alienated the Church and the faithful, the Provisional Government took on the Army as well. As we have seen, Azaña came to office with clear ideas about the ailments of the Army and how to cure them. His diagnosis, incidentally, was correct, and a good many Army officers, if pressed in private, would have conceded as much. The officer corps was simply too large. Eighty generals would have been a normal complement for the sixteen skeleton divisions of Spain's peace-time Army in 1931; instead, there were eight hundred.[15] With tact, diplomacy and a spirit of gradualness, the Army could have been cut down to size without a legacy of resentment. But Azaña couldn't wait. This was his opportunity for an anti-clerical, anti-militarist revolution, and he was determined to seize it without even awaiting the general elections that would have conferred legitimacy and a relative stability on the new régime.

To be fair to Azaña, he did try to keep the officers financially happy. It was the manner rather than the substance of his measures – and the suspected motives behind them – that rankled in the breasts of the men who (as they saw it) had fought for Spain in Morocco. He struck on 26 May – six weeks after the fall of the Monarchy – when he decreed the reduction of the Army from sixteen divisions to six, slashing its officer corps from 26,000 to 7,600, and abolishing the residually political rank of Captain-General. Officers accepting retirement were offered full pay, and indeed a guarantee that their pay would increase periodically, when seniority would normally have brought them promotion. This was a very generous offer since there was nothing to prevent retired officers from taking a job. Not only were they spared financial loss: in many cases they would be better off than they had been.

Money is not everything, however, to Spanish Army officers. The notion of *dignidad*, in particular, is fundamental to the ideas of behaviour of the traditionally minded Spanish officer. To be pensioned off by an anti-militarist War Minister struck them as an affront to their dignity, and many of them, including Mola – the conspirator of 1936 – and Franco, bitterly resented Azaña's reforms. As the king's Director of Security, Mola had applied the concept of discipline – obedience to the State's authority.[16] After Azaña's reforms, he veered to the alternative concept of obedience to the *patria* or nation, even if this involved indiscipline in relation to the State. The Republican Government, he wrote in *The Past, Azaña and the Future* (1933), had acted in a destructive and vindictive spirit, with the intention of smashing the Army morally as well as physically.[17] He now decided that 'Indiscipline is justified when the abuses of power constitute vexations and opprobrium and lead the nation into ruin.'[18]

In 1931, however, Mola kept quiet, at least in public. Franco, on the other hand, gave a public demonstration of discipline in the service of the State, although he had a personal grievance against the Republic in addition to the general grievance of the traditional officers against Azaña for his sweeping reforms. For Azaña, not content with drastically reducing the overblown Army, went on to order the closure of the Saragossa Academy. This measure was, of course, consistent with the Provisional Government's aim to create a small and Republican Army. But as Franco saw it, Azaña's decision meant that a stroke of the pen had wiped out the intensive and patient work he had put in over the past three years.

General Franco had strong reasons, moreover, for supposing that the closure of the Academy was more than a mere adjunct to Azaña's reform programme and, indeed, that it was aimed at him personally. In his ambiguous way, he had stuck his neck out in his letter to *ABC*, correcting its report that he was being sent to Morocco. For the Government attached greater weight to its veiled expressions of loyalty to the departed sovereign than to its reassurances of obedience to the existing authorities. With what was generally known of his good relations with Alfonso, and his willingness to defend General Berenguer, this was enough to make him suspect in the eyes of Azaña and his colleagues.

Though Franco thought these things, he kept them to himself. On 14 July, he brought cadets and staff together for a farewell party. His speech recalled the work of the past three years. He then added: 'We must rise above and overcome in silence our intense sadness over the disappearance of our work, thinking altruistically: the machine is being dismantled, but the work remains – for you are our work . . .' There followed his habitual praise for the military virtues, with a significant variation, for he now singled out discipline as the most important of the soldier's qualities: 'Discipline! Which does not confer merit when the character of an order is agreeable or tolerable to us. Discipline! Which takes on its true value when our thoughts, counsel the opposite of what we are ordered to do, when our hearts struggle to rise in intimate rebellion, or when an order is marked by arbitrariness or error. This is the discipline we practise. This is the example we offer you. (Full text in Appendix 1.)

'Lift up your thoughts towards the motherland and sacrifice everything for it, for while the ordinary citizen has his freedom of will, those who receive in sacred trust the arms of the nation do not, and must dedicate all their actions to its service.'[19]

Although these words were not in themselves subversive, they barely concealed Franco's dissatisfaction with the government's policy, while his references to discipline clearly suggested that it took an act of will to obey orders which any military officer would naturally prefer to defy. Certainly the government interpreted his speech as a call for indiscipline. Azaña summoned Franco to the War Ministry and said to him: 'I have just read your extraordinary Order to the students and I should like to think that you did not believe what you wrote.'

'*Señor Ministro*,' Franco replied, 'I don't write anything which I have not thought out beforehand.'[20]

On 22 August, the War Ministry sent Franco a Note expressing 'displeasure' at his speech, 'in which were formulated opinions and considerations which, although in covert form and under shelter of sentimental motives, contain a censure against certain measures taken by the Government, and which reveal scant respect for discipline. You shall refrain in future from making similar demonstrations, and subordinate your conduct to the elementary exigencies of discipline, which failed you in this address.'[21]

Franco was still at the Military Academy, when this unpleasant communication reached him. The cadets had been the first to go. Then one by one the officers who had constituted the teaching staff took their leave. Some of them wanted his advice: should they accept the government's retirement offer or opt for continued service? To these Franco gave an invariable reply: 'Do what suits you best. But don't forget that the military man must serve his country above all other considerations, and that he may be more useful to it inside the Army than by abandoning it.'

When the last of the teachers had left, Franco expected to be given instructions about handing over the deserted building to some new authority. The days went by without a word, however. He kept himself busy supervising a pet project of his, the construction of a Basque pelota court. One day somebody asked him: 'Why worry about it?' and he answered: 'Whether those who come here to play pelota are cadets of some new Academy or soldiers, isn't in the least important. They are bound to be young Spaniards who will come to acquire dexterity and agility in this particular sport. And besides, since I have still not handed over the premises of the Academy, my duty is to leave the work in progress as far advanced as possible.'

In time, the War Ministry notified Franco that the Academy was to be used as a barracks. No special assignment had been made for Franco himself, so he decided to take his wife to her home town, Oviedo, and await further instructions. These were a long time coming, so he resumed his long-interrupted studies of history and economics.[22]

We broke the strict chronology of this narrative to lend continuity to Franco's brush with the authorities on the issue of Azaña's reforms. The Provisional Government's initial decree and the closure of the Academy were, however, separated by an important event: the general elections of 28 June 1931. Surprisingly, the campaign and the voting took place almost entirely without violence. The resulting Cortes was dominated by the Socialists and left-wing Republicans, although the moderate Lerroux obtained the largest number of votes of any single candidate – 133,425. Many distinguished intellectuals, including those ferocious critics of the dictatorship, Unamuno and Ortega y Gasset, were re-elected. Among the Socialist intellectuals who became deputies was a politically obscure Professor of Physiology, Juan Negrín, who was to be Prime Minister of the Republic in the days of its agony. The dictator's former Finance Minister, Calvo Sotelo, later to provide the dissident Nationalists with their first martyr, was returned for Orense, but the result was declared invalid a few weeks later.[23] The charismatic Colonel Maciá, leader of the Catalan *Esquerra* (Left), topped the poll in Barcelona, with 107,447 votes. Let us record, in passing, that the Communist Party's candidate polled under 3,000 votes in Madrid, and under 13,000 in Barcelona. At this stage, the communist threat, though potential, was scarcely visible.

A crazy plot to seize the land and hand it over to the peasants had been timed for election day, but the Provisional Government had had wind of it, and sent General Sanjurjo, the Civil Guard Commander, to Seville, where the plotters had been meeting, to nip it in the bud.[24] In perspective, this was ironical, since Sanjurjo himself was to lead an unsuccessful revolt in the same city not long after. But at that time, he was still a defender of Republican law and order. On the opposite side was Colonel Ramón Franco, whose accomplices in this latest conspiracy were the Anarchists of the CNT trade unions. Frustrated by Sanjurjo's presence, the plotters delayed action until 20 July, when they broke into agricultural estates and started parcelling out lots among the peasants. Simultaneously, a general strike broke out in Seville, spreading rapidly to cities all over Spain, including Barcelona, Malaga, Valencia, Vizcaya and Corunna. In Seville itself, a state of siege was proclaimed and twenty-two lives were lost, with some two hundred wounded, in clashes between the revolutionaries and the Civil Guard. A fortnight earlier, the Provisional Government (which was still in power pending the adoption of a Constitution) had been faced with a nation-wide strike of telephone workers. Alarmed, it had created a new body, the Assault Guards, to enforce public order; and the Director-General of Security had ordered them to fire without warning on people committing acts of sabotage. The Republic, then, had gone from one extreme to the other: from the complacent contemplation of violence to panicky measures for its repression.

It was against this anarchic background that the constitutional committee of the new Cortes sat down to its labours. It emerged on 28 August with a draft fundamental law for the Cortes to consider. As it stood, the draft provided for a democratically elected lay Republic, a single-Chamber parliament, disestablishment of the Roman Catholic Church, and important reserve powers – including the nomination of a head of government, veto over legislation, and dissolution of the Cortes. The Catalan question had already been solved – or so it seemed – by a referendum held on 2 August, which overwhelmingly approved a statute conferring autonomy on this strongly nationalist region. (The fiery Maciá, who had tried to jump the gun by creating an independent Generalidad in the first few days of the Republic, received a conqueror's ovation in Barcelona.)

Once again, however, Azaña had tried to move too fast. Encouraged, perhaps, by the relative calm that had greeted his first body-blows at the Army, he tried to destroy the organized power of the

Church under two articles of the draft constitution. Article 3 swept aside the 1851 Concordat, by simply declaring that Spain had no official religion. Article 26 abolished the State subsidy to the clergy, dissolved the convents and monasteries and closed all religious schools except the seminaries. In effect, this meant that the religious orders would be allowed to train priests, but would lose the right to educate boys and girls for non-religious careers.

From Azaña's viewpoint, Article 26, together with the anti-military decrees, was what the Republic was all about. He wanted a Jacobin Republic, in which the twin pillars of reaction in Spain – the Army and the Church – would be smashed for ever. Article 26 was revolutionary, and he knew it: his lay revolution was to be accomplished by a clause in a draft constitution. Although the majority of the Cortes favoured Article 26, it occasioned a long, stormy and passionate debate which, in the end, impressed even Azaña. Without surrendering his Jacobin principles, he sought to take some of the venom out of Article 26 by proposing that only the Society of Jesus need be abolished (yet again!). The other orders could remain, and the State would continue to subsidise the Church for two years.

These concessions made the Jacobins feel they had been generous, but failed to placate the conservatives. Although the modified Article 26 was duly passed, it was more than Alcalá Zamora, the Prime Minister, could stomach, and he resigned. With him went Miguel Maura the Minister of the Interior who had vainly advocated the use of force against the incendiaries of 11 May. The most indignant group in the constituent Cortes, however, were the Basques deputies, who walked out and boycotted parliament from that point on.

Even Gerald Brenan, a persistent defender of 'Azaña's greatness', comments: 'The unwisdom of this measure is today evident.'[25] Indeed, it split the nation as well as the founders of the Republic, provided a rallying cry for discouraged opponents of the new order, left tens of thousands of children without education – and even did the Jesuits less harm than Azaña had hoped to inflict, since the Jesuit Fathers had wisely invested most of their money under other names and were able to continue teaching once they had nominally ceased, by virtue of the new constitution, to belong to a religious order.[26]

Article 26, on the other hand, brought its architect, Manuel Azaña, to power as Prime Minister. He took over from Alcalá Zamora in the early hours of 14 October 1931, by decision of the

7a The Republic's first President, Alcalá Zamora (*centre*).

7b President Azaña with the speaker of the Cortes, Martinez Barrio.

8a Franco with an old friend, the much wounded Colonel Millán Astray, founder of the Spanish Foreign Legion.

8b Franco in Morocco in July 1936.

Cortes. It was more logical this way: Azaña had exercised power behind the scenes and by the force of his personality and oratory. The new constitution was, in effect, his baby, and it was only fair that he should hold it. Alcalá Zamora, however, was to have a place in the new order, and this, too, was logical: he had presided over the Republic's birth-pangs, and now, on 2 December, the Cortes unanimously elected him President. He accepted the burden in the hope of reversing Azaña's anti-clerical legislation. But in this, as in other commendable hopes, he aimed too high. Niceto Alcalá Zamora was a nice man, but no match for the Jacobin of the Second Republic.

Let us return now to Franco and the Army's clash with the Republic. Azaña's first blows to the Army had been delivered on 22 April, when the Republic was only a week old, with a decree calling on officers to take the oath to the Republic and undertake to defend it against all enemies. The decree streamlining the Army had been announced on 26 May, and the Military Academy had been abolished on 29 June, the day after the general elections; and physically closed down – bar Franco's lingering presence – on 14 July. Several months now elapsed – with Franco still in Oviedo and out of a job – while Manuel Azaña carefully prepared yet another blow. When it fell, it did more than all his other anti-military decrees put together to justify General Mola's accusations of vindictiveness and deliberate intent to demoralize the Army. For under a draft law, announced on 3 May 1931 (and adopted on 12 September of that year), Azaña now invalidated all military promotions for war merits. Henceforth, in the egalitarian and anti-militarist Army of the Republic (which, under its new constitution, had abolished war as an instrument of policy, at the optimistic suggestion of Salvador de Madariaga), promotion was to be by strict order of seniority.

This new measure, while it rewarded mediocrity and time-serving, penalized bravery and other military virtues. It fell with particular force on officers like General Franco and the friends of his Moroccan days, whose lives were dedicated to the Army and whose valour and qualities of leadership had been rewarded by accelerated promotion. In Franco's case, it meant that he was demoted from the top position among brigadier-generals, in line for promotion to major-general, to the bottom third of the list. Simultaneously, and strictly in accordance with his reduced place in the military hierarchy,

F

General Franco was appointed Commander of a Brigade stationed in Corunna.

Although deeply offended by Azaña's latest sign of hostility towards the Army, Franco took up his new duties without comment. It was, after all, a job, and his forced inactivity at Oviedo had begun to pall. Besides, he was now back in his native Galicia, a local hero still, and able to breathe once again the salty tang of his first love, the sea.

Not all higher Army officers were so docile, at this time of animosity from the civil power. One who was not was Franco's old chief, and at that time, Spain's most famous general, José Sanjurjo, 'Lion of the Rif', and an impetuous man of action. More notable for bravery than for intelligence or judgment, Sanjurjo decided in mid-1932 that he, for one, had had enough of his secular and anti-militarist Republic. Unhappily, with his poverty of political sense, he allowed friends to persuade him that he was Spain's potential saviour, a role traditionally attractive to Spanish generals. Those who flattered him and deluded themselves in this way included the Carlist leader Fal Conde and sundry other monarchists. For some time now, Sanjurjo's name had been mentioned as the possible leader of a coup, and as soon as the rumour reached him, Azaña dropped Sanjurjo as Chief of the Civil Guard and gave him the minor job of chief of the Customs police. The general's personal humiliation made him all the more receptive to the siren calls of those who had cast him in a heroic role.

At the beginning of August 1932, General Franco made a quick trip to Madrid on Army business, where rumours of the conspiracy reached him. To those who asked him what he thought of the idea, he expressed a strong negative. It would be, he said, a blunder (*un disparate*) to go ahead with any plan to overthrow the Republic, under conditions as they then were. He was therefore not invited to join the conspirators; nor was he, in any precise sense, informed of their intentions. This is Franco's own version of his negative part in the Sanjurjo affair, as given to me in 1966 in a written answer to a question.*

Franco's refusal to join Sanjurjo is important in several respects.

---

* It is therefore misleading to say, as Jackson does (p. 76) that the conspirators had 'counted' on Franco to rise in Corunna, although this may have been their *hope*.

He was a friend and admirer of Sanjurjo's, but he was a cautious man and a shrewder observer than the 'Lion of the Rif'. It would never have occurred to him to ignore his own better judgment for the sake of loyalty in a matter in which he was a free agent. In the wider context of history, the dismal failure of Sanjurjo's uprising – for such it was – shows how little fitted he was to lead a national movement. Four years later, a plane crash was to cost Sanjurjo his life after the Nationalist conspirators had asked him to be their leader. His death cleared the way for Franco's rapid ascent within the Nationalist movement; but the proved clarity of Franco's pessimistic judgment of 1932 played its part in his success.

Franco's aloofness in 1932 seems nevertheless to have puzzled and disappointed some of his admirers, who have since explained the way Franco's mind was working in 1932. One of them was General Millán Astray, the founder of the Spanish Foreign Legion, who declared:

Franco does not wish to intervene in national politics and never thought of rising on 10 August [the day of Sanjurjo's rising], but I know that he would do so if he saw that the Government of the Republic was about to dissolve the Civil Guard, or that the hour of communism had come. That day only, with many others, or few, he would take the field.[27]

This informal exegesis echoes the view that had reached Lerroux a year earlier, that Franco would intervene only when he saw 'power lying helpless in the streets'. His view in 1932 was that the mass of the Spanish people had not yet been stripped of their illusions with the Republic, and that the organizations that supported the régime had not yet turned against it. His forebodings were therefore heavy when he returned to Corunna. He was due for leave on his return, and was to have started on a pleasure trip through Galicia. But the divisional commander of the region deferred his leave, doubtless for fear that Franco would take advantage of it to join Sanjurjo. He need not have worried.

Another worried man on 10 August, when news of the uprising came in, was Manuel Azaña, who swung round in his chair and asked: 'Where's Franco?' Told that Franco was at his post in Corunna, Azaña expressed his relief.[28]

In fact, Franco's worst misgivings were soon confirmed. From the planning standpoint, the plotters had done quite well. Where they showed themselves inept was over security (in outline their project was public knowledge) and political judgment: as Franco had anticipated, they entirely lacked popular support.[29] In Madrid, the rebels tried to seize the General Post Office and the War Ministry, but were beaten down within a few hours. In Seville, Sanjurjo issued a *pronunciamiento*, which brought the garrison out on his side but fell flat with the citizenry. When news came that loyal garrisons from neighbouring towns were on their way, he lost his nerve and started fleeing towards Portugal, then thought better of it and gave himself up. He was taken to Madrid, tried and condemned to death. Azaña, however, sided with those of his colleagues who saw no point in making a martyr of Sanjurjo and his friends, and commuted the sentence. The unsuccessful caudillo was sent to prison with common criminals and in felon's garb.

One of his fellow-plotters, Colonel Varela, twice decorated with the Laurels of San Fernando which had eluded Franco, was detained in the Castle of Santa Catalina and later in Guadalajara. In both places, he was surrounded by Carlists who won him over to their ideas. This was the ironical origin of the Carlist militia or *requetés*, which was to play a leading part in the Nationalist war against the Republic a few years later.[30] In 1932, however, the Republic had shown that it was still stronger than the Army, and the master in its own house.

Azaña was surprised, delighted and, on reflection, grateful that Franco had not joined in the Sanjurjo plot. To show his gratitude, he dropped in on the garrison at Corunna. Catching sight of Franco, he called him over and suggested that they should be pictured together for the benefit of the press photographers present. Franco, whose aloofness from the conspirators by no means implied support for Azaña, tried to make excuses on the ground that he was not the senior general present. To his embarrassment, Azaña insisted and invited Franco to stand next to him. At that moment, the Divisional General – Franco's superior – drew near, and Franco nimbly stepped aside as the photographers' bulbs flashed.[31]

From Franco's negative reaction to the 10 August affair, and from his personal impressions on his Corunna visit, Azaña seems to have concluded that Franco, though potentially dangerous, was non-political and primarily interested in his personal advancement within his chosen military career. He sought at one and the same time to reward Franco's discipline and put him out of harm's way, and appointed Franco as General Officer Commanding, Balearic Islands – a post that was senior to Franco's reduced position in the Army hierarchy. To be on the safe side, however, he appointed as Franco's Chief of Staff a colonel said to be a Freemason whose principal mission, according to Franco's friends, was to keep an eye on the General for Azaña's benefit.[32] The Republic, however, did not have anything to fear from Franco. Not yet, at any rate. On 16 March 1933, General Franco arrived at Palma de Mallorca to take up his new duties.

3 Defender of the Republic

Violence marked the end, as it had marked the beginning, of the Azaña phase of the Second Republic. In September and October 1932, a wave of strikes swept over various provinces, and in November and December, bands of peasants seized estates in or near Badajoz and Saragossa, Toledo and Seville, Avila and Cordoba. Bombs exploded, that violent autumn, in Seville, Barcelona, Saragossa and Madrid; and gunmen picked out their political victims, with a remarkably high level of accuracy, in a dozen Spanish cities.[1] In most cases, the Anarchists or Anarcho-Syndicalists were behind these disturbances; but the Socialists and the fledgling Communist Party had a hand in them.

The new year began with Anarchist risings in Catalonia, Levante and Andalusia. It continued, in February, with the tragic violence of Casas Viejas, the bitter repercussions of which brought down the Azaña cabinet. Few Spaniards, let alone foreigners, had heard of Casas Viejas at the beginning of 1933. Not long after, the name of this poverty-stricken village in Cadiz province was on everybody's lips – a symbol of popular resentment and a term of opprobrium. About two thousand people lived there, in deep and degrading poverty. About five hundred of the men were listed as able-bodied farmhands, but not more than a hundred of them had anything like steady employment, and then only for six months of the year. They were the lucky ones: most of the villagers lived – in the sense that breath remained in their bodies – on a pitifully inadequate public dole: one peseta a day if single, two if married.[2]

To this forsaken spot came orders from the Anarchist secret society, FAI – the *Federación Anarquista Ibérica*. All over Spain, said the order, peasants and workers were rising to proclaim 'libertarian communism'. This was the millennium, and for Casas Viejas, too, the hour had come. These were simple peasants, whose companion was hunger and whose minds were uncluttered by learning. Hopefully, and with apparent good will, they raised the black and red Anarchist flag, brought out the pistols and shotguns they had long kept hidden, and marched to the local headquarters of the *Guardia Civil*. 'We have come to tell you that libertarian communism has been proclaimed and that we are all equal,' said their spokesman. Unmoved, the *Guardia Civil* sergeant they were addressing replied that he was there to defend the Republic unto death. At this, the euphoric good will of the peasants evaporated. Opening fire, they gravely wounded the sergeant and two of his companions.

The exalted villagers proclaimed themselves masters. Soon, however, the *Guardia Civil* was reinforced by some ninety members of the rival, staunchly Republican Assault Guards. One by one, the Anarchists were driven out of the houses they had occupied. But there was one curiously stubborn exception. A sixty-year-old Anarchist, known as Six Fingers (*Seisdedos*), shut himself up in a hut with a handful of friends and relatives, including two women and a boy aged thirteen; and refused to surrender. The *Guardias de Asalto*, under the nervy Captain Rojas, surrounded the hut, arming themselves with a machine-gun and hand grenades. At nightfall, old Seisdedos still refused to surrender. At dawn, however, came a message from the Governor of Cadiz, saying: 'By categorical order Minister Interior, raze house which rebels have fortified.' The Minister who gave the order was Casares Quiroga.

On receipt of the message, Captain Rojas ordered wads of material to be soaked in petrol from the official cars. These were wrapped around stones, thrown on to the roof of the rebel hut and set alight. The roof being of dry branches and leaves, the whole hut was soon ablaze. The boy and one of the women came out, enveloped in flames. The charred bodies of Seisdedos and his other companions were found in the blackened ruin.

A thrill of horror swept over the nation at the news from Casas
Viejas, which recalled – as a negative recalls a positive – the twin
horror of Castilblanco where, two years earlier, the villagers had
overwhelmed the local *Guardias Civiles*, gouging out their eyes and
savagely mutilating them. The end result of the confrontation of
revolutionaries and repressors, it seemed, could only be death.
And it made no difference whether a monarchist or a republican
régime gave the orders.

The Casas Viejas affair shook the Azaña government beyond
recovery, tarring the Socialist party with the same brush of guilt for
the death of starving peasants. Although the government survived
the ensuing Cortes debate, it had a rough passage. Municipal elections in April brought proof that the parties of the Left were losing
their erstwhile popularity. Azaña did not, however, resign until
8 September and only when pressed to do so by President Alcalá
Zamora. By then, he had had further anti-religious bills enacted and
indeed had completed the ambitious legislative programme that
sought to add flesh to the bones of the Constitution.

It should not be thought that all was bad in Azaña's two-year
reign. Home rule for Catalonia, although anathema to the centralists,
was not a bad working compromise with the extremist advocates of
Catalan independence. Civil marriage had been legalized and divorce
simplified; and Largo Caballero, as Minister of Labour, had found
time, when not playing left-wing politics, to bring in some advanced
legislation, especially on the introduction of labour contracts. In
themselves, and in an abstract world of reasonable men, these were
admirable measures. The same could even be said of some, though
by no means all, of the anti-Army and anti-Church laws. But this was
not an academic experiment in theoretically ideal conditions: it was
an attempt at a peaceful revolution in an atmosphere of endemic
anarchy and among a deeply divided people, many of whom saw the
physical liquidation of their adversaries as a positive benefit to
humanity.

One can hardly do better, then, for a summing up of the work of
the Constituent Cortes under Azaña's guidance than to quote the
sad verdict of his admirer and defender, Gerald Brenan:

The last Government of the Constituent Cortes resigned in
September 1933 in deep unpopularity. The prisons were full –

there were said to be nine thousand of the CNT alone in them. The country was packed with armed police – half as many again as in Primo de Rivera's time. The unemployment was as great as ever. Capital was lying idle in the banks and strikes and labour disputes were incessant. It was not the extreme Right and Left which protested: it was a man of the Centre, Martínez Barrio, one little given to rhetorical exaggerations, who declared that this was a Republic of mud, blood and tears.[3]

In the days of gloom and discouragement that followed Sanjurjo's tragi-comic attempted coup, Franco toyed with the idea of resigning his commission and entering politics. This was what he told his intimate friends at a time when his own military career seemed blocked and the future of the Army he had known and helped to build looked problematical. But they dissuaded him, with the argument that his presence in the Army was the ultimate guarantee against revolutionary anarchy.[4]

His official biographers go on to say that shortly after the fall of the Azaña government, a delegate of the Right-wing Catholic party *Acción Popular*, came to see him in Palma de Mallorca to propose that he should stand for election under its banner – a proposal he is said to have politely but firmly declined, having by then decided that his friends were right in wishing him to stay in the Army. José-María Gil Robles, who was prominent in *Acción Popular* at the time, flatly denied in conversation with me that there was any truth in this story. There is, however, nothing inherently improbable in it, and I cannot see what advantage Joaquín Arrarás, Franco's first biographer, could have derived from inventing it.[5] On the other hand, Gil Robles, now one of the most courageous members of Spain's illegal democratic opposition, must have little taste for an anecdote that appears to associate him with Franco at a time when there was no pressing need for any such association. Of the possible conclusions that could be drawn from this conflicting evidence, the one that seems fairest both to Gil Robles and to Arrarás is that *Acción Popular* did indeed approach Franco in 1933, but that Gil Robles knew nothing about it.

Whatever the truth, it is certain that once in command of the Balearics, Franco devoted all his considerable energies to strictly military activities. He was happier than he had been at Corunna, for though he missed his native Galicia, he was now first, instead of second, in command and could feel that despite the anti-militarist views of the government in power, he had at least resumed his own career in reasonably promising circumstances.

He had made the challenging discovery that nobody had given the slightest thought to the possible defence of the islands in case of war. Another discovery was that the library of the General Officer Commanding, at Palma, contained full and fascinating accounts of the conquest of the island by James the Conqueror, in the thirteenth century. Having devoured these, he decided that the problems any defenders would face now were much the same as those faced by the defenders of seven centuries ago. And he set out to produce a plan to repulse all comers.

For the next few weeks, Franco rose every morning at dawn and set forth on horseback to cover systematically every square inch of the islands, often lunching with his famished and exhausted companions as late as 4 p.m. From these studies and observations emerged a defence plan, to which, during the Civil War, Franco directed the attention of the then commander, by radio, when a group of Catalan Republicans landed on Mallorca. Doing as he was told, the Nationalist Commander found Franco's plan intact in a drawer in his former office and made successful use of it.[6]

The man who accepted Franco's plan for the defence of the Balearics was, in fact, Gil Robles, after he had become War Minister in 1935. From the autumn of 1933, this young, energetic and intelligent barrister from Salamanca, was the man of the hour in Republican Spain. Unfortunately for him – and just possibly for Spain, though this is a far more debatable proposition – he was never given the opportunity to exercise the power that was his by democratic right. Unfortunately also, he was young – thirty-six in 1933 – and had greatness, of a kind, thrust on him too fast for his own good. Intoxicated, perhaps, by this rapid fame, he succeeded in projecting simultaneously a number of contradictory images, made too many enemies and in the end ruined his own chances. He has been called a clerical reactionary (possibly the truest of his labels) and a fascist, and he has been accused of plotting to seize power by force. Neither the fascist label nor the accusation of plotting can be sustained. But he was partly to blame for the label and the charge; and the fact that both were accepted as true by the entire Left – Socialists, Anarchists and Communists – was one of the major causes of the Civil War.

The son of an eminent jurist, Gil Robles had been a brilliant stud-
ent at the Salesian college at Salamanca and had joined the staff of the
Jesuit paper *El Debate* – one of the newspapers suppressed under
Azaña (another was the monarchist *ABC*). The editor of *El Debate*,
Angel Herrera, was one of the leaders of the Catholic party, *Acción
Popular*, which was intended, as are the present-day Christian
Democratic parties of Germany, Italy and other countries, to be a
party of worshipping masses as well as of the organized Church.
Herrera wanted *Acción Popular* to make way for a larger organization
that would better fill the role of a mass party with clerical affiliations;
and he sponsored Gil Robles as the new party's leader.[7]

Everything went off as planned. Smaller Catholic groups duly
merged with *Acción Popular* to constitute a new party, which was
called the Confederation of Autonomous Rightist Parties, or CEDA
(*Confederación de Derechas Autónomas*). Taking advantage of the new
electoral law passed by the Constituent Cortes, which favoured
coalitions as against individual parties in an attempt to reproduce a
Westminster-type two-party system, CEDA formed an electoral
alliance with the Monarchists, Carlists, Basque Nationalists and
Agrarians. It was a brilliantly successful recipe, for CEDA topped the
poll in the general elections of November 1933, bringing Gil Robles
to parliament with 110 deputies.

Azaña's Left Republicans were smashed, with only five seats. The
Socialists, wishing to disentangle themselves from their alliance with
Azaña to regain a standing with the workers that had been damaged
by the Casas Viejas affair, made the electoral mistake of fighting the
elections alone. The result was that, although they lost no votes, they
returned only 58 deputies to parliament – a drop of fifty per cent.
Lerroux's centre Radicals finished second to CEDA, with 102 seats.
There was one Communist deputy.

It was CEDA's misfortune that it lacked an absolute majority
although it was the strongest party in parliament. By rights, however, Gil Robles ought to have been invited to form a government.
But President Alcalá Zamora had little liking for the young Catholic
leader and felt bound to lend weight to the fact that he was feared
and detested on the Left. He therefore gave the Premiership to old
Lerroux.

There were a number of reasons for the distrust Gil Robles
aroused, not only on the Left but even among mild conservatives like

Alcalá Zamora who sincerely believed in the Republican idea. He was 'in' with the Jesuits, who had suffered from Azaña's anti-clerical Republic and were credited with the ambition of destroying the constitution. He had married into a rich and influential family and his party was subsidized by monarchist and other landlords. He had been impressed by Hitler whom he had seen and heard at the Nuremberg rally, and later by the Austrian fascist, Dolfuss. (He was soon disillusioned with the Nazis, when they started persecuting the Church, but retained his admiration for Dolfuss's corporative ideas.) And his public defence of the Republic had been curiously ambiguous. Alcalá evidently thought that it was safer to let Lerroux form a government with CEDA support, than Gil Robles, with Radical votes. Whether or not this was a mistake on Alcalá Zamora's part is hard to say, for by this time the die appeared to have been cast, and both sides – Right and Left alike – seemed hell-bent on a collision course.

On the Right – or more strictly the Centre-Right – Lerroux formed a cabinet without the CEDA but beholden to it for parliamentary support, and immediately set about destroying the work of Azaña's two years. Largo Caballero's labour laws were repealed or ignored; Sanjurjo was amnestied (though banished to Portugal) and his fellow-plotters were reinstated with back pay; grandees whose estates had been confiscated had them returned and peasants who had been settled on expropriated land under Azaña's agrarian reform plan were evicted.[8] More surprisingly, from this government of the once anti-clerical Radical party, the secular laws of Azaña and his Jacobins were blocked: for instance, the replacement of religious by lay schools was indefinitely postponed.

On the Left, the Anarchists, who had boycotted the elections, immediately declared war on the new government, and on 8 December, on Anarchist orders, *comunismo libertario* was proclaimed in Aragonese villages, with strikes and church burnings in other provinces to make the point clearer. The Socialists afraid as always, of losing ground to the Anarchists, now openly advocated violent revolution. In January 1934, Largo Caballero called for street fighting, and in February his rival, Indalecio Prieto, exclaimed: 'If it is necessary to shed blood, it must be shed!'[9]

Thus began the *Bienio Negro* – the two black years – as the Left called the period that began with Gil Robles's electoral victory.

From Franco's point of view, the advent of the Centre-Right brought a rapid improvement in his professional fortunes. To a large extent, this was due to the extraordinary impression he made on Lerroux's War Minister, Diego Hidalgo. The two men met for the first time in February 1934, in Madrid, where Franco had gone to spend a short leave at a time when his Moroccan war wound was giving him some discomfort.

The first fruit of Hidalgo's nascent admiration for the general – and of the advent of the Centre-Right – came the following month, when the War Minister promoted Franco to Divisional General, thereby raising him to a rank appropriate to his actual command in the Balearics and restoring him to the position in the hierarchy which he would have occupied had he not been demoted under Azaña's decrees.

Not long afterwards, the War Minister – a lawyer by profession and a liberal in his views – visited the Balearics on a tour of inspection. He returned full of enthusiasm for General Franco and recorded his views both in a book, *Por qué fui Lanzado del Ministerio de la Guerra?*, and in an interview in the London *Sunday Express* of 15 May 1938. In the former, Diego Hidalgo wrote an extended eulogy of which the following are selected passages:

> Of his virtues, the highest is deliberateness in examining, analysing, inquiring into and developing problems: but a deliberateness that impels him to be painstaking over details, accurate in service, correct in observation, hard in command, and demanding, while at the same time understanding, calm and decisive.
>
> He is one of the few men I know who never wander from the point. The conversations I had with him on military subjects, during my stay in those islands, revealed to me, moreover, his extraordinary knowledge . . .
>
> And Franco, in the silence of his office, has devoted many years, the years of peace, documenting himself. This study has borne fruit, and today one may well assert that there are no secrets for this soldier in the art of war, elevated into a science by the ingenuity of men.[10]

From the *Sunday Express* interview, I have already quoted an anecdote in the first chapter of this book, recounting Franco's refusal to grant a pardon to an officer who had slapped a private, in defiance of

Hidalgo's order that his visit should be marked by a discharge of all military detainees. 'It was this quality of Franco's, the only chief who had dared to turn down, and justifiably, a petition from a War Minister, that made me admire him and become friendly with him,' said Hidalgo.

It was during Franco's short leave in Madrid in 1934 that his mother died there. It was 28 February and she was on her way to Rome on a pilgrimage. She had caught cold on leaving church after Mass. Pneumonia developed and carried her off in a few days. Franco, whose puritanism owed so much to the moral example of this sad and virtuous woman, stayed on in Madrid to bury her, then returned to the islands.

Though outwardly impassive, as usual, he was feeling depressed, both by his mother's death and by the many outward signs to be seen in Madrid, that the political climate was deteriorating beyond hope of redemption. On 9 February, a few days before Franco arrived from Mallorca, a young medical student, Matías Montero, was shot three times in the Calle de Mendizábal, one of Madrid's central streets, and died. This was no ordinary murder: the shots were fired by a young Socialist, Francisco Tello (later sentenced to $23\frac{1}{2}$ years' gaol).[11] And it was the third such murder in less than a month. Each time, the young victim had been a member of *Falange Española*. Matías Montero, the victim of 9 February, had been selling the Falange's paper, *F.E.*

Here was something new – a *Spanish* fascist party. It is permissible to emphasize the 'Spanish', for though the Falange was an authentic fascist party, it was quite distinct from its Italian prototype or its Nazi contemporary. For one thing, the founder and leader, José Antonio Primo de Rivera, was a very different man from Mussolini or Hitler. The eldest son of the dictator, Miguel Primo de Rivera, José Antonio – as he was soon universally known – was a tall, good-looking young man of considerable charm, to which even his enemies were sensitive, and an unfascist sense of humour. His manners were those of a *señorito* from Andalusia and he was a barrister. He had sworn to rehabilitate the memory of his father and aspired to lead a movement that would unite the whole nation.

It was a vision that was not without a certain naïve nobility, and he expressed it in exalting phrases and with a natural eloquence that always secured him a hearing. On 9 October 1933, he had addressed the inaugural meeting of his new movement in the Comedia Theatre in Madrid, in these terms:

The motherland [*patria* was the word he used] is a total unity, in which are integrated the individuals and all the classes: the motherland cannot be in the hands of the strongest class nor of the best organized party. The motherland is a transcendent synthesis, an indivisible synthesis, with its own ends to accomplish, and what we want is that today's movement and the State it will create should be the effective, authoritarian instrument in the service of an indisputable unity, of that permanent unity, of that irrevocable unity, that calls itself the motherland.[12]

This was heady stuff, words to arouse enthusiasm. It was also – although José Antonio seemed quite unaware of it – a dangerously explosive message for people to hear, in Spain of all countries and in 1933 of all years, when the Right was about to triumph and the Left to threaten revolution. Moreover, it was accompanied, in the same speech of 9 October, by a provocative attack on the economic liberalism that allowed men to starve, without respect for their souls, and on Marxism for its materialism. For this was the fundamental difference between Spanish fascism and fascism in Italy or Germany: José Antonio and his followers were Catholics who saw religion as the spiritual foundation of their ideal State.

This, too, was explosive in the tense autumn of 1933, for here was a movement that attacked capitalism – as Marxism did – but denounced class warfare as well and the atheist materialism of communism.[13] The birth of *Falange Española* was thus a red rag to the bull of Socialism. The answer could only be the undeclared war of the streets that carried off the young vendors of *F.E.* And when, on 4 March 1934, in Valladolid, *Falange Española* merged with a similar group, the JONS (*Juntas de Ofensiva Nacional-Sindicalista*), it became evident that violence would answer violence.

José Antonio himself deplored violence – another way in which he differed from Mussolini and Hitler. When Matías Montero was killed, he wrote to the press, saying: '*Falange Española* in no way resembles a criminal organization, and it does not intend to copy the methods of such organizations, no matter how many provocations it may receive.' His followers, however, did not share this abnegatory approach, and soon the street murders became an uncontrollable street war, with reprisals and counter-reprisals *ad infinitum*.[14]

This, indeed, was the birth-time of new political extremes in Spain, for it was now, in 1933 and 1934, that the Spanish Communist Party first began to make its weight felt. The Party had, in fact, been founded in 1920 by dissident Socialists, under the influence of two Comintern agents, the Russian Borodin and the Indian Roy. But it was not till April 1933, when a new Central Committee of the party, resulting from various Moscow-directed purges and expulsions, met in Madrid, that the Spanish Communists acquired a coherent and effective policy. To a large extent, this was the work of two later Comintern agents, the enormously fat Argentino of Italian birth, Vittorio Codovila, and the sinister Hungarian, Ernö Gerö, who was boss of the Hungarian Communist Party in 1956 when the Hungarian people made their tragic bid to overthrow their Stalinist rulers.[15] Indeed, throughout its stormy history, the Spanish Communist Party has been the instrument of Soviet policy, even after every allowance has been made for deviations caused by Spanish individualism. In the period that concerns us, however, the main *Spanish* executants of Moscow's will, as interpreted by the Comintern, were José Díaz, who started his working life as a baker in Seville and was the plodding type of communist leader who obeys orders without question; and Dolores Ibarruri, the famous *Pasionaria*, whose oratory did so much to fan the flames of violence in the late 1930s.

Fortunately for Moscow, but tragically for Spain, the Spanish Communist Party was reorganized about the time when Largo Caballero took his fateful decision to dissociate himself from the moderate Republicans and opt for revolutionary violence. In 1933, Communist propaganda was still describing Largo Caballero as a 'Social Fascist'.[16] But in December of that year, Moscow launched the policy of alliances between communists and other 'non-fascist' parties that came to be known as the 'Popular Front'. And Largo Caballero's new revolutionary policy made him and his Socialists receptive to Communist overtures. It was shortly after this – and not by coincidence – that Moscow's propaganda machine started flattering Largo by calling him 'the Lenin of Spain'. Ideally, from Moscow's point of view, the *Communists* should have been preaching revolution, with Largo Caballero trailing along. But the increasing violence of Largo's speeches forced them to take an even more incendiary line. Largo's personal responsibility for the Civil War is thus a particularly heavy one, heavier perhaps than that of any other individual.

From Mallorca, General Franco continued to follow the gyrations and intricacies of Comintern policy, as he had since 1928. He had never been among those who dismissed the Spanish Communists because of their numerical weakness. True enough, the party had been minute when the monarchy fell. But it was growing, and had reached 25,000 members in 1933.[17] More important than its growing numbers, however, were the tightness of the party's organization, the dedication of its leaders to Marxist policies serving Moscow's ends, and its capacity to influence the working class movement. Franco noted the facts as they occurred: in May 1934, Largo Caballero had called for a 'revolutionary army'; in July, Largo's name was acclaimed at the Moscow Congress of Youth against War and Fascism; and on 12 September, the Spanish Communist Party entered Largo's *Alianzas Obreras*, after having spurned Largo's invitation to join them for the past five months. The following day, the Communist Party's paper, *Mundo Obrero*, declared: 'The Communist Party joins the Alianzas with the intention of convincing the socialist workers that unity is indispensable for the triumph of the revolution.'[18]

If any room for doubt had existed in Franco's mind, it now evaporated: a communist revolution was on its way in Spain, and Largo Caballero would lead it, with Moscow's approval and support. He was confirmed in his view by news of the proliferating 'front' organizations that had been springing up in Spain during the past few months, under such names as Association of Friends of the Soviet Union of Communist Students, Association of Revolutionary Proletarian Writers and Artists, International Struggle Committee against War and Fascism, and the Revolutionary Atheist League.

Both sides were, indeed, lining up for a showdown. On the Left, the Anarchists, Socialists and Communists were arming and drilling their youth groups for revolutionary armies. In Catalonia, Maciá's *Estat Català* had created a small military organization known as the *escamots*, who wore green shirts. On the Right, the Falangist gunmen were organizing for reprisals against Leftist sharpshooters. Nor were the Falangists alone, for Colonel Varela, emerging from gaol under Lerroux's amnesty, was training and organizing the Carlist *Requetés*, who had been promised arms and money by Mussolini. It was about this time, too, that young Army officers began to join a conspiratorial group known as the *Unión Militar Española* (UME), which was dedicated to overthrowing the Republic and restoring order. Already, then, in 1934, the outlines of the future contending forces, and of the foreign interventionists, could be clearly discerned.

Franco was not the only man who could see the turn events were taking. On 24 September, José Antonio wrote a rather plaintive letter to Franco, which he entrusted to Ramón Serrano Súñer, Franco's brother-in-law, who was still at that time a member of Gil Robles's CEDA and had not yet joined the Falange. In it, José Antonio complained that the revolutionaries were arming themselves and forecast a red revolution and Catalonia's secession.[19] He explained that he was writing to General Franco because the politicians were unworthy, and offered the services of his followers to the general in the event of a civil war. Nearly four years later, on 28 July 1938, General Franco revealed in a speech that his 'instructions', in reply to José Antonio's letter, were 'to wait watchfully without losing faith in the Army'. When the time came, and the revolution had broken out, Falangists were to resort to the military authorities in the certainty that their services would be welcomed. This was not exactly a rebuff; but it could scarcely have been more non-committal.[20]

Largo Caballero and his followers were looking for a pretext to start their trumpeted revolution, and they found it in the autumn of 1934. Lerroux had resigned in a huff over Alcalá Zamora's use of Presidential prerogatives, to be succeeded by Ricardo Samper, an inept fellow-Radical, who was quite unable to cope with the mounting disorders that afflicted the Republic, and resigned on 1 October when Gil Robles's CEDA withdrew its parliamentary support.

By all the normal rules of parliamentary life, the President ought now to have sent for Gil Robles and invited him to form a government. Distaste and fear, however, still held his hand. Distaste for Gil Robles, who had stolen the thunder he had once thought of as rightfully his by rallying and organizing conservative opinion in Spain. And fear of the consequences of provoking the Left by appointing as Prime Minister a man widely (though wrongly) denounced as a fascist in disguise. Gil Robles himself had been pressing for a majority of portfolios in the next government. Since the CEDA was the strongest party in the Cortes, this was a perfectly reasonable request to make.

After long hesitation, Alcalá Zamora sought to compromise by inviting Lerroux to form a government with three minor posts reserved for the CEDA. In so doing, he was, of course, well within his constitutional rights, though the compromise failed to satisfy either Gil Robles or the Left. It is hard, however, to agree with Brenan's verdict that 'all the disasters that have followed for Spain may be traced to this one unhappy decision'.[21] For the Socialists and their allies were quite determined to have their revolution. Largo Caballero had been working up to it for a long time; and Indalecio Prieto, not to be outdone, had been smuggling weapons into Asturias, with which to arm the workers.[22] With or without Alcalá's timid offer to the CEDA, the revolution would have come. True, the Left had warned the President that they would regard the entry of the CEDA in the government as a declaration of war. But a dissolution of the Cortes, which the Left wanted, would at best have delayed the evil day, given the enormous appeal Gil Robles had at that time for many Spanish voters.

At any rate, on 5 October – the day after Lerroux had formed his new government – the Socialist UGT declared a general strike. Next day, Luis Companys (who had succeeded the Quixotic Colonel Maciá as the leader of Catalan nationalism after the latter's death some months earlier) proclaimed Catalonia's independence within a Spanish Federal Republic.

In Asturias, the Socialists, Communists and Anarchists, sinking their differences for once, led the coal miners into action, seizing the city of Oviedo and a number of smaller towns.

Here, then, was the revolution.

Had it broken out a day or two later, Franco would have found himself in the thick of it, for he had just been granted permission to spend a few days' leave at Oviedo, his former garrison town and *patria chica* of his wife and her family. Diego Hidalgo, who had remained War Minister under Samper, had asked Franco to accompany him as a personal adviser on an inspection of military manœuvres in Leon province. It was on their return that Franco asked him and was given leave. No sooner were they back, however, than the crisis caused by the fall of the Samper government broke out, followed almost immediately by the revolution of 5 October.

Re-appointed War Minister in Lerroux's new cabinet, Hidalgo thought at once of Franco. With him as special military adviser, he reasoned, the War Ministry would have gained the services of the most technically competent Spanish general, and one, moreover, who knew Asturias intimately. Where, however, was Franco? If he had already left for Oviedo, it might take some time to find him. Anxiously, Hidalgo sent out messages to Franco summoning him urgently to the War Ministry.

As it happened, Franco was still in Madrid. As he was ushered into the Minister's office, Hidalgo exclaimed: 'I was getting really impatient. I'd sent a number of emissaries to find you. I need you.'

'I am at your orders,' said Franco, who was wearing mufti.

Diego Hidalgo handed him a thick sheaf of telegrams that had been reaching him from various parts of the country. They told of strikes and street fights, of the *Generalidad*'s order to the local Commander, General Batet, to submit with his troops, of the uprising of the well-armed Asturian miners, who at that moment were marching on the two main cities of the province, Oviedo and Gijon.

As Franco was reading, Hidalgo watched for signs of emotion. There were none until Franco reached the account of the Asturian events. At this point, he exclaimed: 'This is bad. There are no forces in Oviedo to face up to the insurrection.'[23]

Indeed, as the messages said, twenty or thirty thousand men, mostly miners, had already seized a dozen towns or villages, were threatening Oviedo and Gijon and knew every inch of the terrain. Facing them were the garrisons of the two main cities, totalling at most sixteen hundred men. It wasn't going to be easy to find reinforcements, garrisons having been reduced to the barest minimum under Azaña's anti-militarist policy. To rob Peter to pay Paul would be to expose Peter – that is, any denuded garrison town – to revolutionary action. Moreover, communications between Asturias and the rest of Spain, bad enough in normal times, had been made really precarious by the cutting of the railway and of the North-South road linking Oviedo with Leon.[24]

Faced with this desperate situation, which he had been outlining to the Minister, Franco proposed that troops should be brought over from Africa. Much criticism has been heaped on this request, notably by Gerald Brenan, who found the use of Foreign Legionaries and Moorish troops in Spain unprecedented and barbarous.[25] The same troops, however, had been called in by Azaña himself to help put down the Sanjurjo uprising.[26] And it is difficult to see what else Franco could have done, short of turning down Diego Hidalgo's appeal for help. In any case, the actual decision to send for African troops was not, of course, Franco's but Lerroux's. The Prime Minister also consulted General Goded – like Franco one of the future leaders of the Nationalist uprising – and from him also received the advice to call in the Foreign Legion and the Moorish *Regulares*.

For the next fortnight or so, Franco became in fact, though not in title, Chief of Staff to the War Ministry. In recognition of the fact, his admirer Diego Hidalgo had handed over his own office to the general, and found him a room to sleep in, next to his own.[27] The actual Chief of the Central General Staff, Colonel Masquelet, was a personal friend of Azaña's and his office, which was in the same building, was said to be 'a Masonic lodge'.[28] While Franco was there, however, it was he who gave the orders, by-passing Masquelet as though he did not exist. For reasons of security as well as of efficiency, Franco appointed his own staff of four, two of whom were naval officers: Captains Francisco Moreno Fernández and Pablo Ruiz Marset, his personal aide-de-camp and cousin, Lieutenant-Colonel Franco Salgado-Araujo, and an NCO, Jesús Sánchez Posada.[29] The Minister's telecommunications room was at Franco's disposal, but as the technicians who worked there were regarded as sympathizers with the revolutionaries, Franco's staff were under orders to take all telephone calls, for fear that vital messages might not reach him or, worse still, reach him deliberately garbled.

Franco, who had changed back into military uniform, was in his element, constantly on the alert, issuing orders to the three armed forces, seeing personally to every detail of the operations he had planned or improvised. From Hidalgo's office, Franco gave orders to quell the street fights in Madrid, reprimanded General Batet in Barcelona by telephone for indecision and ordered the removal of the Commander of the Military airfield at Leon, Major Ricardo de la Puente Bahamonde, who happened to be another of Franco's cousins.[30] Let us note in passing that the cousin's dismissal was justified by his Leftist sentiments, while the reprimand to Batet was perhaps unjust: when Franco telephoned him, at 2 a.m. on 7 October to ask why he hadn't yet crushed Companys's rebellion, he said he was waiting until dawn to save lives. And indeed, three hours later the terms of Companys's surrender were arranged. The Catalan revolt was doomed to failure by the refusal of the powerful Anarchist CNT to join it, and – less importantly – by the inaction of the green-shirted *escamots*. In Madrid, too, the revolt collapsed ignominiously. Only in Asturias did the revolution take root, and indeed turn into the bloodiest chapter of the Second Republic's story until the Civil War itself.

On 6 October, the day after Franco had moved into the War Ministry, about 8,000 revolutionary miners, armed with dynamite and little else, moved into Oviedo. Within the next two days, they had captured two small arms factories, several businesses and the government offices. Having done this, the revolutionary leadership, consisting of Socialists and communists, had instituted food rationing. In the Gijon area, where the Anarchists were strongest, 'libertarian communism' was proclaimed.

The news that reached Franco in his office in the Palacio de Buenavista – which housed the War Ministry in Madrid – was worrying. On 7 October, the messages recorded the capture of the Asturian mines and of the Trubia arms factory, while General Bosch's column, marching from Leon to relieve Oviedo, found itself isolated.[31] In Oviedo, the revolutionaries, by now armed with cannon and machine-guns, were attacking the railway station of the Norte. The Carabineros' barracks surrendered. In the evening, the revolutionaries started to bombard the Cathedral. Much damage was done, but the soldiers defending it held out.

In Gijon, the revolutionaries had invaded the Cimadevilla quarter. By radio, Franco gave direct instructions to the Commander of the cruiser *Libertad* for the disembarkation of a battalion sent from Franco's birthplace, El Ferrol. It was to have landed them at Aviles, but the revolutionaries had blocked the harbour entrance, so the cruiser had to go on to Gijon.

On 8 October, Franco learned that the insurgents had seized the high ground around the hospital, from which they dominated the park and the centre of the city. That day also brought news that one of Franco's former Legion subordinates, Major Carlos Silva, had had a leg amputated after sustaining a severe wound while leading assault troops against the revolutionary forces.

The next day – a Wednesday – brought news of severe street fighting in Oviedo, with the revolutionaries wresting building after building from the forces of order. The rebels captured the Santa Clara barracks and the telephone exchange, and were fighting for the Pelayo barracks.

In Gijon the news, from Franco's viewpoint, was better, the *Libertad* having successfully bombarded the Cimadevilla district. Franco ordered the landing of a column of Marines from the ironclad *Jaime I* and the mobilization of officers who had taken advantage of Azaña's retirement scheme. General Bosch's column was hemmed in in Vega del Rey; and an artillery group was in a similar plight at Campomanes. From Aviles, a relief battalion – a much depleted one, numbering under two hundred men – was marching towards Oviedo under the direct command of General López de Ochoa, whom Diego Hidalgo had appointed as overall commander of the active forces suppressing the revolution.

By this time, the Moorish *Regulares* and the *Tercio* Legionaries whom Franco was bringing over from Africa were nearing the Asturian shores. A message had reached Franco shortly after their departure from Ceuta to say that Lieutenant-Colonel López Bravo, in command of a battalion of the 8th African Alpine Regiment, was unreliable. He had told a group of friends on board that his troops would never fire on their brothers. Franco immediately notified Diego Hidalgo, who ordered that he was to be relieved of his command. The War Minister spent eight hours in his office that day, while efforts were made to locate Colonel López before the ships reached Asturias. At first, he was said to be in the *Segarra*, but couldn't be found on board. Eventually, he was traced to the *Miguel de Cervantes* whose captain was ordered to tie up at Corunna and hand him over to the local garrison commander.[32]

Another of Franco's preoccupations on 8 and 9 October was the appointment of an officer to command the African troops. His choice was the rumbustious Lieutenant-Colonel Juan Yagüe, a former Foreign Legion companion, who was found to be in the village of San Leonardo in the Soria mountains and was summoned urgently to Madrid, where the War Minister formally appointed him on Franco's recommendation.[33] In the meantime, Franco had laid on a plane, an autogyro which landed him safely on the road between the harbour of El Musel and Gijon, whither he was conveyed in an army truck, on the morning of 10 October.

Some hours before, at 5 a.m., the first troops from Africa had been landed at El Musel: the Alpine battalion, the 5th and 6th *Banderas* of the Legion, and a *Tabor* of *Regulares*. The last-named was commanded by Major Ruiz Marset, whose brother, Captain Pablo Ruiz Marset, was a member of Franco's emergency staff in Madrid. Two days later, on the 12 October, the naval officer suddenly remarked to his companions in the telecommunications room in the Palacio de Buenavista that he was sure his brother would die on reaching Oviedo. An instant later, a message from Oviedo starting coming over the wire. Looking anxiously over the operator's shoulder, the naval officer read these words:

LOSSES OF THE COLUMN: INFANTRY MAJOR RUIZ MARSET, CHIEF OF REGULARES, KILLED ON ENTERING OVIEDO AT THE HEAD OF HIS TABOR.[34]

'What gave you this presentiment?' asked Captain Francisco Moreno, greatly moved.

'My brother,' answered the sailor, 'had never commanded assault troops and was waiting for the chance to show that he could do justice to the honour of commanding the *Regulares*. I felt certain that he would enter Oviedo, as the message says, only to die.'

Diego Hidalgo, shaken by the incident, asked Franco what he thought about it. 'It is our duty to die,' was the characteristic reply.

By the evening of 10 October, Yagüe's shock force from Africa had mastered the situation in Gijon. Marching all the next day, they reached the outskirts of Oviedo, to be joined on 12 October by General López de Ochoa's columns from Aviles. There was an immediate clash of wills between the two commanders. López de Ochoa, a Freemason, was a convinced defender of the Republic, bent only on restoring the threatened area to the Republic's authority. Yagüe, an opponent of the Republic who later joined the Falange, wanted not merely to restore order, but to punish those who had disturbed it. When he objected to López de Ochoa's tactical decisions, the latter sternly reminded him who was in command.[35] By one of the tragic ironies of contemporary Spanish history, López de

Ochoa was later executed by the Republicans for his part in repressing the Oviedo uprising. (In contrast, General Batet, who had put down the Barcelona coup virtually without bloodshed, was executed by the Nationalists for refusing to join their 'crusade'.)[36] Colonel Yagüe, of course, became one of the leading Nationalist generals.

As the forces of order were converging on Oviedo, Franco – having, as we have seen, replaced his Leftist cousin in the Leon air base – ordered planes out to bomb the rebel positions in the Asturian capital. Once López de Ochoa and Yagüe reached the scene, the end was in sight. Furious street fighting followed, during which the revolutionaries blew up the University. The miners' last stronghold, at Mieres – where the revolution had started on 5 October – surrendered on 18 October, after prolonged personal negotiations between López de Ochoa and the revolutionary leader, Belarmino Tomás, who was secretary-general of the Asturian miners' *sindicato*.

López de Ochoa had solemnly promised the miners' leader that there would be no reprisals if the surrender conditions were observed by the revolutionaries.[37] In fact, reprisals of vengeful frightfulness were taken. For this, however, López de Ochoa can hardly be blamed. Many of the rebellious miners defied the surrender agreement and fought on, so that on 20 October – two days after the terms had been agreed with Belarmino Tomás – even the humane general was obliged to threaten summary execution for persons found to be hoarding arms.[38] This, however, did not constitute reprisals. What did were the orgy of shooting and rape by Yagüe's Moors, the execution of thousands of prisoners by the *Guardia Civil*, and the sadistic tortures inflicted on captured miners by a police major named Doval.[39]

The man chiefly responsible for these horrors, at least in the first instance, was Lt-Col Yagüe who, in a furious quarrel with López de Ochoa, reproached him with softness amounting to complicity with the revolutionaries, and sent complaints to this effect to Franco.[40] Since Franco had appointed Yagüe in the first place, had sanctioned the use of Moorish troops and allowed Yagüe virtually to supersede López de Ochoa, he himself cannot be acquitted of responsibility for the savagery with which the revolution was suppressed.

On the Right, the methods used in the repression were held to be justified by the alleged atrocities of the revolutionaries. It is now generally admitted, however, that most of the miners' 'atrocities' were pure inventions by right-wing newspapers and propagandists. This was established by independent inquiries, and even so ardent a supporter of Franco as the Nationalist historian Joaquín Arrarás records – to his honour – that the atrocity stories could not be confirmed, except for the burning alive of a security guard and the trampling to death of three girls.[41]

On 24 October, General Franco accompanied the Minister of War, Justice and Public Works on a visit of inspection to Oviedo. It was a sorry sight: the insurgents had destroyed the University and whole streets had been turned into smoking ruins, while the Cathedral was a shell. Diego Hidalgo publicly praised the city's defenders, and Franco, interviewed by a reporter, made a statement that amounted to a political declaration: 'The war of Morocco,' he said, 'with the *Regulares* and the *Tercio*, had a certain romantic air, an air of reconquest. But this war is a frontier war, and the fronts are Socialism, Communism and any other forms that attack civilization to replace it by barbarism.'[42]

It had been a costly little revolution. More than seven hundred buildings had been destroyed. The Army had lost 47 officers and NCOs and 173 men, with 743 wounded and 46 unaccounted for. Civilian losses were given officially as 850 killed and 1,450 wounded, but were certainly much higher if the unknown number of those shot after the miners' surrender are included. In addition, some 30,000 were in gaol; these included Largo Caballero and Manuel Azaña, but not Indalecio Prieto, who slipped across the border into France.

When all the accusing things have been said about the cruelty and folly of the retribution enacted by the Right – for in office Lerroux's nominally centre-right administration had turned sharply rightward – it still remains that there would have been no reprisals if there had not been a revolution from the Left in the first instance. The horse must be put where it belongs, before the cart. After Asturias, there was no hope whatever of averting civil war in Spain. In Gerald Brenan's eyes, the guilt for 1934 fell unequivocally on the Right, and above all on Gil Robles whom he accuses of planning to destroy the constitution; but he makes no mention of the public admission of guilt made eight years after the tragic events of 1934 by the outstanding leader of the Left in Republican Spain: Indalecio Prieto.

Speaking in his Mexican exile on May Day 1942, Prieto said: 'I declare myself guilty before my conscience, before the Socialist

Party and before all Spain, for my participation in that revolutionary movement. I declare it as guilt, as a sin, not as a glory. I am free of responsibility in the genesis of that movement; but I take full responsibility for its preparation and development.'[43]

The most impartial Spanish observer of all, Salvador de Madariaga, supports this belated view, and absolves Gil Robles of guilt, in a verdict of memorable wisdom:

> The revolt of 1934 is unpardonable. The decision of the President in calling the CEDA to share in the government was not only unimpeachable, not only unavoidable, but long overdue. The argument that Señor Gil Robles intended to bring in Fascism was both hypocritical and demonstrably untrue. It was hypocritical because everybody knew that the Socialists of Largo Caballero were dragging the other Socialists to a rebellion and in the teeth of Azaña's opposition to such a desperate course; demonstrably untrue because, had Señor Gil Robles meant to destroy the Constitution by violent means, the defeat of the rebellion of 1934 gave him a golden opportunity to do so – and he did not take it. In fact, Señor Gil Robles was a convinced parliamentarian too deeply committed to a Republican Parliamentarian mode of life to be in any way acceptable to Fascism or susceptible to it . . .'[44]

And Madariaga added: 'With the rebellion of 1934, the Left lost every shred of moral authority to condemn the rebellion of 1936.' This, be it remembered, from a distinguished Spaniard who refused to support either side during the Civil War and who has never wavered in his condemnation of Franco's régime.

Whatever may be thought of Franco's tolerance of Yagüe's methods in Asturias, it is a matter of historical record that he was the hero of the hour in the eyes of the government of the Republic, to the extent that Diego Hidalgo wryly remarked: 'Everybody has expressed esteem for the meritorious and effective work of this general . . . but nobody has had a single word of praise for the Minister who appointed him.'[45]

In recognition of the General's services, Lerroux conferred on him the Grand Cross of Military Merit. Then, in February 1935, he appointed Franco Commander-in-Chief of the armed forces in Morocco. He had intended to go further still and appoint him High Commissioner as well, but was dissuaded from doing so by President

Alcalá Zamora.[46] Franco had remained in Madrid. He now sailed again for Ceuta, to take up his new appointment, having travelled a long way since his first crossing as junior officer twenty-three years earlier.

4 Mortal Sickness of the Republic

Franco was not in North Africa long enough to accomplish anything. Arriving in February 1935, he was recalled in May for a bigger job still – that of Chief of the Central General Staff – in critical political circumstances that need to be explained.

The smashing of the Asturian revolution had left the Right triumphant and exultant, and the Left, defeated but bitterly defiant and already planning revenge. The Right, knowing the enemy was on the ground, wanted, if possible, to kick him to death. And the enemy meant not only the embattled miners and their immediate leaders, but the politicians who had been in power during the first two years of the Republic. Prieto had slipped through the police net, but Largo Caballero had been caught, and so had Manuel Azaña.

The Azaña case became a kind of *cause célèbre*. The former Prime Minister happened to be in Barcelona when the revolt broke out in that city. Immobilized by the general strike, he was arrested on suspicion of having instigated the Barcelona rebellion, and interned in a prison ship in the harbour of the Catalan capital. Although it was soon plain even to Azaña's interrogators that he had nothing to do with planning rebellion, and indeed had tried to dissuade the *Generalidad* from any separatist action, the government refused to release him until late in December.[1] And the Right, especially the Monarchists, then tried to impeach him for general responsibility for most of the ills of the Republic and, in particular, for the Barcelona rebellion and the delivering of arms to Asturias. In the end, Azaña was released for lack of evidence, his popularity having soared as a result of the obvious injustice to which he was being subjected. Largo Caballero, whose responsibility for recent events was far greater than Azaña's, was also released, while Companys, of the *Generalidad*, was sentenced to thirty years' gaol – a sentence which everybody rightly guessed would never be carried out to the bitter end. (He was later executed by the Franco government.) Thirty death sentences of actual leaders of the revolution were passed, but only two were carried out. In fact, and despite the fearsome allegations of the Left, the Right in power were as magnanimous towards the revolutionaries as the Left had been towards Sanjurjo and his plotters two years earlier. One should add that the reprieves were ordered by President Alcalá Zamora, against the advice of Gil Robles and his CEDA, who wanted to make examples of the rebels. Thus the personal clash between the two men continued.

It was against this background that Gil Robles now insisted on a greater share in the government. His opposition to the commuting of the death sentences had brought the Lerroux administration down. Lerroux nevertheless succeeded as Prime Minister himself, and Gil Robles at last entered the government, as War Minister. At this time, the CEDA leader gave absolute precedence to the need to rebuild the Army which, as we have seen, had been decimated and demoralized by Azaña's reforms. As soon as he took over his new office, he summoned all the divisional generals, including Franco, to an urgent fact-finding conference on the state of the armed forces. The picture that emerged was of a dissolution already far enough advanced to please Azaña. The Army lacked arms, ammunition and even uniforms for recruits. The Air Force was still making do with 1918 aircraft, whose bomb capacity was limited to eleven pounds. With the exception of the Army of Africa, the troops were ill-trained as well as ill-equipped.[2] As for the officers, the most technically competent or valorous among them had been demoted or pushed to one side, to be replaced by time-servers who owed their promotion to having the right friends in Left-wing parties or in the Masonic lodges.*

To put things right, Gil Robles turned, as his predecessor Diego Hidalgo had done, to General Franco, and on 17 May 1935, appointed him Chief of the Central General Staff. High posts were also given to two other right-wing generals: Fanjul, who became Under-Secretary for War, and Goded (whom Lerroux had called in for advice during the Asturian uprising), who was put in charge of the Air Force.

---

* To say this is not, however, to accept the conspiratorial right-wing theory attributing most of Spain's ills to the recondite machinations of international Freemasonry.

It would not have been possible to give Franco a job more to his taste, and he threw himself into it with characteristic energy and thoroughness. He was at his desk at the un-Spanish hour of 9 a.m., working through till 3.30 p.m. when he walked home for lunch. Back in his office at the War Ministry at 5.30, he would work until 11 p.m. On Sundays and Feast days, he allowed himself to rest in the afternoon, but worked in the deserted Ministry from 11 in the morning – after attending Mass – until lunch time.

In effect, Gil Robles had given Franco a free hand, and he set himself two clear but related objectives: to rebuild the morale of the armed forces, and to modernize their equipment. The first was possibly easier than the second. Azaña had republicanized and emasculated the Army. Though there is no evidence that Franco deliberately set out to build an anti-republican Army, this was undoubtedly the effect of the measures he took in 1935, since he and Gil Robles removed officers who had profited from the republican reforms and brought back officers who had suffered from them. Thus Generals Miaja and Riquelme, promoted by Azaña, were among those now removed; and it is scarcely surprising that they later turned up as the high commanders of the republican Army against the military uprising of 1936. On the other hand, General Mola, who had been without a job since the advent of the Republic, was charged with preparing a detailed contingency plan for mobilization. Its success was such that he was appointed General Officer Commanding in Morocco. Colonel Varela, who had been gaoled for his part in the Sanjurjo affair, was rehabilitated and promoted to General. Colonel Yagüe was awarded the Military Medal for his part in repressing the Asturian revolution.

President Alcalá viewed these changes with dismay.

'I notice,' he said one day to the War Minister, 'that all those favoured with promotion or reinstatement are enemies of the Republic.'

'All the appointees are excellent soldiers,' Gil Robles replied.

'Of the eighty chiefs appointed to posts of command,' the President insisted, 'only eight have thanked me . . . I have the list here.'

'Without doubt,' Gil Robles answered, 'they are unaware of protocol.'[3]

While restoring men, Franco also restored institutions, principally the Tribunals of Honour, which Azaña had abolished. The Army thus regained the right to rid itself of officers who had been guilty of breaches of discipline, or of conduct unbecoming an officer. Simultaneously, on Franco's recommendation, the government revised the Azaña decrees on redundancy of military personnel.

General Fanjul was charged with the economic needs of the Army, and plans were drawn up for the removal of discrepancies in pay. General Orgaz – another of the jobless officers – was ordered to prepare a plan for military co-operatives.

General Franco now turned his attention to the twin problems of subversion and security. He organized a special information service, whose principal purpose was to study the political beliefs of recruits to the armed forces. Alarmingly, though not surprisingly, it was found that no fewer than 25 per cent of the draftees were 'revolutionaries', many of them in the service, though not necessarily in the pay, of the Comintern. In the ordnance factories, the penetration was even greater.

Armed with this information, Franco helped to draft a bill on espionage and proposed measures to encourage voluntary service in the Army, as a step towards eliminating subversion in the barracks. As for factories serving both the Army and the Air Force, a new decree placed them under direct military control, all employees being forbidden to join listed 'revolutionary organizations'.

The deficiencies of equipment were so vast that they could not be made good overnight. It was not until the beginning of December that patents for the construction of fighter and bomber aircraft were taken out, and plans were ready for their manufacture in Guadalajara. Competitive tenders were invited for the construction of twenty-five anti-aircraft batteries. The munitions facilities, principally at Toledo, were greatly expanded, and studies ordered on the manufacture of toxic gases and the education of the public in preventive measures in the event of chemical warfare. More modestly, steel helmets – long overdue – were issued to the troops. Simultaneously, the Army was streamlined at the divisional level and firepower increased, while plans were drawn up for the creation of two motorized divisions.

On the strategic side, General Franco turned his attention to two problems: an internal one and an external. Internally, the Asturian rising had shown how easily Oviedo could be isolated, once the harbour of Pajares had been blocked. On 21 July 1935, Franco –

flanked by Generals Goded and Fanjul – directed manœuvres designed to find out how Oviedo could be supplied with Pajares out of commission.

The external problem arose from the dramatic worsening of Anglo-Italian relations that attended the Ethiopian crisis in the autumn of 1935. There was no reason to suppose that Spain would be dragged into hostilities, but the Spaniards could hardly be indifferent to any potential threat to the Mediterranean. Franco ordered the construction of new fortifications at Cartagena and in the Balearics – in fulfilment of the plans he had drawn up while in command of the islands.

It was clear enough that these measures, in sum, would prove costly, and doubtful whether, when it came to action, money would be found for them. In mid-December, an extraordinary military budget, providing for the expenditure of 1,100 million pesetas over three years, was presented to the Council of Ministers, which approved it. Nothing came of it, however, for the Centre-Right coalition collapsed and Gil Robles found himself out of office.

Shady old Lerroux himself had been forced to resign at the end of October in the wash of the so-called *estraperlo* scandal – an affair of rigged roulette tables in which his adopted son was involved.* A further scandal in December, involving friends of Lerroux's who had allegedly enriched themselves through colonial Army supply contracts broke the Radical party, and therefore the coalition. Gil Robles now claimed power for his own CEDA party, but –stubborn to the end – Alcalá Zamora withheld his consent. A dissolution was now the only prospect and, after a short-lived minority government, it duly came on 7 January 1936. General elections were to be held on 16 February.

Thus ended the *Bienio Negro*. It had been a period that brought little credit to any Spanish politicians who lived through it. Gil Robles's party had been denied its logical and democratic right to rule, though it had participated in the Centre-Right coalition. Legislatively, the *Bienio* had been a desert of negatives: nothing of value had been achieved, though the trend of Azaña's rule had been reversed (if only temporarily). There had been a premature revolution

* *Estraperlo* – a corruption of Straperlo – formed from the first syllables of the names of the two adventurers who exploited the system, Strauss and Perl – has passed into the Spanish tongue as a synonym for official corruption.

from the Left, and a brutal repression from the Right. The trend towards political extremism and violence had been accentuated, and the two years had ended in scandal and the annihilation of the Centre. If Azaña's revolution had shown the absurdity of parliamentary democracy in Spain, the anti-Azaña governments that followed had demonstrated that lunacy was hardly too strong a word for a system which neither national temper nor historical tradition justified.

On 19 December 1935, the generals of the Central Staff and all members of the departing War Minister's staff gathered around Gil Robles to bid him farewell. It was an emotional occasion, for the generals felt that with the departure of the Right-wing Catholic leader went their last chance of rebuilding an Army capable of saving Spain from revolutionary anarchy. In the name of the officers present, General Franco made the following little speech.

> We cannot but say at this time that our sorrow is sincere. Never has the Army felt itself better led than during this phase. Honour, discipline, basic concepts have been re-established.
> To show to what extent rectitude has been the only guiding principle of the War Minister, all that is needed is to tell a simple anecdote. A proposal for an appointment was being studied. Three names were being proposed, those of three officers whose background was the same and whose merits were equal. The War Minister had to decide between the three. I indicated to him that any of the three was capable and could brilliantly discharge the appointment, but in all fairness, I told him that one of the three officers was being recommended by almost the whole of the Minister's own party, by the Chamber and by personalities of the Army. The Minister replied: 'Leaving that to one side, which of them would *you* pick?' I answered: 'The three have equal qualifications. I would pick the most senior.' The Minister, without hesitating, ordered me to pick the most senior one. This is the kind of man our War Minister was.[4]

In Madrid, thirty-one years after this farewell, I reminded Gil Robles of Franco's words, and he commented: 'I called in Franco purely as a technician. Our relations were correct.'

On 25 January 1936, in the midst of the most feverish electoral campaign the Spanish Republic had known, Franco – who had remained Chief of Staff under the caretaker government of the moderate Portela Valladares·· was sent to London to represent the Republic at the funeral of King George V. He was received by Edward VIII and stayed at Claridge's Hotel, where doubtless his path must have crossed that of Litvinov, the Soviet Foreign Commissar, who was shortly to denounce him in the Palace of Nations in Geneva.[5] At the funeral procession itself, Franco walked behind Marshal Tukhachevsky, who represented the Soviet Union and who was shortly to die in one of the most sensational of Stalin's purges.[6] It is a safe guess that Franco's mind was neither on the deathless nature of the British monarchy, nor even on the transience of the Spanish Republic, but on the Seventh Congress of the Third International, which – as Franco well knew – was largely devoted to Spain.

The Spanish Civil War, of course, was the inevitable consequence of Spain's exacerbated but purely indigenous social antagonisms. It is worth noting that international communist plans to take control of the impending Spanish revolution were already far advanced by the time of the general elections of 1936. The Comintern's Seventh Congress had begun its meeting in Moscow on 23 July 1935. It had examined the causes of the failure of the Asturian revolution. And it had launched the idea and slogan of the 'Popular Front' – defined as an electoral alliance of the 'working class parties' with 'bourgeois anti-fascist elements'. So that there should be no doubt about the ultimate purpose of this tactic, Georgi Dimitrov, who was in the chair as a reward for his defiance of the German judges in the Reichstag fire trial, explained:

> Comrades, you will remember the ancient tale of the capture of Troy. The attacking army was unable to achieve victory until, with the aid of the Trojan Horse, it penetrated to the very heart of the enemy camp. We, revolutionary workers, should not be shy of using the same tactics.[7]

Among those who listened were the secretary-general of the Spanish Communist Party, José Díaz, and La Pasionaria. Also present was the Argentine Italian Comintern agent in Spain, Vittorio Codovila.

Although Franco knew all this, as he walked in procession behind Marshal Tukhachevsky, he was not, at that stage, unduly worried.

G

His equanimity was not, however, entirely due to a naturally tranquil disposition. For one thing, though the party had grown considerably during the Republic, it was still small, with some 30,000 members, at the time of the 1936 elections.[8] For another, there was still, in January, every reason to believe that Gil Robles's CEDA would sweep the board on polling day. He seemed to have both the mass following and the dynamic organization to ensure victory. His portrait was everywhere, in particular covering an entire façade in Madrids' Puerta del Sol, against a background of seething faces, and carrying the legend: 'These are my powers.' Another slogan said: 'Give me the absolute majority and I shall give you a Spain that is great.'[9]

Doubtless this is why Franco told Dr Gregorio Marañón, the distinguished physician and supporter of the Republic, in Paris on his way back to Madrid that everything would calm down in Spain within a few weeks.[10] This is what he and many other Spaniards hoped, and indeed expected. But between 5 February, when Franco returned to Madrid after four days in Paris, and polling day on 16 February, it became clear that the results of the elections were no longer a foregone conclusion. An important reason for this change of outlook was the decision of the Anarchists to vote *en masse* for the Popular Front, whereas they had boycotted previous elections. The smaller group of Trotskyists, shortly to call themselves the *Partido Obrero de Unificación Marxista* or POUM, also decided to support the Popular Front. Late in the day, Gil Robles himself realized that the electoral law, which in 1933 had favoured him against the Socialists, might now favour the Popular Front against his CEDA; and he looked around for allies. But there was no question of a right-wing equivalent of the Popular Front, that is, of an alliance between the clerical Right of the CEDA and José Antonio's Falange, which CEDA viewed with deep distrust despite the allegations of fascism heaped on Gil Robles by the Left.

When the votes were counted it was found that the Popular Front had indeed gained a sweeping victory in parliamentary terms, though much less of a triumph in electoral terms. In the new Cortes, the Front had 258 seats (later revised upward to 277), against 152 for the Right (later revised downward to 132), and only 62 for the Centre (again, revised downward to only 32). In voting terms, there was much less to choose between the groups, for the Left came out with 4,206,156 votes, against a combined total of 4,464,600 for the Right (3,783,600) and Centre (681,000).* In terms of the popular will, these figures were open to all manner of interpretations. In terms of practical politics, they simply meant that the Popular Front had won.

The man of the hour, however, was neither Largo Caballero nor Prieto, but Manuel Azaña, for not only had his non-Marxist Left Centre polled far more votes than the Socialists and Communists combined, but his dignified bearing and constitutional righteousness during his recent trial had greatly enhanced his stature and popularity.

From complacent expectation, Franco now turned to alarm. The results coming in on the evening of 16 February could only mean, as he saw the situation, a return to revolutionary anarchy, with the added danger of an alliance embracing Azaña – the arch-enemy of the Army – as well as the Anarchists, Communists and Socialists. The middle classes and landlords, terrified of the prospect of 'communism' – under which they lumped Socialists, Communists, Anarchists and Trotskyists as well as Azaña and his followers – hopefully looked to Franco, as the hero of the Asturias repression, as their champion.

At this stage, however, the general had not yet begun to think on *pronunciamiento* lines. Preoccupied, as always, with the concept of order, he looked to the provisional authorities of the Republic to call on the Army to enforce it. His idea was to get action taken while he was still Chief of Staff and before the worst – that is, the Popular Front's take-over – had happened. If this were done, in his view, constitutional propriety (and discipline) would be respected and he himself would emerge as the defender of order and the natural leader of all Spaniards who feared anarchy, while no one could honestly accuse him of dictatorial ambitions of his own.

In anticipation of trouble, and while the electoral campaign was still in progress, Franco had sent Lieutenant-Colonel González Badía to General Mola in Morocco to tell him to be prepared to send reinforcements to the Spanish mainland at short notice. Mola's reply was a laconic: 'Everything is ready.'[11]

On the evening of 16 February, Franco decided there was no time

* Anybody interested in psephology should read Madariaga's fascinating analysis of the results in *Spain*, Book Two, Chapter 6, from which these figures are quoted.

left. Accordingly, he telephoned General Pozas, Director-General of the *Guardia Civil*, who had been appointed by the caretaker government and whom he had known slightly in Morocco. Several versions exist of the subsequent conversation, but the differences are of wording, not substance. According to Joaquín Arrarás's account,[12] this is what was said:

FRANCO   I suppose you know what's going on.

POZAS   I don't think anything's happening.

FRANCO   That's why I'm ringing you, to inform you that the masses are in the streets, and that things are going to come out of these elections, of a revolutionary kind, that are not at all implicit in the results, and I'm afraid that here and in the provinces there are going to be disorders, if they haven't begun already.

POZAS   I think your fears are exaggerated.

FRANCO   Let's hope you're right, but if you're not, I remind you that we live under constitutional legality, which I accept and which obliges us to accept the result of the ballot-boxes even if it is contrary to the system. But if anybody wants to go beyond the results by as much as a millimetre, then this would be unacceptable by virtue of this same electoral and democratic system.

POZAS   Nobody will go beyond, I can assure you.

FRANCO   I think you are promising something you won't be able to accomplish. A more effective way would be for the persons of responsibility and those of us who occupy certain posts in the service of the State and of the constituted system, to make the necessary contact so that the masses do not overwhelm us.

POZAS   I repeat that this thing isn't as important as you think. As far as I can see, what is happening is just a legitimate expansion of republican rejoicing. I don't think there are grounds for fearing anything serious.

It was clear that there was nothing more to be expected from this quarter.

After nightfall, news reached Franco of disorders in various places, and at three in the morning, he decided to telephone his temporary political chief, the caretaker War Minister, General Molero. The Minister, not unnaturally, was asleep. Reaching the telephone heavy with interrupted slumber, he listened to Franco without excitement, and asked:

'And what do you think I can do?'

'To begin with,' Franco answered, 'get the Cabinet to declare a state of war.'

'Does Portela know about this?'

'I shall tell him straightaway,' said Franco, and hung up.

Next morning, the harassed Portela government decided to proclaim a state of war, and communicated its decision to Franco at the War Ministry, who immediately alerted the provincial garrisons. In Saragossa, Valencia and Oviedo, the civil authorities handed over power to the military. In the first of these cities, the CNT had called for a general strike. In Oviedo, Alicante, Burgos, Santona, Cartagena, Barcelona and Gijon, mobs gathered threateningly before the prison gates. In Madrid, the streets were crowded with excited Popular Front supporters. Rumours of a military coup were in the air.

Portela, who was old and unambitious, had one thought only: to get out and hand over to Azaña. But President Alcalá Zamora said he must stay at his post until the results of the second ballot were known. In mid-afternoon – still 17 February – the President added to the confusion by countermanding the order proclaiming a state of war.[13]

The Prime Minister telephoned Franco urgently to explain what had happened and to say that the President had vetoed the proclamation because he thought it was a provocation to the people.

'And you – what do you think?' asked Franco.

'I . . .' stammered Portela, 'I just obey the President's orders.'

By the next morning, Franco's worst fears seemed to be coming true. From province after province came news of street clashes, arson and rioting. He decided to seek a personal interview with Portela, through a liberal ex-Minister of his acquaintance, Natalio Rivas.

The meeting took place at midday in the Prime Minister's office. Franco came straight to the point, declaring that the situation was even graver than he had feared. It was the Prime Minister's duty, he exclaimed, to proclaim a state of war, regardless of the President.

Portela shook his head: 'I am old, I am old,' he said in a broken voice. 'The course you propose is beyond my strength. However, I will say that you are the only person who has made me hesitate . . . But, no . . . This is for a man with more energy than I have.'

'You people have brought the country to this pass, and it is your duty to save it,' Franco insisted.

'And why not the Army?' countered Portela.

'The Army,' was Franco's carefully worded reply, 'lacks even the moral unity necessary to accomplish this task. Your intervention is necessary, for you have authority over Pozas and can rely on the unlimited resources of the State, with the public forces at your orders, together with the collaboration which I can promise you and which will not let you down.'

Poor Portela, badly shaken, said he would sleep on it, using the familiar Spanish expression, 'consult with the pillow' (*consultar con la almohada*), which Franco turned against the Prime Minister with the comment: 'I already know what it will say: No. And the urgency is such that both consultations and delays are out of place.'

Portela could only repeat: 'Let me think it over.'[14]

That evening, Generals Goded, Fanjul and Rodríguez Barrio called on Franco and proposed that if the government still refused to proclaim a state of war, a military coup should be attempted. Franco, still cautious, suggested that before going that far they should find out what the state of feeling was among the garrisons. (It turned out later, as he must have guessed, that it was negative.)

The sight of Goded and the others calling on Franco, was however, enough to feed the wildest rumours. On the morning of 19 February *El Socialista* screamed the news that Franco and Goded were about to launch a coup.

At midday, Portela went to the Ministry of the Interior and, from there, sent for Franco. He had been suffering from insomnia and was in a highly agitated state.

As soon as Franco stepped into the office he was using, he said: 'I am no longer the head of government. I have just resigned.'

Taken aback, Franco exclaimed with considerable energy: 'You have deceived us, Mr Prime Minister! Yesterday you were taking quite a different line.'

'I can swear to you,' replied Portela, 'that I have not deceived you. I am a Republican but I am not a Communist, and I have loyally served the institutions in governments in which I took part or over which I presided. I am not a traitor. I proposed the solution to the President of the Republic: it was Alcalá Zamora himself who was opposed to a declaration of a state of war.'

Franco made a supreme attempt: 'And yet, despite everything and as it is your duty not to allow anarchy and communism to take over in the country, there is still time, and you have the means to do what you ought. While you occupy this table and have these telephones at arm's reach . . .'

Portela interrupted him to say: 'Behind this table, there is nothing.'

'There are the *Guardia Civil*, the Assault forces . . .'

'There is nothing,' repeated Portela. 'Last night Martínez Barrio was here. During our interview, Generals Pozas and Núñez del Prado came in to tell me that you and Goded were preparing a military insurrection. I answered that I had better reasons than anybody to know that this was not true. Martínez Barrio asked me to stay put . . . If there was any repression of disorders to be done, he wanted me to do it. He also told me that Pozas, the Inspector-General [*sic*] of the *Guardia Civil*, and the chief of the Assault Forces had offered themselves to the government of the Popular Front that is being formed.'

And he added bitterly: 'You see now that behind this table there is nothing.'[15]

Franco's Nationalist biographers have made much of the meeting between Portela and Martínez Barrio, both of whom were Freemasons, but the point seems to me excessively laboured. There is no need to seek to explain Portela's negative behaviour by some plot of international Freemasonry. The verdict of the polls was that the Popular Front had won; and the President of the Republic opposed a resort to martial law. It would have taken a stronger and bolder man than Portela to hand the country over to the generals at this juncture. Whether this would have averted civil war is an unanswerable hypothetical question.

That night at 10 o'clock, Manuel Azaña presented his ministerial list to the President of the Republic: the Popular Front was in power, although the Socialists – for reasons which we shall examine later – did not take part in the government.

On 21 February, Azaña decided to put Franco and Goded out of harm's way. He announced Franco's transfer to the Canary Islands and Goded's to the Balearics, each as Military Commander. Later, Azaña got into the habit of saying that he had delivered the two generals from temptation.

Before leaving Madrid, Franco called on President Alcalá Zamora and Azaña, in that order. His interview with the President was long and discursive; with the Prime Minister, brief and bitter.

The general told Alcalá that great dangers surrounded Spain and that he feared the country lacked people who could stand up to the triumphant revolution.

The President smiled tolerantly: 'We defeated the revolution in Asturias,' he remarked.

'Remember what it cost to contain it in Asturias,' Franco retorted. 'If the assault is repeated in the whole country, it will be pretty difficult to snuff it out. Because the Army is now short of the right people and because already generals who don't want the revolution to be defeated are back in their old jobs.* Gold braid is nothing when the man wearing it lacks the authority, the prestige and the competence, that are indispensable if one is to be obeyed.'

It was clear that the General and the President were on different wavelengths. Franco rose, and Alcalá Zamora said to him in farewell 'Don't worry, General, don't worry. There will be no communism in Spain.'

'Of that I am certain,' retorted Franco. 'And I can answer that whatever contingencies may arise here, wherever I am there shall be no communism.'

Azaña, in his turn, heard Franco's speech of impending doom, and smiled sardonically.

'You are wrong to send me away,' said Franco, 'for here in Madrid I could be more useful to the Army and the tranquillity of Spain.'

Azaña answered: 'We don't fear uprisings. I knew about Sanjurjo's and I could have avoided it, but I preferred to see it fail.'

This was not, of course, the kind of uprising Franco had in mind. Foreboding weighed heavily on him as he left for the Canaries.

Let us waste no time speculating whether Azaña could have done anything to avert the explosion that was now only five months away. That he himself was not a man of violence, nor one to offend against 'legality' is not in question. The important point is that events were entirely out of his control. Spain had already ceased to be a

* A reference to the appointment of the Republican Generals Masquelet as War Minister and Miaja to the Madrid command.

governable entity, and the February elections merely confirmed the obvious.

Let us rather record, as briefly as is compatible with sense, the main events of the spring and summer of 1936.

The Socialists had stayed out of Azaña's government, thus getting the benefit of his popularity without incurring any of the odium that looked like being his as he tried to rule this unruly country. The split between Prieto and Largo Caballero grew wider and more bitter, with the rival papers of the two Socialist factions hurling insults at each other's leaders, and rival followers clashing in the streets, sometimes with fists, too often with guns. Prieto, a moderate at heart, wanted a planned, constitutional advance towards socialism. Caballero preached violent revolution in terms that terrified the middle class which heard itself almost daily threatened with extinction. During his months in gaol, aged sixty-seven, he had read Marx and Lenin for the first time, and he gloried in the flattering picture of him, sedulously cultivated by the Communists, as the 'Lenin of Spain'. He was not really a Communist, but saw himself as the man who would beat the Communists to the post with revolution.

The Communists themselves were playing a strange double or treble game. Ostensibly, they were applying the Popular Front policy, implying support for the non-Marxist Republican, Azaña, and for Prieto, who believed in the Popular Front. But covertly they worked through Álvarez del Vayo, the crypto-communist in the Caballero faction of the Socialists, who was emerging, with Luis Araquistáin, as the theoretician of the 'new Left'. Through him, the Communists were spreading the notion that Azaña was the Kerensky of the Spanish revolution, to be swamped and pushed aside by the revolution when the time was ripe. When that had happened, of course the 'Lenin of Spain' could take over, and do the Communists' work for them.

If the Left was split, so too was the Right. Despite the large number of voters he had attracted, Gil Robles's stock was falling. Many felt his constitutional approach was demonstrably ineffective, leaving violence as the only way to restore order – that is, smash the revolution. The trend towards violence was fed on the Right by the powerful and eloquent voice of Gil Robles's monarchist rival, Calvo Sotelo, Primo de Rivera's former Finance Minister, whose speeches, though effective, were provocative to the point of foolhardiness. On the extreme Right (if that is an appropriate label for a party that wanted to give power to the workers), José Antonio had lost all ability to steer his followers away from the path of violence. In the climate of extremism that had developed, the Falange was growing fast. Though it was not the Falangists who had started the firing, they continued it with a vengeance. On 14 March, the Falange was, however, outlawed and José Antonio gaoled.

Azaña, in the Centre, was bent only on resuming his interrupted Jacobin revolution. With a complacency almost unbelievable in the orgy of rioting, strikes, murder and arson that was devouring Spain, he resettled tens of thousands of peasants in Extremadura – an admirable piece of legislation but romantic in the total absence of public order. On 10 May, he had replaced Alcalá Zamora as President of the Republic, as a result of a free vote in which all parties joined to depose the man whose handling of presidential powers had irritated them without exception. He himself was succeeded as Prime Minister by Casares Quiroga, a sick man.

Against this background of anarchy and ineptitude, the Army was conspiring and organizing in the shadows. We shall take a closer look at what it was doing in the next chapter.

The climax came in a short series of dramatic happenings in which the following dates stand out:

13 APRIL. A judge was shot dead in the streets of Madrid. He had imposed a sentence of thirty years on a Falangist for the murder of a Socialist newspaper boy.

14 APRIL. A lieutenant of the Civil Guard was shot dead by Socialists during a Republic Day parade. The Falangists started firing on the Socialists and a street battle developed during which a Left-wing lieutenant of the Assault Guards named Castillo greatly distinguished himself.

16 JUNE. In a powerful speech in the Cortes, much quoted since, Gil Robles denounced the government's complacency in the face of outrages that had taken place between 16 February and 15 June, and which he listed as: churches totally destroyed, 160; churches set on fire with intent to destroy them, 251; murders, 269; wounded, 1,287; attempted assault, 215 cases; serious assaults, 138; political and private quarters destroyed, 69; attempts to destroy similar premises, 312; general strikes, 113; partial strikes, 228; newspaper

offices sacked, 10. He was followed by Calvo Sotelo, who in a speech of notable vehemence, indicted the government for leading the country to anarchy and revolution. Uproar punctuated his speech, and as he sat down, *La Pasionaria*, now a deputy, rose – strikingly pale in her black robes – pointed a finger at him, and shouted: 'That is your last speech.' And so it turned out.

1 2 J U LY. Lieutenant Castillo of the Assault Guards was shot dead by three Falangists.

1 3 J U LY. In the small hours – for this was the night of Castillo's murder, Assault Guards in uniform seized Calvo Sotelo in his bedroom, murdered him in a police truck and dumped his body in the cemetery. (It is hard, perhaps, to convey the enormity of this deed, for it is almost impossible to transpose it to other countries and different circumstances. Sir Alec Douglas-Home kidnapped and murdered by Special Branch detectives? Senator Robert Kennedy kidnapped and murdered by the FBI? Unthinkable, one might say. And that is the point: in Spain, in the summer of 1936, the unthinkable had become normal.)

1 7 J U LY. The Nationalist uprising, known to the Republican side as the military rebellion, began.

PART IV

Civil War

❈

1 *The Conspirators*

Even after his farewell meetings with the President and the Prime Minister, and disappointing though they were, Franco had still not committed himself to the idea of a military uprising against the Republic. Until the end of June 1936, indeed, he clung to the hope that the Republic, faced with visibly worsening anarchy, would call in the Army to restore order.* Nevertheless, before leaving Madrid for his Canaries exile, he attended two meetings whose purpose was certainly conspiratorial. Too much should not be read into this fact. Franco was not conspiring early in March 1936. But others were, and hoped to draw him in. He, on his side, wanted to know what was going on, but declined to commit himself. He was well aware that his intervention could be decisive, for by now – with General Sanjurjo in exile – no other general could equal him in prestige. Just as in August 1932, at the Sanjurjo coup, Azaña had swung round in his chair to ask: 'Where's Franco?', so in March 1936, everybody was asking: 'Where does Franco stand?' But when Franco left for the Canaries on 9 March, nobody knew. Prudent to the end, he kept his own counsel.

The chronology of the short period between 21 February, when Franco's posting to the Canaries was announced, and 9 March, when he left Madrid, is confused. Participants in the conspiratorial events that took place at that time have left contradictory accounts, in which dates and lists of those present are at variance. What is

---

* Thomas, I think, goes too far when he writes (pp. 141–2) that at this stage, 'Franco seems to have almost finally committed himself to the idea of a military rising "to save Spain"'. Payne is nearer the mark with the view that 'the attitude of the very prudent and extremely influential General Franco remained in doubt until late in the day'. (p. 102).

certain is that early in March, Franco attended a meeting of conspiring generals and had a private talk with José Antonio Primo de Rivera, who was to be arrested a few days later.

The meeting of generals took place in the home of a money broker, José Delgado. The most important man there, in the context of the moment, was not Franco but Mola. By an unaccountable error of judgment on Manuel Azaña's part, this able, intelligent and highly literate general, Azaña's arch-enemy since the reforms of 1931, adept, moreover, in the techniques of conspiracy which he knew from the inside as Alfonso's last Director General of Security, had been brought back to the Spanish mainland under the same decision that sent Franco and Goded to distant places. As we have seen, General Mola had been appointed to the Moroccan Command when Gil Robles was Minister. Now Azaña had him brought back as Military Commander in Pamplona – a demotion, to be sure, but a crucial error, too. For in Pamplona, Mola was in the heart of the fiercely anti-Republican Carlist country, a natural centre for conspiracy.

Apart from Franco and Mola, the following generals were present at the meeting: Orgaz, Villegas, Fanjul, Rodríguez del Barrio, Ponte, Saliquet, García de la Herrán, Varela and González Carrasco.[1] So was Lieutenant-Colonel Valentín Galarza, the highly efficient leader of the officers' secret organization, the UME. General Goded was not there: he had apparently left for the Balearics just before the meeting took place. It is indeed difficult to reconstitute Goded's precise part in the conspiracy, for he disgraced himself in Nationalist eyes by surrendering to the Republicans in Barcelona during the first week of the uprising and has since been virtually an unperson in official histories and biographies. Goded's son Manuel, however, writing with an eye to restoring his father's reputation, claimed the General had attended a number of conspiratorial meetings while Gil Robles was still War Minister.[2] He even claimed that it was General Goded who persuaded José Antonio Primo de Rivera to bring the Falange into the conspiracy; though this is doubtful on the evidence, and Manuel Goded does not favour us with dates.

Whatever Goded's part, it is known that at the meeting of generals, Franco adopted an entirely non-committal attitude, while Mola emerged as the natural leader of the conspiracy, with Colonel Galarza as the '*técnico*', the man to make sure that everything would be all right 'on the night'. The hot-heads, especially Varela and Orgaz, favoured a sudden move that would take the Republican government by surprise. Mola, deeply conscious of the drawbacks of sudden moves made without adequate preparation – like Sanjurjo's – favoured minute planning, and action only after the garrisons had been won over, one by one, to the anti-Republican cause. He argued that if the Army had wanted to act swiftly, the only time to have done it was during the electoral campaign, when a provisional government was in power. Once the elections had taken place, the chance for quick action had been lost. His advice prevailed.

It was agreed, however, that precipitate action might, in fact, become inescapable, in the event of certain contingencies. One of Mola's followers, the Carlist Félix Maíz, summed up the decisions of the meeting, as follows:

> The drill unanimously agreed was to make sure the garrisons were ready as soon as possible. But in any case, it was necessary to rise with whatever was available if the government inopportunely decreed the dissolution of the *Guardia Civil*, the disbanding of the Army, the dissolution of the officers' corps, or even if the Communists rebelled against the public authorities and launched the projected revolution. Again, in the event that one of the garrisons should be obliged to rise, it would be necessary, in order not to leave it in the lurch, to force the pace of events.[3]

General Mola was entrusted with organizing the movement and ensuring that even the remotest provincial garrisons lined up behind it. Colonel Galarza now took on a job that might be described as Chief of Staff to Mola, who from that point on became known as 'the Director'.[4] As for Franco, it was simply agreed that he should be kept informed of developments.

On 8 March, almost immediately after the meeting of the generals, Franco met José Antonio at the house of the former's brother-in-law, Ramón Serrano Súñer.* The suggestion for a meeting had come from Serrano who, at about this time, began to collaborate with the

---

* Thomas says (p. 142) that this meeting took place on 13 March, but by that date, Franco was in Tenerife. See Serrano Súñer, *Entre Hendaya y Gibraltar*, p. 18.

Falange, bringing the green-shirted youths of the Catholic Youth Movement (JAP) with him.[5] Nothing of substance came of the meeting. José Antonio explained in some detail what resources the Falange had at its disposal, in Madrid and the provinces, for such time as they might be needed, making it plain that this was a hypothetical situation. Franco, on his side, invited José Antonio to keep in touch with him through Lieutenant-Colonel Yagüe – the successful counter-revolutionary of Asturias – whom Primo de Rivera knew and who was to become a leading Falangist general.[6] Franco, in fact, had decided to make Yagüe, who worshipped him, his man of confidence, to keep in touch with Mola, the Carlists, the Falange and the situation in general, and to keep him informed.

This was General Franco's last important meeting in Madrid. Next day, an impressive group of high officers of the Army and Navy gathered at Madrid's Mediodía station to bid him farewell. Among them were two of the major conspirators, Generals Fanjul and García de la Herrán.[7] Franco embraced them and other intimates, Spanish-style, then boarded his first-class carriage, en route for Cadiz. With him were his wife and daughter and his adjutant, Lieutenant-Colonel Franco Salgado, who thus found himself once again, as he had been during the Asturian crisis, uniquely placed to be Boswell to Franco's Johnson.*

When the train stopped at Seville, Franco learned of a series of grave disturbances that were in progress at his port of embarkation, Cadiz. Revolutionary mobs had set fire to at least seven churches or convents, stormed the German consulate and pulled down the Nazi flag. Franco heard the news with his usual impassivity, but was pensive during the last lap of the journey.

At Cadiz Station, an Army officer stepped forward to greet Franco and his entourage with a salute, introducing himself with these words: 'I am the Colonel and acting Military Governor of the city and I come to offer my services to Your Excellency should you need anything.'

His face expressionless, Franco said: 'I cannot offer you my hand because a colonel of the Spanish Army must not permit a church to be burned in the vicinity of the barracks, as happened yesterday. A

* The anecdotes that follow are in fact taken from the biography which Franco Salgado helped the journalist Luis de Galinsoga to write, *Centinela de Occidente* – minus the lyrical and adulatory tone of the original.

soldier of honour must not tolerate such things, and that is why I refuse to shake hands with you.'

'*Mi General*,' replied the colonel, greatly agitated, 'my superior officers have given me standing orders not to intervene in such incidents.'

Franco raised his voice. 'Those orders must not be obeyed,' he declared, 'because nobody may order a soldier to be indifferent when a crime is committed next to him, and moreover, when it is a sacrilege such as you tolerated by allowing the military guard of your regiment to remain passive and indifferent in the face of what happened before its eyes.'

In a cutting tone, he added: 'You may dismiss.'

At the docks, Franco and his group ran into a Popular Front demonstration, to the strains of the *Internationale*.

'What's happening?' asked Doña Carmen.

'Perhaps some prominent Republican is also on his way to the Canaries,' answered Franco.

His guess was right. In fact, the demonstrators were greeting the new Civil Governor of Las Palmas who, in common with the new Military Commander of the islands, was about to board the steamship *Domine*, of the Trasmediterranea Company.

The crossing was rough, and Franco was among the few passengers who turned up for dinner that evening. He spent the next two days in his state-room, reading or attending to his family. At La Luz, the Civil Governor took his leave of Franco ('like a subordinate', as Galinsoga and Franco Salgado put it) and Franco went ashore to take a look at the Canary Islands, which he had never before visited.

On 12 March, the *Domine* reached Tenerife. As Franco emerged on deck to walk down the gangway, he noticed a commotion on the quay. It was immediately plain that it was a hostile demonstration and that he was the object of it. The shouts that reached him and the fists raised in his direction left no possible doubt. The general, however, didn't hesitate for a moment, but walked down slowly and calmly, with a smile. Still smiling, he saluted as he reached the quay, then waved to the crowd, which had fallen silent as it watched him. Now, by one of those sudden changes of mood with which General de Gaulle, who has faced similar situations, is familiar, smiles and shouts of welcome took the place of clenched fists and screams of hatred. A minute earlier, he had been the 'fascist general' of Popular

Front propaganda – a label that has shown itself reluctant to die. Now he was accepted. This was authority.

Once in command, Franco resumed the routine he had adopted in a similar situation in the Balearics. That is, he made an intensive study of the military needs of the islands. He began by familiarizing himself with existing fortifications and the condition of the barracks, and followed this up by inspection of the garrisons of Tenerife and Grand Canary.

While Franco carried out these self-imposed duties with his usual meticulous professional competence, however, he was increasingly concerned with events on the Spanish mainland. Was he 'in' the conspiracy or not? Everybody wanted to know, but the answer remained in doubt. He was 'in', of course, in the sense that he was being kept informed of events and that nobody doubted that he would participate in an uprising when the time came. But he had neither claimed the leadership of the movement, nor spelt out in so many words what he was prepared to do.

In April, a group of right-wing politicians invited him to present himself as a candidate for a by-election at Cuenca, where the general election voting had been declared void because of disturbances. Also on the right-wing list was José Antonio Primo de Rivera. There are conflicting versions of this incident. The Nationalists say that he hesitated, not because he fancied entering politics but because he was sensitive to the argument that if elected, he would be in Madrid, in touch with events and – as a deputy – enjoying immunity from arrest; but in the end he decided that he would be more useful in a crisis as a soldier than as a deputy. Arrarás, reporting the decision, goes on to attribute to him a remark that is no doubt authentic and provides an interesting insight into his attitude towards the political process, as it then was: 'When the funds of the workers' organizations are allocated to political subversion, to the purchase of arms and munitions and the hiring of gunmen and murderers, democracy, as represented by universal suffrage, has ceased to exist.'[8]

That Franco did refuse to stand for election at Cuenca is not in dispute. But the version of the facts that is current among the right-wing politicians of that period throws a different light on Franco's motivation. As this version has it, José Antonio, who was, of course, in gaol, was furious when he heard about the Cuenca plan, and let it be known that he would withdraw his name from the list if it also included Franco's, on the ground that he refused to be associated with the military clique.[9]

There are strong reasons for supposing that this unofficial version of the facts is the correct one. For one thing, Franco had twice disappointed José Antonio, first when the latter had appealed to him to save Spain in October 1934, and secondly when he had met José Antonio at Serrano Súñer's flat just before leaving for the Canaries. But there is more to it than this. On 21 February, in a circular to Falange leaders throughout Spain, José Antonio had given warning against 'all blandishments for taking part in conspiracies, projects of *coup d'état*, alliances with forces of "order" and other things of a similar nature.'[10]

Indeed, he had gone further still – as far as to say that one could not rely on serving soldiers, who were chicken-hearted, with Franco the most chicken-hearted of all.[11] Then there is the evidence of the Carlist conspirator Maíz, who records that Serrano Súñer himself flew to Tenerife to persuade Franco to withdraw his candidacy.[12] The curious fact for leftists to face is that Franco, the 'fascist general', was hardly *persona grata* to José Antonio, the leader of Spanish fascism.

The Cuenca affair seems to have disappointed some of Franco's followers. Conversely, it relieved the Left. On May Day, Indalecio Prieto expressed this relief in the course of an important speech, and went on with a tribute to Franco in which could be detected more than a tinge of apprehension:

> I haven't even half a word to say in depreciation of this military chief. I have seen him fighting in Africa, and for me General Franco reaches the supreme definition of valour: the man who is serene in the midst of the struggle. I must pay this homage to truth. [Prieto went on to speak of military centres of subversion against the Republic.] General Franco, by his youth, by his gifts, by his network of friends in the Army, is a man who, at a given moment, could lead with the maximum of chances of success . . . a movement of this kind. I do not venture to attribute to General Franco proposals of this nature. I accept as it stands his declaration that he will keep out of politics. Ah! But what cannot be denied is that those elements who, with or without his authority, wished to include him among the candidates in Cuenca were hoping for his public exaltation, so that, once invested with parliamentary

immunity, he might . . . become the leader of a military subversion.[13]

Many of the military plotters, who shared Prieto's admiration for
Franco, though for quite different reasons, were increasingly puzzled
at his apparent lack of optimism regarding the outcome of the projected uprising, for which they foresaw rapid success. The difference
between them and Franco amounted to this. They were so certain
that the Republic would crumble within days that they wanted to
move as soon as possible; whereas he would have preferred not to
move at all than move prematurely and court disaster. Except that
Mola had committed himself, and was now beyond the point of no
return, whereas Franco retained the chance of opting out, Franco's
views on the need for long and careful preparation coincided with
Mola's.

About this time, General Franco used to say to his intimate circle
in Tenerife, including his cousin Franco Salgado: 'How wrong
people are who think that the military uprising is going to be brief!
On the contrary, it is going to be very difficult and very bloody and
will last quite a time.'[14] By now, Franco, in common with a number
of Nationalist leaders, was convinced that the Soviet Union had
prepared precise plans for a communist uprising, and Franco Salgado
quotes him as saying that despite all the difficulties that lay ahead, a
military uprising was the only way left to forestall a communist
take-over.

It is hard to say, in the late 1960s, to what extent the 'communist
plot' accusations were genuinely accepted among the conspirators,
and how far they may have been a *post facto* justification of the
Nationalist case. Let us, however, be quite clear what we are talking
about. In a general sense, there *was* an international communist
policy for Spain. Its main lines were laid down in Moscow and its
details overseen in Spain by Comintern agents. This much is beyond
dispute.

Beyond this, however, some Spanish Nationalists, and some of
their foreign supporters, have alleged that there was a precise plot
by the Spanish Communist Party to overthrow the 'bourgeois'
Republic and replace it by a 'Soviet' under the Presidency of Largo
Caballero. It is claimed that the communist coup was to have taken
place between 11 May and 29 June, but was postponed until

1 August, and that the Nationalists struck in order to forestall the Communists. Documents purporting to prove these allegations were said to have been discovered. Copies were published by Sir Arthur Loveday, former head of the British Chamber of Commerce in Spain, in his books *World War in Spain* (1939) and *Spain 1923–1948* (1949), and have since been reproduced in the press and in other books.

A fierce controversy has raged over the authenticity of these documents.* I do not propose to enter into it, because I consider the documents unimportant, even if genuine, and in any case of little relevance to what happened in Spain in July 1936. The Nationalists began conspiring at the beginning of March, long before the existence of a precise communist plot was suspected. In a more general sense, of course, they did fear a communist revolution, or at any rate revolutionary anarchy, and that fear was one of their reasons for conspiring. The rapid deterioration of law and order after the advent of the Popular Front strengthened their view that military action had to be taken.

All this would have happened even if no documents had been discovered. But in any case, the accepted Nationalist version of the facts is now that the documents were found by Nationalist forces in various places *after the July uprising had started*.[15] It is therefore no longer argued that the uprising was timed to forestall a communist coup (foreign supporters of the Nationalist were, in any case, freer with this argument than the Nationalists themselves). As Joaquín Arrarás comments: 'The documents, apocryphal or authentic, were always insignificant.'[16]

The point that interests us here is that Franco himself was among the leading figures on the Nationalist side who believed that precise communist plans existed for the liquidation of all Army officers and men, of whatever rank, known to be anti-communist, in the event of a 'conflagration'. A copy of communist orders to this effect, dated 6 June, is said to have fallen into the hands of the Army's intelligence service and to have reached Franco in the Canaries. He took them seriously enough to double the guard at his headquarters and order additional security measures.[17]

* For ingenious and weighty refutations of their authenticity, see K. W. Watkins, *Britain Divided*, pp. 32–45, and Jackson, pp. 514–17. Hugh Thomas originally accepted the documents as genuine but changed his mind (*The Spanish Civil War*, Penguin Edition, 1965, p. 150, n.).

An inner gate led to twin steps linking Franco's sleeping quarters to the garden. On this gate, Franco posted four men under an NCO. One night their fire dispersed three prowlers who had entered the garden. Within a few minutes, the Civil Governor, the Mayor and various officials were on the spot, a fact which Franco Salgado evidently found sinister. They were refused entry. As for Franco, awakened by the shots, he inquired what was happening, was told, and went back to sleep.

In his assessment of the chances for a successful military rebellion, the state of mind of the Navy was a key factor, if only because, in the absence of a co-operative Navy, Franco's own return to the mainland at the head of the Africa forces would be problematical. He knew that most of the Naval officers were anti-Republican, but he wanted precise discussions and assurances before committing himself. A chance to obtain these came on 11 May, when a naval squadron on exercises tied up at Santa Cruz de Tenerife, under the command of Admiral Javier de Salas. In a private talk with the Admiral, Franco obtained from him a personal assurance that, should this be needed, the Navy would transport the Army of Africa to the Spanish mainland.[18]

That evening, Franco was able to test the feelings of Naval officers at a 'wine of honour' which he offered them at his headquarters. The ceremony ended with a patriotic harangue from Franco himself, who concluded with cries '*Viva España!*' The Civil Governor, who was present, tried a timid '*Viva la República!*' According to one account, Franco hissed: 'Quiet, whippersnapper!'[19] The atmosphere, which had chilled palpably, broke into sudden animation when young officers rushed forward and tried to hoist Franco shoulder-high, shouting: 'Embark on the squadron, now!' Cautious as ever, Franco 'resisted arrest'.

Two months later, most of the officers present at the Tenerife ceremony had been murdered by their crews.

Another who was to be murdered was Franco's cousin, Captain Hermenegildo Franco Salgado, of the cruiser *Libertad*. Franco had been hoping to see him in Tenerife in a second squadron that was supposed to call there after the departure of the first. However, the naval exercises were abruptly called off by the Republican authorities when news of the 'wine of honour' incident reached them; so that the meeting with Franco's cousin never took place.[20]

Locally, the incident caused some commotion. Government officials signed a petition to Madrid calling for the removal of Franco, 'the fascist general', from the command of the islands. 'Franco Out!' slogans were painted on local walls. On the other hand, many written pledges of support reached the general. In the Canaries, too, the pre-civil war was on.

The officers of the garrison chose this moment to demonstrate their solidarity with their commanding general, and invited him to a lunch on Mount Esperanza, a pine-covered beauty spot with a panoramic view of Tenerife. Franco accepted, on condition that all should attend – NCOs and privates as well as officers – and that all should eat the same menu, to consist of a *paella* and one other dish. A picture of the occasion shows a smiling Franco seated at a table at the cigar end of the meal, flanked by colleagues reflecting festive enjoyment. For this was not a conspiratorial occasion.

The conspiracy, however, went on, Franco's part in it still being consultative, not executive. Messages from the mainland reached him, brought sometimes by his brother-in-law, Serrano Súñer, sometimes by Colonel Valentín Galarza, but most frequently by Captain Bartolomé Barba Hernández, an energetic young officer who was one of the founders of the UME. From these men Franco learned of Mola's difficulties and successes. One major success was the decision of General Queipo de Llano, the swashbuckling hero of a pro-Republican plot in the decaying phase of the monarchy,* to join the conspiracy. (In this, he was helped by Queipo's indignation at the ousting of President Alcalá Zamora, a relative by marriage.) The difficulties arose out of the suspicions of the government, by now thoroughly aroused, and of the endless haggling that was going on to form a united movement with the Falangists and the Carlists. On 3 June, the Director-General of Security, Alonso Mallol, had turned up in Pamplona, summoned Mola to the town hall and accused him of plotting against the Republic. But it was not for nothing that Mola had held the same job as the man who now accused him. With skilfully simulated indignation, he diverted the charge: the only threat to the security of the State, he argued, came from the government's failure to maintain order.[21]

On one of his visits to Tenerife, Captain Barba brought a message

* The *Cuatro Vientos* affair: see Part III, Chapter 1.

from some of the conspiring generals, proposing that Franco should put himself at the head of the movement. Goded, in particular, said Barba, had remarked that Franco alone would be equal to 'half a cavalry corps in the rearguard'.[22] Still cautious, Franco neither accepted nor refused. Instead, he entrusted Barba with a number of letters to various friends, in which he outlined measures he had taken and others he proposed to take. Despite this non-committal approach, Barba seems to have returned to Spain under the impression that everything was all right, since 'the affair was now in the hands of Franquito' – a phrase popularized years before by Millán Astray during the Moroccan war.

Even at this late hour, however, Franco had not quite given up the idea that the government might yet come to its senses and call on the Army to restore order, thus obviating any need for an uprising and the long, hazardous and bloody sequel he sombrely envisaged. This is the real sense of a long letter General Franco sent on 23 June 1936, to the Prime Minister, Casares Quiroga.* In it, Franco analysed the discontent within the Army, attributing it to acts encouraging indiscipline, such as the reinstatement of officers previously sentenced for their part in the 1934 rebellion in Catalonia; and to the removal of meritorious officers and their replacement by mediocrities. Recalling the injustices of 1917, which had led to the creation of the *Juntas de Defensa*, he pointed to such symptoms of the Army's disquiet as the existence of two clandestine organizations – the UME and the UMR or *Unión Militar Republicana*, which had sprung up among Republican Army and Assault Guards officers in response to the UME's challenge. There followed a solemn warning:

> I do not hide from you the danger inherent in this collective state of mind at the present moment, in which professional anxieties rejoin those of all good Spaniards, before the grave dangers of the mother country.

This was plain enough. Franco would not have been Franco, however, if this important letter had not also contained a cryptic passage, the purport of which – in the light of the information that was certainly reaching him at the time – can only have been to deceive:

* For full text, see Appendix 2.

Those who represent the Army as disaffected from the Republic are being untruthful. Those who imagine plots in accordance with their passions are lying. Those who adulterate or impugn the dignity and patriotism of the officers' corps, attributing to it symptoms of conspiracy and disaffection, are doing a poor service to the mother country.

Deception or not, however, the letter was a last appeal to the Republic to call in the Army while there was still time. After recalling his own dedication to discipline, Franco signed himself 'Your most affectionate subordinate: Francisco Franco'.

The warning fell on the deaf ears of a sick and distraught man, for Casares Quiroga, ravaged by consumption and faced by problems well beyond his capacity to solve them, did not wish to believe that the Republic was in danger. His main worry was not the security of the State but the paralysing effects of the general strike of building workers then in progress in Madrid. When Prieto warned him of the dangers of a military coup, he quipped that these were just 'fantasies of the male menopause'. Indeed, he went further and publicly proclaimed his confidence in General Mola.[23]

General Mola, however, was still attracting attention. On 5 July, General Batet, Mola's hierarchical superior, arrived in Pamplona. The two men had several talks, in one of which Batet requested Mola's word of honour that he would not take part in an uprising. Mola gave it, calming his conscience with the thought that the interests and indeed the life of Spain were more important than his pledge.[24]

Now events were moving faster. On 6 July, General Fanjul who had been looking after the Madrid end of the conspiracy, visited Mola in Pamplona, and was given a full list of job allocations: Queipo de Llano in Andalusia; Franco, Africa; Mola, Navarre and Burgos; Villegas, Madrid; González Carrasco, Catalonia; and Goded, Valencia. On 11 July, Mola conferred with the Air Force General Kindelán and handed him messages which were later transmitted to Fanjul, Galarza and Álvarez Rementería in Madrid; and to Franco and Yagüe in the Canaries and Morocco, respectively.[25]

For by this time, Franco's prolonged season of doubt had ended, Casares Quiroga's failure to respond to his appeal of 23 June having finally convinced him that the Army would have to act against the

Republic since the Republic would not call in the Army of its own accord.

But if Franco was now in, the Carlists were still giving trouble. Indeed the Falangists, too, and even the UME, had stubbornly held views of their own. Now that action was impending, each group in the conspiracy wanted a major say in determining the kind of State that was to replace the Republic. Sanjurjo's political ideas, as they had filtered through from his Lisbon exile, were primitive: all he could envisage was a 'straight' military dictatorship. Mola wanted to set up a military directory, leading to a State not far different from Primo de Rivera's. These plans were good enough for the UME, but Mola had some trouble talking them out of prior guarantees that all Republican politicians would be shot for treason.

The Falangists, however, wanted a corporative and syndicalist State. Eventually, José Antonio agreed to bring his *milicias* in without firm political guarantees, but he maintained massive reservations. From a maximum security gaol in Alicante, to which he had been transferred on 5 June, the leader of the Falange twice circularized his movement's provincial chiefs – on 24 June and 29 June – warning them against making arrangements with the military without his express permission, and ordering them, whatever happened, to maintain the identity of Falange units, down to their distinctive shirts, emblems and flags.[26]

The Carlists – or *Comunión Tradicionalista* – on their side wanted absolute guarantees that the new State would be anti-democratic, and so exasperated Mola with their haggling that he wrote: 'The traditionalist movement is ruining Spain by its intransigence as surely as is the Popular Front.'[27] Sanjurjo, who was Carlist in sympathy, tried to mediate between Mola and the Traditionalists, at first without success. And as late as 12 July the Secretary of the *Comunión*, Manuel Fal Conde, ordered his followers 'not to second a movement that is not exclusively our own'.[28] Mola, who had planned to launch the uprising on 14 July, was obliged to postpone it, and it was not until 15 July that the Carlists finally accepted the Mola-Sanjurjo programme, in a letter signed by Fal Conde and the Carlist Pretender, Javier de Borbón Parma.[29]

Apart from José Antonio, the only civilian politician of any consequence who had joined the conspiracy was Calvo Sotelo, who had agreed at the end of June that he would invite Gil Robles to lunch at the last moment – on 14 July – to try and win over the CEDA leader. On 12 July, however, Calvo Sotelo was murdered, as we have seen, so the lunch never took place.

The postponement of the uprising at least served the important purpose of allowing time to complete arrangements to convey Franco from the Canaries to Morocco, where he was to take command of the insurgent forces in Africa. The fact that these arrangements had been left until so late in the day reflects the protracted time it took the general to make up his mind to commit himself to the uprising. As Jackson says,[30] the conspirators had decided to go ahead without him. However, now that Franco had made up his mind, it was necessary to find a way to enable him physically to play his full part in the uprising. This was when the fantastic story of the *Dragon Rapide* began.* It was an Hispano-British operation, though strictly a private enterprise one. On the Spanish side, those involved were two leading Monarchists – de la Cierva – son of the statesman and inventor of the autogyro – and the Marquess Luca de Tena, proprietor of the newspaper *ABC*; and Luis Bolín, who at that time was the *ABC*'s London correspondent. On the British side, Douglas Jerrold, the publisher and historian; Major Hugh Pollard, an expert on firearms with varied experience of revolutions; Captain C. W. H. Bebb, of Olley Airways at Croydon; and two English girls, who have been described as 'beautiful blondes'. One was Pollard's daughter Diana; the other, his daughter's friend, Dorothy Watson.

Luca de Tena instructed Luis Bolín to charter a British plane to convey Franco to Morocco. Over lunch at Simpson's in the Strand, Bolín enlisted Jerrold's help. Jerrold, in turn, enlisted Pollard's, and Pollard found the plane – a twin-engined *Dragon Rapide* biplane – and the pilot, Captain Bebb. Pollard knew only that there was some political purpose in the journey, but the young ladies didn't even know this, the idea being that the three of them must appear to be British tourists in search of African sunshine. Bebb knew the trip was important but not why.

The *Dragon Rapide* took off with Bolín, Pollard, his daughter and her friend on 11 July – the day when Mola and Kindelán were meeting in Navarre. After stops in France, Portugal, Casablanca –

* The story has been told by a number of writers, but all accounts are superseded by that of Señor Luis Bolín, who made the arrangements, in *Spain: the Vital Years* (1967), Chapters 1 to 5.

where Bolín stayed on alone – and Tangier, Captain Bebb landed safely at Gando, on Grand Canary, on 15 July – the day the Carlists accepted Mola's terms. Captain Bebb and his passengers were ferried to Tenerife, where Pollard presented himself at the surgery of Dr Gabarda, who had sometimes transmitted messages to Franco. Greeting the doctor, Pollard used the agreed password: 'Galicia salutes France.' To his dismay, Dr Gabarda, who had not been acquainted with this formula, sent him on his way.

Later, however, the doctor, on an afterthought, telephoned the local Army headquarters to say what had happened. The mix-up was sorted out and Pollard, comforted by apologies, went off on his well-deserved holiday, with daughter and friend. As for Bebb, he was instructed to wait at Las Palmas, to which he returned.

All arrangements for the uprising were now complete. The murder of Calvo Sotelo has sometimes been presented as the final cause or pretext for launching the insurrection a few days earlier than the final deadline of 20 July, and it may indeed have made Mola decide that there was no time left. But the most important factor in the timing was undoubtedly the agreement reached with the Carlists on 15 July. Carlist intransigence had been the last obstacle. Now it had been removed, action could follow. Accordingly, Mola now sent out directives to all other Generals in the conspiracy: 'The 17th at 17' – meaning that they were to rise on 17 July at 5 p.m.

Franco's problem was, first to get to Las Palmas without arousing Republican suspicions, and secondly to get to Morocco and to take command of the Africa troops. An accident played into his hands: the military commander of Las Palmas, General Amado Balmes, accidentally shot himself to death with a revolver while at target practice. Franco now telephoned the War Ministry in Madrid and obtained permission to go to Las Palmas to attend the funeral. That day – 16 July – the diplomat José Antonio de Sangróniz visited Franco at Santa Cruz de Tenerife to give him the latest details of the conspiracy, including Mola's order for zero hour. The two men agreed on a cryptic formula for communications, consisting of variations on the agricultural theme: 'The grape juice is maturing' (or not, as the case might be).[31] Sangróniz then gave Franco his diplomatic passport, into which the General stuck his own photograph.

Franco spent the next few hours, until dinner time, in his office, destroying compromising papers, and drafting orders to his Chief of Staff for the 'state of war' that was to be proclaimed in Tenerife and Grand Canary. At a quarter to midnight, Franco, accompanied by his wife and daughter, boarded the ferry. His adjutant, Franco Salgado, and eight or ten officers of his staff travelled with them. At the harbour of La Luz, he was greeted formally by the Republican authorities, and went to the Hotel Madrid, at Las Palmas, emerging for the funeral of General Balmes. In the afternoon, as though nothing were afoot, he and his party strolled through the town like any group of tourists. This left Franco time in the evening to do some more drafting of proclamations and planning of conspiratorial details. The Francos and his adjutant went to bed immediately after a typically late Spanish dinner.

At three on the morning of 18 July, Franco Salgado knocked on Franco's door, and handed him a telegram he had just received from Tenerife, where the radio station had picked it up. It said:

MELILLA. – GENERAL SOLANS TO GENERAL FRANCO: THIS ARMY RISEN IN ARMS AGAINST THE GOVERNMENT HAVING SEIZED ALL INSTRUMENTS OF COMMAND. VIVA ESPANA!

Franco immediately dressed himself, in civilian clothes, and walked to military headquarters. During two hours of decisive activity, he issued orders to all command posts in the Canaries to rise against the civil authorities and telegraphed all divisional generals, in Melilla and throughout Spain, calling on them to rally to the movement. These messages all ended with the phrase *Fe ciega en el triunfo* ('Blind faith in victory') that was to become the rallying cry of the Nationalist cause during the next three years. During those two hours Franco also had all vital centres on the islands occupied – including communications and radio stations, power houses and reservoirs – and requisitioned cars and lorries. He asked for, and obtained, the co-operation of the warships at that time in La Luz harbour, the gunboats *Canalejas* and *Guad Acila*. He asked for, but was refused, the co-operation of the chiefs of the *Guardia Civil* and *Guardias de Asalto*.

At 5 a.m., a company of the Infantry Regiment of Las Palmas proclaimed a state of war, and a few minutes later the local office of the Socialist labour unions – the UGT – announced a general strike. At 5.15 a.m., Radio Tenerife broadcast an important text, which had been drafted by General Franco before his departure from Santa Cruz, and in which he outlined the reasons for the uprising and promised justice and equality before the law, 'liberty and fraternity without libertinage and tyranny; work for all; social justice, accomplished without rancour or violence, and an equitable and progressive distribution of wealth without destroying or jeopardizing the Spanish economy'. More ominously, the proclamation added that before all this could happen there would be 'war without quarter on the exploiters of politics, on the deceivers of the honest worker, on the foreigners and foreign-orientated people who openly or deceitfully endeavour to destroy Spain'.* The text ended with the slogan of the French Revolution, rearranged: 'FRATERNITY, LIBERTY and EQUALITY'.

This extraordinary document – now known as the 'Manifesto of Las Palmas' because Franco was there when it was issued, although it was broadcast from Tenerife – calls for some comments, even at the risk of interrupting this narrative.

For one thing, it was the nearest thing to a *pronunciamiento* yielded by the first phase of the Civil War. In retrospect, it reads like a proclamation by the leader, not merely of an army, but of a whole nation, as though Franco, even in the first hours of the uprising felt confident that he would lead the Army to victory and bring a new order to the Spanish people. Indeed it is addressed simply to 'Spaniards!' And yet, in contrast to previous *pronunciamientos* in Spanish history, it does not bear Franco's name, being signed merely '*Comandante General de Canarias*'. Bear in mind, too, that when Franco drafted his 'Manifesto', Sanjurjo was still supposed to be the Commander-in-Chief of the uprising, while Mola, who had done the organizing, was still known as 'the Director'. But on 20 July – only two days after the 'Manifesto' was broadcast, Sanjurjo crashed to his death; and less than a year later Mola also died in a plane crash, leaving Franco the undisputed master of the Nationalists. Franco's failure to sign his 'Manifesto' or to use the first person singular at any point must be attributed to his deference to those who had committed themselves from the first, and to his awareness that he himself had taken his time to think out the implications of possible action. It was

* For full text, see Appendix 4. A photocopy of the Spanish original appears in *Crónica de la Guerra Española* (Buenos Aires, 1966), No. 7.

typical of his character, however, that protracted meditation was followed by urgent and decisive action; and of his self-confidence that he wrote, from the first, as the natural leader of the National Movement. One should add, incidentally, that there was nothing in the document to please the Falange, apart from the reference to 'social justice', and nothing at all for the Carlists. When the hour of victory came, neither group could point to the Manifesto and complain of broken promises. For of pledges to them, there were none.

That morning, a menacing crowd of Popular Front militants gathered before the Civil Governor's offices in the Calle Triana and started marching in the direction of the Military Governor's building, which Franco was occupying. Franco ordered his cousin to disperse the mob; which he did by firing in the air. Later the militants returned in strength and this time were stopped by live fire.

Franco decided to go to the airfield by sea and boarded a tugboat at 11 a.m. Before leaving he kissed his wife and daughter good-bye and handed them over to Lieutenant-Colonel Martínez de Fuset with instructions that they should proceed to France or Germany in the German steamer *Waldi*, which was leaving next day. Fuset, however, thought the General's family would be safer on board a war vessel and entrusted them to the officers of the coastal patrol boat *Arcila*, little knowing that most Naval crews were about to turn on their officers and murder them. Fortunately, however, the crew of the *Arcila* behaved themselves, and Franco's wife and daughter, whose identity was known only to the officers, came to no harm.

Franco reached the airfield at 2 p.m. and announced himself with outstretched hand to Captain Bebb as 'General Franco'. It was the first clue the pilot had had about the purpose of his mysterious assignment. For days he had stayed at a good hotel, receiving cryptic visits, orders and counter-orders. Now he met his passenger and was told to take him to Casablanca.

During the flight, Franco removed his uniform, changed into Arab dress, complete with turban, placed the uniform, together with various papers in a suitcase and threw it into the sea.

At Casablanca, they were met by Luis Bolín, who – with the advantage of a bilingual upbringing – had been passing himself off as an English tourist. Bolín took Franco, Bebb and the other passengers

– a captain, a telegraphist and the inevitable Franco Salgado – to an hotel for dinner and a short rest. They touched down at 9.30 p.m. and nobody seems to have asked for their documents. At 4 a.m. on the morning of 19 July they were back at Casablanca airport. This time, they *were* asked for their passports. Franco produced Sangróniz's diplomatic one and was waved through, the officials not appearing to notice that if the description given of the holder was correct he must have lost several inches in height on his journey. Franco Salgado, who had no passport, said Luis Bolín had it, and he too was waved through.

An hour after take-off, Franco changed into General's uniform. At dawn a city came into view, and Franco who had remained expressionless and silent throughout the trip, suddenly exclaimed: 'Tetuan!' on recognizing the familiar minarets of his youth.

As the *Dragon Rapide* lost height over the military airport, Franco scanned the expanding faces of the large group of officers waiting below. One of them was familiar: Colonel Sáenz de Buruaga. 'It's all right,' said Franco to Bebb, 'you may land.'

As Franco alighted, Sáenz greeted him with the words: 'Nothing new in Morocco, *mi General.*'

It was the agreed Nationalist password.

2 *Franco's 'Original Sin'*

General Franco arrived in Morocco to find the local situation well under control. But his problems were only beginning, and he was soon to discover that they were worse than his most pessimistic guess could have foreseen.

In Tetuan itself, as the welcoming presence of Colonel Sáenz de Buruaga told him, the Nationalists were in control. The previous evening, 18 July, a Republican Fokker plane had bombed the Arab quarters, killing fifteen and wounding forty, and the furious Moors, not knowing what was afoot, had rioted against the military. They were calmed by the Grand Vizir, Sidi Ahmed el Ganmia – to such effect that one of Franco's first actions on arriving was to confer on him the Cross of San Fernando with Laurels. A Moor was thus the

9a The turbulent Republic: Popular Front demonstration, Madrid 1936.

9b The turbulent Republic: Valencia strikers overturn a tram.

10a The wayward brother: Major Ramón Franco, hero and adventurer.

10b Impartial witness : Salvador de Madariaga.

10c The Radical leader and demagogue, Alejandro Lerroux.

10d Gil Robles, Christian Democrat leader, now in opposition.

first recipient during the Civil War of Spain's highest decoration, which, as we have seen, had eluded Franco himself during his years of fighting in Morocco.

Colonels Yagüe, Solans Lavedán and Bautista Sánchez had mastered situations of varying difficulty in Ceuta, Melilla and Villa Cisneros, respectively; and the Moroccan Major, Mohammed el Mizzian – son of Franco's former opponent of the Moroccan War – and his *Regulares* had taken part in the Nationalist march on Melilla. The Army of Africa was intact and at Franco's orders. At Tetuan itself, on his arrival, and at Ceuta and Dar Riffien, which he visited on the afternoon of 19 July, he was wildly acclaimed both by the troops and the local population. Indeed as soon as his Orders of the Day had been received in Morocco, on the evening of 17 July and during the night, they had been re-broadcast. His call for 'blind faith in victory' still echoed in the ears of the men who had heard it and now thought, on seeing him, that their faith would indeed work miracles.

From the Spanish mainland, however, the news was only inter-mittently good, from Franco's viewpoint. Nearly everywhere, the Army had risen in arms against the Republic on 17 or 18 July. Mola had an easy run in Navarre. Not only had the Carlist *Requetés* rallied to his call, but entire villages had enrolled, to fight, as they had a century earlier, 'for God, Fatherland and King'. In Seville, the ebul-lient Queipo de Llano had bluffed his way to an astonishing success. The ravages of Republican reform had left only 130 men under arms in that great southern city. Queipo, however, personally arrested Republican-minded officers, and struck terror into local breasts by sending his soldiers out on raids with their faces smeared in walnut juice to make it look as though the Moors had come – a fiction he strengthened by declaring on the radio. which he had seized, that indeed they *had* come. Impressed, the Civil Guard and even the Assault Guards allowed themselves to be disarmed, and Queipo carried on with what was to be a long and extraordinary series of broadcasts, for which his individual flavouring of venom, oaths, insults and mordant humour always guaranteed an audience. Against this, the workers mounted a general strike and burned down eleven churches. But Queipo was the victor.[1]

In Old Castile, as in traditional Navarre, the Nationalists tri-umphed. In Burgos, they arrested the Republican General Batet. In

H

Salamanca, Segovia, Avila and Zamora, they met little resistance. In Valladolid, too, the Movement was victorious, largely owing to the co-operation of Onésimo Redondo, founder of the Fascist JONS, and partner of José Antonio's in the enlarged Falange party.

In Aragon, the most striking news was that old General Miguel Cabanellas, though a Republican and a Freemason, rallied to the Movement in Saragossa and had the workers disarmed. His change of heart had, in fact, been one of Mola's diplomatic successes, but his past had made some of the anti-Republican conspirators doubt whether he would play the part expected of him when the hour struck. In Galicia, the Nationalists had to overcome Popular Front resistance in El Ferrol – Franco's birthplace – and Vigo, but captured Corunna without trouble. Alava, one of the most Catholic provinces of Spain, rallied to the Movement with the capture of Vitoria by Colonel Alonso Vega, one of the officers who had graduated with Franco from the Toledo Military Academy and later fought with him in Morocco.

This list just about completed the good news that awaited Franco in Tetuan on 19 July or reached him shortly afterwards. Against the successes were to be set uncertainties and crushing failures. Queipo de Llano's Sevillian success had been matched in Cadiz

Cordoba and Granada; but the countryside was in the hands of roaming Anarchist bands. Bilbao and San Sebastian had stayed loyal to the Republic. Oviedo, the Asturian capital, had been taken over by the Nationalists, but was besieged by the miners, who had not forgotten or forgiven the repression of 1934. In the south, Jaen and Malaga remained in Popular Front hands.

But the most shattering news of all came from Madrid and Barcelona. In the capital, General Fanjul soon found himself and his men outnumbered, and took refuge in the Montaña barracks. On the morning of 20 July, the Assault Guards, reinforced by artillery and the Air Force, stormed the barracks, shooting most of the defending officers in the courtyard. Fanjul himself was captured. In Barcelona, a similar fate had befallen General Goded. Though ranked with Franco as Spain's most brilliant General, Goded was less cautious than his Galician colleague. Originally picked to lead the insurgents in Valencia, he had opted for the more difficult assignment of Barcelona. His troops, however, were overwhelmed by loyal Civil and Assault Guards reinforced by numerous Anarchist workers who had been armed by the *Generalidad*. On 20 July, Goded himself was captured, and went before the microphone to appeal to his followers, including possible reinforcements from Mallorca, to desist. 'Destiny,' he said in a sad but dignified voice, 'has been adverse and I have fallen prisoner, for which reason I release from their obligations towards me all those who have followed me.'[2] These words did not save him, however, for soon afterwards both he and Fanjul were executed by their captors.

The 20 July also brought news nobody could have expected. On that day, General Sanjurjo, greatly to the alarm of the young monarchist pilot who was to take him to Spain from his Portuguese exile, boarded the aircraft with a huge and very heavy suitcase. When the pilot, Juan Antonio Ansaldo, discreetly remonstrated, the General explained that the suitcase contained his full dress uniforms, as he could hardly arrive in Burgos without anything to wear on the eve of his triumphant entry into Madrid. Still apprehensive, but not daring to question the authority of the presumptive Chief of State, Ansaldo accepted the baggage as well as the passenger. The Portuguese authorities, who wanted the take-off to be as unobtrusive as possible, had relegated the Spaniards to a small field fringed at one end with pine trees. Unfortunately, the prevailing wind forced

Ansaldo to take off facing the trees. He did clear them, though only just, but immediately afterwards, the propeller suddenly went dead. The light plane lost height rapidly but he was unable to make a crash-landing because of a low stone wall that lay ahead, and into which the plane crashed, bursting into flames. He himself got out, having tried in vain to release Sanjurjo from his safety belt. The impact, however, seems to have killed the general instantly. Ansaldo later told the story in a long, rambling, violently anti-Franco book.[3] He did not rule out sabotage by communist agents, but was inclined to think it was an accident. His book does, however, scotch – by implication – the inevitable later rumours that Franco had thought up this elaborate way of ridding himself of a potential rival.

Militarily, Sanjurjo's death was bad news for Franco, no provision having been made for a successor. Within three days of the *Alzamiento*, the insurgents were left without a head, so that Mola, Queipo de Llano and Franco himself were so many independent war-lords, acting singly where cohesion should have been essential. Politically, on the other hand, Sanjurjo's removal was an unexpected stroke of luck for the Movement as a whole, and Franco in particular, for whatever Sanjurjo might have had to offer in the sense of courage and tactical skill, his judgment was nil and his political ideas non-existent. There is no record of Franco's reaction to the death of Sanjurjo, and this fact alone may be significant. It is not improbable that he heaved an inner sigh of relief, only mildly moderated by apprehension for the immediate military prospect.

While these tragic or dramatic events were happening, the Prime Minister, Casares Quiroga, found himself under increasing pressure to distribute arms to the 'people'. Exhausted but strictly constitutional to the last, he resigned rather than comply. This was on 18 July. That evening, President Azaña called on the President of the Cortes – the moderate and conciliatory Martínez Barrio – to form a government. Martínez Barrio took on the job, and one of the first things he did was to get Mola on the telephone and offer him a portfolio in his government, some say the Ministry of War. But it was too late, and Mola turned the offer down.[4] Indeed, Martínez Barrio would have been quite incapable of staying in power in a government that included Mola. As it was, the trade unionists were demonstrating against him and he gave up his attempt to form a government before it had really begun. In the meantime, young officers had been distributing arms to the workers anyway, and Azaña now appointed José Giral as Prime Minister. In the prevailing circumstances, it must be admitted that Giral had many of the qualifications needed. In 1933, he had been one of the fiercest advocates of the death penalty for Sanjurjo and his fellow officers. In Casares Quiroga's cabinet, in which he had been Minister of the Navy, he had favoured arming the 'people'. Now as Prime Minister, he did the job thoroughly and officially. It was, in retrospect, a fateful decision. Until then, the Popular Front government had been an administration of more or less radical middle class men, quite incapable of controlling the turbulent masses in whose name they thought they spoke. Now the government was arming the revolution; and it will be seen that this is no mere figure of speech.

Giral, indeed, had yet another qualification in the eyes of the Popular Front's mass following. As Minister of the Navy, he had had his orders disobeyed by most of the principal warships on the outbreak of the *Alzamiento*. He had then officially dismissed them and transferred their authority to the chief machinists. As Hugh Thomas rightly says,[5] in so doing, he was 'merely following strict procedural etiquette in a situation without precedent'. The immediate result of his order, however, was that the junior officers and seamen turned on the admirals and captains, arresting the lucky ones and murdering the others. No fewer than seventy per cent of all Spanish naval officers lost their lives within the next few hours. Giral thus came to be known among the Nationalists as the butcher of the Navy. It is known, incidentally, that the naval crews included many Communists pardoned by the Republican authorities after being dismissed during the *Bienio Negro*, and that they had formed cells in the ships to which they had been posted. It is unlikely that Giral's orders alone would account for the simultaneous murder of officers in such large numbers, and it must be presumed that a prearranged communist plan existed to deal with just this situation.

This brings us to what was undoubtedly Franco's most worrying problem during the second half of July 1936: the almost total breakdown of the arrangements he had made with Admiral Salas for the Navy's co-operation in ferrying the Army of Africa across the Strait to the Spanish mainland. The murder of the officers by their crews left a yawning gap in his plans.

On or about 21 July, one of Franco's assistants asked him what he proposed to do, now that there was no fleet to transport the Army of Africa to Spain.

'Everything that might be feasible and necessary,' was Franco's reply. 'Everything, except surrender.'[6]

This was all very well, but for the time being, there was nothing promising on the horizon. Almost the only contribution the Navy had been able to make to the *Alzamiento* was on 19 July, when the destroyer *Churruca*, sent to Ceuta from Madrid to combat the insurrection, ignored orders, embarked a *Tabor* of *Regulares* and ferried them across to Cadiz, where they joined the Movement. Immediately afterwards, however, the *Churruca's* crew overpowered the Commander and other officers, locked them up in their cabins, and landed them at Malaga, where, shortly afterwards, they were shot.[7] Apart from this, the Nationalists disposed of the cruiser *Almirante Cervera*, the destroyer *Velasco*, both in El Ferrol at the time of the uprising; and sundry small ships in Moroccan or Canaries harbours. Against this, the Republicans could muster overwhelming naval strength, including the battleship *Jaime I*, the cruisers *Libertad, Miguel de Cervantes* and *Méndez Núñez*, no fewer than fourteen destroyers, together with three coastal patrol ships, six submarines and small craft.[8]

For some anxious days, most of the telegrams reaching Franco brought bad news, from the defection of the *Churruca* and the mass murder of naval officers to the surrenders of Fanjul and Goded. As each message reached the general, he read it with a smile on his lips, crumpled it up and put it in his trouser pocket. If anybody asked him what was happening, he would say, without emotion: 'I win or I die.'[9] Nobody could have guessed that, on paper, the chances of success now looked very slender.

True, the *Churruca's* initial success had been followed by the ferrying to Spain of more than 2,000 men, in the gunboat *Dato*, in fishing boats and in the handful of antiquated planes that had fallen into Nationalist hands. But Franco and the men under his command must have wondered what the future held when Indalecio Prieto went on the air after the naval officers had been overwhelmed, to say: 'I don't understand what the rebels are after. They are mad. Who do they think is going to save them? We have in our power the most important cities, politically speaking, the industrial centres, all the gold and silver of the Bank of Spain, inexhaustible reserves of men, the Fleet . . . Do you hear? We have the Fleet!'

As a matter of fact, the failure of the fleet to defect to the Movement was beginning to look like a positive menace instead of a negative disappointment. One by one, the ships of the Republican Navy, led by the battleship *Jaime I*, were steaming towards Tangier. Once anchored there, they might make it impossible for the Army of Africa to cross the Strait. Franco took the view that the presence of the Republican warships in Tangier harbour violated the International Zone's neutrality, as laid down in the Statute of 1923. Accordingly, on 21 July, Franco sent a letter to the International Control Committee, warning it that *force majeure* might make it necessary to take measures to prevent 'pirate ships' from using Tangier for belligerent purposes; in which case, he undertook to respect the lives and property of the inhabitants.

He followed this initial warning with a second one on 22 July, and further notes on 25 and 26 July, and 4 and 7 August. The last was an ultimatum, giving the Control Committee forty-eight hours to get rid of the Republican fleet or face the consequences.* The Committee, however, had already taken alarm and written to Madrid requesting the removal of the warships, the British member of the Control Committee siding with the Italian on this issue.

On 9 August, the last Republican warships steamed out of Tangier.

This was a relief, but it did nothing towards conveying troops across the water. Franco had already decided, however, that there was only one possible solution: an airlift with the assistance of the Axis Powers. His first impulse was to turn to Mussolini. There were good reasons for this. In 1934, the Carlists and Alfonsists had temporarily sunk their differences to send a joint mission to Italy, where Mussolini – mildly amused that the Monarchists couldn't even agree on the identity of the next king of Spain – had promised 20,000 rifles and 200 machine-guns in the event of an anti-Republican rising. Later, he had arranged to train young Carlists, who passed themselves off as 'Peruvian officers' for passport purposes.[10] General Sanjurjo, from his exile in Portugal, had approved of these developments, though he had never, for his part, seriously thought that large purchases of arms would be necessary, being convinced – in contrast

* For texts of the first, second and last of these Notes, see Appendices 6, 7 and 8.

to Franco and Mola – that the Republic would collapse in a few days.

From Franco's viewpoint, however, it seemed natural to continue what had been initiated. So as early as 19 July, the day of his arrival in Tetuan, he sent Luis Bolín – still on the *Dragon Rapide*, and still piloted by Captain Bebb – to Rome, to ask for twelve bombers and three fighters. Bolín's itinerary took him to Lisbon, where he obtained Sanjurjo's counter-signature to Franco's formal request to Mussolini.[11] This was Sanjurjo's last act of consequence before the plane crash that took his life the following day.

The *Dragon Rapide* then went to Biarritz, where Bolín met his Editor, Luca de Tena. Bebb then flew Bolín to Marseilles, where the two men parted, and Bolín completed his trip to Rome in another plane, arriving on 21 July.

A number of writers have conveyed the impression that Mussolini's help to Spain's rebel generals was freely and promptly given. This, however, is not true. Bolín found the Foreign Minister, Count Ciano, in a receptive mood; but Ciano's voice was not the decisive one, and his father-in-law, the Duce, was distinctly cool to the idea of an involvement in the Spanish troubles. Later, Ciano told Roberto Cantalupo, Fascist Italy's first Ambassador to Nationalist Spain, that on receiving an advance telegram from the Italian Consul in Tangier, transmitting Franco's request for twelve Italian aircraft, he had scribbled on it, in blue pencil: 'No.'[12]

On hearing of this unexpected setback, Mola dispatched Antonio Goicoechea to Rome to remind Mussolini that on the last day of March 1934, the Duce had promised arms and money to the Spanish Monarchists. It was Goicoechea who had led the joint Alfonsist–Carlist delegation to Mussolini two years earlier. Goicoechea now boarded the *Dragon Rapide* at Biarritz and flew to Rome on the afternoon of 24 July.* He saw Ciano next morning and cleared up what had been a confused picture in Mussolini's mind: if the Monarchists, the Falangists and Franco were all fighting together, with a corporative State in prospect, then indeed, he would do what was asked of him.[13] Nevertheless, although Mussolini had committed himself on 25 July, he continued to hesitate, probably waiting to see whether the Nazis would also help the military insurgents.[14] It was not until

---

* Also in Rome was the Mallorcan financier Juan March, once gaoled for fraud by the Republic, who helped finance the Nationalist cause.

30 July that twelve Italian three-engined Savoia-Marchetti 81s took off for Morocco. Not only was this first gesture slightly belated, it was also technically unimpressive, for one of the planes crashed into the sea, while two others made forced landings in French Morocco.

One is bound to wonder, writing thirty years after the event, whether it occurred to Franco, in those anxious days of July 1936, when the fate of the movement to which he had committed himself after his long hesitation was in the balance, that he was about to commit the 'original sin' that was to condemn Spain to isolation in a hostile world of parliamentary and communist victors after the Second World War? Quite certainly, the answer is that it did not. The thought that dominated Franco's actions in late July was how to get his army across the water to Spain. It was a technical problem of logistics which he, as the General Officer Commanding the Army of Africa, had to solve, or all was lost. It was out of the question to turn to the western democracies. In France, the Popular Front was in power – a less virulent Popular Front than the one that had completed Spain's descent into anarchy, but an alliance that was supported by the Communists. In fact, as Franco knew, the Giral government of Republican Spain had already asked the Blum government in France for aid. The appeal was made on the night of 19 July, as soon as he had become Prime Minister. Historically then, the Republic's appeal for foreign help was made two or three days before Franco appealed to Mussolini; but too much should not be made of this: in the situation in which either side found itself, appeals to foreign Powers were inevitable, and a day or two either way was neither here nor there.

If Franco could not appeal to France, nor could he, with any chance of success, turn to England. True, the Baldwin government, then in power, was broadly in sympathy with the desire of the Spanish generals to impose order on the unruly Spain of the Popular Front. But the deepest desire of the British Prime Minister, and of the great majority of the British people, was certainly to keep out of international trouble. In fact, though not yet in name, appeasement was in the air; but though appeasement came to mean making concessions to fascist dictators, it never meant actually helping a foreign military rebellion.

All this was plain enough to Franco. The only rulers likely to help him were the dynamic, adventurous and authoritarian dictators of

Italy and Germany. This was – one repeats – 1936. World war was not an immediate prospect. In any case, whether war came or not, the dominant Power in Europe seemed likely to be Germany, with Italy trailing behind as a junior partner. Moreover, both Mussolini and Hitler, whatever reservations Franco might have about their policies towards the Churches, had shown that they knew how to deal with their local Communist Parties. All these arguments must have flashed through Franco's mind on 22 July. But the only one that really counted was that he needed planes; and that, since even Mussolini seemed to be hesitating, Hitler was the only likely supplier. It is certain that Mola shared this view, and indeed probable that he was more enthusiastic about the German connection than Franco. It is sometimes overlooked that Mola, despite his reputation for relative liberalism, had gone as far as to praise Hitler's anti-Jewish policy.[15]

And so, Franco asked Hitler for aid. It was as fateful a decision, in its way, as the Republican decision to arm the masses. On one side, Azaña's bourgeois Republic slipped ever faster towards Communism; on the other, the diverse forces of authoritarian Spain acquired a tinge of fascism as persistent as the stain of blood on Lady Macbeth's hand.

Once the decision had been taken, Franco's problem was how to convey the message to Hitler. As with Mussolini, he tried several approaches. First, he turned to his friend of Moroccan war days, the gifted Arabist, Colonel Juan Beigbeder Atienza. Beigbeder had spent years in Berlin as Spanish Military Attaché, and had many Nazi acquaintances, although by inclination a liberal. On 17 July, he had gone to Melilla, where he had played an important part in the uprising. Now, five days later, Beigbeder, at Franco's behest, sent an urgent request to the German Military Attaché in Paris, General Kuhlenthal, for ten large transport aircraft, which were to be bought through German private firms and ferried to Spanish Morocco by German pilots.[16]

Simultaneously, Franco remembered that among the crowd that had gathered at Tetuan airfield to greet him on 19 July, was a local Nazi, Johannes Bernhardt, who had seemed singularly eager to help the Nationalists. Johannes Bernhardt was a businessman as well as a Nazi: he hoped to make money out of a deal with the Spanish generals; and did.[17] Also in Tetuan at that time was one Adolf Langenheim, the head of the local Nazi party.

That evening – 22 July – Bernhardt and Langenheim, accompanied
by a Nationalist Air Force officer, Captain Francisco Arranz, took
off for Berlin in a Lufthansa Junkers requisitioned at Las Palmas.[18]
They arrived on 25 July, having done the last lap of the trip by train
from Stuttgart. The two Germans went on to Bayreuth, where the
Führer was listening to Wagner. He saw them on Sunday, 26 July,
and read two letters from Franco which Bernhardt had been carrying.
One was addressed to him and the other to Goering, the Air Minister.
Hitler then summoned Goering and General von Blomberg, the
War Minister. That evening, it was agreed in principle that the
Spanish insurgents should be supported.[19] A key factor in this
decision, which was taken against the advice of the German Foreign
Ministry, was the opinion of Admiral Canaris, the head of German
Military Intelligence, who was on friendly terms with Franco and
had a high opinion of his ability.[20]

On 28 July, Franco, confident by now that he had solved his
logistics problem, flew across to Seville to confer with Queipo de
Llano. The Republican authorities evidently got wind of his trip,
for their planes bombed the airfield of Tablada, outside Seville,
about the time he was due to land. The luck that never deserted
Franco, however, once again came to his rescue, for his plane came
in to land a few minutes after the bombing had ceased.

The two generals exchanged views on the feasibility of a military
attack on Madrid. As with all other plans at that time, everything
was contingent upon getting the Army of Africa across the water.
Back in Tetuan that evening, he called in the relatively few high
naval officers who had managed to join him, and outlined a plan
to send a naval convoy across to Spain, whether or not Italian and
German aircraft reached Morocco. The sailors shook their heads
knowingly, and observed that the operation was impossible since
the Nationalist fleet and air force were heavily outnumbered. Franco
countered with these words: 'The Red fleet is not a normal fleet. Its
crews lack morale and leadership and have no taste for sacrifice. I
have only two boats and a handful of planes, but they are commanded and served by men of honour with an ideal, whereas the Red
boats and planes are under murderers, and murderers are cowards.'

When the naval officers continued to object, Franco changed his
tone, and said cuttingly: 'All right, all right! I haven't called you
here for you to say such things, but to tell you that the convoy of

troops and material must get across as soon as possible. And I assure you that it *will* get across.'[21]

Next day, Bernhardt and Langenheim returned to Tetuan with the news that German planes were on their way. Reporting to Goering on the conversation he then had with Franco, Langenheim made an extraordinary revelation: 'The future Nationalist government of Spain,' he wrote, 'has been organized in the form of a directorate of the three Generals, Franco, Queipo de Llano and Mola, with General Franco presiding.'[22] This message, which went out from Tangier on 29 July provides a revealing and precocious insight into General Franco's ultimate ambitions. For it is as certain as anything in this confused period can be that Mola, for one, had not been consulted about any plan to set up a directorate; and most improbable that if he had been, he would have agreed to Franco's being its president.

As a matter of fact, only a week earlier – on 22 July – Mola had set up his own National Defence Committee or *Junta* in Burgos, with old Cabanellas as President. The other members were Mola himself, Generals Saliquet, Ponte, and Dávila, and Colonels Montaner and Moreno Calderón. Initially, Franco was not a member, though it was vaguely understood that he and Queipo would join once the three armies they commanded had linked in the field. Communication was, in fact, established on 11 August, when units of the Army of the South, commanded by Colonel Yagüe, reached Merida and made contact with the Army of the North. It was then, as Franco himself remembers the situation, that he 'must have been included in the *Junta*'. Nevertheless, as late as mid-August, when Franco was operating from Seville, Mola and he, though apparently on cordial terms, were acting quite independently of each other, to the annoyance of the Germans.* During this initial period, the authority of the National Defence Committee was confined to Mola's fief in the

---

* See *Documents on German Foreign Policy*, Series D, Vol. III, Seydel to Foreign Ministry, August 16, 1936, No. 43, pp. 42–3. Sir Robert Hodgson, the British agent with Franco's administration, states incorrectly (*Spain Resurgent*, p. 45) that the Burgos *Junta* was set up on 23 July and that it included Franco. Page 1 of the volume of German Documents quoted above declares that the *Junta* was organized at Burgos on 25 July, and that Franco became a member early in August. These details have found their way into a number of books, including those of Hugh Thomas (*The Spanish Civil War*, p. 238, which, however, gives the date as the 24 July), and Gabriel Jackson (*The Spanish Republic and the Civil War*, p. 294). The facts given in my text were contained in a written reply to a question of mine, from Franco's military household, quoting Franco himself.

North, although it was already being referred to as a 'provisional government'.

Hitler's first planes – twenty JU 52 maximum capacity transports and six Heinkel 51 fighters – started coming in shortly after the return of the Nazi envoys. Indeed, the Lufthansa Junkers that had taken Bernhardt and Langenheim to Berlin and back went into action on the evening of their return, ferrying a first contingent of troops across to Seville.[23] When the other Junkers transports arrived, the pace of Franco's improvised ferry service was stepped up. Together with the Italian Savoia-Marchettis, the Junkers transported up to 500 men and 15 tons of material a day across the Strait. Within a few weeks, some 15,000 men had reached the Spanish mainland.

In the meantime – and though the Republican naval blockade was still effective – Franco decided to go ahead with the convoy plan which his naval staff had opposed. His order was that the operation should begin at dawn on 5 August. It had to be postponed for a few hours, however, because of the presence in Gibraltar harbour of the Republican destroyer *Lepanto*, which was undergoing repairs for damage caused by Nationalist bombing. On learning this, Franco sent an urgent message to the Governor of Gibraltar, requesting the expulsion of the destroyer, on the ground that she was a pirate ship whose crew had murdered their officers. The Governor 'chivalrously' agreed[24] to send the *Lepanto* on her way, and she sailed towards Malaga, removing the threat to Franco's operation.

The Nationalist convoy then set off from Ceuta, at 5 p.m. It consisted of the gunship *Dato* (1,300 tons), the coastal patrol ship *Uad Kert*, a tugboat and three merchantmen. In them were 3,000 troops, 2 million rounds of ammunition, 2,000 hand grenades and 12 tons of dynamite. At 7 p.m., the convoy ran into artillery fire from the Republican destroyer *Alcalá Galiano* (1,950 tons). For a quarter of an hour, the destroyer's 120 mm guns and the *Dato*'s 101·6s exchanged compliments. Then the Nationalist Air Force – consisting of six

---

Further details given were that the *Junta* was formed at exactly 10 p.m. on 22 July 1936, and recorded in a General Order of 24 July, reproduced in the Supplement to the *Official Daily* of the War Ministry, published in Tetuan on Saturday, 25 July, 1936. The news that the *Junta* had appointed Franco 'Chief of the Armies of Africa and the South of Spain' appeared in *La Gaceta de Africa* – a Spanish-Moroccan daily published in Tetuan – on Sunday 26 July, 1936 (No. 1,260).

Bréguet XIXs, two Newports, three Fokkers and three Savoias –
joined in, putting the *Alcalá Galiano* to flight.[25]

That morning before dawn, Franco had prayed at the shrine of the
Virgin of Africa at Ceuta. After breakfast, he had climbed Monte
Hacho to direct the operation, accompanied by General Orgaz, an
officer of the *Guardia Civil*, and two aides. It was there that the Air
Force General Kindelán had brought him news of the presence of
the *Lepanto* at Gibraltar. When the operation started, Franco engaged
his companions in animated conversation about trivialities. At 8 p.m.
came the news that the convoy had safely reached Algeciras.

Smiling, Franco said to his assistants: 'Well, the time went quickly,
talking to you.'

One of them replied: 'Not for me, *mi General*. For me, these were
the longest hours of my life.'

Franco went down to Ceuta, where, says Franco Salgado, he
offered a second prayer to the Virgin of Africa.[26] A prayer of thanks
for victory.

A cool nerve and his 'original sin' had indeed won the battle of the
Strait.

3 *Franco's Apotheosis*

Within two months of winning the Battle of the Strait, General
Franco was to be proclaimed Chief of State and Generalissimo of the
armed forces of Nationalist Spain, after a triumphal string of military
successes, culminating in the relief of the Toledo Alcazar. Before the
end of the year – 1936 – he was to know the bitterness of his first
failure to conquer Madrid – the direct consequence of his decision
to relieve the defenders of the Alcazar. And with failure came the
certain knowledge of something he had felt in his bones: that this
was to be a war of attrition, not a walkover campaign.

Franco had already given warning that the struggle for supremacy
in Spain would be long and bloody. And now, before leaving
Morocco for the peninsula, he told General Kindelán: 'I haven't the
slightest doubt that we will win, nor have I doubted it a single instant.
But it is going to be long and costly.'[1]

On 6 August, General Franco flew to Seville and set up his head-quarters in the Palace of the Marchioness of Yanduri. His relations with the ebullient Queipo de Llano were very cordial. As things then stood, no precise hierarchy of command had been established, and the two generals appeared in public together, to enthusiastic applause from the Sevillians. The military problems they faced were clear: to complete the conquest of Andalusia, to join forces with General Mola to the north, to secure control of the border with friendly Portugal, and if possible with hostile France; and to capture Madrid. The first and third of these objectives were partially achieved within a few weeks, and the second was satisfactorily fulfilled. But the fourth proved elusive.

The disciplined and well-equipped Army of Africa – a term that included the Moorish *Regulares* and the *Tercio* or Foreign Legion – soon proved more than a match for the enthusiastic rabble General Miaja threw against Cordoba and Granada. On 11 August, Colonel Yagüe and his Legionaries and Moors occupied Merida (Extrema-dura) and drove on towards Badajoz, which he took after fierce fighting on 14 August. Within a few days of this feat of arms, Yagüe controlled the whole Portuguese border and had joined forces with Mola's northern army.

On 13 August, Mola flew down to Seville to confer with Franco and Queipo. There news reached the three generals that their colleagues, Goded and Burriel, had been executed in Barcelona's Fortress of Montjuich, the grim scene of repressive tortures a generation earlier. This news could only mean that the fight Franco and his friends had started was a fight unto death or victory, for to surrender was to die. And this was how the three men interpreted the situation.

While Mola was in Seville, his soldiers, pushing towards the Pyrenean border town of Irun, felt a sudden stiffening of resistance and learned that they were fighting the first foreign volunteers to join the Republicans – young men who had answered a call to arms by the French Communist Party. Irun did fall, however, but not until 5 September, when the Nationalists found that the retreating Anarchists who were defending the city itself had set it on fire. This victory effectively cut off the Republican forces in Catalonia from those in the Basque provinces.

By mid-August, it had already become clear that the key to victory lay in the tough and disciplined Army of Africa, which Franco himself had done so much to create in his brilliant military youth. Neither the depleted units under Queipo de Llano nor Mola's large but disparate force could hold a candle to the *Regulares* or *Tercio*. And since Franco controlled this impressive weapon, he was already, in fact if not in name, the Supreme Commander. The tactical successes of Colonel Yagüe, of which Franco was the strategist, brought jubilation to the Nationalist camp and an aura of glory around Franco.

On 15 August, he presided over the hoisting of the Nationalist flag over Seville's town hall. Against the advice of Mola – who did not wish to anticipate the future constitutional form of the Spanish State – Franco had decided that the flag to be hoisted should be the red and gold banner of traditional Spain. And as it rose, he shouted to the cheering crowd: 'It's yours!'[2]

Next day, in Burgos, and in Mola's company, Franco again basked in the noisy enthusiasm of the vast crowd that gathered to greet the two generals as they made their way to the great Cathedral to hear mass. The business part of the visit, as distinct from the symbolical, was to make contact with Mola's Defence *Junta*; and this he did.

General Franco now prepared for what looked like a great victory within reach: the conquest of Madrid. The bustle of Seville was distracting and too remote from the troops – his troops – who were doing the fighting. To be within closer reach and devote his time and energy unreservedly to the organization of victory, Franco and his military staff moved to Caceres, setting up headquarters in the mediaeval Palace of Los Golfines de Arriba. His elder brother Nicolás had now joined him as political secretary.

Once again, as in the feverish days that followed his arrival in Tetuan, and as it had been during the repression of the Asturian revolution, Franco was in his element. At his desk at 8 a.m., he studied maps and battle reports. Some days were spent on military planning. But more often than not, he would have himself driven to various places in the Tagus Valley where he could talk with Yagüe and see for himself how the advance was progressing, taking refuge on one occasion under a bridge to escape Republican bombs.

By now, several European powers had made it clear that they proposed to exploit the Spanish civil war for their own ends. Although, on 24 August, Germany, Italy and Portugal had accepted the principle of non-intervention, there was clearly no intention on their part of translating principle into practice. German and Italian material had already been sent and now Italian pilots were beginning to arrive in Seville. Portugal, too, was helping Franco, both by making ports and railways available for Nationalist supplies, and by sending volunteers to fight in Spain.[3]

On the other side, too, help was coming in. News had been brought to Franco of planes taking off from Toulouse airport on their way to Republican Spain. On 1 August, five Potez bombers left Toulouse bound for Spain, and six Dewoitine on 5 August. On 14 August, seventeen more planes reached Barcelona from France.[4] A more sinister intervention, however, was that of the Soviet Union. As early as 21 July, a joint meeting of the Presidium of the Supreme Soviet, the Comintern and the Profintern (the trade union international) was held in Moscow to discuss the implications for Soviet policy of the Spanish *Alzamiento*.[5] A further meeting, this time of European Communist Parties affiliated to the Comintern and Profintern, was held in Prague on 26 July, when it was decided to set up a fund of 1,000 million French francs, ninety per cent of which was to be provided by Russia, and create an international corps of 5,000 men to fight for the Republic. The fund was to be administered by the French party boss Thorez, the Italian Togliatti, and the Spaniards Largo Caballero, José Díaz and *'La Pasionaria'*.[6]

Aware, as he was, of the internationalization of the war, Franco did not deceive himself into supposing that the fall of Madrid would mean the immediate end of the fighting. He did, however, think that Madrid could be taken fairly easily, and calculated – no doubt rightly – that its fall would bring immense psychological advantages to the Nationalists, who would then be able to proclaim a government in the 'liberated' capital of Spain. At the beginning of September 1936, this did not seem too much to hope. In numbers, there was not, at that stage, much to choose between the two armies on the Madrid front. The Nationalists had 6,000 men and the Republicans 7,000, but these included 2,000 Anarchists who refused to take orders from General Riquelme.[7] In fighting quality and leadership, the Nationalists were immeasurably superior. Nor was the enthusiasm of the Republicans a match for the discipline of the Nationalists: the Republicans were liable to veer from martial fury to panic despair, and on one occasion, the Fourth *Bandera* of the Legion made prisoners of an entire column of 600 men, with all their arms and equipment.

Franco summoned Yagüe at the end of August, to congratulate him on his spectacular successes and to give him his next battle orders. Between 1 and 3 September, Yagüe routed Riquelme's forces, despite the fourteen heavy batteries the Republicans had at their disposal. When the Republican Under-Secretary of War, Hernández Sarabia, telephoned Talavera, the last important town before Madrid, a Moorish voice answered. The *Regulares* had come.

Riquelme's accumulated failures now brought about his dismissal, but his successor, Colonel Asensio Torrado, fared no better: his counter-attack ended in disaster and the retreating Republicans left 500 dead and large quantities of material on the battlefield. Next day, the *Regulares* advanced fifteen miles, and on 8 September, Colonel Monasterio, commanding the Nationalist Army of the Centre, joined forces with Yagüe's Army of Africa. Yagüe's left flank was now covered and there seemed to be nothing to stop him from conquering Madrid.

On 21 September, indeed, he inflicted a further retreat on the Republicans.

Madrid, however, did not fall, for at this stage, General Franco

halted the advance, and ordered his army to strike south, in the direction of Toledo.

If military grounds alone were considered, this would be an incomprehensible decision for Franco to have taken, when the capital of Spain lay open and within his grasp. Military considerations alone, however, never monopolized Franco's thinking during the Civil War. Other motives, especially patriotic ones, in the broadest sense of the term, frequently took precedence. The decision to defer the capture of Madrid was the first time this characteristic became apparent during the Spanish war; but not the last.

Franco had been following with admiration and deepening concern the defence of the besieged Alcazar of Toledo. The story – one of the authentic instances of heroism during the Civil War – had begun on 21 July, when a mixed Nationalist force, after fluctuating street battles, took refuge in the Alcazar, a massive fortress set on high ground dominating the Tagus. The defenders were commanded by Colonel José Moscardó. They numbered 1,300, including 600 Civil Guards, 242 officers and NCOs of the Military Academy and 60 Falangists. With them were 500 civilian refugees, most of them wives and children of the defenders. There were, in fact, 210 children; and three more were born during the 68 days of the siege.[8]

The defenders were not exactly short of food, having stored about three tons of wheat for the siege. For a while, they had toasted wheat in lieu of bread. Then an ingenious mechanic rigged up a mill worked by a motorcycle, and a daily ration of bread was instituted. Meat, though also rationed, was plentiful, for with the defenders in the fortress on 21 July were the 170 horses and mules of the Military Academy, and 27 belonging to the local Civil Guard – a supply soon depleted by the daily slaughter. There were two meals a day – at 10.30 a.m. and 5.30 p.m. There being no sugar, coffee was not on the menu.

For news, the defenders and their families had a cyclostyled daily, *El Alcazar*, which ran from 26 July until 27 September. For entertainment, there was a circus. There *was* some need for relaxation, for the Alcazar was under constant Republican bombardment – from land and air, and in the final stages from underground mines. When the defenders were relieved, on 28 September, the fortress was a chaos of rubble, craters and smouldering timber.

The best-known story of the siege has passed into legend, but bears retelling.* Repeated calls from Madrid to the Alcazar having failed to persuade Moscardó to lay down arms, a militia chief in Toledo brought Moscardó's captured son to the telephone on 23 July and threatened to have him shot within ten minutes if Moscardó did not surrender. Moscardó said to his son: 'Well, then, my son, commend your soul to God, cry "Long live Christ the King!" and die like a patriot.' Young Luis Moscardó was duly killed, but not as a direct result of this conversation: anti-climactically, but no less permanently, he was shot a month later as a reprisal for a Nationalist air raid.

Less well-known is the story of Franco's promise to the defenders of the Alcazar. Toledo, of course, had symbolic and emotional associations for Franco, partly because he had graduated from its Infantry Academy, in common with many of his leading followers, and partly because it had been the capital of Imperial Spain. On 22 August, Franco sent two messages to the defenders. They were dropped by a Nationalist plane, together with food parcels, at dawn on 23 August, and found by Major Villalba, who immediately took the whole bundle – as he had found it, wrapped in the red and gold flag of traditional Spain – to Colonel Moscardó. The messages were from 'General Chief of the Army of Africa and South of Spain Don Francisco Franco Bahamonde', in case the isolated defenders of the fortress had not heard the news of Franco's responsibilities. As the two messages were almost identical, only the second, which was the more explicit, need be quoted:

> An embrace from this Army to the brave defenders of the Alcazar.
> We are drawing near you. We shall come to the rescue. Meanwhile, resist. For this, we shall give you what little help (*pequeños auxilios*) we may.
> All difficulties having been overcome, our columns are advancing, destroying all resistance.
> Long live Spain! Long live the brave defenders of the Alcazar!
> General Francisco Franco. – August 22, 1936.[9]

Although drawn forward by the military magnet of Madrid, Franco remained obsessed by the Alcazar and his promise to its

* Doubts have been cast on the authenticity of this story, but Hugh Thomas disposes of them (*op. cit.*, pp. 270–1, n.).

defenders. In the end, he took the grave decision to relieve the fortress in the full knowledge that it would probably mean losing Madrid. General Kindelán records the following exchange of views that took place between them on the eve of the decision:

'Do you know, General, that Toledo could cost us Madrid?' said Kindelán.

'Yes, I know,' answered Franco. 'I have long meditated on the consequences of my decision . . . In my place, what would you do?'

'I,' Kindelán replied without hesitating, 'would go for Toledo even if it meant not taking Madrid.'

'Well, that's what I have decided,' answered Franco, 'because I have come to appreciate that in all wars, and above all in civil wars, spiritual factors count to an extraordinary degree. We have to impress the enemy, by convincing him that *whatever we propose to do we achieve* and they can't do anything to stop it. Moreover, I hope that a delay of eight days in the march on Madrid will not bring the consequences you fear. But even if it should, I would not give up the idea of conquering Toledo and liberating the heroic defenders of the Alcazar, which I promised them I would do in my message that was dropped by air.'[10]

On 23 September, General Franco ordered his Army to halt their drive on Madrid and switch to Toledo. The operation was entrusted to General José Enrique Varela, the much-decorated Carlist officer; Yagüe having fallen ill with over-exertion. In a lightning drive Varela did what was asked of him. On the afternoon of 27 September, Moscardó, bearded and haggard, came out into the fading sunlight, saying, as the custom was: 'Nothing new in the Alcazar'. With him came the living ghosts of those who had chosen to defend the fortress. Eighty of the defenders had died in the sixty-eight days of the siege, and four civilians.

On 29 September, General Franco himself went to the Alcazar, where he conferred the Laureate Cross of San Fernando on the defenders – individually on Moscardó, collectively on his men. With him was his old friend the former chief of Legion days, Millán Astray, who was in Argentina when the *Alzamiento* began and had come back to offer his services to the Nationalist cause.

As Franco emerged from the ruins of the fortress, he murmured:

'The liberation of the Alcazar is the thing I wished for most in my life. Now, the war is won.' He was right, but only in a long-term sense of inner conviction that victory was his. In a strictly military sense, the relief of the Alcazar lengthened the war by several months.

Nobody, however, thought of the receding prospect of victory in the euphoria of success at the capture of imperial Toledo. One name was on the lips of all followers of the Movement, whether Carlist or Falangist, Alfonsist or military. That name was Franco's, whose prestige had reached its pinnacle. Neither the spectacular Queipo de Llano nor the subtle and devious Mola, who had directed the military conspiracy in its earlier phase, could compete with him for the leadership of the uprising. And nearly all were agreed that a unified leadership was needed to end the period of feudal improvization on the Nationalist side. The man to lead the united Movement could only be Francisco Franco.

As a matter of fact, this conclusion had already been reached before the relief of the Alcazar, but had been kept secret. General Kindelán has told the story of Franco's elevation to supreme power – of his apotheosis, one might reasonably say – in his book *Mis Cuadernos de Guerra'*.[11] For if Franco was a king-apparent, Kindelán was the king-maker he undoubtedly needed.

For any general to be appointed Supreme Commander in war-time must come as the natural culmination of professional ambition, and a general as professionally dedicated as Franco cannot have been an exception to this rule. It is a matter of record, however, that Franco never openly sought the political power that was now to be conferred on him, along with the supreme military power that was manifestly his legitimate reward. And Kindelán's account makes it clear that Franco resisted even the proposition that he should be the Supreme Commander. Was this a formal resistance of the kind that traditionally imposes on the elected Speaker of the House of Commons the duty to resist the ushers who lead him to his Chair? It is hard to say. Kindelán attributes Franco's evasive attitude to his 'natural modesty', 'his fear that the thing was not sufficiently ripe and that any imprudent pressure might break the cordial relations that prevailed among the chiefs of the Army', and perhaps also 'to reluctance to give up the command of the Army of Africa'. All three of these points are consistent with Franco's character; the second may well have been the strongest. For if one thing is certain about Franco, it is that he has never rushed into an important decision, or allowed himself to be rushed by others.

At any rate, when Kindelán told him that he was about to propose Franco's candidacy as Supreme Commander, Franco refused to commit himself. Kindelán then appealed to Franco's brother Nicolás, a naval engineer by profession and at that time Franco's political adviser, to persuade the general to accept. From him Franco learned that his strongest supporters, among the top Nationalist military leaders, were Kindelán himself, Generals Orgaz (who had succeeded Franco in Morocco) and Millán Astray, and Colonel Yagüe. A strong reason for Franco's reticence may well have been the feeling that he would need additional reliable voices in his favour before exposing himself to the possibility of a humiliating vote.

Finally, to overcome Franco's resistance, Kindelán proposed that the leading military chiefs should meet in committee at Burgos and thrash the whole thing out. Even then, Franco would not give an answer. He asked for forty-eight hours of reflection, at the end of which, he agreed to Kindelán's suggestion.

The generals met at 11 o'clock on 12 September, in a small wooden hut that served as the office of San Fernando aerodrome outside Salamanca. The aerodrome itself had been improvised on a field in the estate of Antonio Pérez Tabernero. Those present were: Generals Franco, Kindelán, Queipo de Llano, Orgaz, Gil Yuste, Saliquet, Mola, Dávila and Cabanellas, and two staff Colonels, Montaner and Moreno Calderón. The twelve men seated themselves on uncomfortable rustic chairs at a large table. It was unanimously agreed that General Cabanellas, who was seventy-five, should take the chair by reason of seniority.

The first question to be resolved was whether or not there should be a united command. When Kindelán and Orgaz proposed to table this issue, however, they ran into procedural objections from some of those present. Three and a half hours were wasted on the procedural wrangle, and the Nationalist leaders adjourned for lunch as guests of Pérez Tabernero.

When the session was resumed in the afternoon, Mola vigorously supported the proposal of Kindelán and Orgaz that the committee should immediately decide on the issue of the Supreme Command. Cabanellas objected, and Mola impatiently exclaimed: 'If within eight days, a Generalissimo has not been appointed, I'm not going on. I say if things stay as they are, I'm off!'

Old Cabanellas – who, of course, had been a supporter of the Republic and had a natural taste for committee rule – commented: 'A war can be run just as well by a generalissimo, or by a directory or committee.'

Kindelán took up the point: 'As you say, there are two ways of running a war: by a generalissimo or by a directory. The first way you win; the second way, you lose.'

Cabanellas said he would put the matter to the vote. He was the only one to vote against the appointment of a generalissimo.

Next thing was to appoint the right man. Once again, Kindelán took the initiative, and proposed Franco. Mola and Orgaz immediately and cordially agreed, followed, one by one, by all others present, except Cabanellas, who argued that as he was against the principle of a single Supreme Commander, he could not vote for any particular candidate. The others crowded around Franco, shaking him by the hand and congratulating him. It was agreed, however, to keep the decision secret until the National Defence *Junta* at Burgos should be able to meet and make a public announcement.

In the meantime, the war went on. Mola captured Guipuzcoa, and Franco launched the operation to relieve the Alcazar, thus achieving new heights of popularity which served the further designs of General Kindelán. For Kindelán wanted his king-apparent to be Chief of State as well as Generalissimo, so that both political and military power should be concentrated in his hands. Kindelán discussed the idea with Nicolás Franco, Yagüe, who had started his rest from the battlefield, and Millán Astray. The four then put the idea to General Franco, who, this time, does not appear to have demurred. A further meeting of military leaders was called, to discuss the powers of the Generalissimo and the appointment of a Chief of State. In preparation for what the promoters of the occasion confidently felt was to be Francisco's apotheosis, Nicolás arranged that the Falange and the Traditionalist Communion should each send a hundred of their fighting men to honour the new Caudillo of Spain at the meeting, which was to be held, as the first one had been, at San Fernando aerodrome, on 29 September.

There was nothing secret about this second meeting, for the two hundred Falangists and *Requetés* were at the aerodrome, as arranged.

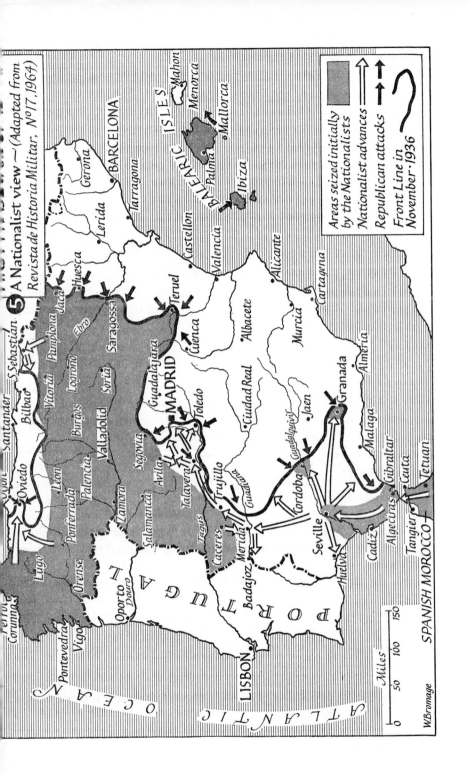

5 A Nationalist view ~ (Adapted from Revista de Historia Militar, Nº17, 1964)

Areas seized initially by the Nationalists

Nationalist advances

Republican attacks

Front Line in November·1936

W.Bromage

Miles
0   50   100   150

ATLANTIC OCEAN

BALEARIC ISLES
Mahon
Menorca
·Palma
Mallorca·
Ibiza

BARCELONA
Gerona
Lerida
Tarragona
Castellon
Valencia
Alicante
Cartagena
Murcia
Albacete
Cuenca
Teruel
Saragossa
Huesca
Jaca
Pamplona
S.Sebastián
Santander
Bilbao
Vitoria
Logroño
Soria
Burgos
Valladolid
Palencia
Segovia
Avila
MADRID
Guadalajara
Toledo
Ciudad Real
Jaen
Granada
Almeria
Malaga
Gibraltar
Ceuta
Tetuan
Tangier
Algeciras
Cadiz
Seville
Huelva
Kordoba
Guadalquivir
Guadiana
Merida
Badajoz
Caceres
Trujillo
Talavera
Tagus
Salamanca
Zamora
Leon
Ponferrada
Orense
Lugo
Oviedo
Coruña
Pontevedra
Vigo
Oporto
Douro
LISBON
PORTUGAL
SPANISH MOROCCO
Ebro

Franco himself, however, was absent – partly no doubt to spare himself the embarrassment of listening to a possibly acrimonious discussion on the kingmakers' proposal to confer new powers on him; but also because he wanted to greet the defenders of the Alcazar that day. The previous evening, he had announced the news of the relief of the fortress to a cheering crowd outside his headquarters at the Palace of Los Golfines in Caceres. When Cabanellas, at the head of the table at San Fernando, had called the meeting to order on 29 September, Kindelán rose and read the text of the proposed decree defining the powers of the Generalissimo and Chief of State, which he and Nicolás Franco had drafted the previous day. It read as follows:

ARTICLE 1   All Land, Sea and Air forces that collaborate or will collaborate in future with the Movement shall be subordinated to a single Command, which should be filled by a divisional general or a vice-admiral.

ARTICLE 2   The man named will be styled Generalissimo and will have the highest place in the military hierarchy, military and naval officers of the highest rank being subordinate to him.

ARTICLE 3   The post of Generalissimo will be combined with the office of Chief of State *for the duration of the war*, and in the latter capacity, his authority will extend over all national activities: political, economic, social, cultural, etc.*

ARTICLE 4   Any provisions contrary to these shall be superseded.

Article 3 aroused instant and noisy disapproval. Mola, who had warmly supported Franco's appointment as Supreme Commander, strongly criticized the proposal that he should be given political powers as well, on the ground that he would have enough to do in running the war effort without also being burdened with matters of State.

An angry Kindelán sprang to his feet to say he was surprised at Mola's attitude since the draft text had been shown to him and had met with his approval. Others, however, supported Mola. Even Orgaz – one of those who had proposed Franco's appointment as Generalissimo – only reluctantly supported his simultaneous appointment as Chief of State.

It is not difficult to guess at some of the motives that animated the dissident generals that twenty-eighth of September. It is fair to sur-

* Author's italics.

mise that Mola may have seen himself in the part of Chief of State, or at least Head of Government. Another motive for dissension on his part was probably the profound disillusionment with the monarchy which he had developed as Security Chief during King Alfonso's last reigning years. He suspected Franco of being fundamentally monarchist and credited him with a desire to restore a discredited institution. In this he was not alone, for Cabanellas and Queipo de Llano, although they had turned against the chaotic Second Republic, remained Republicans at heart in the sense that they would probably have opted for a Republican Constitution in the new Spain of tomorrow. In any case, the suspicions of the anti-monarchists had been thoroughly aroused by the fact that Franco's candidature was being proposed by Kindelán, who was known to be a staunch partisan of restoration.

One of the unsolved questions of the Civil War is how the opposition to Franco as Chief of State was transmuted into support by the afternoon of 29 September. Kindelán himself, so prodigal with other details, merely writes that 'the purest gold of patriotism and disinterest shone in the eyes of those present' – at the luncheon offered for the participants by Antonio Pérez Tabernero. Certainly Kindelán did a lot of talking and was eloquently persuasive. Did this eloquence consist, as Hugh Thomas puts it, of 'a mixture of veiled menace and flattery'?[12] I know of no strong evidence that it did.

Whatever was said at the lunch, the guests reassembled on their rustic chairs ready, at least, to vote for a compromise form of words. The following day, General Cabanellas, as Chairman of the National Defence Committee at Burgos, signed a Decree, the crucial first two Articles of which read:

ARTICLE 1 In fulfilment of the agreement adopted by the National Defence Committee, His Excellency Don Francisco Franco Bahamonde has been appointed Head of the *Government** of the Spanish State and will assume all the powers of the New State.

ARTICLE 2 He is likewise appointed Generalissimo of the National Land, Sea and Air Forces, and the post of Chief General of the Operational Armies is conferred upon him.

So in the end, General Franco's sponsors had obtained more or less what they had asked for. True, Article 1 described him as Head of

* Author's italics.

the 'Government' not 'Chief of State'; but the rider that he would 'assume all the powers of the New State' was sweeping enough to override any limitations implied by the fact that in a formal sense, he had not been proclaimed Chief of State. And indeed, he immediately began to issue decrees as Chief of State, and nobody was heard to contradict him. In that sense, the events of September 1936 amounted to one of the subtlest *coups d'état* in contemporary history, rivalling de Gaulle's in 1958. Indeed there was a final subtlety, which some of those who listened as the Decree of 29 September was read out in the throne room of the ornate *Capitanía-General* of Burgos on 1 October, must have noticed. The original stipulation in the Kindelán-Nicolás Franco draft decree, that Franco would become Chief of State 'for the duration of the war' had been dropped altogether in the final text. It is said that there were some long faces in the throne room that day. But how many of those present could have supposed that today, more than twenty-eight years after the end of the Civil War, General Franco would still be Chief of State?*

* This reconstruction of the events of September 1936 fits the known facts, but it is worth pointing out that the facts are not easy to obtain. The main published source, Kindelán's *Mis Cuadernos de Guerra*, is unfortunately inconsistent. It gives two dates for the first meeting of generals at San Fernando aerodrome—12 and 21 September. The second, apparently a misprint of the first, has been adopted by a number of writers. In the same book, Kindelán gives 31 September for the second meeting (p. 54)! Since the Burgos Decree was dated 29 September (and appeared in the National Defence Committee's Official Bulletin of 30 September), most writers have assumed that the second meeting of generals took place on 28 September. Luis Bolín, on the other hand, in his *Spain: the Vital Years* (Cassell, 1967) gives the date as 27 September (p. 293). I am indebted to Lieutenant-General Franco Salgado-Araújo, General Franco's Military Secretary, for documentary proof that the meetings took place on 12 and 29 September, and for the fact that Franco was not present at the second. Incidentally, the official text of the Burgos Decree disposes of a 'canard': the story that Nicolás Franco sent a messenger on a motor-cycle to the Burgos printer to delete the reference to Franco as 'Head of Government' and substitute 'Head of State' cannot possibly be true, since the official text reads 'Head of the Government of the Spanish State', damaging though this form of words is to Franco's supporters. Hugh Thomas reproduces the story on p. 365 of *The Spanish Civil War*, attributing it to Jean Créac'h in *Le Coeur et l'Epée*. Indeed, the story does seem to have originated with Créac'h, who carries a slightly different version of it on p. 182 of his book. But the official text of the decree shows that it could not be true, good story though it is. More important is the omission of a time-limit on Franco's tenure of power, as mentioned above in this chapter. It is only fair to add that when I checked Créac'h's story with Nicolás Franco in Madrid in April 1967, he said: 'Yes, this is probably what

Unabashed by any unexpressed reservations on the part of a minority of his listeners at Burgos on 1 October, General Franco addressed Cabanellas – who was presiding over the ceremony – and the assembled generals:

> General, and Generals: You may be proud of yourselves. You received a broken Spain and you are giving me a Spain united in a unanimous and grandiose ideal. Victory is on our side. You deliver Spain to me, and I assure you that my grip shall not falter, that my hand shall always be firm. I shall lead the Fatherland to its highest point or die in the attempt. I want your collaboration. The National Defence Committee will follow at my side. Long Live Spain! Long live Spain! Long Live Spain!

From an enthusiastic crowd in the square outside cheers and shouts of 'Fran-co' broke out a few minutes later when the Generalissimo appeared on the balcony. This was the apotheosis – achieved, according to his followers, 'by the grace of God', as the coins later put it, but with a good deal of help from mortal men.

General Franco was forty-three. Despite his active life and frugal habits, he had put on weight since those days when he had first sighted Africa as a slim-faced youth. Now he was round in shape and, with his Legionary's forage cap and tassel, a hostile cartoonist's delight. His enemies were additionally served by the fact that it became fashionable to refer to Franco as the *Caudillo*: a term which linguistic purists deprecate but which means roughly the same as *Führer* and *Duce*. Franco was henceforth labelled a 'fascist dictator' in all parliamentary countries and in communist Russia.

There was, indeed, a distinctly fascist note in his very first speech as Chief of State, delivered that day in Burgos, in which he promised a totalitarian and authoritarian State, and guaranteed the absolute right to work. Conversely, parasites would not be tolerated. On the other hand, there was an embryonic Keynesian flavour about references, in the same speech, to the need to improve productivity and create more wealth. As usual, Franco did not lend himself all that easily to classification.

---

happened. The Secretary of the Junta had decided to cut out the words "of the Government" in the text of the Decree.' But when I showed him the published text, which includes these three words, he commented: 'Well, in that case, the alteration can't have been made.'

4 *Franco in Salamanca*

We have been looking at the Spanish Civil War, through Franco's eyes. Let us pause now, to take a quick look at what went on inside and outside Spain in the shadow of the fighting. If one avoids partisanship one has to record the fact that it was a vicious and nasty business, on both sides of the barricades. On the Republican side, the armed 'people' murdered with gusto and abandon; on the Nationalist side, with calculated ferocity. For my part, I find it an unprofitable exercise to give either category of slaughter a moral margin over the other. Let us simply, and impartially, distinguish between the motives of the killers. The revolutionaries massacred the bourgeoisie because this, as they saw it, was their mystical and exalted class duty. The counter-revolutionaries killed because the 'Marxists' whose death they ordained represented 'anti-Spain'. Neither side doubted its own righteousness.

The proletarians who battered their way into the Montaña barracks in Madrid on 20 July 1936, threw the military defenders out of windows, tore them to pieces, shot them into extinction. Yagüe's Moors and Legionaries massacred many hundreds of disarmed militiamen in the bull-ring of Badajoz after capturing the town in mid-August. (Since Franco congratulated Yagüe on his military successes and did not, as far as is known, reprove him for these excesses, it must be presumed that he approved of them.) These scenes were duplicated in towns and villages throughout Spain, the labelling of the killers and the killed being determined by the success or failure of the uprisings in this place or that.*

The massacres in the Popular Front areas accompanied a far-reaching social revolution which varied in character according to whether Socialist-Communist, or Anarchist, influence predominated. In Madrid, the ruling powers were the Socialist UGT unions and the joint Socialist-Communist youth movement. In Barcelona, the Anarchist CNT ruled supreme. In both cities, churches were burnt

* For fuller details, see Jackson, *op. cit.*, Chapters 16 and 17, and Thomas, *op. cit.*, Book II, Chapters 18 and 19.

systematically, and to wear a tie was to court death. In the Basque provinces, in contrast, the churches were mostly left intact, Catholics having joined the Republican side through regional aspirations that had little to do with revolution. In the rural areas, 'libertarian communism' was the usual pattern. In some cities, for a time, and in villages for longer, money vanished, to be replaced by work vouchers.

With the social revolution came a rapid, secret and extraordinarily successful international communist attempt to take over the Spanish Republic from the inside. Largo Caballero, 'the Spanish Lenin', succeeded Giral as Prime Minister on 5 September 1936. There were only two avowed Communists in his Cabinet, with the relatively unimportant portfolios of Education and Agriculture. But appearances were deceptive: Stalin's policy was faithfully served within the Large Caballero government by two men who were nominally Socialists. One was Álvarez del Vayo, the Foreign Minister, who headed the Commissariat for War and whose control of the Foreign Press Bureau prevented any references to the revolution in Republican Spain from reaching the outside world at a time when the myth that the Republic was still a democracy had to be kept up to maintain sympathy in Britain, France and the United States. The other *de facto* agent of Moscow was Dr Juan Negrín, the Minister of Finance, who had been a professor of physiology and whose personable charm was a great asset to the Republic. Negrín, who later replaced Caballero as Prime Minister, took advice from the Soviet trade representative, Arthur Stashevsky, and had more than half the Republic's gold reserves – worth more than $500 million – shipped to the Soviet Union, thus placing the Republic in bondage to Moscow. Such eminent figures of the international communist world as Togliatti (Italy), André Marty (France), and the Hungarians Laszlo Rajk and Ernö Gerö played important roles in Spanish affairs from the late summer of 1936.*

What is there left to say about the ill-fated Non-Intervention Committee? Let us simply recall that in August 1936, twenty-seven nations adhered to the Non-Intervention Agreement, but that this made no difference to those bold enough or hypocritical enough to

* It is impossible in this necessarily restricted biography of Franco, to deal in any detail with the all-important Communist take-over bid. By far the best account of it is in Burnett Bolloten, *The Grand Camouflage* (Hollis & Carter, London, 1961).

flout their own signatures. True, aid from France to the Republic was soon reduced to a trickle. But aid from Germany, Italy and Portugal to the Nationalists, and from Russia and Mexico to the Republic, swelled to a flood. Soviet tanks were in action on the Madrid front towards the end of October, and German and Italian bombers were bombing the capital. The famous Communist-controlled International Brigades, whose fighting men were idealists from many countries, started going into action early in November; shortly afterwards, the Nazi Condor Legion began assembling in Seville, and Italian infantrymen left Naples for Spain in December. The Spanish war had become an international free-for-all.

During the phase of internationalization of the conflict, Franco conducted operations from Salamanca, where he had set up headquarters in the Bishop's Palace on being appointed Supreme Commander of the Nationalist forces. There, he settled down to a strenuous routine, rising at 8, attending Mass and seating himself at his desk at 9.30, when he began studying reports from the various battle fronts. After that, he dictated letters or memoranda until 11, when he conferred with his Chief of Staff and with various operational commanders. Having heard their views, he would study wall maps, then give orders. At 12.30, he would see the General Officer Commanding the artillery forces, followed by other specialist commanders. This went on until lunch, the hour of which was never fixed but varied according to the work in hand. If there was relatively little work, lunch was served at 3 p.m. But on busy days, Franco and his staff might delay their meal until 5 or 6 p.m. After lunch, and weather permitting, he would stroll about the gardens of his residence, in the company of some officer or technical assistant whom he had not been able to fit into his morning routine. Then back to the office, where he worked until dinner at 11 p.m. After dinner, he returned yet again to his desk, working until 2 a.m.[1]

There was much to do, not only because the running of a sprawling, untidy war like Spain's was exacting work, but also because Franco, in his new and dual capacity, had to give attention to political as well as military matters. It was at Salamanca, for instance, that he first studied the statutes of the Falange.[2] His time-table being crowded, however, he leaned heavily on his brother Nicolás, who continued to hold the post of Political Secretary.

Other influences entered his life at this time – and all within the

11a José Antonio Primo de Rivera *(speaking)*, founder of the Falange – later executed in a Republican gaol.

b The Monarchist leader, Calvo Sotelo, 1935; his murder by Republican police ʒ following year was a landmark in the litary conspiracy.

11c Anti-Republican plotter freed: General Sanjurjo *(second from left)*.

12a Nationalist Generals Goded (*left*) and Burriel, being sentenced to death in Barcelona.

12b 29 September, 1936: Franco meets the defender of the Alcazar, Toledo, Colonel (later General) Moscardó.

family circle. His wife's was undoubtedly one. After the long parting that had started with her departure from the Canaries on 18 July, she had come to Caceres, with their daughter, to join her husband, when he was still working in the Palace of Los Golfines de Arriba. (It is said that Franco was in conference when they arrived and kept his wife waiting for an hour before they could meet.³) Much had happened since the two had parted. In mid-July, everything was uncertain; the future was a question-mark over hazardous possibilities. Now Franco was Generalissimo and, in fact if not in formal title, Chief of State.

Doña Carmen was a profoundly pious woman, ambitious on her husband's behalf, aware – as nobody else seems to have been – of his own ambitions and determined that they should not only lead him to the highest pinnacles of power, but keep him there. And already, under his wife's influence, Franco – who had never been particularly noted for piety – had begun to attend Mass with becoming regularity. At Caceres, and now at Salamanca, Doña Carmen encouraged him to believe what she herself undoubtedly accepted: that a divine hand guided his destiny; that God had chosen him as saviour of Christian Spain. Priests, too, began to influence him at this time; and none seems to have raised doubts about the divine nature of his mission. Nor, on the other hand, is there any evidence that he himself had yet accepted the theory that God had a special interest in his success. There was, in any case, much to do and little time for meditation. But the natural corollary to the theory was one which Franco had no difficulty in accepting: that since God had chosen him as Spain's saviour, there was no special need for haste in restoring the Mon-archy.

The first priest one hears of, in the summer of 1936, is Father Bulart, the Francos' private chaplain, whom the General's hostile biographer, Ramírez, describes as 'well-meaning but weak-willed and unenlightened' and inclined to inflate Doña Carmen's dreams.⁴ Ramírez, however, is not the only chronicler to mention the influence of priests in Franco's *entourage*. Another is von Stohrer, Nazi Ger-many's second Ambassador to Nationalist Spain, who drew attention to the Vatican's influence over Franco through the Jesuit Father, Menéndez Reigada and the Apostolic Administrator of the Basque Diocese, Monsignor Luzurika.⁵ Of the three, the most influential was probably Menéndez Reigada, who became Franco's confessor, and who first popularized the notion that the Nationalist uprising was a Crusade against anti-Spain and anti-Christ.

Though Franco was now Head of Government – and was already having himself described as 'Chief of State' – he was in no hurry to constitute a government as such. For the time being, and indeed until the beginning of 1938, he was content to use the Technical *Junta* of the National Defence Committee in Burgos, which was under the effective direction of a competent staff officer, General Dávila. In effect, the Technical *Junta* was a 'cabinet' of technicians. Two outstanding members were former assistants of the late Calvo Sotelo during his period as Primo de Rivera's Finance Minister: Joaquín Bau, who administered industrial, commercial and supply problems, and Andrés Amado, who looked after finances. José Sangróniz, the diplomat who had lent Franco his passport when the General left the Canaries, was head of the 'diplomatic cabinet' – in effect, Franco's Foreign Minister. Nicolás Franco, as Political Secretary, acted as liaison man between the *Junta* and Franco, and might almost have been called Prime Minister if Franco had not been, among other things, Head of Government.

In fact, Franco was still paying little attention to politics. The untidiness of the 'war lords' situation having been resolved – in his favour – and political issues shelved – under his titular direction – he was able to concentrate on military matters. Of these, an important long-term aspect was the creation of the expanded army that was to be his instrument for victory. Under the direction of General Luis Orgaz, the Nationalists opened crash training courses for temporary junior officers, known as *alfereces provisionales*, whose emergence in large numbers powerfully contributed to the technical superiority of the Nationalist Army over that of the Popular Front.[6]

For the immediate future, however, Franco's main preoccupation, now that Toledo had been 'liberated' was to prepare for what was to be the final assault on Madrid. But a more urgent preoccupation still, while plans for Madrid were perfected, was the relief of the Asturian capital, Oviedo, the scene of two repressions in which Franco had taken part – the scene also of his youthful meetings with Carmen Polo. In Oviedo, as in Gijon, the local commander had opted for the uprising. The action of the Oviedo commander, Colonel Aranda, had, as it happened, come as a surprise, for he had the reputation of being a Republican, and had not taken part in the military conspiracy. He had, however, been converted by Franco himself to the idea of rising against the Republic. When the 1936 elections brought the Popular Front to power, Azaña had ordered the reduction of the Oviedo garrison. Aranda had gone to Madrid to plead with Azaña to leave things as they were, pointing out the damage that had been done in Oviedo by armed revolutionaries in 1934, but Azaña had refused to budge. While in Madrid, he bumped into Franco and told him what had happened. Franco, cautious though he still was at this stage, had remarked: 'There's only one way, and that is, that at the right moment each military chief should energetically declare a state of war in the area under his jurisdiction. Then we shall see how to organize a common action.'[7]

On 17 July, Aranda learned in a telephone conversation with his wife, who was in Morocco, that the Army of Africa had risen. Next day, four thousand armed miners had appeared in Oviedo, burning to defend the Republic. With considerable guile, Aranda had persuaded the civil governor to suggest to the miners' leaders that they send half their force to Madrid to defend the Republic's capital. The miners agreed and two thousand of them went off – although they never reached Madrid, being intercepted by the Nationalists at Leon. The threat having been reduced, Aranda concentrated all the Civil Guards of the province and proclaimed a state of war. Much the same – minus the guile – happened in Gijon under Colonel Pinilla.

The failure of the Basque provinces to join the *Alzamiento*, however, left the Asturian cities isolated, and in both Oviedo and Gijon the Nationalists found themselves under siege. At Gijon, Pinilla and his men had taken refuge in Simancas barracks, where they fought off a much more numerous Republican force for a month. On 21 August, when further resistance seemed hopeless, Pinilla sent the following message to the cruiser *Cervera*, at that time off Gijon:

FIRE ON US. WE HAVE THE ENEMY INSIDE. DEFENCE IS BECOMING IMPOSSIBLE FOR THE BUILDING IS BURNING AND THE ENEMY ARE ENTERING. FIRE ON US, I REPEAT.[8]

Having taken Gijon in these dramatic circumstances, the Asturian miners turned their full fury on Oviedo. Aranda had 3,300 defenders under his orders, including about a thousand armed civilians. In all, the Republican attackers, by this time, numbered fourteen thousand. By early October the city was without light or running water and typhoid cases had broken out. Aranda, an ebullient character who reminded some people of Queipo de Llano, broadcast cheerful and unjustifiably optimistic talks every day, and morale remained high.

One of Franco's first actions on becoming Supreme Commander was to promote Aranda to General. He then sent a *Bandera* of the Foreign Legion and a *Tabor* of Moors, plus three other units, to help Mola's Galician troops who were attempting to relieve Oviedo. Before they could get there, Aranda, his ammunition low and his optimism now deserting him, sent a message to Mola, saying: 'The only thing left is for us to die like Spaniards.'

On the night of 16 October, however, the Moors reached Mount Naranco, which dominates Oviedo, and started firing on the attackers. The following evening, Aranda and his men were relieved, after a siege which had lasted ninety days. The jubilant Mola exclaimed: 'Hardly a month ago, we liberated the Alcázar. Today we have liberated Oviedo. I assure you that within a few days we shall enter Madrid.'[9]

Franco shared this optimism. Count Du Moulin-Eckart, the Nazi Counsellor in Lisbon, who had gone to Salamanca to bring Hitler's congratulations to Franco on becoming Chief of State, reported to Berlin that the Generalissimo had shown himself 'very optimistic as to the military situation, counting on taking Madrid in the near future'.[10] This remark was made at a dinner for Du Moulin-Eckart on 3 October, which Nicolás Franco and General Kindelán attended. Given the purpose of the occasion, it is scarcely surprising that Franco also thanked Hitler for his aid and declared that he felt complete admiration for Hitler and the new Germany. In time, however, the Germans were to discover that the Caudillo could be an awkward man to deal with when it came to questions affecting Spain's independence.

As things stood in early October, however, Franco had no reason to suppose that he would need much more German help than the planes and pilots he had already received. On 6 October, the first day of Franco's new offensive against Madrid, General Masquelet's defence line was broken to the south, bringing the Army of the South to within some thirty miles of the capital. Yagüe, recovered now from his illness, took command of two of General Varela's columns, one of which, advancing fast from Toledo, reached a point twenty miles from Madrid on 17 October. Twelve days later, after a relatively heavy engagement in this war of small forces, the Nationalists cut the Aranjuez–Madrid road.

Now all Madrid's communications, except those to the East, were in Franco's hands. Cautious as usual, however, he wanted to make absolutely sure of success, and brought Mola down from the North to command what was to be the final assault. The ex-'Director' of the conspiracy was overjoyed at his part in what he felt would be a historic battle. If anything, he was even more optimistic than Franco, and he had expressed the fact earlier in a phrase that has passed into many languages. He was optimistic, he told foreign journalists, because not only were four Nationalist columns marching on Madrid but a 'fifth column' of secret supporters inside the city would rise in support of the attackers when the time came.

The four columns, now under Mola's orders, were those of Castejón, Asensio, Barrón and Monasterio. (These are the 'accepted' four columns, although other Nationalist Colonels – Delgado Serrano and Tella – were also pushing towards Madrid at that time.) In the first days of November, each had taken up positions on the outskirts of Madrid. The great attack, however, was delayed until 8 November and when it was launched, it came too late. The consensus of later opinion is that if the Nationalists had attacked on 6 November, they would have captured the city. That day Largo Caballero and his cabinet – against the dissenting voices of four Anarchist Ministers who had just joined the government – decided that the administration should immediately evacuate Madrid for Valencia. Caballero handed over the defence of the capital to General Miaja. While the Ministers and civil servants, with their files and office equipment, piled into caravans on the road to Valencia, the Communists and their Russian and other foreign advisers took over the administrative posts left vacant.

On the night of 6 November, the guards of the Model Prison, disregarding orders to evacuate the inmates to Valencia, lined them up alongside freshly dug trenches and mowed them down. More than a thousand died this way.[11] On 8 November, as Varela attacked, the first 3,000-strong unit of the International Brigades entered Madrid. Superbly trained and disciplined, their presence was to turn the tide in the Republic's favour. Only in the air were the Nationalist forces superior: Soviet tanks, which had been in action on the Madrid front since late October contributed to Popular Front superiority on the ground. From Madrid, the famous cry, '*No pasarán*', went out.

For once, Franco had spoken too soon and acted too late. On 20 October, he had issued a general order for the capture of Madrid, and on 5 November he had announced that the liberation of the capital was at hand, telling Madrid's citizens to keep to their houses, which would be respected by 'our noble and disciplined troops'.[12] That day, too, Franco had threatened those guilty of crimes. Everything was ready for victory, and the German and Italian governments were preparing to recognize Franco's régime the day after his presumed entry into Madrid.[13] But the attack was delayed and Franco did not enter Madrid.

Instead, the battle raged, mainly in and around Madrid's University City, for ten days. Franco, who had followed the news anxiously from Salamanca, now came to Leganes, outside Madrid, where he examined the situation with Mola, Varela and Saliquet. It was there, on 17 November, that Franco decided to suspend the offensive against Madrid. Both sides started digging themselves into trenches and protecting themselves with barbed wire.

Next day, Germany and Italy (and, quaintly, distant Guatemala) recognized Nationalist Spain after all. For the crestfallen Nationalists, this was a tonic, for it meant that in Berlin and Rome a long-term view of aid to the Generalissimo's forces was being taken.

For any Spanish Nationalist, but more for Franco than for any other, the necessity in which he found himself of requesting foreign aid was deeply humiliating. He was, however, in no position to remain aloof, or even to reject the particularly distasteful conditions the Germans sought to impose on him. As early as 30 October, the Germans told Franco that if he wanted more substantial military aid than he had until then received, he would have to agree that the German units should be under German command.[14] True, the Germans agreed that the German commander would be responsible to Franco – so that the man most closely affected by this condition was General Kindelán, the Air Force Commander. It remains that the stipulation was offensive to Spanish pride. General Franco nevertheless swallowed his objections and accepted it.

The result was the formation of the German Condor division – a formidable mixed air force unit commanded by General Sperrle, which formally came into being on 7 November, but was not brought to full strength until towards the end of December.

On 28 November, Franco concluded a secret alliance with Mussolini[15] which, in effect, committed the Duce to aiding Franco Spain for the duration of the Civil War. That day, General von Faupel, who had been colonel of the first World War regiment in which a certain Corporal Hitler had served, arrived in Salamanca as Nazi Germany's first *chargé d'affaires*. His only evident qualification for the job was his knowledge of Spanish, which he had learnt during a long stay in South America. He was, however, a fairly typical Nazi – limited, unsubtle and arrogant. On 30 November, Faupel and Franco had a long talk, during which Franco outlined the military situation as he saw it. The conversation left Faupel pessimistic. Franco was 'likeable' and 'ruthlessly brave'; but his estimate of the situation was 'frivolous'. He added that the generalissimo's 'military training and experience do not fit him for the direction of operations on their present scale'.[16] He was the first, but not the last, foreign diplomat to underestimate the man he was dealing with.

5 *Franco's difficult Allies*

Frustrated before Madrid, General Franco resigned himself to a war of attrition. Politically, 1937 was a year of masterly consolidation: Franco welded his variegated supporters into a single ruling party. But militarily, it was a difficult year for Franco and the Nationalist forces.

The frontal assault on Madrid had failed, but Franco consoled himself with the thought that if he could cut the capital's remaining communications – with Valencia to the east and Republican-held Málaga to the south – he could sap the defenders' will to resist. He had counted without the discipline and martial spirit of the International Brigades; the superiority of Soviet equipment over the material that had reached his side in the early stages from Italy, and even Germany; and the fighting inferiority of the Italian infantry. He was also handicapped by inevitable but debilitating differences of opinion with his German and Italian allies, and between the Nazis and Fascists themselves.

The Germans were highly critical of the conduct of the abortive assault on Madrid, and not entirely without reason. When plans were being drawn up for the formation of the Condor Division, they had insisted that all German units in Spain should be led by German officers responsible to General Franco but to nobody else. At the beginning of 1937, however, they proposed that a joint German-Italian general staff should be set up, and Franco gave his approval.[1]

Humiliating though this was, Franco was still in no position to argue: he needed German and Italian equipment and knew there was a price to pay for it. At the same time, he took advantage of the fact that there were differences between the Germans and Italians. For the immediate future, his ideas coincided with those of the Germans – with the Italians in disagreement. Franco wanted to cut Madrid's communications with the north-west and south-west; the Germans supported this, but under command conditions that would have placed the newly arrived Italian infantry under their orders. The Italians, for their part, wanted to have a front of their own.[2]

Franco's way out of this situation was to give in to the Italian demand without abandoning his own plan for a pincer movement against Madrid. The newly arrived Italian *voluntiare*, under General Roatta, should take part in the attack on Málaga, which, it was rightly reckoned, would give them an easy and encouraging victory. Immediately afterwards, however, the Spaniards, under General Orgaz, were to try to cut the Madrid–Valencia road, in an attack starting from the Jarama Valley; General Roatta's forces were to try to cut the main road from Madrid to Saragossa and Barcelona, in the Guadalajara area.

Such was the plan, as Mussolini's son-in-law and Foreign Minister, Count Ciano, explained it to Italy's first Ambassador to Franco's régime, Roberto Cantalupo, on the eve of the latter's departure for Salamanca.[3] With that optimistic bombast that was typical of Fascist Italy, he went on to explain that once these military moves had been executed, the Red front would collapse, Madrid would fall and all that would be left to do would be to mop up in the separatist northern provinces. By and large, the military plan Ciano outlined was put into effect; but the results fell far short of Italian expectations.

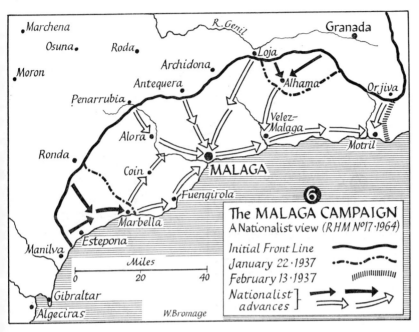

The MALAGA CAMPAIGN
A Nationalist view (RHM Nº17·1964)

Initial Front Line
January 22·1937
February 13·1937
Nationalist advances

W.Bromage

In the south, Franco struck on 10 January. A month later, a mixed force of Moors and *Requetés*, under the command of Queipo de Llano, and of Italians under Roatta, took Málaga. This prosperous seaside town had been the scene of sporadic Republican massacres; and these now yielded to savage Nationalist reprisals – so savage that the Italians were shocked and Cantalupo was given orders to raise the matter with General Franco. The Generalissimo recognized that the Nationalist tribunals had been severe and hinted that it was difficult for him to control local reprisals.[4]

The final assault on Malaga had been accomplished with great speed, and the Republican General Villalba had fled so precipitately that he had left behind in his room a suitcase containing the hand of Saint Teresa, which had been stolen from the saint's birthplace at Avila. This curious discovery led to much fruitless speculation whether the 'Red' General could possibly have been a saint-worshipper. The hand, meanwhile, was conveyed to General Franco as a personal gift, and has remained with him ever since, accompanying him on all journeys.[5]

The Jarama offensive, designed to cut Madrid's road link with

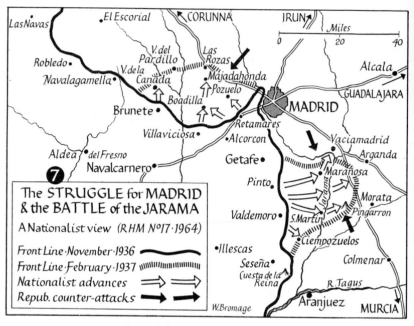

The STRUGGLE for MADRID
& the BATTLE of the JARAMA

A Nationalist view (RHM Nº17·1964)

Front Line·November·1936
Front Line·February·1937
Nationalist advances
Repub. counter-attacks

W.Bromage

Valencia – where Largo Caballero's government now functioned – was launched on 6 February, four days before the capture of Málaga. General Varela, who had been wounded during the siege of Madrid but had now recovered, was put in command of the operation. For three days, the Moors and Legionaries under his orders advanced against strong Republican resistance, reaching positions from which the Madrid–Valencia highway came under their fire. Then they ran into formidable counter-attacks by the International Brigades under the command of 'the Hungarian General Emil Kléber', who, the wits claimed, was neither a General nor a Hungarian, nor properly named Kléber – a *nom de guerre* he had borrowed from a glorious French Revolutionary figure.[6] Whatever his origins, he seems to have joined the Red Army in Russia in 1917; and whatever his rank, he was an able military man, whose counter-attacks brought Varela's offensive to a halt with very heavy losses, some units losing as many as forty per cent of their numbers. On the Brigades' side, too, losses were heavy; and both sides paused for breath.

In a rare outburst of measured praise for his enemy, Franco confided to Cantalupo that Kléber's Spanish Commander-in-Chief,

General Miaja, 'was a good general, that the International Brigades had given proof that they knew how to die and that he considered that they were as ready to give their lives as if their soldiers were Spaniards'. This, at any rate, was how Cantalupo quoted the Generalissimo's words in his report to Mussolini. Coming from Franco, there could be no higher praise.

Franco does not, however, seem to have been as downcast as Mussolini's envoy expected, after the costly stalemate that was the only outcome of Varela's attack. If we accept, as I think we must, the important testimony of Cantalupo, to whom Franco's arguments came as an evident surprise, the Generalissimo's strategic ideas at that time by no means coincided with the Italians'. Nor did he share the facile optimism that was the order of the day not only among Roatta's troops but even among his own military followers at Salamanca. Referring to 'operation Guadalajara', in which the Italians were to bear the brunt of the fighting, Franco declared that its object was not – as Ciano had supposed – to complete the encirclement of Madrid and therefore its fall, but simply to relieve the constant pressure against General Orgaz's forces to the south. Victory, said the Generalissimo, was sure, but nobody should think it would be rapid. He refused to commit himself as to the duration of the war, but 'if he had wished to say something, it would not be in support of brevity'.

Franco added that he had prepared precise war plans for 1937 which amounted to a real calendar; and he hoped the facts would bear him out. The battle of Guadalajara had its place in the calendar; it was destined to destroy a part of the international forces. Next would come, not the capture of Madrid, but the conquest of the Basque country, Santander and Asturias, and the isolation of Catalonia from the rest of Spain by the capture of part of the Mediterranean coast north of Valencia. Once isolated, Catalonia would have to be pacified. Only then would Madrid's hour come.[7]

Nobody else in Salamanca in March 1937 seems to have shared this typically cautious view of immediate prospects. There, all the talk was of the final offensive that was to bring the war of liberation – the 'Crusade' as it was now being called – to a victorious end within weeks. So overpowering was local optimism, indeed, that talk was quite unrestrained, with the result that General Miaja had ample warning of what was in store and plenty of time to make his defensive plans.

Starting from Sigüenza to the north-east, General Roatta's divisions – numbering 50,000 well-armed troops with 250 tanks – drove towards Guadalajara, flanked on the right by a mixed brigade of Moors, Legionaries and *Requetés* under General (as he now was) Moscardó, the defender of the Alcazar. It was 7 March. Until 11 March, the Italians and Nationalists advanced rapidly. They then ran into icy rain interspersed with snow storms which, between them, converted the airfields into quagmires and grounded the Italian air force. On 13 March, Miaja, having brought up reinforcements from the inactive Jarama front, counter-attacked in strength, with a battalion of Spaniards and the XII International Brigade. The Italians were driven back several miles, recovered, then collapsed. By 22 March, the retreat had become a rout.

During the early stages of the Popular Front counter-offensive, Luigi Longo (now, thirty years later, boss of the Italian Communist Party) and a number of others appealed to the Italians by leaflet and loudspeaker not to fire on their brother workers, but to desert and join the International Brigades.[8] Some, but not many, of their compatriots, gave in to this temptation. This did not prevent the

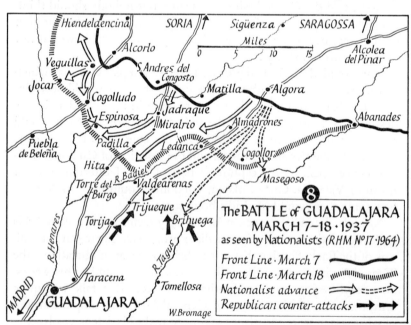

The BATTLE of GUADALAJARA
MARCH 7–18 · 1937
as seen by Nationalists (RHM Nº17 ·1964)

Front Line · March 7
Front Line · March 18
Nationalist advance
Republican counter-attacks

W. Bromage

enormously efficient communist propaganda apparatus, both in Spain and outside, claiming with suitable fanfares that the Italian Fascists had suffered 'another Caporetto'. But at Caporetto in 1917, the Italian army lost 300,000 men and 3,000 cannon. At Guadalajara, twenty years later, the Italians lost 1,375 killed, 2,400 wounded and 300 prisoners, against 450 prisoners, 3,500 wounded and 2,000 killed on the Republican side. These are Nationalist figures, but even allowing for some understatement of Italian losses and overstatement of Popular Front ones, they show that Guadalajara was in no sense another Caporetto. It should be added that the Nationalists, having advanced up to twenty miles, only retreated up to ten miles. If Guadalajara was a defeat, then, it was so only in a relative sense. More accurately, it was a costly stalemate, such as the Jarama Valley drive had been.

There is no doubt, however, that, from the standpoint of the Italians who had expected easy victories and been encouraged in this expectation by their walkover at Malaga, the retreat at Guadalajara was a humiliating moment. Mussolini was wounded where it hurt most . . . in the prestige of an aspirant conqueror. To make matters worse, the Spanish Nationalists took little care to conceal their pleasure at their Italian ally's discomfiture – a pleasure that derived as much from the cocksure superiority affected by the Italian officers as to the fact that they had not bothered to keep the Spaniards informed of their movements. In fact, Nationalist officers drank to the defeat of the Italian legionaries, and on both sides of the fighting, it was pointed out that 'CTV', which meant *'Corpo Truppe Voluntarie'*, in Italian, could also mean – in Spanish – *'Cuando te vas?'* ('When are you going home?')[9]

For his part, Franco took the Italian setback as calmly as he took most things, remarking to a major on his staff: 'This falls well, for now we can go ahead with the operation on the northern front, which is so important strategically.'[10]

Franco was, however, concerned lest Mussolini should withdraw his 'volunteers' in a fit of pique over their unfortunate performance. For weeks, he himself did his best to soothe the ruffled feelings of the Italian staff officers at Salamanca. In the same spirit, he called in Roberto Cantalupo on 23 March to give him an appreciation of the military situation as he now saw it, in terms that were diplomatically tactful for thin-skinned Italians.[11] He dismissed the failed offensive as no more than an unfortunate episode without grave consequences for the war as a whole. He recognized that Orgaz and Varela had been in the wrong not to have warned Roatta that their troops were too exhausted to counter-attack in support of the Italians. For this reason, he added, he had relieved both men of their commands, although they retained his personal esteem.

As for the future, Franco thought that the undoubted material superiority which the 'Reds' enjoyed at that time would not last long. He was, he explained, asking Germany and Italy to send enough war material to restore Nationalist superiority, without worrying too much about the Non-Intervention Committee. To this end, he was sending a personal letter to Mussolini, which he was entrusting to one of his men of confidence, Captain Villegas. The time had come, he added, to give Spanish public opinion the brilliant operation for which it hungered.

Mussolini, in fact, had committed himself too far in Spain to withdraw on the morrow of a defeat. On 28 March, he instructed Cantalupo by telegram to announce to Franco that he could count on continuing aid from Fascist Italy.[12]

Franco had already heard the news from Captain Villegas. But when Cantalupo called on him on 29 March to read out Mussolini's telegram, the Generalissimo, apparently savouring the occasion, asked him to read it out a second time, then a third. After that, wrote Cantalupo in his report to Mussolini, Franco, in a spontaneous movement – 'very rare, for him' – asked his visitor to express to Mussolini 'his deep satisfaction, his liveliest pleasure over the rightness of the decisions that had been taken, his gratification at finding himself understood and appreciated, and his gratitude for the assurance which Your Excellency is giving that National Spain can count on Italy's aid.'

Relieved of anxiety about military supplies, Franco was now able to turn to his campaign to complete the conquest of north-west Spain.

It should not be thought that General Franco had spent the six months or so since his appointment as Generalissimo chained to his desk in the Bishop's Palace at Salamanca. He was, in fact, a highly mobile supreme commander, visiting the battle fronts as frequently as he was able, and managing to keep an eye on minor operations whose import was symbolical rather than strategic. His disregard for his own safety – a product both of an innate incapacity for physical fear and of

a growing conviction that God had a special interest in his survival –
was often the despair of those whose job was to keep him alive and safe.
We have seen how his concern over the defenders of the Alcazar
had cost him Madrid. He felt much the same about two other isolated
stories of heroism – the defence of Simancas, where the local commander had called on the Nationalist fleet to fire on the defenders;
and the siege of Santa María de la Cabeza at Jaen, in Andalusia. With
the exception of Madrid on the Republican side, the defence of Santa
María de la Cabeza was the longest siege of the Civil War. It began
on 22 August 1936, when Captain Santiago Cortés González of the
Civil Guard took refuge with his men, their wives and children –
nearly 2,000 people in all – in the Monastery of Santa María. It
ended more than eight months later, on 1 May 1937, with the mortal
wounding of Captain Cortés, the overrunning of the improvised
fortress by the Republicans, and the slaughter of the defenders.

Although it proved physically impossible to relieve Santa María
de la Cabeza as the Alcazar had been relieved, Franco tried to prolong
the resistance by having arms and food dropped from the air. On
many occasions he sent his personal plane, a Douglas, piloted by
Captain Haya of the Air Force, to Jean with supplies for Cortés
Gonzáles and his charges.

One of these occasions almost cost the Generalissimo his life, and
indeed might easily have changed the course of the war by delivering
Franco into his enemies' hands. It happened towards the end of 1936.
Franco had to make a sudden trip to Escalona, in Toledo province, to
confer with General Varela. That morning, Franco had sent Captain
Haya with his Douglas to Santa María de la Cabeza, saying, as he
always did, that he would take whatever plane happened to be handy.

On the outward trip, the pilot revealed that he had had no experience of night flying and suggested that, for safety's sake, since
the December nights were lengthening, the party should start on the
return journey not later than 3 p.m. At lunch, however, Franco's
discussions with Varela showed signs of dragging on past danger
point, and Colonel Franco Salgado, who – as usual – accompanied
the Generalissimo, repeatedly tried to persuade Franco to take his
leave. Franco, deep in conversation, brushed him aside, so that it
was about 5 p.m. when the party left.

Shortly after take-off, night started closing in. Phlegmatic as
usual, Franco told the second pilot, a sergeant, to swap seats with

him. Seated next to the very nervous first pilot, Franco gave him instructions in his calm, high voice: 'A little to the left here,' or 'You'll need to rise a bit now – the Gredos mountains are ahead of you!' While this was going on, the second pilot, relegated to the back seat, showed signs of extreme agitation, which other members of the party attributed to nervousness at the unorthodox navigation of the distinguished temporary second pilot.

Once over the mountains, Franco said: 'You see that light over there? Those are the last rays of the setting sun. Head straight for the light and you'll come to Salamanca which is due west of where we are now.' The pilot obeyed and successfully landed the plane at San Fernando airfield in total darkness, to everybody's relief.

This was not, however, the end of the story. Next morning, the second pilot boarded the plane that had taken Franco to Toledo province and back, on the excuse of making a practice flight, took off and headed straight for Alcalá de Henares, Cervantes's home town, due east of Madrid, where he joined the Republican forces, complete with plane. The reason for his extreme agitation of the night before now seemed clear: he had been planning to take advantage of his senior colleague's inexperience to suggest that he should take over, and in that event would have landed at Alcalá – with the Generalissimo. This, at any rate, is how the survivors interpret this curious incident.*

6 *Franco imposes Unity*

Franco now took command of politics, as he had taken command of the armed forces, and for much the same reasons. The war could not be won by feudal war-lords intent on the private pursuit of regional power, even if all fought the common enemy. Neither, as he saw it, could the war be won by vociferously discordant political or ideological groups in pursuit of incompatible ultimate aims, even if all

* A slightly different version of this incident will be found in *Centinela de Occidente,* pp. 263–6. My version of it was given to me by Lieutenant-Colonel Eusebio Torres Liarte, who, as a junior officer, was in the plane with Franco and Franco Salgado.

were agreed on the need to fight 'communism' and 'freemasonry'. Armed, as he now was, with supreme political power, he decided to weld all supporters of the National Movement – Carlists, Falangists and the rest – into a single political party. To suppose, however, that this was a purely political operation would be to misunderstand it utterly. Its purpose, motive and procedures were fundamentally *military*. To be sure, Franco acted in his capacity as 'Chief of State' or 'Head of the government of the Spanish State' – whichever version is considered legitimate – but this way of seeing things, though formally correct, is misleading. It would be truer to say that in April 1937, General Franco became 'Generalissimo of the political forces', just as in October 1936 he had become Generalissimo of the armed forces. More simply, civilians and soldiers alike, on the Nationalist side, henceforth had one *Caudillo* and only one: Francisco Franco Bahamonde.

The widespread and persistent impression that what Franco created in April 1937 was a 'fascist' party has led to endless confusion outside Spain. It suited – and still suits – leftists everywhere that this should be thought, for 'fascism' is a recognized bogey-word, a legitimate object of hatred. Conversely, Franco's association with 'fascism' has embarrassed potential Right-wing supporters of his rule in many countries, and for the same reasons. 'Fascism' was only marginally a rude word among British Conservatives and French conservatives in the 1930s; but the monstrous excesses of the German variety were more indigestible. And in the end, Nazism becomes the common enemy of the West, with Fascism – Italian-style – its willing junior ally. By association, the Franco régime, too, came to stand for 'fascism': its victory in the Civil War was attributed to its Nazi and Fascist allies and it was almost universally, but quite mistakenly, assumed that Franco was content with the role of satellite to the larger fascist powers.

The truth of the matter is that Franco is a singularly un-ideological leader, who acted as he did because of the circumstances that prevailed in Spain in 1936 and 1937. To describe his behaviour as opportunism, however, would be to tell a half-truth. Franco was always a man of principle, not ideology. Whether or not one agrees with his principles is irrelevant. That he had them cannot be doubted. Their names were Duty, Discipline and Order. He was anti-liberal and anti-parliamentary because parliamentary liberalism in Spain had led to indiscipline and disorder, and discouraged the observance of military duty as he conceived it. If parliamentary liberalism had preserved order, maintained discipline and encouraged a sense of duty, it is likely that the summit of his ambition would have been to become Supreme Commander of Spain's armed forces. But this is a hypothesis, for parliamentary liberalism in Spain did none of these things. It had led, on the contrary, to revolutionary anarchy. Since Carlists and Alfonsists opposed revolutionary anarchy, Franco would accept their support, though he himself was always a conditional monarchist. It was as a monarchy that Spain had achieved greatness, and he therefore favoured a monarchical form of government. But it was unthinkable to say so in 1937, since the monarchists themselves could not agree on a candidate for the throne, and since the Falangists were fundamentally anti-monarchical. The constitutional issue could therefore be saved for the future.

As for the Falangists – the only group on the Nationalist side that could legitimately be called 'fascist' – they presented Franco with a problem; or rather with a number of problems. Since they had indulged in street fighting, they could hardly be said to have contributed to public order. On the other hand, *they* hadn't started the shooting; their ideology, which he had belatedly studied, favoured an authoritarian form of government and national unity, both in the sense that they opposed regional separatism and that they rejected the Marxist concept of the class war. They were, moreover, willing to fight and die for Franco's concept of Spain, and their popular following had grown rapidly after the formation of the Popular Front. Nor did they reject religion, as the Communists (and for that matter, the Nazis and Fascists) did; and the Church was, or ought to be a pillar of stability and order, and an essential strand in the fabric of the Spanish tradition. A place of choice must therefore, as Franco undoubtedly reasoned, be reserved for the Falange in the new order that would follow the Nationalist victory.

These were the factors in the political equation that faced General Franco on his assumption of supreme political and military power in October 1936. There was, however, no time for the untidiness of individual groups in his camp. If unity and order were the national objectives – and they were certainly his own – it was intolerable that his followers should squabble among themselves or, worse still, stake out individual claims of political power. Whether they liked it or not, all of them, whatever their distinctive aspirations, would have to sink their differences under a common political label.

It was as the outcome of this reasoning that Franco created the ruling party of Spain, whose inevitably cumbrous title was *Falange Española Tradicionalista y de las Juntas Ofensivas Nacional-Sindicalistas*, usually shortened to FET. A fascist party? Yes and No. Certainly it included the fascists. But it could equally be said that its creation condemned Spanish fascism to slow death by strangulation.*

So acute an observer as Dr Franz Borkenau, writing in 1937, not long after the creation of the FET, distinguished between German and Italian fascism on the one hand, and the Franco régime on the other, and pointed to the deep disagreement between Franco and the Falange. At that time, as Borkenau noted, the Falange Press carefully avoided calling Franco the 'chief' or the 'leader'; they simply called him the Generalissimo, which indicated that they accepted his temporary dictatorship only as a war measure. Not all Borkenau's judgments have stood the test of time, but here is one that did: 'There can be no real fascism, then, in the Franco camp, because the Fascist party is against the general-leader who, himself, has no political party at his orders. All this is not changed, in the (very) least, by the superficial unification of Carlists and Falangists recently brought about by Franco.'[1]

To understand what Franco did in April 1937, and why it was possible, one must go back a few months. The *coup d'état* of September-October 1936, which had given Franco political as well as military power, had taken place in the absence of the Carlist leader, Fal Conde, who, together with other leading Carlists, had rushed to Vienna on learning of the death there of the old Pretender, Alfonso Carlos. On their return from the funeral, they found it hard to conceal their distaste for the accomplished fact of Franco's assumption of political power. Their discontent crystallized two months later in an attempt to create their own 'Royal Military Academy'.[2] In itself, there was nothing particularly subversive about this project. It was obvious, however, that had it gone forward, it would have created a Carlist-slanted officers' corps with autonomous loyalties independent of the Generalissimo's overall

---

* Stanley G. Payne reaches much the same conclusion in his brilliant history of Spanish fascism, *Falange* (Stanford and Oxford, 1962).

authority. Moreover – and this was the rub – the Carlists had neglected to consult Franco about their plan. Coldly furious, Franco
summoned Count de Rodezno, one of the leading Carlists, and
reprimanded him. On further thought, he decided that the Carlist
initiative was part and parcel of an attempt to restore the monarchy
in defiance of his supreme authority, and therefore amounted to an
attempted *coup d'état*. One by one, he summoned leading Carlists –
except Fal Conde, the top leader – who all dissociated themselves
from the Academy project. He therefore concluded that the initiative
was entirely Fal Conde's.

Franco later told Faupel, the German envoy, that he had been on
the point of having Fal Conde tried for high treason before a military
tribunal, but decided against it both because of Fal Conde's undoubted services to the Movement, and of the effect his execution
would have had on the morale of the *Requetés*.[3] Instead, he gave Fal
Conde forty-eight hours to get out of the country, and the Carlist
leader took refuge in Lisbon.

It was a measure of General Franco's authority, even in December
1936, that he was able to get away with exiling the political leader of
the largest, most combative and most genuinely popular group of
opponents of the Spanish Republic. Further political trouble was
brewing, however – this time from the Falange.

The small extremist party created from the fusion in 1934 of the
original Falange and the earlier JONS had grown enormously, and
its militias were making a substantial contribution to Nationalist
military strength. But Spanish fascism had become a body without a
head. Nobody knew what had happened to José Antonio (who, in
fact, had been executed on 20 November 1936, by order of the newly
appointed communist civil governor of Alicante, where the young
Falange chief was gaoled). Had José Antonio lived, Franco would
have had to contend with a formidable challenger to his political
power. But he did not, and though nobody knew for certain that he
was dead, his charisma made itself felt in the early days of Franco's
régime at Salamanca, when it became customary to refer to him as
el Ausente – 'the absent one'. The cult of José Antonio did not officially begin until 16 November 1938, when a decree proclaimed that
the anniversary of his death was to be a day of national mourning.

Not only had José Antonio vanished, but his colleagues of the
JONS, Onésimo Redondo and Ledesma Ramos, had both lost their

lives – the former in battle and the latter in a massacre of political prisoners by the Republicans. The relatively minor figures who now tried to run the Falange in the absence of José Antonio were deeply divided. The strongest of the factions was that of Manuel Hedilla, an ex-mechanic from Santander, who was honest and dedicated to social reform, but lacked the personality of a leader. A second faction, under Agustín Aznar wanted to preserve the pure spirit of *José Antonismo*, even if José Antonio himself should never return. Yet another faction – a numerous one – consisted of the Right-wing conservatives of various shades who had deserted Gil Robles's CEDA in Popular Front days, and of opportunists who thought a Falange party badge might be useful. This third faction became known as the 'new shirts' as distinct from the 'old shirts' (*camisas viejas*) who had been with José Antonio or the JONS from the start.

Franco's elder brother, Nicolás, had tried, but utterly without success, to create a united party, under the General's leadership, out of the conservative groups that supported the *Alzamiento*. The *Falangistas* themselves, however, scoffed at the idea of associating themselves with capitalists and reactionaries. (The myth that the Falange was a party of the Right was, of course, perpetuated by the Communists; in fact, it was a revolutionary party of the Left, and José Antonio's posthumous papers called for an opening to the left and a government that would have included Prieto.)[4]

To Franco, the squabbles of the Falangist factions, both among themselves and with their Carlist rivals, were a constant source of irritation. Apart from exiling Fal Conde, however, he had done nothing about it when, towards the end of February 1937, his brother-in-law, Ramón Serrano Súñer, turned up in Salamanca, after a perilous escape from Madrid, where the Republicans had executed his two brothers and he himself had tricked death by taking refuge in the Dutch embassy. Within a few weeks – in fact if not in name – he supplanted Nicolás Franco as the Generalissimo's political adviser.

The arrival of this talented personality, indeed, transformed the political outlook in Franco's camp. Before, all was aimless confusion and dissension; after, a sense of purpose and direction manifested itself. Ambitious, subtle and intelligent, Serrano Súñer was a born politician. A persuader rather than a leader, he had the charm that soothes offended feelings, and the intellectual agility – derived from a Jesuit education and a legal training – that overcomes objections by argument. In temperament and appearance, however, he presented a striking contrast to Franco, for he was slight, nervous, emotional, prematurely grey and blue-eyed.

Serrano's greatest political asset was undoubtedly the lucky circumstances that his wife and Franco's were sisters. But he had others. One was that he had been a close personal friend of José Antonio's, although he had never joined the Falange, as he disapproved of its revolutionary syndicalism. Another was that as organizer of the CEDA's youth movement, JAP (*Juventudes de Acción Popular*), he had many contacts in the clerical, conservative and monarchist world that had put Gil Robles forward in 1933 as the leader of a mass Catholic party.

One fine afternoon, he strolled with General Franco in the gardens of the Bishop's Palace at Salamanca and expounded his ideas to the Generalissimo. Spain, he argued, now had an almost unprecedented chance of creating a new State that would be modern, socially progressive yet conservatively sound, and juridically based. Carlism was too old-fashioned to be the foundation of such a State, but the Falange, suitably expanded and reorganized, could fill this purpose.[5] As for the Army, important though it was, a military régime could only be temporary.

Serrano Súñer was not the only person advising Franco to form a strong ruling party. Faupel, the German ambassador, with typical bluntness, was saying that a decision to this end must be taken immediately.[6] On 11 April, Franco discussed the matter with him at length. The old parliamentary system, he declared, was thoroughly discredited. The Falange, on the other hand, had grown rapidly in importance since the war. Unfortunately, since the death of José Antonio – which, said Franco, could no longer be doubted – the party lacked a leader. His successor, Hedilla, lacked the necessary qualities. He was surrounded by ambitious young men who influenced him, whereas he ought to be leading them.

It was in this conversation that Franco revealed to Faupel the fact that he had almost had Fal Conde condemned to death for attempting to restore the monarchy. The only way to resolve the differences and rivalries between the Monarchists and Falangists was to unite them in a new party under his own leadership. In this party, the Falange, whose programme was sounder and whose adherents were more numerous, would be the dominant element. A *Junta* would be formed to help him – Franco – lead the new party; it would probably consist of four representatives of the Falange and two monarchists.[7]

Hedilla had neither the stature, nor the cunning nor the following necessary to stand up to the *coup d'état* which, in effect, was what Franco and Serrano Súñer were now plotting. Yet this was just what he was foolhardy enough to attempt. In February he himself had attempted to negotiate a united party with Fal Conde, who, of course, was still in Portugal. The negotiations had broken down on the issue of the monarchy. On 12 April, a group of Falange dissidents had tried to depose Hedilla, but he had stood firm. On 14 April, his own followers had tried to patch things up with the dissidents,but a meeting for this purpose had ended with two men killed and with the arrest of the survivors by the Civil Guard. Hedilla's leadership was however narrowly confirmed at a meeting of the National Council of the Falange on Sunday, 18 April. That evening, Hedilla called to see Franco, who apparently congratulated him on his re-election and appeared briefly with him on the balcony of the Bishop's Palace, to the cheers of a small group of Falangists. No mention, of course, was made of the impending move that was to deprive Hedilla's re-election of all meaning.*

Franco now moved fast. Serrano Súñer had been drafting a decree uniting the Carlists and Falangists. Generals Mola and Queipo de Llano were urgently summoned to General Headquarters at Salamanca and shown the draft, which they duly approved – with what reservations it is not known. On the evening of 19 April – the day after his meeting with Hedilla – General Franco delivered a major speech on the Nationalist radio in which he announced the creation of the new united party – the FET. The tone of his speech was firm and uncompromising.

He declared:

> This unification which I insist upon in the name of Spain and in the sacred name of our dead does not mean a conglomeration of forces or of governmental concentrations . . . what I ask of you is in no sense inorganic, fugitive or ephemeral . . .
>
> Abandoning doctrinal preoccupations we oppose the verbal and formalistic democracy of the liberal State which has failed in

* The most detailed account of the Hedilla affair appears in Payne, *op. cit.*, Chapter XIII.

all its parts, by an effective democracy, which gives the people
that which is truly of interest to them: to see themselves and feel
themselves governed in a spirit aspiring to integral justice, both
in the order of moral values and in that of economic and social
factors . . . The liberal exploitation of Spaniards will be succeeded
by the rational participation of all Spaniards in the management
of the State through the medium of their family, municipal and
syndical functions.

The decree enshrining the new order was published at midnight
on the same day – 19 April 1937. The *Comunión Tradicionalista* and the
Falange Española y de las JONS were duly merged, and Franco was
declared 'National Chief' of the new party thus created. All other
parties were abolished, and the *Requetés* and Falange militias were
merged (to blur the former distinction between them, the militiamen
of the new party were ordered to wear the Falange's blue shirt *and*
the red beret or *boina* of the *Requetés*).

From all over Spain came messages of loyalty to Franco, who told
Faupel on 5 May that he had received 60,000 telegrams of support
and congratulation.[8] Poor Hedilla woke up to find he had no party
behind him. As a sop to him, however, he was named Chairman of
the new Political Junta of the FET, but he stubbornly refused the
job. On 25 April, Franco suddenly lost patience with him and had
him arrested on a charge of attempted rebellion. He was sentenced to
death, but reprieved after pleas from Faupel (who thought his
execution would affect the morale of the Falangists) and Serrano
Súñer, and spent the next four years in solitary confinement in the
Canary Islands. He was moved to comfortable quarters in Mallorca
in 1941, still unbroken in body or spirit.[9] A number of other
Falangists were gaoled in connection with the Hedilla affair, but
released within two or three years. As a purger of dissidents, Franco
was always rather mild, compared to other totalitarian dictators of
the twentieth century.

That his ideas at that time *were* totalitarian, however, cannot be
doubted, for he himself said so, in an interview with the monarchist
newspaper *ABC* on 19 July 1937. And the point was driven home in
a further decree, published on 4 August of the same year, which
officially adopted the 26 Statutes of the Falange as State doctrine.
Point 6 read:

Our State shall be a totalitarian instrument dedicated to the service of the national integrity. All the Spanish people will participate in the State through the families, municipalities and syndicates. No one shall participate through the mediation of a political party. We shall radically abolish the political party system with all its consequences: inorganic suffrage, representation by warring parties, and a parliament of the kind that is only too well known.

If any doubt remained about the absolute power now achieved by Franco, it was dispelled in the following passage of the same decree:

As the author of the historical epoch during which Spain achieved its historic destiny, while at the same time obtaining the goals of the Movement, the Chief (or *Caudillo*) exercises the most absolute authority to its fullest extent. The *Caudillo* is responsible before God and History.

It was in this strange form of words that the notion that God and history were on Franco's side became State doctrine in Spain. Henceforth, Franco was not merely the giver of the word and maker of the law, but in effect above the law.

7 *The Conquest of the North*

After the Italian setback at Guadalajara, Franco felt free to devote the major part of his military effort to the conquest of north-western Spain. Strategically, the operation made sense, for if successful it would give Nationalist Spain the industrial base it lacked. There was no question in Franco's mind, however, of indulging in the lightning moves – the *Blitzkrieg* – which the Germans would have liked to see. For as he told Roberto Cantalupo, he was 'liberating Spain, not making war on her'.

Mussolini's envoy had become so pessimistic after Guadalajara that the Duce recalled him and about 18 April he had a farewell talk with Franco, who outlined his plans to him in explicit detail.[1] This is the way Cantalupo recorded the Generalissimo's words:

I must not exterminate the enemy, nor destroy the cities, the countryside, industries and production. For that reason, I must not be in a hurry. *If I were in a hurry, I should be a bad Spaniard. If I were in a hurry, I should not be a patriot but would be behaving like a foreigner.**

To liberate, Franco went on, also meant to reclaim or rehabilitate. If he did not do this, he would not have accomplished anything. To recapture cities held by the Reds was relatively easy; but he also had to save the Reds themselves. There was a necessarily slow job of redemption and pacification to be done, without which the military occupation would be largely useless. The moral redemption of zones already occupied was bound to be slow and difficult, for the roots of anarchy in Spain were old and deep. Nor was it simply a question, as Cantalupo feared, of restoring the old Spain, but of ushering in the Spain of tomorrow. He went on:

The tactics of the Spanish war are a function of the policy I have just explained. I need gradual stages corresponding to the means at my disposal . . . I shall occupy city after city, village after village, railway line after railway line. The thwarted offensives on Madrid have taught me that I have to abandon my programme of total, grandiose and immediate liberation. Region after region, success after success: the people on the other side will understand and will know how to wait. No amount of argument will make me depart from this gradual programme. There will be less glory but more internal peace, afterwards. After each of my successes there will be fewer Reds in front of me, and behind me as well. Seen in this light, this civil war could last another year, two or perhaps three. . . .

It would be very dangerous, Franco added, to get to Madrid too soon as the result of a big-scale military action. He would not get there an hour sooner than was necessary: before doing so, he would have to be certain that he was able to found a new régime there, and establish the capital of the new Spain.

In conclusion, Franco asked Cantalupo to warn Mussolini's government, which was in a great hurry – a haste which he under-

* The italicized words appear in French in Cantalupo's text, Franco having spoken in a mixture of French and Spanish.

stood because of the sacrifices Mussolini had made for the Nationalist victory – that he would not modify his plans:

> Give me planes, give me artillery, give me tanks and ammunition, give me your diplomatic support, and I shall be very grateful. . . . But above all do not make me hurry, do not oblige me to win at top speed, for this would mean killing more Spaniards, destroying a greater part of the national wealth, and, in consequence, to make the foundations of my government ever more unsteady.

This important testimony from the departing Italian ambassador undoubtedly reflected Franco's military and political thinking at the time, although – as we shall see – he did, at least once more, allow himself to be tempted by the prospect of a decisive blow against Madrid. By and large, however, and in the face of mounting pressure from his allies – sometimes in favour of faster action, sometimes in favour of a negotiated peace – the Generalissimo stuck to his programme of gradual reconquest and consolidation. As Gabriel Jackson – a strong opponent of the Nationalist side in the Civil War – comments, after summarizing Cantalupo's report:

The iron will, the idealism, and the absolute centering of the
cause in his own person were clear to Cantalupo. They became
increasingly clear to all Spaniards and many foreigners in the further course of the Civil War. No Falangist leader, no other general,
and no figure of the traditional Right compared remotely with
Franco in power and determination.[2]

When Roberto Cantalupo had his farewell talk with Franco, the
offensive against Bilbao was eighteen days old. It had begun on 31
March 1937, with an attack in the Vitoria sector. Mola was in overall
command of the operation, with General Solchaga in the field. On
the Nationalist side were 50,000 men, mainly the Navarre Brigades,
with a small Italo-Spanish reserve. The defenders numbered some
10,000 more; they were protected by mountains and by an intricate
complex of trenches to which the name of 'iron belt' had been given.
When Franco examined reconnaissance pictures of these fortifications,
however, he exclaimed: 'What a mistake! What a tremendous mistake!' The lines of trenches indeed were so long that they would have
required far more men to man them than the Basque soldiers disposed of. Moreover, observation posts and firing points had been
arranged without regard to their military utility.[3]

The first phase of the Nationalist advance, however, was slow,
owing partly to torrential rains, and partly to desperate Republican
resistance. On 29 April, the Nationalists entered the Basque town
of Guernica, which was found to be totally destroyed. So deep-
rooted is the belief that the destruction was the work of German
bombers of the autonomous Condor division that it is not easy even
to admit the possibility that this might not be the archetypal example
of Nazi frightfulness which I, for one, had always assumed it to be –
being encouraged in this belief by the considerable success of Picasso's painting, *Guernica*. The facts, however, are in dispute; and Luis
Bolín, in *Spain: the Vital Years*, has collected powerful evidence in
an Appendix (pp. 355–60) to suggest that the major part of the
destruction was caused by the retreating Republicans, who dyna-
mited most of the buildings. Since the evidence consists mainly of
Nationalist field reports that were not intended for publication, due
weight must be given to it. Whatever the proportionate degree of
responsibility, it is clear that neither Franco nor Mola was consulted
or informed about any German decision to bomb the town. It is,

however, by no means certain that the Germans bombed Guernica at all; that they did not is the likeliest inference to be drawn from an exchange of telegrams found in the captured German archives.[4] Nationalist planes did, however, bomb the railway station and an arms factory – both legitimate military targets. Ironically, the balance of probability seems to me to indicate that the Nazis – who have had so much to answer for – were wrongly blamed for the destruction of Guernica. But German and Nationalist denials notwithstanding, Guernica became a symbol of Nazi terror from the air, and the whole affair did more to damage the Nationalist cause abroad than any previous incident in the Civil War.

Within a day or so of the destruction of Guernica, the Nationalists completed their preliminary objectives – the occupation of a semi-circle of territory running from south of Bilbao to the coastal village of Bermeo, north-east of the City. The second – and last – phase of the offensive was to be the assault on Bilbao's 'iron belt'. Franco flew up north to discuss the timing of the operation with Mola, and the two generals agreed on a pause to regroup their forces.

Taking advantage of the lull, the Basques launched furious counter-attacks which, for a time, cut off Bermeo from the rest of the Nationalist semi-circle. Not long before, the Basque government had sent out feelers to Franco, proposing a separate peace on condition that the Nationalists promised the Basques limited autonomy.[5] Since Franco's war aims included a firm insistence on the unity of the Spanish State, these proposals were rejected. Now, with their temporary success on the Bermeo front, the Basques felt optimistic, and prematurely proclaimed the imminence of a new Guadalajara.

They spoke too soon, for almost immediately – early in May – the Nationalists resumed their advance, again in heavy and continuous rain. Although they did not know it, there were still several weeks of heavy fighting ahead of them; and before Bilbao could be taken, an unexpected event deeply shocked Nationalist morale.

On 3 June, General Mola took off by air from the front, for Burgos, where he was to confer with the Generalissimo on the final details of the assault on Bilbao. His pilot, Chamorro, had often made the trip before. A heavy and deceptive mist, however, made him lose his bearings and the plane crashed into the side of a hill near Castile de Peones, in Burgos Province. The pilot, Mola and the other passengers were all killed.

It is well known that General Franco heard the news of his old friend's death with surprising equanimity, and even – according to Faupel – with relief. His remark to Kindelán, who brought the news, about the loss of Mola's *peace-time* talents has already been mentioned. Faupel described his reaction in these words:

> . . . the Generalissimo undoubtedly feels relieved by the death of General Mola. He told me recently: 'Mola was a stubborn fellow, and when I gave him directives which differed from his own proposals he often asked me: "Don't you trust my leadership any more?" '[6]

These reactions have been put forward to support the rumour that Franco had ordered a time-bomb to be placed in Mola's plane before take-off – just as it had been alleged that he had caused Sanjurjo's plane to be sabotaged before the death crash of 20 July 1936. It is, of course, quite impossible to throw precise juridical light on these events of thirty years ago. But to have committed either deed would have been utterly out of character. Ruthless though he was towards the 'Reds' of 'anti-Spain', Franco never liquidated his friends, even when they turned against him, much less when their presence was merely inconvenient, and less still on the eve of an important battle. Even Hedilla was reprieved. For former companions-in-arms who plotted against him punishment was often astonishingly light: reprimand, a posting abroad, demotion – even promotion in the sense of 'kicking upstairs'. But not death. Moreover, there was no need for Franco to remove Mola in June 1937, for whatever his private feelings, the former 'Director' of the *Alzamiento* had accepted Franco as Generalissimo, 'swallowed' his assumption of supreme political power, and acquiesced in the creation of a ruling party at the Caudillo's orders.

The fact remains that Mola's death removed the last figure with prestige and intelligence to compare with Franco's own. (Queipo de Llano was hardly of comparable calibre.) Politically, the Caudillo's astonishing run of luck continued (or, as his more sycophantic biographers would put it, the finger of God went on interceding on his behalf). The only two soldiers who could have challenged him – Sanjurjo and Mola – had died. The only two civilians who might have reached the top in politics were gone – Calvo Sotelo, murdered;

José Antonio Primo de Rivera, executed. Even the minor prophets of fascism, Redondo and Ledesma Ramos, had been killed. And Franco himself had removed the minor challengers to his power: Fal Conde, in exile; and Hedilla in solitary confinement. More than ever, the little general cast a giant shadow on a flat landscape of Nationalist mediocrity.

Mola's sudden death, convenient though it might have been in one sense, was nevertheless extremely unfortunate in the military circumstances of June 1937. For the time being, Franco himself, having transferred his headquarters from Salamanca to Burgos, directed the Bilbao operations. On the eve of the final attack, however, he appointed one of his staff officers, General Dávila, to succeed General Mola as Commander of the Army of the North. On 19 June, General Dávila's forces entered Bilbao, and started distributing food to the population, which had greatly suffered from a prolonged naval blockade. Between 20,000 and 30,000 Republicans had lost their lives; 14,000 prisoners were in Nationalist hands.

The capture of Bilbao was one of the decisive victories of the Civil War. It gave Franco his first major industrial centre, iron ore, and a

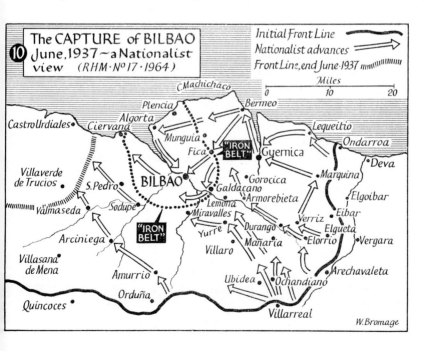

The CAPTURE of BILBAO
June, 1937 — a Nationalist view   (RHM·Nº 17·1964)

Initial Front Line
Nationalist advances
Front Line, end June 1937

W. Bromage

first-class port. It brought the number of provincial capitals in Nationalist hands to thirty-four – out of fifty. From now on, final victory seemed assured.

General Faupel, the Nazi envoy, however, took a sour view of Franco's success, pointing out that it had taken the Nationalists eleven weeks to cover forty kilometres, whereas with better assault troops, they should have been able to do it in three. He attributed this slow progress, in part, to Franco's differences with the Italian General Doria. Franco had wanted to use the two available Italian divisions for some easy operation to condition them for battle, but Doria had refused, insisting that his troops be used 'only for a decisive action which promised great success'. Franco, on the other hand, had rightly taken the stand that another military reverse for the Italians – who had also been responsible for the temporary setback at Bermeo, was intolerable. As a result, the bulk of the Italians had remained inactive.[7]

In the same interesting report, Faupel observed that General Franco, evidently having learned from the experience of the 'senseless shootings' in Málaga, had forbidden large troop detachments from entering and remaining in Bilbao, 'and thus avoided possible excesses'.

Franco was about to regroup his troops for a further offensive, this time against Santander – on the Cantabrian coast due west of Bilbao – when a telegram from the Madrid front informed him that General Miaja had launched a powerful offensive in the Brunete sector, about twelve miles west of the capital. It was 6 July, and Miaja had attacked during the night. Franco immediately suspended operations on the northern front and ordered all available planes to fly to airfields in the centre.

The situation looked critical, for Miaja had thrown 60,000 men against weakly defended Nationalist positions. With the defenders were 20 artillery batteries, 128 tanks and 150 planes. Varela was put in charge of the Nationalist defence. Meanwhile, Franco mobilized fleets of lorries and commandeered trains to transport reinforcements from Aranda de Duero, Salamanca, Caceres and the northern front. In torrid summer heat, the Nationalists were pushed back with heavy losses.

On 12 July, Franco moved into a property at Villa del Prado,

where he set up battle headquarters, making frequent visits to
Varela's headquarters at Sevilla la Nueva, and often turning up
unexpectedly at points uncomfortably close to the fighting. So close,
indeed, that one day Varela gently chided him, using the familiar
'*tu*', for exposing himself to enemy fire: 'What are you doing here,
mi General? Don't you understand that if anything happens to you,
I'll be held responsible?'

Franco hesitated, then gave in and left.[8]

Varela launched his counter-attack on 18 July, but it was not until
24 July, when he threw in his Moroccan reserves, that the Republicans began to be driven back. By that time, the German pilots on the
Nationalist side had established complete air superiority. Next day,
the Battle of Brunete ended with a Nationalist victory. The 25 July,
as Franco pointed out, was the Feast Day of Santiago Apóstol, patron
saint of Spain. It was at this time that Franco really began to believe
that God was intervening on his behalf.[9]

Victory though it was, Brunete had been costly, for Nationalist
casualties amounted to more than 12,000. For the Republicans, however, Brunete was a Verdun – a frightful blood-letting in which the
élite of the International Brigades lost their lives. The Republican
casualty list reached 25,000.[10] About a hundred Republican planes
had been brought down, for the loss of twenty-three Nationalist
aircraft.

Elated by his hard-won victory, General Varela wanted to pursue
the retreating enemy, and reduce the Escorial salient to the North.
Once that was done, he argued, Madrid would be wide open. Franco,
however, turned down this proposal in the following words:
'Santander has to be captured so that we can finish off the war in the
North, and I have only a few weeks left, for after that the fogs will
be coming, the rains, and the snows on the heights. I get the point
that we could destroy the Escorial salient, but this would mean
delaying *sine die* the victory in the Cantabrian region.'[11]

Thus Franco stuck to the strategic plan he had outlined to
Cantalupo. Ordering Varela to fortify the gains made at Brunete, he
went back to Salamanca and started attending to the logistics of the
Santander operation. For once, the impending onset of the autumn
made him think in *Blitzkrieg* terms. On 14 August, General Dávila,
in tactical command, launched three Navarrese brigades towards the
coast with the object of cutting off the Popular Front forces from

K

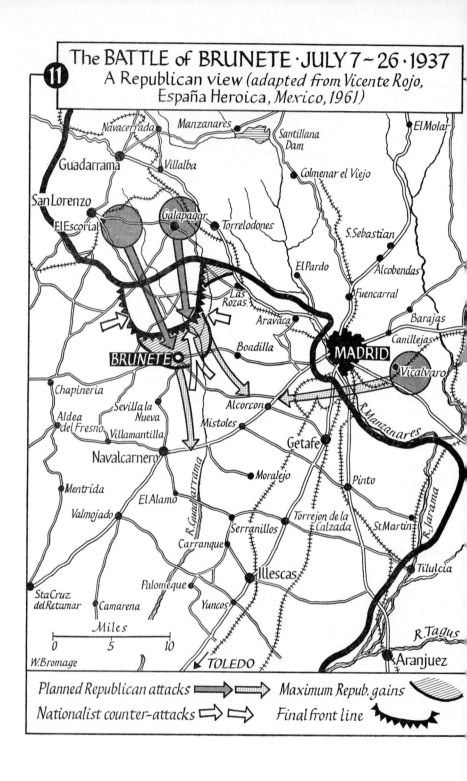

The BATTLE of BRUNETE · JULY 7 ~ 26 · 1937
A Republican view (adapted from Vicente Rojo,
España Heroica, Mexico, 1961)

Planned Republican attacks ➡ ➡ Maximum Repub. gains
Nationalist counter-attacks ⇨ ⇨ Final front line

Miles
0   5   10

W.Bromage

Asturias. All told, he had 106 battalions at his orders, including twenty Italian units – purged of officers and men deemed insufficiently combative – Basques and Castilians, and six mixed Italian and Spanish battalions, known as 'Black Arrows'. Facing them was General Gamir Ulibarri with sixty battalions.

Franco had moved to battle headquarters at Aguilar de Campo, some fifty miles from the coast. This time, Popular Front resistance was brief. By 18 July, the Republicans were demoralized, and three leading officers had fled for Bayonne by air. On 26 July, Dávila and the Italian General Bastico entered Santander. General Ulibarri had fled to safety in a submarine, in the company of his staff and local Republican politicians.

The Generalissimo was so elated by the fall of Santander, that he forgot his customary reserve on hearing the news, flung open his office door and shouted: 'We've taken Santander! Santander is ours! *Arriba España!*'[12]

A week later, L. M. Lojendio, a member of the Caudillo's recently constituted press office, prepared a report for Franco on the importance of the latest victory, under the title of *Los Efectos de la Liberación de Santander*.[13] He summarized the consequences under three headings:

1 COMMERCIAL AND ECONOMIC Santander was the second great port on the Cantabrian Sea to fall into Nationalist hands. With Bilbao it was one of the two main export points for iron ore. It would now, therefore, be possible to trade with England, and this in turn would benefit Nationalist Spain's commercial balance. The mineral riches of Santander Province were considerable and the large metallurgical works at Reinosa in the south-west was an important potential base for a war industry. Until the fall of Bilbao and Santander, the Nationalists were superior to the 'Reds' in agriculture but inferior in industry; now the imbalance was rectified.

2 STRATEGIC The fall of Santander left the 'Reds' with only two ports in the region – Gijon and Aviles. It would now be correspondingly easier than it had been to blockade the Cantabrian coast.

3 MILITARY A 'Red' army of 75,000 to 80,000 men, under General Gamir Ulibarri, had been defeated. Enough war material had been captured to supply an entire army. Captured cannon alone numbered 38, and between 50,000 and 55,000 prisoners had been

taken, most of whom had joined the Nationalist Army in battle formation with all their equipment.

The most significant consequence of the fall of Santander to the Nationalists, however, was one that Franco worked out for himself: he was now strong enough to begin to stand up to the Germans – especially in resisting the economic demands they continued to make. The time for a direct clash with the Germans had not quite come however: before that, Franco reckoned he would have to take the Asturian stronghold of Gijon. Meanwhile, he could demonstrate his new commercial independence. As Lojendio had pointed out, possession of Santander meant that Nationalist Spain could start exporting iron ore to Britain. And this Franco now proceeded to do, on a considerable scale, using the foreign exchange so earned to buy American vehicles in preference to German and Italian ones.

The reactivation of mineral production in the Cantabrian provinces over the next year was indeed a minor economic miracle and a major factor in Franco's victory. In Vizcaya province, the output of iron ore in the first year of Nationalist rule was three times as high as it had been under the Republic during the first year of the war; and indeed higher than the average of the previous five years. Exports of ore from Bilbao to Germany increased considerably, as compared with the Republican period; but exports to Britain remained much greater, as Nationalist commentators recorded, with apparent approval.[14] In 1936, the monthly average of iron ore exports to Germany and Britain respectively were 2,000 and 51,416 metric tons; for 1937, the corresponding figures were 10,917 and 42,000 In March 1938, for the sake of comparison, 9,732 tons of ore were exported to Germany and 46,615 to Britain.

In general, the economic situation in Nationalist Spain improved fast during the second half of 1937, and towards the end of September, Franco's staff was reporting to him that the National peseta was still being exchanged on the Paris money market at the rate of 100 for 180 French francs – the value to which the Republican peseta had fallen ten days after the outbreak of the Civil War (from an official rate of 207.5); whereas 100 Valencian pesetas now fetched only 50 francs – a loss of 85 per cent of their par value.[15]

A week later, the Caudillo's staff estimated that prices of everyday commodities were now four to ten times as high in the 'Red' zones as in the Nationalist ones, though it was admitted that lack of data made such calculations hazardous.[16] To a large extent, this satisfactory situation reflected the competence of Franco's economic advisers, Joaquín Bau (Trade and Industry) and Andrés Amado (Finance). But above all, it reflected international confidence in the Franco régime, despite the military scepticism of the Germans.

Now Franco really did feel strong enough to defy the Germans. With typical caution and cunning, however, he chose, not a direct confrontation but a measure that did not appear to be aimed at the Germans in particular. The Technical *Junta*, now under the chairmanship of General Count Gómez Jordana (soon to become Franco's Foreign Minister) drew up a decree, in the drafting of which Joaquín Bau played an important part. Franco approved it, and it was published on 9 October. The decree simply abolished all mining concessions granted since the beginning of the Civil War and limited foreign capital holdings in Spanish enterprises to twenty-five per cent, stipulating that control was to remain in Spanish hands.

Although the decree was couched in such general terms, it was clearly aimed at the Germans. Within less than two weeks of the outbreak of the Civil War, Bernhardt, the Tetuan Nazi who had acted as Franco's messenger to Hitler in July 1936, had been rewarded by being made head of a new Hispano-German export-import company, known cumbrously as HISMA-ROWAK (*Compañía Hispano-Marroquí de Transportes/Rohstoffe und Waren Einkaufsgesellschaft*). Under this arrangement, Germany as a country and Bernhardt as an individual had benefited enormously, mainly from the export to Germany of ore from the Anglo-French Riff mines, which were expropriated by the Nationalists. On 20 March 1937, the Germans and Spaniards had signed a secret protocol at Salamanca, providing for co-operation against communism and intensified economic relations.[17] In July, the Germans confidently expected that Germany would get nearly all the output of the iron mines around Bilbao and negotiated three secret protocols with Franco's régime, the purpose of which was to obtain a favoured place for Germany in trade and investment in the Spanish market.[18]

And now came the Decree of 9 October, together with the news – disquieting to German ears – of forthcoming British economic negotiations with Spain. Only three days later, on 12 October, General Franco felt bold enough to make a speech proclaiming that 'Spain does not admit speculations on its sovereignty.'[19] He had chosen a day which the Nationalists had set aside as the Festival of the (Spanish) Race; but the irony of the compliment to Nazi racialism implicit in this form of words was brutally apparent. The speech itself was aimed at the Germans, and they knew it.

By this time, Franco's army had fought off a massive but inefficient diversionary offensive on the Aragon front – the principal objective of which, had it succeeded, would have been Saragossa – and had launched his own final offensive in Asturias. On 21 October, Gijon – the scene of fierce fighting in the miner's revolution of 1934 – fell to the Nationalists, whole battalions of the Republican Army changing sides amidst scenes of 'indescribable emotion'.[20] Apart from mopping up – which proved much tougher than Franco had expected – Asturias belonged to Franco, bringing up to 62 per cent the proportion of Spain's total area under Nationalist control. By now, only 10 million people or so remained under Republican rule; 13,560,000 lived in the Nationalist zones.[21]

The German Foreign Ministry followed all these developments with a jaundiced eye. General Faupel had been removed from Salamanca at the end of August and replaced a few weeks later by

von Stohrer, an amiable career diplomat of enormous stature. Von Stohrer soon showed that he attached less importance to following the political intrigues in Salamanca than his predecessor, and more to improving Germany's economic stake in Spain. He sought, and obtained, reassurances from Franco that his régime's economic negotiations with Britain – which had now yielded a consular agreement – did not mean that German interests were forgotten.[22]

A further démarche by Stohrer, this time about the 9 October Decree, brought an evasive reply from the Caudillo, who declared that 'the decree had been issued because of the danger that the Red Government might sell out everything, and that German interests would be protected'.[23] The new German Ambassador's report, however, entirely failed to satisfy Goering, who had begun to take a personal interest in the question. The 'Colonel General' as Goering then was, exploded. His 'unusually great personal assistance to General Franco,' he told his underlings, 'gave him the right to make very definite demands with regard to the safeguarding of the German "war booty".' He therefore proposed to send a special envoy to Salamanca to 'hold a pistol to General Franco's breast'. He was however, talked out of this drastic, if figurative, step.[24]

By then a new and unexpected factor had appeared in the equation: the Chamberlain government in London had been quietly negotiating *de facto* diplomatic relations with Franco's régime, and on 16 November, Sir Robert Hodgson was appointed British 'agent' in Nationalist Spain – a gesture which the Nationalists returned six days later by accrediting the duke of Alba as their agent in London. This news aroused misgivings in Berlin, which subsequent developments did little to justify. Sir Robert Hodgson and his staff did not arrive in Salamanca until 16 December 1937, and soon found that they were 'exceedingly unpopular' among the Nationalists.[25]

Stohrer was nevertheless instructed to complain to Salamanca that according to 'reliable information' in German hands Franco's concessions to England exceeded those he had admitted; and to tell him that Germany would reconsider her policy unless guarantees were given for vital German economic interests.[26] We next find Stohrer complaining to Sangróniz – who, in effect, was Franco's Foreign Minister in the Technical *Junta* – about unreasonable delays on the Spanish side in granting seventy-three mining concessions which the Germans had requested. On 16 December, Stohrer reported that

Sangróniz – evidently well briefed by the canny Caudillo – had countered his pleas with the following arguments:

- The question was of the greatest importance for Spain and therefore could not be disposed of in a hurry.

- The Spanish government was a provisional one which could not proceed precipitately in such matters.

- Each of the 73 concessions had to be examined separately.

- Any arrangements 'had to be compatible with the general stipulations of Spanish law.'[27]

Stohrer was not, in fact, within sight of getting satisfaction from Franco; though he was not to know this at the time.

As for the Italians, they were never to get full compensation, or anything like it, for the impressive military supplies they had sent to Nationalist Spain. Through SAFNI – a joint Italo–Spanish trading company set up in August 1936 – the Nationalists exported brown coal, woollen goods and olive oil to Italy, in part-payment for Italian military deliveries. To the Spaniards' annoyance, the Italians re-bottled the olive oil and sold it abroad as Italian.[28] By November 1937, the Nationalist war debt to Italy had reached 3,000 million lire, but Mussolini could hardly have supposed that he would ever get repaid. In any event, he was so committed by now that money or no money, he was in it for the duration.

What annoyed the Italians far more than any mere quarrel over finance, however, was General Franco's refusal to allocate to Italian troops the glorious role which Mussolini thought should be theirs by right. On 3 December 1937, von Stohrer reported that he knew from eye-witnesses that 'a violent scene' had occurred between Franco and the former Italian commander-in-chief, General Bastico.* Franco, he said, had spoken disparagingly about Italian military aid and about the failure of military operations because of quarrels on the Italian side 'over matters of vanity and prestige'.[29] On their side, too, the Italians were full of complaints.

---

* The name 'Bastico' appears as 'Bastiani' in the text of Document No. 477, *Documents on German Foreign Policy*, Series D, Vol. III – doubtless a slip on Stohrer's part.

Now, more than ever, the Caudillo might reflect that friends could be more difficult than enemies. He was not, however, a man to allow himself to be thrown off course by hostile criticism when convinced that time would prove him right. When it came to it, it was he who laughed longest and last.

8 Franco 'blends' a Government

In the spring of 1937, the battlefields of north-western Spain were not the only place where Spaniards were killing Spaniards with political intent. On 3 May, and for four or five days after, an obscure but vicious little civil war took place in the streets of Barcelona, while the wider Civil War went on far from Catalonia. It began when the Catalan government police chief raided the telephone building, which was under the control of the Anarchist CNT. The police chief, Rodríguez Salas, was a prominent man in the *Partido Socialista Unificado de Cataluña* or PSUC – the joint Socialist–Communist party of Catalonia.

The firing started. Some of those who fired knew why they were firing and at whom; some just fired because others were firing, or in self-defence. Broadly speaking, the anti-Stalinist Marxist party, POUM (*Partido Obrero de Unificación Marxista*), supported the CNT against the PSUC. But it was an untidy little war, for in the end order was restored by Assault Guards commanded by a CNT member. The dead numbered five hundred or more, with twice that number wounded.

The importance of Barcelona's little civil war, however, did not lie in the number of dead so much as in the fact that it gave the Communists the chance they had long been waiting for to get rid of Largo Caballero. Like a once-juicy lemon, the old Socialist firebrand had been squeezed and squeezed by the Communists until – as far as their advantage lay – he was dry. At first he had been flattered to be called 'the Lenin of Spain'. Once in power as Prime Minister, however, it had not taken him long to realize that the Communists – from Marcel Rosenberg, the Soviet Ambassador, to the Spaniard José Díaz – wanted to use him for their own ends. He fiercely

resisted communist demands for the unification of the Socialist and
Communist parties. On 17 April 1937, he approved a decree placing
the predominantly communist political commissars in the Republican
Army under his personal control. He dissolved the communist-
controlled Madrid defence *Junta*. And for good measure, he had
Marcel Rosenberg recalled to Moscow.

The Communists did not propose to stand for such independence.
Skilfully, Rosenberg, while he was still in Valencia, Díaz and the
Argentine-Italian Codovilla cultivated good relations with Largo
Caballero's great Socialist rival, Indalecio Prieto. For reasons of his
own, principally the desire to get rid of Largo, Prieto proved surprisingly amenable to communist suasions – ready, for instance, to
agree to the fusion of the Socialist and Communist parties.[1]

On 13 May, the Spanish Communist Party brought matters to a
crisis. The two Communist ministers in Caballero's cabinet called on
him to dissolve the POUM. Caballero refused, and after a stormy
meeting, the Communists walked out of the Cabinet meeting.
Simultaneously, the Russians let it be known that they would not
provide aircraft for an offensive in Extremadura, which Largo
Caballero had long been planning. In the ensuing ministerial crisis,
the moderate Socialists sided with the Communists and Largo
Caballero was forced out of office. The road was now clear for the
appointment by President Azaña of the man the Communists wanted
as Prime Minister – Juan Negrín. And on 17 May, Negrín duly took
over.

But why Negrín? Why a moderate Socialist instead of a revolutionary firebrand? In fact, the Communists – from Stalin in Moscow
to his agents in Spain – wanted less revolution, not more. They
wanted to reassure liberal supporters of the Republic in various
countries, who might have been scared by the course of events in
Republican territory. For such purposes, the easy-going, prosperous,
easy-living Negrín was a perfect choice. Later, the then Soviet
Intelligence chief in western Europe, General Krivitsky, was to tell
the story in detail. It was Stashevsky, the Soviet trade representative
in Spain, who had picked Negrín for the premiership. And indeed,
as Krivitsky observed:

He was just the type to suit Stalin's needs . . . He would impress
the outside world with the 'sanity' and 'propriety' of the Spanish

Republican cause; he would frighten nobody by revolutionary remarks . . .

Doctor Negrín, of course, saw the only salvation of his country in close co-operation with the Soviet Union. It had become obvious that active support could come only from that source. He was ready to go along with Stalin in everything, sacrificing all other considerations to secure this aid.[2]

A savage, Communist-organized persecution of the POUM now began, culminating in the murder of its leader Andrés Nin. The Communists did not, however, succeed in dominating the first Negrín cabinet as completely as they had hoped, for Prieto, who had become Defence Minister, behaved in office much as Largo Caballero had, as far as the Communists were concerned, resisting most of their demands and going so far – on 18 November – as to remove Álvarez del Vayo as head of the Political Commissariat, and indeed abolishing the system of commissars entirely. For this, the Russians did to Prieto as Defence Minister what they had done earlier to Largo Caballero as Prime Minister: they reduced their military supplies to the Republican forces.[3]

Partly because of this calculated parsimony, and partly because Franco, on his side, was regrouping and reorganizing his forces, there was a lull in the fighting during the autumn of 1937. By the end of the year, the Nationalist Army had grown to 582,000 men (including 50,000 to 60,000 Moroccans), in comparison with 492,000 men on the Popular Front side.[4] The success of the Nationalist build-up, together with the conclusive nature of Franco's victories in the Basque provinces and the relative inactivity on the Republican side, led the Generalissimo to reconsider the plan for a war of attrition which he had outlined to Ambassador Cantalupo. Once again, he was thinking of bringing the war to an end with a massive assault on Madrid.

Mopping up in the Asturian mountains, where some 18,000 troops had taken refuge, took a good six weeks. Then bad weather set in on the Madrid front. While Franco was waiting for more encouraging conditions, the Republicans took him by surprise with a powerful offensive against Teruel, due east of Madrid and about one hundred miles inland from the Mediterranean. It was 15 December. Once again, General Franco had to abandon the tempting idea of entering the capital of Spain.

Militarily, the Teruel offensive made sense. Perched on a rocky promontory above the Guadalaviar river, the town was weakly defended by a garrison of fewer than 6,000 men. Against them, the Republican General Hernández Sarabia was able to muster 100,000 troops. His aim was to encircle Teruel, cutting it off from its communications with Saragossa, then move in for the kill. In the interests of surprise, he had ordered his men forward in deep snow and without attempting to bomb the city from the air. It was a successful manœuvre, and by the end of the first day the town was isolated.

Caught off balance, Franco listened to advice from his staff officers, then discarded it. They were advising him to strike much closer to Madrid, between Alcala de Henares and Guadalajara, with the object of drawing off some of the troops attacking Teruel. His decision, however, was to go straight to the rescue of the Teruel garrison. In so doing, he had two reasons, which were typical of Franco's way of thinking. One was military: he wanted to grasp the chance of destroying a large Republican force (thereby disproving Ciano's facile theory that he was interested in gaining ground, not annihilating the enemy). The other reason was human and psychological: Franco had vowed to himself that he would never allow a town or city that had joined the Nationalist cause to fall into 'Red' hands, because of the near certainty of reprisals on the population, and because the Nationalist Army must never be defeated, even if it could not always be victorious.[5] This way, as he knew, morale would always remain high on his side, and low on the Popular Front side.

Franco therefore rapidly organized a force for the relief of Teruel, which he entrusted to General Dávila, with General Varela in operational command of forces drawn from the Madrid front, and General Aranda of troops from the Huesca–Saragossa sector.

Benefiting from surprise, the Republican forces soon reached Teruel, and on 22 December, the Spanish and Catalan newspapers in Barcelona – where the government had moved from Valencia at the end of October – proclaimed the capture of the town in banner headlines. The news was premature, for the garrison continued to resist until mid-January, some of the defenders having laid down their arms on 7 January 1938.[6]

On the Nationalist side, too, optimism got the better of veracity. On 31 December 1937, the Generalissimo, in an order of the day from Salamanca, proclaimed that the Nationalist forces had arrived at Teruel, putting the Reds to flight amidst indescribable enthusiasm.[7] The Nationalists had indeed reached the scene that day, but they ran into a terrible snowstorm with the thermometer plunging to minus 2° F – 34 degrees of frost – which slowed down their effort. When it became evident that a long, hard battle was in prospect, Franco moved to a Special Operations Section near the front, consisting of two sleeper carriages, a dining car and another carriage that had been equipped as an office. It was still intensely cold, and the office carriage was coupled to a locomotive kept under steam so that the carriage temperature could be raised to a 'working' level.[8]

Teruel was not recaptured until 23 February. It was a dismal victory, for the entering Nationalists found the town totally ruined, with 98 per cent of the buildings destroyed: in the grim chaos of stones there reigned 'bestial filth and repugnant fetidness'.[9]

Dismal though the scene was, however, Franco had won yet another victory. The famous Communist guerrilla specialist *El Campesino* (Valentín González) had fled, and nearly 17,000 prisoners (actually 16,298) had been captured in the last seventeen days of the Nationalist offensive. In addition, as the Generalissimo's press office recorded for home consumption, 9,753 'Marxist bodies' had been 'piously buried'. Who, one might ask, were these 'Marxist bodies'? There were Assault Guards among them, members of the Washington and Lincoln battalions of the American International Brigade, and soldiers of the notorious Lister Brigade – 'famous for its crimes and barbarism' – which, at last, had been smashed.[10] (In fact, however, the Lister Brigade was soon in action again.)

On the military side, as we have seen, the last month of 1937 and the first two months of 1938 had been a very busy and even anxious time for Franco. But politically, too, he and his staff were extended. While he was reacting to the new military threat at Teruel, he was also finding time to transform the Burgos *Juntas* into his first government. No doubt the energetic Serrano Súñer – already referred to in jest as the *Cuñadísimo* (or 'brother-in-law to the Nth power') – was doing most of the paper work. But in the end, then as always, all decisions had to be referred to the Caudillo; and it was he, and no one else, who made the appointments.

If, as I have suggested, the Generalissimo's creation of a single

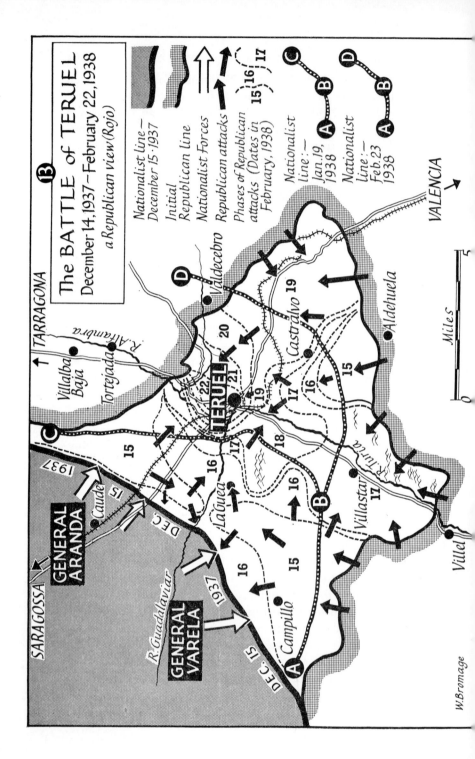

13

The BATTLE of TERUEL
December 14, 1937–February 22, 1938
a Republican view (Rojo)

Nationalist line —
December 15 · 1937

Initial
Republican line

Nationalist Forces

Republican attacks

Phases of Republican
attacks (Dates in
February, 1938)

Nationalist
line: —
Jan. 19,
1938

Nationalist
line: —
Feb. 23
1938

SARAGOSSA

TARRAGONA

GENERAL ARANDA

GENERAL VARELA

Caudé

Villalba Baja

Tortajada

R. Alfambra

Valdecebro

Castralvo

Aldehuela

TERUEL

La Guea

Campillo

Villastar

R. Turia

Villel

VALENCIA

R. Guadalaviar

DEC. 15 1937

DEC 15 1937

Miles

0   5

W. Bromage

ruling party was primarily a *military* operation, here was his first truly *political* exercise. It makes a fascinating and instructive study, for it set the pattern for Franco's continuing hold on power. The main secret was a careful, almost pharmaceutically measured, blend of the political ingredients in Franco's camp, so that none should feel left out and none should be dominant. But there were other secrets too, as will emerge.

General Franco published his list of ministers on 30 January 1938, during a lull in the Battle of Teruel. There was something for every-body: for the Alfonsists and the Carlists, for the *camisas viejas* of the old Falange and for the new Falangists of the FET; and finally, for the Army itself – the main prop of Franco's power. There was indeed and conveniently, some overlapping, since the same man could, of course, be both a general and a monarchist, thus strengthening Franco's hand on both counts.

The two most important appointments were those of Ramón Serrano Súñer as Minister of the Interior and General Count Gómez Jordana as Foreign Minister and deputy Prime Minister. Serrano, of course, represented the new Falange; but he was flanked by old Falangists, such as Raimundo Fernández Cuesta – the most obvious political rival of the *Cuñadísimo*. Fernández Cuesta was forty-one in 1938. Like Serrano Súñer, he had had a legal training, and indeed had been a member of the Corps of Naval Lawyers. Like Serrano, too, he was a friend of José Antonio's; but unlike Serrano, he had actually joined José Antonio's party, and *el Ausente* had appointed him National Secretary of the Falange in 1934. After several stays in Republican gaols, he was released when Franco exchanged him for a Republican prisoner. It is typical of Franco's policy of never allowing any of his supporters to acquire too much power that in December 1937, when Serrano Súñer was resented for behaving as though he were the boss of the FET, Franco appointed Fernández Cuesta as Secretary-general of the ruling party and first Secretary of its Political *Junta*. Now, in January 1938, he joined Franco's first cabinet as Minister of Agriculture. And this, too, was typical, for while Fernández Cuesta had become more powerful than Serrano within the FET, the Ministry of Agriculture naturally carried considerably less weight than the Ministry of the Interior, which had been given to Serrano. Another old Falangist, Pedro Sainz Rodríguez, was also appointed to the new cabinet, as Minister of Education; but Pedro

González Bueno, a new Falangist (newer, at any rate, than Saínz and Fernández Cuesta) was also in, as Minister of the Syndicates (trade unions).

On the Monarchist and military side, two generals joined the government. One, as we have seen, was Jordana as Foreign Minister; and the other was Martínez Anido, who now became Minister of Public Order. Jordana, who was to display qualities of exceptional statesmanship during the Second World War, was already over sixty in 1938, having graduated from the General Military Academy in 1892, the year of Franco's birth. He served in Cuba and Morocco and in 1923 became a member of Primo de Rivera's Military Directorate. King Alfonso conferred an earldom on him in 1925 for his part in the Alhucemas Bay landing. Three years later, he was appointed High Commissioner in Morocco, but was gaoled on the advent of the Republic. Tiny in stature and calm in demeanour, he was a man of great professional integrity and personal probity (who, appropriately, died penniless), and drew sincere tributes from the British agent in Salamanca and Burgos, Sir Robert Hodgson; the British Ambassador, Sir Samuel Hoare (Lord Templewood); and the American Ambassador, Mr Carlton Hayes, in their respective books.

The other monarchist general, Martínez Anido, was a man of very different stamp. He had repressed the Anarchists in Barcelona in 1920 with shocking brutality, and had become Minister of the Interior under Primo de Rivera. Fittingly, he was now made Minister of Public Order, lest the unruly should forget that Franco's war aims included its restoration and maintenance. A more purely military appointment was that of General Dávila, commander of the Army of the North – and at the time of the announcement, in command of the Nationalist forces before Teruel – as Minister of Defence. An unpolitical soldier, Dávila was unconditionally loyal to Franco.

The Carlists were not forgotten. Franco himself had invited Fal Conde, the Carlist leader whom he had exiled to Lisbon, to become a member of the FET's National Council in November 1937. Fal Conde refused, and the offer was finally withdrawn on 6 March 1938.[11] Count de Rodezno, who stood next to Fal Conde in prominence among the Carlists, was, however, appointed Minister of Justice in Franco's 1938 government.

Other portfolios went to men who should properly be regarded as technicians with no particular political allegiance. One was the industrialist Juan Antonio Suanzes, a childhood friend of Franco's, who became Minister of Industry and Commerce. Others were Alfonso Peña Boeuf (Public Works), and Andrés Amado (Finance). This was the mixture. Two other appointments made at this time, however, also set a pattern for the future. Nicolás Franco – the Caudillo's brother – was sent to Lisbon as Ambassador; and José Sangróniz, the diplomat, was appointed Ambassador in Caracas. This, too, was to be one of the secrets of Franco's permanent hold on power (a secret which, of course, he shares with other successful practitioners of the art of ruling): when a man's presence has become inconvenient, post him abroad. Nicolás Franco's presence had become inconvenient because of the rivalry between him and Serrano Súñer; Sangróniz's because, as *de facto* Foreign Minister in the Burgos National Defence *Junta*, he had given the Axis representatives the impression of being excessively pro-British.

There was yet another secret (if it may be called a secret), and it emerged for the first time and for the discerning few, when the new ministers took the oath of office. This was no simple ceremony, streamlined to the needs of a new State. It was, wrote Serrano Súñer, 'intimate, fervent and devout, like a vigil in arms'.[12] It was held, with bated breath and deep solemnity, in the old monastery of Las Huelgas near Burgos, in an atmosphere that deliberately recalled that of the Catholic kings of Spain. This, then, was Franco's third secret: he had already decided that Spain was to be a kingdom without a king, and himself a king without a crown. This, however, the monarchists did not suspect at the time. Nor were they meant to; and later that year (on 15 December) when Franco's government restored King Alfonso's citizenship and returned his family properties to him, they were encouraged to suppose that it would not be long before their absent king – or another claimant, in the case of the Carlists – would come back to reign over them. It was left, however, to Serrano Súñer to point out what he called 'the first juridical characteristic' of the new government – the fact that Franco had combined in his person the offices of Head of Government and Chief of State.[13] He had now, at last, assumed the executive office reserved for him by the Decree of 29 September 1936, as 'Head of the Government of the State of Spain', which he had hitherto disdained to take, preferring the more powerful title of 'Chief of State', which the Decree had *not* conferred on him. His *coup d'état* was now complete.

It will be seen that Franco's first government was a very different and more complex creation than the 'fascist' or totalitarian fantasy of liberal and left-wing propaganda. This was true in more ways than one, as two superficially contradictory examples of the work of Franco's press office will show. On 26 February 1938, for instance, the typewritten *Noticiero de España* – which was at once Franco's quick weekly guide to events, and the ruling party's guide to thought and action – reported Hitler's latest speech in lyrical terms, praising his absolute disinterest in acquiring territory through his military aid for Spain, and his acceptance of the Nationalist uprising as a crusade of the nation against Communism. Had supporters of the Republic been able to read this report at the time, they might well have taken it as 'proof' of the Nazi character of Franco's régime.

But was it? For in its issue of 8 January, the same improvised publication carried an erudite and humane article on the Jews, by the great novelist, Pío Baroja, who calmly and methodically refuted Hitler's anti-Semitic race theories (though without once mentioning either Hitler or the Nazis).

The message of these articles was contradictory only to those who had done their labelling without considering the evidence. Franco was accepting German help and knew he was going to need more of it before he was through with the Civil War. It was therefore good politics to create a Nazi-looking party and take the title of Caudillo. But this did not mean that he would accept dictation from the Nazis, and still less that his régime would absorb patently nonsensical theories about Jews and Aryans.

Another indication of Franco's thinking at this time came in *Noticiero* No. 28 for 26 March 1938, which quoted with approval a speech by Neville Chamberlain in the House of Commons on 16 March. In this the British Prime Minister had dismissed the view of the Opposition leader, Clement Attlee, that the triumph of Franco would mean that Spain would fall under the control of Germany and Italy. So often wrong, Mr Chamberlain has been proved right on this occasion. (Attlee was being satirized at that time in the *Noticiero* in connection with the visit to the Popular Front lines he had paid in December 1937.)

.   .   .   .   .

Having blended his government, Franco had to do something to keep each of the groups that composed it happy, in the sense of making them feel that he had their aspirations in mind. For the time being, the Alfonsists would have to rest content with the outward signs that tomorrow's Spain was likely to be a Monarchy. The Carlists were, by definition, more troublesome, since it was not possible to concede their dynastic claims as well as the Alfonsists'. Moreover, Franco had found it necessary to exile their leader, and they could not be brushed aside, since their *Requetés* were doing some of the toughest fighting in the Civil War. One thing, however, Franco could do for them, and did: this was to restore the Church's traditional hold on Spanish life, which had been destroyed by the Republic.

In his Manifesto of Las Palmas, Franco had said nothing about religion or the Church. But with his new conviction of divine guidance had come a deep piety. Moreover, since so many of the Republic's disorders and outrages had been directed at the Church, it was natural that the Church should benefit from Franco's 'crusade'. More than ever, since the outbreak of the Civil War, the Spanish Republic had stood in the eyes of Franco's half of the Spanish nation as 'anti-Christ' as well as 'anti-Spain'. Nearly 7,000 religious people had been murdered in the Popular Front zones, including twelve bishops and 4,000 priests. Many of the dead had been sadistically tortured before death.[14] Small wonder, then, that on 1 July 1937, nearly all the Spanish bishops signed a collective letter supporting the Nationalist cause, or that, in October, Pope Pius XI appointed a Nuncio to Franco's régime.

The support of the Church and the hopes of Spanish believers had to be rewarded and fulfilled. Hence, shortly after Franco's first government had taken office, it decreed compulsory religious instruction in all schools, banned civil marriages and suspended the Republic's divorce laws. Then on 3 May 1938, the much-banned Society of Jesus was allowed to resume all its activities.

The Falange – old and new – had also to be conciliated. This was not an easy task. Franco himself had always been interested in such concepts as 'social justice' and the reduction of inequalities of wealth. In 1935, for instance, he used to say: 'For the good of Spain, I should like there to be rather fewer rich people and rather fewer poor.'[15] Unlike religion, the theme of social justice had been given special emphasis in the Manifesto of Las Palmas. On general political grounds, however, Franco was deeply aware of the need to offer something to the Spanish workers on the land and in the factories, after their years of exposure to Marxist ideas, culminating in the tragedy of the Civil War.

To inaugurate a labour policy, however, did not necessarily mean following the old Falangists all the way with their exalted ideas for a national-syndicalist State. Moreover, if Franco was interested in the welfare of the Spanish workers – as indeed he was – he was also aware that both landed proprietors and industrialists placed hopes in the outcome of his forthcoming military victory. Since the interests of the workers, the employers, the landlords and the Falange – old and new – could not simultaneously be satisfied, Franco and Serrano Súñer drafted a document that would at least have something in it for each of the interests that needed to be considered.

The outcome was the Labour Charter of 9 March 1938. Let us see, briefly, what there was in it for each of the interested groups:

For the workers: annual holidays with pay, stability of employment, a minimum wage and family allowances.

For the employers: the recognition of private enterprise as 'the perennial source of the economic life of the country'.

For both, and for the Falange: the creation of 'vertical' trade unions, representing both employers and workers, under the direction of the Spanish Traditionalist Falange and in the service of the State. (As it turned out, this wasn't really what old Falangists understood by 'national syndicalism', but then, the concept was always vague.)[16]

An article in *Noticiero*, inspired by Serrano Súñer, compared the Labour Charter with similar documents in Germany, Italy, Austria and Portugal, though claiming, no doubt correctly, that it was 'substantially Spanish'. And the Minister of the Interior himself explained that the Charter would resolve once and for all the problem of relations between workers and bosses, and establish a fair balance between the rights of property and the rights of labour. He also emphasized the 'human and Christian sentiments' of the Charter.[17]

The Labour Charter, however, was primarily a declaration of intent, and it remained to be seen how many of its provisions would become reality. In a more practical way, however, *real* social work was being done – not by the male members of the Falange but by

Pilar Primo de Rivera, sister of José Antonio, who was later to become National Chief of the *Sección Femenina* of the FET. From 1937 on she did devoted work in Franco's zones of Spain, creating children's canteens and a nursing service, and distributing food in 'liberated' areas.

Whatever criticism could be made of Franco's government in its early days, it could not be accused of idleness. To have done as much as Franco did in a few months, while conducting the Battle of Teruel and planning the forthcoming campaign in Aragon, was a measure of the energy of the Generalissimo's mature years.

9 *Franco's most difficult Year*

9 March 1938 was a crowded day in Franco's history. In Burgos, the Labour Charter was published. And in Aragon, he launched his greatest offensive.

That same day, Franco set up military headquarters at Pedrola, in Aragon. Five Army corps had been mustered for the offensive, under the overall command of General Dávila. The Generalissimo's plan was to disrupt the Republican front south of the Ebro, attacking to the east and south of Saragossa. Once this was achieved, there were to be further attacks from the north and the south. The southern divisions, in particular, were to aim for the Mediterranean, with the object of cutting Republican territory in two.

Everything went according to plan. By 22 March, 10,000 Republican prisoners had been taken. By 3 April, the northern forces had occupied the great hydro-electric installations of Tremp, thereby depriving Catalonia's industries of power. And by mid-April, the Nationalist forces had reached the Mediterranean on a front of about eighteen miles. Nationalist commentators proclaimed that now 'the great imposture of the so-called Catalan "nationalism" is reaching its end'.[1]

The Second Republic had been reduced to two contrasting zones. To the north, industrial Catalonia, the power-base of the Popular Front's war effort. To the south, the Spain of Madrid and Valencia, the Spain of agriculture. Among the Nationalists and their foreign allies, there reigned the most complete optimism. Franco himself suggested to the Germans that they could now start thinking about withdrawing their volunteers, since the war was reaching its end.[2] And in Rome, Ciano told his *Diary* that the Barcelona government's fate was inevitable.[3] They were, however, all wrong, Franco included: for the end of the war was still nearly a year off.

While the Nationalist troops – which included the Italians – were advancing on the Aragon front in mid-March, Italian bombers carried out a series of air raids on Barcelona – seventeen in all, between 16 and 18 March. Stohrer, not the most aggressive of Germans, was horrified, and reported that the effects had been 'nothing less than terrible'.[4] He added:

> Almost all parts of the city were affected. There was no evidence of any attempt to hit military objectives . . . Hundreds of houses and whole streets are said to have been destroyed by the bombs, which were evidently of a particularly destructive type. So far, 1,000 dead have been counted; it is assumed, however, that many more dead will be found beneath the ruins. The number of wounded is estimated at over 3,000. One bomb is said to have killed a whole group of women waiting in line to get their milk rations, while another one struck a subway entrance and tore to pieces the people who had sought refuge there.

Inevitably, Franco was blamed in the democratic capitals for what was universally condemned as an exhibition of fascist barbarism. The Generalissimo, however, knew nothing about the raids until they had taken place. In 'great indignation', he told the German liaison officer with the Nationalist forces that Mussolini had personally ordered the bombing, which he considered a blunder, for 'the bombing had now strengthened morale and had united diverging interests. Moreover, the population was partly Nationalist'.[5] Mussolini, indeed, boasted of his delight that Italians 'should be horrifying the world by their aggressiveness for a change, instead of charming it by their skill at playing the guitar'.[6]

Protests came in from the Vatican and Paris, and on 31 March, Sir Robert Hodgson delivered a Note to the Spanish Foreign Minister, General Jordana, in which the British government expressed its horror at these 'deliberate attacks on civilian populations'.

Jordana's reply, of course, made no mention of the origin of the bombing raids, seeking only to excuse them by the existence of military targets in Barcelona, and adding that 'General Franco had given repeated proof of his intention to render the war as humane as possible, being compelled to wage it in his own country, and had designated safety zones in various places and towns whose immunity he had guaranteed in advance'.[7]

Bombing raids were not, unfortunately, the only sources of suffering in Barcelona during this troubled and anxious time. The Communists had gained complete control of the *Servicio de Investigación Militar* (SIM), and transformed its original purpose – the investigation of espionage – into the rooting out of defeatists and political opponents. Suspects were tortured into confessions, true or false, and the 'guilty' were summarily shot, usually after being taken for a ride, gangster fashion.

The defeatists, by this time, included some, like President Azaña himself and Indalecio Prieto, the Defence Minister, who were too high to be touched by the SIM. They were not too high, however, to be removed by the Spanish Communist Party – or more accurately, by Moscow. For now, more than ever, Dr Negrín was willing to do Moscow's bidding.

To some extent, no doubt, this was because Moscow's aims and Negrín's coincided. It was an ominous time in Europe, and to many observers, another great war now seemed inevitable. On 14 March, Hitler had arrived in Vienna to take formal possession of Austria. At almost exactly the same time, Léon Blum returned to office for what proved to be a very brief period of Popular Front rule. Negrín happened to be in Paris at the time, and Blum's cabinet, at his request, agreed on 17 March to reopen the Franco-Spanish border. To Negrín, these circumstances encouraged further Republican resistance, and opened up long-term prospects from which he was less ready to shrink than some of his colleagues. Further supplies of war material, with a friendly French presence to the north, would improve Barcelona's bargaining power in the event of negotiations with Franco. Something might after all be saved from the wreckage of the Second Republic. Alternatively, if the Republic could hang on until the inevitable European war – perhaps later that year – Franco might yet be defeated if, as seemed likely, Britain and France found themselves allied with Russia against Germany.

Franco and his government followed these developments with some concern, for if Negrín looked forward to a generalized conflict that would rescue the Republic at the eleventh hour, Franco dreaded it for converse reasons. On 28 March, on instructions from Burgos, the duke of Alba presented a *note verbale* to the British Foreign Office, drawing its attention to recent massive deliveries of men and arms across the Pyrenees.[8] A month later, the duke was instructed to take advantage of the forthcoming visit to London of the new French Prime Minister, M. Daladier, and his Foreign Minister M. Bonnet, to draw the British government's attention to the danger of leaving the Franco–Spanish border open for the passage of military supplies to the Republicans.

The duke's instructions, dated 25 April, were detailed and bore the distinct stamp of Franco's personal attention. He was to give top priority to making the British government understand that Burgos attached greater value to friendship with England than with France. He was to point out that while Spain needed British aid, Britain in turn could obtain advantages in Spain. Moreover, harmonious relations between the two countries would give Britain security of access to the Mediterranean. Turning to the Civil War, the duke was to argue that Red Spain had lost the war and its leaders knew it. The responsibility for the prolongation of the fighting rested entirely on France and in view of the danger of a wider European conflict, the Spanish Nationalist government looked to Britain to make the French understand that it was not in France's ultimate interests to listen to Leftists in either country. The duke of Alba was to suggest that the French Ministers' visit could be the occasion for a friendly call from the British to close the border immediately to military supplies, thus giving France a chance to modify her policy. On no account, however, was the duke to give the impression that Franco was in any degree anxious to open relations with Paris, except under the conditions outlined.[9]

Daladier and Bonnet visited London on 28 and 29 April, and had long discussions with Mr Chamberlain, the Prime Minister, and Lord Halifax, the Foreign Secretary. Whether or not because of the duke of Alba's representations, the French border with Spain was, in fact, closed to military traffic a few weeks later; and in May, Bonnet initiated abortive talks with the Italians.

Doubtless Stalin weighed the prospects of war in Europe very carefully that spring. True, his domestic problems must have taken precedence over foreign affairs, including the embroilment in Spain: in March 1938, Bukharin, Rykov, Yagoda and other Bolsheviks were being tried and executed. The previous summer, Marshal Tukhachevsky and other leading Red Army soldiers had been court-martialled and shot, to the obvious weakening of the armed forces. Stalin could not ignore the fact, however, that in November 1936, Germany and Japan had signed a pact against communism – that is, against the survival of Stalin's State. Nor that since 1935, Russia had been in alliance with France and Czechoslovakia. Meanwhile, in Spain, Russia was already, in effect, at war with the Axis Powers. Whatever Stalin's ultimate purpose in Spain, he could hardly disinterest himself entirely in the fate of the Republic, in the spring of 1938. And whatever his strategic aims, they would best be served by a Spanish government entirely subservient to his will. This fact dictated Soviet tactics in Barcelona.

Negrín, for his part, having decided that continued resistance might pay – or at any rate, that it was too soon to capitulate – naturally sought to rid himself of the defeatists in his company. The most obvious candidate for removal was the Defence Minister, Prieto, who – since the collapse of the Aragon front – had made it plain that he considered all further resistance to be useless. This suited the Russian purpose, both because of the international factors and because Prieto had ceased to co-operate with the Communists.

Faced with the combined pressure of Negrín and the Communists, Prieto resigned at the end of March, rather than accept the ministerial demotion Negrín had in mind for him. By this time, Prieto was a tired man, tired especially of the long fight against communist control of the administration (as he explained in his Book *Como y por qué salí del Ministerio de Defensa Nacional*).

The Spanish Communists, on their side, were having a private quarrel with the Russians, who wanted them to quit Negrín's cabinet – so that public opinion in Britain and France should be more amenable to Soviet plans for an alliance against Hitler.[10] There is, of course, no contradiction between this policy and the Soviet desire to control the Barcelona government: the Russians certainly wanted that control, but they preferred to exercise it through men like Negrín who were respectably 'bourgeois'. The Spanish Communists, on the other hand, were rather enjoying their stay in office and didn't see

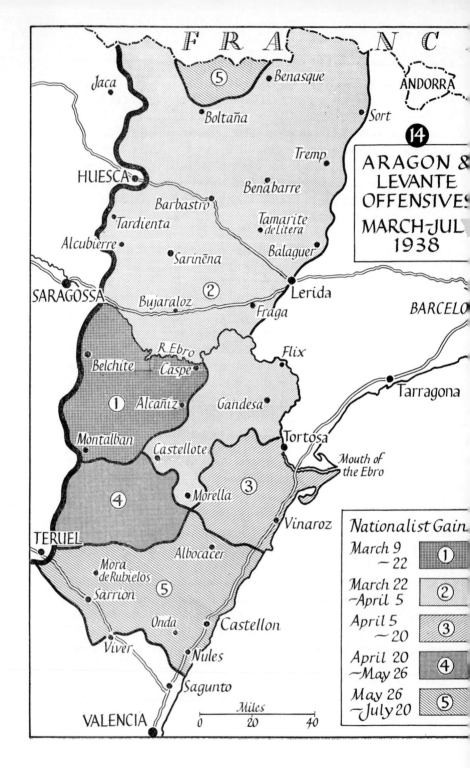

F R A N C E

ANDORRA

Jaca

Benasque

Boltaña

Sort

⑤

14

Tremp

HUESCA

Benabarre

ARAGON &
LEVANTE
OFFENSIVES

Barbastro

Tamarite
de Litera

MARCH–JUL
1938

Tardienta

Alcubierre

Sarinẽna

Balaguer

SARAGOSSA

Bujaraloz

②

Lerida

Fraga

BARCELO

R. Ebro

Flix

Belchite

Caspe

Tarragona

①

Alcañiz

Gandesa

Montalban

Castellote

Tortosa

③

Mouth of
the Ebro

④

Morella

Vinaroz

TERUEL

Albocacer

Mora
de Rubielos

⑤

Sarrion

Onda

Castellon

Viver

Nules

Sagunto

VALENCIA

Miles
0   20   40

Nationalist Gain	
March 9 – 22	①
March 22 – April 5	②
April 5 – 20	③
April 20 – May 26	④
May 26 – July 20	⑤

why they should quit. In the end, Jesús Hernández – one of the two Communist ministers – did leave the Ministry of Education. The other, Uribe, remained Minister of Agriculture. But as Hernández now became Commissar-General of the Armies of the Centre and South, the Spanish Communist Party's hold on power was strengthened, not weakened by the change. Moreover, Álvarez del Vayo returned to the Foreign Ministry, and promptly appointed Communist nominees to key positions on his staff.[11] As for Negrín, he dropped the Ministry of Finance, but took on Prieto's old job as Defence Minister. The outcome of Barcelona's ministerial crisis was thus eminently satisfactory both to the Russians and to the Spanish Communists.

Franco's success in reaching the Mediterranean and cutting the Republic's territory in two did not mean the end of his spring offensive. At this stage, in mid-April, he had no immediate plans for an assault on Catalonia. His territorial aim was Valencia; and his military one, the destruction of General Miaja's Army of the Centre. Valencia, however, could not be taken until the territory lying between Teruel and the sea had been cleared of the enemy.

To this end, Franco started his Levante campaign to complete the Aragon offensive. He diverted the Army Corps of Navarre, under General Solchaga, and General Berti's Italian 'volunteers' to the south. On 13 July, General Varela, who had been inactive during the attacks to the north, attacked in his turn. By 20 July, the Popular Front lines had been broken yet again, and the Nationalists had extended their hold on the Mediterranean to the south of Castellon and within twenty-five miles of Valencia. A pause for regrouping followed.

Before General Franco could resume his advance on Valencia, however, the Republican General Rojo, Miaja's Chief of Staff, launched an offensive of spectacular daring and strength from Catalonia against the Nationalist forces south of the Ebro. The history of previous Republican offensives – Brunete and Teruel – now repeated itself. Immediate tactical successes for the Republicans were followed by a Nationalist counter-attack, a fluctuating battle and, in the end, another Nationalist victory. But this time, everything was on a larger scale than ever before, and the losses on both sides correspondingly greater.

In tactical terms, the Republicans achieved complete surprise in the initial phases of the Ebro offensive. But when the news was brought to General Franco on 25 July, he heard it without visible surprise, telling Colonel Medrano, one of his staff officers, that it was only to be expected that the 'Reds' would do something to divert his forces from the Levante operations. Studying reports of General Rojo's probe south of the Ebro, he exclaimed with a smile: 'They make me want to let them penetrate as deeply as they can, holding back the pivots of the breach, then seal the bulge produced by the enemy's infiltration and give battle there to the Red army with the object of wearing it out and finishing it off at one go.'[12]

Franco moved to mobile headquarters in Alcañiz. These consisted of an austerely equipped office-lorry, which his subordinates promptly christened 'the Terminus'. As Alcañiz was evidently one of General Rojo's primary objectives, the Generalissimo's presence there made his staff nervous for his safety.

As usual, his preparations were deliberate. He did not launch his counter-attack until 6 August, and progress thereafter was slow, each position being taken only after prolonged artillery bombardment and desperate fighting. When liaison and staff officers expressed impatience, Franco would wait until they had gone and exclaim to his intimates: 'They don't understand me, they don't understand me. I have the best of the Red army locked up in an area thirty-five kilometres long, and they don't understand me!'[13] By 19 September, the Nationalist forces had suffered heavy losses for small gains, and German gloom was deepening. Stohrer wrote: 'The military situation must therefore be termed very unsatisfactory at present.' He added the consolatory remark, however, that it was not yet dangerous.[14]

By this time, Franco's dominant worry was political, not military. For Hitler's Sudeten crisis had burst upon Europe and the world. Now a generalized war looked imminent, and Franco's fear was that the final victory that seemed within his grasp would elude him. Conversely, Negrín could allow himself to hope either for a victory snatched from the jaws of defeat, or for a compromise peace. On 1 May, he had issued a thirteen-point programme, modelled on President Wilson's fourteen points, and intended to stand as Republican conditions for peace. He had made a number of attempts to negotiate with Franco, none of which had come to anything.[15] Indeed, Franco had repeatedly made it plain that he was interested, not in a compromise peace, but in the Republic's unconditional surrender.

Franco's fears were of several kinds. German war supplies had suddenly dried up in mid-September because of possible German needs in central Europe. This seemed to suggest that in the event of a wider conflict, Nationalist Spain would be left to its own devices. Moreover, French threats to invade Catalonia and Spanish Morocco if war broke out had been conveyed to Count Jordana.[16] The Germans reassured Franco's Ambassador in Berlin, the Marquess de Magaz, that German supplies of men and weapons would continue.[17] But Franco took his own precautions, by ordering fortifications to be built along the Pyrenees and in Morocco.

The French government, with British support, was, in fact waging a war of nerves on Franco. In Paris, Quiñones de León, Alfonso XIII's former ambassador to France and now Franco's representative there, was summoned to the Quai d'Orsay and told that France would take offensive action against Franco's régime in the event of a European war. In London, the duke of Alba was told by the Foreign Office that the French General Staff would be inclined not to intervene against Nationalist Spain if Franco would declare his neutrality in any European conflict. 'If not,' the duke cabled Burgos, 'France would immediately attack the Pyrenees and Morocco.'[18]

As a matter of fact, Franco had already made up his mind that if neutrality would save his régime, he would be neutral, no matter what the Germans might think of his ingratitude. An indirect message from the French Commander-in-Chief, General Gamelin, had been brought to Franco at 'the Terminus'. It said that if Franco did not enter the now imminent European war on Germany's side, France would send no aid whatever to the Republicans and would maintain strict neutrality in the Spanish Civil War. The message was brought by the head of Franco's Military Information Service, General Ungría. Franco looked him in the eyes and said: 'Right. Tell them that if there is a war, Spain will be neutral so long as they don't break their own undertaking to keep out of *our* war.'[19]

The duke of Alba was instructed to let the British Foreign Office know that Spain proposed to remain neutral in the event of a European war, but the British immediately argued that Spain's neutrality was incompatible with the continued presence of volunteers from other countries on Spanish soil. The duke's report to this effect, in the form of a personal letter to Count Jordana, was followed, on 2 October, by detailed instructions to him from the provisional Foreign Ministry in Burgos. He was to go back to the British and explain that 'National Spain's' position was conditioned by three elements: the frank and determined aid that had been given by Spain's friends (Germany and Italy); Britain's relatively benevolent neutrality; and France's equivocal and almost hostile attitude and persistent belief that after Franco's victory, Spain would be dominated by Germany and Italy, despite the Caudillo's repeated reassurances to the contrary.

The danger of war was now imminent, the duke of Alba's instructions went on. The Spaniards offered the French government, which had caused them such harm, a strict and unconditional neutrality without even asking for reciprocal guarantees. They hoped this attitude would be followed by a change of heart on the part of the French government, marked by discontinuance of aid to the Reds. The duke's mission, he was told, was to bring the British government round entirely to the Nationalist viewpoint; and to prevail upon the British to convince the French of the futility and injustice of further assistance to the Reds. As for the withdrawal of volunteers, as advocated by the Non-Intervention Committee in London, he was to argue that there was no connection between this question and that of Spain's neutrality.[20]

At this time, of course, the duke of Alba was still labouring under the handicap of inadequate status. His presence in London as 'agent' of Franco Spain implied *de facto* not *de jure* recognition, and he did not enjoy diplomatic privilege. He had no office as such, but operated from a flat at 22 Hans Place in Knightsbridge. His *notes verbales,* written on notepaper headed '*Estado Español*' brought only printed acknowledgment slips from the Foreign Office. On the other hand, any personal letter from him, to some politician or official of his acquaintance, usually brought a prompt reply. To add to his difficulties, some of the people he wanted to see were on holiday.

He was able, however, on 5 October, to write a personal letter to Count Jordana, starting, as usual, '*Mi querido amigo*', saying that he had duly told the Foreign Office that the Spaniards saw no connection between the question of the volunteers and Spain's proposed neutrality. For Jordana's benefit, he explained that the British did see a connection, and still wanted to know what Spain proposed to do about the volunteers in the event of a general war.[21] The Munich settlement, however, relieved Franco of pressure to answer this tricky inquiry.

A subsidiary fear in Franco's mind during the Czechoslovak crisis was that the Great Powers would follow up any settlement by an attempt to impose a similar settlement in Spain, without consulting him. Indeed, Hitler's failure either to consult him or to inform him about the Sudeten crisis had infuriated him, and Stohrer asked his Minister on 25 September whether it was possible to give the Franco government further information.[22] Next day, the marquess de Magaz officially informed the Wilhelmstrasse that Spain intended to remain neutral in the event of a European war.[23] Now it was the Germans' turn to be annoyed, and on 3 October, Woermann, the Under-State Secretary at the German Foreign Office, told the Spanish Ambassador that both in Rome and in Berlin 'the handling of the question of neutrality had left somewhat of a nasty taste'. Why, he asked, was it necessary for Franco's government to declare itself neutral so prematurely?[24]

By this time, the Munich agreement – which, in effect, destroyed the Czechoslovak State – had been signed, and conversely, the Republic's last chance of salvation had gone. But if Franco's worst fears had now been removed, there remained the ominous possibility that the Powers might attempt a similar exercise on Spain. At a dinner on 1 October, Franco told Stohrer of his enthusiasm over Hitler's triumph at Munich, 'but, when I remarked that the method of the successful solution of the Czech crisis could become a model for subsequent international conflicts, he avoided relating this in any way to the Spanish crisis and did not pursue the subject further'.[25]

For his part, Stohrer was more pessimistic than ever about Franco's military prospects, and was urging a negotiated settlement, although the Spanish Nationalists rejected any such plan 'with positively nervous intensity'.[26] Well might Franco look back on 1938 as his most difficult year. Stohrer was not alone in his pessimistic criticism. Colonel von Thoma, the commander of the German tank corps in the Condor Division was witheringly scornful of Franco's 'old school' methods at the start of the Aragon offensive and complained that he had to fight to use tanks the way tanks ought to be used – 'in a concentrated way'.[27] Mussolini went further, exclaiming to Ciano: 'Put on record in your book that today, August 29, I prophesy the defeat of Franco.'[28]

Franco also had a good deal of trouble from recalcitrants on his own side in 1938. In June, he had arrested two of the *camisas viejas*, Agustín Aznar and Fernando González Vélez, for alleged plotting (a charge later dropped, though the two men were eventually sentenced to five and a half years' forced labour).[29] Then General Yagüe – Franco's faithful and indispensable commander – had disgraced himself on 19 April by a speech in Burgos praising the bravery of the 'Red' soldiers, and criticizing the administration of justice. For his rashness, he was suspended from his command (though not for very long: he was too valuable to be dispensed with).[30] More serious by far were the clashes between Franco and his generals as the Nationalist counter-offensive on the Ebro got bogged down in September. Violent scenes between the Generalissimo and his commanders, 'who do not carry out orders correctly', were multiplying, reported Stohrer on 19 September; and morale at headquarters was low.[31]

13a The apotheosis: Franco (followed by Mola) at Burgos after being proclaimed Generalissimo of the Nationalist Armed Forces and 'Head of the Government of the State of Spain' in October 1937.

13b Burgos crowd cheers the new Generalissimo.

14a *The Republic's leaders:* Largo Caballero, 'the Lenin of Spain'.

14b Alvarez del Vayo, Comintern contactman in the Republican government.

14c Defender of Madrid: General Riquelme.

14d The Commander-in-Chief, General Miaja (*right*) with International Brigade Commander Lister.

A theme that needled the amiable Von Stohrer constantly in 1938 was that of Nationalist reprisals for crimes allegedly committed by the 'Reds' in 'liberated' zones. This concern for the victims of Nationalist terror was doubtless, in part, inspired by humanitarian motives, for the German Ambassador was hardly a typical Nazi. There were also, however, strictly political motives at work in Stohrer's attitude. Pessimistic as he was about Franco's military chances, Stohrer thought that the negotiated peace which he therefore favoured must be based on a political amnesty in both the fighting zones. But even in the event of a Nationalist victory, unlikely though this seemed to him, the Ambassador argued that Franco would have so many people against him that it was in his own interests to keep reprisals to a minimum. Failing that, he thought, Franco would find it hard to maintain stability.

Thus we find Stohrer, on 19 May, estimating the number of politically unreliable people in 'White Spain' at about forty per cent. Severe reprisals had prevented assassinations and acts of sabotage from getting out of hand; but these, of course, 'produce counteraction'.[32] What Stohrer does not seem to have known is that earlier that month a decree of Franco's had created a special organization – known as the *Delegación del Estado para Recuperación de Documentos* – whose purpose was not, as might appear, archival and historical, but to obtain documentary proof of foreign intervention and war crimes on the Republican side.[33] The ultimate object of this service was clearly to establish the identity of 'Red criminals' with a view to their punishment.

Undoubtedly, there had been countless atrocities on the Republican side – and the *Noticiero de España*, the restricted news-sheet produced by Franco's press office – reported many new cases in 1938. There was therefore, from Franco's standpoint, a good deal of punishing to be done; though one does not need to take at face value the estimate which the Nazis were quoting in June, of a half a million hostages murdered by the Republicans.[34] That the policy of punishment was a deliberate one, approved by Franco, cannot be doubted. Stohrer, however, was shocked by the reign of terror instituted by that old hand at repression, General Martínez Anido, the Nationalist Minister of Public Order, in Burgos in the spring and summer of 1938.[35] On 19 September, he reported Franco as unreceptive to the idea of a general amnesty, and indeed unwilling to make 'even small

L

concessions of the same sort proposed to him by the Reds through the exchange commission of British Field Marshal Chetwode'[36] (a commission for the exchange of civilian prisoners that stayed in Spain from September 1938 to April 1939 without accomplishing much).

Not long afterwards, however, the Ambassador was reporting with approval a radio speech by the Generalissimo in which he had declared that 'all those who had committed no crimes against the common law and sincerely wished to support the cause of Spain had nothing to fear'.[37] But any hopes aroused in Stohrer by this speech were short-lived: on 19 November, he was reporting 'innumerable additional arrests' after an unexplained plot. He added that the local prison (in San Sebastian), though designed for forty persons, was crammed with eighteen hundred. In the same dispatch, Stohrer recorded that he had asked Jordana whether it was true that the Generalissimo had declared that he had a list of two million names of Spanish 'Reds' who had been guilty of some crime or other and would be punished. The Foreign Minister had replied evasively that he did not know whether the Generalissimo had made such a statement, but it was a fact that there was a long list of 'Red criminals who had to be given their just punishment'.[38] It was with evident relief that Stohrer referred three months later to the death of Martínez Anido, whose Ministry of Public Order was being taken over by Serrano Súñer.[39] (In the same dispatch, incidentally, he referred to a fresh 'Russian reign of terror' in what was left of Republican territory.)

From many quarters, then, Franco was under fire. His confidence, however, so exasperating to his critics, never deserted him. Only the Czech crisis, which was entirely beyond his control, had shaken him. Now, in the autumn of 1938, he was determined to go for final victory, whatever the Germans or anybody else might think of him.

10 *Franco's Crushing Victory*

At the beginning of November 1938, the end – in the sense of the complete collapse of Negrín's administration – was nearer than anybody supposed. But in the sense of Franco's final triumph and entry into Madrid, it was further off than Franco himself may have hoped. For the Republic's collapse and Negrín's flight to refuge in France did not mean the immediate end of all resistance. Indeed, the last convulsions of the dying order were as messy and nasty as any since the collapse of the monarchy, for a military coup in Madrid was followed by a Communist rising and yet another civil war within the Civil War.

Before the Generalissimo could launch his *coup de grâce* at the dying Republic, he had to finish off the ghastly and bloody battle of the Ebro. And before he could turn to Catalonia, the power base of the revolution, he knew he would need a further injection of German help and was ready – now that it had become inevitable – to pay the price.

On 24 October, Franco issued a 'General Instruction' ordering the Army Corps of the Maestrazgo to capture the heights south-east of Gandesa. This fiercely defended objective was not attained until 7 November, after a tremendous artillery barrage a week earlier by 175 cannon. This was the death blow: 100,000 Popular Front troops had crossed the Ebro on the forward wave of the offensive, and only 15,000 crossed it on the way back. When the firing had stopped on 16 November, the dreadful arithmetic of the Battle of the Ebro worked out something like this:

REPUBLICANS: 20,000 killed, 20,000 captive, 17,600 gravely wounded, 41,000 lightly wounded.

NATIONALISTS: 33,000 losses of all kinds.[1]

During the latter phase of the Ebro Battle, General Franco appealed to the Germans for fresh arms deliveries to finish off the war. The Germans did not say No, but seized the obvious chance of wringing from Franco the concessions he had so far avoided making.

It had been a long and irritating wait for the Germans. Franco's

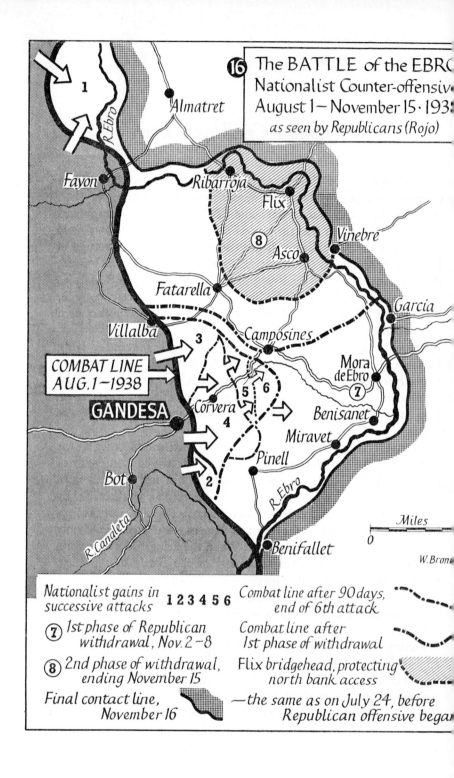

16 The BATTLE of the EBRO
Nationalist Counter-offensive
August 1 – November 15 · 1938
as seen by Republicans (Rojo)

Almatret

R. Ebro

Fayon

Ribarroja

Flix

8 Asco

Vinebre

Fatarella

Garcia

Villalba

Campósines

COMBAT LINE
AUG.1 – 1938

Mora
de Ebro

7

GANDESA

Corvera

3

5 **6**

4

Benisanet

Miravet

Pinell

Bot

2

R. Ebro

R. Candela

Benifallet

Miles

0

W. Bron

Nationalist gains in
successive attacks   **1 2 3 4 5 6**

7 1st phase of Republican
withdrawal, Nov. 2 – 8

8 2nd phase of withdrawal,
ending November 15

Final contact line,
November 16

Combat line after 90 days,
end of 6th attack

Combat line after
1st phase of withdrawal

Flix bridgehead, protecting
north bank access

—the same as on July 24, before
Republican offensive began

only response to prolonged Nazi pressure was to raise the limit on foreign holdings in Spanish enterprises from twenty-five to forty per cent. But he signed the law to this effect at the beginning of June 1938, without previously discussing the text with the Germans, as they had expected. When Stohrer wanted to discuss the matter with Franco, as Berlin had instructed him, he was told that the Generalissimo was too busy to see him. Mortified, he asked himself 'whether I was perhaps no longer *persona grata* with the Generalissimo'.[2]

In October, when the Caudillo started sounding out the Germans about fresh supplies, the Nazi Foreign Office held lengthy discussions about the concessions that might be extracted from Franco. The idea of trying to persuade him to sign a political treaty (binding Spain's foreign policy to Germany's) was discarded for the time being.[3] But Stohrer was instructed to remind Jordana once more that the Spaniards had still not made any definite promise about the extended mining rights the Germans wanted.[4] But discussions with the Spaniards dragged on until 19 December; and even then, the Germans didn't get all they had asked for. On that day, when the Spanish Foreign Ministry, in a 'top secret' Note to the German embassy, announced that German participation in three companies had been raised to seventy-five per cent, and in another to sixty per cent; the German share in a fifth company remained unchanged at forty per cent. The Spaniards also acknowledged their indebtedness to Germany for aid received and to come.[5] It was a victory for Germany; but a very late one. And there was still no political treaty between Germany and Nationalist Spain.

Franco's original request for German supplies was made on 20 October. He asked for 50,000 rifles, 2,000 machine-guns and 100 75-mm. guns.[6] A week later – on 27 October – he told Stohrer that he was considering two new offensives: one towards Catalonia and the other towards the Levante. He hadn't made up his mind, at that time, which one to launch first. Perhaps it was this typical example of Franco's caution that made Stohrer write that – even at this late stage and even if the Germans sent Franco the material he wanted - 'a speedy and victorious conclusion of the war through purely military means is not probable.'[7]

A fortnight later, with the Republicans routed, Franco's prospects looked rosier, although he had still not made up his mind to invade

Catalonia. The balance of military power had shifted invincibly in his favour. Despite the departure of 10,000 Italian 'volunteers' in mid-October, he now had some 300,000 combat troops, against only 220,000 on the Popular Front side.[8] Moreover, his troops were exalted by victory; the 'Reds' were demoralized. Soviet supplies had dwindled; and the French border, reopened by Blum in March, had been closed again in mid-June.

On the political side, too, the balance was tilted in Franco's favour. Whether despite, or because of, the police terror in the Nationalist zone, the territory under his rule was firmly in his iron grip. On the Republican side, the State had begun to disintegrate. In August, Negrín had provoked a crisis with the clear intention of removing the last vestiges of President Azaña's authority. He had called on the Council of Ministers to approve fifty-eight death sentences that were then pending. The government fell, and Azaña called on the opposition leader, Julian Besteiro, to form a cabinet. Negrín threatened to leave Spain, and an obviously prearranged flood of telegrams from communist military commanders, each pledging support for him, were delivered to him. Simultaneously, the Russians staged an impressive display of military might in the streets of Barcelona and the air above. Azaña got the message and approved a cabinet list submitted by Negrín, who was henceforth dictator of what was left of the Spanish Republic.[9]

Early in December, Franco at last made up his mind to drop his alternative plan for a second Levante campaign, and go for Catalonia and victory. He had planned to launch his offensive on 10 December, but bad weather delayed him and he did not give the order to march until 23 December. Only three of the Communist-led units offered any serious resistance. One was Lister's, which the Nationalists thought they had destroyed at Teruel.

As the Nationalist forces drew near Barcelona, half a million people fled the city and other areas in panic, heading for the French border. On 27 January 1939, Yagüe's Moors took Catalonia's capital without a fight. On 6 February, the men of the Republic – Azaña, the intellectual turned unsuccessful statesman; Negrín, the doctor who had become Moscow's tool; Companys, whose Catalan ambitions had led him too far; and Martínez Barrio, an honourable man who had become powerless to influence the course of events – crossed the border into France, together and on foot.

FRANCE

•Tarascon

Perpignan

gneres-Luchon

Viella

ANDORRA

Puigcerda   La Junquera

Port Bou

Sort•

Seo de Urgel

Camprodon•

Figueras•

Rosas

Pobla

Ripoll•   Olot• Besalu•

Tremp•

Berga•

Torroella

enabarre

Basella   Solsona•

Gerona•

La Boronia•

Artesa•   Pons•

Cardona•

Vich•

Palafrugell
Palamos•

Balaguer•

Tora
Calaf•

San
Celoni•

Lerida•

Tarrega

Cervera Monistrol•

Manresa•   La Garriga•

Granollers•

Blanes•

Bellpuig•

Motaro•

ona•

Borjas Blancas
Montblanch•

Sta
Coloma   Martorell•

S.Cugat•

Masnou•

Mequinenza•

Prades•

Valls•

Molins•
Villafranca•

BARCELONA

Flix   Falset•

Reus•

Yendrell•

Prat•

Mora• Cambrills•

Sitges•

ndesa

Tarragona

ortosa•

Hospitalet•
Ametlla•

Amposta•

Mouth of
the Ebro

17

The Nationalist Offensive in
CATALONIA
December 23·1938–February 9·1939
A Nationalist view   (R H M·N°17·1964)

Initial Front Line
Main lines of attack

0   Miles   50

W.Bromage

In three days, the Nationalists' *Auxilio Social* distributed 350,000 rations of bread, 150,000 cold meals and 60,000 hot ones to the starving, cowering people of Barcelona. The churches were reopened; and Barcelona's great newspaper, *La Vanguardia*, reappeared with a slight change of name: it was now *La Vanguardia Española*.[10]

On 21 February, General Franco passed his victorious forces in review in Barcelona. And next day, in the waters off Tarragona, he reviewed the tiny Nationalist fleet. (On 5 March, the Republican Fleet, rebelling this time against the defeated Republic, set sail for the safety of Bizerta.)

Until his arrival in Barcelona, the Generalissimo had followed the course of the Catalonia campaign from Operational headquarters at Castello de Raymat, near Lerida. Now, having reviewed his victorious forces, he returned to Burgos, where he issued a solemn appeal to the remaining Republican forces to lay down their arms.

By all the odds, the appeal should have produced a response. But the pitiless logic of 'unconditional surrender' is that surrender is delayed. A last convulsion was about to afflict the dying body of the Republic.

Negrín had returned to Spain on 26 February, after further abortive efforts to negotiate a compromise peace, and was eager now

to fight to the bitter end. Next day, France and Britain recognized the Nationalist government and Azaña resigned. On paper, then, the Republic had died. But its death twitches gave it an appearance of lingering survival.

Franco had assembled an invincible grand army for the last attack of all: 600,000 men in 58 divisions and 18 army corps – to march on Madrid first and Valencia later. Only the Communist commanders were willing to listen to Negrín's appeal for a fight to the finish. In Madrid on 5 March, Colonel Casado, with the political support of Julián Besteiro, the respected moderate Socialist, who had stayed in Madrid throughout the war, announced that he had formed a National Defence Council and appealed for an honourable peace. The troops under Communist command promptly went into rebellion against the Casado-Besteiro Council, and were subjugated only after several days' hard fighting.*

To the Council's surprise, General Franco invited it to send representatives to Burgos. To their disappointment, once they were there – on 22 March – he merely sent word to them that there were no terms for an armistice, simply an unconditional capitulation. The Council's representatives tried to play for time, and returned to Madrid.

On 26 March, the Generalissimo ordered his troops forward; and on 28 March, they entered Madrid, by the route that led from Casa de Campo to the University City where General Varela's forces had been driven back in 1936.

That day, there was an anti-climax in Burgos: for the first time since the start of the Civil War, Franco fell ill with influenza and took to his bed at his Burgos headquarters. But there was no fight left on the Republican side. The rest of Spain was occupied without a battle.

On 1 April 1939, General Franco issued his last war-time announcement from Burgos. It said:

TODAY, THE RED ARMY HAVING BEEN DISARMED AND CAPTURED, THE NATIONAL TROOPS HAVE REACHED THEIR FINAL MILITARY OBJECTIVES. THE WAR IS OVER.

Franco was master of all Spain; and the doubters had been proved wrong.

* For conflicting accounts of the Casado affair, see Thomas (pp. 742-55), Jackson (pp. 467-76) and Madariaga (pp. 543-7).

11 *Triumph and Retribution*

The defiant capital of Spain, starving and heatless, was Franco's, as was the rest of Spain. It was out of the question, however, for Franco to take formal possession of Madrid immediately after his victory. There was too much to do first to relieve the sufferings of the population.

Once again, as in Barcelona some weeks earlier, Franco's *Auxilio Social* went into swift and effective action, handing out 780,000 rations on 2 April – the day after the Nationalist entry into Madrid – and 750,000 on the next day. Fortunately, the more prosperous agricultural areas had been in Nationalist hands during most of the war, and their produce was now available to feed the deprived cities. With the total exhaustion of reserves, however, the emergency supplies brought in by *Auxilio Social* could do no more than bring temporary relief. Soon, the essentials of Spanish life – bread and olive oil, rice, potatoes and other vegetables, coffee, sugar and meat – had to be rationed. With the arrival of the Nationalists, the worthless Republican peseta was replaced by a more solid currency. Even then, the note issue rapidly doubled. It was not until after the Second World War that black marketing – the *estraperlo* – was finally rooted out.

By mid-May, the most visible pains and scars of the war had been removed from Madrid's face, and on 19 May, Franco staged his grand victory parade. Standing in an open car next to the picturesque, moustachioed General Saliquet, Commander of the Army of the Centre, waving his hand in acknowledgment of the cheers of the large crowd that had gathered along Madrid's broad Paseo de la Castellana, Franco at last reached the reviewing stand. The biggest moment of his life was about to come.

It was not the victory parade as such, but what happened in the reviewing stand, where the diminutive General Jordana, in his capacity as Vice-Premier, read out a long list of the Generalissimo's military feats. For these, he announced, the Grand Cross of San Fernando with Laurels had been conferred on General Francisco Franco Bahamonde.[1] The Grand Cross with Laurels, Spain's highest decoration, which had eluded him in his youthful years of strenuous heroism in Morocco, was at last to be his – self-conferred, no doubt, since no king or president was there to do him such honour, and he was Generalissimo of the Armed Forces, Chief of State and Caudillo of Spain. But his at last. And there to pin the coveted decoration on his breast was the bravest officer of them all, General Varela, himself twice the winner of the Grand Cross with Laurels. . . .

The other military heroes of the Civil War were also there, of course. There was El Mizzian, the Moroccan officer who had joined the Alzamiento the first day and had fought at the head of his *Regulares* throughout the war. Queipo de Llano, conqueror of Seville, known both as 'the radio General' because of his outspoken broadcasts and as 'the social General' because he wanted to expropriate all landlords in favour of their tenant farmers, was there, too. So was Moscardó, the haggard and bearded 'ghost' of the stricken Alcázar. Present, too, were Yagüe who had conquered Extremadura and – right at the end – Barcelona; the Navarrese commanders, Solchaga and García Valiño; Aranda, the victor of Oviedo; Dávila, whose brilliant planning had made a great contribution to Franco's victory; and Asensio and Alonso Vega, later to occupy important posts in Franco's administration. The Italian Gambara was there, too, in a place of choice, at the head of his departing 'Volunteers'; and so was von Richtofen, who in November 1938 had taken over from Sperrle as Commander of the Condor Legion. (The Italians started leaving Spain at the end of May; the Germans on 26 May.)

More important than any of these, in the Generalissimo's eyes, were the marching survivors of the Army that had brought victory to him and to the Movement: the Carlists with their red *boinas* and crucifixes, the fierce and disciplined *Regulares* and the Legionaries of Africa, the conscripts and their *alfereces*, and the proud cavalry.

In his thin, level-toned voice, Franco spoke to them all and to the Madrileno crowd lining the Castellana:

In this martyred Madrid, now liberated from the tyranny of the mob, you have today witnessed the Victory Parade of 120,000 warriors in perfect formation, accompanied by the most modern and efficient war material, representing the million men who formed the rank and file of the National Army . . . Now that the war has ended in victory, I assure you that Spain will overcome all her trials: after what we have already gone through, nothing can make us suffer more.

We love peace because we love Spain, and we prize the blood of our youth, but above all on account of Spain's dignity and independence. Our desire is to collaborate in the task of the pacification of Europe, but it must be understood once and for all that we will not submit to any infringement of our sovereignty or of our political and economic freedom, for which we have in fact fought our war and for which our soldiers fell in battle.

After the triumph, the thanksgiving. On 20 May 1939, General Franco attended a *Te Deum* in Madrid's Church of Santa Barbara. He then laid down his sword before the altar and spoke the following prayer:

> Lord, benevolently accept the effort of this people, which was always Thine, which, with me and in Thy name, has vanquished with heroism the enemy of the truth in this century.
>
> Lord God, in whose hands rest all right and all power, lend me Thy assistance to lead this people to full imperial liberty, for Thy glory and that of Thy Church.
>
> Lord, may all men know that Jesus is the Christ, the living son of God.[2]

One is inclined to doubt whether, in similar circumstances, Hitler or Mussolini would have spoken similar words in a similar place. The wording of Franco's prayer, however, repays careful study, for it spells out the underlying assumption of the Generalissimo's 'Crusade' – that the National Movement was carried out in God's name; and it describes the defeated half of the Spanish people as 'the enemy of the truth'.

One does not have truck with the enemy of the truth, much less sup with him, even with a long spoon: one destroys him. That is why, in Franco's mind, retribution was an inevitable companion to triumph and thanksgiving. Nor did it occur to any of his close companions that magnanimity becomes a victor; or if it did, it was not with sufficient force for the fact to be stated. For the enemy that had been partially destroyed during the years of fighting was 'anti-Spain'. One does not reason with 'anti-Spain' or pardon it, or treat it with psycho-analysis: one destroys it. Since 'Spain' had won and representatives of 'anti-Spain' were still alive in large numbers (apart from those who had fled), the work of the 'War of Liberation' had to be completed, by exterminating those who had survived the fighting. It is not for nothing that years later, in 1951, Fernández Cuesta, at that time Minister Secretary-General of the Movement, was to say: 'Between their Spain and ours there is an abyss that can only be crossed by repentance and submission to our doctrine. Otherwise, may they remain on the other side of the abyss, and if they attempt to cross it surreptitiously, may they perish.'[3]

All this has to be said. But no one should suppose that had 'anti-Spain' defeated 'Spain', things would have been any different, for in that event, too, the victors would have turned executioners; though the victors, it is true, would not have been the same. It is impossible to reach any other conclusion if one looks at the facts of the Popular Front massacres, especially in Madrid, Barcelona and Valencia, and the executions of Goded, Fanjul and José Antonio; if one recalls the hounding of the POUM by the Catalan communists; or if one remembers the grim torture chambers of the *chekas* in Spain's two greatest cities. Nor does it carry conviction to argue, as have some apologists for the Republic, that most of the crimes on the Republican side were committed by enraged mobs within the first few months of the Civil War, while Nationalist reprisals or executions continued throughout the war and after it into the Second World War. For this fact merely reflected the military situation: after the first few months, the Nationalists advanced continuously or held the Republicans to a stalemate. As they advanced, they found fresh evidence of atrocities, and took further reprisals. If the situations had been reversed, Republican reprisals would have been correspondingly greater.

It happens, however, that the Nationalists won the Civil War. And the retributive machinery immediately went into action. As we have seen, formal trials – however summary – had replaced the indiscriminate massacres of the early days. On 9 February 1939, in anticipation of victory, Franco's Government adopted a retroactive Law on Political Responsibilities punishing subversion between 1 October 1934 (the time of the Asturian revolution) and 18 July 1936 (the day of the Nationalist rising); and punishing opposition to the National Movement thereafter. On 14 March of the same year, a special Tribunal of Political Responsibilities was set up to administer the new Law. Simultaneously, military tribunals were set up in towns and cities that had emerged from Republican rule, to which all witnesses of Republican crimes were summoned to give evidence.

As Sir Arthur Loveday – a staunch defender of the Nationalists – has recorded, arrests, trials, imprisonments and executions took place on a vast scale after the Nationalist victory.[4] The alternative, as he wrote, would have been a wholesale settlement of accounts by individuals and groups. And, indeed, this is what happened in France after the Liberation.

How many people were executed or otherwise punished in Spain after the Civil War? It is still impossible to answer this question with absolute conviction, for the subject remains taboo in Nationalist Spain in 1967, twenty-eight years after Franco's victory.

Wildly different figures are given in their respective books by Hugh Thomas and Gabriel Jackson. While I believe that Jackson grossly understates the number of atrocities on the Popular Front side, I am less certain that he overstates the number of Nationalist executions after the war had ended, which he puts at 200,000 (describing them as '"red" prisoner deaths through execution or disease, 1939–43').[5] The late Bernard Malley, of the British Embassy in Madrid, who was in Spain throughout the Second World War, gave me the same figure, though tentatively, in a conversation I had with him not long before his death. He added that there were daily trials and executions throughout 1939, 1940 and 1941; later, trials took place twice a week. Due weight must be given to any information from this honest and well-informed observer, who had sampled the inside of a Republican gaol and whose sympathies were by no means with the Left.

The former Associated Press correspondent in Spain, Charles Foltz, has recorded that an official of the Spanish Ministry of Justice gave him the figure of 192,684 death sentences carried out between April 1939 and June 1944 – not counting special Army executions.[6] Stanley Payne quotes this figure but thinks it 'was probably a considerable exaggeration'.[7] But who is to say?

Certainly the prisons remained inordinately full for years. A simple rule of thumb that guided arrests was that all who had been officials of the Republic, and all who had served in the Republican forces, were to be detained. All who had been responsible for killings, *or who had failed to stop them* when it was in their power to do so, were condemned to death, and nearly all were executed. Ordinary recruits to the armed forces were soon released. But it was assumed that any recruit who had subsequently been promoted must have been guilty of some crime or other, and most were condemned to long prison sentences.[8] Such sentences could, however, be reduced by work on reconstruction projects, each day of work reducing the sentence by two days. The sons of executed 'Reds' were absorbed into the Youth Organization of the FET.[9]

According to statistics which I believe to be correct, prisoners in Spanish gaols numbered 250,719 on 31 December 1940 (compared with a pre-Civil War prison population that fluctuated from a minimum of about 6,000 to a maximum of 12,500 in 1934 after the Asturian rising).[10] Remissions of sentences and amnesties reduced the high initial figure to 139,990 in 1941, 95,601 in 1942, 46,661 in 1943 and 28,077 in 1944.

It was probably Franco's intention that only those actually guilty of crimes should be punished. But the term 'crimes' was very widely interpreted. Moreover, the summary nature of the trials and the speed with which executions had to be carried out gave professional informers dangerous opportunities and led to injustices, as even Loveday concedes. The few spectacular deaths of prominent Republicans suggest that had most of the Republican leaders not successfully found refuge abroad, they would all have been executed or died in Nationalist gaols. For instance, Companys, the Catalan leader, and Zugazagoitia, the Socialist, were executed after Nazi police had picked them up in France and handed them over to Franco. And Besteiro, the moderate Socialist who had tried to negotiate with Franco in the last days of Madrid, died in gaol of untreated tuberculosis. There is no doubt that in the minds of Franco and his friends, the Civil War had indeed been a fight unto death, as they had decided it would have to be in the early days, when Goded and Fanjul were shot by the Republicans.

It is difficult to paint a reliable picture of Franco's attitude to the men he sent to their deaths. Wildly different accounts exist. One of his former followers, for instance, has described him to me as chuckling with glee together with the Assessor-General of the General Staff, Martínez de Fuset,* as they drew up the daily execution lists. On the other hand, José María Doussinague, a former

* The trusted officer who had taken Franco's wife and daughter to safety in 1936.

permanent head of the Spanish Foreign Ministry, tells the following story:

> One day when the American Ambassador, Carlton Hayes, was visiting Franco (probably in 1943, though Doussinague does not say so), he made a tentative reference to the desirability of liquidating the civil war, as regards death sentences. Franco invited him to sit down and showed him a pile of appeals that lay on his desk. The Caudillo then patiently started reading out details of individual cases. Hayes interrupted, with the words: 'In the United States, all these would have been sent to the electric chair.'
>
> 'They are the ones I have pardoned,' was Franco's suave reply.[11]

It is only fair to add that Hayes himself does not refer to this incident in his own book.

The sustained terror of the war-time years forms part of Franco's biography, along with the many constructive achievements. It is against the background of daily executions, casting a shadow of fear on neutral Spain, with all its other miseries, that Part V of this book has to be read.

PART V

World War

✳

1 *Neutrality*

Drained of blood and treasure, Spain was exhausted. Only a long period of peace could restore the country's well-being. Yet peace, as Franco knew, was beyond the bounds of hope in the long hot summer of 1939. He lacked the economic basis and the diplomatic conditions of a positive foreign policy. A victor by the grace of the Nazis and Fascists, he was unwilling to allow Spain to become a satellite of Germany or Italy. Only the Soviet Union and Mexico had failed to recognize his régime, but outside the European dictatorships, he had few friends and many enemies. A fund of international ill-will had built up against him and only the threatening prospect of a second great war diverted unwelcome democratic attentions.

In the threat of war, indeed, lay Franco's opportunity as well as the greatest danger to the fragile structure of his new State. Survival now became his major preoccupation and it would take all his patience, cunning and caution to ensure it. *Hábil prudencia* or 'skilful prudence', he had told the National Council of 5 June 1939, was to be 'the chief feature of our foreign policy'.

What *hábil prudencia* dictated, above all, was neutrality in the great conflict that loomed ahead between the Axis powers, which had helped him to victory, and the western democracies, which had sourly watched him crush the Republic. Spain's exhaustion was only one of the circumstances that made the Caudillo opt for neutrality. Another was the turmoil of emotions that prevailed among the victors of the Civil War. One thing united them: a common detestation of bolshevism, which had become the hated symbol of all they had fought against, from anarcho-syndicalism to the burning of churches. France was deeply unpopular with all groups, with the right-wing Falangists as well as with the Carlists, with the Army as well as the Church and the bourgeoisie, the Blum government being blamed for the contagion of Popular Front ideas and for providing arms for the Republic, while historic memories of the Napoleonic wars were still fresh enough to matter. The British, too, were disliked, if only for their continued hold on Gibraltar; and the fact that Wellington had helped defeat the French in Spain did less to make England popular than to keep hatred of France alive. Nevertheless, a strong section of the bourgeoisie, including many monarchists and industrialists, was mindful of Spain's traditional trading links with Britain and aware that the British – and the Americans – were better placed than the Germans or Italians to provide the capital and the credit Spain desperately needed.

There were mixed feelings about the Germans and Italians. The Falangists, to be sure, were carried away with admiration for National-Socialist drive and efficiency, in which they saw the solution for Spain's sickness and decadence. But even among the Falangists, there was little real warmth for the Germans, whose ambassadors, Faupel and Stohrer, had made little effort to hide their contempt for, or exasperation with, Spanish methods. Nor was the Falange's enthusiasm for Germany widely shared within the Army, which could not forget that Hitler was less interested in helping Franco win than in prolonging the Civil War for Germany's advantage; while the Foreign Minister, Jordana, was pro-British. It was very different with the Italians, for whom warmth, but not admiration, was felt. In the eyes of the Spanish victors, the Italians had several points in their favour. Their behaviour in Spain had been bombastic and self-seeking, but at least they had helped the Nationalists in their hour of military need, as indeed the Germans had. In addition, however, the Italians, unlike the Germans, were Latins and Catholics. So, too, were the Portuguese, and Franco's ideas of Iberian friendship were generally accepted, as was his wider notion of cultivating good relations with the Spanish–American countries in a spirit of *Hispanidad.*

If Franco had been able to follow his own inclinations, he would have turned to the democracies for economic succour, and moved away from Germany. But this was easier said than done: he had to contend not merely with the pro-German policy of his right-hand man, Serrano Súñer, but also with the indignantly anti-Franco sentiments that dominated public opinion in Britain, France and the United States. The essential things were to preserve Spain's independence and territorial integrity and keep out of the impending European war. 'We need a period of peace of at least five years,' he had told the Italian General Gambara in March 1939, and he repeated this remark to Ciano in July.[1]

The sequence of events in 1939 and 1940 reflects both the pressures with which Franco had to contend and the skill with which he avoided undesirable commitments. It also shows clearly enough the narrowness of the limits within which he could manœuvre.

In the spring of 1938, Jordana had refused to sign a secret treaty of friendship with Germany, which would have tied Spanish foreign policy to that of the Nazis after victory. His motive was the fear that any such arrangement would limit Spain's ability to draw closer to Britain, in which he thought her real interest lay. On the morrow of the Nationalist victory in Catalonia, however, Franco overruled his Foreign Minister, while taking care not to bind himself too closely to Hitler.[2] Under the Germano–Spanish Treaty of friendship that was signed in Burgos on 31 March 1939, the two States bound themselves to consult each other in the event of an international crisis, with a view to defending their interests and combating the Comintern. Each was to support the other diplomatically in the event of danger, to refrain from joining any coalition against the other, and not to take any action against the other signatory if the latter were involved in a war against a third Power. Provision was made for closer military, cultural and economic links, to be separately negotiated. Although the mere fact of signing such a Treaty was enough to damn Franco in democratic eyes as a satellite of Hitler's, it will be noticed that his undertakings were purely negative. He had not become Hitler's military ally, and his hands remained relatively free.

The Axis Powers, understandably, wanted more than that from him, and, yielding to their pressure, he brought Spain into the Anti-Comintern Pact with Germany, Italy and Japan. The decision to sign the Treaty and join the Pact had been under discussion for some time and had been approved on 20 February 1939, by the Spanish Cabinet, under General Franco's chairmanship. It was laid down, however, that Spain's adherence to the Pact must be kept secret until the Civil War had ended. Accordingly, it was disclosed only on 7 April, six days after the Nationalists had announced their victory.

This was a delicate time for Franco's representative in London, the duke of Alba. Britain having extended *de jure* recognition to the Nationalist régime, the duke was appointed Ambassador and had to present his credentials. He drew up a memorandum for his own guidance at his first formal meeting with Lord Halifax, the Foreign Secretary, on 9 March 1939, and sent it to Burgos for approval (which it received). He was to emphasize three points:

1 Spain was determined to maintain its independence, despite military aid received from the Axis Powers.

2 He would appeal to Lord Halifax's religious and mystical sense, by explaining 'the lofty Catholic aspect of our noble Crusade'. He would recall the work Lord Halifax's father had done to unite the Churches of England and Rome.

3 The personality of the Caudillo: the duke was to explain that Franco was a humane man and alien to any spirit of vengeance in dealing with his Civil War opponents.[3]

Lord Halifax's reactions to these arguments are not known to me. Shortly afterwards, however, the Foreign Secretary summoned the duke to the Foreign Office, to ask him to explain Franco's motives in joining the Anti-Comintern Pact. On 27 April, the duke reported on the visit in a personal letter to Count Jordana, beginning *'Mi querido amigo'*, in the Ambassador's own hand. Halifax, he wrote, had said he quite understood Spain's motives and the Spanish desire to fight communism. He also understood Spain's lack of sympathy for, and reserve towards, England, in view of England's attitude during the Civil War. What could be done, asked Lord Halifax, to efface bad memories?[4] Britain's first Ambassador to Franco's Spain, Sir Samuel Hoare, was soon to find, however, that to efface the past was far from easy.

In adhering to the Anti-Comintern Pact, Franco was being consistent with himself, for as we have seen, his anti-communist convictions were of very long standing. In practical terms, however, Spain's adherence to the Pact was undoubtedly less significant than the conclusion, four days later, of a Treaty of Friendship and Non-aggression with Portugal; for it then became highly unlikely that Franco would get himself involved in a war on Germany's side against Britain, whose 'oldest ally' was Portugal. Indeed the Hispano-Portuguese Treaty, ratified on 31 March 1939, bound each signatory not to allow its territory to be used for aggressive purposes against the other. In the circumstances of 1939, this was equivalent to a further advance notice of neutrality.

Inevitably, however, German and Italian influences continued to outweigh all others in Burgos. It is hard, otherwise, to explain why Franco, who was deeply aware of his shattered country's need of capital, turned down the offer of a major reconstruction loan made in May by a consortium of Dutch, Belgian and French banks, with British support.[5] Similarly, it was as a concession to Italy (still smarting under the sanctions policy over the Abyssinian incident) that Franco withdrew Spain from the League of Nations, also in May; although the use of the Palace of Nations for Republican diatribes against the Nationalists could not have predisposed the Caudillo in favour of the League.

The most enthusiastic defender of the Italian connection was Serrano Súñer, who accompanied Mussolini's 'volunteers' back to Italy in May and spoke in praise of Italy in Barcelona on 14 June, on his way back. Less than a month later, Ciano returned the visit, meeting Franco at San Sebastian on 19 July, at the end of a Spanish tour. The two men had a long conversation, which Mussolini's son-in-law recorded in detail.[6] Ciano found Franco simple in bearing, calm in judgment and lucid in exposition, disinclined to speculate and with a preference for limiting conversation to actual events and their consequences. The Caudillo argued that he had to treat France with care, in order to recover the wealth exported by the Spanish Reds. As for identifying Spain with the Rome–Berlin Axis, this was his intention, but the conditions had to be right. Spain needed at least five years of peace. He realized, on the other hand, that a Spain that had remained neutral would have a wretched future after an Axis victory, and he thought the survival of his régime after a victory of the democracies would be out of the question. In the meantime, Spain would have to speed up its arms programme. Mussolini had been right in suggesting to Serrano that Spain should start building four battleships. The Air Force, too, had to be reorganized and formed into an autonomous body, detached from the Navy and Army. In both these matters, Italy's help would be appreciated. Finally, the Pyrenees would have to be fortified, and work had already begun.

Ciano was evidently flattered by the clear distinction Franco made, in Italy's favour, between Spain's attitudes towards Italy and Germany. Franco had left Ciano with the impression that he was completely under Mussolini's spell and declared repeatedly that when he met the Duce – as he expected to do shortly – he would be expecting instructions and even directives. The controlled Spanish press, however, was coldly unresponsive to Ciano's public claims that Spain stood side by side with the Axis against the democracies. Neither friendship nor gratitude, in the Caudillo's view, added up to a military alliance with Italy. Indeed his talk with Ciano on the eve of the war, was only the beginning of a long series of tortuous exchanges with the Axis, in which the recurring theme was always the same: an undertaking to enter the war on a date that remained unspecified, and on conditions that seemed likely to remain unfulfilled. Ciano was unaware of this at the time (as Franco intended) but western commentators have often failed to allow for the element of deception in Franco's pro-Axis utterances.[7]

On 23 August, only a few weeks after Ciano's visit, came news that shocked, outraged and bewildered the Spanish Nationalists: the Nazi-Soviet Pact was signed in Moscow. This shattering event, which made instant nonsense of the Anti-Comintern Pact, confirmed Franco's conviction that neutrality was Spain's only course, and greatly strengthened his hand against the advocates – chiefly to be found within the Falange – of an alliance with the Axis. Now Franco's supporters discovered how much more importance he attached to anti-Communism than to friendship with the Nazis. By this time, the pro-western Count Jordana had yielded to Colonel Beigbeder at the Foreign Ministry. This looked like a concession to the Nazis, for Beigbeder had served in Berlin as Military Attaché. But his term in Berlin had ended in a row in which he had been accused of prying into Nazi archives. In any case, Beigbeder was a true Anglophile. Indeed, Sir Samuel Hoare, shortly after taking up his appointment as British Ambassador, found him a 'sympathetic and attractive friend'.[8]

Hitler's attack on Poland was a further shattering blow to the advocates of friendship with the Nazis in Franco's entourage. The Caudillo himself found it incomprehensible that the initiator of the anti-Comintern Pact should have allied himself with the Bolsheviks in preparation for this aggression against a fellow-Catholic country. His first concern was to mediate between the belligerents, with two objects in mind – to save Poland and to avert a general war. His second concern was to keep Spain out of the conflict. Accordingly, Mussolini having failed to bring the Powers to a Munich-type conference to solve the problems of Danzig and the Polish Corridor, Franco tried his own hand as a mediator. On 3 September – the day of the declaration of war on Germany by Britain and France – he wired Mussolini from Burgos to say he wished to co-operate with the Duce in trying to localize the conflict.[9] The same day, he sent a Note to the ambassadors of the belligerent countries, in which he appealed to them in these words:

> With the authority given to me by the fact of having borne during three years the weight of a war to liberate our fatherland, I appeal to the nations that hold in their hands the power of unleashing a catastrophe without precedent in history, to spare the peoples the sufferings and tragedies that affected the Spaniards, in spite of the voluntary limitation of the use of means of destruction, and the horrors that would be multiplied one hundredfold in a new war.

If it was too late to stop the fighting, he went on, at least the belligerents should 'localize the present conflict'.[10]

Not unnaturally, this appeal fell on deaf ears: those of the Nazis, who were bent on conquest and had no wish to hear; and those of the Western Allies, who tended to look on Franco as a satellite-apparent of Hitler's, and who were undeterred by their own manifest inability to stop him from overrunning Poland, whose integrity they had guaranteed.

The following day – 4 September – mediation having failed, Franco ordered Spaniards to observe 'the strictest neutrality' and the press to refrain from all comment. Less than a fortnight later, Franco's worst fears were confirmed, when Hitler's Soviet allies invaded Poland from the east, meeting the advancing Germans two days later – on 19 September – at Brest-Litovsk. On 3 October, Franco told Manuel Aznar, the military historian of the Civil War, that he had done his best to 'avoid the disappearance of Poland'.

'My duty as leader of a Catholic people, and my interest in the fate of Europe,' he went on, 'impelled me to do this.' Now, however, the worst had happened; and with a prescience that was denied at the time to either of the belligerent camps – both of which had tried to woo the Russians – he added: 'The irruption of Russia into Europe is of very deep gravity. This fact cannot be hidden from anybody . . . It is necessary to act quickly so that new and yet graver perils for the European spirit do not come from eastern Europe. And this cannot be done unless peace is restored in the West.'[11]

The day this interview appeared, on 3 October, Franco launched a new attempt to mediate between the belligerents. Admiral Magaz, the Spanish Ambassador in Berlin, called on Ribbentrop to explain that his government was ready to mediate. And a week later, Colonel Beigbeder, in a talk with Stohrer, reiterated that Spain was 'completely and entirely at [Germany's] disposal in respect to the peace question'.[12] It must be assumed that Franco's government made similar overtures to London and Paris, which, however, remained unimpressed. Since Franco's efforts coincided with Hitler's own 'peace offensive' on the morrow of his Polish conquest, the natural tendency was to look upon Madrid's initiative as the junior Axis partner's way of helping the controlling shareholder. There is no reason to accept this view, since Franco's desire for peace and his forebodings about Russia so clearly outweighed his wish to help Hitler consolidate his hold on Catholic Poland.

The phoney war, meanwhile, was setting in, and the Caudillo used it, as far as he was able, to breathe some life into Spain's moribund economy. Towards the end of September, a national loan was floated. Oversubscribed, it brought in well over 5,000 million pesetas. On 7 October, General Franco put before his Ministers in Burgos a ten-year rehabilitation plan designed to reduce Spain's cruel dependence on imports and, by the same token, its chronically deficient balance of trade. The success of the national loan had encouraged him to believe that despite the country's parlous state, a start at least could be made with reconstruction out of her own resources. The plan he outlined aimed at laying the foundations of industrialization, by means of hydro-electric development, and increasing the areas under cultivation by extensive irrigation projects.

And now, on 18 October, the Caudillo left his war-time capital to set up a permanent peace-time administration in Madrid. He had selected as his residence, not the Royal Palace – a choice that would have implied more than his ambitions allowed for – but the more intimate and secluded Royal summer residence of El Pardo, close to Madrid. There, he at once settled down to the routine of work and exercise that has lasted with only minor changes to the present day.

There was much to do, and much to be undone. It is true, but only part of the truth, to say as Dante A. Puzzo says,[13] that 'Franco's victory had secured the political, economic, and social supremacy of the traditional ruling elements in Spanish life – the landed aristocracy, the financial and industrial oligarchy, the Army and the episcopacy'. Traditional Spain had won the Civil War, but traditional Spain was not alone, and its ally, the Falange, was revolutionary in intent, a point that escapes people who use such terms as 'fascist' and 'reactionary' simply as smear words.[14]

All Franco's supporters agreed that the anti-clerical and separatist measures of the Republic had to be undone. But the oligarchs among them were by no means attracted to the national-syndicalist and welfare state ideas of the Falangist old guard. Franco, however, had seen to it that the old guard was only part of the ruling FET (*Falange Española Tradicionalista y de las JONS*), and that the ruling party itself was only one of the pillars of the State – together with the Church and the Army. He could afford, therefore, to undo what everybody wanted undone, while not doing all that the Falange old guard – flushed with victory and the reflected glories of Axis successes – would have liked him to do.

He could cancel all laws passed by the Catalan parliament, as he did in September 1939, annul the 1932 divorce law and restore the payment of stipends to the clergy. He could please the traditionalists by restoring the consultative Council of State – abolished by the Republic – and please everybody by outlawing freemasonry, communism and anarchism, as he did early in 1940. He could delight the *Falangistas* and mildly shock the Vaticanists, by having the body of José Antonio Primo de Rivera re-buried with military pomp on 30 November 1939, in the chapel of the Escorial. He could please the landed gentry by restoring to them most of the lands confiscated by the Republic, and worry them by holding some land back for colonization by the peasants. He could give the *Falangistas* many of the trappings of the totalitarian State they wanted, but damp down their revolutionary fervour by vetoing their plans to control credit and socialize the economy. To all, he gave something; to each never enough.

All these things emerged during the autumn and winter of the phoney war. On 9 September 1939, Franco created the Institute of Political Studies, as a kind of brains trust for the FET, and on the same day, he appointed a National Delegate for the Syndicates, under an ambitious Falangist – Gerardo Salvador Merino, whose mandate was to build up the syndical organization, which existed only in rudimentary form at the end of the Civil War. The first outcome of his labours was the proclamation, on 26 January 1940, of the Law of Syndical Unity, which abolished government representation for private economic interests, reversing the provisions of the 1938 laws. Henceforth, all economic representation, both of the workers and of their employers, was allotted to the 'vertical syndicates' that have remained one of the more enduringly 'fascist' trappings of Franco's State. Towards the end of the year, the Falange's *Secceón Femenina*, which had taken over all Spain's social services with considerable success, was reorganized as a semi-autonomous organization on lines that paralleled those of the Falange itself, and under the direction of Pilar Primo de Rivera, younger sister of José Antonio.

This was the heyday of the party, whose tentacles now stretched in many directions – into the Army, all officers having become members during the Civil War; among the women, to whom the *Sección Feminina* brought a status within the State which they had never previously enjoyed; to the workers and their bosses, now united in enforced amity; and among the students, the Falange student syndicate having a monopoly of their representation. But the FET, powerful though it was, derived its power from Franco himself, who was its *Jefe Nacional* and in that capacity appointed the National Council of the party.

All power, indeed, flowed from Franco and was vested in him. And in foreign affairs as at home, the ultimate decisions were his. At the end of 1939, Juan Peche, the under-Secretary of State at the Foreign Ministry, declared, in a remark quoted by his colleague Doussinague:

> It is the Chief of State who personally holds all responsibility in these questions of international policy. He listens to one and all and meditates at length; and then it is he who takes the decision.[15]

Politically, the circumstances of Franco's victory obliged him to lean towards the Axis; but economically, his need was trade with Spain's traditional partners. A formal military commitment to

Germany would have deprived the country of its life blood. Neutrality kept it flowing. On the outbreak of war, Britain and Spain had exchanged Notes that amounted to a war trade agreement. In March 1940, the two governments signed a formal trade agreement, under which Spain obtained £4 million worth of credits in London and promised not to re-export sterling area purchases. Already, Franco had concluded trade pacts with Portugal (December 1939) and France (January 1940), and reaffirmed previous economic agreements with Germany by means of a protocol (22 December 1939). In March 1940, both sides were reasonably satisfied with Madrid's behaviour. In London, Mr R. A. Butler, then Under-Secretary for Foreign Affairs, told the House of Commons: 'We have no cause to complain of the Spanish government's attitude, which has been one of strict neutrality.' And Hitler, writing to Mussolini from Berlin on 8 March, observed that he had 'no reason to be displeased with the Caudillo, quite the contrary. Furthermore, I understand perfectly the desire experienced by that country, after three years of cruel civil war, not to get caught up in a new conflict'.[16]

Even during the phoney war, however, the weight of Germany was preponderant in Madrid, and as early as 19 October 1939, Stohrer was able to report that Beigbeder, despite his pro-British inclinations, was supplying him with information originating from Spanish diplomatic missions abroad.[17] To be sure, this was a relatively cheap way of keeping in with the then dominant race, since the value of the information made available by the Spaniards does not seem to have been very great.* The real enemy of the western allies in this early war-time period was Serrano Súñer, whose rise to eminence was continuing unchecked. In Spain at that time, if Franco was the fount of all power, Serrano was the man who exercised it.

Already the *Cuñadísimo* was head of the Falange's *Junta Política* and Minister of the Interior. The party, the police and the press were at his orders. His ambition seemed boundless and his abilities were considerable. His nervous energy was inexhaustible. Possessed of a subtle and analytical intelligence, he was fanatically devoted to the

* On 6 September 1940, Franco told Stohrer that he had instructed the Spanish Ambassador in London to ask all Spanish consuls in England for 'detailed reports on the morale of the population and the effects of our [German] attacks by air' (Documents, Series D, Vol. XI, p. 48).

new form of Spanish fascism – which he had largely created, and which was consistent with his devout Catholicism as Nazi paganism could never have been. Yet he was able, when the occasion demanded, to be cautious. He saw himself as the architect of a permanent fascist State, with an unshakable legal and constitutional structure. Looking further ahead, he probably saw a Spain in which Franco, as a figurehead President, would benevolently reign over a State in which he, Serrano, exercised the substance of power. And looking beyond Spain's boundaries, his vision was of a Europe dominated by the victorious Axis Powers, in which an independent Spain, aggrandized perhaps at France's expense in Africa, would play a part consistent with its mighty past.

Franco, for his part, did not see himself as a figurehead, nor had he any taste for rigid constitutional forms that might deprive him of his freedom of manœuvre. The Falange was useful, as the Carlists and other traditionalists had been. But the time might come when it would have to be cut to size, its usefulness exhausted. The time might come, too, when the *Cuñadísimo* would have to be cut to size. But that time had not yet come. This was Serrano's hour.

'He hates and loves impetuously,' said Ciano; and if France was his *bête noire*, as Ciano put it, he had no love for England either.[18] He hated France both on patriotic and on personal grounds – because France was 'the eternal enemy of Greater Spain' and because he thought his two brothers had been put to death 'by French bullets'. Similar considerations governed his slightly milder feelings towards England. The youth of Spain, he told Ciano, lived for the day when England would be pushed into the sea; while he held the British partly to blame for his brothers' death at the hands of the Republicans for turning them away when they asked for asylum at the British Embassy. Sir Samuel Hoare, when he became Britain's Ambassador, was unable to shake this belief although he had gone to great pains to sift the allegation and 'found that there was no shred of evidence in support of it'.[19] Serrano, in fact, still held it when I first met him in Madrid in 1965. As for his loves, he declared in his own book, *Entre Hendaya y Gibraltar*, that he was an Italophile 'spontaneously' and a Germanophile 'reflectively'.[20]

This distinction shows that it would be misleading to simplify his emotions. Hoare, who disliked him and all he stood for, and suffered greatly from his rudeness and obstructiveness, could not find anything good to say about him. It became fashionable, in English histories and works of reference, to dub him 'Germanophile' and leave it at that. His own viewpoint has had less of a hearing, if only because his book of memoirs – one of the liveliest and most fascinating sources of that period – has never appeared in an English translation. He had finished his education in Bologna and felt a Catholic and Latin affinity with the Italians. For the Germans, he felt admiration and fascination, but not love or understanding. He expends a good many words, in his memoirs, unexpectedly defending himself against charges that he was not really pro-German. In 1939 and 1940 (and well beyond) he was convinced the Germans were going to win the war and that the best way of serving Spain's interests was to be 'absolutely friendly' towards the Axis.[21]

What he meant by 'absolutely friendly', as he showed during his time as Minister of the Interior, was to turn the Spanish newspapers into vehicles for unbridled German propaganda, and order the police to give every help to the Nazi agents who swarmed over the capital. Collaboration with the Germans, however, stopped short of praise for the Nazi-Soviet Pact or any sign of tolerance for Bolshevism; and when the Russians invaded Finland at the end of November 1939, the controlled Spanish press energetically denounced the aggression.

Although Franco allowed his brother-in-law a free rein for his pro-German activities, he himself neglected no occasion to further his claims as a mediator and improve his links with the West. He was deeply impressed by Pope Pius XII's appeal for peace in his Christmas message in 1939, and sought to identify Spain with it in his own message to the Spanish people on 31 December, which ended with the following words:

> Our nation, which fought heroically for three years to save Christian civilization from extinction in the West, shares in these moments the sufferings of the other peoples of Europe, and joins its voice to the supreme authority of the Catholic Church, of our beloved Italy and of so many States that are pressing for a cessation of hostilities which, if they go on to the end, will open the way to the West for Asiatic barbarism.

The trade pacts with Britain and France had been one sign of Franco's desire to improve relations with the West, and before the winter was over, he tried to seize what looked like a chance of associating Spain with American peace initiatives. In February 1940, President Roosevelt sent his Under-Secretary of State, Mr Sumner Welles, to Europe on an exploratory mission. Mr Welles was to visit the belligerent countries: Britain and France on the Allied side, and Germany and Italy on the Axis side.

Two things encouraged Franco to think that a settlement of differences was not out of the question. One was a speech by Neville Chamberlain on 24 February, opening the way for a *modus vivendi* with Germany on condition that the independence of Czechoslovakia and Poland was restored. The other was a report known as the 'Dublin document', which purported to represent Germany's peace proposals, as expressed by a senior member of the Nazi Embassy in Dublin. As transmitted to Madrid by the duke of Alba, the 'Dublin document' offered recognition of Czech and Polish independence, a plebiscite in Austria and disarmament under an international Convention.[22] Mr Welles arrived in Rome on 26 February, where he saw Mussolini and Ciano, and went on to Berlin for talks with Hitler, Ribbentrop, Hess and Goering. His itinerary led to London via Paris, and the Spanish Foreign Minister, Beigbeder, instructed the duke of Alba to try to see him in London. He was to explain that Spain and other neutrals were against the annihilation of any belligerent, on the ground that any future peace would require the full economic support of France, England and Germany. Peace must be negotiated, not imposed; and negotiations should be based on the principles stated by the Pope in his Christmas message (which included equality of rights and the recognition of the needs and rights of peoples and minorities, together with agreed disarmament).

Sumner Welles reached London on 11 March, and two days later more precise instructions were sent to the duke of Alba. He was to invite Mr Welles to Madrid for a talk with the Caudillo, with a view to convening a conference of neutral nations – including Spain and the United States – at San Sebastian. Next day, however, came a telegram from the duke, saying Sumner Welles had declined to see him. José M. Doussinague, the then Director-General at the Spanish Foreign Ministry, records the news with indignant bewilderment, in his memoirs, *España Tenía Razón*, finding it hard to understand such an affront to 'the duke of Alba, a Stuart, duke of Berwick, three times a grandee of Spain, knight of the Golden Fleece, peer of England, whom His Britannic Majesty called "cousin", ambassador to the nation that gave its civilization to eighteen American countries and to which belonged three-quarters of the territory of the United States from Florida to Louisiana'.[23] The unimaginable had, however, happened, and later attempts to make contact with Sumner Welles in Paris and Rome, to which he returned before going home, were unavailing. In American eyes, Spain was a satellite of the Axis and Franco a 'fascist dictator'. A further chance of a Spanish–American dialogue did not come until 1942, when President Roosevelt sent Professor Carlton J. H. Hayes to Madrid as Ambassador.

And then, in April 1940, the illusory calm of the phoney war was shattered when Hitler's airborne divisions descended on Norway. An Anglo–French expeditionary force, sent to relieve the Norwegians, was defeated within a fortnight. Hardly had the survivors returned when the Nazi *Blitzkrieg* began against the Low Countries, Luxembourg and France. By mid-June, while Russian forces moved into Estonia, Latvia and Lithuania, Marshal Philippe Petain, called to 'power' in defeated France, was suing for an armistice. The aged soldier had been appointed ambassador to Franco Spain on the eve of the Republican collapse. In the prevailing climate he had accomplished little in Spain. When he took his leave of the Caudillo in June 1940, Franco said, 'Don't go, Marshal. Shelter behind your age. Let those who lost the war liquidate it and sign the peace. Thanks to God, you were here, apart, without any responsibility whatever. You are the victorious soldier of Verdun. Don't allow your name to be linked with what other people have lost.'

'I know, General,' replied the old man. 'But my country is calling me and it is my duty to go. It will perhaps be the last service I can render.'

'He embraced me, very moved,' Franco added, 'and left for the sacrifice.'[24]

2 *Non-Belligerency*

In the dramatic happenings of 1940, Mussolini saw a chance of instant glory and a place in the pantheon of the great conquerors. More practically inclined, Franco saw above all terrible dangers ahead for

Spain, to be avoided if at all possible. The only way to avoid them was to keep Spain out of the war, and the best hope of doing that lay in naming an impossibly high price for Spain's participation at Germany's side, and raising it each time the subject came up. To be sure, he allowed himself to nurse ambitions for colonial expansion at France's expense, and for the recovery of Gibraltar. But such ambitions, when presented as demands, were always hypothetical, and he was always aware that they were. In their different ways, Hitler's demented dreams of territorial grandeur had affected both Mussolini and Serrano Súñer. Though Franco was convinced that German arms were invincible, his feet were more firmly on the ground. Hoare was to find him 'incredibly complacent', but it is hard to agree a quarter-century later, that his self-confidence, in a crushingly difficult situation, was misplaced.

In May 1940, while the Nazi Panzer divisions were pouring through the Ardennes, Mussolini's dominant anxiety was that his chance of glory might be slipping through his grasp. 'We Italians,' he told Ciano, 'are already sufficiently dishonoured. Any delay is inconceivable. We have no time to lose. Within a month I shall declare war.'[1]

He did, on June 10, only a week before France sued for an armistice.

In this situation, Franco did not seek glory in the last hours of somebody else's victory, but needed to show that he supported the Germans without actually fighting on their side. Mussolini's old formula of 'non-belligerency', now discarded, filled the bill, and two days after the Duce's declaration of war, Franco adopted it as his own, in his turn discarding 'neutrality'.

It was in these forbidding circumstances, a week or so before Mussolini's 'stab in the back', that Hoare arrived in Madrid as Britain's 'ambassador on special mission'. He had been preceded by a highly eulogistic account from the duke of Alba, which referred to his anti-Communism (dating back, the duke pointed out, to an intelligence mission to Moscow at the time of the Bolshevik revolution), and to his friendly attitude towards the Nationalist cause during the Civil War, marked among other things by the sending of congratulations on Franco's victory at Teruel.[2]

Although this impressive build-up had been shown to Franco personally (which was not true of all the duke's dispatches), Hoare was kept waiting until 22 June for his first interview with the Spanish

15a 'The radio General': Queipo de Llano of Seville.

15b 'The conspirator': General Mola's last picture.

15c The defeated Republican Premier, Dr Negrín (1938).

16a Chief of State and kingmaker: General Franco and his brother Nicolás.

16b Franco prepares the death blow – Catalan front, 1939.

Chief of State. He naturally seized the occasion to ask Franco what was meant by 'the equivocal and ill-omened status of non-belligerency'. What it did *not* mean, said Franco, was any departure from the general policy of keeping out of the war. On the other hand, the war having reached the Mediterranean, Spain had 'to show its direct interest in what had happened and to be prepared for all emergencies'.[3]

The first of Hoare's exasperated references to Franco's complacency follows:

> We parted, he, completely blind to the moral and material strength of the British Empire; I, astonished at his unshakable complacency and at his evident conviction that he had been marked out by Providence to save his country and to take a leading part in the reconstruction of the new world.

On 14 June, Franco demonstrated the kind of action he had in mind, when his troops occupied Tangier, in the name of the Sultan and with the proclaimed motive of preserving order – a defensible claim, since Italy's entry into the war made nonsense of the Tangier Statute of 1928, under which Italy and Spain shared control of the city with Britain and France. This minor action, however, served two more tangible purposes of foreign policy: it gave notice to Mussolini that Spain, like Italy, was a claimant in any redistribution of Mediterranean spoils, and it could be represented in the Spanish Press – and was – as a victory over the discomfited western allies.

A few weeks later, on 18 July, the Caudillo made a bellicose speech, laying claim to Gibraltar and declaring that two million soldiers were ready to revive Spain's glorious past.[4]

The 'impregnable' Rock, a perpetual thorn in Spain's proud flesh, was of course a natural focus of irredentist claims in the feverish days of expansionism by Franco's dictatorial partners. But the shouts of 'Gibraltar Español' that punctuated a well-drilled march past in the presence of the Diplomatic Corps added to the calculated discomforts inflicted on the stoical Sir Samuel Hoare during his first few days in Madrid.

Franco himself simply puzzled him: 'There was obviously more in him than met the eye,' he wrote, 'or how else could this young officer of Jewish origin, little influence and unimpressive personality have risen to the highest post in the State?'[5] Then came one of Hoare's

M

rare moments of insight. On one point, and one only, there was common ground between them: the desire to keep Spain out of the war. It was therefore important to support him in any resistance he might make to German aggression. 'The mysterious movements of Providence, I reflected, might indeed be providing a dictator for the destruction of other dictators.'

Rare though such insights were, a measure of admiration must be spared for Hoare's behaviour in an oppressive, hostile and provocative atmosphere. Madrid was hungry and the threat of famine hung over the countryside. In his New Year message for 1940, General Franco had presented a crushing list of the country's deficiencies: 500,000 tons of wheat (a quarter of normal consumption), 120,000 tons of root vegetables and rice (a fifth of normal consumption) and 180,000 tons of sugar (more than half the people's needs).[6] Spain, he said, was producing only a quarter of the milk she needed. The situation grew steadily worse during the first winter of the Second World War, and in April, Serrano announced that Spain was short of a million tons of wheat to satisfy normal needs. Britain sent thirty-four wheat ships to Spanish ports, but the bread ration stood at 250 grammes a day and was not always honoured. The 1940 harvest was disastrous. Tobacco, fuel, paper and petrol were in short supply and black marketeering was rife. The *estraperlistas* – or black marketeers – were flourishing and prices were soaring. Starved of raw materials, industry was at a standstill.

Against this background of misery, tensions of diverse kinds gripped the capital. Madrid, wrote Hoare, was like a besieged city, and a small army of official gunmen followed him around. Falangists and Civil Guards, police and troops, patrolled the streets. Malignant rumours, often fostered by the Germans, who virtually controlled the Spanish censorship, spiralled through the cafés and drawing rooms. Any reader of the Spanish Press would have concluded that Britain was starving and on its knees; and anti-British incidents – such as tearing flags off British embassy cars – heightened the ambience of hostility and hysteria.

There was one bright spot, from Sir Samuel Hoare's viewpoint: the almost recklessly demonstrative friendship of Colonel Beigbeder, the Foreign Minister, who, at a time when the Ambassador was most closely watched by the Gestapo, would walk arm in arm with him through the streets.[7] Beigbeder's star, however, was on the wane, and Serrano was determined to snuff it out. From the drama of Dunkirk on 4 June, the two men drew contradictory lessons. Beigbeder noted that 215,000 British troops had been saved, to fight another day; Serrano, exulting in Hitler's victory, accepted the Führer's invitation to the cocktail party he proposed to give in London on 15 September. In Serrano's eyes, Jordana – Beigbeder's predecessor as Foreign Minister – had been old and stupid, and Beigbeder himself was simply mad – a man to be removed from responsibility as soon as possible.[8]

At the time, the logic of events did seem to be on Serrano's side. As he wrote after the war, 'in not much more than half a year, Germany had occupied the whole of the western coast of the Continent, from the Polar Circle to the Gulf of Viscaya' (Bay of Biscay).[9] Indeed on 27 June, the first German forces had reached the Pyrenees. The invincibility of Nazi arms seemed patent, and any outcome other than total victory the purest self-delusion. It was unthinkable, as Serrano wrote, to oppose Germany, and even a 'chemically pure' neutrality would not have saved Spain from German occupation. Only words and gestures of friendship to Germany might avert the catastrophe. He knew for a fact that in July 1940, the British government didn't even dream of surviving until September, and supported the assertion with a reference to a speech in November 1940 by 'that great fighter Churchill'. To be sure, England resisted alone, 'with boldness, with all its strength and heroically, in the unequal fight'.[10] But no relief was in sight, for the entry of the United States in the war seemed unlikely. Even Roosevelt, who supported Churchill, was pessimistic, and prominent Americans, from Senator Vandenberg to Lindbergh and Joseph Kennedy, the ambassador in London, opposed intervention.

Franco fully shared his brother-in-law's reading of the military situation in Europe and of Spain's plight. But he was more realistic than Serrano in his appreciation of the country's need to avoid antagonizing Britain to an extent that might jeopardize desperately needed deliveries. True, he had told Hoare that Spain needed nothing from the British Empire and could import anything it did need from North Africa;[11] but in view of his readiness to sign economic pacts with Britain, it is clear that this was a line calculated to deflate the Ambassador's bargaining power in 'England's finest hour'. When Serrano was advocating at least an unconditional verbal commitment to the Axis, Franco continued to support Beigbeder. It was typical of his approach to government.

In June, when Beigbeder was negotiating an agreement with Portugal, to complement the previous year's Friendship Treaty, Serrano's controlled Press launched a campaign against Portugal as England's ally. The *Cuñadísimo* persuaded Franco, by last minute pressure, to hold up the signing of the final agreement, but Franco, in the end, overruled him and signed.[12] And the following month (24 July), Franco went further and sanctioned a three-way agreement between Britain, Spain and Portugal, providing for commercial exchanges through the sterling area.[13]

The same month, the British Council was allowed to open a British Institute in Madrid. There were other signs, too, of Franco's determination not to be swept off his feet by Hitler's triumphs. For instance, he dismissed General López Pinto, who had called for cheers for the Führer and the Duce at a reception for German officers on the Franco–Spanish border when the Nazi forces reached the Pyrenees. And in July 1940, he offered the palace of La Granja to the children of King Leopold of the Belgians as a residence while the war lasted. [14]

Having thus reasserted his independence and strengthened his western bridges, Franco summoned the German ambassador and stated his terms – as they then stood – for entering the war. Reporting on his talk on 8 August, Stohrer told Berlin that Franco was indeed willing to enter the war. But before doing so, he wanted assurances that Spain would receive Gibraltar, French Morocco and the pre-dominantly Spanish-speaking Oran area of Algeria. Rio de Oro, and the Spanish colonies of the Gulf of Guinea were also to be expanded at France's expense. In addition, Spain would need military and other assistance for playing its part in the war. The economic support Franco expected from Germany included petrol and wheat. Even if Germany made all the required promises, however, the Caudillo thought Spain should not intervene before Germany had landed in Britain – 'to avoid entering the war prematurely, or a war of a duration which the country could not support and which would, in certain conditions, be a source of danger for us.'

A week later, Franco was making a similarly cloudy promise to the Duce in a letter dated 15 August, in which he declared his readiness 'to enter the foreign war at a favourable opportunity in proportion to the means at our disposal'.[15] He appealed to the Duce for support in his claims to territories 'whose present administration is a consequence of that Franco-English policy of domination and exploitation, of which Italy also bears so many scars'.

Mussolini replied on 25 August, inviting Franco not to stand aside from the history of Europe which the victorious Axis Powers were creating.[16] Franco, however, was keeping his own counsel. He had made conditional promises. He now had to find ways of avoiding more precise commitments. Although he did not know it at the time, Hitler – evidently counting on Franco's apparent readiness to enter the war – was about to decide on an assault on Gibraltar, as part of a wider operation designed to give Germany control over the Mediterranean. On 6 September, the Führer summoned Grand Admiral Raeder, Commander-in-Chief of the Navy, and General Jodl, to a conference in Berlin. Preparations for Operation Felix, as it was called, were to begin immediately, for any American intervention must be forestalled. About Gibraltar, Hitler was specific: its conquest 'should not be considered of secondary importance, but *as one of the main blows against Britain*'.[17] Raeder himself italicized the key words.

There is therefore no doubt of the supreme importance Hitler attached at that time to Spain's participation in the war. Although Franco knew nothing of the Berlin conference of 6 September, he sensed the pressures the Germans were about to bring to bear upon him. As the days passed and the German bombing of British targets gathered momentum, Beigbeder's pro-British policy began to look more and more Quixotic and untenable. Serrano had been saying this for some time, and now, at the beginning of September, Franco began to share his view that Beigbeder's period of usefulness was approaching its close. Massive though Germany's representation was in Madrid, Serrano considered Spain's communications with Germany to be inadequate, because the Spanish Ambassador in Berlin, Admiral Magaz, was 'old and tired'.[18] It was essential, writes Serrano in his memoirs, to end Spain's isolation and establish effective contact with a powerful neighbour who might at any moment become the occupying Power.

He, Serrano Súñer, was the man to do this, he told Franco; and Beigbeder must go. Cautious as usual, the Caudillo proposed a compromise. He admitted that Beigbeder was too clearly labelled 'pro-British' to be acceptable in Berlin as a negotiating partner. He agreed, therefore, that Serrano himself should go to Berlin; but Beigbeder could keep his job, at least for the time being. After all, he reasoned, Churchill had not yet conceded defeat.

Preceded by a formal letter from Franco to Hitler, Serrano started on his journey on 13 September, accompanied by Ambassador Stohrer and by a large Spanish retinue whose function was to impress by numbers rather than to perform any useful work. After a day in war-time Paris – sad, deserted and beautiful – the long, slow trip brought the party to Berlin on 16 September. An hour later, the Falange Minister was closeted with Ribbentrop.* Serrano found the Nazi Foreign Minister good-looking but uncongenial – *poco simpático* – neither distinguished nor elegant.[19] Whether by order or by personal inclination, Ribbentrop set out to bully his Spanish visitor. He asked Serrano point-blank when Spain could enter the war. Playing for time, the Falange leader outlined Spain's aspirations and needs – especially the needs, of which he presented a formidable list embracing stated requirements of food, petrol, rubber, cotton, nitrates and transport. Ribbentrop commented that the figures mentioned seemed excessive.

Hurriedly, Serrano changed the subject to Morocco. He gave an exposé of the international agreements under which mandates and zones of influence had been distributed without consideration for Spain's natural rights. This was evidently the right tactic, for Ribbentrop relapsed into a silence which Franco's brother-in-law found significant. The Germans, he thought, had no wish to commit themselves on Morocco, either because of promises to Pétain or because of their own African ambitions. On the Spanish side, there could be no illusions, but the only course was 'to shelter intransigently behind our claims'. Informed of this stand, Franco sent his strong approval.

Serrano felt he had won a verbal battle; but he had not yet won the campaign. Indeed, the Nazi pressure had only begun. A luncheon

---

* My account of Serrano Súñer's talks in Berlin are based, in the main, on his memoirs (*Entre Hendaya y Gibraltar*, pp. 165–94). The much fuller account in the captured German archives differs from Serrano's on a number of points of detail, and even in chronological presentation. Although the German version may well be more accurate, I have thought it more appropriate, for the purposes of this book, to present events through the eyes of the principal Spanish participant.

and reception in honour of Don Ramón and his entourage followed, at which Ribbentrop voiced Hitler's displeasure at Spain's equivocal foreign policy. This amounted to ingratitude, said Ribbentrop, and he went on to accuse the Franco government of harbouring a Minister who was in the service of England – a clear reference to Beigbeder. Serrano Súñer, of course, held no brief for Beigbeder, whom he was hoping to supplant. Nevertheless, he took issue energetically with his host, who withdrew the charge but added in a threatening tone that lack of clarity in Spain's foreign policy might one day make Hitler decide to occupy the peninsula as a security measure, in view of its strategic value. Nor was he able to approve of Spain's friendship with Portugal, which maintained close links with England. Should it ever be known that Spain's friendship with Germany was luke-warm, the British might land in Portugal, as they had in Wellington's day.

Serrano Súñer records that he was 'naturally worried', although he personally thought it would be a good thing for Spain to be on Germany's side, militarily.

In contrast to his Foreign Minister, Hitler seems to have decided to present a paternal image to the Spanish visitors, leaving actual threats to Ribbentrop. At Serrano's first meeting with the Führer, on 17 September, Hitler embarked on one of his theoretical dissertations. Comparing Europe and Africa to America, North and South, he said that the unity of the two parts was essential. He referred only in vague terms to Spain's possible participation in the war. Since Spain was in Europe, Spain must be part of its unity and its system. In this context, Spain's geographical situation had an important contribution to make. Serrano said that if Spain was to capture Gibraltar, she would need 380 mm. guns, knowing as he said it that Germany could not supply them.[20] Evading the issue, however, Hitler replied that technicians from both countries must start talks. As for territorial claims, Hitler reluctantly conceded Morocco to Spain, but 'on condition that they (the Spaniards) assured to Germany, through favourable trade agreements, a part of the raw materials of that region'[21] – an indirect way of saying the Germans would probably lay claim to the whole of Morocco, if they felt like it. One thing was plain to Serrano: had he said 'No', categorically, to Hitler's demands, the Führer, would have developed an irresistible urge to violate Spain's neutrality.[22]

A further disagreeable talk with Ribbentrop followed immediately. Pointing to a wall map, the Nazi Foreign Minister outlined a zone starting at Lake Chad and stretching to Angola and Mozambique, excluding the Portuguese territories but including the Cameroons, French Equatorial Africa, the Congo – French and Belgian – Kenya and Tanganyika. All this, he exclaimed, constituted Germany's sphere of interest. Pointing to Spanish Guinea, Serrano observed that it needed a larger hinterland than it already had. Ribbentrop did not bother to answer, but observed that Germany needed military and air bases in Mogador and Agadir, both in French Morocco.

Suddenly, Ribbentrop dealt Serrano an unexpected body blow. He demanded the cession to Germany of one of the Canary Islands, on which a German military base could be established.* Though taken aback, Serrano replied, sturdily enough: 'Please take account of the fact, Mr Minister, that these islands of which you are speaking form part of our national territory itself; they are a province of our Fatherland.'

'Common necessities of Euro-African defence in the face of American imperialism,' Ribbentrop rejoined, 'call for this. I hope the Generalissimo will see things this way.'

Serrano commented that he could not even transmit such a request to General Franco. He nevertheless sent the Caudillo a special letter by air in the plane the Germans had placed at his disposal. In a reply dated 21 September, Franco congratulated his brother-in-law on his conduct of his second interview with Ribbentrop. Referring to the latter's demand for a base on the Canaries, he added, characteristically, that he could only make an allusion to what had justly provoked Serrano's indignation 'and which the pen is reluctant to write'.[23]

In the meantime, Serrano's tormentor, Ribbentrop, had gone down to Rome, where he arrived on 19 September, to tell Mussolini about the Triple Alliance between Germany, Italy and Japan, of which he considered himself to be the architect. During his conversation with the Duce, the day he arrived, Ribbentrop took a more sanguine view of the prospects for Spain's entry into the war than his exchanges

* Documents on German Foreign Policy, Series D. Vol. XI, No. 63, p. 90. Serrano himself, though he records his indignation, states more mildly (*Entre Hendaya y Gibraltar*, p. 182) that Ribbentrop requested the cession of *a base* on one of the islands, not the island itself. Although the distinction is small, I have preferred, in this instance, the German version, which seems to justify Serrano's indignation more convincingly than his own account does.

with Serrano could have justified. The Führer was, in principle, in favour of giving the Spaniards what they wanted, and the immediate object of Spain's entry would be the occupation of Gibraltar. The German General Staff was already working on plans, and Ribbentrop hoped, on his return to Berlin, to draw up a protocol with Serrano defining the conditions for Spain's entry into the war.[24] He thought Spain would declare war on England in four weeks' time, with the first shot fired on Gibraltar.

Ribbentrop, however, was counting chickens in eggs that did not look like being hatched. And so was his master, for on 18 September – with Serrano still in Germany – Hitler wrote Franco a letter couched in the most cordial terms, in which he took it for granted that Spain would enter the war on the side of the Axis Powers.[25] Indeed, the cordiality arose from this assumption.

Franco read the letter as soon as the German Chargé d'Affaires handed it over, but took two days over his reply. This was hardly surprising, for he had made up his mind to say No without appearing to say it, and the implications of every sentence had to be carefully weighed. In his letter, dated 22 September, he thanked Hitler for the cordial reception his envoy had been given and said that, apart from 'small details', he agreed with the Führer on Spain's part in the war.[26] The 'small details', however, turned into a formidable list. German bases in Morocco, which Ribbentrop had proposed, would be 'unnecessary in peacetime, and superfluous in wartime'. Expelling the British Fleet from the Mediterranean would not solve Spain's supply problem 'since there are many products and raw materials which Spain lacks, and which are not to be found in the Mediterranean basin'. Besides, Franco went on, English naval strength could be seriously impaired only if the Italians were successful in Egypt. And unless it was impaired, Spanish action in the western Mediterranean might not succeed. Then again, it would be difficult for Spain to keep the British out of the Canary Islands unless the Germans helped with dive-bombers. This, it will be seen, was a new element, which has to be considered against the background of the letter Franco had written to Serrano the day before. Since the Germans were asking for bases on the Canaries, Franco countered by asking for German help to keep the British out. Thus the price for Spanish participation in the war rose still higher. In the circumstances, the fact that Franco ended his letter to Hitler with an affirmation of loyalty to the Axis cause should have carried little weight.

By invitation of the Führer, Serrano left Berlin to pay a brief visit to France and Belgium, where he was shown German fortifications and was duly impressed by their apparent efficacy and by the optimism of the German military authorities. Back in Berlin, he had yet another talk with Ribbentrop on 24 September. Hitler's interpreter, Paul Schmidt, who was there, describes Ribbentrop pointing to the wall map of France's colonial empire in Africa and – this time – saying: 'Help yourself!'[27] Ribbentrop according to Schmidt, was eager to sell goods that did not belong to him, for no price was too high for Spanish collaboration. He adds that Ribbentrop requested U-boat bases in Rio de Oro and on the island of Fernando Po, opposite the Cameroons. Serrano was non-committal, but thought bases in Rio de Oro might perhaps be conceded. He declined any concessions on Fernando Po, both for historical reasons and because Spanish public opinion would not stand for it.

Soon, as Schmidt records, Hitler and Mussolini were referring to Serrano as a 'crafty Jesuit'.[28] Serrano, for his part, quotes these words from his diary: 'My reasons seem to them too unilateral and my answers inconvenient. It wouldn't surprise me to learn that what they were looking for was a serf.'[29] Later, Ribbentrop posted a man called Gardemann as his special agent, to the German Embassy in Madrid. There he intrigued against the ambassador and against Serrano himself, stirring up the latter's enemies in the Party.

Serrano's Nazi hosts must indeed have found him an infuriating guest. Faced with all the power and grandeur of Hitler's Reich, and Ribbentrop's bullying, he remained polite but elusive. On 27 September – after ten days in Nazi company – he assisted at the signing of the Triple Alliance, which, as he says in italics in his memoirs, 'we refused to sign'.

He had, in fact, weathered the storm. In a second interview with Hitler, on the day of the signing and before his departure for Rome, Serrano found the Nazi dictator relaxed and cordial. There is no doubt that the young Minister was fascinated by Hitler's monstrous genius – the term he used when I first met him in Madrid twenty-five years after these events. At the time, he found Hitler an extraordinary mixture – at once petty *bourgeois* sentimental, hard, fanatical and

NON-BELLIGERENCY325

childish. But one thing was clear: neither Hitler nor Ribbentrop had obtained the substance of a promise from the Spaniards.

Count Ciano had come to Berlin on 27 September for the signing of the Tripartite Pact. Next day, he too had a talk with Hitler, who looked worried.[30] There now seemed no chance of invading England or blitzing the British into submission, wrote Ciano. The Führer seemed much concerned about Spanish intervention, but now thought it would cost more than it was worth. This was one way of putting it. Franco, said Hitler, had asked Germany to deliver between 400,000 and 700,000 tons of grain for the coming year; all necessary fuel, equipment for the Spanish Army; aircraft and artillery, together with specialists and special weapons for use against Gibraltar; and all this on top of the territorial demands in Africa. The sacrifice was too great for the 'good graces' of the Spaniards.

Warming to his indictment, Hitler observed that without the help of Germany and Italy, there would be no Franco. Ciano picked up the theme. At the beginning of the Civil War, he said, Franco had asked Italy for twelve planes, to win the war in a matter of days, but 'these twelve air planes became more than one thousand airplanes, six thousand dead and fourteen billion lire'.

Hitler revealed that Franco had suggested a personal meeting with him, but before committing himself, he would like to discuss the matter with the Duce.

The Hitler–Mussolini meeting was to take place on the Brenner Pass on 4 October. But, in the meantime, Serrano Súñer arrived in Rome three days earlier. The 'Germanophile' Falange leader was sadly out of temper with his late hosts, and Ciano records that he exploded in 'colourful invectives against the Germans for their absolute lack of tact in dealing with Spain.'[31] Ciano thought he was right but wished he had chosen milder words to express himself, since the Spaniards had been asking for a lot for years and giving nothing in return.

In the formal conversation that followed, Serrano told the Duce and Ciano that Spain was preparing to take up arms to settle its centuries-old account with Great Britain.[32] But he did not name a date for Spain's entry in the war and recapitulated Spain's familiar needs and difficulties. The Duce, bombastic as usual, repeated his conviction that Franco Spain would be unable to stand aside from the great fight. The question now was to settle the time for Spain's declaration of war. Italy, unfortunately, had had a bad harvest and could do nothing to help Spain with grain; on the other hand, air support could be assured here and now.

Serrano, having stayed on in Berlin to see the signing of the Tripartite Pact, now decided to stay on in Rome and hear about Mussolini's meeting with Hitler. The two dictators met in the presence of their Foreign Ministers. The Führer blamed his failure to invade England on the weather and the blocking of French ports with ships the Germans themselves had sunk. Meanwhile the bombing went on 'in the hope of dealing a decisive blow'.[33] This was where Spanish intervention came in. Hitler outlined the protocol the Spaniards had proposed but raised objections to Spain's territorial demands. Gibraltar could be ceded to Spain, but not Morocco, for Germany needed part of the Moroccan coast as a base and had to think of the colonies it would need in West Africa. In any case, it would be dangerous to let it be known that Spain was to get Morocco, for England might be provoked into occupying the Canaries, while North Africa might go over to the Gaullist movement. The Duce suggested that Serrano Súñer should be told they agreed to Spain's claim to Gibraltar; as for Morocco, there was agreement in principle, but precise definition of claims would have to await a peace conference. Hitler assented to this presentation.

The following day, Ciano reported to Serrano on the Brenner meeting as far as Spain was affected and recorded in his *Diary* that the Spaniard was only half satisfied. 'Why hasn't he seen,' Ciano asked himself, 'that the Germans have had an eye on Morocco for a long time?'

3 *Franco v. Hitler, Game One*

The stage was now virtually set for Franco's meeting with Hitler. The wily Caudillo could not see all the cards in the game, but he could see enough of them to know that the Axis Powers were not quite in sight of the victory they kept on trumpeting. September had come and gone without the promised invasion of England, and the British seemed to be standing firm under the repeated blows of the

Luftwaffe. And now autumn was setting in: with every day that passed, a German invasion seemed less likely.

On the Mediterranean front, the Italians, who had invaded Egypt from Libya on 13 September 1940, had got bogged down within a week. Then on 12 October, the Germans started taking over the air defences of the Rumanian oil wells. This new commitment, as Franco saw it, could only increase their problems, both because it *was* a new commitment and because it would inevitably harm German–Soviet relations. The Caudillo was not to know that Mussolini, incensed over Hitler's latest *fait accompli*, was about to try and turn the tables with an invasion of Greece – which, as he told Ciano with glee, Hitler would find out about from the papers.[1] This was one card he couldn't see. But the game was clear enough, for why should the Germans be so insistent on bringing Spain into the war if victory was already theirs?

On his side, Serrano Súñer was now ready to dispatch his rival, Colonel Beigbeder. Though his personal relations with the Germans, and in particular with Ribbentrop, were worse now than before his trip to Berlin, he was still – on ideological grounds – broadly acceptable to the Nazis and Fascists. And in Franco's eyes, he had the merit of having carried out his instructions with precision and intelligence. He had said No while appearing to say Yes. These things seemed clear to everybody but poor Beigbeder, who told Sir Samuel Hoare on 27 September that he now thought he was coming out on top.[2] (Earlier, in May, he had told Doussinague that he could expect to 'live' – that is, to stay in office – only until September;[3] but having survived till the end of that month, he had regained his confidence.) On 15 October, he had been encouraged in this belief by a long and apparently friendly chat with the Caudillo.[4] Then, two days later, without warning or formal notice, he read of his own dismissal in the daily press.

Serrano Súñer now moved into the Foreign Office, announced the beginning of a new era and marked the point by crowding the venerable old building with blue-shirted Falangists and bully-boys. This was Hoare's hour of maximum depression.

Less than a week later, General Franco and his new Foreign Minister boarded the special train that was to take them to Hendaya on the French frontier, for the Caudillo's talk with Hitler. The Spanish railway system, never outstandingly efficient, had been disrupted by the Civil War and the special requirements of Spain's exposed non-belligerency. Even with the Chief of State aboard, it could not make Hendaya by the appointed time. Hitler, who had arrived punctually after meeting Laval on the way down, started pacing the platform with increasing agitation as the quarter-hours ticked by.* The myth-makers later fabricated the flattering story that Franco deliberately arrived late to unnerve the Führer, but this is quite untrue. Though the Caudillo was determined to give nothing away, he knew the interview was going to be difficult and the last thing he wanted was to irritate Hitler unnecessarily. At all events, he arrived eventually, a full hour late, grasped Hitler's right hand in both of his and, squaring his shoulders, walked rather solemnly side by side with the Nazi leader on the red carpet, with his right hand raised in the fascist salute, flanked on either side by a guard of honour and swastika flags – looking in the eyes of the world like a junior partner in the Axis alliance.

There followed the most infuriating hours in Hitler's life, which caused Hitler later to confide to Mussolini that rather than go through it again, he would prefer to have three or four teeth taken out.[5]

Hitler met Franco with two objectives in mind: to bring Spain into the Triple Alliance, and to gain the Caudillo's assent to German plans for an assault on Gibraltar.[6] The Caudillo, for his part, came to the meeting with the single negative, but onerous objective of avoiding all precise commitments of any kind. It is clear that Franco left Hendaya satisfied and relieved; and Hitler, angry and frustrated.

There is unfortunately no full or in other respects satisfactory account of this meeting. For instance, only a fragment of the official German report survives in the captured archives. But the atmosphere was perhaps more interesting than the substantive detail. This was high drama, tense in the clash of rival wills and personalities, but comical too, in the frustration of an outmanœuvred dictator who, but for the stubbornness of a little Galician, held half a continent in his grasp.

Hitler, misinformed perhaps by sycophantic officials, had misjudged his man. How seriously can be seen from his later remarks to Mussolini, to whom he observed that Franco was 'a brave spirit,

* His interpreter, Schmidt, says (p. 193) that the Führer was calm, but newsreels of the incident don't give that impression.

but a man who has become leader only by chance' – and one, moreover, 'not cut out to be a politician or organizer'.[7] Somebody ought,
in kindness, to have told him about Franco's famous impassivity.
But nobody could have, for he expected Franco to be 'Latin' and
excitable. Instead, it was Hitler who got excited, controlling himself
at times with the greatest difficulty, while Franco sat undisturbed,
occasionally directing a carefully timed jet of cold water on Hitler's
flights of strategic fancy.

Hitler's interpreter, Paul Schmidt, paints him as 'short and stout,
dark skinned, with lively black eyes' – an Arab, had he been wearing
a burnous – hesitant and tentative in manner but clearly 'a prudent
negotiator, not to be nailed down'.[8] As Hitler harangued him, declaring England to be decisively beaten though not yet prepared to
admit the fact, Franco sat huddled on his chair, protected by his
impenetrable expression. Was he impressed or not? It was impossible
to tell. Gibraltar, *that* was the key and the prize – the key to England's
final defeat, for it would exclude her from the Mediterranean and
Africa, and the prize for Spain's alliance. Now, said Hitler, now
was the time to conclude a treaty with Germany, and January was
the time for action at Germany's side. When the New Year came,
Spain could declare war on England. On 10 October, the crack
German troops of the *Sturm Abteilung Koch* who had stormed the
Eben Emael fort of Liége with such unexpected dash would seize
Gibraltar. It was all worked out. For some time now, German units
in the south of France had been 'storming' an exact replica of the
Rock. Perfection had been reached and success was inevitable. Once
Gibraltar had been liberated it would be restituted to Spain.

Though specific about Gibraltar, Hitler was studiously vague
about colonial changes in Africa. Franco just listened. Was he
impressed by the promise of Gibraltar, or disappointed by the
vagueness of Hitler's allusions to Morocco? It was hard to tell.

At last, the Führer's opening monologue was over and Franco
began to talk in his high, quiet voice which reminded Schmidt of a
muezzin calling the faithful to prayer. Spain, he said, was hungry and
needed several hundred thousand tons of wheat immediately. Was
Hitler able to oblige? Spain, the Caudillo went on, was short of
modern armaments, and heavy guns would be needed for the
assault on Gibraltar. It was, of course, unthinkable to leave this
mission to foreign troops. Spanish national pride would not stand

for it, nor accept the Rock as a present from others. Only Spaniards could take it. Then again, what about the Canaries and Portugal? If Spain declared war, the English would certainly try to take the Canaries and perhaps land in Portugal as well, or attempt a coastal landing in Spain itself. Anti-aircraft guns and other defensive weapons would be needed. Would Hitler do the necessary?

Another matter, said Franco, was Hitler's argument that Panzer units based on Gibraltar could clear the British from Africa. 'To the edge of the great deserts, very possibly,' said the Caudillo, 'but central Africa would be protected against major attacks by land by the desert belt, in the same way that an island is by the open sea. As an old African campaigner I am quite clear about this.'[9]

Hitler, in growing exasperation as he listened to the tranquil flow of words, had begun drumming his fingers on the side of his seat. When the Caudillo's high-pitched voice was stilled, he resumed his oration. By this time, one can see, Franco had got his measure. Hitler, in full flow against the British, cited Ribbentrop's unsuccessful mission to London in 1937–8 as an example of the bad behaviour of the British, and Franco interrupted him with a laugh, to say: 'In political dealings with the English, one shouldn't try to gallop, Führer! Churchill would never have imposed himself over the moderate Conservatives if Ribbentrop had trotted along in the English way.'[10]

As for England's being defeated, said Franco at another point, this was premature to say the least, for in the first place the British would fight to the last man for their own soil, and in the second, if driven out, the government would continue the fight from Canada. Nor should one forget, added Franco, that behind England stood the United States, with its enormous power.[11]

Hitler's hints of an impending anti-British alliance with France brought another jet of cold water from Franco's corner. This, he said, was pure delusion, for France would never ally herself with Germany to fight England.

On other occasions, Franco added to Hitler's irritation by asking the interpreter to re-translate certain passages which he hadn't fully grasped.[12] At one stage, the exasperated Hitler sprang to his feet and declared that there was no point in going on. But no sooner was he up than he sat down again and asked Franco to proceed.

In the end, Franco said he was prepared to sign a treaty, subject to

the reservations he had already made, and which he now recapitulated.

The two men separated, leaving their Foreign Ministers to discuss
the details of the proposed treaty. It was, however, less a discussion
than an occasion for Ribbentrop to revert to the bullying tactics he
had tried out against Serrano in Berlin. Again, the Spaniard deflected
his shafts by reasoned argument. In Berlin, Ribbentrop, in a rare
expansive moment, had invited Serrano to help himself from
France's African possessions. Now, in the special German Foreign
Office train, he qualified the offer, under Hitler's instructions. Certainly, Spain could be given French colonial possessions, said
Ribbentrop, but only if France could be compensated at Britain's
expense. Serrano nimbly pointed out that this could mean Spain
would get nothing at all.

That evening, Hitler was host to the two Spaniards in his great
banqueting car. After the meal, he made a last attempt to persuade
Franco, but gave it up after two hours. Meanwhile, Ribbentrop was
putting further pressure on Serrano, but to no more avail than for-
merly. Ordered by Ribbentrop to bring back an acceptable text by
8 a.m. Serrano merely sent his Under-Secretary of State, Espinosa
de los Monteros, with a draft that gave Ribbentrop no greater satisfaction than earlier attempts. In the end, Espinosa consented to
minor changes, and Ribbentrop, spluttering with rage (says Schmidt),
left with a protocol providing for Spain's entry into the war at an
unstated date and subject to specific reservations concerning deliveries of food and arms. And even this evasive document was subject to Franco's approval.

Although Franco did not know it for certain, he had seen through
Hitler's bluff at Hendaya. In one of his monologues about England's
fate, the Führer had declared that 'with the first break in the weather'
England was doomed. It is now known, however, that the German
invasion of England had been scheduled for 19 to 26 September, but
had already been indefinitely postponed a fortnight before the
Hendaya meeting.[13]

Here was another card that Franco couldn't see. But this had not
prevented him from winning the first game in his match of wits
against Hitler.

From London, Winston Churchill had followed with anxious concern

Hitler's first and abortive attempt to browbeat Franco. He had expressed a desire to visit the duke of Alba at home, away from official formalities, and have a friendly talk with him. Pressing engagements delayed the meeting until 9 December when the Prime Minister, accompanied by such intimates as Lords Lloyd and Croft, Colonel Moore-Brabazon, Mr Butler and Mr Brendan Bracken,* was the duke's guest at luncheon.

Churchill went out of his way to be pleasant to his host and to remove any ill-feeling that might have been left by his change of attitude towards the Nationalists during the Civil War, when he switched from support to hostility.[14] 'At the beginning of the Spanish Civil War,' said Churchill,† 'I was a supporter of yours, for had I been a Spaniard, either the Reds would have killed me, or without hesitation, I would have served on Franco's side. Later, seeing the intervention of Germany and Italy, as a good English patriot, I thought a Nationalist victory would not be in my country's interest, and for that reason, I even started writing against you. Later still, I became convinced that I had been mistaken, and tried to show it in my speeches in the House. I have been pained, to be sure, that my words were not published in the Spanish press.'

The Prime Minister added that he was ready to help keep Spain supplied, and was prepared to intervene personally to see that she was. A close watch was being kept on Negrín – the last Republican Premier, then in exile in Britain – and the government would not tolerate the slightest political activity on his part.‡

Churchill then asked: 'Will Spain be able to resist German pressure?' and added these reassuring words: 'As far as we are concerned, we wish to have the best and most friendly relations with you, and if these change, you may be sure that it will not be our fault. I detest Communism as much as you do.'

* At the time, Lord Lloyd was Colonial Secretary; Lord Croft, Parliamentary Under-Secretary for War; Colonel Moore-Brabazon, Transport Minister; Mr Butler, Parliamentary Under-Secretary for Foreign Affairs; and Mr Bracken, Information Minister.

† As quoted by the duke of Alba in his dispatch to Madrid: these words are, of course, my re-translation into English from the duke's Spanish.

‡ In November 1940, questions had been asked in Parliament about Dr Negrín, and Claud Cockburn's communist news letter, *The Week*, had carried a story about the refusal of the American government to give Negrín a visa, and about pressure allegedly put on Negrín by Lord Halifax and Mr Attlee, the Leader of the Labour Party, to get the former Premier to leave England.

The duke of Alba's dispatch describing this conversation was, not unnaturally, among those shown to Franco in person. The Prime Minister's friendly approach was to be followed, less than a year later, by a more determined attempt on Churchill's part to buy Franco's friendship.

4 *Franco v. Hitler, Game Two*

Further battles of will followed, first in rapid succession, then at lengthening intervals. For the Führer never gave up his view that Spain's territory was essential to his wider ambitions, and commentators[1] who have suggested that he lost interest in Spain after his armies had invaded Russia have ignored, or been ignorant of, all the facts. The Russian involvement certainly reduced the pressure on Spain. But long after Hitler had given up all hope of bringing Spain into the war on Germany's side, he was hatching schemes or dreams of escalating wildness for invading the country, or even for unseating the Caudillo. These schemes, of course, came to nought. But this does not alter the fact that Franco was never Hitler's unconditional or even willing ally, and that at all stages, he gave no more, though no less, than was necessary to keep the German armies away from Spain and her possessions. Let us, then, follow the story through, at the cost of breaking the even chronology of Franco's biography.

After the exhilarating victories of the spring and summer of 1940, Hitler was entering a time of frustrations, delays and uncertainties. France was beaten and England ought to have been, but refused to admit it. He had counted on Spain's acquiescence in his plans to seize Gibraltar and cross the Strait, but first that 'crafty Jesuit', Ramón Serrano Súñer, and now this insignificant but stubborn little Galician, a Generalissimo by luck, had frustrated or circumvented him. As if this were not enough Mussolini had to face him with the accomplished fact of an attack on Greece, from which folly he himself, the Führer, would probably have to rescue him. Even Pétain and Laval, the representatives of a beaten and demoralized nation, had shown themselves curiously uncooperative in the face of Hitler's suggestion that France should now declare war on England.[2]

Italy's invasion of Greece on 28 October 1940 – on the very day Hitler met Mussolini in Florence – redoubled Hitler's interest in the Mediterranean front. Whether by diplomatic reasoning, by promises or by threats, those stubborn Spaniards must be made to play their part in Operation Felix, the proposed German assault on Gibraltar. Clearly, this was not going to be easy. The disagreeable meetings at Hendaya had been followed by niggling arguments on points of detail in the secret Protocol that was to bring Spain into the Tripartite Pact. On 26 October, two days before Hitler's meeting with Mussolini, Stohrer was transmitting the 'bitter feelings' of Franco and Serrano at the rejection of changes they had proposed in the secret Protocol.[3]

Now November was here and still no definite promise had come from the Spanish side. The next thing, Hitler decided, was to invite the Spanish Foreign Minister for a second round of talks in Germany. As Serrano was driven from Salzburg towards the Führer's chalet at Berchstesgaden in the Austrian Alps on the fine autumn day of 18 November, Spain was heading for a winter famine. Four days earlier, Stohrer had written in cipher to say that the country was now short of grain by 1,250,000 tons – about twice the amount Serrano had requested in Berlin.[4] In parts of Spain, the poorer people were already going without bread for days or weeks on end. Corruption was on the increase, and so was discontent. 'Constantly increasing numbers of people previously favourable to the régime are joining the Red element,' Stohrer noted gloomily. The régime was being openly criticized and, apart from 'certain military and Falangist circles', there was sharp opposition to Spain's entering the war. Unless Germany soon gained control of the Straits and found new food supplies for the Spaniards, Spain could become a heavy burden, Stohrer warned the Foreign Ministry.

Spain's catastrophic grain shortage was increasingly to dominate the Hispano-German contention over entry into the war. The circle was as vicious as circumstances could make it, for Spain, needing British and American food deliveries, would not consider entering the war without a guarantee of 600,000 tons of wheat from Germany; and Germany, lacking a surplus of such dimensions, would not even promise deliveries in realistic quantities until Spain named a date for declaring war on Britain. If Spain did declare war, the sea lanes would be closed; if she didn't, Germany might invade her. Franco's dilemma was starker than ever.

'I have decided to attack Gibraltar,' exclaimed Hitler in the climax of his harangue to the visiting Falange leader.[5] 'I have minutely prepared the operation. The only thing left is to start, and start we must.' Some minutes earlier, he had pointed out, with casual menace, that the German Army now numbered 230 divisions, of which 186 were idle. As for Serrano's objections that a country short of wheat could not fight, and complaints that the secret Protocol was too vague on future territorial rewards in Morocco, Hitler brushed them aside impatiently. Italy, he said, was getting one million tons of coal from Germany, but she wouldn't be getting even 200,000 tons if she were not waging war.[6] All Spain had to do was to declare war; then she would get the wheat she needed. As for recompense in Morocco, this would follow naturally, once Gibraltar had been taken and the German forces had crossed over to North Africa. Once that had happened, there would no longer be any need to fear a possible defection of Morocco to the British side, perhaps on the basis of a secret understanding between Pétain, Laval and de Gaulle.

Arguing to the end, Serrano nevertheless contrived to give the impression that Spain would soon be entering the war – though without mentioning a date – and would use the time at her disposal to build up stocks of wheat from Canada, the United States and Argentina. After a talk with Ribbentrop the following day, which was more cordial than previous ones had been, Serrano returned to Spain.

Hitler must have thought that at last he had the Spaniards where he wanted them. Indeed on 28 November, Stohrer reported with glee, in a 'MOST URGENT, TOP SECRET' telegram, that 'the Generalissimo has agreed to the starting of the preparations which were contemplated'.[7] Alas, next day, Franco seemed to be up to his old tricks again, for Stohrer told his Ministry that while Spain was about to speed up her war preparations as much as possible, these would take time and no definite date could be given for the start of operations against Gibraltar. The Caudillo suggested that a group of German military experts, including 'an officer enjoying the Führer's special confidence', should be sent to Spain for frank discussions.[8]

What was behind this studied vagueness? Was it duplicity? Or legitimate caution? To find out, Hitler decided to send his Intelligence chief, Admiral Canaris, to Madrid in a determined effort to nail down the elusive Caudillo. As for the 'officer enjoying the Führer's special confidence', he was to be General Jodl, Chief of the Wehrmacht Operations Staff. Canaris was to arrive on 8 December, said Ribbentrop in a telegram to Stohrer dated four days earlier, but sent just after midnight on 5 December.[9]

Franco chose this moment to make one of his rare conciliatory gestures. Late on 5 December, Stohrer reported that the Spanish government was now ready to allow German destroyers to be refuelled in secluded bays on the Spanish coast. The timing of this morsel of good news was hardly fortuitous, for the Germans had requested this facility as early as 31 October.[10] To grant it now, Franco reasoned, was to show willing – and perhaps avoid more onerous commitments.

Canaris's mission was clear: it was to dissolve the nebula of vagueness with which the Generalissimo had clouded the whole issue and replace it by a precise undertaking. And indeed, a precise date. The admiral arrived earlier than expected. He was shown into the Caudillo's study at 7.30 p.m. on 7 December, and came straight to the point. The Führer, he said, proposed to send German troops into Spain on 10 January with a view to starting the attack on Gibraltar.[11] As soon as the first troops had crossed the Spanish border, economic assistance would begin.

Calm as usual, the Caudillo listened to Canaris, whom, of course, he had known during the Civil War. Did Canaris, one wonders, remember that years before he had described the man who now faced him as a tested man who 'deserved full trust and support'?[12] Now he listened while Franco declared that it would be impossible for Spain to enter the war on the date mentioned, and went on to enumerate reasons more precise and elaborate than he had mentioned in any previous list. Gibraltar, of course, would be taken immediately, but Guinea and one of the Canary Islands would fall to the British. Then England and the United States would have an excuse to occupy the Azores, Madeira and the Cape Verde Islands. Spain needed a million tons of grain and was short of rolling stock, so that war would bring misery to many provinces. True, grain was being bought in South America and Canada, and so were railway carriages.

Locomotives were being repaired and petrol stations built. But all this would take time.

In mentioning all these difficulties, Franco went on, he was not, of course, thinking of Spain alone, but of Germany also. For if the war were long drawn out, Spain would become a burden to her ally.

This was not at all what Admiral Canaris had bargained for. Well then, he asked the Caudillo, if 10 January is unacceptable, could he name another and later date? Impossible, was the Caudillo's reply, for the removal of the difficulties did not depend on Spain alone. It was advisable, he added, for a German economic adviser to be sent to Spain, and for exploratory studies to continue as discreetly as they had begun. Oh, and would the Admiral please convey to the Führer his most cordial greetings?

Back in Berlin, Jodl was preparing to leave for Madrid 'as soon as the news has been received from Canaris that the Spanish agree with the target date set by us'.[13] When Hitler and Ribbentrop learned how sadly misplaced this confidence had been, Stohrer was instructed to find out just why Canaris's discussions with Franco had turned out to be 'in flagrant contradiction' with the Hendaya meeting and with Serrano's talks in Berchstesgaden.[14] For good measure, Stohrer was requested, for the time being, to keep away from Spanish statesmen – a cryptic instruction that seemed to impose an unnecessary handicap on the ambassador in his search for clarification.

In retrospect, Franco's decision to refuse to allow German troops through Spain – for that is what his 'No' to Canaris meant – must be accounted one of the major turning points of the war. As it turned out, it meant not merely the postponement but the involuntary abandonment by the Germans of Operation Felix. Had the operational plan been carried out, there is little doubt that Hitler's men would have been in French North Africa by the end of January 1940. Though it is difficult to work out in any precise detail the consequences of a German presence in Africa some fourteen months before General Rommel's first brilliant appearance in the spring of 1941, these would clearly have been far-reaching, perhaps more far-reaching than the Führer himself envisaged at that stage. What Hitler had in mind, for a start, was to seal off both ends of the Mediterranean, thus meeting one of the Spanish objections to an operation limited to Gibraltar – that there wasn't much point, as far as Spain was concerned, in taking Gibraltar, unless access to the

Mediterranean through the Suez Canal were also denied to the British fleet.

Despite his encounter with the Caudillo's obstinacy at Hendaya, Hitler had no doubt whatever that Operation Felix would go forward for, on 12 November 1940, he issued a top secret directive giving detailed instructions for the taking of Gibraltar in a wide context that embraced military measures in France's African colonies, possible actions in Portugal and Greece, the defence of the Canary and Cape Verde Islands, an air offensive to close the Suez Canal, and the revival of Operation Sealion (the invasion of England).[15]

Understandably, then, Franco's rebuff to Canaris was followed by frantic attempts on Stohrer's part to find out why things had gone wrong. On 9 December he was reporting a split within the Spanish general staff, with Franco isolated and Serrano Súñer at odds with the military.[16] Two days later, he had decided that the famine in Spain, with people collapsing in the streets of Madrid from undernourishment, was the real reason why Franco had changed his mind. (The possibility that the Caudillo had never intended to bring Spain into the war, and was merely playing for time, does not seem to have occurred to him.) Stohrer was strengthened in his view by reports that Serrano had told the Italian Ambassador that if only Spain had grain she would enter the war immediately.[17]

Though famine was a major reason for Franco's reticence, it was not the only one. More important, perhaps, was his growing scepticism about Germany's ability to bring the war to an early and triumphant conclusion. It was not that he had begun, at this early stage, to doubt Germany's ultimate victory. But his healthy respect for the Royal Navy – born of his family's naval traditions and his own frustrated love for the sea – made him attach greater weight to Britain's capacity to resist than some of his advisers allowed. He did not accept the repeated Nazi claims – by Ribbentrop even more than by Hitler – that the war was as good as won. Had he thought England was about to surrender, he would probably have brought Spain into the war, if only to expand Spain's territories at France's expense and improve his country's chances of independence in Hitler's New Order. Since he didn't share Hitler's optimism, he played for time; and since he doubted Germany's ability to replace Britain as a supplier, he insisted on economic aid as a precondition for Spain's entry into the war.

Hitler, on his side, was not prepared to accept Stohrer's explanation for the Caudillo's reticence, and January 1941 brought even more peremptory instructions to the German Ambassador to nail the elusive Generalissimo down to a definite promise. On 20 January, Stohrer reported that he had urged Franco to enter the war immediately, as instructed, but that Franco had embarked on a long explanation of his country's economic difficulties, and pleaded for time.[18] Next day, Ribbentrop told him, in effect, not to take 'No' for an answer. He was to go back to Franco and read out word for word a strongly drafted message from Ribbentrop reminding Franco that he owed his position to the Führer and the Duce, expressing the Führer's deep disturbance at Spain's 'equivocal and vacillating attitude' and warning him that unless he decided immediately to join the war of the Axis Powers, the end of Nationalist Spain could be foreseen.[19]

Rightly judging that this near-ultimatum – and especially the warning at the end – would strengthen, not weaken, Franco's resolve, Stohrer pleaded for wording less offensive to Spanish susceptibility. Though the evidence is incomplete, it seems that Ribbentrop ignored this appeal, leaving the unfortunate Stohrer to read the message just as he had received it. Stohrer was right, and when he had listened to Ribbentrop's message on 23 January, Franco reacted with anger and – for him – an unusual display of heat. This message was of extreme gravity, he declared, and moreover it was untrue in various ways. When Stohrer protested, the Caudillo 'very heatedly' exclaimed that far from vacillating, he had always been on the side of the Axis, both in gratitude and as a man of honour.[20] Spain *would* enter the war, but it was his responsibility to see that she did not, in her present catastrophic economic condition.

It is of course characteristic that this rare instance of visible anger on Franco's part should have been aroused by remarks that appeared to impugn his own and his country's honour. The reproach of a vacillating policy had really stung him, and he reverted to it time and again during this talk with Stohrer. The fact remained that once again, Ribbentrop's bullying had achieved no more than Hitler's cajoling. Apprised of Franco's reaction, the Reich Foreign Minister immediately wired Stohrer to arrange forthwith for yet another interview with the Caudillo, who was to be told that only Spain's immediate entry into the war was of any use to the Axis.[21] Germany was willing to deliver 100,000 tons of grain stored in Portugal if Franco allowed Germany to name the date for Spain's entry. General Franco was to be asked once more for a clear and final answer.

It was three days before the Ambassador was able to see Franco – on 27 January – but the interview, which lasted an hour, was as fruitless as earlier ones had been. If the Germans doubted Spain's economic plight, said Franco, why didn't they send economic experts to see for themselves, as he had long been urging? Moreover, it would be useful to send some high military person who had the confidence of the Führer. This time – not knowing, apparently, that Jodl had at one time been picked for the job – the Caudillo suggested Field-Marshal Keitel, Chief of the Wehrmacht High Command.[22]

Stohrer's account of this latest frustration brought him a scolding from Ribbentrop, who wanted to know whether he had read his messages to Franco word for word, and asked to know how it was he had allowed Franco to wriggle out of giving a straight answer to a straight question.[23] Now Franco was trying to put the blame on Germany for his own failure to bring Spain into the war. Had he or had he not rejected Germany's request for immediate entry? Though Stohrer duly defended himself against Ribbentrop's unfair aspersions, he was unable to offer him a decision which only Franco could take, and would not.[24]

By this time – 29 January – the first month of the new year had gone and Greece's winter victories over the Italians had made it clear that Hitler must turn his attention to the eastern Mediterranean and eastern Europe. There was, indeed, another and bigger decision looming ahead: Russia. On 12 November 1940, with Soviet troops massed on the Rumanian border, the Soviet Foreign Minister, Molotov, had held a conference with Hitler in Berlin which the Germans regarded as highly unsatisfactory. By the end of the year, Hitler was beginning to give attention to Russia as a potential threat to his dreams of European domination. And in January, during a conference that lasted two days, Hitler and some of his top generals decided that the Russian threat had to be eliminated.[25] Some time between 19 January and 4 February, Hitler seems to have decided to launch Operation Barbarossa – the invasion of Russia – later in the year, and to shelve Operation Felix indefinitely.[26] The plan to bring Spain into the war was still not quite dead, however, for on 19 January, when Hitler met Mussolini at Berghof, he asked the Duce to do his best to persuade Franco to declare war, the Germans having done what they could and failed. But the projected Franco–Mussolini meeting did not take place until 12 February; and Hitler, having meantime decided to drop his Gibraltar plan and prepare for the attack on Russia, wrote Franco a furious letter on 6 February. Belabouring the Caudillo for failing to help Germany and Italy in a battle that was decisive for Spain's national survival, he regretted Franco's refusal to act, since the conquest of Gibraltar 'would at one stroke have changed the entire Mediterranean situation'. In an expression that has turned out to be prophetic, Hitler wrote that the Caudillo would never be forgiven his victory in the Civil War, accomplished with German and Italian help. Less presciently, he added that Franco's régime would survive only in the event of an Axis victory.[27]

Franco duly met Mussolini at Bordighera, in the Genoa area, on the appointed day, but merely countered the Duce's gentle pressure with the old familiar arguments. Then, at his leisure, he wrote a reply to Hitler's diatribe, complaining of Germany's failure to aid Spain, reminding him of the Spanish view that any attack on Gibraltar should coincide with an attack on the Suez Canal, refraining from precise commitments and ending, for what it was worth: 'I . . . declare my readiness to be completely and decidedly on your side, united in a common destiny.'[28]

The date on the letter was 26 February. Though Franco did not know it, he had won the long second round of his battle of wills with the Führer. Ribbentrop had written to Stohrer four days earlier to say it was now quite clear that Franco had no intention at all of bringing Spain into the war, and he (the ambassador) was to stop trying to talk the Spaniards into it.[29]

5 *Franco* v. *Hitler, Game and Match*

Early in 1941, Hitler – convinced by now that he had nothing to expect from Franco – began to think in terms of invading Spain since the Caudillo refused to allow German troops in. A number of contingency plans were drawn up. The Führer's first thought was to capture Gibraltar without using Spanish territory. In January 1941,

General Student, Commander-in-Chief of the Airborne Forces, was instructed to work out a plan to capture the Rock by parachute descent.[1] He did as he was told, but came to the conclusion that parachute forces alone could not do the job, and indeed that Gibraltar could not be taken if Germany respected Spanish neutrality. Almost immediately, a group of German staff officers met in the deepest secrecy, to plan Operation Isabella.*

The outcome of their discussions found its way into a High Command directive, dated 7 May.[2] This was, in the full sense a contingency plan, for it was to go into operation only in the event of a British attempt to take advantage of Germany's forthcoming involvement in Russia to seize Tangier, and possibly land in Portugal. Franco and his Ministers had already begun anxiously to wonder whether Hitler, frustrated by their uncooperative attitude, might take matters into his own hands, for on 4 May – just before the High Command directive on Isabella – Serrano Súñer had expressed the hope that Germany would not resort to military measures in Spain without Spain's consent, forecasting a 'very vigorous' reaction on the part of the Spanish people if this happened. Berlin was aware of Serrano's views, which Stohrer had transmitted, although they had not been expressed to the German ambassador himself.[3]

For Stohrer, who had evidently been kept in the dark about Hitler's Russian plans, this must have been an anxious and frustrating time. Hitler and Ribbentrop had got the message: that Franco was not going to bring Spain into the war. But Stohrer, for his part, was unwilling to believe that his protracted lobbying was not going to bring results; and we find him, as late as 30 May, reporting that it was quite possible that Spain might suddenly, and of its own accord, decide to enter the war.[4] He had convinced himself that Serrano was pressing for immediate entry, against the opposition of the generals, with Franco maintaining an uneasy balance between them. But nobody who reads Serrano's memoirs can doubt that Stohrer was misinformed, or guilty of wishful thinking.[5] And if Serrano's own evidence is discounted, as that of an actor in the drama anxious to improve his position in history, one cannot so easily brush aside the

* Probably in the French Jura, away from prying eyes. See Georges Roux, 'Hitler Contre Franco', in *Miroir de l'Histoire* (Paris), July 1965. This article, though fundamentally on the right lines, is unfortunately replete with inaccuracies.

views of General Jodl, the former Chief of the Wehrmacht Opera-
tions Staff, who wrote in his diary: 'The resistance of the Spanish
Foreign Minister, Señor Serrano Súñer, has ruined and ended
Germany's plan to make Spain enter the war at her side and seize
Gibraltar.'[6] And it was Jodl, again, who told a meeting of Gauleiters
assembled in Munich on 7 September 1943, that the 'Jesuitical'
Spanish Minister had deceived the Germans – an accusation which,
incidentally, Serrano himself has always denied.

Relations between Spain and Germany improved overnight,
however, when Hitler threw his legions against Russia on 22 June
1941. There were two complementary reasons for this improvement:
one was that Germany was now fighting Bolshevism, which Franco
had always considered the main enemy of the West; and the other
that, while the Germans were otherwise engaged on the eastern
front, their pressure on the Spaniards diminished, at first to vanishing
point. Serrano told Stohrer on the day of the invasion, after consulting Franco, that 'the Spanish government had noted with the
greatest satisfaction the beginning of the struggle against Bolshevist
Russia', and offered volunteers to fight on the Russian front 'in
memory of Germany's fraternal assistance during the Civil War'.[7]
This was the germ of the idea that was to turn into the famous (or
notorious, according to the viewpoint) Blue Division. As Serrano
had anticipated, the plan aroused great enthusiasm in Spain, and
forty times the numbers needed volunteered.[8] As finally constituted
the Blue Division numbered more than 18,000 Spanish regulars,
under the command of General Múñoz Grandes, one of Franco's
companions since his Moroccan days.

Late that summer, the Spaniards suggested that they alone should
attack and capture Gibraltar, without German help, but Stohrer –
wiser, perhaps, by now – dismissed this suggestion as an attempt
to sabotage Germany's own plans by the 'Anglophile' General
Varela, whom he described as the leader of the officers who opposed
Spain's entry into the war.[9] Varela, he said, was about to marry into
a rich Bilbao family which feared that they would lose their privileges
when Germany had won the war.

A few days later, on 13 September, the Wehrmacht High Command directed that military action on the Iberian Peninsula should
be shelved while the Russian campaign lasted.[10] It was thought,
optimistically, that the fighting on the eastern front would not end

until the spring of 1942 at the earliest. But it was not till 13 November that a Top Secret directive from Berlin strictly forbade the German Ambassador in Madrid even to discuss Spain's possible entry into the war, or any joint military operations.[11]

Two months later, Hitler told a visiting Spanish General that he was sorry he was not able to do anything about Gibraltar just then, and regretted that Franco hadn't seized the opportunity that had come his way in the spring.[12] Gibraltar, indeed, continued to haunt the Führer, even in the midst of his deepening Russian involvement. In March 1942, while the Germans were still driving forward, the British raid on St Nazaire came as a reminder that England, for all her relative weakness, might yet pull off a successful landing somewhere on the Atlantic seaboard.[13] By the end of April, the guess that came uppermost in Hitler's mind was that the British and Americans might be planning landings in French and Spanish Morocco and on the Iberian Peninsula. If this happened – or if it became certain that it was about to happen – the Germans must be ready with a counterblow or a pre-emptive invasion of their own. The outcome of Hitler's cogitations was Directive 42, issued on 29 May, in which the Führer laid down the 'guiding principles of operations against unoccupied France and the Iberian Peninsula'.[14] Exactly a month later, on 29 June, General Rundstedt was ordered to draw up a new and detailed plan, to replace the discarded Isabella. The new plan, – called Operation Ilona – emerged in the form of a General Directive on 15 July. It was, of course, a contingency plan, for use if the Allies did – or looked like doing – what Hitler feared they would. On paper, at least, the German counterblow looked impressive: the Pyrenees were to be transgressed and Bilbao, Vitoria and Pamplona were to be taken in a first phase. In a second phase, a wide circle ranging from Santander to Saragossa was to be overrun.

For Hitler, this was still a time of euphoria. His armies still looked invincible and he did not yet sense that before the end of the year the tide would begin to turn against him in Russia as well as in North Africa. His exasperation with Franco – and with Serrano Súñer – was mounting. Unlike the European Left, he saw little similarity between Franco's régime and National-Socialism, and the comparisons he drew within his circle of cronies were hardly flattering to the Spaniards. On 7 June, only a week or so after he had issued Directive 42, the Führer proclaimed to his dinner guests that the Spanish State was running towards a fresh disaster.[15] The priests and the monarchists – the same mortal enemies who had opposed the resurgence of the German people – had joined together to seize power in Spain. If civil war broke out afresh, he wouldn't be surprised to see the Falangists compelled to make common cause with the Reds to rid themselves of the 'clerico-monarchical muck'. But alas, in Spain there was always somebody like Serrano, ready to serve the interests of the Church. 'From my first meeting with him,' Hitler declared to the usual silent and respectful group, 'I was conscious of a feeling of revulsion in spite of the fact that our ambassador, with abysmal ignorance of the facts, introduced him to me as the most ardent Germanophile in Spain.'

As for Franco, the Führer mused aloud at dinner a month later, he obviously hadn't the personality to face up to his country's political problems.[16] He himself, and the Duce, had had much tougher problems to tackle, since they not only had to capture the State but also to win over the armed forces. But Franco couldn't cope, even with political and military power concentrated in his own hands. He was clearly incapable of freeing himself from Serrano's influence. Serrano – that 'parson in politics' – was blatantly double-crossing the Axis Powers. In fact, these parsons were too stupid for words, trying to use Serrano to restore the monarchy. But all they would do was to spark off another civil war, which they themselves would never survive.

A crazy idea was germinating in Hitler's mind as his monologue went on. Franco and Serrano stood in his way. Then they must go. The boss of the para-military labour organization, Todt, had told him time and again that the Spanish workers in his factories were not 'Reds' in the German sense. Revolutionaries, yes, but not Reds. They were skilled and industrious. Indeed they had greatly distinguished themselves. In fact, said Hitler, his voice rising, the 40,000 Spanish workers in German camps would be the Nazis' reserves against the day when another civil war should break out in Spain. Together with survivors of the old Falange (as distinct from Johnny-come-latelys like Serrano Súñer), they would constitute 'the most trustworthy force at our disposal'.

After an interval for Jodl and others to say their pieces, Hitler came back to his theme. Now he saw the Blue Division – at that time fighting on the Nazis' side in Russia – as destined to 'play a decisive role, when the hour for the overthrow of this parson-ridden régime strikes'. The Blue Division's Commander, General Múñoz Grandes – now *there* was a man of energy who could master the Spanish situation. Everything said Hitler, had to be done to promote the popularity of General Múñoz Grandes.

As so often with Hitler, there was more to his outburst than mere rhetoric. Even allowing for his 'monstrous genius', one may doubt – though this has been suggested[17] – whether he ever seriously considered the dazzlingly simple solution of indoctrinating the Spanish Republic's exiles and actually sending them back with the mission to overthrow Franco; though it is true that he thought they would serve his designs *if* a new civil war broke out in Spain. In 1942 and 1943, however, he does seem to have tried his worst to find men willing to conspire from within to overthrow Franco. The 'Germanophile' Serrano was likewise marked down for replacement, while still in office.

Serrano alludes in his memoirs to these goings-on and to the intrigues of Ribbentrop's special agent, Gardemann. Not only was Serrano 'that crafty Jesuit', in Nazi eyes, but he had the added demerit of being a new Falangist, whose concept of fascism was unacceptable to the Nazis. It was within the old Falange – in which, wrongly, one suspects, Hitler thought he found a spiritual kinship with National Socialism – that the Nazis were looking for anti-Franco conspirators, and better still, a more amenable successor to Franco.

Ribbentrop, as we have seen, had a hand in this project, and so had Walter Schellenberg, the head of the Nazi Foreign Intelligence Service (*Sicherheitsdienst*),[18] who had built up a formidably pervasive organization in Spain, with tentacles all over the country.[19] In the summer of 1942, while Sir Samuel Hoare continued to lament the régime's 'pro-German' policy, Schellenberg drew up a short list of Spanish politicians thought to be in favour of removing Franco and his brother-in-law. Three names headed the list: General Yagüe, an Old Falangist and former Air Minister; Eduardo Ezquer, another Old Falangist, a landowner who was considered the spokesman of the anti-Franco opposition within the party; and José Luis Arrese, who as Secretary-General of the ruling FET, was the bitterest opponent of its political chief, Serrano Súñer. Nothing, however, came of these German schemes.

On the military side, however, came the General Directive of 15 July 1942, for Operation Ilona; and, for a start, German troops began to concentrate south of Bordeaux, while the Third Air Force was reinforced around Bayonne. But Ilona, too, came to nothing, as Isabella had. It was not that it was abandoned. It was that a combination of circumstances made it either unnecessary or undesirable to pursue it. In Russia, Hitler's Army was heading for the catastrophe of Stalingrad, his attack on which began on 22 August. In the West, a few days earlier, the heavy losses suffered by the British and Canadians in the Dieppe landing seemed to show that the Western Allies were not yet, after all, in any shape to open a second front, even in the Iberian Peninsula. In Africa, Rommel had captured Tobruk, and though checked at El Alamein, he did not seem to be in urgent need of support at the Gibraltar end of the Mediterranean.

Yet another factor was one that probably came to the knowledge of the German High Command: Franco had had wind of Operation Ilona.[20] On his urgent orders, the whole Pyrenean area had been divided into five large defensive regions: fortifications and concrete entrenchments were going up everywhere to prevent any use of roads or passes by the Germans – now Spain's potential enemies.

This news caused alarm and despondency in Berlin, for it destroyed the basic assumption of Ilona, indeed its *sine qua non* – co-operation, or at least acquiescence, on the part of the Spaniards. With Franco's consent, a pre-emptive bid to occupy the Peninsula before the Allies did looked possible; without it, the whole enterprise looked chimerical. Now all that could be done would be to intervene if the Allies landed first, and then only if Franco called for German help.

November 1942 was the great turning point in the Second World War, and as reverses and disasters crowded the calendar, Hitler cast his eyes once more in the direction of Spain. In Africa, General Montgomery had broken Rommel's front and pushed the Germans out of Egypt. Four days earlier, on 8 November, a great Anglo-American invasion force, sailing from Gibraltar, had landed in Morocco and Algeria. At Stalingrad, the guts were being ripped out of Field Marshal von Paulus's invaders.

On 19 November, at the height of the Russian counterblows at Stalingrad, Hitler conferred with Grand Admiral Raeder.[21] The two men agreed – wrongly – that the Iberian Peninsula was the most

N

likely area for an Allied second front in Europe. Operation Ilona –
renamed 'Gisela' because of a security leak – was therefore taken out
of its pigeon hole. By now, circumstances were much less favourable
than they had been some months earlier from the German point of
view. Franco's Pyrenean constructions and Germany's military
losses alike seemed to rule out the massive intervention that had been
projected under Ilona. At this stage, therefore, Gisela was a more
modest plan, confined to defending the Pyrenees against any attack
from the Spanish side.

As 1942 drew to its close, however, the German High Command
became increasingly convinced that the next Allied blow was going
to fall in Spain. The frustration and dilemmas of Germany's over-
extended military machine were never more painfully evident. On
22 December, Raeder spelt it out for Hitler, in agonizing detail.[22] If
the Allies occupied the Iberian Peninsula, he declared, 'Germany
would be deprived of important raw materials'. A million tons of
iron ore would be lost to Germany's war effort, together with
3,500 tons of wolfram, 200 tons of lithium, 1,000 tons of tin, not to
mention mica, beryllium and much else besides. Militarily, an Allied
attack on the Iberian Peninsula would face Germany with an extremely critical situation.

From Germany's standpoint, it was therefore 'of the utmost
strategic importance' to take over the entire Iberian Peninsula. Only
that way could the submarine warfare be intensified; only thus could
the Anglo-American occupation of North Africa be neutralized.
Ah, but there was the rub! The Germans couldn't spare the military
forces or the economic resources for so vast an enterprise. The only
thing was to try and strengthen the neutrality of Spain and Portugal.

But what if the Allies did land, or if the Germans became certain
that this was their intention? In that case there was no escape:

> ... Germany must be ready to seize Spain and Portugal by force
> and integrate them into the economic life of Europe *at the very
> moment* when the danger of an enemy seizure of the Peninsula is
> imminent, even if such a step should entail great economic sacrifices
> for the rest of Continental Europe.[23]

So runs the last paragraph in the official German summary of a
memorandum presented at the conference of 22 December 1942. We
are back, therefore, to the concept of a pre-emptive bid – but only

when Allied plans should be known beyond doubt. One thing was certain: Gisela would have to be activated, and on a grander scale. Hitler, agreeing with Raeder's diagnosis, therefore ordered an urgent expansion of Gisela. This took more than four weeks, and was perfected – on paper – on 1 February 1943.

As the plan now went, the First Regiment of Motorized Artillery of the First Army was to cross the Pyrenees to occupy the whole of the Cantabrian coast from San Sebastian to Vigo. Seven infantry divisions would follow, and concentrate in the Valladolid region. Despite earlier indications of the Spanish attitude, the expanded Gisela plan envisaged Spanish consent to the use of airfields by the Luftwaffe, and an Italian division was to be invited to join in. They were to land in Barcelona, and link up with the German divisions in the Valladolid area.

February and March, however, went by without any sign of an impending Allied landing in Spain or Portugal. And Hitler, who had followed the Gisela project with feverish attention for several weeks, suddenly lost interest in it. On 8 April, he met Mussolini, who urged him to start a fresh African campaign, to be launched from Spain.[24] He replied that he could not spare enough divisions from the Russian front for an operation of this size, and he could not presume that the Spanish government would allow the Germans right of transit.

Whatever Hitler told Mussolini, however, there is no doubt that the Iberian invasion fever gripped the German Army in the spring of 1943. One of the surviving Generals of that period, Freiherr Leo von Geyr von Schweppenburg, who was in charge of the invasion plans, wrote to an old English friend, Captain (now Sir Basil) Liddell Hart, six years later, to recall the situation as he saw it in April 1943, at about the time Hitler saw Mussolini. Though General von Geyr's memory was faulty, his letter makes interesting reading:

I was in command of the XXXVI Army Corps with headquarters at Dax in April 1943. The divisions earmarked for this folly 'Hildegard' (I think this was the covering name) were:

715th (motorized)
3rd and 39th (mechanized)
28th (armoured)
1st Infantry.

The 715th was to race for Bilbao, the rest fanwise, the left wing to central Spain – direction Madrid.

The preparatory talks for this political and military blunder of the first magnitude have been held by myself at Dax.*

Actually, of course, the operation was called 'Gisela', not 'Hildegard' (though this could have been a local name for the same operation); but this confusion of German feminine names is of little moment. Actually, again, the XXXVI Army Corps was in Finland at the time, and General Geyr must have meant the LXXXVI. Then again, there was no 28th Armoured: he could have meant the 26th or 24th Panzer; and the 1st Infantry was in Russia, so he probably meant the 1st Armoured. Let us not, however, quibble. One thing General Geyr didn't forget was that he was supposed to prepare for the invasion of Spain.

About that time, again, on 11 April 1943, Admiral Doenitz, the new Commander-in-Chief of the German Navy, conferred with Hitler and strongly argued in favour of occupying the entire Iberian Peninsula and closing the Straits of Gibraltar.[25] This, as he saw it, was the only way to frustrate the strategic plans of the Anglo-Saxons, even if the whole of Tunisia should fall into their hands. Doenitz assumed the existence of 'an Anglo-Saxon Gisela', with the Allies only waiting for the Germans to attack to put their own invasion plans into operation.

What, then were the Germans waiting for? Once again, the rub was the uncooperative attitude of Franco's government. Doenitz, as his views are reflected in the captured German documents, agreed that the German plan could be carried out only with Spanish consent. 'But the Spanish Government is convinced that the chances for victory are in no wise definitely in Germany's favour. The Spanish people are opposed to participation in the war.' Perhaps, however, the Spaniards could be won over. And the relevant document went on to number off the military and political conditions *sine qua non* for Spanish participation on the German side – a quaintly optimistic list that bears recapitulation here:

1   Definite stabilization on the eastern front.
2   The holding of Tunisia.
3   The publication of German peace aims. This meant 'doing

* This is a direct quotation of von Geyr's English.

something' about the new Europe in Norway, France, Poland, the Baltic countries and the Ukraine.

4 A rapprochement with the Vatican and the Christian churches.

5 A simultaneous assurance that National-Socialism would not change into a 'western form of Bolshevism'.

6 Making large forces available for causes that appealed to Spain, such as preventing the loss of Spanish Morocco, and the conquest of Algeria and French Morocco.

7 Adequate economic guarantees.

The document relating to this conference concluded with a revealing drafting change. As originally drafted, the last paragraph acknowledged that the prerequisites for success were lacking, and ruled out any occupation of the Peninsula *at this time*. Preparations should nevertheless go forward until the time was ripe and it was desirable that the operation should be expanded 'to enable us to occupy the entire Iberian Peninsula and take Gibraltar'.

The whole of that paragraph, however, was crossed out, and the following words were written in by hand: 'The preceding considerations must be taken into account when making decisions and preparations.'

At that time, in fact, Hitler was beset by multiple fears of Allied landings. One day he would be convinced that Norway was threatened. Then, no, it was Denmark; or Holland, or Portugal, or Spain, or the Adriatic – 'in fact, all around the map!' as his Chief of Staff, West, General Blumentritt, told Captain Liddell Hart under interrogation after the war.[26] The generals, however, according to Blumentritt, kept warning Hitler of the formidable difficulties in the way of an invasion of the Iberian countries, not least the fact that the Spanish generals had made it clear that the Spaniards would fight if the Germans tried to occupy their territory.

The point evidently went home, for on 14 May 1943, when Doenitz resumed the attack with the argument that only the occupation of Spain and Gibraltar would ease the British stranglehold on the German submarines operating in the Bay of Biscay, Hitler silenced him by exclaiming that the occupation of Spain without the consent of the Spaniards was out of the question. They were the only tough Latin people, said the Führer, and they would carry on guerrilla warfare in the German rear.[27] On a note of nostalgia, he added that in 1940 it might have been possible to get Spain to accept a German military presence, but the Italian attack on Greece in the autumn had shocked the Spaniards. It did not seem to have occurred to him that Franco was far less shocked by the attack on Greece than by Hitler's pact with Stalin and his invasion of Poland.

Doenitz made one last try, on 31 May, when he proposed a surprise attack on Gibraltar at the end of June with a new Air Force weapon. This time, Hitler turned the proposal down on grounds of security: some of the new weapons might fall on land at Gibraltar, and the British would find out what they were. Moreover, he added, he was doubtful about reaching Gibraltar, since it was becoming increasingly difficult, from a political point of view, to fly over Spain.

This was the end of Gisela, though the plan was not formally abandoned until 14 June 1943. Thereafter, the Pyrenean frontier was guarded by a mere two regiments.

From now on, Franco was safe – at least from Hitler's fury. By sitting tight, he had won the third and final round of his encounter with the Nazi dictator. Or rather, Russia and the Western Allies, between them, had brought rewards to his patience and defiance.

6 *Allied Pressures*

Throughout the Second World War, General Franco was, in effect, his own Foreign Minister, and the incumbent with the title merely carried out his orders. His foreign policy was governed, as all foreign policies are, by a self-centred view of his country's national interests. If his interpretation of these interests seems even more self-centred than is normal, this is because Spain was isolated by her weakness and neutrality. She emerged from the Civil War with Axis friendships that could not, and did not, survive for long her refusal to enter the war on the Axis side. But Franco's frustration of Axis policy did not, as might have seemed logical, win him alternative friendships, which were blocked both by the memories of his Civil War assistance from the Germans and Italians, and by the historical accident that made Russia the West's 'gallant ally'. The irony of this situation is that Spain herself, as we have seen, missed being the West's gallant ally too by the hair's breadth of Hitler's failure to invade Spain, which would have met with fierce Spanish resistance.

The men who executed Franco's foreign policy were appointed for their usefulness in the Caudillo's diplomatic tight-rope act at a given time, and dismissed when their usefulness had ended. The pro-British Beigbeder symbolized Franco's awareness of Spain's dependence on Britain's naval and commercial good will. France's defeat, England's plight and Hitler's early triumphs called for a 'fascist' and Germanophile Foreign Minister, and this was the time of Serrano Súñer's ascendancy. When the difficulties of the Axis partners in North Africa and Russia became patent, Serrano had to go, and the pro-British Jordana – a former Foreign Minister – was brought back. Then Jordana died, in the summer of 1944, and Lequerica was put in charge of the Foreign Office during the difficult last phase of the war. Psychologically, the only jarring note in these appointments was that of Lequerica who, as Spain's former Ambassador to Vichy, could not have been expected to be popular with the western Allies in their forthcoming military triumph. But Lequerica was one of the more pliant instruments of Franco's will: supple and amenable (an *arriviste*, said Sir Samuel Hoare, quoting unnamed Spaniards[1]), he had no particular trouble in adapting himself to a policy of being nicer to the democracies.

Just as the fluctuations of the war governed Franco's policy and his choice of Ministers, so they governed the content of his public pronouncements. The more he evaded or resisted Hitler's demands, the more sneeringly or even viciously anti-western were his speeches. As the Spanish Foreign Office kept saying to the British and American Ambassadors: '*Estamos pagando a Alemania con palabras el precio de nuestra paz*' – 'We are paying Germany in words as the price of our peace.'[2]

One theme and preoccupation was constant: Franco's fear and detestation of Communism. And even that was attenuated in 1944, probably as a show of response to Allied pressures, in his curious remark to the American Ambassador, Carlton Hayes, distinguishing between the 'disciplined' and constructive Communism of Russia and the 'revolutionary' and destructive Communism of political minorities in eastern Europe.[3] Because Franco feared Bolshevism, he opposed the Allied policy of imposing unconditional surrender on Germany, which he saw would bring Soviet power deep into central

Europe. A negotiated peace, on the other hand, would – as he saw it – give the German people a chance to overthrow their Nazi rulers, leaving Germany as a natural bulwark against Stalin's expansionism. In the perspective of the cold war, the division of Germany, the blockade of Berlin and the creation of Nato, there is a quaintly naïve flavour about the spirited defences of Russia that were put up by Hoare and Hayes. It was not they but Franco who showed foresight. After all, what Franco was saying in 1943, Churchill said three years later in his Fulton speech.

Franco's analysis of the communist danger in the post-war world stands up to scrutiny in the hard light of actual events. It is not his strategic vision that can be faulted, but his tactical assumption that the Western Allies could be diverted from their resolution to destroy Nazi Germany, to spare a thought for the shape of a continent that might be held to ransom by the victorious Russians. The distinction he made between the war in the West and the war against Bolshevism, though logically consistent with his own analysis, was bound to be unacceptable to the embattled Allies in the days of strategic bombing and Russia's spectacular advances. Nor could his advice bring anything but snubs. He ought, perhaps, to have seen this, but reasoned that it was worth a try. As for his belief that Hitler could be overthrown, the officers' plot against the Führer in April 1944 – though it failed – showed that the chance of it existed. Whether Hitler's overthrow would have improved the prospect of peace and stability in the post-war world, is a hazardous speculation. But Franco, by now, is far from alone in questioning the wisdom of 'unconditional surrender'.

Let us now look at some of the other pressures General Franco had to contend with while staving off the Germans. England's sea power was a potent source of pressure, despite the increasing strain of the war against the Nazi U-boats. More specifically, the issue or refusal of 'navicerts' (navigation certificates) was a precise mechanism of control, enabling London – or Washington – to permit or deny Spain the wheat or petrol she needed for survival. At the beginning of 1941, the duke of Alba was reporting that delays in issuing navicerts were due not to ill will but to administrative difficulties, Indeed, he said, the British government always showed the best desire to be agreeable and wipe out Spanish memories of Britain's 'equivocal attitude' during the Civil War.[4]

For the next few months, in fact, relations between London and Madrid were reasonably good. 10 April brought the signing in Madrid of a further Anglo–Spanish commercial agreement (supplementing an agreement signed in London on 18 March 1940); Britain granted Spain a loan of £2½ million to be spent as both governments saw fit. Shortly afterwards, the duke of Alba thought it worth reporting that he had spoken with Churchill's secretary, Major Desmond Morton, whom he described as the Prime Minister's *éminence grise* and who, he said, had declared that, looking at France and England he was beginning to realize how dangerous democratic theories were for Europe.[5]

With the German invasion of Russia in June, however, Anglo–Spanish relations took a sudden turn for the worse. Young Falangists were encouraged to stage a disagreeable demonstration before the British embassy, in protest against Churchill's declaration of solidarity with Russia. Not unnaturally, the British Foreign Secretary, Anthony Eden, raised this subject when the duke of Alba called on him to discuss the implications of Hitler's attack on Russia. Alba observed that any attack against Russia was bound to be greeted with enthusiasm by Spanish opinion, which could not forget Spain's frightening experience of Russia's interference before and during the Civil War. Eden replied that he quite understood Spain's attitude, and reiterated his own anti-Bolshevism. There was not, and there never would be, an alliance with Russia. But Hitler's war with Russia was bound to weaken Germany, and the principal objective of the British war effort was the destruction of Hitler and the Nazi régime.[6] (Three months later, the duke recorded a rumour then current among journalists that *The Times* had prepared a leader for Monday, 23 June – the day after Germany's invasion of Russia – arguing against an alliance with Russia and even pointing out the advantages of an understanding with Germany; the galley proofs, however, had been destroyed after Churchill's speech of Sunday, 22 June.)[7]

Until that summer, Franco had said nothing, in public at least, on Britain's delays in issuing navicerts. Now, apparently incensed at the use Britain was making of its power over his country's lifeblood, the Caudillo denounced England's 'inhuman blockade' in a speech before the National Council of the Falange on 17 July 1941. England, he declared, was beaten, anyway.

Slightly puzzled, the duke of Alba reported that Franco's view that the Allies had lost the war had come as a surprise in London, for 'in Great Britain it is firmly believed that the facts do not justify this assertion . . . Nobody believes even remotely that the war could end with England's defeat.'[8] He drew Serrano Súñer's attention to the critical reaction to Franco's speech on the part of the British Foreign Secretary, Anthony Eden, who had commented in the House of Commons that the speech 'displayed a complete misunderstanding not only of the general war situation but also of British economic policy towards Spain'. There had to be goodwill on both sides, Eden had said, and Franco's statement made it appear that he did not wish for further assistance from Britain – a clear threat that Spain would be starved of essential imports if Franco's 'pro-German' policy – as it appeared to be at the time – did not cease.

A week after Franco's offensive speech, a whiff of menace blew in from the Atlantic, with the publication on 25 July in the Spanish Republican exiles' New York paper, *España Libre*, of an article forecasting a pre-emptive seizure by the British and Americans of the Canary Islands, and the Azores and Cape Verde.[9] The existence of such a plan was immediately denied by the State Department, but the Spaniards were not fully reassured, for news reached the Foreign Ministry's Palacio de Santa Cruz that Roosevelt had personally studied the arrangements, which involved the participation of the exiled Republican Generals Miaja and Asensio. Although the United States had not yet entered the war, the main expeditionary force was to be American, says Doussinague, who claims that it was Churchill himself who put up the plan to Roosevelt when they met in mid-ocean on 14 August, to proclaim the Atlantic Charter. Although England was at war and America was not, Churchill did not want to use British troops against the Canaries for fear of provoking a German move against Gibraltar.

The Canaries scare died down but revived in the late summer of 1942, with the formation of a 'Spanish American Division' in Buenos Aires after months of stridently anti-Franco diatribes in the American press. Carlton Hayes records that a precautionary occupation of the Canaries was part of the Allied plan to land in North Africa. Informed of this at the end of September 1942, he protested energetically to Washington, on the ground that an attack on the Canaries would embroil the Allies with Spain at a time when it was essential to have a buffer between the Germans in France and the Allied expeditionary force in Africa.[10] The argument carried in Washington, and on 2 November, Hayes was able to assure Count Jordana – who, by that time, had replaced Serrano Súñer – that Spanish territory would not be violated.

On the Allied side as well as the German, blandishments alternated with threats. Not long after Eden's veiled threat of economic pressure against Spain came a curious attempt by Churchill to win Spain's co-operation by competing with Hitler in offering Spain territorial aggrandizement at France's expense. Little attention has been paid to this episode in London and Washington, because the disclosures on the Spanish side, being highly inconvenient politically, were officially discounted by the British. There is no doubt at all, however, that the offer was made.

It was Serrano Súñer who, in his Memoirs, first disclosed what had happened.[11] The duke of Alba, he wrote, had been host to 'three very important personalities of British politics', the most important of whom had pointed out that if England won the war – which was not in doubt – France would owe her everything, and she nothing to France. She would therefore 'be in a position to exert strong and decisive pressure for France to satisfy Spain's just claim in North Africa'. Spain, indeed, could become the strongest Power in the Mediterranean, with England's help. There was only one condition: '. . . We only ask Spain not to let the Germans pass through her territory.' The only one of the duke of Alba's guests named by Serrano was Sir Samuel Hoare.

The former Spanish Foreign Minister's book was published in Madrid in 1947. In conversation with him eighteen years later, I asked him who the main speaker was and why he had kept his name dark. He expressed surprise that I should not have guessed that it was Churchill himself. He had named Hoare because he was an old enemy, but he had strong personal reasons for not naming Churchill at that time. One was that he regarded Churchill as a friend of Spain and he did not wish to embarrass him in the context of British politics. The other was that Churchill's son, Randolph, had given him a sympathetic hearing during a visit to Spain in 1946, and had later made complimentary references to him in articles in the *Daily Telegraph*. Who, then, I asked, was the third of the 'very important personalities' who had visited the duke of Alba that day? But Serrano couldn't remember whether it was Eden or Butler.

In fact, both Eden and Butler were there, and they were the second and third of the V.I.P.s, Sir Samuel not ranking as such in Serrano's mind. The Caudillo himself, in a speech before the Cortes on 18 May 1949, read out the telegram in which the duke of Alba described the luncheon he had given for Churchill, Eden and Hoare on 2 October 1941, and in which Churchill had made his offer to Spain. The speech brought an instant denial from Lord Templewood (Sir Samuel Hoare) – in a letter to *The Times* of London for 21 May 1949 – that he had attended any such luncheon. And in the House of Commons, on 22 June, Mr Eden, replying to a question, said he was in a position to state in the most categorical terms that no offer had been made to Spain.

Doussinague, however, confirmed in his book that the offer had indeed been made by Churchill.[12] The Spanish Diplomatic Information Bureau, moreover, was able to draw attention to an item in *The Times* Court Circular of 3 October 1941, confirming that the Prime Minister had indeed been the guest of honour at the Spanish Embassy the day before, the other guests including Eden, Butler and Hoare. Whether Churchill actually did offer Spain French territory is, of course, another matter. But there is no doubt that more weight should be attached to the duke of Alba's war-time telegram, the object of which was informative, than to the 1949 denials of British Conservative leaders intent on returning to power after several years of Labour rule.* Indeed, the offer is consistent with Churchill's expressed views about Franco and the Spanish Nationalists before, during and after the Second World War. On the Spanish side, however, the duke of Alba's telegram, though it was taken seriously, was not considered important enough to influence policy, which was determined entirely by Franco's estimate of Spain's needs in the light of his analysis of the fortunes of the war.

* The original cable was in code, and I am unable to reproduce it.

7 *Competing Fears*

Even at the close of Hitler's Russian winter of 1941–2, Franco had not begun to doubt the Nazis' ultimate victory. It was already clear to him, however, that they were in for a long struggle. His natural inclination, now that Hitler's Russian embroilment had reduced the German pressure on Spain, was to improve his links with the 'Anglo-Saxons'. The Canaries scare, however, had given Franco food for thought. Since the Portuguese Azores – as well as the Spanish Canaries – appeared to be threatened, the best course, he reasoned, was to consolidate Spain's friendship with Portugal. For one thing, Portugal – though neutral – retained her traditional friendship with England. For another, Iberian solidarity in the face of the western threat to the peninsula's island possessions seemed to him in the highest degree desirable. Moreover, unlike some of his irredentist brother officers, who had dreamt of reconquering Portugal, Franco had always believed in a good neighbour policy.

It was in this frame of mind that General Franco met his neighbour, the Portuguese Prime Minister, Dr Salazar, at Seville on 12 February 1942.[1] Cordiality prevailed. Years later, Franco revealed in one of his occasional interviews that he considered Salazar 'the most accomplished and worthy of respect of all the statesmen I have known'.[2] Serrano, who accompanied him, shared his master's enthusiasm. Indeed, for once, he saw eye to eye with the British Ambassador, for Sir Samuel Hoare was equally struck by 'this learned and impressive thinker', whom he contrasted disparagingly with 'Franco, the lucky and complacent staff officer'.

Dispensing with an interpreter, Franco talked to Salazar in his own native Gallego dialect, which is so close to Portuguese that communication was easier than it usually is between Iberians of different nationality. Salazar, although disclaiming any deep sympathy for England, professed esteem for her, but complained that the Americans were sabotaging Portugal's interests with their niggardly allocations of navicerts. On the other hand, he feared the Germanization of Europe after a Nazi victory, whereas in his view the

Anglo-Saxon powers, if they won, would leave the German Reich as a bastion against Bolshevism.

Both Serrano and Franco – who was doing most of the talking – demurred. Perhaps with tongues in cheek, they quoted the 'understanding' attitude Hitler had adopted when Spain had refused to enter the war. This, at any rate, is what Stohrer, the German Ambassador,[3] reported to his Foreign Office; but as this was what Serrano had told him, it must be assumed that the Foreign Minister dressed up the occasion for German ears.

On the practical side, the two dictators agreed that they would defend the neutrality of their territories by force of arms, and that they would improve economic relations between their two countries.

From Franco's point of view, the meeting had been highly satisfactory. But he was well aware that the Germans would take an unfavourable view of this rapprochement with a traditional friend of England's. Here, he thought, was another occasion when the price of peace was words. Accordingly, while still in Seville, on 14 February, he made a speech well calculated to please the Germans and infuriate Sir Samuel Hoare. If, he said, the road to Berlin were open to the communist hordes, it would no longer be a mere division of Spanish volunteers fighting on the eastern front, but a million Spaniards who would offer their lives.

As it happens, the pleasure aroused in London by the Franco–Salazar meeting outweighed any anger provoked by Franco's pro-German speech. The duke of Alba reported that in political and diplomatic quarters in London, the meeting had been taken as a sign of Franco's independence from the Axis and of reduced likelihood that Spain would enter the war.[4] As usual, indeed, in Franco's relations with Germany, deeds conspicuously failed to follow words.

The duke of Alba's dispatches, often running to thousands of words and analysing in close detail the fortunes of war as seen in London, were a major factor in Franco's confidence that he was right to stand up to Hitler while publicly appearing to support him. An acute observer, little escaped Alba: from the activities of Dr Negrín in his London exile, to Britain's economic difficulties in the face of Germany's sea blockade. Negrín didn't look like an immediate menace, with Churchill in power; but so long as he enjoyed asylum and ample funds, the duke was supposed to keep an eye on him. On 10 February 1942, he reported the opening in London of the

Hogar Español ('Home for Spaniards') with some 500 anti-Franco members, including Negrín. At this time, he reported, the former Prime Minister was living comfortably in the country, but still kept his flat in London at a rent of about £1,000 a year. Every week-end, he saw the Soviet Ambassador, Maisky. He also often saw the ambassadors of Mexico, Chile and China, and the Minister of Colombia. Negrín, the duke went on, made heavy purchases at expensive shops like Harrods and Fortnum & Mason's, and lived in great luxury. Señora de López was still living with him, with what degree of intimacy nobody knew, and he also saw a lot of the Belgian Mme Blum, and of Señor Azcárate, the former Republican Ambassador in London, and other leading exiles. He was often seen eating out at first-class restaurants. He had recently had a large refrigerator installed, and a safe worth £250. Latterly, he had invited 300 local children to his Bovingdon home; each had been given a present of a box of chocolates.[5] Five months later, he reported that Negrín's mode of life, still in the company of Señoras López and Blum, went on in much the same way.[6]

The duke of Alba's constant warnings to the British about the dangers for Europe of a Russian victory always brought the reply that the Soviets were now nationalists, not internationalists and, besides, would be so broken financially and materially that they would be incapable, after the war, of exerting pressure beyond their borders. As an afterthought, the British officials and politicians the duke of Alba saw would add that should it ever be necessary, the British would fight the Russians with American aid.[7] Shortly afterwards, the duke sent Franco the text of Britain's Treaty of Alliance with the USSR (cmd. 6368) of 26 May 1942, which Eden had told him ten months earlier would never be signed.

Discouraging though this attitude was for the duke of Alba, he never wavered in his admiring appreciation of Winston Churchill's conduct of the war and of his political leadership, just as he never concealed opinions that might be distasteful to his ultimate master, the Caudillo. On 10 July 1942, he reported the Prime Minister's Parliamentary victory in a vote of censure in the following passage:

'The Premier loses the battles and wins the debates,' said the MP Aneurin Bevan in the House of Commons when the vote of censure was discussed. True though Bevan's assertion is, it also constitutes, coming from so exalted a detractor of the Government, the best possible testimony that the debate on the supreme direction of the war ended with a success for Mr Churchill, yet another of those which this tenacious and skilful statesman knows how to prepare and enjoy when, through political vicissitudes or military reverses, he wants to make the country feel that he is the only man with enough nerve and prestige to be at the helm in the tormented storm which today besets the ship of the British Empire.[8]

Soon afterwards, however, he was reporting a drop in British morale following Rommel's victories in Libya and Britain's heavy losses. Coal was short, he wrote, and a hard winter lay ahead. On the other hand, the government had just scored two by-election successes, at Windsor and Salisbury. As soon as things went badly for Britain, he observed, the British voters united in adversity behind their government.[9]

Most of the duke of Alba's contacts were naturally to be found among the mainly right-wing people who had supported Franco's cause during the Civil War. About this time, however, the duke had an unexpected opportunity for a lengthy exchange of views with one of Franco's most vigorous opponents, Ernest Bevin, who was Minister of Labour in Churchill's war cabinet. The two men happened to be guests at the same luncheon and had been placed next to each other. The duke decided to break the ice with appropriate jocular remarks and soon Bevin – with 'his typical accent of the lower classes' – and he, were in animated conversation. The duke steered the talk round to the Russian menace, and Bevin said he thought Bolshevism was dead and there was no longer any possibility of its resurgence after the war, among other things because Russia had always been a hundred years behind Europe. After the war, said Bevin, she would be 150 years behind and would have to rebuild after the enormous destruction she had suffered. Russia's principal preoccupation would be to be accepted in the European concert of nations as a civilized country and to remove existing prejudices against the Kremlin.[10]

Although such arguments did nothing to encourage Franco's hope that Spain might find its salvation in an anti-Soviet front after the war, the duke of Alba's reporting did make it plain that England under Churchill was not in any immediate danger of going under, especially now that America's weight was behind her. And Germany's difficulties in Russia were plain to see. Franco therefore decided the time had come for a change of direction in foreign policy. In this context, Serrano Súñer, in Franco's reasoning, had now outlasted his usefulness. The trend of events called for a Foreign Minister who would be *persona grata* with the western Allies, and Serrano's militantly pro-Axis record disqualified him. He was removed, therefore, and replaced by General Count Jordana, who had preceded Serrano's own predecessor – Beigbeder – in the Palacio of Santa Cruz.

The change took place at the beginning of September, and on 8 September, the American Ambassador, Carlton J. H. Hayes, a history professor plucked by President Roosevelt out of the faculty of Columbia University, made his first call on the new Foreign Minister. Tiny of stature, and sixty-five years old at the time of his reappointment, Count Jordana was a man of courtesy, sincerity and devotion to duty. He assured Hayes of his anxiety to improve relations with the United States; and indeed it was soon apparent that he meant what he said.

It was easier to say this, however, than to accomplish it. The anti-Franco campaign in the American press was at its height, and the reports of plans to attack the Canaries were disquieting. Great play was being given in the American newspapers to charges that Spain was acting as middleman for German purchases, was building submarines for Germany and had leased island bases to the Italians. All this sounded like a build-up for an American aggression against Spanish territory.

In some respects, this was a time of maximum anxiety for Franco. Not only did hostility loom from the Atlantic side, but the news from Germany was far from reassuring. From Berlin the Spanish Ambassador, Count de Mayalde, was reporting that if the German campaign in the Volga and Caucasus succeeded, pressure on Spain to permit the Germans to conquer Gibraltar would immediately be renewed.[11] From his intelligence service, Franco had learnt of Germany's contingency plans to invade Spain, and had ordered the building of fortifications in the Pyrenees.

In a report to the Cabinet on 19 September, Jordana declared that the situation was serious and that it was Spain's duty to improve her defences and modernize her armaments.[12] This was indeed the view of

Franco, who was now more than ever his own Foreign Minister. As Doussinague revealed, Count Jordana submitted all decisions, even on points of detail, to Franco for his approval.[13] Although Franco's domestic preoccupations were pressing, he found time for a personal study of the large sheaf of extracts from diplomatic telegrams, studies of this problem and that, and extensive notes which the diligent Foreign Minister wrote in his own execrable hand.

He thought out a plan of action. The best way to test out Germany's intentions, he thought – and by the same token, to strengthen Spain's defences against a possible Anglo-American attack – was to request German arms for Spain's armed forces.[14] This he did. As regards the national territory, he was prepared to make one concession, and one only: if the Allies attacked Spain, he would allow German troops to pass through Spain to Morocco. But he would not accept assistance from German troops for the defence of Spain itself – for only Spaniards could die for Spain. And if the Germans should invade Spain, then they, too, would be resisted, to the last fighting Spaniard.

Towards the end of the month, President Roosevelt's special representative at the Vatican, Myron Taylor, passed through Madrid on his way to Rome and General Franco asked to see him. He received Taylor on 30 September in his office in the Palace of El Pardo, decorated at that time with a curious triumvirate of photographs: the Pope in the centre, flanked on either side by Hitler and Mussolini.[15] Taylor, with Hayes in attendance, listened to a long and carefully prepared speech, in which Franco argued that the Pacific war was separate and distinct from the war in Europe, which was a struggle against the barbarous Communism of Russia – the common enemy of Britain, the United States, Germany, Italy and indeed all Christendom. As for Hitler, he was an honourable gentleman, who had no quarrel with Great Britain and no thought of impairing its independence.

Point by point, Myron Taylor rebutted Franco's argument, forcing him to admit that the Americans had to fight a war which the entire Axis had started, and not merely Japan, and that it was Germany that had attacked Russia, not *vice versa*. Hayes thought Franco was impressed by Taylor's counter-arguments. Taylor, on his side, was worried by Franco's apparent willingness to swallow Nazi propaganda. But, says Hayes, 'as I was to discover later, the bark of the

Caudillo was worse than his bite, and the bark on that occasion was his worst'.[16]

Although Franco had dismissed Serrano Súñer and was aware of the potential weight of America's industrial power, he still feared Germany more than the Allies. And indeed, until November 1942, the military picture on the Allied side was of unrelieved gloom, for the Germans were still advancing in Russia and North Africa, while the Japanese were subjugating the whole of South-East Asia with lightning speed. An incident that coincided with Myron Taylor's visit to Madrid came as a reminder that even 'non-belligerents' were not immune to Nazi ruthlessness. The Spanish ship *Monte Gorbea* had been sunk off Martinique, with heavy loss of life and the destruction of a precious wheat cargo from Argentina, and it was taken for granted in Madrid that a German submarine had done it as a warning to Spain not to flirt with America – an assumption that was strengthened when Washington formally denied responsibility. Indeed the Germans later admitted they were to blame and paid an indemnity. The point, however, is that not even a hint that Germany might be responsible for the sinking was allowed to appear in the Spanish press.[17] The consequences of offending the Germans were still feared.

Another source of mounting anxiety, however, now began to manifest itself on Spain's own doorstep. Every day, more war vessels and landing craft seemed to appear at Gibraltar, and soon the overflow spread to the Bay of Algeciras. What did this portend? A landing in North Africa, or an attack on Spain? He cabled the duke of Alba in London to find out all he could.

On 25 October, a reassuring reply came from the duke, who reported that he had raised the matter with Churchill, Eden and Sir John Anderson. All three had denied that there were any Allied plans to invade Spain. Churchill, especially, had been emphatic. The duke had also learnt that General Torr, the British military attaché in Madrid, thought that even if the Germans invaded Spain, the British – in their own interest – would not intervene, unless a situation similar to that of 1808 [when Wellington intervened against Napoleon] should arise.

Against this, the duke went on, he had discovered that a section of the British Intelligence Service was in contact with the Spanish 'Reds' for political ends. This was a card in England's hand, to be played should Spain decide to enter the war on the side of the Axis. In that event, the British would support a Republican-type movement, inside and outside Spain. Consolingly, the duke quoted British expert views that it would be very difficult for the Allies to invade the Iberian peninsula because of the distances involved and the probability that in Spain, in contrast to other European countries, they would not be welcomed by the population.[18]

In another message, the duke informed his government – correctly, as it turned out – that the Allies were about to invade North Africa, push towards Algeria and Tunisia, then use the North African seaboard for an invasion of Europe on the Mediterranean side.[19] Spain herself would be left alone.

Franco, however, could not be certain that the duke was right. He had a gnawing fear that the Allies would need to invade the Canaries, and that the Germans would counter with an invasion of Spain. In both respects he was remarkably near the truth. We have seen what the Germans were up to. The Allies, on their side, were indeed planning to take the Canaries in their stride, and Carlton Hayes, when confidentially informed of this intention, protested against it energetically.[20] His protest carried, and on 2 November, he was able to give written assurances to Count Jordana that no action against Spanish territory was contemplated, and that press items advocating a diplomatic break with Spain did not represent American policy.

Even these reassurances, however, did not dispel Spanish anxieties and on 4 November General Jordana outlined the dangers threatening Spain in a special report to the Cabinet.

Four days later, indeed, he thought his worst fears were about to be realized, when Carlton Hayes, preceded by an ominous telephone call from the Spanish Foreign Ministry, dropped in at Count Jordana's residence at 1 a.m. and asked for an immediate interview with General Franco. The object, Hayes explained, was to hand him a personal letter from President Roosevelt. Half-awake in his dressing-gown, and grey with worry, the little Foreign Minister looked so unhappy that the American Ambassador, treating him as 'a trusted friend' decided to take him into his confidence. On listening to a translation of Roosevelt's letter, Jordana's expression changed from intense anxiety to intense relief. 'Ah!' he exclaimed, 'so Spain is not involved.'[21]

By this time, Hayes felt safe, for he knew that Operation Torch – the Allied invasion of North Africa – was already under way. But he, too, had his worries: would the 150,000 troops of Spanish Morocco make common cause with the French? Then these worries, too, were dispelled later that morning when General Franco received him at El Pardo. From Franco's viewpoint, the American President's letter could hardly have been more satisfactory. Its tone was friendly, its message reassuring. 'It is because your nation and mine are friends in the best sense of the word,' wrote Roosevelt, 'and because you and I are sincerely desirous of the continuation of that friendship for our mutual good that I want very simply to tell you of the compelling reasons that have forced me to send a powerful American military force to the assistance of the French possessions in North Africa·' There followed an outline of the reasons for the operation, and a 'full assurance' that Spain had nothing to fear from the Allies.[22] The letter ended with the cordial formula:

I am, my dear General, your sincere friend
                                    FRANKLIN D. ROOSEVELT

Calm and cordial, General Franco expressed admiring interest in the landings and declared that he accepted Roosevelt's assurances. Both the American President's letter and Franco's formal reply to it were 'splashed' in the Spanish press.

While Hayes was with Franco, and by prior arrangement between the two Allied Ambassadors, Sir Samuel Hoare handed Count Jordana a British Note assuring Franco that the operations in North Africa would neither involve Spain nor interfere with trade.[23] In the light of Spain's later ostracism by the United Nations, it is worth quoting the last paragraph of the Note, which read:

His Majesty's Government are in full sympathy with what they understand to be the desire of the Spanish Government to save the Iberian peninsula from the evils of war. Briefly, they wish Spain to have every opportunity to recover from the devastation of the Civil War and to take her due place in the reconstruction of the Europe of the future.

Reassured on the Allied side, Franco turned to the Germans for similar assurances. But the Nazis were less forthcoming. At first, they said no guarantees were needed from friends. When the Spaniards insisted, they gave oral assurances which the Spaniards didn't think worth publishing. Later in the year, alarmed at the rapid successes of the Allies in North Africa, they twice requested free passage for German troops through Spain. Twice, the Spaniards snubbed them.[24] Indeed Franco made it clear to them that if they moved in, Spain would enter the war on the Allied side. And on 7 December – a month after the landings – Count Jordana, stretching the conventions of diplomatic language as far as he could, told Hayes that

> . . . General Franco and his whole Government are determined to pursue a policy of 'impartiality' toward the two sets of belligerents, to maintain the partly mobilized Spanish army strictly on the defensive within present Spanish frontiers, and to resist *forcefully* any attempt by *any* foreign Power to invade Spanish territory.[25]

Since the British and Americans had solemnly assured Spain that she had nothing to fear from them, these words could only mean that Spain would resist any German invasion.

For Von Stohrer, who had worked so hard and so long to soften up Spain for Hitler's embrace, this was the end of the road. He was too soft, stormed the Führer; and replaced him by von Moltke, who, as Germany's Ambassador to Poland, had acquired a properly Nazi reputation for ruthlessness. All von Moltke was able to accomplish, on the political side, however, was a further exhibition of Franco's capacity for pro-German speeches and gestures, while avoiding precise commitments. In January 1943, for instance, the Caudillo sent his cordial wishes for Hitler's success against Communism. And later in the month, he dispatched the Secretary of the Falange, Arrese, to Berlin accompanied by much Nazophile publicity.[26] Simultaneously – on 29 January – Franco told von Moltke: 'If anybody should think of attacking us, we would defend ourselves like a single man with or without arms, for it has already been proved in our war of liberation that, despite the fact that the Madrid Government had the power, the money, the Army and the Navy, thanks to our thrust (*empuje*), and faith in victory, the war was won.'[27] True, he was commenting on von Moltke's remark that Spain would get arms only if she guaranteed to use them against Germany's enemies alone and only if these invaded Spanish territory. But at that

time, the only threat of invasion was from the German side, so
Franco's message was clear. No German arms, incidentally, were
forthcoming, although eight obsolescent planes were sent later.

There is little point in following the rather repetitive story of
Allied irritation with Franco's public gestures and attempts to
counter German propaganda in Spain. Franco's readiness to fight
the Nazis if Spain were invaded is historically of greater importance
than the pro-German tone of his speeches.

8 *One War, or Three?*

Looking at the world war through the eyes of a non-belligerent,
Franco analysed it in ways with which neither the Allies nor the
Axis could have been expected to agree. In his very first meeting with
the Caudillo, on 9 June 1942, Carlton Hayes had been astonished by
Franco's insistence on seeing the war as two distinct conflicts. Spain,
explained Franco, was neutral in the conflict between the western
Powers and the Axis, but emphatically not neutral in the conflict
between the Axis and Russia.[1]

A year later, on 29 July 1943, the Caudillo told Carlton Hayes
that he now saw the world war as consisting of *three* distinct wars.[2]
There was the war between the English-speaking countries and
Germany, in which Spain was neutral and indeed benevolently
neutral towards the Anglo-Saxons. The second war was the one
against the Japanese barbarians, who must be defeated. And the
third was the war against Communism: if Russia got the better of
Germany, she would use the communist cells that honeycombed
Italy and Germany for her own ends and in time dominate the entire
Continent.

In this conversation, Hayes protested against the presence in
Russia of the Spanish Blue Division, expecting an explosive reaction
from Franco.[3] Instead, the calmness of the Caudillo's reply surprised
him. The Spanish Civil War, Franco explained, had involved a
struggle against Communists inspired and directed by Soviet agents.
That was why he had joined the Anti-Comintern Pact. To his
astonishment, however, Hitler started making overtures to Russia.

He had protested to Hitler and to Mussolini and had approached England, France and the Vatican about breaking up the incipient partnership between Berlin and Moscow. Germany's attack on Poland in September 1939 had found Spain deeply sympathetic to Poland, on whose behalf he had made representations to Italy and the Vatican. Then he had watched Germany standing by while communist Russia took over half Poland, and knew that he could never think of Spain's joining Germany. Only the lack of equipment had prevented Spain sending a volunteer division to help the Finns when Russia attacked them. When Germany and Russia fell out he saw his chance of sending volunteers to Russia, not to help Germany against the western Allies, but to fight Communism.

Hayes, though grateful for Franco's explanation of the background, replied that there could now be no possible justification for leaving the Spanish troops in Russia. After all, we would all have to live with Russia after the war. It was at this stage that Franco advanced his theory of 'three wars', which elicited the comment that the Allies would continue to act jointly with Russia after victory.

An account of the American Ambassador's conversation with Franco was sent to the duke of Alba for his information, and he wrote back to say how interesting he had found it. The duke suggested that whenever the subject of the Blue Division was brought up in London, he would use the following arguments:

1   That Spain owed Germany both an economic debt and a debt in blood for the help received at a time of trouble.
2   That the economic debt had already been repaid with usurious interest [a reference to the mining concessions granted to Nazi Germany].
3   That Spain's way of repaying the blood debt was to send the Blue Division to help the Germans fight the Russians.

In the same dispatch, the duke mentioned that Maisky, the Soviet Ambassador, had just been recalled to Moscow. The main losers, he commented, would be Negrín and Azcárate, who used to spend nearly all their weekends with Maisky.[4] (A year later, he was to report that Maisky's successor, Gusev, was only seeing Negrín briefly and infrequently; this was after another year of declining Republican hopes.)[5]

·   ·   ·   ·   ·

Franco made similar efforts to convince Sir Samuel Hoare of the post-war danger from a triumphant Russia. On 6 January 1943, for instance, he caused something of a sensation by taking the British Ambassador to one side after a State banquet, in full view of rival envoys from Germany, Italy and Japan, and holding a prolonged conversation with him.[6] Precise information, said Franco, had reached him of a clash of wills between Churchill and Stalin, in which the British Prime Minister had only with the greatest difficulty persuaded the Soviet dictator to agree to keep his forces east of the Rhine after Germany's defeat, leaving the rest of western Europe under British influence. One could put no faith, however, in Russian promises, said Franco, and if ever the Russians reached the Rhine, they would overrun all continental Europe, leaving England isolated. Would it not be better for England and Germany – between whom there was no deep hatred but only a political antagonism that could change with circumstances – to conclude an honourable peace, thus saving European civilization from Communism?

The doctrine of 'two wars', or 'three wars', and the corollary of a separate peace with Germany were naturally abhorrent to the Western Allies, especially after the surrender of the German armies at Stalingrad at the beginning of February 1943. The common aim of total victory over Germany could be achieved only by maintaining the unity of the anti-Axis Powers. It seemed to follow that the Allies, including Russia, must be jointly responsible for post-war reconstruction and peace-making; and it was an article of faith – especially in President Roosevelt's mind – that the unity forged in battle would be preserved into the peace.

Not surprisingly, then, Franco's efforts were given short shrift in the Allied camp. On 19 February, Hoare presented the British War Cabinet's views in a memorandum to Jordana. The British Government, it emerged, did not admit the existence of a Russian danger to European civilization.[7] The victory would be an Allied, not a Russian victory. And the memorandum added, comfortingly: 'Moreover, M. Stalin declared on 6 November 1942, that it was not the future policy of Russia to interfere in the internal affairs of other countries.' Sir Samuel does not seem, as he read out the memorandum to Count Jordana, to have asked himself what help this passage would bring to the peoples of half Poland and of the Baltic States whose countries had been forcibly incorporated into the Soviet Union.

Two days later – and three weeks after the German defeat at Stalingrad – General Franco returned to the charge, by way of a memorandum from Jordana to Hoare. He pointed out that Spain was not alone in fearing the consequences of a Soviet triumph in Europe.[8] If Russia penetrated deeply into Germany, he asked:

> ... What is the greater danger not only for the Continent but for England herself, a Germany not totally defeated and with sufficient strength to serve as a rampart against Communism, a Germany hated by all her neighbours, which would deprive her of authority though she remained intact, or a Sovietized Germany which would certainly furnish Russia with the added strength of her war preparations, her engineers, her specialized workmen and technicians, which would enable Russia to extend herself, with an empire without precedent, from the Atlantic to the Pacific?
>
> If Germany did not exist [the letter went on], Europeans would have to invent her and it would be ridiculous to think that her place could be taken by a confederation of Lithuanians, Poles, Czechs and Roumanians which would rapidly be converted into so many more states of the Soviet confederation.

Allowing for the fact that Germany was only partly Sovietized, her division having been made possible by the Normandy landings of 1944, the passage I have just quoted is a remarkably accurate prediction of Stalin's Europe after the Second World War. In contrast, Sir Samuel, in a rejoinder dated 25 February 1943, saw a Europe in which Russia would present no danger and in which British influence would be 'stronger than at any time since the fall of Napoleon'.[9] The actual course of events makes comment unnecessary. Hoare, however, was not alone in war-time blindness to the Soviet danger, and at the end of the year Carlton Hayes took up the same theme in a letter to Count Jordana, dated 27 December 1943, in which he declared that 'Russia does not represent and will not represent for Europe and for the world in general a threat comparable with that represented by the unholy alliance of Nazi Germany and pagan Japan'.*

Thwarted on the Allied side, Franco tried, with equal unsuccess, to persuade the other neutrals to join Spain in a general agitation in

* Doussinague, p. 264: my translation from Doussinague's Spanish. Curiously, Hayes does not mention this letter.

favour of peace. He returned to the theme in several speeches in the spring of 1943.

It should not be thought that the Germans encouraged him in such initiatives, on which, indeed, they looked with jaundiced eyes. It was a matter of judgment and analysis. The western Allies, in the enthusiasm of their victorious alliance, saw only harmony in a future Europe relieved of Hitler's tyranny. The Germans, confident still in the might of their military machine, were not yet prepared to concede defeat, as the dispatches of their ambassador in Madrid, von Moltke, clearly showed.[10] Nor was Moltke's successor, Dieckhoff, who took over after Moltke's sudden death in April, given more conciliatory instructions. For on 15 June 1943, Dieckhoff requested an audience with the Spanish Chief of State, to ask him to desist from peace gestures which the Allies might think inspired by the Axis and might interpret as signs of weakness. He explained that Germany, now at the summit of her power, was about to launch an offensive against Russia and was ready for final victory.[11]

The Nazis could not, indeed, have been expected to sympathize with the reasoning behind Franco's campaign for a separate western peace with Germany, had they but known it. The key to it was Franco's belief that Hitlerism could be overthrown, leaving the German armies intact as a rampart against Soviet expansion.

At this time – in the spring of 1943 – readers of the western press 'knew', since this was the only thing they were told, that Franco was hand in glove with the Nazis. Yet Franco chose the audience of 15 June with Dieckhoff to protest energetically against religious persecution in Nazi Germany.[12] In so doing, he had the full support of the Vatican, and indeed was acting in concert with Pope Pius XII. The rather naïve supposition that a separate peace with Germany could be made more palatable to the Allies if only the Nazis would stop persecuting Catholics undoubtedly played a part in the Caudillo's reasoning at that time. When it was made clear to him that the Nazis would go on treating priests and believers as they thought fit, he dropped the idea of a separate peace for a while. He remained, however, convinced that this was the only way to ensure the future peace and stability of Europe and spare the Continent from communism.

Towards the end of 1943, a new development raised Spanish official hopes that Hitler could, after all, be overthrown, in the framework of a separate peace with the western Allies. There was, however, a fly in the ointment: the notion that Heinrich Himmler was the man to rid Germany of Hitler and Nazism. Even with the passage of the years, it is hard to see how this idea could have been seriously entertained in Madrid. But it was.[13]

A German aristocrat, Prince Max Egon Hohenlohe, long resident in Spain and with a Spanish wife, returned to Spain from a German trip in December 1943, bearing startling news. Goering, Ribbentrop and Goebbels, he said, were all discredited and now only Hitler and Himmler counted. But of the two, Himmler was the more powerful. He was prepared to overthrow the Führer to spare Germany from a Soviet invasion; and the most important German financiers and industrialists, together with the German Army, would support him. Once Hitler was overthrown, Himmler would dismantle National-Socialism and the Germans would collaborate with the British and Americans in the reconstruction of Europe. It went without saying that this plan would be launched only if the Western countries agreed to drop their Russian allies in favour of a separate peace with Germany.

Improbably, Count Jordana, presumably on Franco's orders, instructed his Director-General at the Spanish Foreign Office, José M. Doussinague, to sound out some senior British diplomatist about the possible Allied reaction to the Himmler peace plan. He did, in the course of a talk with the then Counsellor at the British Embassy, Arthur Yencken (who died shortly afterwards in a plane crash).

Predictably, Yencken observed: 'There's one thing I can't understand: how can Spain, a Catholic country, advise a negotiation with Himmler?'

Disconcerted, Doussinague countered that there was no question of defending Himmler but simply of pointing out that Himmler held the key to peace in Europe, whether one liked him or not.

Even allowing for the strange and special relationship between Spain and Nazi Germany, it is hard to understand the failure of political psychology which Spanish acceptance of the Himmler peace feelers revealed. More even, perhaps, than Hitler, Himmler was the hated personification of Nazi evil in the eyes of the British and American people, the torturer and executioner of Hitler's Reich. To suppose that the Allies would trust him to rid Germany of Nazism was a grotesque misconception on Franco's part; though to

say this is not necessarily to invalidate his thesis that Germany and
Europe should be saved from Soviet occupation. Nor need one
necessarily rule out the possibility that, with Hitler overthrown, ways
of getting rid of Himmler too could have been found. It is not part
of my purpose to speculate what might have happened in Europe in
that event. Arguments could be found to defend the separate peace
plan. Where Franco's judgment, for once, was badly at fault was in
the supposition that anybody on the Allied side would take Himmler seriously as a negotiating partner. And so it turned out when
Himmler himself later aired the idea.

9 *The Screw Tightens*

As 1943 wore on, and it became clear to the Allies that the tide had
turned in their favour, they resumed and gradually intensified their
pressure on Franco. The new phase began mildly enough with the
American ambassador's talk with Franco on 29 July 1943, in which
Carlton Hayes protested against the continued presence in Russia of
the Spanish Blue Division. It gathered momentum until, at the war's
end, Franco's régime was left isolated and ostracized as though it had
fought on Hitler's side instead of denying right of way to Hitler's
troops.

For Sir Samuel Hoare's taste, Carlton Hayes's protest had been
altogether too mild. The situation, as he saw it, called for toughness –
not so much, perhaps, for the benefit of the Allies as for his own.
Foremost in his mind was the fact that he was due to make his annual
visit to England late that summer.[1] By 'talking tough', he could
impress his constituents and fellow MPs with the forcefulness with
which he was serving the Allied cause in 'fascist' Spain. With this
end in view, he spent weeks gathering material for a Grand Remonstrance, which he solemnly handed to the Spanish Foreign Ministry
in July.[2]

There was admittedly a good deal of substance in Hoare's detailed charges of unneutral acts by the Franco régime under its
guise of 'non-belligerency'. As the Grand Remonstrance put it,
special facilities had been provided in Spain for Axis submarines; the

aircrews of Axis planes that had force-landed had been repatriated,
while British air crews had been detained; Axis spies and saboteurs
had been allowed to operate in Spanish territory and even in the
Spanish-occupied International Zone of Tangier; moreover the
Falange-controlled press had consistently discriminated against
the Allies in its presentation of war news. Last but not least, the
Blue Division was still in Russia.

The Grand Remonstrance remained unanswered, wrote Hoare,
adding peevishly that 'after a considerable delay', the Spaniards
countercharged that British planes had flown over Spanish territory
and Spanish ships been intercepted by the Royal Navy.[3] The next
thing was to see Franco himself and make Britain's complaints face
to face.

It might have seemed logical to time his protest to coincide with
that of Carlton Hayes, since the impact of a double protest would
clearly have been greater. Moreover, it would have been physically
easier to talk to the Caudillo at about the same time as Carlton Hayes
did, since Franco was due to leave Madrid a few days later for his
native Galicia. Hoare, however, was a politician and saw only the
disadvantage of losing his separate share of any credit to be gained
by tough talking. He therefore postponed the interview until 20
August, within a few days of his departure for London. His own
version of the facts does less than justice to the truth. He maintains
an improbable innocence about the domestic political implications of
the interview, and makes no mention of a fact which Carlton Hayes
rightly considered important: the announcement by the British
Embassy in mid-August that the ambassador was about to have a
momentous interview with General Franco, followed by a briefing
for British and American correspondents, who, says Hayes, were
given the text of 'suggested dispatches' they might cable their
newspapers.[4] As Hoare flew off to Corunna in 'overpoweringly hot'
weather, the BBC was broadcasting news of the flight and of its
'high significance'.[5]

If this was not a build-up, one does not know what it can have
been. But all Hoare says is that he left the interview till 20 August in
the belief that his words would carry greater weight if the Sicilian
campaign were over and if he spoke on the eve of his departure for
high-level consultations in London. Indeed, the Allies did overrun
Sicily by 17 August; but this success, though impressive, was hardly

as dramatic as the news of the resignation and arrest of Mussolini on 26 July. To Sir Samuel's surprise, in fact, even this momentous event seems to have left Franco indifferent, and he comments, once again, on the Caudillo's 'almost overwhelming' complacency, as he sat in his comfortable smoking room, four hundred miles from his capital in the midst of a European crisis, ready to switch the conversation from the tremendous happenings of the war to the crops or the weather, so that Sir Samuel Hoare's strong words fizzled out in cotton wool.[6]

Disconcerted, the British Ambassador fell to wondering, not for the first time, what made Franco tick. And he answered his own question: Franco's cunning and the weakness of his rivals.

Discounting any intention of giving particular publicity to the interview, Sir Samuel says the British were nevertheless forced to do so when the Spanish Embassy in Washington issued a statement to the effect that the talk had been friendly and satisfactory. Carlton Hayes, however, puts the facts in a very different light. Since the British Embassy had briefed Allied correspondents about the Ambassador's forthcoming flight to Corunna, it is unlikely that there was no intention to give publicity to the interview. And indeed no sooner was Hoare back in England than the BBC and the press began to report that the Ambassador had 'demanded' the withdrawal from Russia of the Blue Division. This, says Hayes, with some show of irritation, went a good deal further than Sir Samuel himself had gone when describing his interview with Franco in private conversation.[7]

The ineffable Sir Samuel (or some official spokesman in London) had undone the good work Carlton Hayes had accomplished in his own talk with Franco a month earlier. For Franco, who had decided to pull out the Blue Division, now felt that he could not do so if he appeared to be acting under duress. Incensed at the way the British were presenting the story of his talk with Hoare, and beset now with vigorous German protests at his apparent decision to yield to British pressure, Franco decided to leave the Blue Division in Russia for a few weeks longer.

The Allied cause had suffered a small setback. Sir Samuel, however, was basking in the words of praise for his toughness.

Carlton Hayes was not, on the other hand, entirely deprived of the satisfaction of a job well done, for immediately after his talk with

Franco on 29 July, the Caudillo issued directives to the Spanish press to observe impartiality between the Axis and the Allies in its presentation of the news. Soon the Spanish papers were publishing more news and pictures from the Allies than from the Axis. And on 1 October – the 'Day of the Caudillo' on which he received diplomats and high officials – Franco formally reaffirmed Spain's neutrality, thus, by implication, burying 'non-belligerency'. The previous year, Hayes noted, he had worn the Falange uniform on this occasion. Now he discarded it to don the uniform of an Admiral of the Fleet.[8]

Franco did, in fact, begin shortly afterwards to move the Blue Division away from the Russian front. But the process did not begin until 12 October – at an honourably long interval after the Corunna talk. And it happened quietly, at first, so that Hayes was deprived of the full enjoyment of the diplomatic triumph Sir Samuel had delayed.

As late as 22 October, Winston Churchill was remonstrating with the duke of Alba about the continued presence of Spanish soldiers on the Russian front. On that day, the Prime Minister was the duke's guest at luncheon. When the duke, complying with his instructions from Madrid, explained how difficult it was for the Spaniards to withdraw their troops, Churchill said he understood all that, but it was in Spain's own interests 'to put an end to the presence of these troops, whose action in Russia may be a motive for very serious clashes and difficulties with that great military power'.[9]

At the same lunch, Churchill adopted a severe tone when referring to the Falange, for which, wrote the duke, the Prime Minister had no affection. 'I don't want to use excessively strong words,' said Churchill, taking up one of the themes of Hoare's Grand Remonstrance, 'but we have grievances, very serious complaints and very frequent vexations with it.'* He referred to the Italian ships interned in Spanish ports since the armistice and declared: 'I should much wish that you would let them leave, the warships as well as the merchantmen, although those especially.'

On the general subject of 'the Russian menace' – which the duke of Alba was under standing instructions to raise every time an occasion presented itself – Churchill said: 'The Soviet régime seems to be evolving. However, I am still as anti-Communist as ever and if

---

* These passages inevitably suffer from being my own retranslations into English of the duke's quotations, themselves a translation into Spanish of Churchill's words.

17 Generals Yagüe and Asensio march into fallen Barcelona.

18 The hour of victory: Franco in April 1939.

Communism should be a danger for Europe I shall fight against it, as I have done all my life, with all my strength.'*

Some days earlier – in fact on the very day the Blue Division began to be relieved by German troops, although the British Ambassador in Madrid was unaware of it – Sir Samuel Hoare officially informed Count Jordana that the Portuguese government had granted Britain air and naval bases in the Azores, and reiterated Britain's guarantees to Spain.[10] The Foreign Minister immediately called in the German Ambassador to express the view that the Anglo-Portuguese agreement was no reason to bring the war to the Iberian Peninsula. Dieckhoff listened bleakly, but made no comment. In the evening, General Franco turned to the Portuguese Ambassador, after a Columbus Day dinner, and remarked that the Portuguese need have no fear for their back door, for 'it will be guarded by Spain'.

By the time Franco recalled the Blue Division, the trend of the World War had begun to swing unmistakably in the Allies' favour. On 23 August, the advancing Russians had captured Kharkov, and on 3 September, the western Allies, having completed their occupation of Sicily, crossed the Straits of Messina to begin their invasion of the Italian mainland. Only five days later, Marshal Badoglio, in the name of Italy, surrendered unconditionally; and though Mussolini, dramatically rescued by Nazi paratroopers a week later, proclaimed a Social Republican Government, Franco withheld recognition from it. Looking back on the early days of the World War and on Mussolini's advice to him not to stand aside from the History of Europe, he could well feel that it was he, not Mussolini, who had remained in step with history.

More trials were on the way, however, for the western Allies, emboldened by Russia's successes and their own, began to step up their pressures on the Spaniards.

In this later summer of 1943, the issue that gripped the belligerent chancelleries in Spain concerned neither spies nor battles, neither

---

* At the end of the year, the duke of Alba, reporting on the Prime Minister's grave illness, said Churchill had written to the king suggesting that should anything happen to him, His Majesty should send for Lord Woolton, the Food Minister. He recovered, however, and the letter was never delivered.

o

neutrality nor propaganda. For this was the time of the great
Wolfram Fever. This worthless ore, as it had seemed in the outbreak
of the World War, now fetched £7,500 a ton on the open markets of
the Iberian Peninsula. For the Germans, it had become an essential
ingredient in their war machine, the touch of alchemy that transformed ordinary steel into high-grade steel for their more sophisti-
cated weapons.

As a neutral, Spain was entitled to sell to the highest bidder, as
Turkey sold her chrome and Sweden her iron ore. And since the
Allies were determined to collar the supplies by outbidding the
Germans – a policy known as pre-emptive buying – the price soared
until the Nazis were apparently priced out of the market. By August
1943, the Nazis seemed to have had enough, and stopped buying.

In London, New York and Washington, the strategists of economic
warfare felt entitled to rub their hands, for already the Germans had
been driven out of the Spanish market in woollen goods, fleece-lined
gloves and other exports of value to an army that was soon to face
a third winter in the Russian snows.

The Germans, however, had merely called a halt in the wolfram
battle. The real reason they had stopped buying was not the high
price of the ore but their inability to pay eight million pesetas in
Spanish taxes on accumulated stocks. By November, the German
buyers were back. The stratagem they had found to raise the tax
money was ingenious. They simply presented the Spaniards with a
bill for the contributions made to the Nationalist armed forces
during the Civil War. From this they deducted a relatively small sum
to cover the expenses of the Blue Division in Russia.[11] This left a
large surplus, which enabled the Nazis to pay off their tax arrears and
resume purchasing. To supplement their favourable balance, however, they began pouring exports into Spain. As winter closed in,
forgetting their own needs, the Germans sent wheat, barley and
potatoes to Spain, and in January 1944 alone, 20,000 tons of German
wheat reached the Spanish market. This was the measure of Germany's wolfram hunger.

In October, during the lull in German purchases, Carlton Hayes
had thought to bring mild pressure on the Spaniards to stop or
greatly reduce their exports to Germany, especially their re-exports
of goods received from the United States in the normal course of
war-time trade. There was no question, at that stage, of an Allied

ultimatum to Spain. The memorandum which the American Ambassador presented to Count Jordana on 22 October was empty of overt threats. It simply pointed out that as the war entered its final phases, American needs, of oil in particular, would increase, and the United States could hardly be expected to keep on supplying countries that continued to trade with Germany.[12] The Spanish reaction was cautiously favourable, and Carlton Hayes was hoping that a plan could be worked out to persuade the Franco régime to modify its trading policy – when the so-called Laurel incident blew up in his face and put conciliation out of reach.

José Laurel was a Filipino judge whom the conquering Japanese had set up in office as a puppet President of the Philippines – still in 1943, at least on paper, a colony of the United States. At the end of October, however, the Spanish government had sent Laurel a congratulatory telegram. The decision to do so appears to have been taken by a Spanish Foreign Office official without much thought for the possible consequences. Franco had no intention of recognizing the Laurel régime, and his ambassador in Washington, Señor Cárdenas, called on the State Department on 29 October, and again the following day, to say so.

Washington, however, was not to be appeased. *PM*, and other American newspapers of the Left, were up in arms, and a public clamour grew for a showdown with Franco.

Until that moment, the British and American governments had acted in concert in the wolfram crisis, as in other matters of Allied concern, such as the closing of the German consulate at Tangier, the denial of facilities for German spies and saboteurs, and the use for German purposes of Italian ships in Spanish harbours. The Laurel incident, however, was a specifically American case of wounded *amour propre*, and the State Department, goaded by the American press and public opinion, instructed Carlton Hayes on 6 November, to demand a 'complete and immediate embargo' on Spanish exports of wolfram to Germany, without any *quid pro quo*. The opinion of the British government had not been sought.

It was, in fact, difficult in other ways for the two Allies to act in unison in the wolfram crisis. The British, who imported iron ore, brown coal and potash from Spain, needed Spanish trade more than the Americans did. And there was a further cause of divergence in the anomalous fact that Portugal sent at least as much wolfram to

Germany as Spain did. Since Portugal was, in historical tradition at least, Britain's ally, and had lately granted Britain air bases in the Azores, the British were reluctant to force a total embargo on Spain which might have to be extended to Portugal.

The Americans, however, were less consistent on this issue than the British. Although Portugal continued to export wolfram to Germany, and in the event of a Spanish embargo could easily have made up Germany's loss, the Americans were unwilling to contemplate putting pressure on Dr Salazar's government to stop sending wolfram to Germany.[13] The reason, as Hayes learned, was that the Americans were secretly negotiating with the Portuguese for their own bases on the Azores. The negotiations dragged on for months, while the Portuguese went merrily on shipping wolfram to Germany. Dr Salazar, however, similar though his régime was in various respect to Franco's, was free of the stigma of having come to power with German arms, and it was against Franco that the United States directed its fury.

Curiously little understanding was shown on the American side, during the whole wolfram crisis, of the stubborn pride that lies at the heart of the Spanish character, and of Franco's. It is clear enough that a partial embargo – that is, a considerable reduction of exports to Germany – could have been achieved in the autumn of 1943 by diplomatic bargaining and persuasion. But to demand a 'complete and immediate embargo', as Washington did, was to court Spanish resistance to *any* kind of embargo. Carlton Hayes himself, who well understood the situation, was by-passed, for the State Department summoned Ambassador Cárdenas to demand the immediate embargo, together with the release of Italian warships and merchant ships, the expulsion of German agents from Tangier and landing rights for American planes.

The outcome of this 'tough' approach, as Hayes had anticipated, was a fresh example of the delaying tactics Franco had shown himself to be a master of during his dealings with Hitler. The position of Count Jordana himself was placed in jeopardy, for his pro-Axis colleagues seized the opportunity of taxing him with having brought Spain to a pretty pass with his pro-Western policies. Poor Carlton Hayes patiently pointed out to his chiefs that an immediate embargo would cost Spain her main source of sterling and dollar earnings, cut off a major source of revenue in the form of the export tax on wolfram, provoke the opposition of the wolfram producers, expose Madrid to further German pressure and antagonize the Spanish armed forces, since the wolfram shipments paid for imports of arms, which Spain could obtain only from Germany. Having sent this reasoned explanation by telegram, the Ambassador went to Washington on 11 November to argue the case for gradual methods by word of mouth.

It was, however, too late. Washington, inflamed by the Laurel incident – which Jordana recognized as a blunder but thought the Americans were taking too seriously – had made up its mind to force the issue. Franco, for his part, decided to play for time. He was ready to make concessions on other issues, but not to do anything about wolfram. He approved the American request for landing rights for American commercial airlines, agreed to release all Italian merchantmen, except two that were to be kept in compensation for Spanish ships sunk by Italian submarines, and promised to put the trickier question of the Italian warships before his legal advisers.

By the turn of the year, it was clear that Franco had no intention of yielding on the wolfram issue. When Carlton Hayes complained to Jordana about the inordinate delay in replying to the American proposals, the Foreign Minister replied that 'there was too much pressure from the United States'. The more the Americans got, the more they asked, he declared.

Privately, Hayes could see the point. But Washington was asking for action. The next step could only be sanctions, which in turn could only mean an immediate ban on oil shipments to Spain. Sir Samuel Hoare was against sanctions – at least until the Allies had successfully landed in France, for, as he argued, there was still a danger that the Germans, afraid to lose the wolfram they vitally needed, would strike at Spain across the Pyrenees. However, on hearing that the Spanish Treasury had granted Germany a credit of 425 million pesetas, mainly for the purchase of wolfram, he changed his mind.

On 27 January 1944, Sir Samuel called on General Franco at the Pardo, finding once again 'the usual atmosphere of complete un-concern', while Franco – to his obvious irritation – spoke to him 'in the still small voice of a family doctor who wished to reassure an excited patient'.[14] Not to be deflected from his chosen course, Sir

Samuel doggedly read through a prepared memorandum of particular 'toughness'. Wolfram, of course, dominated the Ambassador's list of complaints. But it was a long list. He had heard that the Falange was enlisting men for a German Foreign Legion and wanted immediate reassurance that such plans would not go forward. Espionage and sabotage by German agents must cease forthwith, and the German consulate at Tangier – one of the chief centres for such German activities – must be closed down. There was more in this vein, with detailed supporting evidence.

For once, Franco seemed to be impressed, and indeed taken aback. He promised action against German agents. As for wolfram, while avoiding any promise of a complete or permanent embargo, he committed himself to suspending further exports while current negotiations with the British and Americans went on. The British Ambassador emerged from the interview with the impression that Franco was, in principle, willing to give the Allies satisfaction, but at a moment of his own choosing that would avoid a showdown with the Germans.

Whether his hopes were well or ill founded, however, Sir Samuel had no means of knowing, for almost immediately they were dashed by the kind of leak with which a democratic press and radio can occasionally wreck secret diplomacy. An American news agency carried a report that the American government had imposed an oil embargo on Spain. The BBC and the press of the United States and Britain gleefully seized on what any journalist would naturally consider a first-class news story. Besieged by curious newsmen, both Anthony Eden in England and Cordell Hull in America rose to the occasion with firm declarations that their respective governments had indeed banned shipments of oil to Spain because they were dissatisfied with Spanish responses to Allied grievances. For the left-wing or merely liberal press, these statements were the signal to unleash vehement and uncompromising attacks on Franco.

The Caudillo's reaction was predictable, and indeed both Hayes and Hoare had foreseen it with impotent apprehension. A distressed Count Jordana complained to Hayes on the evening of 29 January that the Americans seem to have no understanding at all of the Spanish character. Attacks from abroad made the Spaniards resentful and stubborn, not compliant or docile. Nothing could be achieved if Spain was seen to be acting under duress. This kind of thing simply played into the hands of the Germans. Could not the Ambassador do something to stem the flow of words?

Equally distressed, Carlton Hayes said he would do what he could, and indeed the American Office of War Information was able to silence the vociferous critics within days. Hoare on his side was less successful, and the BBC went on pouring oil on the flames with inconsequential gusto.

Unwilling now to go too far to meet the Allies, the Spanish Foreign Office, on Franco's instructions, proposed on 5 February that Spain might limit her exports of wolfram to 720 tons for 1944, including the 300 tons that had already reached the Germans in January. Sir Samuel thought this an acceptable figure, and so apparently did Hayes, but once again Washington said No. Nothing less than an immediate and complete embargo would satisfy the United States government, said the State Department on 9 February, and until such an embargo was forthcoming, tanker loading would be suspended.

Until the story leaked, the intention had been merely to impose a ban during February, and without publicity. Now the ban was to be of indefinite duration.

Franco immediately slashed the petrol ration to domestic consumers. Private cars and motorcycles vanished, except the rare vehicles adorned, as one saw in England just after the war, with the unwieldy gas contraptions known in Spanish as *gasogenos*. Taxis and lorries thinned down to half the previous number and buses almost disappeared, as did fishing boats and tractors.

Throughout the prolonged crisis that followed, the views of London and Washington continued to diverge, until at last after two personal appeals from Winston Churchill to President Roosevelt, the Americans climbed down. The second of Churchill's approaches, on 25 April, was indeed a threat rather than an appeal. Unless the Americans went along with him, said the Prime Minister, Britain would conclude a separate 'peace' with Franco and provide the missing oil. The prospect of public exposure of the rift between the West's major combatants was too much for the State Department, which capitulated.

On 2 May 1944, Mr Eden announced in the House of Commons that agreement had been reached between the British, Americans and Spaniards. Wolfram exports to Germany were to be drastically cut (though not completely stopped: Spain was to limit shipments to 40 tons a month). All but two of the Italian merchant ships were to be released and the question of the Italian warships would be submitted to arbitration. As for the German Consulate at Tangier, it was to be closed, and all German spies and saboteurs were to be expelled from Spanish territory.

In this way the Allies gained most of the points they had sought. But Franco, on his side, was left with the satisfaction of knowing that he had not given in to an ultimatum.

In time, perhaps, some impartial historian will tell the full story of the refugees from Nazi tyranny who poured into Spain in their thousands, and eventually in their tens of thousands in 1942 and 1943. There were Frenchmen and Dutch and Belgians, Hungarians and Poles, Czechs and Austrians. Hungry and destitute, they crowded into camps that soon became insanitary through overcrowding. For the Spanish government they were not merely a financial burden, but a grave embarrassment, since the Germans could argue, and did, that any who were allowed to pass through Spain into Allied hands might take up arms as belligerents against Germany.

Sir Samuel Hoare and members of his Embassy devoted much of their time to helping them and to putting pressure on the Spanish authorities both to improve conditions and to give transit rights to those who might be regarded simply as refugees and not as potential combatants. His account of the refugee problem is, however, so transparently biased and indeed dishonest that it calls for correction.

Any reader relying solely on Sir Samuel's account, for instance, would gain the impression that the Spaniards ruthlessly arrested all refugees who did not manage to find their way secretly to a British consulate or to the Embassy in Madrid. Those arrested, he would learn, were brutally treated and herded into prisons or concentration camps in inhuman conditions.[15] He would be told of the almost intolerable delays that frustrated the British Ambassador's attempts to get the prisoners liberated.[16]

From Carlton Hayes's more objective account, on the other hand, he would learn that the sudden influx of refugees from France in the winter of 1942 to 1943, when Spain herself was short of food and supplies of all kinds placed an intolerable strain on existing reception and transit facilities; and that there were indeed delays due to

Spanish inter-ministerial wrangles and German bullying.[17] The reader is also told, however, that Jordana assured Hayes that Spain would resist German pressure or threats of aggression designed to prevent the release of prisoners who might be useful to the Allies; that the Spanish and Portuguese authorities did, in fact, provide facilities for the evacuation of refugees from Spain across the Portuguese border to western ships; and indeed that:

> Altogether, 16,000 Frenchmen, with Spain's active help, were transported to North Africa in the course of 1943 and incorporated with Allied armed forces.[18]

As for Spanish obstructiveness, Hayes wrote:

> The Spanish Government had not closed its frontiers to refugees but had allowed them to enter and cross the country with considerable freedom. Their 'travel documents' were not too meticulously inspected.[19]

It is characteristic of Hoare's pettiness and lack of generosity that he avoided any mention of Spanish help in the refugees question, apart from a passing reference to support from Beigbeder and Jordana against German pressure in two specific cases.[20]

But there was more. Many of the unfortunates who crossed the Pyrenees in deep snow were stateless Jews. Those who were anti-Nazi Germans and Austrians were presumed to include a number of planted German agents, and no Allied country would have them. Eventually, they found their way to special reception camps in North Africa. A more bizarre case was that of the Sephardic Jews from Salonika, who had been expelled by the Nazis in 1942 and now tried to make their way back to Spain, their original home. Four and a half centuries earlier, in 1490, the ancestors of this same community had been expelled from Spain; yet still, after 452 years of exile, they spoke pure, though slightly archaic, Castilian Spanish.

Sir Samuel Hoare's account of their plight, though moving, is almost impertinently misleading. The Franco government, he wrote, went as far as to put obstacles in the way of the admission of the Sephardic community and was deaf to his appeal that since they had never abandoned their Spanish nationality, they had an automatic right of admission.[21]

A fairer man would have said something about the Franco government's sustained efforts to give the Sephardic community the protection of Spanish citizenship against German persecution. Count Jordana secured the release of an initial batch of three hundred Sephardim, and in time more than a thousand Jews were freed from the Nazis, 'by direct intervention of the Spanish government,' as Carlton Hayes duly recorded.*

10 *Spain Ostracized*

A brief honeymoon between Spain and the western Allies followed the conclusion of the wolfram agreement. In the House of Commons on 25 May 1944, Mr Winston Churchill praised General Franco's government for its refusal to yield to German blandishments and pressures. If it had, he said, the Straits of Gibraltar would have been closed, access to Malta denied and the Spanish coast become a nesting place for the U-boats. Moreover, the Spaniards had contributed to the success of Operation Torch – the invasion of North Africa – by their friendliness and tranquillity at a time when 'Spain's power to injure us was at its very highest'.

* See Carlton J. H. Hayes, *Wartime Mission in Spain*, p. 124. On this page, Hayes refers to the creation, in March 1943, of a fictitious Spanish citizenship for Sephardic Jews, with the specific purpose of interceding with the Germans to free the Sephardic community. This is not quite right. General Primo de Rivera, under a decree of 20 December 1924, offered the Sephardim the right to re-acquire Spanish citizenship on completion of certain formalities. From 1940 on, General Franco, through his representatives in Vichy France, Rumania, Greece and French Morocco, made repeated efforts to get local Sephardic Jews to register as Spanish citizens, whether or not they had claimed their rights under the 1924 decree, so that they could be protected against Nazi-inspired discriminatory laws. A formal offer of citizenship to Sephardim who had availed themselves of Spanish protection during the war was made under a further decree signed by Franco on 29 December 1948. Factual details will be found in *España y los Judíos*, Oficina de Información Diplomática, Madrid 1949.

That Franco did indeed help many Jewish victims of Nazi tyranny was confirmed to me in private conversation by the late Mr Bernard Malley ('Don Bernado') of the British Embassy in Madrid, who, though he had been Sir Samuel Hoare's Private Secretary, never let his undoubted loyalty to his former chief blind him to objective facts.

A delighted duke of Alba recorded some of the untold background to Churchill's speech. He had been the Prime Minister's guest for luncheon on 26 July 1943. After coffee, and 'in the charming garden' of 10 Downing Street, he had had a long talk with Churchill, in which the Prime Minister 'loyally recognized the importance of our neutrality and the difficulties we had in defending it and promised, at my request, to take an opportunity to make public the truth on this question'. He had intended to do so shortly afterwards, but was dissuaded by his colleagues. Later, he had fallen ill, and Eden had made his own statement on Spain. It was not until the long negotiations on wolfram had been successfully concluded that Churchill was at last able to keep his word and make his statement.[1]

After Churchill had made his speech, the duke of Alba saw Eden, who remarked that it had brought only feeble reactions from the Left, except in certain papers, and not much even in America. He asked the Ambassador to convey his compliments to Count Jordana and added: 'You are aware that everything would have been settled more easily between us, but at times the Americans were difficult.'

In the same report, the duke referred to a statement made to diplomatic correspondents by Mr Brendan Bracken, the Minister of Information, saying how short memories were, since what Churchill had now said was just what he had said in the House of Commons on 8 October 1940, which had passed almost unnoticed by the Spanish press. (Churchill, indeed, had expressed his disappointment at this neglect, when lunching at the Spanish Embassy.)

A few days after Churchill's speech, the Spanish Ambassador had a talk with his opposite number, Sir Samuel Hoare, who had arrived in London. He found Sir Samuel in a much more amiable mood than might be concluded from Hoare's later references to this period in his memoirs. Sir Samuel declared that he was very pleased with the present state of relations between their two countries, and Alba, carried away perhaps by his affinity with another staunch monarchist on Spain's behalf, made this comment in his report: 'I personally believe that we could not have in Madrid a British Ambassador who would be better for us than Sir Samuel, bearing in mind present circumstances.'

After some of the difficult times he had undergone, the duke seems to have enjoyed the present atmosphere of benevolent relaxation; and in the same dispatch, he mentioned the friendly attitude of Sir

Leslie Hore-Belisha, the former War Minister, who, he said, was of Spanish-Jewish origin, and had been making speeches stressing the importance of friendship with Spain.

Even the obsessive problem of Russia seemed less menacing than usual, and he quoted without comment some remarks Stalin had made to Eden: 'I am a practical man and I differ from Hitler in that the latter did not know how to limit his ambitions, but I do: I shall always know how far I can go without entering the domain of madness as did the German Führer.'

From the American side, too, all seemed sweetness. In an unprecedented show of trust, Washington instructed Carlton Hayes to inform the Spanish government that the Normandy landings were impending – though without actually disclosing the date of D-Day.[2] He requested facilities for the evacuation of Allied casualties through Barcelona, and for the establishment of Barcelona as a free port for supplies to civilians in southern France. To both these requests, General Franco agreed.

Within weeks, the Germans pulled back their forces from the Pyrenees to reinforce the Normandy defenders, and Franco – if visible events only were the criterion – should have felt able to breathe more freely. Churchill's speech seemed to show that all was well. He had weathered the alternating storms of Axis and Allied pressure, and in the end given satisfaction to the Allies when the hard-pressed Germans were no longer in a position to put the squeeze on Spain.

But the Caudillo felt less secure, in fact, than the ordinary public could have suspected, for even before D-Day, proof came to him that the Americans did not share Churchill's views, with a sharp reminder that even if Spain emerged unscathed from the Second World War, she would soon enter a period of isolation in the midst of hostility. On 27 May – three days after Churchill's speech – the Spanish Foreign Minister drafted a startling Note to the American Ambassador. The Note, which appears to have been delivered on 5 June, contained allegations of American plans for clandestine action in Spain.

For some time, the Note said, groups of Spanish refugees had been trained in North Africa under United States Army direction. They were shown how to blow up buildings and derail trains; they were taught espionage techniques and instructed in the art of forming cells of informants and accomplices. Once in Spain they were to make contact with Communists and other enemies of the régime.[3]

Some landings had already been made, and captured raiders had given full details to the police. While in North Africa, the Note went on, the Spaniards wore United States Army uniforms and were paid on the scale of an American NCO. Once in Spain, trainees who had been assigned to the Communist Party and its affiliated organizations would work exclusively under Communist orders. Others would report back to the Americans in Algeria as agents of 'the North American Secret Service'.

The Spanish security services knew what was going on, partly through information given by one 'Feliciano', who was ready to accept American money to bring down Franco and restore the Republic, but drew the line at spying for the United States; and from the statements of prisoners – especially one Salvador Rodríguez Santana, a radio-operator who was executed not long afterwards, his testimony having failed to save his life. In the end the Spaniards built up a three-volume report on 'United States complicity with the clandestine communist organization in Spain'. The secret Communist apparatus in Melilla had provided the hard core of the trainees who had offered their services to the Americans, said the report. One group of raiders had instructions to destroy a high tension cable in the Pyrenees that served French heavy industries. Others were to set up 'Red guerrillas' and arm them with tommy-guns.

Doussinague, however, on quoting from Jordana's Note to Carlton Hayes, exonerates the higher American authorities from collusion with these clandestine activities, which he attributes to the independent machinations of the secret services. At all events, he adds, once the Americans had received Jordana's complaint, which was supported by the Spanish Ambassador in Washington, both the spying and the American support to Spanish Communists diminished considerably.

There is nothing inherently improbable in these Spanish allegations. In the disastrous closing phase of President Roosevelt's life, America's chief executive does seem to have put greater trust in Stalin than in Churchill. The menace Roosevelt saw, or thought he saw, on the horizon was not Bolshevism but imperialism and reaction. If at all possible, the western imperial powers were to be prevented from reasserting their control over their colonies. As for Spain, whatever Franco might have done to resist Hitler, he was a 'fascist dictator', brought to power with Axis arms and spiritually in league with the Nazis. It was intolerable that his régime should survive into the brave new democratic world of Roosevelt's vision.

Since Franco must go, who were the men most likely to bring him down? Clearly, his most determined enemies, the Spanish Communists. So at a time when the American Office for Strategic Services (OSS) was making its first tentative contacts with an obscure Vietnamese Communist leader called Ho Chi Minh, similar contacts were being made with Spanish communists in North Africa.

For Franco now, in any case, the only sensible course was 'benevolent neutrality' – benevolent, of course, to the Allies. His High Commissioner in Morocco, General Orgaz, agreed to stop Spanish batteries firing at Allied planes that violated Spanish neutrality in pursuit of German submarines. Temporary embargoes were placed on the export to Germany of Spanish woollen goods, skins and olive oil.[4] To all practical purposes, since the Nazis were being forced out of France, they ceased to benefit from Spanish supplies from the time of the Normandy landings.

On 6 July – a month to the day after the landings – Carlton Hayes made a farewell call on General Franco before returning to Washington for consultations. As soon as he entered the Caudillo's study at the Pardo, the Ambassador noticed a sign that times had changed. At an earlier visit, large autographed pictures of Hitler and Mussolini flanked a likeness of Pius XII. Now the Pope had lost his inappropriate companions.[5]

The Caudillo was in a talkative and conciliatory mood. He gave details of Spanish measures to prevent the smuggling of wolfram to Germany and expressed the view that the Germans would be defeated within a year. The generals, he said, would acknowledge defeat before the fanatical Nazis, and sue for peace.

It was the post-war period that seemed to worry Franco most. Only a military occupation for five years of the countries into which the Allied forces entered could prevent civil war in some of them. In tune with the trend of events, he softened the tone of his references to Communism. It was during this interview that he referred to a 'disciplined' popular Communism in Russia and a 'revolutionary'

Communism in other countries of Europe.* But he continued to foresee dangers for the West in the fate of a defeated Germany. Once the Allies were victorious, he suggested, could they not save Germany both from Russia and from the German Communists? His information was that a large section of the Nazi Party was fundamentally in sympathy with Communism and would prefer Germany to be occupied by Russia than by England or America.

As with much of Franco's information and many of his judgments of this period, this view of Germany's perilous future now seems curiously prophetic, as the whole history of the Soviet Zone of Germany and its transformation into the German Democratic Republic, with the collaboration of ex-Nazis, bears witness.

Carlton Hayes does not, however, record his reactions on hearing the Caudillo express these views on 6 July 1944. Before he took his leave, Franco expressed regret at the painful fate that awaited Finland, Rumania and Poland, occupied now by the hated Germans and facing occupation by the equally hated Russians, with civil strife in prospect between the supporters and opponents of Communism.

Count Jordana, who was present at the interview, heard Carlton Hayes praise his constantly helpful efforts in favour of good relations between Spain and the United States. It was the last time the Ambassador saw the Foreign Minister, who collapsed and died at San Sebastian, the summer capital, on 3 August, when Hayes was in New York. Sir Samuel Hoare, who was in San Sebastian at the time, seems to have felt Jordana's loss keenly. According to him, Franco himself felt it less, for he records that the Caudillo went to a cocktail party the day Jordana died and did not attend the funeral in Madrid on 5 August.

Between 6 July, when Carlton Hayes had seen Franco, and 3 August, when Jordana died, the duke of Alba was summoned by Eden, who complained that despite the agreement of 2 May, thirty of the original forty-two German agents were still in Spanish Morocco. The meeting took place on 19 July. Eden accompanied his complaint with a friendly plea: 'You know,' he said, 'that the enemies of the Spanish Government are fairly numerous in the House, and there is no point in giving them grounds for souring our relations.'[6]

* See Chapter 6 above.

Alba counter-attacked with a complaint of his own, about viciously anti-Franco broadcasts that were being heard in Spain at that time, and which he attributed to the British. The Foreign Secretary doubted whether the offending radio station was in fact British. The duke, however, reported that he had since received a letter from Sir Alexander Cadogan, the Permanent Under-Secretary at the Foreign Office, saying that the station was indeed British and he was looking into the matter.

About that time, Lord Selborne lunched with Alba, expressed his sympathy for Spain and made proposals for improving Anglo-Spanish trade after the war. Existing agreements, he said, would be honoured; but the Americans would raise difficulties if any wolfram smuggling went on.

In his dispatch reporting these conversations, the duke of Alba enclosed an extract from *Hansard* (cols 1131–4, 1944) recording a statement in which Eden – hard-pressed by a group of left-wing MPs* – refuted Soviet radio allegations that Franco was giving the Germans facilities at Pamplona for testing explosives and pilotless planes; for the use of Spanish shipyards for war production; for the organization of nitrogen factories by German engineers, and for the training in Spain of Luftwaffe personnel. It was also alleged that Spain continued to export iron ore, tin and zinc to Germany. The Foreign Secretary pointed out that no communication on these lines had been received from the Soviet government – implying that if there had been any substance to the allegations, the Russians would have put them in writing. 'I am satisfied that these reports are without foundation,' he said. The Spaniards were not providing assistance for enemy scientific research. Two nitrate factories were being built in Spain for which machinery had been delivered from Germany. German engineers were working there, but there was no training of Luftwaffe personnel.

The appointment of Señor Lequerica, the former Ambassador to Vichy, as Jordana's successor, aroused apprehension in London and Washington, and provoked another comment from Hoare about Franco's 'inhuman complacency'.[7] But the new Foreign Minister, who had studied both in Paris and in London, soon showed that all he wanted was to carry out Franco's policy of 'benevolent neutrality'

* Messrs Leach, Shinwell, Driberg, Strauss and Pritt.

in favour of the Allies. He removed censorship restrictions on Allied correspondents, and gave instructions for the internment of German ships seeking refuge in Spanish ports.

As 1944 wore to its close, Franco's neutrality indeed became increasingly benevolent. In September, he closed down the German consulate in Tangier and expelled a number of German agents.[8] And on 31 October, he recognized General de Gaulle's Provisional Government. Prudently, Vichy's Ambassador to Madrid, M. Piétri, had announced in August that he considered his mission to be at an end.

Little did these measures do, however, to save Franco's Spain from the pent-up gall and fury of the European Left. At the beginning of October, the duke of Alba gave Franco a candid warning of what was in store for him from the British side. A violent press campaign against the régime was about to be launched, he wrote. It would not be promoted directly by the British government; however, since the press was free, and it was no longer possible to appeal for journalistic discretion on the grounds of patriotism, there was nothing the government could do about it. In any case, the duke pointed out, the government was irritated by hints that had appeared in Spain's controlled press about difficulties between the British and Americans – which hurt all the more for being true.

He thought the campaign was unlikely to be launched before the American Presidential elections in November; possibly it would be the French press that would start the ball rolling once the French Provisional Government had gained recognition. The theme would be the impossibility of tolerating – after the triumph of the democracies in Europe – a totalitarian State in which were preserved, like an island of refuge, the fascist doctrines and national-socialist methods whose extirpation from the world had cost the Allies so many efforts and so much blood.

There followed an astonishing indictment of Franco's régime which showed that bitterness against the general was by no means confined to the European Left. It was unfortunately true, wrote the duke of Alba, that during the early years of the Second World War and even later, there was plenty of anti-Allied material in the Spanish press that could be exploited by journalists and cartoonists. For example, the duke reminded Lequerica – and through him, Franco – the Spanish press had reiterated its faith in an Axis victory, had rejoiced over the first air bombardments of England and identified 'our Movement' with Germanic or totalitarian ideals. Very recently, the press had expressed hopes for the efficacy of the German flying bombs. To all this should be added the official instructions to the metropolitan and provincial papers, about the timing and manner of anti-Allied press campaigns. These were realities that could not be denied; and, the duke added, though he did not like the role of Cassandra, he had to point them out.[9]

The press campaign came, as the duke had foreseen; but there were deeds as well as words. As the German forces withdrew from south-western France, the Maquis moved in. It was a time of terror and revolutionary anarchy, which few Frenchmen now look back on with pride. As in Malaya a year later, in the wake of the defeated Japanese, the Communists – who had been the hardest core of the Resistance – seized villages and towns and took justice into their hands in the name of the 'people'. Toulouse, Carcassonne and Perpignan were among the cities that fell into the hands of the revolutionary Maquis, who soon rounded up 'collaborators' – some of whom were merely patriotic 'class enemies' – for summary execution.

What followed, in that autumn of 1944, was a spectacular example of the gullibility and capacity for self-deception of the Left. Thousands of Catalan and other Spanish exiles, many of them Communists or Anarchists, had enlisted in the French Maquis. With their French comrades, they thirsted for the blood of their arch-reactionary, Franco. This, they felt, was their hour. The Nazis had left, and their trembling protégé across the Pyrenees was ripe for toppling.

General Franco, screamed Toulouse radio, knew the 'jig was up'.[10] He was on his way to the Pyrenees to give himself up to Maura's Republican government in exile. In his despair at the departure of his beloved Nazi allies, and in a thirteenth hour effort to stem their retreat, he was shipping vast quantities of oil, food and arms to the besieged German garrisons on the southern French coasts. In Fleet Street, eager monitors picked up this sensational news, with which, for days, they regaled the readers of the London and New York newspapers.

What fire was there behind this left-wing smoke? The stories about Spanish shipments to the Germans were simply untrue, fabrications of Moscow's propaganda machine, which fed it into a feverish radio news room in Toulouse. Franco's impending fall belonged to a slightly different category of fabrication. The local people and the foreigners in Barcelona were surprised to learn from Toulouse Radio that there was rioting in their city, and indeed, that 1,500 had died there in street fighting. For this was not what their eyes told them. Equally puzzled were the people of Bilbao and Seville, where ghostly radio armies fought for possession of the bricks and mortar. Málaga, it seemed, had fallen to 'loyalist' guerrillas, but the good people of Málaga knew nothing of the drama in the newscasts.

The truth was tamer and more disappointing to the exiles. A guerrilla 'army' did indeed cross the border into Spain. Hayes underestimates their number when he writes that 'a few hundred . . . did attempt to get over'.[11] A few thousand would be nearer the mark. One authority, by no means favourable to the Republicans, puts the figure of those who gathered at the frontier at 10,000, although only about half that number seems to have crossed into Spain.[12] The invaders entered by the Hospitalet Pass, next to the Republic of Andorra. Exalted by their own propaganda and by their memories of a heroic struggle which, for them, had taken place only yesterday, they expected the local population to rise as one man and greet them as liberators. But nothing of the kind happened. For the ordinary people of Spain, the Civil War was a nightmare, to be buried in disgust and horror, not revived in a new show of heroics. Nobody lifted a finger to help the invaders, much less flocked to their revolutionary colours. Indeed in some villages, the peasants denounced them to the authorities or fired on them.

General Yagüe, who was in command of the Pyrenean region, had no trouble in rounding up or forcing back the pitiful bands. Some – the bulk of them – crossed back into France with their war trophies: the sheep and cattle they had seized from uncooperative peasants. Others stayed on in the hills to conduct a desultory guerrilla war.

What worried Franco, in this miserable episode, was not the attempted invasion, which in itself was of little moment, but the evidence it had brought of French and Soviet hostility towards his régime. Nazi Germany was on the verge of destruction; fascist Italy was defeated and Mussolini a spent force. Moreover the incident of the landings by American-trained exiles has shown that, for all Carlton Hayes' personal goodwill, the Americans, too, were hostile, and indeed willing to use Spanish Communists as the tools of an anti-Franquist policy. It was already apparent to him that 'benevolent neutrality', though it might blunt the edge of American hostility, would not be enough – at least in the first post-war phase – to transform that hostility into goodwill.

Where, then, was he to turn for support in a friendless world? The only friendly words for Franco's Spain from a democratic statesman had been those uttered by Churchill on 25 May 1944, and it was to Churchill that Franco naturally turned.

There was a good deal of sense in this decision, in terms of both *Realpolitik* and chances of success. Franco's interest was in the survival of the 'true' Spain, as he conceived it, which had won the Civil War under his leadership and which, under his guidance, had negotiated the competing perils of the Second World War. He knew, with experience to support him, that he was competent to continue to guide Spain into the peace; nor was it apparent that anybody else, or any group but the disparate Movement he had created, was equally competent to do so. His personal survival in power was therefore an essential element in his plans for Spain, and he rightly reasoned that his and Spain's difficulties would be greatest if his régime emerged utterly friendless into the post-war world. In the early days of the World War, when the Nazi war machine had seemed invincible, he had envisaged an authoritarian post-war world in which his régime would have looked similar enough to the Nazi and Fascist model to enable him to preserve independence from actual German control. Even then, he had managed to resist Nazi pressure for Spain's entry into the war.

Now, however, the situation had reversed itself. The parliamentary democracies were winning the war. Though he had no sympathy with liberal democracy, which had failed in Spain, he was willing to – and later did – discard the unwanted and more offensive trappings of his authoritarian State. But he was aware that though this, in time, might bring dividends, it would not be enough to ensure external support in the years ahead. Churchill, however, had always seemed reasonably well disposed towards the Spanish Nationalist cause. Had he not declared, as early as 21 August 1936: 'It seems certain that a majority of Spaniards are on the rebel side'? And had he not written five months later with a prophetic insight which British commentators have wrongly denigrated: 'It does not ... follow that if General Franco wins he will be grateful to his Nazi and Fascist allies. On the contrary, the probability is that the first thought of all patriotic Spaniards, once delivered from their awful plight, will be to escort their rescuers to the nearest seaport'?[13] And the man who had been right then had spoken up seven years later – in 1944 – in praise of Franco's attitude during the Second World War.

Moreover, Franco reasoned, there seemed every chance that Churchill, the probable victor, would emerge as the dominant political leader in post-war Britain. A Britain led by Churchill would be the natural protector of Spain. Moreover, Franco was not unaware of Churchill's long history of hostility toward Communism, from the days of the ill-fated Archangel expedition of 1917 to the present. Though the British statesman had been quick off the mark in offering support to Stalin when Hitler struck at Russia, Franco foresaw the fragility of the war-time alliance. So far, all his warnings about the dangers of a Sovietized Europe had fallen on deaf ears in a situation in which Stalin's Russia was the West's glorious ally. But a final appeal to Churchill – a personal appeal from one Head of Government to another – might yet carry the necessary weight.

As Franco himself told me twenty-one years later, he made no attempt to prepare the ground by diplomatic soundings, and did not consult the duke of Alba. Had he done so, it is at least possible that he would have spared himself the painful rebuff that followed. But to have used an intermediary would have been inconsistent with his assessment and with his plan. For the plan stood or fell on Churchill's response to the man-to-man approach, at the summit. Franco was confident enough to suppose that Churchill's reply would be consistent with his speech of 25 May and with his utterances of seven or eight years earlier, during the non-intervention phase of the Civil War.

In this he was, of course, wrong. But circumstances do, to some extent, extenuate his error of judgment. The factors he had considered seemed solid enough. True, he was aware that his name was coupled with Hitler's, however unjustly, and that he was personally unpopular throughout the democratic world. He knew, in particular, that he was the object of concentrated venom on the part of the mass of the British Labour Party. What he didn't know was the extent to which Churchill's own Conservative colleagues had been shocked by the Prime Minister's friendly references to Spain on 25 May. Nor could he have known that the Prime Minister had felt the need to defend

himself against vicious American press criticisms of his speech in a
personal letter to President Roosevelt on 4 June 1944, in which he
wrote:

> I see some of your newspapers are upset at my references in the
> House of Commons to Spain. This is very unfair, as all I have done
> is to repeat my declaration of October 1940. I only mentioned
> Franco's name to show how silly it was to identify Spain with
> him or him with Spain by means of caricatures. I do not care about
> Franco, but I do not wish to have the Iberian peninsula hostile to
> the British after the war. I do not know how I can depend on a de
> Gaullist France. Germany would have to be held down by main
> force, and we have a twenty-year alliance with Russia. You must
> remember that we are very near to all this pleasant outlook.
>
> We should not be able to agree here in attacking countries which
> have not molested us because we dislike their totalitarian form of
> government. I do not know whether there is more freedom in
> Stalin's Russia than in Franco's Spain. I have no intention to seek
> a quarrel with either.[14]

The Caudillo himself, was quite unaware of such considerations
as he sat down on 18 October 1944, to write a long communication
to the duke of Alba, with instructions that it should be handed
personally to the Prime Minister.

Sir Samuel Hoare quotes the letter in full as the best example he
could find of 'the Caudillo's unconscionable self-complacency' (thus
varying the adjective that accompanies his favourite word for
Franco). True enough, the image of Spain which Franco presented
was not exactly self-derogatory. To read both Franco's letter and
Churchill's reply more than twenty years later, however, is to find
that Franco's stands up better by the test of time.

He began with a polite reference to Churchill's 'noble words'
about Spain, which he linked with 'another gesture in his youth
when he unselfishly served in the Spanish ranks' – a reference to
Churchill's youthful service in Cuba in 1895. He went on to offer
the following analysis of the post-war world situation:

> Since we cannot believe in the good faith of Communist Russia,
> and since we know the insidious power of Bolshevism, we must
> take account of the fact that the weakening or destruction of her

neighbours will greatly increase Russia's ambition and powers, making necessary more than ever an intelligent and understanding attitude on the part of the Western countries. The events in liberated Italy, and the serious situation in France, where the government orders are ignored and *maquis* groups impudently proclaim their aim of setting up a Soviet Republic – for which they claim to have the support of the USSR, speak for themselves. . . .

Once Germany is destroyed and Russia has consolidated her preponderant position in Europe and Asia, and once the United States has consolidated her position in the Atlantic and the Pacific, thus becoming the most powerful nation in the universe, European interests will suffer their most serious and dangerous crisis in a shattered Europe. I understand quite well that military reasons of an immediate character will not permit Englishmen in positions of responsibility to make any comments on this aspect of the world struggle, but the reality exists and the menace remains. After the terrific test Europe has gone through, those who have shown themselves strong and virile among the nations great in population and resources are England, Spain and Germany.

But, once Germany is destroyed, England will have only one country left in Europe towards which she can turn her eyes – Spain. The French and Italian defeats, and the internal decomposition of those countries, will probably not allow anything solid to be built upon them for many years to come. To do so would bring the same tragic surprise which England and Germany had to suffer in the present war. What we deduce from that is clear – reciprocal friendship between England and Spain is desirable.

Franco went on to lament the unsatisfactory state of Anglo-Spanish relations, which he attributed to the hostility of the Press and the activities of the British Secret Service.

Hoare found this letter 'incredible' and commented that it 'would be impossible to imagine a more objectionable communication to make to the government of a country that had made the Anglo-Russian alliance a foundation of its policy and was pledged to restore the greatness of France'.[15] But if Franco's letter overestimated the relative weight of Spain in the future Europe, his view of the Soviet danger was being echoed in Churchill's Fulton speech when Hoare's book was in the press in 1946. As for France's 'greatness', it was restored, in the end, less by a deliberate act of British policy than by the allocation of Marshall Aid (which Spain was denied) and, in time, by the return to power of an anti-British de Gaulle.

Hoare had hoped, with some show of expectant relish, to have the Prime Minister's reply for delivery in person to Franco at his farewell interview.[16] But the Foreign Secretary was held up in Moscow, and Churchill had more urgent matters to deal with, so Lord Templewood (as Sir Samuel now was) went back to Madrid without it. It is clear that Churchill would have liked to send Franco a milder or more conciliatory reply than in fact he did. Indeed, it may be surmised that if Churchill had been in a position to override the views of his colleagues in the war cabinet and of his American allies he would have responded with some sympathy to the Caudillo's approach and to his analysis, with major aspects of which he must have agreed.

There are strong pieces of evidence to support this view. On 8 December, for instance (as the duke of Alba reported in a dispatch that also noted the cold reception given to an anti-Franco speech by Lord Templewood in the House of Lords),[17] Churchill had defended his earlier statement on Spain in the Commons against Left-wing MPs – especially Shinwell, whom the Prime Minister teased for making faces as though he had swallowed a bitter medicine. More significantly, Churchill recorded his comments on a draft of the proposed reply to Franco submitted to him by Mr Anthony Eden, then Foreign Secretary, on 11 December 1944. These are some of Churchill's comments:

> I do not think the balance of help and hindrance given us by Spain in the war is fairly stated. The supreme services of not intervening in 1940 or interfering with the use of the airfield and Algeciras Bay in the month before 'Torch' in 1942 outweigh the minor irritations which are so meticulously set forth.[18]

The Prime Minister went on to call for a reduction in the list of grievances and for changes in wording 'compatible with justice and consistency'. Even he, however, reminded the Foreign Secretary that the Cabinet would wish some reference to the Falange and dictatorship, and instructed Eden to look into it.

These passages show clearly enough the pressures to which Churchill was subjected, despite his great personal prestige. Indeed, as the war seemed to near its victorious end, and the politicians at

Westminster began to think of the electoral battle ahead, it was inevitable that they should try to identify themselves with the prevailing mood which, quite understandably in the emotional climate of the war, was anti-Franco.

The final draft of Churchill's reply, dated 15 January, shows that he only partly got his way in his argument with Eden over the 'balance of help and hindrance' that was to be presented. Hoare, evidently shocked by Churchill's House of Commons speech of 25 May, saw in the January letter a confirmation of his view that Churchill hadn't really meant what he said in Parliament and was now stating his true view of 'a régime he cordially detested'.[19] But the evidence of Churchill's own memoirs, and of his references to Spain before and after the January letter, strongly suggests that the letter represented a concensus of the war cabinet's views rather than Churchill's own.

The Prime Minister's letter began, not unexpectedly, by expressing surprise at Franco's attribution of current Anglo-Spanish difficulties to British political opinion and the activities of British agents, which he dismissed as without foundation. He went on to say that he had not forgotten that Spain did not oppose Britain at two critical moments of the war: the collapse of France in 1940 and during the Anglo-American invasion of North Africa in 1942. But he also recalled the fact that Spain had allowed German influence to hinder the Allied war effort and had sent a division 'to help our German enemies against our Russian allies', and had committed many unneutral acts.

Paragraph 4 might almost have been drafted by Sir Samuel Hoare, and indeed the Ambassador must have had some say in it. His Majesty's Government, wrote Churchill, could not overlook the past record of the Spanish government nor the consistently hostile activity of the Falangist Party, officially recognized as the basis of the present political structure of Spain, nor the fact that the Falange had maintained a close relationship with the Nazi dictatorial party in Germany and with the Italian Fascists. He wanted to remove obstacles in the way of cordial Anglo-Spanish relations, but the changes in Spanish policy towards Britain which had begun when General Jordana took office, though welcome, were not sufficient. As long as the barriers (which Churchill did not specify) were not removed, it was out of the question for the British Government to support Spanish aspirations to participate in the future peace settlements. Nor did he think Spain would be invited to join the future world organization.

It was Paragraph 5 of Churchill's letter, however, that seems least consistent with his own historic vision and his known misgivings about the future of Europe. He wished, he said, to remove from Franco's mind the idea that Britain would be ready to consider any bloc of Powers based on hostility to her Russian allies, or on any assumed need of defence against them: 'His Majesty's Government's policy is firmly based on the Anglo-Soviet Treaty of 1942, and considers permanent Anglo-Russian collaboration within the framework of the future world organization as essential, not only to her own interests, but also to the future peace and prosperity of Europe as a whole.'

This, of course, was what Churchill wrote, but it was not what he believed. Within a few weeks, Churchill knew that 'Soviet Russia had become a mortal danger to the free world'. As he put it in his war memoirs:

> The destruction of German military power had brought with it a fundamental change in the relations between Communist Russia and the Western democracies. They had lost their common enemy, which was almost their sole bond of union. Henceforward Russian imperialism and the Communist creed saw and set no bounds to their progress and ultimate dominion, and more than two years were to pass before they were confronted again with an equal will-power.[20]

This passage refers to Churchill's feelings in March 1945, only two months after his letter to Franco saying almost the opposite. But there can be no doubt which passage truly expresses the Prime Minister's appreciation of the situation in Europe, and no reason to question his sincerity when he adds:

> I should not tell this tale now when all is plain in glaring light if I had not known it and felt it when all was dim and when abounding triumph only intensified the inner darkness of human affairs.

Indeed on 12 May, Churchill wrote to President Truman to express his deep anxiety over the Russians 'because of their misinterpretation of the Yalta decisions, their attitude towards Poland, their overwhelming influence in the Balkans, excepting Greece, the difficulties they make about Vienna, the combination of Russian power and the territories under their control or occupied, coupled with the Communist technique in so many other countries, and above all their power to maintain very large armies in the field for a long time'. It was in this letter that Churchill coined a phrase that became famous: 'An iron curtain,' he wrote, 'is drawn down upon their front.'[21]

And towards the end of his memoirs, Churchill complains that the Americans, and to a lesser extent the British, pulled back their troops, 'thus giving the heart and a great mass of Germany over to the Russians'.[22] He was unable to get American support for the view that no western withdrawals should be made until Russian intentions had been tested; and his election defeat made it impossible to settle the fate of Europe, as he had hoped, in a final confrontation with Stalin.

I have not, of course, quoted Churchill at such length merely to prove how right he was, but to demonstrate that in fact his view of the dangers that faced Europe was almost identical with Franco's. Only Franco expressed similar fears much earlier, but went unheard because of the processes of thought that associated his name with Hitler's.

To say that Churchill's rebuff to Franco – a rebuff from his only potential friend – discouraged him would be to misunderstand the man. It would be more correct to say that it made him realize that nothing more was to be expected from Britain or Britain's allies. From now on, he had to settle down to a long siege, which would certainly be conducted on the diplomatic front, and might be on the military. He did make a few internal concessions to the prevailing external climate of victorious democracy, though none to that of victorious Communism. But he would make no further overtures to the West. He had invaded his own homeland in the early days of the Civil War, against odds that seemed insuperable. He had kept Spain out of the war in the face of pressures that looked irresistible. The problem now was survival in the face of general hostility: his personal survival and national survival, which in his mind were synonymous, since the second depended on the first. In time, he was confident, the West would come to him. And until then, he would no longer try to go to the West.

He had rightly interpreted Churchill's forbidding words as a
warning of bad weather ahead. But when the storm broke it surprised
him by its ferocity. What neither he nor Churchill had guessed was
that the victorious leader himself, the man of Dunkirk and the
saviour of his people in their darkest and finest hour, would be cast
aside by the British voters on the morrow of victory. A Conservative
government might have tempered its initial hostility towards the
'surviving fascist régime'. This could hardly be expected of a Labour
government, whose leader, the mild and apparently moderate Mr
Attlee, had inspected the International Brigades in Spain during the
Civil War, and greeted them with the clenched fist salute.

Churchill's electoral defeat in July 1945 was in fact the rejection of
a Conservative leader, not of Churchill as such. Labour's victory was
part of the general landslide to the left in Europe. Everywhere, the
climate of opinion was hostile towards conservatism, which was held
responsible both for the miseries of the Depression and for the
failure to prevent the rise of fascism and the outbreak of world war.
All over occupied Europe, but especially in France, Italy, Greece
and Jugoslavia, the Communists had played, at least in the later
phases, a major part in the resistance to the Nazis and Fascists. Now,
with victory, they were clamouring for the political rewards of their
courage and resourcefulness. And one of the major, and to them self-
evident, rewards was the liquidation of the Franco régime. The
Communists were not alone in demanding his removal. The international Communist movement, as the instrument of Stalin's foreign
policy, had suffered a major reverse with the defeat of the Republic
in the Civil War. To its adherents, the post-war climate of hostility
towards 'fascism' was an opportunity to reverse the defeat of 1939.
But to the emotional non-Communist Left, and even to liberal and
moderate conservative opinion, it was unthinkable that Franco's
'fascist' régime should be allowed to survive the defeat of the
dictatorial régimes that had, as they reasoned, brought him to power.

Many felt hostile towards Franco, but not all for the same reasons.
There were those who felt the war was not won while a single
fascist régime remained in power. Disapproving of fascism on moral
grounds, they were not concerned with subtleties of analysis about
the special nature of Spanish fascism; nor did it occur to them to
ask whether Franco himself was a fascist. For the hostile, it was
enough that Franco had accepted fascist help and given a fascist

party a special place in the Spanish State. If they looked beyond his overthrow it was to the restoration of a Republic which they saw in their own democratic image and not as the Left-totalitarian polity it had become.

For the Communists, it mattered little whether their anti-fascists allies had the same end-objectives in mind as they had. The essential thing was to bring down Franco, and to this end they employed every resource and expedient of Stalin's international network, from the State power of the Soviet Union as a victorious Power, to the ability of every little Communist group to persuade the non-Communist Left to join them in passing anti-Franco resolutions.

Once again, but on an international scale, the capacity of the Left for self-deception was seen at its most intense and most absurd. Living in a world of their own conception, remote from the Spanish reality, the Leftists of the world believed in 1945, as Maura and his Spanish exiles did in 1944, that it was enough to blow on Franco's castle for it to collapse like a pack of cards. The true Communists, on the other hand, had no such belief. But they welcomed the support of those who held it. What they aimed at was to create a situation in which the very existence of the Franco régime would appear to be a threat to world peace, so that diplomatic, economic, and if necessary military, action could legitimately be taken against it. And for this appearance to emerge and crystallize, the support of the emotional and the gullible was essential.

To be sure, there were statesmen and governments that refused to be led up the violent path of intervention in Spain, men like Ernest Bevin, the Labour Foreign Secretary, who resisted the pressure of the irresponsible Left; or Churchill himself; or Mr Byrnes, of the United States; and governments such as those of Colombia, Cuba, Ecuador and Argentina. In time, the views of the clear-sighted came to prevail over the hysteria of the irresponsible or the ill-will of the Communists. But on more than one occasion, the situation facing Franco was ugly with danger. And throughout the period of post-war hostility, it was more than the political reputation of even the calmest of non-interventionist statesmen was worth to express anything but detestation of Franco Spain.

The opening shots in the cold war against Franco were fired at San Francisco, on 20 June 1945, when the delegate of Mexico, where so many Spanish Republicans had found a refuge, proposed that

Franco's Spain should be kept out of the new world organization then being created. Although his proposal that words to this effect should be written into the Charter of the new world body was rejected, the Allied delegations announced that they intended to 'ban from the world organizations those nations whose régimes have been established with the help of the armed forces of countries having fought against the United Nations so long as those régimes should remain in power'.

The Big Four, meeting at Potsdam shortly afterwards, went further still. Further, no doubt, than Churchill would have liked had he remained in power throughout the conference. This we know, for even before his defeat in the 1945 elections, he managed to get one of Stalin's more blatantly self-interested proposals rejected. 'Stalin,' he writes, 'wanted the United Nations to break off all relations with Franco "and help the democratic forces in Spain" to establish a régime "agreeable to the Spanish people". I resisted this suggestion, and eventually the subject was dismissed.'[23] Churchill, for one, knew his semantics and, in particular, the special connotation, in Communist jargon, of expressions like 'democratic forces' and 'the people'.

On 28 July, however, Clement Attlee sat in Churchill's vacant seat, and raised no objection to Franco's formal excommunication, in this passage from the Potsdam Declaration:

> The three governments, so far as they are concerned, will support applications for membership from those States which have remained neutral during the war and which fulfil the qualifications set out above.
>
> The three governments feel bound, however, to make it clear that they for their part would not favour any application for membership put forward by the present Spanish government which, having been founded with the support of the Axis Powers, does not, in view of its origins, its nature, its record and its close association with the aggressor States, possess the necessary qualifications to justify such membership.

That distinguished opponent of the Franco régime, Salvador de Madariaga, found this condemnation peculiarly distasteful, for as he noted, 'Franco was kept out as a totalitarian and aggressor by Stalin, the arch-aggressor and arch-totalitarian'.[24]

Little would such strictures have worried Stalin. Franco Spain was excommunicated from the United Nations, while Russia had become a founder member. This was what mattered.

Franco, for his part, approved the text of an official comment, couched in those terms of slightly pompous dignity that so irritated Sir Samuel Hoare:

> Spain [it ran], following the rule of discretion and good will which it has adopted in the face of foreign errors that will not affect her directly, did not wish to express its reservations with respect to the agreements of San Francisco, taken in the absence of almost all the European countries. However, on seeing herself so unjustly treated, she is obliged to declare that she will not beg a seat in international conferences and would not accept any position that would not be consonant with her history, her population and her services to peace and culture.

What was more worrying to Stalin than such exchanges was the apparent unwillingness of Russia's allies, for all their hostile words, to take any action to bring down Franco. In France, General de Gaulle's government, although it included Communists, had rejected a unanimous recommendation of the Foreign Affairs committee of the National Assembly on 25 May, to ask France's allies to demand that General Franco should step down.

Then again, on 5 December, Bevin duly told the House of Commons that his government detested Franco's régime, but was not prepared to take any steps that would promote civil war in Spain. This was not at all what Stalin had in mind. Ideally, the Spanish Republican guerrillas who had crossed the border a year earlier should have stirred violent opposition to Franco, so that a threat to international peace could be shown to exist, and intervention justified. But regrettably, the guerrillas had utterly failed to win popular support.

There were, however, other ways of creating a *casus belli* in Spain, as the Communists were to prove in the spring of 1946. Two Spanish Communists, Santiago Álvarez and Salvador Zapiraín, were sent secretly over the Franco-Spanish border, where they were duly arrested.[25] Another Spanish Communist, Cristino García, who had fought in the French Maquis, was among the former Republicans executed in Spain at this time. This was what the French Communist Party was waiting for, and the party itself, together with the communist-dominated CGT, now called on the French government to break diplomatic relations with the Franco régime. By this time, General de Gaulle had retired to sulk in his tent, and the Socialist Prime Minister, Félix Gouin, immediately sought to give satisfaction to the Communists in his government by closing the Pyrenean border on 28 February. The aim was clearly to impose a form of economic sanctions on Spain and force Franco to quit. Franco, however, 'jumped the gun' by closing the border himself throughout its length on 27 February, and strengthening its defences. A few days later, on 4 March, the American and British governments joined the French in declaring that 'so long as General Franco continues in control of Spain, the Spanish people cannot anticipate full and cordial association with the victorious Powers'. The hope was then expressed that 'leading patriotic and liberal-minded Spaniards may soon find the means to bring about a peaceful withdrawal of Franco'.

This was still not what Stalin wanted, but he had further stratagems in reserve, and the UN Security Council debate on Spain in April 1946 gave him a chance for further action. Characteristically, it was not the Soviet but the Polish delegate, Oscar Lange, who was charged with leading the new offensive. Two hundred thousand armed Germans, he declared dramatically, were camping in Spain. Worse still, German scientists, led by one Bergman von Segerslay, were working in the laboratories at Ocana on the production of an atomic bomb. These extravagant charges did not take in the British delegate, Sir Alexander Cadogan, even though he, too, expressed distaste for the Franco régime.

What de Madariaga has called the 'indignant insincerity' of the Communists had begun, in fact, to pall, and the debate on Spain soon degenerated into a confused, sterile and acrimonious wrangle, with Gromyko threatening the veto if strong action were not taken, and the British and American delegates trying to stem the interventionist tide while continuing to 'detest' Franco and all he stood for. In the end, Franco Spain was again – as at Potsdam, but more solemnly and with the weight of the United Nations in support – excommunicated from the peace-loving community of States, with the resolution of 12 December 1946, in which the General Assembly barred Franco's government not merely from membership of the UN but even from participation in any of its subsidiary bodies or in its conferences. For good measure, the resolution added that if

9a The beginning of Hitler's ordeal at Franco's hands, in the Führer's carriage at Hendaya, on 23 October 1940.

9b Franco with Mussolini and Serrano Súñer at Bordighera (1941).

9c Franco with his old friend Marshal Pétain, at Montpellier, on his way back from Bordighera, February 1941.

20a The late John Foster Dulles, Secretary of State, in the Pardo Palace, November 1955.

20b President Eisenhower parts from Franco with a Spanish *abrazo,* December 1959.

'within a reasonable time' an elected government were not formed, the Security Council would 'consider adequate measures'. Meanwhile, all members of the United Nations were to withdraw their heads of mission from Madrid.

General Franco heard the news of Spain's expulsion from the world community with his customary calm. The day the UN passed its resolution, he told one of his Ministers that he had spent the afternoon painting. 'Really,' he added, 'every day I have more and more taste for painting.'[26]

Whether or not this story is apocryphal, the Caudillo did feel he had good reason to be calm. On 9 December, three days earlier – for he had anticipated the UN resolution, as he had struck first in closing the Pyrenees – one of the greatest crowds ever seen in Spanish history had gathered before the Royal Palace in Madrid to shout their support and defiance of foreign interference. It was of course an 'official' demonstration, since the Chief of State himself was flanked by various Falange and other functionaries, but the vast Plaza de Oriente was black with people.

Salvador de Madariaga commented that 'demonstrations are easily arranged by dictatorships';[27] and so they are. But a newsreel of the occasion, which I have seen, suggests that it far transcended the scope of an arranged demonstration. Some of the enthusiasm may have been dutiful. Most of it was wildly, almost terrifyingly sincere. Similar mass demonstrations took place in Barcelona, Valencia and other cities. Franco was no longer simply Caudillo by the Grace of God, and the force of arms, but now by the acclaim of the Spanish people. Nothing, indeed, could have done more to consolidate his power than the hostility of those who condemned his régime.

As he looked down on the great multitude – which probably exceeded half a million in numbers – from the balcony of the Palace of the Kings of Spain, the uncrowned monarch of the Spaniards found words that matched their mood of indignation and defiance:

We Spaniards [he said] must not be surprised at what has happened in the UNO, for a wave of Communist terror is devastating Europe and violations, crimes and persecutions, of the same order as many of you suffered or witnessed, preside, unpunished, over the life of twelve nations, independent until yesterday.

[In these conditions], we should not be surprised that the sons

of Giral and *La Pasionaria* should find support with the official
representatives of these unhappy peoples.

The peaceful spirit of Spain has been sufficiently demonstrated.
Her interests are not in conflict with the honest interests of other
countries. Our country serves these as it serves ourselves. If our
freedom and our sovereignty were in danger, we should become
a real apple of discord. Just as they defend and administer their
peace, we shall administer and defend our victory.

As for the UN, he chose a vein of savage irony that might, but for
a fundamental difference in political outlook, commend itself to that
disenchanted Spanish satirist, Luis Buñuel, when he exclaimed: 'So
long as the concert of the world's nations shall rest on the respect of
each people's sovereignty, no one – except in the event of some
international fascism that would dictate its decisions and unify them –
has the right to interfere in the private business of each nation.'

If to rule is to sense the mood of the ruled, Franco had proved his
mastery of the art of wielding power. More soberly, however, he had
carefully assessed the realities of the situation and concluded that 'his'
Spain had nothing to fear from the surrounding wrath. He had carefully read Bevin's speech of 5 December 1945 – a year earlier – and
noted the Labour Foreign Secretary's opposition to intervention in
Spain. He had read one sentence with particular attention: 'The
British government,' Bevin had declared, 'believes that any foreign
intervention in the Spanish question will strengthen General Franco.'
Now, in the frenzied acclamations of the crowd in the Plaza de
Oriente, he saw and heard the proof of Bevin's assessment.

Similarly, he had read with pleasure and interest the meticulous
demolition of Oscar Lange's accusations by Sir Alexander Cadogan
in the Security Council debate in April 1946. It had not escaped him
that a Labour government in power is not the same thing as a
Labour Party aspiring to exercise power. Nor that the American
government, for all the fervour of its opposition to 'fascism', was
hardly likely to join France and the Soviet Union in imposing, or
attempting to impose, another government on Spain.

Besides, there were increasing signs that his assessment of the
post-war world was coming true. The peace-time strains on the
unity of the wartime alliance were beginning to tell. Stalin's idea of a
democratic Poland was hardly Mr Attlee's or Mr Truman's. In

Greece and Iran, the British had faced the challenge of take-over bids by the Communists. Already, any joint action in Spain by the Communist Powers and the Democracies had become unthinkable. Soon, he reasoned, the necessity of Spain to the non-Communist world would become apparent.

Another point, too, had been noted by the cautious man in the Pardo. When the resolution of 12 December had been put to the vote in the General Assembly, Britain, France and the United States had voted with the Communist countries; but six Latin American countries had voted against, and there had been twelve abstentions, including those of the Arab countries. There, thought Franco, in Hispano-America and the Arab world, lay an opportunity to end the isolation that now encompassed Spain.

As for the recall of the ambassadors from Madrid, it proved a damp squib. Of the major Powers only Britain had an Ambassador in Spain at the time: Sir Victor Mallet, who had replaced Lord Templewood a year earlier. Sir Victor was duly recalled, as were the ambassadors of Holland and Turkey. The United States had not named a successor to Carlton Hayes who, like Lord Templewood, had resigned in December 1944. Argentina, which had voted against the UN resolution, now appointed an ambassador in defiance of it. Meanwhile, the headless foreign missions continued to function as though nothing had happened, under *chargés d'affaires*.[28]

No wonder Franco was calm.

11 *Divide and Rule*

Throughout the World War, General Franco faced challenges to his authority, some of them open, others clandestine. Broadly speaking, the clandestine ones came from discontented Falangists who could see he was not going to build the fascist State they had envisaged, and from Nazis in Madrid who were under orders to find a Caudillo more amenable to Hitler's will. The open challenges tended to be from monarchists who thought he was being too slow in restoring the monarchy.

Neither singly nor in groups were the plotters or the discontented a match for the Caudillo, who demolished them by isolation, or exile, promotion or demotion, as the case might be. In extreme cases, a few men were gaoled. Only one was excuted and then not for treason but black-marketeering. Franco ordered or sanctioned the execution of many Republicans, though not necessarily for their Republicanism. Harsh though these punishments were, unlike Stalin he did not kill his own followers when they turned against him. His way was 'divide and rule'.

He had emerged from the Civil War with the prestige of victory and the self-attributed title of Chief of State. Once, Mussolini had suggested to Serrano that Franco should leave the actual governing of the country to others; and years later Franco confided to Martín Artajo that he was not interested in the part of mother-in-law.[1] Indeed all civil and military power was concentrated in his hands, without any provision that he should hand it over to a constituted body or another individual. But among his followers there were many who had their own ideas about the future of the Spanish State. The old Falangists or *camisas viejas* (old shirts), as they were known, thought the hour had come for them to claim their reward for having been the original companions of José Antonio. With peace restored in a shattered Spain, they saw, or thought they saw, their chance of building the national-syndicalist revolution of their dreams. The Alfonsists reasoned that Franco had done his job by crushing the Republic; he should now go and make room for their Pretender, Don Juan. The Carlists or Traditionalists, of course, wanted no truck with Don Juan, nor for that matter with national-syndicalism or anything that smacked of revolution. Their main objective was to put the Falangists in their place – even though they had consented to cohabit with the Falangists in the FET.

These divisions, of course, played into Franco's hands, in that they made it relatively easy for him to remain in power by balancing one faction against another. But it would be too simple to suppose that staying in power was his only ambition, though it was the first, since it was only by staying in power that he could achieve his other ambitions. He wanted a traditional Spain that would also be united. This implied giving the workers, and perhaps the peasants, a stake in the country's welfare which they had never enjoyed in the traditional Spain of the past. For this reason, he went part of the way with the revolutionary syndicalism of the Falange, but only part of the way. He visualized 'unity' in regional as well as social terms, and therefore had no time for the naïve regionalist aspirations of the Carlists, though willing to give them what they wanted in matters concerning the Church and education.

In all this, Franco's motivation was his sense of order and of what was fitting in a State. Ideology was foreign to his nature. This, of course, offended both the old and the new Falangists, who wanted to give the new State a firm ideological basis.

Thus, while the disunity of his enemies served Franco's wish to stay in power, it ill served his wider desire for a united Nation and Movement. Above all, Franco wanted a government and a State that *worked*. And this could not be achieved if all factions were pulling in different directions. On the home front, then, the essence of his dilemma was that he knew he had to divide and rule, but that he must not allow divisions to run too deep, or working government would become impossible. By and large, he resolved this dilemma.

Franco's first concern after the Civil War, was to clip the wings of the *camisas viejas*. One of them, Raimundo Fernández Cuesta, was still Secretary-General of the FET. A mild and relatively undynamic man, he stood in the way of Ramón Serrano Súñer, whose flame was burning bright. Serrano, of course, was a new Falange man, whom the old guard resented both because he was new and because he so obviously enjoyed Franco's personal favour. It suited Franco at that time to lean on his *cuñadísimo*, since he wanted to keep the old guard in its place. He would have liked to put Serrano in Fernández Cuesta's job, but when the old guard made it clear that there was nothing they would like less, Serrano himself didn't insist.[2] Franco found a solution for this and other problems in a cabinet reshuffle he announced on 9 August 1939, not long after the Civil War had ended. Fernández Cuesta was sent to Rio de Janeiro as Ambassador, and replaced not by Serrano but by Franco's old companion-in-arms, General Muñoz Grandes. In Franco's eyes, Muñoz Grandes had three major qualifications for the key post of party boss: he was a friend and confidant; he was an Army officer and as such preferable to the civilian he had replaced; and since his associations with the Falange were of long standing, he was more acceptable to the *camisas viejas* than Serrano would have been. He was hardly a *camisa vieja* himself, however, so that his appointment left the old guard without a representative in the Cabinet. As for Serrano, he kept his job as

Minister of the Interior, but was given a new party post that would enable him to be, in reality, though not in title, the party boss: he became Chairman of the FET's *Junta Política*.

The old guard, however, were not entirely forgotten. Many of them, having emerged from Republican gaols, became unconditional supporters of Franco's new order. Since Serrano was Franco's coming man, they agreed to support him instead of Fernández Cuesta, and were rewarded with various junior posts. One of the most prominent, Rafael Sánchez Mazas, was appointed Minister without Portfolio.

The new Cabinet as a whole was a judicious mixture of civil and military, of party and Army, with at least a few crumbs for each group of supporters. Muñoz Grandes and Serrano Súñer balanced each other in the party. A Traditionalist, Esteban Bilbao, was given the portfolio of Justice; Finance and Agriculture went to technicians without political affiliation; Education to a Catholic Falangist, Ibáñez Martín; and Industry and Commerce to Lieutenant-Colonel Alarcón de la Lastra, who had made a good job of supplying Madrid when the Nationalists took over.[3]

General Franco removed General Jordana from the Cabinet and abolished the post of Vice-Premier, which he had held along with the Foreign Ministry. The single Defence Ministry, which had played its part during the Civil War, was abolished also and replaced by separate Service ministries. General Varela, a Carlist, became Minister of the Army; General Yagüe, a Falangist, took the Air Ministry; and Admiral Moreno, who had made sure of the Navy's loyalty to the Nationalists at El Ferrol in the first days of the *Alzamiento*, took the Navy. Another military man, Colonel Beigbeder, a liberal Monarchist who at that time was High Commissioner in Morocco, was brought back to Madrid to replace Jordana as Foreign Minister.

The Army, therefore, was present in strength in the Cabinet, albeit with a careful dosage of divergent tendencies. But not all the higher officers who had helped Franco to defeat the Republic were to be rewarded with offices of power. One whom the Caudillo thought prudent to remove was the talkative General Queipo de Llano, who had made an anti-Franco speech in Seville and who had earlier told an Italian officer that once 'two persons' had blotted their copy-book in Madrid, he would be happy to go there. The two persons were Franco and Mola.[4] There was no question of 'liquidating' Queipo, whose services to the Nationalist cause had been considerable, but simply of putting him out of harm's way. Franco thought at first of sending him to Buenos Aires, but in the end posted him to Rome as head of the Spanish military mission there – an honourable post reasonably far from the seat of power.[5]

Having, in effect, stifled the *camisas viejas*, Franco turned to the task of making sure that none of the Falange's autonomous organizations should become strong enough to challenge the authority of the State. This meant, principally, bringing the militia, the students, the syndicates and the ideologists under control.

Doubtless many of the more exalted Falangists had visions of their war-time militia as a peace-time force equivalent in power to the Nazis' Brownshirts of the SS and SA, an autonomous instrument for the enforcement of their theories of national-syndicalism. But Franco was an Army officer, not a political demagogue like Hitler. As far as he was concerned, the militia had served its purpose. The FET was a useful instrument for the enforcement of *his* State power, but it was not to be allowed to have an instrument of its own. The Army came first. Accordingly, shortly after the Civil War had ended, he re-grouped the militia in the ex-combatants' organization, under José Antonio Girón, later to become his labour boss. On 2 July 1940, the Caudillo signed a decree creating an official Falange militia. But there was little of the Falange about it, except the title: all the key jobs went to regular Army men.[6]

The students and syndicates were, in some respects, tougher nuts to crack, for each threw up an energetic and ambitious natural leader. Enrique Sotomayor was only nineteen in 1939, when he made a bid for the leadership of the Falange student syndicate, the SEU. For the past two years, he had come to public notice by his part in producing the SEU review, *Haz*. Now he and his friends wanted to reform the SEU and create a Front of Youth Organizations (*Frente de Juventudes*) to spread José Antonio's ideas in the minds of tomorrow's leaders. According to Stanley Payne, the Caudillo himself gave an audience to Sotomayor and two of his friends and was favourably impressed by them. Muñoz Grandes, however, was alarmed lest these wild and eloquent young men should get out of hand, and on reflection, Franco offered Sotomayor the job of Secretary-General of the SEU, on condition that he should serve under one of the loyal, recently released *camisas viejas*, José Miguel Guitarte, who was to be *Jefe*

Nacional.[7] As Muñoz Grandes had hoped, this combination effectively stifled young Sotomayor, who took the job in August 1939, but resigned after three months in utter frustration; he was killed two years later in Russia, fighting in the Blue Division.

Syndicalism was part of the price Franco knew he had to pay for the support of the old Falangists. But his aims were less revolutionary than theirs. Those Falangists who were most loyal to the memory of José Antonio saw the syndicates – which could not be organized on a national scale so long as the Civil War lasted – as the way to bring fulfilment to the working men and smash the power of the bankers and capitalists. This was not at all Franco's idea of what syndicates should do. He saw them as a convenient medium for supervised collective bargaining, leaving the bankers and capitalists with their wealth, while bringing certain measures of welfare and social security to the workers. The *camisas viejas* thought the *sindicatos* would complete the social revolution; Franco merely wanted them to ensure social stability.

There was no obvious candidate for boss of the *sindicatos*. Franco, who had other things to think of, seems to have delegated the job of selecting one to Serrano Súñer and Pedro Gamero del Castillo, a close friend of Serrano's and Vice-Secretary General of the FET under Muñoz Grandes. The best candidate Serrano and Gamero could see on the horizon was a Falangist called Gerardo Salvador Merino.[8] True, he had been rather too fervent of the middle class when serving as *Jefe Provincial* of Corunna during the Civil War, but latterly he had kept very quiet. True again, he had been appointed to his earlier post by Manuel Hedilla, José Antonio's successor. But this was hardly Merino's fault. At any rate, his interest in syndical matters was well known; he was a *camisa vieja*; and he seemed to have a capacity for organization. So on 9 September 1939, Salvador Merino was duly appointed National Delegate in charge of the syndicates.

Considering the scale of his ambitions, which soon became only too visible, he had a good innings: nearly two years. He began cautiously enough by organizing industry-wide National Syndicates, with the approval of the traditional Right, which saw the value of order and simplicity under authoritarian control. By the end of 1939, Merino had gone far enough in his work for the new power of the syndicates to be defined in decrees. On paper, these powers were to be considerable. Under the 1938 laws, private enterprise had had its own government representation. Now the syndicates became the only organizations in which economic interests of any kind could be represented. Workers and managements alike were lumped together in the National Syndicates, there to work out their shares of the national cake, under party control. On 3 May, the power of the *sindicatos* was increased still further, when it was announced that henceforth, prices and economic standards were to be fixed by these giant trade unions. Until then, they had been determined by a Regulative Commission.

So far, there was nothing to which the bankers and employers could possibly object. In the end, everything came back to the Caudillo, who had the power to appoint the National Delegate as well as each *sindicato* chief; and they trusted Franco not to fall for the revolutionary line of the old guard. This trust was not, of course, misplaced. But now, in the spring of 1940, Salvador Merino began to alarm his potential enemies by offering them startling confirmation of their suspicion that his real aim was to use the syndicates as an instrument of personal power on behalf of the proletarian masses. He chose Victory Day, the first anniversary of the end of the Civil War, on 31 March 1940, to muster his workers in thousands for a monster parade down Madrid's majestic Paseo de la Castellana. The Carlist War Minister, General Varela, was incensed and swore he would have Merino removed.

After other such demonstrations, Serrano got worried and offered Merino the Ministry of Labour, as one way of getting him out of the syndical organization. But Merino loftily replied that the only job he would consider apart from his present one was that of Secretary-General of the FET, and even then, only on condition that he also became Minister of the Interior. Exasperated, Serrano Súñer, who had only just surrendered the Ministry of the Interior himself, exclaimed that Merino was hopelessly ambitious.

Merino's enemies now began to move in for the kill. Varela was the main one, of course; but there were others, including the ex-Carlist Esteban Bilbao and the industrialist and financier Demetrio Carceller. Bilbao and Carceller were members of the party's *Junta Politica*, and therefore powerful. Biding their time, they waited till he left Madrid, in July 1941, for his honeymoon, then spread the accusation that he had been a Freemason. As soon as he and his bride came back, Franco banished him to the Balearics.

From then on, there was no nonsense about revolutionary syndicalism. Franco handed the job of trade union boss to José Antonio Girón, who had lately been appointed Labour Minister. Now the syndicates became what Franco and the Right wanted them to be: organizations of social stability, not centres of mass unrest.

The ideologists of the party might also have been a source of trouble to Franco, had they interpreted their job as seeing that the 'New Spain' conformed to José Antonio's precepts. But they were given little chance of doing anything of the kind. Franco had no intention of being burdened with ideology, and he soon made it clear that the Institute of Political Studies, which he created on 9 September 1939, was to fashion ideology in the image of his authoritarian State. The State, then, was to dominate the ideology, not the other way round.

The Institute's most important ideologist, in the early days, was Juan Beneyto Pérez, whose first assignment was to express the principle of *Caudillaje* in ideological terms.[9] In those days, 1939 to 1940, Nazism and Italian Fascism were in the ascendant, and liberal democracy was 'decadent'; and Beneyto Pérez duly praised the totalitarian features of Franco's Spain. Later, as the fortunes of the Axis waned, the totalitarian aspects of Falange ideology were played down and timid words of semi-praise for liberalism even found their way into the party publications. All this was shocking to the 'pure' followers of José Antonio, but there was nothing they could do about it. Whatever the international Left might say about the 'fascist dictator', Franco was a fascist only when it suited him. And it did not suit him for very long.

Not unnaturally, the gradual awareness that they had been saddled with a strictly non-ideological Caudillo caused discontent in the ranks of the original Falange. Soon they began to plot his removal. Towards the end of 1939, says Payne, on the basis of talks with leading figures of the conspiracy, the discontented Falangists formed a secret *Junta Política* in Madrid under the Presidency of Colonel Emilio Tarduchy, whose background combined Falange and Right-wing Army activities in the *Union Militar Española*.[10] A Sevillian *camisa vieja*, Patricio Canales, was the secretary, and there were regional representatives from Asturias, Galicia, Santander, Catalonia, the Levante, the Canaries and Morocco.

For military support at the top level, the plotters turned to the arch-intriguer of the military Falange, General Yagüe. With Yagüe 'in', they reasoned, they could bring in most of the officers who were dissatisfied with the kind of state Franco was setting up. There was also a good chance of bringing in Yagüe's friend Girón who, in turn, could bring in the *ex-combatientes* of the key region, Castile, where, as things then stood, the conspiracy was weak.

Yagüe, however, was cautious, and Girón said he wouldn't commit himself without Yagüe. The plotters then decided to turn to the Nazis for support. Throughout 1940 and until February 1941, they had talks from time to time with Thomson, the Nazi Party man at the German Embassy. As the *Junta Política* had guessed, the Nazis were interested in the chance of setting up a thoroughgoing national syndicalist régime in Spain. As they should have guessed but did not, however, the Nazi price for help was excessively high: if paid, it would have turned Spain into a soulless satellite of the Third Reich.

Meanwhile, Yagüe's own machinations were denounced to Franco, who called him in and gave him so severe a reprimand that he emerged in tears. The Caudillo knew better, however, than to make a martyr of him. Instead, he *promoted* Yagüe, who thus became useless to the conspirators.

Deprived of Yagüe, and therefore of Girón, and unwilling to become quislings en masse to the Nazis, the plotters thought now of a bold stroke – assassination. At first, they had thought of assassinating Serrano, the upstart who had sullied the pristine purity of José Antonio's Falange. But the logic of their train of thought made them see that anybody, even Serrano Súñer, was replaceable so long as Franco had supreme power. There was no other way, then: Franco himself would have to be killed.

This conclusion, though logical, was easier to reach than to achieve. It would take steady nerves and painstaking organization. But when it came to it, the dispirited plotters couldn't face it. They met in Madrid one day in March 1941, and put the matter to the vote. The issue was: 'Do we assassinate the Caudillo or accept his authority?' By four votes to none, with one abstention, they voted to bow down.

Now the conspiracy was over. The secret *Junta* dissolved itself. It was only now, late in the day, that the security service learned about the plot. Once again, however, Franco was magnanimous, for the plotters having rallied to him, he decided to leave them alone. (One irreconcilable, Eduardo Ezquer, who had once been expelled from the Falange by José himself, went on plotting in Catalonia. For his pains, he was arrested in 1942, and his schemes came to nothing.) The men of 'anti-Spain', Communists, Freemasons and such like, were fair game for liquidation. But not patriots who had strayed from the fold. In this, as in many other respects, Franco differed from the totalitarian dictators of the twentieth century.

The Nazis at the German Embassy had learnt nothing from their failure to find quislings with the weight to carry out a *coup d'état*. (They *had* found some quislings, in fact, but only minor ones.) Their appetite had merely been whetted. As time passed and their exasperation with the prevarication of the Spanish leaders grew, so did their determination to rid themselves of Serrano and Franco. Schellenberg, the Nazi intelligence chief, had drawn up a list of top Spaniards thought likely to collaborate in a coup against Franco and his brother-in-law. In this as in other espionage efforts in Spain, the Germans were remarkably obtuse, since, despite the lesson of 1940–41, Yagüe headed the list. Ezquer, who was also on the list, was certainly a 'possible' in that he remained in opposition; but the smallness of his following, and especially its local character in Catalonia, suggested that he would not have been of much use. José Luis Arrese, who by that time had replaced Muñoz Grandes as Secretary-General of the FET, was certainly an opponent of Serrano's, but not to the extent of plotting against the Caudillo, to whom he was rigidly loyal.

There is in fact no evidence that Yagüe, Arrese, or any other highly placed personage of the régime was prepared to collaborate with the Nazis against their Chief of State. At the 'small fry' level, there were plenty of Spaniards in the pay of the Germans, and Doussinague records that the Spanish police were on the track of some of them in the summer of 1942.[11] One day, he writes, an attaché at the German Embassy (whom he does not name) was driving to the French border and stopped for lunch at Burgos. There, he exchanged views with a companion about the German plot against Franco. A German-speaking Spanish agent, who heard what was said, passed on the details to the police. Once the attaché had crossed the border into France, the Spaniards refused to allow him to return, in the face of strong protests from the German Embassy.

A few days later, on 15 August 1942, Carlist *requetés* and Falangist youths clashed outside the church of the Virgen de Begoña, patron saint of Bilbao, and a young Falangist named Domínguez threw a hand grenade into the crowd as they were leaving the church.* Now, General Varela, the Carlist Minister of War and anti-Falangist, was in the church at the time, and the Carlists immediately accused the Falange of trying to assassinate him, even though he himself is said to have told Franco, who telephoned him for news, that he thought it was just a street incident.[12] Varela was unhurt, but there were several dozen killed or injured.

The Bilbao incident had dramatic political consequences in Spain. The point that concerns us here is that Domínguez, the youth who threw the bomb, was in the pay of the Germans. It is a tenable theory that the Nazis put a bomb into Domínguez's hands in the hope that the resulting outrage would set the Army against Falange, to their ultimate advantage. The smouldering feuds behind the façade of the régime certainly erupted with the explosion of the Virgen de Begoña, but the Germans were unable to put events to their profit, perhaps because the Nazi attaché who was in the know was prevented from returning to Spain when the crisis came.

The attempt on Varela's life – if that is what the Bilbao outrage was – brought Serrano Súñer down from his pinnacle of power, and indirectly led to the dismissal of the German Ambassador, von Stohrer. His successor, von Molkte, arrived in Madrid early in January 1943, and shortly after was mixed up in a curious little crisis in German-Spanish relations, in which the little group of Nazi conspirators in his Embassy tried to use him for their own ends.

This, of course, was the time when Hitler's feverish preparations for Operation Gisela – the invasion of Spain – were at their height. Alarming reports were reaching the Spanish Security Service: Spanish-speaking German officers and men were being transferred from Berlin to the Pau region of the Pyrenees; intercepted telephone conversations in the Perpignan region spoke of the arrival of five

---

* As so often in contemporary Spanish history, it is difficult to establish dates with certainty. Payne (*Falange*, p. 234) gives 16 August. Martin gives 15 August on p. 223 of the French edition of his biography of Franco, and 14 August on p. 397 of the Spanish edition. Hoare adds variety by making it 15 August (*Ambassador on Special Mission*, p. 165).

divisions; in Montpellier, 2,000 rooms had been requisitioned for members of the German forces.[13] On 31 January, the Spanish Foreign Ministry had in its hands a precise report of German plans to cross the Pyrenees at 5 a.m. the following day, and the Spanish Ambassador in Berlin was instructed to see Hitler, if possible, or Ribbentrop, if not, and declare with all the energy at his command that the Spaniards would defend themselves with armed force against any attempt to violate their territory.

At 6 a.m., the German Embassy telephoned the Foreign Ministry to say that von Moltke requested an immediate interview with Count Jordana. The official on duty raised objections in view of the early hour and the interview took place two or three hours later. von Moltke declared that he had been requested by Berlin to deny categorically all rumours of a projected invasion of Spain by the German forces.

The Spaniards later learned the background to this slightly feverish *démarche*. At 4 a.m. that day, the German Ambassador himself had summoned his three Armed Forces attachés and other subordinates, to tell them he had just received a telegram from the Wilhelmstrasse ordering him to seek an immediate interview with Jordana to deny the invasion rumours. His staff objected that this was surely an excessively melodramatic way of doing things, reminiscent of the American Ambassador's visit to Jordana in the middle of the night to give him President Roosevelt's reassurances about Operation Torch. Better wait a little, they counselled. And he did, but only until 6 a.m.

A few days later, on 6 February 1943, Doussinague, the Permanent Head of the Spanish Foreign Ministry, went to bed at 11 p.m., exhausted after a tiring day. He had scarcely dropped off to sleep when the telephone rang. It was Lazar, the Press Officer at the German Embassy, and he wanted Doussinague to confirm or deny a sensational piece of news. Was it or was it not true, he asked that General Franco had gone to Lisbon that morning to meet Winston Churchill?

Puzzled, the Foreign Office chief said there was not a word of truth in the story. Next morning, Lazar dropped in with an apology and an explanation. He himself, he said, had been summoned to the Ambassador's office at 11 p.m. the previous night, and had found Moltke with the Armed Services attachés and several other diplomatic officials. Von Moltke held a sheaf of papers in one hand, while the other rested on his telephone, as though he were about to make a call.

The papers, it turned out, were a report by embassy officials concerning the movements of the British Prime Minister and the Spanish Chief of State. Between 14 and 24 January, Churchill had conferred in Casablanca with President Roosevelt. He had gone on to Cairo and then to Turkey where, at Adana on 2 February, he had had important talks with President Ismet Inönü. These had caused a disagreeable sensation in Berlin, where it was seen that they signalled a change in Turkey's neutrality, in favour of the Allies. On his way home, Churchill had spent a night at Lisbon. At 5.30 the following morning, the Caudillo had been seen in his car, speeding towards Barajas airport. The report stated the time of his arrival at Barajas, and of his landing at Lisbon. It went on to mention that Swiss Radio had reported Churchill's conversation with Franco.

The little group of Nazis had been urging Von Moltke, on the strength of their report, to telephone the news to Berlin, with the comment that it clearly showed Franco to have gone over to the British. When Lazar entered the office, the Ambassador took his hand away from the telephone, explained the circumstances and asked the Press Officer's opinion. Lazar hesitated, then said it seemed strange that anybody could recognize the Caudillo in a car at 5.30 on a winter's morning, when it was still dark. The Ambassador asked him to make inquiries. And Lazar successively telephoned Doussinague, Esteban Bilbao, the President of the Cortes, and General Franco Salgado, the Caudillo's cousin and vice-chief of the Military Household. In all cases, the answer was a firm and instant denial.

It seemed unlikely that the people contacted could have concerted their answers. Shaken, and mindful of his predecessor's failures, von Moltke opted for caution and refrained from telephoning Berlin.

This, it turned out, spelled the collapse of the Nazi plotters' hopes. On the basis of Lazar's account and of the Security Service reports, Doussinague deduced that the plotters wanted to provoke Hitler into an immediate invasion of Spain and thought the best way to do it was to persuade the Ambassador to telephone the phoney news of the Franco-Churchill interview. Once the Germans had crossed the border, and whether or not the Spanish forces resisted, they reckoned that the men on their list of potential quislings would overthrow

Franco and provide another 'Serrano Súñer' more receptive to Nazi pressures. Franco's successor and Serrano's, they reasoned, would then bring Spain into the war on Germany's side.

The flaw in their plan was that no Spaniard of any prominence, whatever his views about Franco, would have done Hitler's work with Nazi troops on Spanish soil. At any rate, the plot collapsed, and so did Hitler's chances of unseating the Caudillo. Shortly after, the group of Nazis who had urged von Moltke to call Berlin were sacked and sent to fight on the Eastern front.

Let us now return to the Falange's troubles and resentments. General Muñoz Grandes, close though he was to the Caudillo, had neither administrative talent nor aptitude for intrigue. Both were needed, at that time, for the key post of Secretary-General of the FET, and when it became clear to him and to others that he lacked both qualifications, he resigned.[14] This was on 15 March 1940.

Since no successor was named, the running of the party was left to Muñoz Grandes' assistant, Pedro Gamero del Castillo, with Serrano, as political boss and Minister of the Interior, actually giving the orders. Gamero, whose position was invidious, made do as best he could by allocating spoils to those he thought it necessary to conciliate. This brought him a few friendships but did nothing to reduce the smouldering resentment of the *camisas viejas* against Serrano Súñer. They enlisted the support of Pilar Primo de Rivera, José Antonio's sister and head of the FET's *Sección Femenina*, and early in 1941 presented the *cuñadísimo* with a virtual ultimatum. Either be one of us, they said in effect, and give the party its rightful place in the State; or stop pretending and come out in the open as a reactionary.

But Serrano said neither Yes nor No. By then he was Foreign Minister and there seemed no stopping him. The frustrated Old Guard watched his continual rise in fascinated impotence until, suddenly, in May 1941, the smouldering crisis within the régime burst into flames.

Intent on improving the Army's share of power, which had diminished through Muñoz Grandes's resignation, Franco appointed the anti-Falangist Colonel Valentín Galarza – the 'technician' of the 1936 conspiracy – to Serrano's vacant post of Minister of the Interior. This was on 5 May, and it was too much for the Old Guard. Within a few days, José Antonio's brother Miguel resigned as *Jefe Provincial* in Madrid and half a dozen other provincial bosses followed suit.

Arriba, the party newspaper, made matters worse by carrying an anonymous article entitled 'The Man and the Pipsqueak', in which the 'pipsqueak', though unnamed, could only have been Galarza.

Now, it seemed, the fat was really in the fire. But this was just the kind of crisis Franco was adept at handling. Calm as usual, he called for a full report. The *Arriba* article, it turned out, had been written by the fiery young poet, Dionisio Ridruejo, who was still, as he had been in Serrano's day, Propaganda Chief in the Ministry of the Interior, and therefore Galarza's subordinate. But it was Antonio Tóvar, Press Sub-secretary of the Falange, who oversaw the contents of *Arriba*, and he took full responsibility.

Galarza and other indignant Army officers besieged the Pardo Palace, clamouring for the political heads of the guilty young men. It was awkward, for both Tóvar and Ridruejo were known to be personal protégés of the *cuñadísimo*. Franco, however, never forgot that the Army was the ultimate source of his power. Without bothering to consult his brother-in-law, he dismissed both Tóvar and Ridruejo.

Furious and dismayed, Serrano, it is said, privately wrote to the Caudillo, tendering his resignation. The Caudillo, however, was ready for this one, too. So the Falange was offended? Then he would give the top administrative job in the FET to a *camisa vieja*. Moreover, he would give it to a personal enemy of Colonel Galarza.

The man he had in mind was José Luis Arrese. One of the better products of the original Falange, Arrese was loyal, honest, sincere and energetic. He enjoyed the prestige of one who had married into the Primo de Rivera family, but suffered – or so he feared – from the handicap of having twice blotted his copy-book. The first blot came when he was arrested during the 1937 purge – the Hedilla affair. He had effaced it by hard and efficient work as *Jefe Provincial* in Málaga. But now he had added a second blot to the record, for, outraged at Galarza's appointment as Minister of the Interior and unwilling to take orders from him, he had resigned as *Jefe Provincial*. Now, his conscience clear but uncertain of the future – Spain's or his own – he came to Madrid to find out what was going on. To his surprise, he was called to the Caudillo's office and learned that he was appointed Secretary-General of the FET.

His answer was a qualified yes. He would take on the job, but his appointment alone was insufficient to balance that of Galarza. If this was the price to be paid for a contented old guard, Franco was willing to pay it. He invited Arrese to call a meeting of top Falangists and submit proposals for improving the party's representation in the government.

The Falangists duly met in Arrese's home, and drew up plans which Franco accepted with alacrity. Two more top Falangists ascended to the Cabinet: José Antonio Girón, who became Minister of Labour, and *the* José Antonio's surviving brother, Miguel, who was appointed Minister of Agriculture. The Press and Propaganda services, whose young incumbents, Tóvar and Ridruejo, had precipitated the crisis with their criticisms of Galarza, were removed from the Ministry of the Interior and transferred to the FET itself.

This ought to have been the end of the crisis, but it wasn't – quite. Serrano Súñer had attended the meeting of top Falangists at Arrese's home, anxious both to see that the party was given its due in the Cabinet, and to ensure that his own power should not be diminished in the reshuffle. Inevitably, he was less successful in the second of these objectives than the first. Arrese was in the strong position of having been invited to make his own terms for his own appointment. Serrano, in the relatively weak one of having had two of his protégés dismissed under his nose and without a by-your-leave.

He and Arrese immediately clashed over the division of power and responsibilities between their two posts – Serrano's as chief of the Political Junta and Arrese's as Secretary-General. To the general surprise of those, including Hoare, who had supposed Serrano Súñer's power to be inviolable, Franco sided with Arrese. The 1941 crisis, in fact, marked the beginning of the *cuñadísimo*'s decline. By virtue of his office, foreign affairs claimed more and more of his time and he was inevitably less well placed to keep the Falange within his grip than when he had been Minister of the Interior.

Before his eyes, but beyond his power to stop it, the State was evolving in a direction neither he nor the *camisas viejas* had foreseen. 'We were idealists,' he told me years after these events, 'and thought we could change society. But we were wrong.' His hopes of giving the new Spain an unshakable legal foundation, with the enlarged party the ultimate power in it, stronger than Franco, stronger than the Cabinet, whose functions it would duplicate behind the scenes –

these hopes were collapsing. He could see, for no one has questioned his percipience, that Franco had used him to defuse the original Falange by diluting its revolutionary fervour. And he could perceive that his usefulness might be running to an end.

One thing only he had in common with Arrese: both men were fervent Catholics who, in a real clash between fascist and Christian principles, would opt for religion. Serrano's theoretical turn of mind impelled him to attempt a synthesis between religion and the corporate State. Arrese was a practical man who would not try to bend facts to fit theories.

Serrano was ambitious and self-seeking, to such an extent that Franco came to feel that his brother-in-law's ambitions took precedence over loyalty to the Chief of State. Arrese's ambitions were limited. As a *camisa vieja* who had fallen under the late José Antonio's spell, he would have liked to sweep capitalism from the face of Spain and turn the party into the instrument of the national-syndical will. But this was so clearly not what Franco wanted that he did not insist. Loyalty to the Caudillo came first, and the Caudillo wanted unity, calm and Catholic authority. Accepting the Generalissimo's Messianic role, he had neither taste nor talent for intrigue, and worked to give Franco the tamed party he wanted. In this, he was highly successful. A good deal of the credit for the gradual tranquillizing of Spanish public life during the Second World War must go to this able administrator.[15]

November 1941 brought a purge of the anti-Franquist hotheads within the party (none of whom lost life or liberty) and, on 28 November, the abolition by decree of the party's twelve National Services created in 1938. With the decree went Serrano's last hope of setting up a party structure parallel to the State's and in control of it. Franco himself had decided to discard the whole idea. Instead, he divorced the party from the administration, replacing the twelve Services with four Vice-Secretariats responsible for party organization, syndical and veteran affairs, propaganda and other activities.

It was against this background that the Begoña incident at Bilbao took place. The young ruffian Domínguez who threw the bomb while General Varela was in the Church of the Virgen de Begoña could hardly have guessed what he was starting. The leading anti-Falangists in the Cabinet, General Varela himself and Colonel Galarza, the

Minister of the Interior, sent joint messages to the Army Captains-General all over Spain, seeking support against Falange insolence.

   This independent initiative ill-accorded with the Caudillo's sense of discipline, and he summarily dismissed both men. For good measure, he dismissed Serrano Súñer as well, rather unfairly since Serrano had had nothing to do with the Bilbao incident and had supported Franco in opposing Arrese's plea for clemency to Domínguez, who had been sentenced to death.[16] From the Caudillo's point of view, however, the Bilbao crisis provided a useful pretext to dispense with his brother-in-law. He had lost confidence in Serrano in party terms, but Serrano's dismissal had nothing to do with the party or with Bilbao. The plain fact is that his overtly pro-Axis attitude had become an embarrassment to the Caudillo at a time when the fortunes of war were beginning to turn against Hitler and Mussolini. Once again, Franco had decided to vary the mixture according to the outside temperature. Varela was pro-British and he had gone; then Serrano, who was anti-British, would have to go as well. But Serrano's supporters would have to be reassured; so he brought in a former protégé of the *cuñadísimo*, Blas Pérez González, as Minister of the Interior. This left room for an Anglophile; so old General Jordana was brought back as Foreign Minister.

   Broadly speaking, Franco had no more trouble from the Falange, as such. Even Queipo de Llano, back from Rome, rallied to his chief. Side by side, the two companions in arms knelt, as they had in 1936, at the foot of the Virgin of Macarena in the Alcazar at Seville.[17] It was now May 1943, and Franco could reflect that in a world at war, he had at least achieved internal peace.

   He had not, however, counted with the monarchists. These did not, of course, form a cohesive group, for the Carlists had no desire for a restoration of Alfonso XIII's branch of the Bourbon dynasty; and even the Carlists were divided among themselves between Traditionalists and Legitimists, according to the identity of the Pretender they favoured. To the bulk of Spaniards calling themselves monarchists, however, if the Monarchy were restored, the king could only be Don Juan, Count of Barcelona. This, at least, was their position from that day in February 1941 when the dying King Alfonso had renounced his rights to the throne in favour of Don Juan.

   In 1939, on the morrow of the Civil War, the situation was less clear-cut. Alfonso was still alive and he had few supporters, for even staunch monarchists conceded that he had discredited himself by the scuttle of 1931. Franco's supporters were deeply divided. The old Falangists were as opposed to a restoration as they were to the return of a liberal democracy. Some of the generals were Monarchists, but not all. Kindelán, the Air Force commander, wanted a king; and so did Vigón, who had been Alfonso's aide-de-camp. But Queipo de Llano was said to be against a restoration, and so was the Falangist General Yagüe.[18]

Franco himself was well aware of the many precedents in Spanish history, not least the dictatorship of Primo de Rivera, for the co-existence of a king and a military strongman. He had loyally served both the Monarchy and the Republic, and his taste for tradition and authority inclined him towards a restoration. He was, however, in no hurry. To bring back a discredited monarch, who had fled without abdicating, seemed to him highly undesirable. Above all, he was interested in unity within his Movement. It was clear that a hurried restoration would divide his followers even more than a 'suspended' one. He chose, therefore, to let it be known that he favoured the Monarchy, but without actually allowing a king to sit on the Spanish throne.

For Don Juan, the situation was embarrassing and frustrating. He had pleaded with Franco to be allowed to serve with the Nationalist forces during the Civil War, but this offer had been spurned.[19] His father's dying wish that he should succeed him revived his hopes. Franco's government had proclaimed 28 February, the day of Alfonso's death, as a national day of mourning. And the Count of Barcelona, addressing Spanish grandees who had gone to Rome for the funeral, quoted a letter he had written to his late father, referring to the Civil War as 'this great national crusade'.[20] But there was no response from the Pardo.

As the months went on, and Don Juan's frustration deepened, he sought to spur Franco in the right direction by declarations to the press. On 11 November 1942, for instance, he declared in the *Journal de Genève* that though he was not the head of a conspiracy, he was the 'legitimate depository of the secular political inheritance of the Spanish Monarchy' which he was sure would be restored 'as soon as the interests of Spain demand it'.[21] Still, no invitation came from the Pardo.

In the eyes of the monarchists, Franco's ambiguous attitude was simply not good enough. Nor was it, in those of Sir Samuel Hoare, who saw himself as a kingmaker who might rid Spain of Franco and build a bridge of Anglo-Spanish friendship under a monarch of his choosing. Sir Samuel's choice was, of course, Don Juan, whose British education and service in the Royal Navy made him 'one of my boys'.[22] In fact, wrote Carlton Hayes, his British colleague 'wanted, for all countries of western Europe, governments which would collaborate closely with Great Britain as in a British "sphere of influence", and to this end he wanted a monarchical restoration in Spain and a régime in France of only such Frenchmen as were habitually and vigorously pro-British'.[23]

In the aristocratic and monarchical circles in which Sir Samuel naturally moved, there was no lack of men ready to listen to him, though it would be foolish to suppose that these men decided to act merely because a Spanish monarchy would be more acceptable to His Majesty's Ambassador than a military-Falangist régime. Many of these prominent monarchists were members of the rubber-stamp Cortes or Parliament created by Franco on 17 March 1943. On inauguration day, they had heard the Caudillo refer to the Bourbon dynasty as having ceased to exist. In the same speech, he had reiterated his repudiation of liberalism, but in ambiguous terms that suggested there might, after all, be some good in it.[24] Two or three weeks earlier, on 1 March, the Chief of State had invited the entire diplomatic corps to a solemn requiem mass at the Escorial, for 'all the Kings of Spain', and Madrileño cynics were quick to observe that it sounded like a requiem for the Monarchy itself.

The gulf between the Caudillo and the monarchists seemed, in fact, to be deepening. On 9 April, in a dispatch from London, the duke of Alba had dropped a heavy hint, which the Caudillo had not deigned to notice. The duke had reported that he had had a talk with King George VI at a palace reception. The king had asked about the prospects for a restoration of the Monarchy in Spain, and, said the duke, 'I replied that many Spaniards were enthusiastically in favour and that the Caudillo had always said this would be the pinnacle of his work.' The king had commented that he understood that this restoration would have to await an opportune moment.[25]

Within days of his talk with the king, the duke of Alba gave a ball in Seville for his daughter's *début*, which the flower of the Monarchists attended. Hayes records, however, that Franco and the Falangists stayed away – or were not invited.[26] 'Two weeks later,' he added, 'as a kind of counter-demonstration, the Caudillo made a State tour through Andalusia attended by cheering crowds whom the Falange mobilized along the way.'

In July, the duke of Alba and twenty-six other prominent Monarchists signed a memorial addressed to the Chief of State and respectfully requesting Spain's immediate return to 'the traditional Catholic monarchy' as the only way to bring back political stability and heal the wounds of bitterness between Spaniards.[27]

This was an open challenge to Franco's authority and known reluctance to restore the monarchy in the immediate future, and his response to it was characteristic. Five of the signatories were Falangists, and the Caudillo decided to make an example of them. A few days after the memorial had reached him, Arrese announced the dismissal of the five from all official posts. They included Professor Valdecasas, the former companion of José Antonio who was the first head of the Institute of Political Studies, and Gamero del Castillo, the former Vice Secretary-General of the FET. As for the non-Falange signatories, he simply left them alone. Franco didn't particularly mind Monarchists expressing Monarchist sentiments; but he didn't want Falangists to join them, for he saw the Falange, among other things, as a safeguard against an early restoration.

The Caudillo did not, as might be guessed, bother to reply to the memorialists. Instead, on 17 July, in a speech before the National Council of Falange, he circuitously suggested that one day Spain might again have the régime she possessed 'in the days of her glory'.[28] This was evidently the extent of the change the Monarchists were going to get out of Franco, and they were unwilling to admit that it was enough. On 15 October, a group of generals petitioned Franco in favour of a prompt restoration;[29] and two or three weeks later, the text was disclosed in a letter from Gil Robles, the Christian Democrat leader who had once been Franco's departmental chief and was now in exile in Portugal. Gil Robles had written to General Asensio, the War Minister, calling on Franco to stand down in favour of a restored monarch.

Franco ignored these importunities, but in March 1944, he exiled four out of a hundred university professors who had signed a petition for the restoration of the monarchy, to forced residence in the provinces.

To Don Juan in his exile, Franco's unwillingness to commit himself to a definite date for the restoration and his castigation of selected monarchists seemed to show that so long as he was Caudillo by the Grace of God, Don Juan's chances of claiming his father's vacant throne were non-existent. But as the world war drew to its close, the general detestation in which Franco's régime appeared to be held on the winning side seemed to offer him hope. The Great Powers wanted Franco out of the way, and so did he. In March 1945, he sought, in a Manifesto issued in Lausanne, to harness his cause to the mood of the victorious Allies. There was no more need, he thought, to pay tribute to Franco's 'glorious crusade'. The time for denunciation had come. 'The régime established by General Franco,' he proclaimed, 'which was modelled on the totalitarian systems of the Axis Powers and which is entirely contrary to the character and tradition of our people, is quite incompatible with the conditions prevailing in the world as a result of the present war.' He now raised his voice and solemnly required of General Franco 'that he should recognize the failure of his conception of a totalitarian State, surrender his power and allow the restoration of Spain's traditional régime, which is the only one capable of guaranteeing religion, order and liberty'.[30]

Almost immediately, the duke of Alba resigned as Spain's Ambassador in London, on the ground that he could do nothing to improve relations between Britain and Spain so long as Franco's régime lasted.

To say that Franco took no notice at all of all this Monarchist indignation would be an exaggeration. In June 1945, he announced that a Council of State would soon be established and charged with deciding the question of the monarchy 'when necessity arises'.[31] And this, for the time being, was where the constitutional issue stood. Franco was not against the monarchy; but he didn't actually want a king.

PART VI

'Spanish Peace'

✸

1 *Franco Consolidates*

General Franco set out to silence his critics by giving the Spaniards a bill of rights, by demonstrating that he ruled with popular support and by formally declaring Spain to be a monarchy, while shelving indefinitely the issue of who was to sit on the throne. Since he has never been in a hurry, these three distinct processes were spread over two years, from mid-1945 to mid-1947.

Needless to say, they did not, in fact, silence the critics or enemies of his régime. But they helped to reduce the force of their hostile arguments. At the beginning of the two-year period, the régime was threatened from without and resented within. By the end of it, the external threat had receded, and the worst internal resentments had been stilled and transmuted into resigned acceptance. Franco was beginning to look like an institution, to be lived with if not loved.

In all three of the initiatives, Franco acted within those limits of what he considered necessary and possible. In different circumstances, he would have acted differently. Though pragmatic to the edge of cynicism he remained true both to his principles and to his past experience. The circumstances that prevailed after the Second World War could not have been foreseen in 1936, when he assumed supreme political power, or in 1935, when he created the ruling FET. Had the Europe of 1945 been a continent of defeated democracies and exulting fascist dictatorships, Franco would have strengthened the 'fascist' trimmings of his New State. Since the democracies had won, anything that reminded the world of his 'original sin' had to be attenuated or put out of sight. But it is doubtful whether the reality of power in Spain would have been any different if the Nazis had won the war. There would have been more 'Nuremburg-style' rallies, and economic concessions to Germany would have had to be made; but political, and even ideological, concessions would have been kept to a minimum. The Falange might have been given a more visible part in policy-making, but Franco would have stuck to his diluted mass party and kept all power within his own hands.

As it was, he pushed the Falange further into the background and abolished the Roman salute. And he sprinkled his 'bill of rights' – the Charter of the Spaniards (*Fuero de los Españoles*) – with democratic-sounding phrases. But the reality of power remained unchanged, as did the substance of the 'rights' and 'duties' he was conceding to, or imposing on, the Spanish people. The Caudillo's adaptation to circumstances was thus superficial and illusory: there was nothing in his Charter of the Spaniards that was incompatible with the Manifesto of Las Palmas.

The document itself – the Charter of the Spaniards – was dated 16 July 1945, and published the following day in the *Boletín Oficial del Estado*. Proclaiming 'respect for the dignity, integrity and liberty of the human person', it added prudently that Spaniards owed 'loyalty to the Chief of State'. Spaniards were declared equal before the law 'without class preference'; they were promised freedom from arbitrary arrest and a guarantee that within 72 hours, anybody arrested would be 'set free or turned over to the judicial authorities'. On the social side, the rights to education and work were guaranteed, as were those of 'security in distress' and inviolability of property. The Catholic Church's rights were specifically and exclusively stated: nobody was to be 'molested because of his religious beliefs or the *private* exercise of his creed' (my italics); but the only 'external ceremonies' permitted were those of the Catholic religion.

Other rights were defined, but in some cases with modifying or even nullifying phrases, which I italicize in the following examples:

ARTICLE 12   All Spaniards may freely express their ideas, *so long as these do not prejudice the fundamental principles of the State.*
ARTICLE 16   Spaniards may assemble and associate freely *for lawful purposes and in accordance with the law.*

There were, however, two catches in the *Fuero de los Españoles*, in successive articles in Part II, 'on the exercise and guarantees of the rights'. Article 34 stated that the Cortes would 'vote the necessary laws for the exercise of the rights recognized by this Charter'; and Article 35 gave the government the right 'temporarily' to suspend certain articles – all concerned with the freedom of the individual. The snag about Article 35 needs no elaboration. The snag about Article 34 became apparent as the years accumulated and remarkably few of the laws that might have breathed life into the still-born clauses of the Charter were ever passed. Nevertheless, the *Fuero* stands as one of the Organic Laws of the Spanish State.

Having defined, as he saw fit, his people's rights and duties, Franco decided to give his government a subtly different look. To be sure, the new mixture presented on 25 July 1945 was much the same as the old, but the dosages of Monarchism and Catholicism were marginally strengthened; and the FET was noticeably reduced in importance. The anti-Monarchist Arrese was removed as Minister and Secretary-General of the Movement, and the post itself was significantly left vacant. The War Minister, the Falange General Asensio, was replaced by the 'non-denominational' General Dávila. The party continued to be represented in the government, but not in positions of maximum power. Girón remained as Labour Minister, and Fernández Cuesta, one of the founders of the Falange, became Minister of Justice. The monarchists, strengthened negatively by Arrese's removal, were strengthened positively by the appointment as Air Minister, of Eduardo González Gallarza, who had seen Alfonso XIII off at Cartagena when his exile began.

The most significant change, however, was in the conduct of foreign affairs. Lequerica was dismissed as Foreign Minister, and in his stead Franco appointed Alberto Martín Artajo, a lawyer and former leader writer on the Christian Democratic paper *El Debate*, who had many years of militant activity in Catholic Action behind him. In Martín Artajo, Franco now had a Foreign Minister who was singularly free of the taint of 'fascism' or even of Lequerica's 'sin' of having been Franco's representative at Vichy. His Christian Democratic past was calculated to make him *persona grata* among the groups of similar persuasion that were emerging in post-war Western Europe. And within a few years, he was to show – as Franco had hoped he would – that he was an acceptable negotiating partner in the United States.

A short month after Franco had reshuffled his government, the pathetic but persistently hopeful remains of the Republican Cortes met in Mexico City. It was 17 August 1945, and the Republican government-in-exile, like Franco's, was reshuffling itself. Martínez Barrio was elected President of the defunct Republic; Negrín resigned and José Giral – the man who, as Minister of the Navy, had dismissed the rebellious naval officers in July 1936 – replaced him as 'Prime Minister'. Did these men really think that the defeat of the Axis would be followed, as day follows night, by the eviction of 'the only surviving fascist dictator'?

Some of them apparently did. But the realistic ones among them, especially Indalecio Prieto, thought the only promising way of getting rid of Franco would be through a reconciliation of Republicans and Monarchists, leading to a referendum in which the Spanish people would be asked to choose their own constitutional future. The biggest obstacle Prieto could see – apart from the inconvenient presence of General Franco in supreme power – was the attitude of the Spanish Pretender, Don Juan, who, if his pretension was serious, could hardly relish the idea of risking the monarchic principle in a popular vote. He himself, Prieto, was too compromised by his Popular Front past to qualify as a mediator between the exiled Republic and the exiled Monarchy. Better qualified would be Gil Robles, who, though he had risen to political prominence under the Republic, was known for his sound Catholic connections and his support for a restoration. Prieto therefore envisaged a programme in three parts: an understanding between Gil Robles and Don Juan, followed by an agreement between the Monarchists and the Popular Front to set up a common opposition party; and finally, a constitutional referendum. To this end, Prieto and Gil Robles started 'secret' negotiations in Paris and London.[1]

Such negotiations were bound, by their nature, to be delicate and therefore lengthy. Franco got wind of Prieto's plan and decided to pre-empt it by opting for a Monarchy (without, for the time being, a king), thus facing Don Juan, Prieto and Gil Robles with an accomplished fact. On 31 March 1947, he announced that Spain was shortly to be declared a Monarchy, but that there would be no king while the present Chief of State was alive.

For Don Juan, this was a bitter pill to swallow. His 'Manifesto of Lausanne', two years earlier, having fallen flat, he had gone to live in Estoril, to be near at hand for the day of his triumphal return to

Spain. When he began his Portuguese exile, his followers – as mistakenly optimistic as the Republicans – thought this day could hardly be long delayed. And now, in March 1947, Captain Carrero Blanco of the Spanish Navy (later to become something of an *éminence grise* to Franco) came to see him in Estoril to show him a copy of the draft Law of Succession. Bitterly angry, the Pretender saw that he had been outmanœuvred. Perhaps, however, the power of international opinion could still bring Franco down. In that hope, Don Juan issued another scathing denunciation of Franco's régime and of his usurpation of royal rights. Franco's response was to sequester the royal properties in Spain, cut the State's allowance to the widowed Queen Mother in Switzerland, and unleash a campaign of insults against Don Juan in the controlled press.

On 7 June 1947, Franco's Law of Succession was published. Its first article, as he had foreshadowed, declared Spain to be a kingdom; but the second article was chillingly unmonarchical:

> The office of Chief of State is held by the Caudillo of Spain and of the Crusade, Generalissimo of the Spanish Armies, Don Francisco Franco Bahamonde.

So it had been in the beginning – in 1936 – so it was now and so it was to be, if not forever and ever, then for as long as it pleased the Caudillo to remain in power. Should, however, the office of Chief of State fall vacant, its powers were to be exercised by a Regency Council consisting of the President of the Cortes, the highest prelate of the Church and the top Army officer. Should the Caudillo tire of office, he could, 'at any moment', pick a king or regent to succeed him. If ever a king or regent were picked, he would have to be Spanish, male, at least thirty, and a Catholic. More significantly, he would have to swear to respect the Fundamental Laws and the Principles of the National Movement. Moreover, let no Pretender think that his claims were necessarily inviolable, for the Chief of State could propose 'the exclusion from succession of those persons of royal blood who lack the necessary capacity to govern or, because of their noted indifference to the basic principles of the State or because of their actions, have forfeited their rights to the succession as established by this law'.

Undeterred by this pre-emptive reminder of the realities of power in Spain, Indalecio Prieto and Gil Robles went ahead with their agreement, with the blessing of Ernest Bevin, Britain's Labour Foreign Secretary, who in October 1947 received the two men with great cordiality. A previously drafted statement was issued, to meet the anti-Franco requirements of the three-Power declaration of 4 March 1946 (see Part V, Chapter 10) and the United Nations resolution of 12 December of that year. Spain, it said, was to have a provisional government; once a referendum had established its definitive form, Spain would be admitted to the Brussels Treaty.[2]

Even without help from his enemies, Franco would probably have stayed in power; but his enemies did, in fact, help him. For the 'agreement' between the Spanish Socialists and Monarchists was not, it turned out, an agreement. From his exile in Estoril, the Count of Barcelona, who clearly feared the taint of association with the 'Reds' of the Popular Front, declared that Gil Robles did not act with his authority. And Gil Robles, on returning to his own Portuguese exile, explained that he was against a government of 'concentration' and could never agree to the 4 March formula.[3]

Once again, Franco knew that he had only to sit tight, leaving his enemies, both Spanish and foreign, to fall out among themselves. In any case, he was already two moves ahead. The Law of Succession was one; the other, which followed almost immediately, on 6 July, was a referendum on the same Law. Franco went on the air to appeal for a solid vote in favour, using an argument well-calculated to appeal both to the good sense and to the war-weariness of the Spanish voters. 'If our country's present is in my hands,' he observed, 'I cannot serve her beyond death; for this reason, her future is in your hands.' The reasoning was incontrovertible, at least for those who were not particularly interested in the present or who feared a return to the past. On the day, 14,145,163 Spaniards voted in favour of the Law – that is for Franco's rule at Franco's pleasure – out of 17,178,812 voters. The Noes totalled 722,565, and the blank returns, 335,592. Perhaps, indeed, the dictatorial completeness of this triumph showed that Franco need not have bothered to appeal to the voters. But either way – whether the figures were true or faked – it was clear that his hold on power was complete. If anything, the huffing and puffing of his enemies had strengthened the foundations of his house, leaving them (the enemies) breathless and unhappy.

2 Franco almost Clubbable – I

Even in the darkest hours of isolation, Franco's Spain had never been entirely without friends. In the Arab world and in Latin America, there were governments that were neutral, or well-disposed towards him, or positively helpful. Among the latter was General Juan Domingo Perón's government in Argentina. Perón had, or thought he had, a number of things in common with Franco. Both were Army men who had achieved supreme political power. And both had a 'social' policy: for though there was little real similarity between Perón's irresponsible populism and Franco's concept of order, *Peronismo* obviously owed some of its inspiration to the fascism of the original Falange.

In the UN's anti-Franco debates in the autumn of 1945, the Argentine delegate, Dr Arce, had emerged as the Caudillo's champion against his parliamentary and Communist detractors. In October of that year, Perón's government granted the Spanish government a credit of 350 million Argentine pesos, enough to import sufficient wheat to avert near-famine. Perón's reward was the overwhelming reception that awaited the Argentine dictator's wife, Eva Perón when she visited Spain the following year. Later came further Argentine credits, at only 2¾ per cent interest, which enabled Franco to import 1,500,000 tons of wheat, 500,000 tons of maize and 8,000 tons of oil. It is hardly an exaggeration to say that Perón's help ensured the survival of Franco's régime at a critical time. Had it not come, hunger might well have led to the revolutionary situation which the Communists and other Franco-haters were hoping for.

As it happened, however, the second line of Argentine credits was relatively short-lived and was withdrawn after acrimonious disputes marked by personal insults from Eva Perón to José María de Areílza, the Spanish Ambassador in Buenos Aires. But this anti-climactic change was not held against Perón himself when he was overthrown in 1955, and he was granted political asylum in Spain.

In 1948, however, it was still chilly in the great world outside Spain. When the American Secretary of State, General George C.

Marshall, launched his famous plan of economic assistance to war-ravaged Europe – which became the European Recovery Programme in April 1948 – Spain was excluded from it, Franco's 'original sin', thus being visited on the Spanish people. The Soviet Union and her European satellites, however, had opted out of the Marshall Plan, and Franco drew comfort from this fact. For here was an important sign, among others, that the unnatural war-time alliance between the parliamentary democracies and Stalin's anti-parliamentary régime had ceased to exist. The cold war, which Winston Churchill had diagnosed in its infancy in his Fulton speech two years before, was now a hard reality which, as Franco reasoned, would sooner or later make the Americans, if not their European allies, discern the strategic value of a solidly anti-Communist Spain.

Strategic reality, however, was not of itself enough to achieve the thawing of relations with the United States which Franco knew was his best way of ending Spain's isolation. Skilled diplomacy was also needed. And Franco had a skilled diplomatist in reserve, in José Felix de Lequerica. With his Basque dynamism, his command of English, and his experience as a lawyer and businessman to supplement his official career as Ambassador to Vichy France and as Foreign Minister, Lequerica seemed just the man. It was not for nothing that Franco had dismissed him in 1945; for now, under Franco's orders and with Martín Artajo's guidance from the Foreign Ministry, Lequerica was available.

Franco's original plan had been to send Lequerica to Washington as Ambassador. But it was frustrated when President Truman's Administration refused him *agrément* because of his war-time association with Vichy and the Nazis.[1] Unabashed, the Caudillo forced Lequerica on Truman anyway, by sending him to Washington as Inspector of Embassies and Legations. Once he was there, he stayed there. Well endowed with charm and fluency, and well supplied with convertible pesetas, he set out to woo the Americans most likely to become Franco's friends. On 27 December 1950, his work and Franco's patience brought him the best of rewards, for he was at last accepted as Spain's Ambassador to the United States.

By then, the ever grimmer realities of the cold war had brought the right Americans out of their shell of reserve; and as they emerged, Lequerica was there to wine and dine them. In July 1948, only two months after Lequerica's arrival in Washington, the Russians began their blockade of Berlin; the rape of Czechoslovakia also came that year. In October 1949, Mao Tse-tung and his Communist Party took over in China, and in June 1950, the communist army of North Korea invaded the south. Of these events, the Korean War was the decisive one in Washington's change of heart towards Franco. But long before that, the logic of events was modifying the climate of opinion in America. As early as 30 March 1948, for instance, the House of Representatives had voted by 149 to 52 in favour of extending the Marshall Plan to Spain – a measure which President Truman vetoed, though he let it be known that he would not object to private banking credits to that country.[2]

Shortly after that, the first trickle of what was to be a long stream of prominent Americans began to visit Madrid to see for themselves whether Spain was indeed the 'fascist' country it was said to be. There were the Senators: Tom Connally of Texas, Pat MacCarran of Nevada, Owen Brewster of Maine and Dennis Chavez of New Mexico. There was Vice-President Albert William Barkley, there were journalists and professors, and Admirals Sherman and Connolly. Admiral Forrest Sherman, especially, was to exert a decisive influence in Hispano-American relations. Benjamin Welles has recalled that the Admiral's son-in-law, Lieutenant-Commander John Fitzpatrick, had been stationed in Madrid as Assistant Naval Attaché from 1947, and that Mrs Sherman, on her visits to Spain, was charmed by Spanish courtesy and kindness.[3] Admiral Sherman himself, as Commander-in-Chief of the US Sixth Fleet, stationed in the Mediterranean, later made a number of official friendships in Spain and invited the Spaniards – among others – to send units to the Sixth Fleet for training courses. His Spanish and Mediterranean experience was to prove important when, in 1949, he was appointed Chief of Naval Operations in Washington.

For Sherman and other visitors, the ritual audience at the Pardo Palace was the climax to their self-educative exercise. The smiling Caudillo, already milder and more benevolent than the stern soldier of the Civil War and after, gave them all his standard lecture on Communism, pointing out that his own anti-Communism was already of twenty years' standing and had not been tempered by war-time association with Russia. Without him, he could convincingly argue, Communism would have taken over in Spain and the Russians would have gained access to the Mediterranean. For good measure, he

Q

could add that his neutrality had kept the Germans from Gibraltar and allowed the Allied build-up that preceded the successful North African landings of 1943.

As if to echo him, came the influential voice of Winston Churchill, who, in a speech in the House of Commons on 10 December 1948, when he was still Leader of the Opposition, attacked the concept that Spaniards should be treated as outcasts.

Soon, a majority of sovereign governments were thinking the way Churchill was. On 5 November 1950, the UN General Assembly rescinded its 1946 resolution calling for the withdrawal of Heads of Mission from Madrid (forthrightly, the Americans voted in favour of rescinding; evasively, the British and French abstained). Once again, Franco's patience and obduracy had paid off. And he celebrated his triumph on 1 March 1951, when he stood in the Throne room of the Royal Palace in Madrid, beside the vacant throne reserved for Spain's hypothetical king, to receive President Truman's Ambassador, Stanton Griffis. It was a moment to remember, for it meant that Spain's isolation was over, and one by one new ambassadors came to Madrid to fill the chairs left vacant by their departed predecessors.

Did it yet mean, however, that Franco had become 'clubbable'? Apparently not. At a time when Soviet military power threatened western Europe, strategic logic suggested that Spain should have been invited to join the North Atlantic Treaty Alliance. But Nato's logic was selective and discriminatory. The democratic preamble of the Treaty had been stretched to accommodate Portugal, which was under a dictatorship no less repressive than Franco's, and which had sent volunteers to fight for Franco during the Spanish Civil War. But Salazar, though a dictator, was free of the taint of association with Hitler. Franco, though no more a dictator than Salazar, was not and remained distinctly unclubbable in Nato circles.

To suppose that Franco was indifferent to this blackballing would be quite wrong. Nothing would have made him happier than a cordial readiness on the part of the democracies to forget the past and start afresh. But he had never had any illusions about the difficulties his régime would face if it survived a Nazi defeat. Outwardly, his attitude was of calm acceptance of undeniable facts, one of which was that he was not wanted in the Nato club. When an American correspondent raised the subject of Spain's entry into Nato, Franco replied: 'A direct understanding with the United

States would be much less complicated, much better and more satisfactory.'[4]

By this time, many Americans had become converted to Admiral Sherman's views and were eager, indeed impatient, for an understanding with Franco. One of the hardest to convince was the most important of all, President Truman himself, who had no more liking for dictators than for kings. But in the end, even Truman was persuaded, and gave in to Sherman with the words: 'I don't like Franco and I never will, but I won't let my personal feelings override the convictions of you military men.'[5]

It was now July 1951. On the sixteenth, Franco received Sherman and Griffis in the Pardo and an agreement, in principle, on the establishment of US bases in Spain, was rapidly reached. At this point, however, fate intervened, for Sherman dropped dead of a heart attack two days later. The disappearance of Franco's most powerful American advocate inevitably delayed the conclusion of a formal agreement. Moreover, when serious negotiations began, the Americans soon found, as other impatient people had found before them, that Franco was in no particular hurry. He wanted an agreement, certainly, but not at a price that might undermine Spain's sovereignty. The Americans had wanted to rent bases: this, said Franco, was just what he meant by undermining Spain's sovereignty. He did not want any more Gibraltars; one was quite enough.

And so the negotiations dragged on, until General Eisenhower's victory in the 1952 Presidential elections brought to power a man who did not need to be told how vital Spanish bases were to American and western defence. In April 1953, a new American Ambassador, James Dunn, arrived in Madrid with orders to speed things up. But final agreement was not reached until the summer. By that time Franco was in Corunna for his holidays. He summoned his Ministers there and handed them a text that showed – yet again – the benefits to be derived from patience and firmness. The bases were to remain under Spanish sovereignty and the Spanish flag was to fly over them. Outside the base areas, American personnel were to change into civilian clothes. The bases, however, were to be described as 'joint'. There would be three air bases: at Torrejon, Saragossa and Moron de la Frontera; an air supply depot near Seville; a naval base at Rota; seven radar installations; and a vast complex of auxiliary arrangements, including a 485-mile fuel pipeline connecting

Rota with Saragossa, *via* Moron and Torrejon. In one respect only had Franco failed to get his way: economic aid – disguised under the usual euphemism of 'defence support' – was fixed at $85 million, far less than he had hoped for. It was, however, a start, and with it came $191 million for improving the Spanish Army's armament and equipment, together with the stimulating prospect of orders to be placed in Spain for thirty per cent of the materials needed for the construction of the bases, and of employment for thousands of Spanish workers.

On 26 September, the interminable process ended happily when the Spanish Foreign Minister, Martín Artajo, and the American Ambassador, James Dunn, signed the agreements in Madrid's Palacio de Santa Cruz. Franco was still not quite clubbable; but he had acquired a powerful friend, and an ally in all but name.

3 *Franco's Masterly Inertia*

Masterly inertia had long established itself as Franco's way of ruling, though some called it 'immobilism'. At the outset of the Second World War, he himself had defined it as *hábil prudencia*, and essentially, these terms stand for the same combination of cleverness, patience, caution and timing. As the impatient Axis generals discovered during the Civil War, Franco would always prefer to delay action than to act unsuccessfully. It was when he had violated his own rules – as in his repeated attempts to storm Madrid – that failure stared him in the face. But in the end, and by a circuitous route, Madrid was his.

It was the same thereafter. He had outsat Hitler, and outstared the hostile post-war world. He had resisted the impatient pleas of advisers who wanted him to agree immediately to the American terms for military bases in Spain, for the sake of rapid economic benefits. And in the end, *his* terms had been accepted, though it had taken him two years and more to get his own way.

At home, masterly inertia implied patience – the patience to wait for a situation to mature to the point where decision became viable. Sometimes, this meant waiting until time had eroded opposition, or tempted an opponent to play his hand prematurely. By the time the world war had ended, Franco's enemies had ceased to be a danger: they were in exile, or had died, or been liquidated. But if 'anti-Spain' was no longer a problem, the same was not true of the groups and individuals who had fought in the 'Crusade' and who constituted the National Movement in its broadest sense.* For each of Franco's supporters is, in some senses, his enemy. The Carlists support him for restoring the Church to its traditional position, but resent him for totally ignoring their dynastic claims. The Alfonsists could hardly not support him when he declared Spain to be a monarchy, but resent his presence near the vacant throne. Both sets of Monarchists resent his tolerance of the anti-Monarchist Falangists. The Falange, in turn, owes him gratitude for creating the 'vertical' trade unions, and for the spoils of office; but cannot forgive him for shattering the bright young dream of José Antonio, for stunting the political potential of the *sindicatos* and allowing capitalism to flourish. Of all the supporting groups, the Army has perhaps the most to be thankful for; but the Army itself is not a political entity. There are Alfonsist officers, and Carlist officers and Falangist officers; and each set shares the resentments of civilians in the same set. Though Franco's power ultimately rests on the Army, then, he cannot take the Army's unanimous support for granted.

Fortunately for Franco, the selective enmity of each group of his supporters is outweighed at any stage by the inherent mutual hostility of all. At home, therefore, Franco's masterly inertia has consisted of knowing when to give one of the groups something to keep it quiet, while stopping short of the full satisfaction that would provoke other groups to excess. That way, the sum of reasons for satisfaction always outweighs that of reasons for hostility. Masterly inertia however, does not exclude direct action against individual recalcitrants who do not seem to know when they are well off. But the removal of an obstreporous supporter – as distinct from an 'anti-Spain' enemy – does not involve physical liquidation.

Nobody else, except perhaps Mola, could have carried out this

* A prominent 'old Falangist' told me in Madrid in 1955 to be careful not to confuse the 'party' and the 'Movement'. He was speaking as a *camisa vieja*, and indeed one should not confuse Falange with FET, the heterogeneous party created by Franco in 1937. The term 'Movement', however, is often and properly used to mean the FET; though it can also mean the Spanish Nationalists as a whole.

sustained exercise in political skill and craft. And Franco demonstrated, in September 1936, how easily, when it came to it, he could
outmanœuvre even so wily a customer as Mola. Sanjurjo's rashness,
ignorance and unwisdom would have brought about his early
downfall no less surely than Ansaldo's defective plane. José Antonio's essential idealism would have driven him either to fanatical
extremes or to despair. For all Serrano Súñer's cleverness, Franco
showed him up, in the end, as a political man-of-straw. Juan III's
likeable liberalism – had Don Juan become king – would have been
quite incapable of coping with the problems of an innately anarchic
country during and after the Second World War.

It would be wrong, however, to suppose that Franco's only
interest has been to stay in power. No doubt he enjoys the exercise
of supreme authority, which in his case, has never ruled out the
simple pleasures of hunting, fishing, painting and family life. But his
dominant emotion has always been patriotism, and power has been
his means of indulging it. In this he deeply resembles Charles de
Gaulle, though his identification with the nation is less complete
than the Frenchman's, and his patriotism therefore less narcissistic.
But it would not occur to either man to doubt the essential rightness
of what he was doing or his essential right to do it. Like Joan of Arc,
it is said, de Gaulle hears voices. Franco, for his part, acts by
Providential Dispensation.

Irony apart, Franco's long-term objective has always been to
modernize Spain's economy and improve the living standards of its
people. Though he had come to power in very different circumstances
from those that made a dictator of Miguel Primo de Rivera, a lesson
of Franco's youth was that much can be accomplished materially,
even in Spain, when order and stability are assured. The Republic
taught him the converse lesson – or rather, drove the first one home:
that material progress is impossible where disorder reigns. To put it
another way, the connection between order and economic growth
had not escaped him. It seemed to him self-evident that politics
had to be neutralized if Spain was ever to emerge from her centuries
of poverty and stagnation. Since only he was capable of neutralizing
politics, it followed that he had to remain in power if Spain was to
make economic progress. Masterly inertia was thus a condition of
material improvement.

Don Juan had been outmanœuvred and frustrated. To the general surprise, and to the special dismay of his followers, the Pretender shortly afterwards spent several hours in Franco's company. The chosen meeting place was discreet, uncontroversial and congenial to both men: the high seas. On 25 August 1948, Franco's yacht *Azor* sailed out from San Sebastian. At a prearranged spot, she stopped and was joined by Don Juan's yacht, *Saltillo*. The Pretender then boarded *Azor*, and the discussions began.

Don Juan knew the subject to be discussed was the education of his son Don Juan Carlos, but if he thought he might take advantage of the occasion to further his own claims to ascend the throne in the near future, he was soon disillusioned. It was agreed that the boy should continue his education in Spain, and indeed the royal father could hardly refuse so patriotic a request on Franco's part. Franco refused, however, to be drawn on the issue of the restoration. It was painfully clear to the Pretender that the political cards were heavily stacked against him, though he drew consolation from what seemed to be a demonstration that the Caudillo *needed* the monarchy. What may have escaped him was the fact that he had given Franco an easy way of keeping hope alive in the breasts of the Monarchists in the Army and in industry, commerce and banking, while failing to obtain even the faintest of guarantees in return.

Franco, indeed, had 'solved' the constitutional issue in his own fashion by his Law of Succession. Having reduced Don Juan to impotence, Franco nevertheless felt the need to meet him from time to time. The second meeting took place in December 1954, at the country home of the Count de Ruiseñada, a prominent Monarchist who had fought at Franco's side in the Civil War. Once again, the education of Don Juan Carlos was discussed, and it was agreed that he should be entered for the Military Academy at Saragossa. This time, however, the Pretender let fly at Franco, with an explosion of complaints against the repressive aspects of the régime, and called on him to institute press freedom, free the courts from government control, and allow free trade unions and political parties. Franco is said to have merely commented: 'I do not find the burden of rule heavy. Spain is easy to govern.'[1]

Between the second and third meetings, Franco inflicted heavy fines on a group of Monarchists calling itself *Unión Española*, which had met and denounced the régimes at a Madrid banquet on

29 January 1959. The participants included the outspoken lawyer, Joaquín Satrústegui, Gil Robles and Professor Tierno Galván. Well to the left of the Carlists, and even of Don Juan, *Unión Española* favours political parties and co-operation with such Socialists as may be won over from nostalgic attachment to the Republic. The Madrid banquet appears to have angered Don Juan as a needless provocation of Franco.[2]

Partly as a reaction against the activities of 'unofficial Monarchists', the count of Barcelona injected new life into his *Consejo Privado*, a body he had set up in 1944 to prepare for what then seemed likely to be his early ascent to the throne of his ancestors. Failure and frustration had made the *Consejo* degenerate into squabbling futility. At the beginning of 1960, the Pretender made his attempt to revitalize it; and though the limitations of a primarily consultative body are obvious, the *Consejo Privado* has managed at times to be an effective body for Monarchist propaganda.

Not unnaturally, the competitive virtues and failings of Don Juan's *Consejo Privado* and Franco's *Consejo del Reino* (a body created under the 1947 Law of Succession) were the subject of heated debate when Don Juan next met Franco, in the Ruiseñada country home in March 1960. The Caudillo is said to have 'permitted himself the ghost of a smile' when the count of Barcelona asked him whether Spain was to be saddled indefinitely with 'one bad political party' – the ruling FET.[3]

After a long day of argument, the only concrete decision was that Juan Carlos would enter Madrid University. This, however, was a victory for Franco, not the young man's father. Benjamin Welles records that Don Juan had intended to withhold permission for his son to continue his education in Spain unless Franco recognized the young man as prince of Asturias (that is, the undoubted heir to the throne), while conceding at the same time that his own claims to the throne were not prejudiced. He had drawn up a communiqué to that effect, and thought, when Franco grumblingly relieved him of the text, that the Caudillo had accepted both his conditions. It was in this belief that he had agreed to send the young Prince back to Spain. It turned out, however, that Franco was merely up to one more of his tricks. When the communiqué appeared in the Madrid press, Don Juan found to his anger that it had been altered in several material respects without his consent. The title of 'Prince of Asturias' had been deleted; a reference to 'the achievements of the National Movement' had been inserted; and Don Juan's claims to the throne had been blurred by a reference to the Law of Succession.

The prince of Asturias was nevertheless sent to Madrid University shortly after his father's third meeting; and was rewarded for his father's conformity by the gift of the Zarzuela Palace outside Madrid.[4]

As with the Monarchists, so with the Falangists. Franco had smothered José Antonio's Falange in 1937, by swamping it with other elements to create the FET. For the sake of convenience, the monster party that emerged from this gestation has sometimes been described in these pages as 'the ruling FET'. But it was not even the ruling party for very long. True, it appointed the *alcaldes* or mayors throughout Spain, subject of course to the approval of the *Jefe Nacional* – Franco – but this scarcely gave it a monopoly of political power. By 1945, the greatest privilege of the FET was a monopoly of another kind – that of patronage and graft. In the cabinet reshuffle of that year, Franco smashed any lingering illusions among the *camisas viejas* that political power was theirs by right. The bitterest pill of all for them to swallow was Franco's decision to leave the office of Minister Secretary-General of the Movement vacant, after dismissing Arrese.

One of Franco's objectives at that time was to improve his support among the Monarchists. By 1948, however, the Monarchists had become tiresomely restive and pressing. The best way of cutting them down to size again was to improve the relative position of the FET. This he did, on 5 November 1948, by the simple expedient of re-appointing the Minister of Justice, Raimundo Fernández Cuesta, to the vacant post of Secretary-General of the Movement, which he had held before. But if Fernández Cuesta, or any other old Falangist, thought for a moment that this was a step in the direction of power, they soon found out they were mistaken. Franco had merely wanted to scare the Monarchists, not encourage the Falangists.

The years went by. They were the years of subsistence – living on Argentine credits, of economic stagnation and international isolation. They were not, however, entirely wasted years, from the point of view of the *camisas viejas*. True power might be out of reach; and so too was the national-syndicalist dream of younger days. But much could be done, against a background of private and state capitalism, to create something of the workers' welfare state the original Falangists had dreamt of. This ambitious task fell to one of the biggest men (in size as well as in ability) thrown up by the Falange: José Antonio Girón, who was Minister of Labour from 1941 to 1957. Under Girón, Spanish workers gained absolute security of tenure (a device that substituted subsidized underemployment for unemployment), and Spaniards as a whole gained benefits for old age and ill-health, maternity grants and other devices made familiar on the grander scale of a richer economy under Britain's Labour government of the late 1940s. The workers, though denied the right to strike, could console themselves with the magnificent Labour Universities, and Workers' holiday homes and recreation grounds built out of the Movement's share of public funds. Girón's workers were the aristocrats of the new Spain. With all this came considerable popularity. The reverse of Girón's medal, however, was that his experiments in proletarian contentment contributed to Spain's prolonged economic stagnation (since featherbedding goes with high costs and inefficiency), and in the end to runaway inflation.

On 19 July 1951, Franco decided to mark the resumption of cordial relations with the United States by reshuffling his cabinet with a view to making the best use of the opportunities that had now arisen for co-operation with the Americans. This – and the performances of individual ministers – were his only guiding principles. There was no question of automatically turning to the Falange for ministerial plums. In fact, a Carlist, Antonio Iturmendi, was appointed Minister of Justice, and Fernández Cuesta, who had held this job, was told to concentrate on his work as Secretary-General of the Movement. Girón – at that time the one really successful Falangist Minister – was kept on at the Labour Ministry; but so was the non-Falangist Martín Artajo as Foreign Minister. In each case, retention of the job was due to competence, not ideology. Two 'pro-Americans' were given high appointments: Joaquín Planell, who had been military attaché in the Spanish Embassy in Washington, became Minister of Industry; and a banker, Manuel Arburúa, was appointed Minister of Commerce.

For the Falange, the lesson was clear: it was there – within the wider Movement – simply to carry out Franco's orders; of power it had none. By 1955, the party, as distinct from some individuals, such as Girón and the burly Andalusian lawyer José Solís Ruiz, who was boss of the *Sindicatos*, had reached the nadir of unpopularity. In

February, the party paper, *Arriba* interviewed the Chief of State with a series of questions that might have trapped a lesser man into denigrating the memory of Spain's last king, Alfonso XIII, and of the Monarchy as an institution.[5] The labyrinth of interminable clauses that came in reply, however, was designed to make the interviewer and the reader lose their sense of direction; and did. In sum, it even emerged from Franco's replies that the Falange defended the Monarchy, although it had not occurred to the Falange to suppose so. Moreover, Franco rubbed the lesson of his general displeasure home by making it clear that the Falange, however worthy, was only one component part of the Movement, and not necessarily the most important.

On 20 November of the same year, Franco turned up at the Escorial, as usual, for the annual memorial mass for José Antonio Primo de Rivera, Founder of the Falange. What was unusual was that for the first time, he arrived wearing, not the uniform of the Movement – white jacket and blue shirt – which the Falange regards as peculiarly its own, but the military garb of a Captain-General. This was unprecedented; and so was the reception that awaited him from the hundred young Falangists who constituted his guard of honour and who could not refrain from rebellious murmurs and even subdued boos. Franco retaliated by dismissing the entire leadership of the Falangist Youth Front.[6]

It was probably in the universities, however, that the FET's unpopularity was deepest, for the students deeply resented party control over the only legal students' union. Early in 1956, the renegade Falangist, Dionisio Ridruejo, organized a dissident students' club, *Nuevo Tiempo*. Tension between the students and young Falangists of the *Frente de Juventudes* erupted in fights between rival groups in Madrid University. After the police had done their usual job of hitting young rioters over the head and arresting them, Franco reacted by dismissing the unfortunate Fernández Cuesta, who had been out of Madrid when the disturbances began.

In this respect and others, 1956 was a bad year both for Franco and for the frustrated Falange. In April, Girón persuaded Franco to decree a twenty-five per cent increase in basic wages – a proposal he accepted not because the workers were excessively poor but because Girón had argued that public order would be in jeopardy if wages remained static at a time of economic expansion, rising prices and corruption in high places. As might have been guessed, the sweeping rise triggered a vicious spiral of wages chasing prices and never catching up. In October a further wage increase of fifteen per cent was decreed, with equally undesirable side-effects.[7]

In place of the discomfited Fernández Cuesta, Franco had brought back the able José Luis Arrese. The discontent of the Falange old guard was now at its height. The true heirs of José Antonio – as the *camisas viejas* thought of themselves – gathered around Arrese, bubbling with the notion that for them, it was now or never. Either they made a successful bid for a share of power, or their identity was lost without trace.

The idea of actually attempting to overthrow Franco apparently did not enter their heads. What they were concerned about was the future – after Franco had died or retired. They envisaged a renovated Falange, purged of its extraneous elements – Monarchists and the like – while giving it a constitutional right of veto over the future king's choice of a Prime Minister. For months Arrese and his friends were at work drafting new Fundamental Laws incorporating these principles and others to their taste – to the consternation of Army officers, Churchmen, Carlists and others who feared they were being pushed out into the cold.[8]

Franco, inundated with the protests of non-Falangists, summoned Arrese and reminded him that the Law of Succession already made adequate provisions for the transition to a monarchy, through the creation of the Council of the Kingdom. The indignant Arrese handed in his resignation, which Franco coldly turned down. On 27 February 1957, to show the Minister Secretary-General who was boss, and the Falange that it counted for nothing, Franco appointed Arrese Minister of Housing, and gave Arrese's old job to Solís, a Falangist who had shown that he accepted Franco's brand of highly diluted Falangism. As, by this time, the Secretary-Generalship was hardly a full-time job for a man of Solís's energy, he remained National Delegate of the *Sindicatos*.

Since the body-blow of Arrese's removal in February 1967, Franco has never been seriously challenged by the old guard of the Falange – though illegal leaflets and occasional demonstrations have demonstrated their continuing dissatisfaction. On 17 May 1958, he issued a Law on the Principles of the National Movement, which said nothing new, made no reference to the Falange, or even to the

FET (using simply the term 'National Movement'), and stands as a monument to Franco's skilful command of platitudes and impenetrable prose.

By now, the divorce between Franco and the followers of José Antonio was almost complete, although there was no formal separation. The spring of 1959 brought a scandalously appropriate occasion for a public row: the reburial of José Antonio's remains. This was the second reburial. The first, on 30 November 1939, had come as the grand and solemn climax of a procession covering the 300 miles between Alicante – where the young man had been buried in a common grave after his execution by the Republicans – and the monastery of El Escorial, where his remains had been interred at the foot of the altar of the chapel of the kings. This first reburial had flattered the Falangists and shocked the Monarchists.

The second burial, however, removed a Monarchist grievance but offended the Falangists. A second funeral procession took place on 30 March 1959. It was a shorter one, covering only the few miles from El Escorial to the newly completed mausoleum of the 'million dead' who had died 'for God and Spain' in the Civil War – the Valley of the Fallen. Nothing, it might be thought, could have been more fitting than this second inhumation, for where else should the mortal remains of the Falange's demi-god find peace but in this pantheon of the fighting dead? To the thousands of Falangists who flocked to the basilica in the living rock, however, the solemn gesture represented a victory for the Monarchists, and therefore a slight to the Falange and to the memory of the Founder.

To make matters worse, Franco himself did not bother to attend, but sent the Under-Secretary of the Presidency, Luis Carrero Blanco, and it was on him that the assembled Falangists directed their hisses and boos. This time, however, Franco took no action. He himself had not been insulted; and the gesture was accomplished – from the Escorial, the monument of the Spanish kings, to the Valley of the Fallen, his own monument, could hardly be a step down, whatever the Falangists might say. Meanwhile, José Antonio had found his last resting-place, and there was nothing the *camisas viejas* could do about it.

As if any doubts remained that Franco had no intention of reviving Falange hopes, they were removed by Franco's speeches before the National Council of the FET, in March 1963, and again in April

1964. On each occasion, Falange pretensions to a constitutional share of power were simply ignored.

Whatever else Franco might have failed to do, one thing was plain: he had smashed Spanish fascism.

4 *Towards Affluence*

The Civil War had hardly ended – indeed, the government was still in Burgos – when Franco announced his long-term plans for the Spanish economy in these words:

> We must lift up and rebuild Spain, and make our national revolution effective, improving the living conditions of our peoples' middle class.

'Produce, produce, produce' was the slogan he launched, and he made it clear that it would not be enough just to produce, for what Spain needed was goods that other people would buy. And all this was to be accomplished while maintaining the purchasing power of the peseta.

These were brave words to speak on 5 June 1939, in a Spain poor by nature, and devastated by war. The solution, as Franco saw it, lay in industrialization, which he described as 'not a caprice but a necessity'.

Not long afterwards, the Second World War put paid to any hopes of foreign capital for Spain. Private capitalism was not going to be big or strong enough for reconstruction and industrial growth: State capitalism would be needed as well. As it happened, this view fitted in with the climate of opinion of the early war years, dominated by the Falange and strongly influenced by Nazi ideas of autarky. There was therefore no opposition when, in 1941, Franco created the *Instituto Nacional de Industria* (INI) as a public instrument for creating and managing new industries.

To launch and run the INI, Franco picked a lifelong friend and confidant, Juan Antonio Suanzes. A naval engineer by profession, Suanzes was what would nowadays be called a technocrat, though the term had not yet become fashionable. He had taught at the Naval Military School and had later directed the shipbuilding yards of Cartagena and Franco's birthplace, El Ferrol. Having criticized the Republican governments, he had lost his official jobs and had gone into private industry in Madrid. Arrested during the revolutionary strikes of 1936, he was freed on the eve of the Civil War – on 10 July – took refuge in a foreign embassy, and found his way to the Nationalist lines. He later enrolled in the Corps of Engineers in the exiguous Nationalist Fleet.

Under Suanzes's energetic guidance, INI became a sprawling economic octopus, spreading its tentacles outward, until, in the mid-1950s, it owned or shared in some seventy enterprises. It even made a profit – estimated in 1957 at 11 per cent. Inevitably, the growth of this State economic monster brought corruption, nepotism and graft in its train. But its contribution to Spain's economic growth was prodigious. Nor did its emergence inhibit a parallel growth of private industry, encouraged by aggressively expansionist policies on the part of the commercial banks. A further fillip came in 1953 with the American bases agreements. High profits had led to rapid capital formation, and investment bounded ahead. Between 1951 and 1958, industrial production doubled.*

With peace, order, profits and the driving energy of Suanzes, Spain's 'economic miracle' began. Dams were built, and the output of hydro-electric power soared from 3,687 million kilowatt-hours in 1940 to 11,225 million in 1956. Twenty thousand workers used a million and a half tons of concrete to throw up a massive steel works at Aviles, in north-western Spain. Oil refineries sprang up at Escombreras and Puertollano. In 1957, a modest but rapidly growing automobile industry was created in Barcelona, when the *Sociedad Española de Automóviles de Turismo* (SEAT) began to manufacture the Italian Fiat range under licence.

Nor was the poverty-stricken land neglected. In 1950 alone, the recently created *Instituto Nacional de Colonización* purchased 296 neglected properties and settled 23,517 peasant-farmers on them.

* It is beyond the scope of this biography to deal exhaustively with Spain's 'economic miracle'. Many excellent studies have been made of it. One of the most sober, concise and informative is an article by Richard Comyns Carr, 'Spain in Transition', which appeared in *Lloyds Bank Review* for April 1965. Spanish speakers should not neglect Claude Martin's *Franco, Saldado y Estadista*, Part III, Chapter VIII.

With fertilizers and tractors imported under American credits, production of wheat, rice and cotton improved rapidly. Huge schemes of reafforestation were launched in Extremadura, Jaen, Málaga and Aragon. The most spectacular of the agricultural schemes, in Badajoz, is reclaiming tens of thousands of hectares of fallow land and creating new model villages and towns of settlers.

Inflation, the familiar disease of expanding economies, raged unchecked in the mid-1950s, and was indeed stimulated by the dramatic pay increases decreed in 1956. Between 1945 and 1956, prices trebled. In 1952, Spain already had a foreign trade deficit of $114 million. Six years later, it stood at $387 million and Spain was virtually bankrupt on external account: reserves of gold and hard currencies had dwindled to $65 million, while actual and prospective liabilities in 1958 and 1959 totalled $118 million.

By the beginning of 1957, Franco had begun to wonder whether, as technocrats go, Suanzes was not looking a little old-fashioned. He was not quite certain of his ground, however. Suanzes, after all, had impressive successes to his credit, and while it appeared that the INI could not be entirely absolved of blame for Spain's descent to bankruptcy, nor was it, on the other hand, entirely to blame. Franco decided to keep Suanzes, while bringing newer technocrats into his administration. He found his men in the world of banking and academic economics. One of the most remarkable of them was Alberto Ullastres Calvo, who had been teaching world economic history in Madrid University, and who now – on 25 February 1957 – joined Franco's cabinet as Minister of Commerce, replacing Arburúa, who was widely blamed for Spain's unfavourable balance of trade.

Of equal calibre was a young professor of administrative law, Laureano López Rodó, who was appointed Technical Secretary-General to the Presidency – that is, to the office that carries out the orders Franco gives in his capacity as Spain's permanent Prime Minister. At the time of his appointment, López Rodó was only thirty-seven, a quiet man of unusual intellectual clarity. A year earlier, he had written an interesting article on administrative reforms which had been drawn to Franco's attention. Now he got a chance to carry out such reforms as were compatible with Spanish realities.

Other new men included Mariano Navarro Rubio, administrator of the Banco Popular and a former officer of the military Juridical Corps, who was appointed Minister of Finance. Another was

Fernando-María Castiella, a young Professor of Law at Madrid University, who became Foreign Minister, in place of Martín Artajo, whose able and fruitful tenure of office had lasted twelve years. Castiella was a controversial choice. His ability was not in doubt, but he had a past that was likely to cause him difficulties in his new appointment; and in time, did. He had fought against Russia in the Blue Division, and he was co-author of a book, entitled *Reivindicaciones de España* (*Spain's Claims*), which – quite properly, from a Spanish point of view, but unfortunately, coming from the new head of Spain's diplomacy – was strongly anti-British in its passages on Gibraltar. It could also be considered unfortunate that he had been, for a while, Director of the FET's Institute of Political Studies, which labelled him – wrongly, as it happened – a 'fascist ideologist'. On the other hand, he had studied in France and Britain, and had a reputation, which events later justified, as a 'European' and a 'liberal' (in the British, not the American, sense of this abused word). He was Ambassador to the Vatican when transferred to the venerable *Palacio de Santa Cruz*, Spain's Foreign Ministry.

Yet another academic who joined Franco's team in February 1957 was Pedro Gual Villalbi, a Professor of Political and Economic Science from Barcelona, who became Minister without Portfolio and Chairman of the National Economic Council.

The point about the 1957 cabinet that attracted most attention, at first in Spain and later in other countries, was neither Castiella's past nor the appointment of three university men. It was the fact that López Rodó and two of the new Ministers – Ullastres and Navarro Rubio – were members of the *Sociedad Sacerdotal de la Santa Cruz y del Opus Dei*, usually shortened to '*Opus Dei*'. For the past two years or so, this Roman Catholic lay order had been a topic of conversation at Madrid parties; I myself first heard about it at a Madrid dinner early in 1955, from the eloquent Irish lips of Professor Walter Starkie of the British Council. In fact, it was founded as early as 1928 by a Spanish priest, José-María Escrivá de Balaguer, but it did not emerge from its initial obscurity for many years. In one fundamental respect, it differed from the many religious orders that have been established in Spain for centuries, notably from the much persecuted Society of Jesus. The Jesuits, Dominicans, Franciscans and others were priestly or monastic orders, whose members wore religious robes or habits of one kind or another. Opus Dei, in contrast, was for civilians.

Its members were not supposed to withdraw from the world, or to dedicate themselves to a uniform pursuit, but to go forth into the world, serving God by excelling in whatever their calling might be. A good follower of Monseñor Escrivá (as he now is) does not shelter behind the traditional humility of Christianity, or refer problems to his parish priest, as Spanish tradition encourages. On the contrary, he tackles problems himself and solves them. Opus Dei thus teaches an un-Spanish philosophy of success, offering the puritanical alternative of hard work in place of the passive acceptance of God's will which has often relieved pious Spaniards from the urge to toil. Not unnaturally, this alien and dynamic approach to life, allied with the discretion verging on secrecy of the Order's methods, has aroused suspicion and antagonism in Spain and abroad, not least among older-established Orders, such as the Jesuits. It is often referred to as a new kind of Freemasonry, a club of the 'ins' that makes sure the 'outs' stay out. That the Society – as the sum of its members – has grown rich and powerful cannot be denied. It has its own University, the *Estudio General de Navarra*, at Pamplona, and controls a bank (Navarro Rubio's *Banco Popular*), a news agency and many publications, including newspapers. It has also, however, been suggested that it has gained political power, through the presence of its members in the innermost councils of Franco's régime. This needs careful examination.

The charge that Opus Dei had been aiming at political power, and had achieved it at last, was heard in February 1957, when Ullastres and Navarro Rubio joined Franco's cabinet. In this bare form, the charge seems to be unfounded because based on a misconception of what Opus Dei is. It is not, as its enemies either think or want others to think, a political party; nor is it a political pressure group. Nor, for that matter, is it a kind of super labour-exchange for politicians. In February 1957, Franco did not turn, as one would almost conclude from reading hostile comment, to Opus Dei's leadership, saying, in effect: 'I have vacancies for a couple of technocrats. Send me some candidates and I shall make my choice.' This would not have been Franco's way, even if it had been Opus Dei's ambition. What happened was more pragmatic and less sinister. Franco had heard of the intellectual and technical merits of Ullastres and Navarro Rubio and sent for them; they happened to be members of Opus Dei. On the same occasion, he had heard of the technical and intellectual merits of Castiella and Gual Villalbi and sent for them; but Castiella and Gual Villalbi happened *not* to be members of Opus Dei.

In other words, Opus Dei was not a group to be conciliated by being given a share in power, as the Monarchists were, or the Falange or the Army. It had played no part, as such, in the National uprising, and had no special title to Franco's gratitude. As it happens, every Franco cabinet since 1957 has included members of Opus Dei; but it would be misleading to say that Opus Dei is 'represented' in Franco's government, and even more misleading to suggest that Opus Dei has any prescriptive right, other than the talents of gifted individual members, to be so represented. The charge that Opus Dei is a kind of Freemasonry, on the other hand, has some basis: Opus Dei men, once in office, tend to appoint other Opus Dei men.

If Opus Dei is neither a political party nor a pressure group, it is clear, on the other hand, that it is an intellectual forcing ground, tending by natural selection to produce an élite, not merely in politics, but in all walks of life, especially the professions. It does this in two ways, both by attracting men whose natural talents and drive make them impatient of mediocrity; and by encouraging those who do join to dedicate themselves unabashedly to success in the service of God as the Order sees it – with vows of chastity and poverty to reinforce their dedication. (In practice, the vow of poverty means that a member's wealth belongs to Opus Dei, which makes him an allowance consistent with his status in ordinary life.) It would be surprising if this combination of circumstances did not throw up a natural élite. While Opus Dei has no right to representation, as such, therefore, one need be neither astonished not outraged if its members should continue to be in demand on their merits, long after Franco has gone. The only thing that could vitiate this prophecy would be a determination on the part of the Order's many enemies, who are found in the Falange as well as among opposition Christian Democrats of Gil Robles's school, to persecute Opus Dei and hound it out of public life. This, of course, cannot be ruled out. In the meantime, Opus Dei offers a remarkable diversity of opinions: for instance, Rafael Calvo Serer, one of the Order's leading thinkers, is an enthusiastic Monarchist, while Ullastres is cool towards a restoration. Other shades of opinion range from the authoritarian Right to the Christian Social Left. Even the supposed economic aims of the Order have confused observers, for a simple reason that may have escaped them: the Order, as such, has no economic aims. Nevertheless, one sees Opus Dei described as 'economically liberal' and as preaching 'a heavy-handed economic doctrine', by two American writers, each serious in intent and with an affection for accuracy.* The fact is that there is not, as far as I am aware, an Opus Dei economic doctrine, or a political doctrine either. There are, on the other hand, a number of Opus Dei members in the financial and banking world. Each is entitled to his own views, and some may choose to write these down for publication, and it is therefore hardly surprising that the views expressed by articulate Opus Dei members should be those that are current in Spanish business quarters. Such men have gained enormously from the stability conferred on Spain by Franco's authoritarian régime, and they feel neither love for Communism, nor nostalgia for the Spanish Second Republic. But too much should not be read into the fact that men who hold such opinions happen to be members of Opus Dei, for so do many men who do not happen to be members.

At first, however, in the grave economic crisis of the late 1950s, the Opus Dei technocrats seemed powerless to stem the tide of inflation and accumulating foreign debts. They had inherited a costly, inefficient, featherbedded, uncompetitive economy. They had also, thanks to Suanzes, inherited an industry that could be made to expand and improve, if steps were taken to prune it of the dead branches that were strangling its effective growth. This was far from easy. For one thing, Suanzes was still there, defending to the last the right of his baby, the INI, to support more people than it could afford to, entrenched behind the State's protective arms.

Here was one problem that time could not solve, and indeed far from solving, could only make worse. While the peseta plummeted and gold reserves dwindled ominously, Franco's masterly inertia, for once, seemed irrelevant. The new technocrats advised him to seek aid abroad. No advice could have gone more against the grain. It was one thing accepting American aid after prolonged negotiations that had led to agreements in which Spanish conditions had been met. A rescue operation was quite another thing. This was no longer

---

* The first quotation is from Benjamin Welles, in *Spain: the Gentle Anarchy* (p. 31); the second, from Stanley G. Payne, in *Falange* (p. 262). Payne, in particular, misunderstands the situation, I believe, when he says that in 1957, 'Franco turned to the "grupo Opus"' as a logical alternative to the discredited FET.

a matter of negotiations between equals. Spain was proud, but Spain was sick. Calling in foreign doctors implied a prior commitment to swallow whatever medicine was prescribed. In the end, the Caudillo is said to have exclaimed impatiently: '*Hagan lo que les de la gana*' – 'Do whatever you feel like doing!' or more succinctly: 'All right! Have it your own way.'[1]

It was now late in 1958. Soon, two teams of foreign 'doctors' came to Spain. One was sent by the Organization for European Economic Co-operation (OEEC) and came in December; the other was sponsored by the International Monetary Fund (IMF) and arrived in February 1959. Both teams agreed about the medicine to be administered. It was going to be hard to swallow and unpleasant in its side-effects, though the name given to it – the 'stabilization plan' – sounded reassuring, sedative, indeed almost Franco-ish in its tranquillizing promise.

Still, the doctors promised, if the patient did swallow the plan, there would be all manner of benefits: the peseta would be stabilized, and there would be aid from the United States government and the American commercial banks, and from the IMF and OEEC themselves. Strongly supported by the austere economists of the Opus Dei, the plan was formally accepted by Franco's government in July 1959. Immediately, Spain was raised from associate to full membership of the OEEC. The peseta was devalued from 42 to 60 to the US dollar, and the previous system of multiple exchange rates – depending on the kind of exchange being transacted – was abolished.

Against the State-subsidized expansionism of Suanzes, López Rodó, Ullastres and Navarro Rubio had been preaching 'orthodox' economics – that is, a strong dose of deflation, with a credit squeeze and cuts in government spending. But to force their policies through against the entrenched opposition of those who were afraid of getting hurt had proved impossible until Franco himself had decided to take the plunge and had called in the foreigners. Now the Spanish technocrats got their way, for the stabilization plan carried with it a built-in dose of deflation, as massive as they could have wished. Ceilings on government spending for 1959 and 1960 were laid down; government borrowing was to be slashed; severe limits were imposed on credits to private industry. To prevent frivolous or speculative imports, importers were told they must deposit twenty-five per cent of the cost of goods purchased abroad.

This, then, was the medicine. The benefits, as the foreign and native technocrats had forecast, were immediate – indeed, spectacular. The peseta, which had been threatened with the fate that has overcome so many Latin American currencies, took its place among the world's strongest monetary units at its new and realistic exchange rate. The deficit of $50 million in the 1958 balance of payments was transformed into an $80 million surplus the following year. Suddenly, prices stopped rising. Where goods had been scarce, they became abundant almost overnight, as hoarded stocks were released on a market that had ceased to offer rising rewards to the speculator.

The side-effects, too, as the economists had feared, were felt immediately. Speculators were driven out of business, and no tears were shed for them; but many small business men were ruined or impoverished. Tens of thousands found themselves jobless and tens of thousands more lost the overtime pay and incentive bonuses that had made their living standards rise despite the inflation of the past two or three years. After the first buying spree that had followed the release of hoarded goods, retail trade creaked to a standstill. Spain was a depressed country: this was orthodox economics with a vengeance.

The patient, however, was alive and cured of his fever. It remained to breathe new life and energy into him. Rehabilitation being by nature more delicate than emergency treatment, the Opus Dei Ministers went about it cautiously. 'Reactivation' was the slogan for 1960. It began with mild increases in government spending, the easing of credit restrictions and taxation reliefs as an incentive to industry.

At first, recovery was slow. But in 1961, industrial output soared by eleven per cent; Spaniards consumed twelve per cent more electricity than in 1960 and produced twenty per cent more steel. The year of recovery was 1962, with investment booming, new jobs opening up and retail trade expanding. This was the moment for Solís's vertical syndicates to do their work, and Franco ordered them into action. Industry by industry, new wage contracts were negotiated.

With reflation came more of the old troubles, but in a rapidly changing setting. Exports remained sluggish while imports boomed; and Spain's commercial balance went out of gear again. This time, however, less harm was done because of two new developments that helped to redress Spain's balance of payments even though the balance of trade, as such, remained unfavourable. One was the increasing volume of remittances to Spain from a growing number of Spaniards who left their homeland to work in the more affluent labour markets of western Europe – Switzerland, West Germany, France and Britain. The other was the early signs of what was to become a prodigious tourist boom. The yearly percentage rises in the tourist trade made astonishing reading. In 1961, 21 per cent; 1962, 16 per cent; 1963, 22 per cent; 1964, 28·8 per cent. In 1964 some 14 million tourists – nearly half of Spain's own population – spent $1,000 million enjoying Spain's beaches, visiting her grand and austere monuments or watching the swirling skirts and clicking heels of the flamenco dancers.

Meanwhile, the technocrats were preparing for Phase 3 of their economic programme. After deflation and reactivation, Spain's industry had to be modernized and made competitive. For the country's future, as the technocrats saw it, lay within the wider European market opening up among the more advanced countries of the West. But the price of entry into the European Economic Community – assuming that the hostility born of Franco's past could be overcome – was greater efficiency, and the technocrats knew it.

Once again, the foreign experts were called in for advice. This time, they came from the Organization for Economic Co-operation and Development (or OECD, as the OEEC has been renamed) and from the International Bank for Reconstruction and Development, usually shortened to 'World Bank'. Their respective reports were published in 1962. The World Bank's massive report,* in particular, opened encouraging vistas of economic expansion.

This was where López Rodó, the brilliant Opus Dei backroom boy who had taken over the technical side of Franco's government, came into the open, and into his own. For some time, he had been working on an economic plan designed to lift Spain into the mid-twentieth century. Now, in July 1962, Franco appointed him Commissioner for the Four-Year Plan, as part of a further reorganization of his government. In a sense, the 'new' technocrats had been put on trial in 1957; and they had come out of the test with

* A useful summary of which was published in various languages by the Spanish Information Service (Economic Documents 1).

flying colours. The time had come to give them their head. On 18 July 1962, Franco dropped three Falange mediocrities from his cabinet, confirmed Ullastres and Navarro Rubio as Ministers of Commerce and Finance respectively, and brought in yet another Opus Dei technocrat, Gregorio López Bravo de Castro, as Minister of Industry.

Once again, however, Franco remembered the sources of his power. He had not, as many observers supposed, handed power over to Opus Dei; he had merely hired the ablest technicians on offer, four of whom happened to belong to the Order. But the 1962 cabinet reshuffle was just as notable for other appointments. One was that of his trusted old friend, General Muñoz Grandes, as Vice-Premier – a new post created for him, which showed, if this needed further demonstration, that if anything were to remove Franco from the scene, he would be the man to take over and ensure the continuance of order. Only two years younger than Franco, and in indifferent health, Muñoz Grandes was an austerely honest man. Franco had made him a Captain-General in 1957; and since he was the only man, apart from Franco himself, to hold this rank, he was automatically a member of the Consejo del Reino, whose function was to ensure the transition of Spain from a theoretical to a real Monarchy in the event of Franco's death or incapacity. Another old friend who entered the cabinet at this time, as Minister for the Navy, was Vice-Admiral Nieto Antúñez; and in the background, another naval man, Vice-Admiral Carrero Blanco (the man who had taken a copy of Franco's Law of Succession to Don Juan in 1947), played an important part as Under-Secretary to the cabinet. Both Nieto Antúñez and Carrero Blanco – the latter perhaps the most conventionally 'right-wing' of Franco's Ministers – have been spoken of as candidates for supreme power after the Caudillo's departure.

Yet another important appointment to the 1962 cabinet was a young technocrat who – to the confusion of the analysts – was not a member of Opus Dei. This was Manuel Fraga Iribarne, a professor of Law at Madrid University, who had won some renown as a kind of miracle exam-passing machine, the holder of numerous degrees and competition successes that were the fruit of a prodigious facility and capacity for work, allied with a phenomenal memory. Fraga's new post was Minister of Information and Tourism, a double charge he tackled with breath-taking energy and – in his early years – an unduly optimistic view of the speed of change in Franco's rejuvenated régime.

Well aided by several dozen experts, López Rodó toiled throughout 1963, to produce a veritable encyclopaedia of an Economic and Social Development Plan, running to thirty-one volumes. As I heard him explain it during a brief visit he made to London in 1963, the Plan set Spain objectives that were modest enough to be within range, yet ambitious enough, if achieved, to lift the country to within sight of an economic take-off. The Plan was to begin in 1964 (and did). Productivity was given high priority, and López Rodó hoped it would rise by five per cent per year. Gross National Product – the sum of all the goods and services, measured in value – was supposed to rise six per cent per year; and income *per capita* from $360 to a still inadequate $470. Private firms that moved into backward areas were to get considerable tax cuts and easy credits. The move of workers from country to city was expected to continue and increase. With rising purchasing power, car production was expected to be doubled – to 200,000 private cars and 50,000 commercial vehicles – during the four years of the Plan.

By and large, these expectations look like being fulfilled.

If 1964 was the first year of the Four-Year Plan, it was also the year when colourful posters began to appear all over Spain, proclaiming – against the red and gold background of the Spanish flag – the completion of *25 años de Paz Española* – '25 years of Spanish Peace'. A quarter-century had indeed elapsed since that day in April 1939 when Generalissimo Franco had announced that all fighting was over. His 'skilful prudence' had kept Spain out of the Second World War, against a background of police terror at home and threats from outside. But in the end the firing squads had been silenced and peace of a kind had settled over the violent land. Not far from Madrid, the huge and austerely beautiful monument to the fallen of both sides during the 'War of Liberation of Spain' had been erected, mainly by prisoners of the defeated side, and its massive cross seemed to promise reconciliation, in time, though meanwhile the Press and the régime's propaganda machine kept alive the obsessive fears of an earlier day of chaos and hate. With lengthening peace, crimes of violence had dramatically diminished and startling changes had been wrought in a land of torpor and impatient action. To be sure, the old habits died hard, and *Madrileños* still insisted on their three-hour lunch break and their fancifully late dinners, even when the new-found discipline of the technocrats started bringing them into work at 9 a.m. But the will to produce was there and mountains of concrete testified to unleashed energies.

More important still, perhaps, Spanish workers had gone abroad in their tens of thousands, coming into contact not only with the higher living standards of richer countries that had made an earlier start than Spain in the industrial revolution, but with the freedoms of parliamentary democracy. Was it possible to liberalize the economy, as the technocrats were doing, and keep the Spanish people – relatively speaking – muzzled and guarded? To an increasing degree, in the 1960s, this became the central problem of Franco's slowly evolving régime.

It was, perhaps, less easy a problem to solve than the foreign critics supposed. Within hail of Franco's twenty-five years of Spanish Peace, several events reminded him of unpleasant things he might have preferred to keep out of his mind: his own mortality, for one, and the violent challenges of the recent past.

On Christmas Eve, 1961, Franco was out hunting when his shotgun exploded, wounding him in the left hand. It was the first time he had been wounded since that distant day in 1916, when he was almost left for dead on a Moroccan battlefield. This time, the accidental wound was far from mortal, but an operation was necessary and a general anaesthetic was advised. Strong though the patient's heart was known to be, the possibility of sudden death could not be ruled out, and this prospect produced a flurry of consultations. The interesting point, however, is that of the three high personages designated as the Regency Council under the Succession Law of 1947, the Caudillo summoned only one – Captain-General Muñoz Grandes. The others – the Cardinal Primate and the President of the Cortes – were ignored. With Muñoz Grandes came other old military friends of Franco's.[2] The Generalissimo's preoccupation was therefore not with legal niceties but with the maintenance of order in a transitional phase of possible panic and agitation. Army men maintain order; Cardinals and Assembly Chairmen do not.

It is probable that until his accident – which occurred a few days after his sixty-ninth birthday – Franco had given only the most casual thought to the possibility that he might one day be removed from the Spanish scene. The 1947 Law of Succession, though it did reflect his conviction that the Spain of the future would have to be a Monarchy, had been timed to take the wind out of the sails of plotting Monarchists, not with any intent to restore the Monarchy during his lifetime. Although Franco emerged from the anaesthetic with his strength unimpaired (and, to the surprise of the surgeons who were at his bedside, ready to correct them over figures of his blood count and pulse rate),[3] he did, from that time on, give more serious attention to transitional arrangements for that day when death or incapacity might bring power to other hands. Characteristically, however, five more years elapsed before the Organic Law of the State was published and submitted to the Spanish people by referendum.

The other events that troubled Franco during this period all occurred in 1962. The first was a wave of strikes among Spain's best-paid workers – the coal miners of Asturias – in April. The Asturian miners have long memories of Franco, and Franco of them. The passions of 1917 and 1934 might well have come bubbling to the surface again; yet they did not. There was no violence on either side. Strike funds, provided by the Communists, the Socialists of France and Belgium, and the International Confederation of Free Trade Unions, were lavish. Support also came from the left-wing Catholic *Hermandades Oberas de Acción Católica* (HOAC), whose status might be described as legally tolerated but officially disapproved of.[4]

The wind of change that blew in from the Vatican after the advent of Pope John XXIII in 1958 had a profound effect on the Spanish Church's attitude towards social problems. At the time of the Asturian strikes, it was not merely the lowly Basque priests who supported the strikers, but even – by clear implication of spoken words – the hierarchy of the Church. The aged Cardinal Primate of Spain, Monseñor Pla y Deniel of Toledo, publicly called for improvements in workers' wages and for a strict observance of Christian values on the part of the rich. So, with variations of phrase and emphasis, did the Cardinal Archbishop of Seville, Monseñor Bueno Monreal; the Archbishop of Valencia, Monseñor Olaechea; and the Bishop of Bilbao, Monseñor Pablo Urpide.[5] It was a chorus which Franco could not ignore, even though he turned down Pla y

Deniel's pleas for leniency on behalf of HOAC members caught in subversive activities. The Pope's 1961 Encyclical, *Mater et Magistra*, which was widely interpreted as sanctioning the moral right of workers to strike, undoubtedly played an important part – allowing for the usual time lag for reflection and gestation – in Franco's 1966 bill legalizing strikes for strictly industrial purposes, however illiberally this measure may have been interpreted judicially.

In the end, the 1962 strikes were settled when José Solís Ruiz, the boss of the *Sindicatos*, flew to Oviedo to reconcile the interests of the mine-owners and the workers. The former were allowed to increase the selling price of coal, to finance wage increases for the latter. This restored serenity.

The next jolt to Franco's régime came in June, with the so-called Munich affair. More than a hundred opponents of his régime gathered in Munich. There – over a symbolical handshake of reconciliation between two former political opponents, Gil Robles and the Socialist Rodolfo Llopis – a Manifesto was issued, calling on the six countries of the European Common Market to refuse to admit Spain until certain democratic reforms had been introduced.

The Munich affair brought a new round of unfavourable publicity down on Franco's head. Spain's application for association with the European Economic Community had in fact been officially entered in February 1962; and it is more than likely that the Munich affair made it politically more difficult for governments that favoured the Spanish application to press it on those – principally the Dutch and Belgian – that did not. For the Opposition, the Munich affair brought some personal discomfort or inconvenience. Gil Robles and others were arrested on their return to Madrid. Gil Robles went into exile in Geneva; some of the others were deported to the Canary Islands.

A further splash of bad publicity for Franco Spain came with the Grimau affair. Julián Grimau García, a Communist, was arrested in Madrid on 8 November 1962, and charged with crimes allegedly committed during the Civil War. He was said to have been a member of the notorious Barcelona *chekas* and to have ordered, and taken part in, tortures and executions. Under interrogation, he admitted that he had returned to Spain from exile in 1959, under orders from the clandestine Spanish Communist Party, to organize subversion. In an attempt to escape, he jumped from the first floor of the Dirección-

General de Seguridad, and broke his skull and both wrists. After hospital treatment, he was tried by a military tribunal and sentenced to death on 18 April 1963.

It is known that a heated and protracted cabinet meeting was held to consider whether the death sentence should be carried out. It is just possible that Franco would have exercised his prerogative of mercy, but a personal cable to him from the Soviet Premier, Khrushchev, appealing for clemency, tilted the scales against the accused. A majority of the cabinet had been in favour of execution anyway, and the sentence was duly carried out.

As the Foreign Minister, Castiella – one of those favouring a reprieve – had said it would, the execution aroused liberal as well as left-wing opinion against Spain in many parts of the world. To this extent, and to the extent that it raised further obstacles in the path of Franco's desire to be accepted in the western community, the decision to carry out the sentence was a political error. It should be added that given a choice between doing something fundamentally derogatory to Spanish pride – such as accepting an appeal from the leader of international Communism for mercy to one of his acknowledged agents – and improving his image in the world's press, Franco would invariably avoid the easy way out. For my part, I cannot believe that Khrushchev actually wanted to save Grimau's life though this would have given him a propaganda success. He probably calculated that his cable would force Franco to refuse clemency, thus giving the Soviet Communist Party, and the large majority of Communist Parties that were still, at that time, ready to accept Moscow's leadership – and even those that did not – ready-made material for a propaganda blow against 'fascism'.

For this reason among others, while willing to concede that Franco would have gained more from reprieving Grimau than having him executed, I am unable to share the general moral disapproval which the manner of his death aroused. I wish he had had a fairer trial, and in a civil not a military court, but I have little doubt that he was guilty of the atrocities with which he was charged. And I am no more convinced that time had eroded his guilt than I am in the case of the Nazi criminals who still turn up from time to time. Moreover, he was well aware that in returning to Spain for subversive purposes, he was risking death. Would a Spanish 'fascist' agent have fared any better if arrested in similar circumstances in Russia?*

To many, however, the execution of Grimau was a sudden and sickening return to the terrors of the 1940s; perhaps the more so because it followed a period of two years in which nobody at all had been executed in Spain, for political or criminal offences. To rub in the fact that the Civil War was still not really over, two anarchists were also executed in 1963. Their crime, at least, was new: they had deposited a time-bomb in the passport office of the Security building, and its explosion had seriously injured a number of innocent people.

Despite these incidents, 1963 was a landmark in the liquidation of the Civil War in that trial by military tribunals for political offences was at last abolished. A decree to that effect had been on the agenda for some months before the Grimau affair, but was passed too late to help him.† Like most forms of 'peace', the Spanish Peace was relative.

5 *Franco almost Clubbable – II*

Franco's 'original sin' still bedevils his attempts to gain universal acceptance of his régime. Though Spain is a *de facto* member of Nato through her bilateral military pacts with America, her formal entry into the Atlantic alliance is barred – largely through the hostile recollections of well-meaning people in Belgium, Holland, Norway and Britain who are unwilling to discard the irrelevant associations of twenty or thirty years ago. Such emotional fixations tend to be immutable: neither Franco's skills nor the facts of a changing world can shift them. And there, no doubt, they will stay, until Franco and his generation of enemies die out.

With two able men – Martín Artajo, followed by Castiella – to

* I expressed such views in a BBC Spanish-language broadcast to Spain at the time (in a series in which I often criticized the continuing illiberalism of Franco's régime), and I see no good reason for modifying them now.

† Benjamin Welles claims that the decree was due for discussion on 19 April 1963, when Grimau's sentence came up for review, but was shelved so that the execution could be carried out without juridical embarrassment (*Spain: The Gentle Anarchy*, p. 72).

execute his policies, Franco has nevertheless scored considerable diplomatic successes during the post-war years. The greatest breakthrough was certainly the signing of the Hispano-American bases agreements of 1953. But the same year also brought Spain's Concordat with the Vatican, which was a success that was far from negligible, since it could be taken, both in Spain and in the Catholic areas of Europe and Latin America, as a long-delayed sign of the Holy See's moral approval.

It was indeed difficult for the Vatican not to reach agreement with Franco, sooner or later. The military uprising of 1936 would certainly have collapsed had it not been widely supported by Spanish Catholics outraged by the Republic's treatment of their Church. Under Franco, the Spanish State had restored the Church's traditional rights, lifted the ban on the Society of Jesus, abrogated the Republic's divorce law and banned civil marriage. The study of religion had been made compulsory in schools and universities and the State was subsidizing the Clergy.

The negotiations with the Vatican were nevertheless protracted, for much had happened since the Concordat of 1851, which the Republic had abrogated. In the end, agreement was reached on 21 August 1953, after prolonged discussions, conducted in Madrid by the Papal Nuncio, Monsignor Cicognani, and Martín Artajo; and in Rome by the man who was to succeed Artajo as Foreign Minister, Castiella – then Ambassador to the Vatican – and Monsignor Tardini, pro-Secretary of State.

God and Caesar, it might be said, had equal hands in the Concordat of 1953.[1] God's Church had its traditional rights reaffirmed. Caesar's State, on the other hand, was given the right to propose and veto Papal nominations of Spanish Bishops. In other respects, perhaps, the Church did better than the State out of the Concordat. The State's censorship service was placed at the disposition of the Church to exclude heretical opinions and prevent the publication of books on the Vatican's Index; the Church's publication, *Ecclesia*, on the other hand, was exempt from Franco's censorship, although only on condition that it was not offered for public sale. A further major privilege conceded to the Church – under Article XXXIV – was that it was allowed to conduct its 'apostolate' through Catholic Action, which thereby became something of a political party. This particular privilege inherently harboured the seeds of conflict between Church

and State which came into the open at the time of the Asturian
strikes of 1962, through the involvement of Catholic Action's
HOAC workers' organization in support of the strikers.

Though he remained *persona non grata* in the exclusive western clubs
of international politics, Franco did achieve membership of that
less exclusive club – the United Nations. This came in stages. In
1953, Spain became a member of UNESCO (the United Nations
Educational, Scientific and Cultural Organization). In January 1955,
the Spaniards were given the status of permanent observers at the
UN, and Dr Hammarskjöld, the Secretary-General, sent an invitation
to this effect to Areílza, Franco's Ambassador in Washington. Nearly
a year later, on 7 December 1955, Spain was voted a full member of
the UN, by the overwhelmingly favourable vote of the General
Assembly's *ad hoc* Political Committee.

This should have been one of Franco's greatest moments of
triumph, since Spain's admission was a tacit recognition of the
fatuity of the UN's anti-Franco resolution of 12 December 1946.
In the event, however, UN politics had denied him the joy of a singular victory, for Spain was admitted only as part of a package deal
between the great Powers, involving the admission of sixteen
countries in all. While it was true, therefore, that 'even the USSR'
voted for Spain's entry, as Spanish official publications put it,[2] this
was hardly the whole truth.

As far as the UN was concerned, Spain had been in Coventry for
nine years. This did not, however, stop Franco from entertaining
visitors at home, as it were, since he could not invite them to the
club. Eva Perón had come in 1947, representing the most important
of the Latin American countries that had spoken up for Spain in the
UN debates (others, of course – especially Mexico and Uruguay –
had been very hostile towards Madrid). Latin America was indeed a
natural field for Spanish diplomatic endeavour. Franco needed,
however, to live down the war-time excesses of the Council of
Hispanity, which he had created in 1941 in the fascist exuberance of
Serrano Súñer's heyday, and which expended Spain's energies and
goodwill during the Second World War by making propaganda for
the Nazis and their allies. After the war, Franco realized that this was
yet another Falangist liability, and he abolished the Council of
Hispanity, replacing it by an Institute of Hispanic Culture without

21a Franco votes in municipal elections, 1966.

21b Franco receives first councillors of the Spanish Sahara, July 1963.

22a and b Two moods of
General Franco.

any imperialist pretensions other than the export of Cervantes, Lope de Vega, Calderón and similar manifestations of Hispanic genius. Since the days of Spain's ostracism, dual nationality treaties have been concluded with a number of Latin American countries, whereby citizens of one country may obtain citizenship of the other without losing their own.

If Latin America was one natural field to explore, the other was the Arab world. King Abdullah of Jordan, the Regent of Irak, Moulay Hassan of Morocco (now King Hassan II) and various Egyptian Ministers were among the Arab notabilities who visited Spain during the period of the UN boycott. Martín Artajo returned these attentions in 1952 in a successful tour of the Near East, which took him, among other places, to Amman, Cairo and Baghdad. In each of these capitals the Spanish Foreign Minister was given a warm welcome. In each, the Arabs told him they resented American policy, since they found it impossible to give serious credence to the view that the distant Russians were enemies; their true enemies, they said, being the western imperialists on their doorstep.[3]

The Arab argument, and the unanimity with which it was preached, was doubly useful to Franco at that time. On the one hand, it confirmed his own view of the strategic value to the United States of a genuinely anti-Communist Spain, in comparison with the Arab countries, at a time when the negotiations for the American bases agreement were still in progress. Had any doubts remained whether his terms would be accepted, Martín Artajo's trip removed them. On the other hand, the trip brought home the fact that Spain herself, though accepted as a friend in the Arab world, was also tarred with the 'colonialist' brush through her presence on Moroccan soil.

During the Second World War Franco had thought it natural to demand imperial recompense at France's expense as the price for participation in the fighting at Germany's side. In the sober, anti-colonial light of the post-war world, such dreams were neither fashionable nor feasible. A Falangist Spain would not, however, have abandoned them as easily as Franco did. Nothing, indeed, more clearly demonstrates the pragmatic nature of his policy and its hard-headed realism, than his adaptation to the anti-colonial trend of world opinion after 1945. Writers who have noted that Franco Spain differs from 'other' fascist dictatorships in not being expansionist or imperialist have missed the point, which is that Spain under Franco

R

is *not* a fascist country. It is a traditional, conservative and authoritarian régime, in which the fascist element – always a minority even at the height of its influence – has been firmly pushed down where it belongs: away from any control over policy.

In 1952, Franco had promised wide autonomy for the Spanish zone of the Protectorate; without, at that time, thinking of independence as anything but a distant prospect. He was incensed when, in August 1953, the French government – with Georges Bidault as Foreign Minister – deported the Sultan, Mohammed ben-Yussef, without so much as informing the Spaniards of its intentions. Franco retaliated by refusing to recognize Moulay ben-Arafa, the puppet Sultan installed by the French, and by welcoming Moroccan Nationalists, such as Allal el-Fassi and Ahmed Balafrej, to Madrid.

At this stage, the colonial policy of authoritarian Spain could be regarded as distinctly more 'progressive' than that of democratic France. Once again, as in so many actions of his life, Franco's motive force had been patriotism, or, if you prefer, nationalism. Spain was in northern Morocco, to 'protect' the Sultan, and had earned her right to stay there by the blood and tears of the Moroccan war, in which Franco himself had played so notable a part. It followed that the Sultan should not have been removed without Spain's consent; and that Mohammed ben-Yussef's deportation was therefore an intolerable insult to Spain and her Chief of State. To mark his disapproval, Franco ordered his High Commissioner in Morocco, General García Valiño, to make an anti-French policy speech. This was done on 21 January 1954, before the assembled Moorish notables in Tetuan and in terms of considerable violence. A few days later, Franco received a Moroccan delegation led by the Grand Vizier of the Califate, Ahmed el-Haddan, and told them that Spain would 'resolutely defend Moroccan unity'. Since that unity had been broken by France's action in deporting the man who was not merely the temporal but the spiritual ruler of the Moroccans, Franco now formally 'detached' the Spanish zone from French Morocco. And this, in turn, brought a strong protest from the French Ambassador in Madrid.

By adopting – for reasons of offended pride – a position as champion of Moroccan nationalism against French colonialism, Franco had, of course, deprived himself of any room to manœuvre should French policy change, as it did abruptly later in 1954 with the advent of a series of French governments – starting with that of M. Mendès-France – that were anxious to rid France of costly colonial burdens. Was this an uncharacteristic case of lack of foresight on Franco's part? To the extent that he had gone further than he probably needed to in encouraging Moroccan nationalism, it probably was. But Bidault's unilateral action had left him with little choice. Besides, in any conflict between Spain's interests, as measured by material advantage, and Spanish pride, Franco has always given precedence to pride.

At any rate, when the Edgar Faure government hit on the magic formula of 'independence within interdependence' for Morocco, Franco tried hard, but in vain, to concert a common policy with the French. France's recognition of Morocco's independence – with Sultan ben-Yussef duly restored – on 2 March 1956, caught Franco on the wrong foot again. Three years earlier, he had looked dangerously 'progressive'; now he was being made to look a reactionary imperialist. In fact, Spain's position as a protecting Power had now become an anachronism, and it fell to Franco, who had first won military glory in Spain's service in Morocco, to recognize the fact. It was a painful decision for him to make, but he did not hesitate for long. On 4 April 1956 he went to Barajas airport, outside Madrid, complete with a Moorish guard of honour, to welcome the Sultan. Three days later, Spain too had recognized Morocco's independence and the Spanish zone reverted to the Sultan's sovereign rule. Spain, however, held on to Ceuta and Melilla, the Spanish *presidios* on the northern coast, and to the Ifni region in the deep south.

By his policy of the early 1950s, Franco thought that at least he had won Morocco's friendship and consolidated his 'Arab' policy. He was to be disillusioned on both counts in late 1957, when the 'Moroccan Liberation Army' invaded Spanish Ifni. Ironically, this guerilla force had originally been armed and trained by the Spaniards with anti-French intent during the Sultan's exile. Now its remnants were being incited by independent Morocco to have a go at Spain. In the end, just as in 1925, a joint Franco-Spanish punitive expedition restored order in February 1958. Hispano-Moroccan friendship had been shown to be fragile; and Franco marked the fact by disbanding his Moorish Palace guard – the last symbolic link with the faithful force that had helped bring him to political power in 1936.

Hispano-French friendship, on the other hand, had been forged anew on the Saharan battlefield. It was not, however, till General de Gaulle's return to power – which Franco, pushing back memories of his old friend Pétain, publicly welcomed – that Spain could make much of the opportunities opening to the north with the development of the European Economic Community. And it was not till the economic stabilization policy of 1959 had borne fruit that Spain felt strong enough to request association with the EEC. Not unnaturally, since Franco Spain was still notably short of friends in western Europe, the approach to the Community was first made in a letter from the Spanish Foreign Minister, Castiella, to his French opposite number, Couve de Murville, on 9 February 1962.

French friendship, however, was not enough to get Franco into a club that was more jealously exclusive even than NATO. The initial response was chillingly negative: the silence of lost causes. Castiella repeated the request two years later, on 14 February 1964. And on 2 June, at last, a procedurally favourable reply came from the Belgian Foreign Minister, Paul-Henri Spaak, himself one of the European Socialists who had not overcome his distaste for Spain's 'fascist' dictator. It said: 'The Council [of Ministers of the EEC] is disposed to authorize the Commission to initiate with the Spanish government, conversations whose object will be to examine the economic problems that are raised for Spain by the development of the European Economic Community, and seek appropriate solutions.'[4] When these lines were written, however, in the spring of 1967, Spain was still knocking at the door of the Common Market.

On a bilateral basis, on the other hand, Spain's friendship with France has produced more tangible results. French and Spanish Ministers have exchanged visits: Franco-Spanish naval co-operation has become a regular routine; the defences of the two countries have been, in some particulars, co-ordinated; a $150-million French credit was granted to Spain in 1963; and France is building a nuclear power station for Spain.

Friendship with America, however, remained the corner-stone of Franco's foreign policy. In November 1955, the then American Secretary of State, John Foster Dulles, had started what was to be a habit of dropping into Madrid on his way back from NATO gatherings in Paris to brief the Caudillo about the defence decisions of the western alliance to which Spain did not quite belong. On 21 December 1959, a bigger fish altogether – President Eisenhower – was attracted into Spanish waters. It was a great moment for Franco, and despite the barriers of language and temperament, the two generals got on famously. Franco helped break the ice by telling a story that seemed to him appropriate, about a young French major who was having a bullet removed from his brain when a messenger from Napoleon brought the news that he had been promoted to general. The hero jumped off the operating table and on to his horse. When the surgeon protested, the young man shouted as he galloped away: 'I'm a general now; I don't need brains any more!'[5] History does not record which of the generals present, if any, Franco's story was aimed at. At all events, Eisenhower and Franco parted with a spontaneous farewell *abrazo*.

On Franco's side, however, – and no doubt on the American side as well – the friendship was never unconditional. In 1958, when Italy and France – the Americans' NATO partners – had refused landing rights to American aircraft on errands connected with the crisis in the Lebanon, Spain granted them. This was friendship. But in 1961, Franco's controlled Press unanimously condemned President Kennedy's Bay of Pigs expedition against Cuba. Indeed, Spain has continued to trade with Cuba and in other ways maintain good relations with Havana, in defiance of the American boycott. This is, of course, a paradoxical situation, since Cuba is under a Communist régime. Blood and history, however, are thicker than the water of ideology. Fidel Castro's forebears come from Franco's part of Galicia; and Cuba, the first and richest of Spain's colonies, was the scene of the humiliating disaster of 1898, inflicted on Spanish arms, by, as the Spaniards see it, the upstart imperialism of North America.

As the initial ten years of the American bases agreement started drawing to a close, Franco began to show signs of dissatisfaction with what had always seemed to him a cut-price alliance – in the sense that the agreements, as they stood, appeared to be not much more than a property contract between a sovereign landlord and a sovereign tenant who happened to be richer than the landlord. Even in the matter of economic aid, the agreements hardly made amends for the regretted failure to include Spain in the Marshall Plan; for, as the Spaniards pointed out, Spain stood only ninth in the list of European recipients of American aid – after Germany and Italy, which countries, unlike Spain, had been at war with the United States.

Franco dropped a hint that the whole project needed to be thought out afresh, in a speech at Burgos on 1 October 1961, when he declared: 'Now that four-fifths of the time laid down for our agreements has elapsed, they need to be studied afresh and brought up to date in accordance with the new situation.'

The new situation Franco had in mind was the advent of the Polaris nuclear missiles, and Spain's possible willingness, in contrast to many other countries, to harbour them on Spanish soil – for instance at Rota, the powerful American air-naval base on Spain's southern Atlantic coast; and Spain's increasing acceptability as an ally, as distinct from a host to American transients. His warning to the Americans – for this is what he intended it to be – went unheeded for more than a year, however. There is no need to follow the ensuing negotiations in every detail* but Franco's way of conducting them merits attention.

At first, all was confusion. Competing Spanish Service Chiefs presented separate lists of arms requirements which, in total, came to $500 million. Captain-General Muñoz Grandes streamlined this massive 'bill', cutting it by half; but without consulting the Foreign Minister, Castiella. The Americans filed this figure away without any apparent intention of doing anything about it. They then counter-attacked – by this time, it was January 1963 – by calling on Spain to purchase $85 million worth of American arms each year for three years, as part of a global attempt on Washington's part to 'off-set' the yearly drain of gold from US coffers. The Spaniards said 'No' and Franco, through Castiella, formally notified the United States that they wished to re-negotiate the 1953 agreements, which were due to expire on 26 September 1963. Until then, no formal notification to this effect had gone out from Madrid.

When the Americans countered by saying they proposed to send a high official to Madrid to sign the 'off-set' agreements which the Spaniards had already turned down, the Spaniards let it be known that none of the Ministers the high official wished to see – the Vice-Premier, the Foreign Minister and the Finance Minister – would be available. General Franco, in fact, had invited them to come hunting with him. The official's trip was cancelled. By now it was March, and Hispano-American relations were in full crisis.

Franco's masterly inertia was beginning to look as though it would

* An excellent account of them appears in Welles, *op. cit.*, pp. 292–308.

simply drive the Americans out of Spain, with nothing to show on either side but wounded feelings. At this stage, writes Welles, the Spanish Ambassador in Washington wrote a long memorandum to Franco asking for *carte blanche* to negotiate, calling on the Caudillo to keep the Spanish military out of the discussions and proposing that Spain should drop any demand for military hardware, insisting instead on the need for a military alliance; or, failing this, on firm defence guarantees from Washington.

The diplomat who was bold enough to make such sweeping proposals to Franco was not, in the conventional sense, a diplomat. He was a lawyer named Antonio Garrigues, whom Franco had appointed to Washington in 1962, on Castiella's advice. The appointment itself was a striking instance of Franco's unideological criteria for selecting executants of his policy. If ideology had played a part in Franco's thinking, Garrigues would have been ruled out for his liberal monarchism and for his general background of quiet disapproval of the régime. Garrigues, on the other hand, had an unrivalled range of contacts in the American business world and a high professional reputation as a lawyer.

Franco called Garrigues home for consultations and sent him back to Washington in June with written instructions and full and exclusive authority to negotiate on Spain's behalf. This unprecedented mark of confidence was rewarded by the conclusion of an agreement that fell short of Spain's maximum demands but which Franco nevertheless accepted, against the wishes of the military members of his cabinet.

In fact, the new agreement did give Franco the essence of what he wanted. It consisted of a number of documents, including a joint declaration, two joint communiqués, two exchanges of Notes and a letter from the American Secretary of State, Dean Rusk, to the President of the US Export-Import Bank, dealing with economic loans for Spain. The two most important passages were these:

1 The government of the United States reaffirms its recognition of the importance of Spain for the security, well-being and development of the Atlantic and Mediterranean zones. The two Governments recognize that the security and integrity of Spain as well as of the United States are necessary for the common security. A threat to either of the two countries, to the joint installations which each contributes for the common defence,

would jointly affect both countries, and each country would adopt whatever action might be considered appropriate in accordance with its constitutional processes. (Extract from the Joint Declaration.)

2   The proposed Consultative Hispano-American Committee was empowered, should the need arise, to recommend solutions 'to those problems that might arise in connection with the use of the installations in Spain . . . matters that may arise in the application of the Aid Agreement for Mutual Defence, and *whatever other matters* which one or the other of the two Governments may submit to the Committee for consideration.' (Italics added; extract of Note from American Secretary of State to Spanish Foreign Minister.)*

What Franco had gained, therefore, was the transformation of a simple military lease agreement between theoretical equals into an alliance in all but name, without limits on consultation. On the economic side, the American commitment was, on the other hand, relatively meagre: Spain was to be granted credits of up to $100 million 'during the next few years'. On the military side, the Americans would provide $100 million worth of arms and equipment for the Spanish forces, and the Spaniards would buy $50 million worth on their own account.

Once again, masterly inertia had triumphed, but only when Franco was goaded into last-minute action by the able man he had sent to Washington. For Castiella, who had supervised the protracted negotiations, the renewed agreement, which was to last five years, was a major achievement. Though still barred from the major western clubs, Franco Spain had become the indispensable ally of the West's dominant Power. In the end, Franco had conceded nothing but a reduction in exorbitant initial demands.

Successful though the Spanish Foreign Minister had been in the vital matter of the *de facto* alliance with the United States, he has had little to show but bitterness in his handling of relations with one of Spain's oldest and best customers, Britain. To be fair, the British are at least as much to blame as the Spaniards for this state of affairs.

* My translation from Spanish text: *Alianza*, pp. 67–75.

There is, of course, one dispute, and one only, between Spain and Britain: Gibraltar. There are, however, residual ideological objections to Franco on the British side, which bedevil any attempt to solve real problems while Franco is alive and in power.

Let us look at each side's actions from the other side's viewpoint. What emerges is something like this:

FRANCO'S SIDE

Franco remembers that the Leader of the British Labour Party gave aid and comfort to the 'Reds' by visiting the International Brigades, and, it is said, giving the clenched fist salute. The writers and cartoonists of his semi-private *Noticiero de España* attached and satirized Clement Attlee for it.

Franco remembers the actions of the British Foreign Secretary, when the Labour Party was in power after the Second World War, to put 'his' Spain beyond the pale. Nor can he forget Ernest Bevin's efforts to bring his Monarchist and Socialist opponents together, with a view to unseating him. He doesn't need to remember all the anti-Franco pamphlets, speeches, resolutions and declarations emanating from various British bodies, principally the British Labour Party. The other memories will do.

Franco has his own views about Gibraltar. (In this he is not alone: most patriotic Spaniards have.) True, he did say, once, that Gibraltar was not worth a war. But it needles him, as it needles all Spaniards: after all, why should Britain give independence to vast territories, such as India and Pakistan, and hang on to a rock and its approaches, about the size of Hyde Park? Would England like it if the Spanish Armada had not gone down to defeat and if Spain, in consequence, still held on to Land's End?

Still, Franco is a cautious man, aware of British susceptibilities. Did he not confide to Mussolini's Ambassador, as long ago as 1937:

> . . . I have to be careful of the British. England has ancient and traditional interests here. Gibraltar can be the cause of grave discords with Spain, but meanwhile it is by the nature of things a bond. Be careful that it is not a paradox. You know that English recognition of my government is something I have very much at heart.[6]

Moreover, did he not – by his mulish and unreasonable insistence during the Second World War, that only Spanish troops could take Gibraltar – keep the Rock out of Hitler's hands?

BRITAIN'S SIDE

This is less easy to define than Franco's side, since on Franco's side, when all is said and done, there is only one pair of eyes that matters; whereas on the British side, there are Conservative eyes, and Labour eyes, and Liberal eyes and indifferent eyes. Since the present phase of worsening relations with Spain began in 1964, the Labour eyes are the most important ones. And this means Harold Wilson's eyes.

On 16 June 1964, Mr Wilson, winding up for the Opposition at the end of a two-day debate in the House of Commons, asked whether Britain had to sell drawings and details of frigates to 'a fascist country' for a few million pounds. (Mr Wilson was referring to negotiations then in progress for the building in Spanish shipyards of a 6,500-ton light cruiser, four frigates of 2,700 tons each and two submarines, using British licences, materials and techniques.) On that occasion, Mr Wilson also wanted the Foreign Secretary to tell him if the Franco government had withdrawn its claim to Gibraltar in return for the arms deal.

Now, Mr Wilson, as the Leader of the Labour Party, is the heir to the deeds and words of past Leaders. The heir, for instance, to Mr Attlee's prank with the International Brigades. The heir, too, to the decision of Mr Attlee's government, in 1951, to refuse *agrément* to Franco's nominee to the post of Ambassador to the Court of St James, who, as it happens, was Fernando María Castiella, now Spain's Foreign Minister. The explanation usually given for this refusal was that the Attlee government objected to the nomination of a man who had expressed himself intemperately in print on Spain's claim to Gibraltar and who had fought against Britain's gallant war-time ally, Russia, on the side of Britain's war-time enemy, Nazi Germany. In the circumstances, the refusal of *agrément* was perfectly understandable; but unfortunate, for both sides, in the crisis of the late 1960s.

It was also, on the other hand, understandable, that Franco was so incensed by Wilson's remarks of June 1964, that he called a cabinet meeting to consider the frigates deal negotiations and abruptly cancelled them on 30 June. The orders, worth some £11 million to the British economy, were later placed with France and the United States.

Against this background, it is hardly surprising that Anglo-Spanish relations were at a low ebb when Mr Wilson came to power in October 1964; or that they have deteriorated still further since then. It would be wrong, however, to think that Franco merely wanted to make things awkward for the British Labour Party when he imposed new restrictions on the passage of people, cars and goods in the month of Mr Wilson's appointment as Prime Minister; or when, on 25 October 1966, he closed the Spanish frontier to all vehicular traffic from Gibraltar. Gibraltar was, indeed, as Franco's advisers would have pointed out had he not noticed it, a non-party issue in Britain despite differences of approach among the political parties. In fact, it is one of the elements in a situation that offers no prospect of an early solution that neither of the main British political parties is disposed to negotiate with Spain on Gibraltar's constitutional future (as distinct from discussing the harm done by Spanish restrictions). Labour does not want to, because Spain is under a 'fascist dictatorship'; and the Conservatives, because the Rock of Gibraltar is one of the few remaining symbols of a vanished empire; neither Party does, because one does not lightly dispose of the political future of people, however disparate their origin and few their numbers, who appear to want to remain 'British'. The furthest the British will go is to concede that the future of Gibraltar can only be settled in conjunction with Spain.

Against this, Franco is an old man, conscious of his place in history, aware that the restoration of Spain's sovereignty over Gibraltar would be acclaimed by friend and foe alike, and mindful of the fact that the slow processes of masterly inertia may be too slow to bring results within his lifetime. It is no part of my purpose to discuss the relative merits of the British and Spanish positions. I have simply tried to explain how Franco's mind works. This problem will remain insoluble until the British change their minds, or Franco goes.

6 *Franco looks to the Future*

From the gallery of the Cortes, he looked smaller than ever, and old, his bald cranium shrunken and the flesh of his neck – once plump and firm – now slack and worn. *'Se hace viejo'* – 'He is getting old,' my neighbour, Lieutenant-General Antonio Barroso, murmured to me. And he added, reflectively: 'He has done so much for Spain.' The man next to me, who had known Franco since they were cadets together at Toledo, is in fact only eight months younger than the Spanish Chief of State, but the cares of his various public offices had been relatively slight, and he looked ten years younger than his chief.

The gallery had been filling up for half an hour, and so had the assembly benches of the round and noble old Chamber, with its faded blue and gold adornments. Most of the men entering the Cortes – its *Procuradores* about to hear the 'Caudillo of Spain and of the Crusade' – wore the white tunics and dark blue shirts of the *Movimiento*; a few were in military uniform; some wore the more spectacular robes of the Sahara, whose provinces they represented. Familiar faces had been appearing one by one as their owners – Muñoz Grandes, Castiella, Carrero Blanco, Martín Artajo – took their seats on either side of the President's rostrum, seats of honour reserved for cabinet ministers and members of the Council of the Kingdom.

Outside and on the route from the Royal Palace to the Cortes, mounted police and Civil Guards ensured the Chief of State's Rolls-Royce an unimpeded passage. Security, by British or American standards, was slack: individuals slipped without difficulty through the police cordons and the balconies were packed with onlookers – doubtless screened, but well placed to shoot or throw a hand grenade should this have been anybody's wish. There had never, however, been an authenticated attempt on Franco's life, and none was expected on 22 November 1966, the day of the extraordinary session of the Cortes, summoned to hear the Chief of State present the much awaited Organic Law of the State.

The old man, in his uniform of Captain-General, walked the last part of the journey on his sturdy legs, acknowledging the cheers, then climbed the steps of the Cortes building. As he entered the

Chamber, all present stood and acclaimed him. It was about three minutes before silence was restored. He glanced at his text, then looked around him and upwards with that unchanging opaque gaze, impenetrable as ever. It was a long speech, and he began it with modest oratorical effects, using both hands to emphasize points. Soon, however, only the right hand was in rhetorical use; and presently, neither. By then his voice had settled in its high-pitched monotone, his Gallego accent more pronounced, it seemed to me, than ever. He was a sick man, the rumours said, suffering from mild arteriosclerosis and capable of only intermittent concentration. But, for a non-orator, there was nothing wrong with his performance. Without a pause, he read steadily for fifty-five minutes, not bothering, in the last half-hour, to look up from his text. After a while, communication ceased and although each word was individually clear, meaning was lost.

So true is this that some foreign correspondents, who had evidently been listening to the speech on their radio sets, reported that the Chief of State had spoken for two hours. After the round of cheers, the President of the Cortes, Antonio Iturmendi, had read out the text of the Organic Law, and this, too, had taken an hour. Then after a few more words from Franco, there were more cheers and the extraordinary session of the Cortes dispersed, the President having announced that the Law had just been adopted by acclamation.

It was only later, on studying the text of Franco's speech, that one realized he had been saying important things. He had reminded his audience that 1966 had brought the thirtieth anniversary of his assumption of supreme powers and of the National Movement. He had alluded to the lack of understanding of the victors in the Second World War, to the ruin and dishonour which the rule of political parties had inflicted on the nation and the economic desert he had inherited at the end of a cruel internal war.

Two sentences, in particular, deserve quotation, for they sum up the man's profound and sceptical understanding of his people and his paternalistic will to protect the Spaniards from themselves:

Let Spaniards remember that each people is always haunted by its familiar demons, which are different for each of them. Those of Spain are called: anarchical spirit, negative criticism, lack of solidarity between men, extremism and mutual enmity.

He rattled off figures of schools, pupils, universities and graduates, to demonstrate the progress accomplished by the nation under his guidance. There followed some philosophizing about political systems. 'Well interpreted,' he remarked, democracy was the most precious civilizing legacy of western culture. But parties were not an essential element in democracy; there had been frequent democratic experiments in history, and the phenomenon of political parties was a relatively recent one. What Spain needed was an 'authentic, ordered and effective' democracy, not a party democracy in which the parties became platforms for the class struggle and for the disintegration of national unity.

He recapitulated previous fundamental laws – the Labour Charter of 1938, which he could not recall without emotion, for it was the first, and passed at a time of mortal struggle; the Act of 1942 creating the Spanish Cortes; the Charter of the Spaniards of 1945; the Referendum Act of the same year; the Law of Succession of 1947; and the Law on the Principles of the National Movement of 1958. He then announced that there would be changes in four of these – the Charter of the Spaniards, the Labour Charter, the Act of the Cortes, and the Law of Succession.

When the text of the Organic Law became available, it was found to provide for a number of important changes – each of which would need legislative or executive action before becoming a reality. The most striking proposal was that the functions of Chief of State and Head of Government, which Franco had exercised since 1936, should be separated. While this implied an alleviation of Franco's burdens, however, it did not signify a reduction of his power, for it was up to him, as Chief of State, to pick a Prime Minister. True, he was to do this from three names presented to him by the Council of the Kingdom – the top advisory body created under the Law of Succession of 1947. But it must be assumed (although the new Organic Law didn't actually say so) that the Council of the Kingdom would not submit names of men without being sure in advance that each was, in one way or another, acceptable to Franco. Moreover, Franco retained the right to dismiss the Head of Government.

Next to the provision for a Prime Minister, the most important innovation of the Organic Law was the provision for a very modest injection of free elections into the corporate body of the Cortes. Under a law to be passed later, each province was to elect two representatives of families, elected by heads of family and married women; the rest of the Cortes was to be much the same mixture as before, of 'representatives' of the Movement, the universities, the professions, the *Sindicatos* and so forth. It was not much, but it was a step in the direction of a representative legislature as it is understood in the western world.

A greater measure of religious freedom was foreshadowed by a drafting change in Article 6 of the Charter of the Spaniards, removing the ban on non-Catholic ritual and inserting a clause guaranteeing State protection for religious freedom. There was also an interesting minor change in the Labour Charter. The original text had banned 'individual or collective actions which in any manner perturb normal production or threaten it'. The revised text inserted the word 'illegal' before 'individual or collective'; this appeared to give constitutional protection of the right to strike, which had already been granted by a recent law and had therefore become 'legal' – though only for strictly industrial and non-political purposes.

Other changes affected the Law of Succession. The Council of the Kingdom was enlarged and declared to have precedence over other consultative bodies. There were also elaborate new provisions for voting for a king or regent in the event of the death or retirement of the Chief of State. Franco retained his own right to choose a king or change his mind about a candidate previously proposed and accepted by the Cortes (a right which would enable Franco, if he so elected, to 'choose' the Pretender, Don Juan, as king, then change his mind and pick his son, Don Juan Carlos, instead). Moreover, if anything, the duty of the prospective king or regent, to swear loyalty to the Fundamental Laws of Franco's State as a condition of appointment, was further strengthened. Since Article VIII of the Law on the Principles of the National Movement (which a kingly aspirant is specifically bound to honour) declares illegal all political parties outside the existing institutions of the State, this seemed to extend, well beyond the grave, Franco's ban on parliamentary democracy.

It remained to put the Organic Law of the State to the test of a national referendum, and if this were successful, to transform its provisions into realities. Only once before had the entire adult population of Franco Spain been called upon to vote – in 1947, when a majority of more than twelve to one had approved the Law of Succession and in effect declared their confidence in Franco as their ruler for life. Now they were being asked to vote 'Yes' to Franco's Organic Law.

It was a tremendous exhibition of mobilized official efficiency. For weeks on end the vast resources of the Ministry of Information and Tourism, under the Minister, Fraga Iribarne, and the devoted guidance of his brother-in-law the Director-General of Information, Carlos Robles Piquer, were brought into play. A quarter-million pictures of Franco – 50,000 of them in colour – went out to all parts of Spain. Posters sprang up everywhere – nearly all of them variations on the central themes of peace, stability and security. Spaniards were urged to vote 'Yes' for the future of their children, for the prosperity of their country, for the stability of their homes. One of the posters showed children playing with ABC blocks saying 'Vote Yes,' while a caption explained that 'They don't vote, YOU do'.

Girón, Franco's Minister of Labour for seventeen years, left his convalescent bed after a major operation to appeal for a 'Yes' with his thunderous voice over the television network. Other personalities of the régime – from Navarro Rubio to Martín Artajo – did their bit. The newspapers explained and exhorted; nobody was left in doubt that the key to Spain's future was in the hands of the Spaniards themselves.

In all this clamour, a few strangled cries were heard from the opposition. The Christian Democratic review *Cuadernos para el Diálogo* was allowed to carry a series of dissident opinions. Isolated anti-Franco posters appeared here and there; in Pamplona, two Professors of the University of Navarre and several students were arrested for posting bills without proper authority. The Communists managed to distribute leaflets in considerable numbers, calling on Spanish voters to abstain in the referendum.

Two days before the vote, General Franco himself made a final appeal to his compatriots. 'You all know me,' he said in familiar tones on radio and television, and added words which cynics considered hypocritical:

Never have I been moved by the ambition to command. Ever since I was very young, responsibilities heavier than my age or job have fallen on my shoulders. I should have liked to enjoy life like other Spaniards; but the service of the fatherland filled my hours and occupied my life. I have had thirty years at the helm of the ship of State, saving the nation from the storms of the world today; but, in spite of everything, here I am still at the foot of the cannon, with the same spirit of service of my youthful years, employing what is left in me of useful life in your service. Is it too much to demand what I ask of you, in my turn, your support for the laws which for your exclusive benefit and that of the nation are to be submitted to a referendum?

Though Franco's disclaimer of personal ambition rang more strangely than his reminder of his willingness to assume heavy burdens in the name of duty, his appeal – and the overwhelming resources of his State – did what was expected of them. On the appointed day – 14 December 1966 – more than nineteen million Spaniards, or nearly 89 per cent of those entitled to vote, went to the polls. More than eighteen million of those who voted (nearly 96 per cent) said 'Yes'; only 1·79 per cent – under 350,000 – said 'No'. Fewer than half a million had spoilt their votes. It was hard to tell how many of the two and a half million abstainers stayed away because they had better things to do and how many because the Communists had told them to.

Was Franco's triumph as overwhelming as it looked on paper? Possibly not quite. Officially inspired stories spoke of the embarrass-ment of officials at the completeness of the Caudillo's victory, since a smaller percentage would have looked more convincing. The profession of embarrassment could have been sincere; or equally, it could have been a clever double-bluff. Foreign correspondents and others who visited polling booths at random reported that every-thing seemed normal, and that the voting papers were duly burnt after counting. There were virtually no incidents. Why, however, were the Barcelona results held up for several hours after the Madrid ones had been declared? Because they were embarrassingly low? Or embarrassingly high in one of the Republic's former citadels and in the stronghold of Catalan separatism? Did the Asturian miners really vote for Franco?

It is hard to answer such questions. What can be said with confi-dence, however, is that by and large – and even allowing for the possibility of faked figures in Catalonia and Asturias – the Spanish people gave Franco an overwhelming vote of confidence. As in 1947, the referendum was, in reality, a personal plebiscite. This is the true meaning of 14 December 1966, and there is no need to waste time on well-known arguments about the value of referenda in democratic terms. Clearly a vote of 'Yes' or 'No', on a long and complicated law, which requires hours of study for minimal comprehension, and without an alternative choice, is of limited value. But it is beyond question that the Spanish people voted for Franco as the man who has given them peace and prosperity, and into whose hands, not anybody else's, they would entrust their future.

For Franco indeed, the occasion must have brought wry satisfaction. He had been feared, then tolerated, then accepted. Now, it seemed, he had attracted a kind of loving. This may seem paradoxical in the face of the many evidences of dissatisfaction in Spain, from strikes to student riots and the veiled criticisms in the press. But it is clear that, with the exception of the irreconcilable (and illegal) opposition, the dissatisfaction is with the régime, not the man at the head of it. Franco is popular, as the warmth of the crowds that greet him shows – even in Barcelona, with its natural prejudice against the central control he symbolises. He is popular because his presence spells stability and is a guarantee against domination by any of the mutually antagonistic groups in his government.

The régime itself is less popular, because it provokes the envy of those who have not benefited from its patronage and because the régime – without Franco – implies a scramble for power with unpredictable consequences. While Franco is there, for instance, Monarchists can tolerate a monarchy without a King; they would resent and resist any attempt to perpetuate a kingless monarchy after the Caudillo's departure.

For his part, General Franco was determined that his régime – essentially a permanent coalition of parties conventionally termed 'Right-wing' but including the revolutionary Left of the original Falange – should survive him in perpetuity. He saw his Organic Law, together with the other Fundamental Laws which it superseded or complemented, as a permanent constitution for the nation he had guided for thirty years. This was why, on 21 April 1967, the texts of all the Fundamental Laws, revised to conform with the Organic Law, were published in the Official Bulletin of the State.

Nor was this the end of it. The Organic Law itself generated a whole series of individual Laws, each designed to provide a specific legal basis for its individual provisions. Draft laws on Family Representation, on the Movement and its National Council, on

Religious Freedom and other matters showered on the Cortes, and each was subject to intensive debate, emerging extensively amended. For Franco, the months that followed the referendum were absorbingly busy. It was as though the Caudillo were trying to rival Napoleon as law-giver as well as soldier. His brother Nicolás told me he had complained to Francisco that he was doing too much work. 'Why don't you hand this over to a secretary?' he had asked one evening, finding the Chief of State drawing up an elaborate programme for the next day's activities.

Franco did indeed dictate his speeches and draft texts to secretaries, but much of his time was spent alone in his study. Not that recreation was neglected. He still spent most week-ends shooting, either on the Pardo estate or on the *fincas* of some aristocratic host, though rigorously observing seasonal restrictions. Fishing was, in the main, reserved for the summer months, in the rivers of Galicia.

His capacity for self-abstraction continued to surprise his visitors and his hosts. But those who thought he had fallen asleep were usually wrong: he was merely husbanding his energies. When in the mood, he would reminisce at length; but only before his family and a handful of intimate friends, before whom he could drop the double barrier of shyness and stately aloofness. At such times, however, he would never talk politics. Nobody – not even his brother Nicolás, or the faithful and efficient executant of his policies, Admiral Carrero Blanco – would claim to be in his confidence as regards political intentions. Weekday afternoons are reserved for Ministers who want to discuss their problems with him. But what takes place is hardly a 'discussion'. Franco listens patiently, jotting down points of interest in a note-book. Either then, or later, he makes his decision known; and he will have reached it alone. Not for nothing did he tell a visiting 'Establishment' journalist: 'The trouble with you, F—, is that you dabble too much in politics. Take a tip from me: I've never bothered with them.'

To the end, indeed, he was the soldier not the politician. There was something curiously military about the minor concession to human weakness he started making in 1966. Until then, cabinet meetings went on without a break until all business was dispatched. Now Franco allows a break for supper at 10 p.m. He himself dines with his family; the Ministers are given a cold dish. Work is resumed at 10.30 promptly. Franco's State is a disciplined State.

PART VII

'Before God and History'

✳

1 *Spain*

According to the fundamental laws of Spain, General Francisco Franco Bahamonde is responsible 'before God and history'. It would be presumptuous to guess how Franco stands in the sight of God. Nor is it possible, in the inadequate perspective of 1967, to assess his place in history. For one thing, the last chapter cannot yet be drafted, since the subject was still alive when these lines were written. And it will be a very important last chapter, for if his Organic Law of the State of 1966 ensures a peaceful transition to a régime as stable as his and more normal, it is clear that his place in the history books will be immensely improved; whereas if the arrangements fail or usher in a further period of violence, it may be said of Franco that he merely gave Spain a breathing space.

The assessment that follows is therefore, by its nature, provisional. The most a biographer can do, at this stage, is to indicate, tentatively and incompletely, some points that will have to be considered when, in time, a definitive assessment is attempted. In one sense, then, this is a *pre*-assessment. But in another, it is a *re*-assessment, for the preconceptions of 1936–9, when Franco first imposed himself on the world's awareness, and of 1945, when he was condemned by most of the civilized world, have only a remote connection with the evolving reality of Franco's Spain.

The most persistent of these preconceptions is that Franco is a 'fascist dictator' and that the régime he created is a fascist State. Before leaving London for Madrid to continue and complete this work, I cut two extracts from the London press:

1 Paul Johnson, in his *London Diary* (*New Statesman*, 13 May 1966),

commenting on the news that the British government was about to begin talks on Gibraltar with the Spanish authorities: '. . . It might seem inconceivable that a Labour government should be prepared to hand over to a *fascist dictator* the lives and liberties of this small democratic community . . .' (my italics)

2 From the *Madrid correspondent* of *The Times*, in a story dated 26 June 1966: '. . . Today Falangists, *dissatisfied with the present régime* and the National Movement, and preoccupied about the future, clashed with the police in the Alcalá, Madrid's central thoroughfare . . .' (my italics)

Question: Since the Falangists, who are Spain's original fascists, are dissatisfied with Franco's régime, can Franco be a fascist dictator?

As if to underline the irony and fallacy of the Left's favourite label for Franco, *Le Monde* of 5 June 1966, reported the closing by the police of the José Antonio Centre in Madrid, which attempts to perpetuate the principles of the founder of Spanish fascism, José Antonio Primo de Rivera. The Centre had invited police action by publishing violent attacks on Franco's government and on the policy of the National Movement, which is still widely – and very misleadingly – called the Falange.

Such incidents are revealing but hardly surprising. They represent the whimperings of Spanish fascism in its death throes. Paradoxically, then, one of Franco's outstanding achievements has been to break fascism in Spain – a remarkable feat if one considers his indebtedness to fascist and Nazi aid during the Civil War and the apparent predominance achieved by the Falange in the National Movement. Certainly fascism is much less menacing in Spain today than it was during the first half of 1936 under the Popular Front government of the Second Republic. It has been isolated and emasculated; and its capacity to use violence has practically vanished. If logic were a guiding principle of the Left, it would gratefully acknowledge its debt to Franco for having done what the Republic failed to do.

The Right, too, has its stereotypes, some of which may induce nausea in the uncommitted. There was the famous remark by the British Conservative, Sir Henry Page Croft: 'I recognize General Franco to be a gallant Christian gentleman, and I believe his word.' There was Douglas Jerrold's much quoted description of Franco in *Georgian Adventure* (Collins, 1937): 'Having talked with him, I realized, as everyone does, that that in itself is a privilege. He may or may not be a great man as the world judges, but he is certainly something a thousand times more important – a supremely good man, a hero possibly; possibly a saint.'

My own favourite example of long-play sycophancy is the late Luis de Galinsoga's *Centinela de Occidente*. For instance:

'On Guard, Sentinel!' The Sentinel of the West was there at, one and the same time defending hill by hill the Spanish positions on the Ebro front and, with watchful eye and sagacious gaze, attending to international happenings of such obvious bearing on the development of our campaign. 'I am the sentinel who never goes off duty, the one who watches while others sleep.'

Exact words, newly applicable to that occasion (from p. 308)!

To many on the Left, Franco's Spain is 'worrying'. They see it as the surviving 'fascist' Power, a refuge for German Nazis, as repressive as any régime in eastern Europe, with a single ruling party and no freedom of speech or political gathering.

Such arguments rest partly on half-truth and irrelevancy. It is true, for instance, but irrelevant, that Spain is a refuge for many Nazis. So are Brazil, Argentina and the Republic of Ireland. Does that make them worrying? It is simply untrue that Spain is as repressive as any régime in eastern Europe. Ask Andrei Sinyavsky of Russia, or Milovan Djilas of Yugoslavia to compare notes with Dionisio Ridruejo, the dissident Falangist writer. Or consider the case of Viktor Khustov, the young Soviet citizen sentenced in February 1967 to three years in a strict régime labour camp under a recent law making it an offence to tell political jokes. Does he, I wonder, feel less repressed than the students who rioted in Madrid and Barcelona in January 1967? Or reflect on the case of José-María Gil Robles, the Christian Democratic leader of the 1930s. Gil Robles has a prosperous law practice in Madrid and Paris. He was harried for many years by Franco's régime, and had to go into exile for attending the Munich rally of Spanish opposition leaders in 1962. An issue of the magazine *Actualidad Española* was confiscated early in 1967 for carrying an interview with him criticizing the referendum and the Organic Law. On the other hand, a book entitled *Letters from the Spanish People*, prepared by a study group under his direction, though banned in July 1966, was later allowed to appear and has since become something of a best seller. Now clearly the liberty enjoyed by Gil Robles is minimal, compared to that enjoyed by political dissidents in Britain or the United States. But it greatly exceeds the degree of freedom allowed to Soviet, East German, Rumanian, Bulgarian, Czech and Albanian dissidents. Sinyavsky was given a savage sentence; Tarsis was locked up in a mental home before being allowed to go into permanent exile.

As repressive as any régime in Eastern Europe? Does Madrid have a wall around it, with armed guards to shoot at those who try to cross it? Spaniards can come and go as they please. Can Russians or East Germans?

As repressive as any régime in Eastern Europe? In June 1966, General Rojo Lluch, former Chief of Staff of the Republican armies during the Spanish Civil War, died in Madrid. He had gone into exile at the end of the war, but returned to Spain, without any special restrictions, in 1957, after General Franco had granted his personal request for permission to do so.

It is a half-truth to describe Spain as a one-party State or to assert that there is no freedom of speech or political gathering. The National Movement is hardly a party at all: in Stanley Payne's words, the *Falange Española Tradicionalista y de las JONS* is now 'a bureaucratic arm of the State, stripped of political power'. As for freedom of speech, Spaniards have long enjoyed a quite remarkable freedom to say what they think, bearing in mind the supposedly totalitarian nature of the régime.

Not that they have yet achieved freedoms comparable to those of other West European countries – far from it. After the revised Press Law of 1966, the freedom of the press to say what it thought did increase to a degree that confounded the cynics; though there were limits, as the case of *Actualidad Española*, mentioned above, showed. But for some months at least, it was possible, as it never had been before under Franco's rule, for Spaniards to keep reasonably well-informed about what was happening in their own country, by reading their own newspapers. Opinions critical of the régime were finding their way into the Spanish press, previously so dully conformist. A striking instance was the decision of the editors of *ABC*, the Monarchist daily, to publish a long letter from the Spanish exile Miguel Sánchez-Mazas, in its issue of 2 February 1967, complaining in detail about the judicial procedures that had culminated in a sentence of twelve years' gaol on him for having published two anti-régime articles abroad in 1957. For my part, incidentally, I consider this sentence to be wildly, even absurdly, disproportionate to the 'offence'. An interesting point, however, emerged from Sánchez-Mazas's letter. He was allowed to return to Spain for three days in October 1966, to bury his father; he was neither informed of the charges pending against him, nor prevented from returning to his Swiss exile. Would he have been allowed to escape the course of 'justice' in Eastern Europe?

It is sad to have to add that only a week after *ABC*'s daring publication of this letter, a commission of the Cortes started discussing an amendment to the Spanish Penal Code – since adopted – to impose penalties of one to six months' gaol and a fine of up to £300 for infringing the Press Law and publishing untrue information. Dire penalties are also in store for those 'lacking a proper respect for institutions or persons in criticizing political or administrative activities'. Almost immediately it became known that these penalties were under discussion, the Spanish press reverted to its dull conformism. But not for long: the papers are, on balance, much livelier than they used to be.

Though Spain will not, I think, gain the liberal freedoms during Franco's lifetime, it is not a truly totalitarian country; and that is the point of this argument. It is possible, in Spain, to *opt out* of politics in a way that is denied to Soviet citizens, and it is utterly unthinkable in a truly totalitarian country like Mao Tse-tung's China. The trouble, in Spain, begins when you want to 'opt in' to politics and don't happen to agree with the régime. At this point, the régime's rather unpredictable and not always efficient security police come into play.

Objectively speaking, then, Spain is not a 'worrying' country. Russia *is* a problem; and so is China, because they are powerful, Messianic countries which export their ideologies and subvert independent governments. Franco Spain is not a powerful country, nor a Messianic one; it lives at peace with its neighbours, Portugal and France; it does not export its 'ideology' (partly because it is fundamentally, as we have seen, an unideological régime), nor does it subvert other countries. This is what I mean by a non-problem.

In an otherwise perceptive article* which uses some of the

* In a stimulating special number of *Holiday* magazine (April 1965) devoted to Spain.

left-wing arguments we have been considering, Mr V. S. Pritchett quotes with approval a Spanish waiter's opinion that the country's economic miracle was due, not to Franco's twenty-five years of peace, nor to American aid, but to the tourists in their millions. This raises an interesting point. It is true, as I have pointed out, that Spain's 'miracle' falls short of economic soundness. In 1966, for instance, Spain had a trade deficit of £830 million. Tourism normally wipes out the deficit and is therefore a very important element in Spain's total economic picture. It is, of course, subject, at least in part, to unpredictable factors beyond Spain's control: the prosperity of western Europe, for instance, and the tastes and inclinations of the tourist themselves. But that is not all. Tourism does not just happen: tourists have to be encouraged and attracted. Spain's sunny climate is a fixed asset. But Franco's government must be given an important share of the credit for attracting tourists in ever greater numbers. Under Fraga Iribarne's direction the State has provided first-class hotels in attractive surroundings – the *Paradores* and *Albergues Nacionales*. Although the cost of living rose sixteen per cent in 1966, Spain still offers cheaper holidays than most other parts of Europe. But a fundamental background to the tourist explosion, as well as to the Spanish 'miracle' as a whole, is the order and stability of Franco's Spain.

'Order,' writes Professor Raymond Carr on page 694 of *Spain, 1808–1939*, 'was the indubitable achievement of General Franco's rule.' But order is not an end in itself; nor is it, as Professor Gabriel Jackson seems to think, a rather tiresome Right-wing obsession.* It is an essential condition of economic progress. If in doubt, compare the economic performance of the Spanish Republic with that of Franco Spain. Or, to pick contemporary examples, of Sukarno's Indonesia – potentially one of the richest countries in the world – with that of Japan, an overcrowded country poor in natural resources.

Franco's achievement, therefore, though it may start with order, transcends it. Before wealth can be distributed to social purpose, it must be created. What Franco has done is to create the public preconditions of economic well-being; and, not content with these, to drag Spain into the technological revolution. These are great and good achievements, both in absolute and relative terms.

In absolute terms, the changes wrought in Spain under Franco's

* See p. 32, *The Spanish Republic and the Civil War*.

rule are there for all to see and need not be laboured. But history, by which Franco asks to be judged, needs perspective and implies relativity. Spain must be judged by standards that apply to her; and those of liberal western Europe do not. It is true, but not particularly relevant, that Spaniards enjoy fewer civil liberties than Britons or Americans. It is true that Spain's living standards are low in comparison with Sweden's, but so are Greece's, so it is not particularly apposite to say so. It is true that a Spaniard still runs a far greater risk of arbitrary arrest and imprisonment than an Englishman; but there has probably never been a time when this was not true, so the fact has little to do with our assessment of Franco's rule.

Franco Spain, indeed, must be judged by the standards of Spain's own history. How does his régime compare with other Spanish régimes in modern history? How does it compare with the Republic? Has he left Spain a better place than he found it?

In all material senses, the average Spaniard, of all classes, is far better off than he was during the Republic. In welfare and amenities for the worker, this is equally true: the Republic attempted much but accomplished little. Agriculture is still a black spot, but here again Franco's régime has accomplished more than the Republic did.

In quantitative terms, education has made considerable strides under Franco (although Spain remains one of the most backward countries of western Europe in this respect). In qualitative terms, the picture is less satisfactory: the hold of the Church on education is not, in certain respects, conducive to the enlightenment of the pupils. It was not, on the other hand, politically possible – even if it had been his personal inclination – for Franco to accept the important aid of the Carlists during the Civil War and not restore the Church's rights when it had ended in victory. Azaña had gone too far and too fast in laicizing the State; to restore what he had undone was therefore one of the principal war aims of the National Movement; not to have done so would have been unthinkable in view of the physical horrors inflicted on the Church and its representatives under the Republic's complacent gaze.

In general cultural terms, the Republic undoubtedly comes out better than Franco's régime. True, the visual arts continue to flourish. But the censorship, even now that pre-censorship has been abolished, lays a heavy hand on creative freedom. This, too, has been part of the price Spain is paying for the calm and order Franco has given her. It should not, however, be thought that the Republic was a consistent defender of publishing freedom. It may not have censored the newspapers, but it often suppressed them; the Monarchist *ABC* and the Catholic *El Debate* were the most prominent, but by no means the only newspapers that suffered suspension for carrying opinions of which the Republican authorities disapproved.

The regions, of course, are unhappier than they used to be. The Republic did not tackle the regional problem so much as simply give in to Basque and Catalan demands for autonomy and even independence. Since this was one of the causes of the Civil War, the restoration of a centralized and unitary State was one of the war aims of the victorious side. In consequence, the suppression of Basque and Catalan culture, as well as political aspirations, was carried to great lengths – possibly much too far. Now a new linguistic freedom in both areas is the rule: if this, in turn, goes too far and leads to further nationalistic agitation, a further dose of repression will be inevitable.

An important aspect of Franco's ordered State has been a great improvement in the average citizen's freedom from fear. This may seem paradoxical in a country that is still, to a reduced extent, a police State; but it is true. The average Spaniard has learnt not to be particularly interested in politics. If they *are* interested in politics, they face the limited choice of conformist activity through the all-embracing Movement, or perilous dissidence. If they choose the latter, they are in some danger of being locked up or fined; but much less so than years ago, and incomparably less so than in the years of retribution against the defeated side in the Civil War. On the other hand, their chances of being shot down in the street by political opponents, or kidnapped and murdered by the police, as happened to the unfortunate Calvo Sotelo, are insignificant. On balance, the gain is considerable.

The price of Spain's prosperity and of the improvement in freedom from fear has been the loss of freedom of association for political purposes. Under Franco, the price has been paid in full, and the net result has been a public gain. The old political associations – Christian Democrats, Socialists, Basque and Catalan nationalists among them – continue under the surface, however; and it is not certain that

Franco's successor will have the strength of will to keep them there. This uncertainty is indeed one of the factors in Franco's determination to stay in power to the end. In the meantime, the illegal Spanish Communist Party, though divided, probably fares better than other groups because its history and training have conditioned it to clandestinity.

The price of Spain's welfare system has been acquiescence in the Falangist 'vertical unions', in which the State and the employers, as well as the workers, play a part. Under men like Girón and Solís these *Sindicatos* have done more for the Spanish worker than foreign Communists and Social-Democrats may find it convenient to admit. But recent strikes and student demonstrations have disclosed a spreading reluctance to accept 'official' unions. A symptom of this latent discontent has been the emergence of illegal, but occasionally tolerated, *comisiones obreras*, which are freely elected trade unions within the *Sindicatos*. Many prominent members of the *comisiones obreras* are 'left-wing Falangists' – spiritual brothers of the *camisas viejas* who fought and dreamed with José Antonio; the *comisiones* also include an unknown number of Communists, trained in Czechoslovakia, France and other places.

Will the syndical organization prove flexible enough to meet the demands of workers and students for greater freedom in representation? It is hard to say. But it would be going a long way to state a preference for a return to the violent free-for-all of Spanish trade unionism in the days of the Anarchist CNT and Largo Caballero's UGT. There, too, on balance, is a net gain for Franco's State.

What of the corruption, which, it is alleged, is widespread among officials of the régime, and even in Franco's own family? (Nobody has suggested that Franco himself is corrupt; but then this was generally supposed to be true of Ngo Dinh Diem and, before 1949, Chiang Kai-shek, both of whom presided over notoriously corrupt régimes.) British libel laws make it difficult to give precise details of allegations, which in the nature of things, tend to come from political exiles and to be difficult to prove or disprove. That there has been corruption is certain. But it is equally certain that this is not particularly characteristic of the Franco régime. The Republic had its scandals of graft and corruption; and nobody who reads pages 589 to 591 of Salvador de Madariaga's *Spain*, and some of the extracts from the duke of Alba's dispatches quoted in this book can doubt that Dr Negrín did well financially out of the fall of the Second Republic, whose destinies he had guided in the last stages.

What is one to say of comparative standards of justice in Franco Spain and under the Republic? For a long time, Franco's justice was arbitrary and harsh. The retroactive 1939 Law on Political Responsibilities was a sweeping instrument for the settling of old scores, which brought many injustices in its train. The use of Military Courts for the trial of political offenders in effect kept the whole country under martial law until 1962, when various categories of offences were taken out of military jurisdiction. Article 29 of the 1966 Organic Law proclaims the absolute independence of the judiciary, but it remains to be seen whether such independence will be achieved. For old habits die hard, and too often, still, workers who exercise their new found right to strike, and editors their new freedom to publish, find themselves in trouble with the law.

Since one is comparing like with like, however, one should not imagine that the administration of justice was exemplary under the Republic. The Left suffered injustices when the Right was in power, and the Right was persecuted when the Left ruled. Franco's justice is still repressive (though far less than it used to be) but less capricious than the Republic's; as even Manuel Azaña, the ex-Prime Minister held for months on non-existent evidence on the orders of a right-wing (but Republican) Minister of Justice, might have testified.

It became dangerous to go to Church during the Republic's untrammelled lifetime, and suicidal or simply impossible in the areas under Republican control after July 1936. Since Spain remained a Catholic country, despite Azaña's anti-clericalism and Anarchist and Communist disapproval, this amounted to denying a fundamental freedom to the majority of the population. Under Franco, this freedom has been restored; and though compulsory religious instruction smacks of totalitarianism, Spaniards have not lost their alternative freedom of *not* attending Mass if they so choose. It must be added that until 1967, Spain's religious minorities (Protestants, Jews and Moslems), representing slightly more than one-tenth of one per cent of the population, were denied full freedom of worship. An admittedly inadequate bill on religious freedom was, however, passed by the Cortes in June 1967; so that, in this as in many other respects, Franco has at last provided a reform where it was needed.

Individual examples and broad comparisons can never, of course, in themselves be conclusive. But the Second Republic, for all the hopes it aroused initially in the minds of intellectual democrats and the breasts of the untutored, was a time of disorder and increasing violence, culminating in civil war. It will be remembered not as a brave experiment but as a dreadful failure. In comparison, and for all its undeniable defects, Franco's régime will stand recorded as the longest period of peace, stability and progress in modern Spanish history. The only comparable period during the past 150 years began in 1876 with the Bourbon Restoration and the promulgation of a new Constitution. It lasted sixteen years, until the beginning of Anarchist terrorism in Barcelona; or twenty-one years, if one extends it until 1897, when the great statesman Cánovas del Castillo was assassinated; or at the most twenty-two years if one stretches it still further until the Spanish-American War. This was the time of the liberal experiment in pre-arranged alternations of power, known as *turnismo* and invented by Cánovas. But it was also the heyday of landlord tyranny over the peasants and of official corruption on the grand scale; and it ended in failure and further violence.

That Franco has beaten Cánovas del Castillo's record of peace and quiet at the price of intellectual dullness is true enough. It may seem absurd that at a time when Spain is requesting association with the European Economic Community, it is still not possible for Spaniards to read and write what they please and associate with the like-minded outside the *Movimiento*. No doubt many Spaniards, especially the young, thankful though they might be to Franco for having given them peace, now feel it is time for a change and for more freedom. But this is not an argument Franco could listen to with any sympathy. To give freedom to the untutored, he might say, is to give the demagogue *carte blanche* to incite the mob to murder for the sake of a millennium that cannot come. The Spaniard is not ready for freedom; even the technological revolution comes as a shock to men and women who see the twentieth century around them but are not yet fully conditioned to make it work. Give them freedom – only the mildest dose – and look what happens: strikes and student riots. Thinking this way, and knowing what is best for his people – and indeed he has never doubted whether he knew – Franco is not the man to open the floodgates. And perhaps he is right: even now, even in 1967. Spain has made a great and enduring contribution to European and world civilization; but she stands slightly apart from

Western Europe, in some respects backwards, in others simply aloof in her uniqueness.

No amount of criticism on philosophical or doctrinal grounds can obscure the central fact of Franco's achievement in giving Spain more than a quarter-century of stability and material progress. Of all Spain's statesmen of the past 150 years, only Cánovas del Castillo and Miguel Primo de Rivera challenge him in stature. But his achievements are greater than theirs.

2 *The World*

As the undiluted Nationalist myth has it, Franco saved not only Spain but the West as a whole from Communism. Since this is so clearly an over-simplification, the myth needs to be looked at more closely.

The Nationalist myth asserts that Spain was heading for Communism when the uprising began; and that the *Alzamiento*, for whose success General Franco was responsible, made sure that the destination was not reached. It is, I think, difficult to test the truth of such assertions without attempting to answer some hypothetical questions:

– Would Spain have become a Communist country if there had been no military uprising?

– Would Spain have gone Communist, once the Civil War had begun, if Franco's side had been defeated?

– What would have happened if Franco had remained in a subordinate position while the conflict lasted?

The Nationalists confuse the issue by lumping all their Republican opponents together – Communists, Anarchists, Socialists, Freemasons and liberals – and calling them 'Reds' (while complaining about the other side's habit of lumping Franco's supporters together and calling them 'fascists'). What Spain was heading for in 1936 was not 'communism' but revolutionary anarchy. Stalin had his plans for Spain, and the Spanish Communists were at his disposal, but these plans probably did not include an attempt to seize power. This is not to say, however, that some form of Communist revolution was an unthinkable prospect. The first of our hypothetical questions assumes

23a The Francos 'at home'.

23b Franco with one of his grandchildren.

24 Franco presents his Organic Law to the Cortes, 22 November 1966.

– a large assumption – a situation in which the armed forces refrained from intervening. But even on this unlikely assumption, Spain would have had a civil war. The 1936 elections had damaged the Centre parties and enhanced the power of the Right, the Left and the extremes at both ends. There was a sharp and accelerating descent into disorder and violence, in which the Army, as such, played no part. Had there been no military uprising in July, the most likely outcome of this situation would have been a general settlement of accounts, in which the Falange, outnumbered by the combined forces of the Communists, Socialists and Anarchists, would have been wiped out. (Indeed it was the fear of just such an outcome that made José Antonio Primo de Rivera decide, though with great reluctance, to put his *milicias* at the disposal of the military conspirators.) This in turn would most likely have been followed by *ad hoc* regional revolutions – Anarchists in Barcelona, and certain agricultural areas, especially Andalusia; and Socialists in Madrid and other cities – in which the middle class and aristocracy would have been massacred in large numbers. These revolutions would have given the well-disciplined and fast-growing Communist Party a chance to take over power, in coalition with the Socialists, and quite possibly to attempt to restore order in the outer provinces in the name of the Republic.

Long before this, however, our hypothesis would have collapsed, for it is unthinkable to suppose that the Army would have stood idly by and allowed all this to happen. In a sense, therefore – the sense that emerges from this paragraph – the military uprising did indeed save Spain from 'Communism'. But it is not quite in this sense that the Nationalists would like their myth to be accepted.

Our second question is perhaps easier to answer with confidence. Once the Civil War had started, the Communists rapidly extended their influence; and in May 1937, when Negrín came to power after Largo Caballero had been ousted, they controlled what was left of the Republican State. A year later, having destroyed their Trotskyist rivals in Barcelona, their hold was more or less complete, though indirectly exercised.

The Munich crisis was the turning point for Spanish Communism. After Munich, the heart went out of the Republican forces and – more important still – Soviet supplies dwindled, so that a Nationalist victory became inevitable. One of the great and unanswerable questions of contemporary history will always be whether Chamberlain and Daladier were right or wrong to buy time at Munich by giving in to Hitler's demands. I am not concerned here with the wider implications of this question, but with the bearing it has on the Spanish situation. If Chamberlain and Daladier had picked up Hitler's gauntlet in 1938, it seems highly probable that Hitler and Mussolini would have withdrawn their forces from Spain; and not improbable that the Russians would have resumed their supplies to the Republic, with the help and encouragement of France and, at least, the approval of Britain. In these circumstances, Franco would presumably have been defeated and the Republic – dominated by the Communists – would have been victorious. In that event, the Prague technique of Communist take-over might have been tried out in Spain a decade earlier than it was.

To ask what would have happened if Franco had remained in a relatively subordinate position is to assume what almost did, in fact, happen, since it was Sanjurjo's death at the outset of the uprising that made Franco's rapid rise possible. Had Sanjurjo lived to lead the Nationalist forces, it is of course just possible that he would have carried them through to victory. And in that case, one must assume that the Monarchy would have been quickly restored, possibly to the satisfaction of the Carlists. Before that happened, there would probably have been a division of spoils, with Sanjurjo as Acting Chief of State and Franco as Commander-in-Chief.

I find it extremely difficult, for my part, to suppose that things would ever have got that far, even if Sanjurjo had survived. Whatever his military ability, the man was totally devoid of political instinct. Quite early in the game, he would have been faced with the political need – given Nazi and Fascist help – to lean towards the Falange at the expense of his supporters, the Carlists. He would have lacked the political skill to resolve the fundamental differences between his supporters, and most likely Franco's admirers would have found a way of bringing him to power, as they did against the wishes of Mola, politically a far more formidable enemy than Sanjurjo. What this amounts to saying is that when it came to a crisis, Franco soon stood out as superior to the others in all departments, and would have got to the top anyway. He was lucky, but luck alone does not account for his success.

·   ·   ·   ·   ·

Let us now build on the foundation of a hypothetical Republican victory in the Civil War. As I have said, the Communists, who already controlled the State in 1938, would have been better placed than any other political group to consolidate their hold on it after a Republican victory made possible by Soviet arms. (In a similar situation, Franco resisted the pressures of his Nazi and Fascist allies; the Communists, not being Nationalists, would have had no such compunction in their dealings with the Soviet Union.) In any case, since we are postulating a general European War in 1938 instead of 1939, there would have been no time for the Franco-Soviet pact to decay, or for the Nazi-Soviet pact to be signed. From the start, Russia would have been the West's 'gallant ally', and so would a Communist or near-Communist Spain.

Having disposed of France (and quite possibly of Britain, which was ill-prepared for conflict in 1938), Hitler would have invaded Spain and captured Gibraltar: there would have been no Franco to tangle him in double-talk. The Allied campaigns in North Africa would therefore almost certainly have become impossible. And America might well have stayed out of the European war.

Assuming, however, that Hitler had refrained from invading Spain, the West's alliance with the Soviet Union would have provided the ideal international climate for the consolidation of the Communists' hold on the Spanish Republic. Had the Allies nevertheless emerged the victors, Stalin's hold on Spain would have given him a forward base from which to strike at France and Italy. The Atlantic Alliance might have been impossible.

These situations are, of course, hypothetical. Two factual points do, however, emerge. One is that there *was* a Communist danger in Spain before the Civil War, and a greatly increased danger after it had started. Franco's victory removed it. In so doing – and this is the second point – it removed the probability that Hitler would strike at Gibraltar. A victorious Republic could have resisted Hitler – with all the force of an exhausted Army and its inferior equipment. It could not have stalled, as Franco did, until Hitler was forced to call the whole thing off.

It was not for nothing that General Alfred Jodl, Chief of the Operations Staff of the German High Command, told the Nuremburg tribunal after the war that 'General Franco's repeated refusal to allow German armed forces to pass through Spain to take Gibraltar' had been one of the major causes of Germany's defeat. This is what Winston Churchill was aware of when he made his speech in praise of Franco's neutrality, on 25 May 1944.

Churchill's appreciation of the Spanish tragedy varied in perceptiveness. There were flashes of insight and moments of patriotic doubt. In an article published in January 1937, he had written, prophetically: 'It does not ... follow that if General Franco wins he will be grateful to his Nazi and Fascist allies. On the contrary, the probability is that the first thought of all patriotic Spaniards, once delivered from their awful plight, will be to escort their rescuers to the nearest seaport.'[1] But on 30 December 1938, when convinced of the inevitability of a European war, he wrote of the danger of a totalitarian victory in Spain, and added: 'The victory of the Spanish Republicans would ... be a strategic security for British Imperial communications through the Mediterranean ...'[2] Churchill's earlier estimate turned out to be the correct one.

Though Franco acted as he did, during the Second World War, for purely Spanish motives, it is impossible to exaggerate the contribution his skill and patience made to the Allied victory. A Republican victory in the Civil War – or a Nationalist victory under less skilled guidance than Franco's – would have been disastrous for the West. The democracies therefore stand deeply – and however paradoxically – in debt to Franco's authoritarian and initially fascist-tainted régime. This is the measure of his importance in contemporary history.

While I prefer, as I have suggested, to leave it to a divinely qualified judge to decide on the moral issues involved in Franco's seizure and exercise of power, I cannot refrain from a few remarks on the subject. One important point is that Franco himself had virtually no responsibility for the state of affairs that led to the Civil War. In suppressing the Asturian revolution of 1934, he acted as the technical executant of the then Republican government's policy. He warned successive governments of the danger the State was running through their failure to maintain order, and offered his services to restore it. Had they accepted the offer, there would probably not have been a civil war. Finally, he took no part in the military conspiracy – to the extent that Mola and the others decided to go ahead without him.

And then, belatedly, he joined the uprising, with a call to action that far transcended the usual limits of a *pronunciamiento*. He was, I think, justified in doing so. The facts do not, in my view, support the opinion expressed by Gerald Brenan in his Preface to the second edition of his indispensable *The Spanish Labyrinth*: 'Of the folly and wickedness of the Military rising, dependent as it was upon foreign assistance, there can today be no two opinions.' There can, indeed, be two opinions. My own is that the government of the day – that of Casares Quiroga – ought to have seen that the State was breaking down, and ought to have heeded Franco's warning and called in the Army to restore order. A period of calm, even at the cost of relatively few lives, might have prevented the terrible tragedy that followed. It might even, ironically, have avoided the prolonged period of authoritarian rule which Spain has had under Franco.

Franco's attitude towards his enemies was ruthless and vindictive. It was, however, a typically Spanish attitude, whether of the Right or the Left. There are, of course, many exceptions; but often a dialogue with a Spaniard is, in fact, not a dialogue at all but two separate monologues. You make your speech, while the Spaniard listens politely. Then he makes his, which is unaffected by what you have just said. And so forth. V. S. Pritchett in the article to which I referred in the last chapter put it in these words, when describing an argument between two Spaniards:

> The whole performance illustrated the blindness of Spanish egotism. The speaker stares at you with a prolonged dramatic stare that goes through you. He stares because he is trying to get into his head the impossible proposition that you exist. He does not listen to you. He never discusses. He asserts. Only *he* exists.

This is profoundly true. The Spaniards are a deeply Manichean people, singularly unqualified for democracy (though this could change with literacy and affluence). There is good and there is evil; there is black and there is white; there is Spain and there is anti-Spain. In this respect, as in certain others, Franco is deeply Spanish, as were his enemies of 'anti-Spain'. They killed with the joy of removing class enemies of *their* anti-Spain. He killed his enemies because their removal would purify a poisoned and corrupted country. He killed, too – in the sense of sanctioning the numerous executions that followed the Nationalist victory – in a spirit of cold retribution. His enemies, on their side, would have killed on a mass scale, had they won; just as Fidel Castro's Left-wing victors killed Batista's followers on a shocking scale in Cuba after the *Fidelistas* had won. This was a Hispanic reaction. It was not – or is no longer – the Anglo-Saxon thing to do. But it is Spain we are writing about, not England or America. To point this out is not to express a moral judgment in favour of Franco's dreadful retribution, but to state matters that are fundamental to an understanding of Spain's history.

But to see Franco and his work whole, one cannot consider only the repressive side. If it is true that he virtually handed over State power to the fascists, it is also true that he broke the fascists when they had outlived their usefulness. And if it is true that he long kept his people deprived of civil liberties, it is also true that he has gradually liberalized his régime. There are still true reactionaries in his cabinet – men like Alonso Vega, the Minister of the Interior, and the Under-Secretary of the Cabinet, Carrero Blanco. But there are also men like Fraga Iribarne, the Minister of Information, and Castiella, the Foreign Minister who, though not true liberals, are relatively liberal. And it was Castiella's view, not the reactionaries', that prevailed early in 1967 when the draft Law on Religious Freedom was discussed at the Pardo Palace. Nor did Franco suppress opposition merely for the sake of suppression; for he used the order he had created for the sake of bringing the technological revolution to Spain. It is for all his works, and not his sins alone that he is responsible 'before God and History'.

Appendices

The texts that follow illustrate Franco's progression from military discontent to dissidence and political leadership. Most of the documents are not readily available elsewhere in English. The translations are by Isobel Crozier, revised by the author. Fidelity to Franco's involved and sometimes wilfully obscure style has been preferred to the tempting elegance of a translated paraphrase.

APPENDIX 1

Franco's talk to the Cadets of the Saragossa Military Academy, 14 July 1931*

Gentlemen Cadets: I should like to celebrate this farewell ceremony with the solemnity of former years, in which, to the strains of the National Anthem, we would unfurl our flag for the last time, and, like yesterday, you would kiss its rich colours, the chill of emotion passing over your bodies and clouding your eyes with the entreaty of the glories incarnated by it; but lack of an official flag restricts our fiesta to those emotional moments in which, making yourselves the object of our farewell, you receive my final advice in a lesson on military morals.

The General Military Academy has had three years of life and its splendid sun is now nearing its setting. Years that we lived at your side, educating you and instructing you and endeavouring to forge for Spain the most competent and virtuous body of officers which any nation could come to possess.

We derive intimate satisfaction from our thorny path when the best-qualified foreign technicians lavish the warmest praise on our work, studying and applauding our systems and pointing them out as a model among modern institutions of military teaching. Intimate

---

* There are several marginally different versions of this speech. The one used here appeared in *ABC* of 1 October 1966, in a supplement on the thirtieth anniversary of the Burgos decree proclaiming Franco 'Head of the Government of the State of Spain'.

satisfactions which we offer to Spain, proud of our work and sure of its finest products.

We studied our Army, its virtues and its vices, and, correcting the latter, we have enhanced the former to the extent that we were registering a real evolution in procedures and systems. Thus we saw rigid and archaic text-books give way before the thrust of a modern professorship conscious of its mission and at loggerheads with such bastard interests. . . .

The entrance examinations, now automatic and anonymous, before, a field rich with intrigues and influences, were not bastardised by recommendations and favour, and today you may be proud of your progress without being made to blush by the old vicious and obsolete procedures. There has been a profound revolution in military teaching, which used to carry with it, like an enforced corollary, the intrigues and passions of those who found profit in the maintenance of such pernicious systems.

Our Ten Commandments for the Cadet drew all that was most pure and salutary from our wise statutes to offer you as an indispensable creed that your life should follow; and in this day and age, in which chivalry and nobility are constantly in eclipse, we have endeavoured to guarantee your integrity as gentlemen, maintaining among yourselves a lofty spirituality.

At this time, therefore, when the reforms and new military dispositions close the doors of this centre, we must rise above and overcome in silence our intense sadness over the disappearance of our work, thinking altruistically: 'the machine is being dismantled, but the work remains' – for you are our work, the 720 officers who tomorrow are going to be in contact with the soldier, those who are going to care for and direct him, those who, constituting a large nucleus of the professional Army, must be, without wavering, paladins of loyalty, chivalry, discipline, the fulfilment of duty, and the spirit of sacrifice for the Fatherland, all of which qualities are inherent in the true soldier, and of these, discipline, that sublime virtue, indispensable to the life of armies, that you must look after like the most precious of your garments, takes first place.

Discipline! Never well-defined and understood. Discipline! Which does not confer merit when the character of an order is agreeable or tolerable to us. Discipline! Which takes on its true value when our thoughts counsel the opposite of what we are ordered to do, when our hearts struggle to rise in intimate rebellion, or when an order is marked by arbitrariness or error. This is the discipline we practise. This is the example we offer you.

Lift up your thoughts towards the motherland and sacrifice everything for it, for while the ordinary citizen has his freedom of will, those who receive in sacred trust the arms of the nation do not, and must dedicate all their actions to its service.

I want the comradeship born in these first times of military life spent together to last through the passing of the years, and your love for your chosen career of arms will always have as its guide the well-being of the Fatherland and consideration and mutual affection among the components of the Army, for, if you need each other in wartime, in peacetime it is indispensable to have learnt mutual understanding and esteem.

A companionship which entails help to the comrade in disgrace, happiness in his progress, applause for the outstanding and also energy to help the misguided or lost; but your generous feelings must be restained by a high concept of honour, so that you prevent those who transgress from day to day abusing the benevolence—that is, the complicity – of their companions, and who tomorrow may be promoted by chance, from becoming a pernicious example of immorality and injustice in the Army.

The concept of honour, which is not exclusive to a regiment, Service or corps, is the inheritance of the Army and is subject to the traditional rules of chivalry and nobility: he who hopes to protect the good reputation of his corps by snatching from another what he himself couldn't make use of, is committing a grave sin.

This is something that occurs so frequently that I must not stay silent about it, although there will be no tomorrow for further advice to you.

I cannot now tell you, as before, that you are leaving your own hearth here, as today it is going to disappear; but what I can assure you is that, once you are scattered around Spain, you leave it in our hearts and that in your future action we put our hopes and dreams; that when the passing of the years whitens your temples and your professional competence makes you masters, you will have to appreciate how great and lofty our bearing is, and then the memory of you and your serene judgment must be our most precious reward.

Let us feel today, in taking our leave of you, the satisfaction of duty fulfilled, and let us unite our feelings and aspirations for the greatness of the Fatherland, shouting together: 'Long Live Spain'.

Your General and Director, Francisco Franco.

APPENDIX 2

Letter from Franco to Casares Quiroga, Prime Minister, 23 June 1936*

Respected Minister,

The state of unrest which the latest military measures are causing in the souls of the Officers' Corps, is so serious that I would incur a grave responsibility and would be lacking due loyalty, if I did not impart to you my impressions on the military state of affairs and the dangers which it embodies for the discipline of the Army; such a lack of internal contentment and state of moral and material unrest does one perceive, although it is 'without outward manifestation' in the corps of officers and NCOs.

The recent measures reintegrating into the Army the Commanding Officers and officers sentenced in Catalonia (in 1934), and since the military movement of June 1917 has hardly changed – together with the recent promotions, aroused uneasiness within the greater part of the Army.†

The news of the incidents at Alcalá de Henares, with their fore-runners of provocations and aggressions on the part of extremist elements, linked together with the dislocation of garrisons, have, without doubt, produced a feeling of disgust, unhappily and clumsily made manifest in a moment of confusion, and, interpreted as a collective offence, it had the most serious consequences for the Commanding Officers and officers who took part in these deeds, and caused sadness and regrets in the military community.

All this, Sir, apparently demonstrates the faulty information which in this respect must be reaching Your Excellency; or, the ignorance which the collaborating military elements may have of the internal and moral problems of the military community. I would not wish that this letter should denigrate the good reputation which he who gives you information and advice on military matters possesses: he may sin through ignorance; but I permit myself to ensure, with the responsibility of my command and the seriousness of my past, that

---

* Source: *Centinelo*, p. 203.

† This sentence is very obscure in the original which reads:

Las recientes disposiciones que integran al Ejército los jefes y oficiales sentenciados en Cataluña y hoy dejados al arbitrio ministerial, que desde el movimiento militar de junio de 1917 no se había apenas alterado, así como las recientes promociones, despertaron la inquietud de una gran mayoría del Ejército.

the published arrangements allow the interpretation that the information which may have motivated them is unrealistic and sometimes contrary to patriotic interests, attributing to the Army, in your view, characteristics and vices very far removed from reality. Recently deprived of their commands were Commanding Officers, for the most part with brilliant pasts and exalted standing in the Army, who had to yield their posts – of the greatest distinction and responsibility – usually to someone, who, in the opinion of ninety per cent of his colleagues, is very poor in virtues. Those who approach the Institutions to fawn on them and to receive favour, have no more feeling for them, and are no more loyal to them because of their services of collaboration; these same men, in years past, made themselves conspicuous under the Dictatorship and the Monarchy.

Those who represent the Army as disaffected from the Republic are being untruthful. Those who imagine plots in accordance with their passions are lying. Those who adulterate or impugn the dignity and patriotism of the officers' corps, attributing to it symptoms of conspiracy and disaffection, are doing a poor service to the mother country.

The lack of dignity and justice of the civil powers in the administration of the Army in 1917 caused the emergence of the Military Juntas of Defence. Today one could almost say that the Military Juntas are [again] in existence.

The writings which clandestinely appear with the initials UME and UMR* are evident signs of their existence and harbingers of future civil disturbances, if you do not try to avoid them, a thing which I consider easy with measures of equity and justice.

The movement of collective indiscipline in 1917 was motivated in a large part by favouritism and arbitrariness in the question of transfers; it was produced in similar circumstances, but, however, to a lesser degree than those that prevail today in the corps of the Army.

I do not hide from you the danger inherent in the collective state of mind at the present moment, in which professional anxieties rejoin those of all good Spaniards, before the grave dangers of the Fatherland.

Even though I am many miles from the Peninsula, news which reveals that such a state of affairs exists, equally, or perhaps to a greater extent, in the Peninsular garrisons, including the military forces of public order, manages to reach me here.

Well-versed in discipline, to the preservation of which I have

* *Unión Militar Española* (anti-Republican) and *Unión Militar Republicana*.

dedicated myself during many years, I can assure you that such is the spirit of justice which reigns in our commissioned ranks, that any unjustifiedly violent measure would produce counterproductive effects in the general mass of the forces, who feel themselves at the mercy of anonymous actions and calumnious charges.

I consider it a duty to inform you of what I believe to be of such grave importance for military discipline, and this Your Excellency can personally prove, informing himself through those Generals and Commanding Officers, who, exempt from political passions, live in contact, and concern themselves with the intimate problems and feelings of their subordinates.

Very attentively, your most affectionate subordinate,
Francisco Franco.

APPENDIX 3

*Franco's Proclamation, 17 July 1936**

I, Francisco Franco Bahamonde, General, Commander-in-Chief of the forces of Morocco, make known that:

Once again the Army, united with the other forces of the nation has seen itself obliged to take the initiative from the great majority of Spaniards, who, with infinite bitterness, witnessed the disappearance of the object that united them in a common ideal: Spain.

It means re-establishing the rule of order inside the Republic, not only in its outward appearances and signs, but also in its very essence; for this, it is necessary to labour with justice, which does not distinguish between classes or social categories; these should be immune from both flattery and persecution, so that the country ceases to be divided into two groups: that of those who enjoy power and that of those whose rights are trampled underfoot; even in the case of laws made by the very same people who violated them.

* Source: *Crónica*, No. 7. Although this is known as the '2nd Proclamation', it was the first to be issued of the numerous documents drafted by Franco in the Canaries on 16 and 17 July 1936. The 1st Proclamation (not reproduced here, but declaring a State of War and prohibiting meetings and imposing censorship) was posted in the streets of Las Palmas early on the 18th. The 2nd Proclamation, under which Franco assumed command of dissident forces in Morocco, was read publicly in General Marina Street, Melilla, at 6 p.m. on 17 July, by Lt-Col Bartomeu, who was flanked by an escort of fifty men and a band of trumpets and drums. There followed the Manifesto of Las Palmas (Appendix 4), a message of greetings and encouragement to the General Officer Commanding, Melilla (not reproduced here), and a General Call to arms (Appendix 5).

The behaviour of each man will be a guide to the behaviour of Authority towards him. Authority is another element which has disappeared from our nation, but which is indispensable to every human community, whether it is a democratic régime or a Soviet one, in which it attains maximum harshness. The re-establishment of this principle of authority, forgotten in these last years, inexorably demands that the punishments be exemplary by the severity with which they are imposed and the rapidity with which they are carried out, without hesitation or vacillations.

As regards the working-class element, freedom to work remains guaranteed: coercion from one party or another will not be tolerated.

The aspirations of employers and workers will be studied and resolved with the greatest possible justice, in a plan of co-operation, trusting in the common sense of the latter and the charity of the former; fraternizing in reason, justice and patriotism, they will learn how to carry their social struggles into a common ground of understanding, to the benefit of all and of the country. He who voluntarily refuses to co-operate or impedes the achievement of these ends will be he who first and foremost will suffer the consequences.

[*Martial Law regulations are enumerated at this point.*]

Finally: I hope for the active co-operation of all patriotic people, lovers of order and peace, who were hoping for this movement, without necessarily being specially called upon to serve it, seeing that these people are without doubt the majority; by complacency, lack of civic valour, or absence of a bond to unite the efforts of all, we have been dominated up to now by audacious minorities, and subject to international orders of various kinds, but all equally anti-Spanish; for this reason I finish with a single cry, which I hope will be felt in all hearts and repeated by those of all persuasions: Long Live Spain!

APPENDIX 4

*Manifesto of Las Palmas**

SPANIARDS! To whomsoever feels a sacred love for Spain; to those of you, who in the ranks of the Army and Navy have made a profession of your faith in the service of the Mother Country; to those of you who swore to resist your enemies even unto death: the nation calls to her defence.

* Source: *Crónica*, No. 7. An English translation of this important text appeared in *Coles*, pp. 175-7. This is a fresh translation from the original.

The situation in Spain is becoming more critical with every day that passes; Anarchy reigns in most of her villages and fields; government-appointed authorities preside over the revolts, when they are not actually fomenting them. Differences are settled by pistol-shots and with machine-guns among the mobs of townspeople, who, traitorously and treacherously, kill each other, without the public authorities imposing peace and justice.

Revolutionary strikes of all kinds are paralysing the life of the nation, dissipating and destroying its sources of wealth, and creating a state of hunger that will drive working men to desperation.

Our monuments and artistic treasures are the object of the most virulent attacks from revolutionary hordes obeying orders which they receive from foreign elements who can count on the complicity or negligence of governors and petty officials.

The gravest crimes are committed in the cities and countryside, while the forces of public order remain quartered, corroded by the despair which provokes a blind obedience to leaders who mean to dishonour them. The Army, the Navy and other Service institutions are the target of the most vile and calumnious attacks, coming from those very people who ought to have upheld their prestige.

Emergency regulations merely serve to muzzle the people and ensure that Spain ignores what is happening outside the gates of her towns and cities, as well as to imprison her presumed political adversaries.

The Constitution, suspended and impaired for all, is suffering a total eclipse: neither equality before the Law, nor Liberty, shackled by tyranny; nor Fraternity, when hatred and crime have replaced mutual respect; nor unity of the Mother Country, menaced by the rending asunder of our land – which the powers themselves foment – rather than by regionalism; nor integrity and defence of our frontiers, when in the heart of Spain one hears foreign broadcasts predicting the destruction and partition of our soil.

The Judiciary, whose independence the Constitution guarantees, likewise suffers persecutions which weaken or divide it, and indeed, its independence receives the hardest blows.

Electoral pacts made at the cost of the integrity of the Mother Country itself, together with attacks on local authorities and safes, in order to falsify the records, constitute the mask of legality which rules over us. Nothing has checked the lust for power; the illegal dismissal of moderating elements; glorification of the Asturian and Catalan revolutions, the one and the other violating the Constitution, which, in the name of the people, was the fundamental Code of our Institutions.

To the revolutionary and unheeding spirit of the masses hoaxed and exploited by the Soviet agents who veil the bloody reality of that régime which sacrificed twenty-five million people in order to exist, are joined the maliciousness and negligence of authorities of all kinds, who, sheltered by a crippled power, lack the authority and prestige.

Can we consent one day longer to the shameful spectacle we are presenting to the world?

Can we abandon Spain to the enemies of the Mother Country, handing her over without a struggle and without resistance, by our cowardly and traitorous behaviour?

No; that we cannot do! Let the traitors do that, but not we who have sworn to defend her.

Justice and Equality before the law we offer you; peace and love between Spaniards. Liberty and Fraternity without libertinage and tyranny. Work for all. Social justice, accomplished without rancour or violence, and an equitable and progressive distribution of wealth without destroying or jeopardizing the Spanish economy.

But face to face with this, a war without quarter on the exploiters of politics, on the deceivers of the honest worker, on the foreigners and foreign-oriented people who openly or deceitfully endeavour to destroy Spain.

In these moments it is all of Spain which is risen seeking peace, fraternity and justice; in every region, the Army, the Navy and forces of public order are rushing to defend the Mother Country. The energy expended in the maintenance of order will be commensurate with the magnitude of the resistance offered it.

Our impulse is not determined by the defence of some bastard interests; nor by the desire to retrace our steps in the road of history: because the Institutions, be they what they may, must guarantee a minimum of conviviality between citizens, who, despite the illusions cherished by so many Spaniards, have seen themselves cheated, despite the transigence and indulgence of all the national organisms, by an anarchic reply whose reality is unfathomable.

As the purity of our intentions restrains us from choking off those conquests which represent an advance in politico-social betterment, and the spirit of hate and vengeance has no sanctuary in our breasts, we shall know how to salvage as much as is compatible with Spain's internal peace and her aspired greatness from the wreckage that will afflict some of our legislative experiments, making realities in our country, for the first time, and in this order, of the trilogy of Fraternity, Liberty and Equality.

Spaniards: Long live Spain! ! !

Long live the honourable Spanish people! ! !

> Commanding General of the Canary Islands,
> Santa Cruz de Tenerife, at 5.15 a.m., 18 July 1936.*

APPENDIX 5

General Call. Santa Cruz de Teneriffe,
18 July 1936, at 7.10 a.m.†

The General, Military Commander of the Canary Islands to the General Officer Commanding, the 1st, 2nd, 3rd, 4th, 5th, 6th, 7th and 8th Organic Divisions in Madrid, Seville, Valencia, Barcelona, Saragossa, Burgos, Valladolid, Corunna; to the Military Commander of the Balearics; to the General Officer Commanding, the Cavalry Division, Madrid; to the Head of the Military Regions of Ceuta and Larache; to the Commander of the military forces of Morocco, and to the Admirals Commanding, the naval bases of El Ferrol, Cadiz, and Cartagena.

In a radiogram of today's date I say the following to the General Commanding, the Eastern Military Region of Africa: Glory to the heroic Army of Africa: Spain above all. An enthusiastic greeting to those garrisons which join you and other Peninsular companions in these historic moments. Blind faith in victory. Long Live Spain with Honour. This I say for Your Excellency's information.

APPENDIX 6

Telegram to International Control Committee (Tangier),
21 July 1936‡

I have the honour of informing Your Excellency that the crews of the ships of the Spanish battle fleet anchored in the Bay of Tangier, which are in a state of mutiny because their officers have been

---

* The *Manifesto of Las Palmas* was broadcast over Tetuan Radio (Morocco) on the night of the 17th, no indication of its origin being given to listeners.

† Source: *Crónica*, No. 7.

‡ Source: *Centinela*, p. 245.

forcibly arrested on board the *Tofiño*, have shown their intention of attacking the open cities of this zone, as well as the places under Spanish sovereignty. Acceptance of this de facto situation would amount to admitting the principle that pirate ships can take refuge in Tangier and use its port as a base for provisioning and operations against the Moroccan, Spanish and Portuguese coasts, and Gibraltar. In consequence, cannon, machine-guns, and air-dropped bombs may make themselves heard in these places. In anticipation of any incident involving *force majeure* that would oblige me to take measures to anticipate (*sic*) this eventuality, I declare myself always disposed to respect the Statute of Tangier, as well as the life and properties of its inhabitants.

I have the honour of appealing to your authority in the International Zone, so that, as far as possible, the said naval units be placed in a state of neutrality, especially as their possible acts of violence could cause harm among the civil population; though they will have no influence whatever on my resolution strictly to maintain the order and discipline of these territories.

APPENDIX 7

Telegram to International Control Committee (Tangier), 22 July 1936*

I have once again the honour of drawing Your Excellency's attention to the dangerous activities that are taking place in Tangier at the present time, with the complicity of Sr Prieto del Río. Thus, four vehicles of the Tetuán–Tangier mail line have been detained on your initiative, obliging me to interrupt a service of public benefit. According to my information, one of the mutinous warships of the Spanish squadron anchored in Tangier has weighed anchor with the intention of bringing a cargo of arms, which, also under the protection of Sr Prieto del Río, is to be distributed among the revolutionary elements of the International Zone. A mob of this kind, armed and excited by the prospect of pillage, constitutes, more for Tangier than the Spanish Zone, a danger the gravity of which needs no exaggeration. I am convinced that the Control Committee will not take upon itself the responsibility of tolerating the organization of violence and banditry on a large scale in Tangier, and that it will put an end to

* Source: *Centinela*, p. 246.

these disturbances and intrigues, which are only possible through the abuse of diplomatic privileges and the hostility of those in the International Zone.

APPENDIX 8

Telegram to International Control Committee (Tangier), 7 August 1936. *

Further to my note Number 1,393, of the 4th instant, I have the honour to point out to Your Excellency that, in spite of the agreements reached by the Control Committee, the Communist units of the Spanish squadron make use, with complete safety, of the roads of Tangier as a base for operations and supplies. The *Tolfiño*, moored to the quay, has converted itself into the flagship of this squadron, and its Headquarters and Command are to be found there; on its orders attacks are made on the security and commercial freedom of the Spanish Zone by brutal and sporadic acts which violate the principle of the open door as laid down under the Act of Algeciras. Your Excellency will find in the attached memorandum proof of the role played by the *Tolfiño* in international waters and its barefaced way of violating the Act of Algeciras and the Statute of Tangier. In addition, here is confirmation of the intrigues which I had previously denounced to the Control Committee, of Sr Prieto and of one Cerdeira in the former Consulate General of Spain in Tangier.

On the nights of the 5th and 6th instant, bands of fifty Red Militiamen, equipped with pistols, submachine-guns and various other arms furnished by the pirate squadron and distributed in the Consulate General of Spain, invaded the Kehla del Fahs and organized watch patrols facing the Spanish posts of Bordj and the International Bridge. In view of the gravity of such a violation of Tangier's neutrality and principally of Article 10 of its Statute, and in view of this threat to the Spanish Zone, I ask Your Excellency to advise the Control Committee and the Administration of Tangier, that if within a period of 48 hours they have not taken effective measures for the definitive withdrawal of the *Tofiño* and all the pirate warships in international waters, and for the disarming, dispersing and punishing of the bands established in the hinterland of this zone, I decline all responsibility as to the inevitable consequences of this state of

* Source: *Centinela*, p. 247.

affairs, which is absolutely contrary to prevailing treaties. As the Statute has been violated by the Administration of Tangier, and there is no guarantee whatever as to the neutrality of the International Zone, I shall consider myself at liberty to take my own measures to guarantee the security and peace of the Spanish Zone against the aggressions schemed in Tangier.

Notes on sources

Journalists conceal sources, and historians reveal them. Since this book partakes of journalism as well as history, revelation must compete with concealment, especially where informants would prefer their identities to remain unstated.

Broadly speaking, the 'journalistic' sections are Part I, 1, and the whole of Parts VI and VII. On the other hand, Parts II, III, IV and V deal with events of which I had no journalistic experience, and constitute the 'historical' sections of this biography. Many facts unearthed by research have, of course, been checked with surviving participants in the events described; but this 'journalistic' device was popularized by Thucydides and therefore bears an honourable historical stamp.

In writing Parts IV and V, which deal respectively with Franco's role in the Spanish Civil War and the Second World War, I drew heavily on three important collections of documents, one of them neglected, the other two, as far as I know, previously untapped. The neglected source consists of the hitherto unpublished documents captured from the German Archives at the end of the World War, and covering the period from the end of 1941, which is as far as the published *Documents on German Foreign Policy* go. The documents that remain unpublished throw a new light on Franco's relations with Hitler and provide important evidence on the German Führer's plans to invade Spain. I have been able, in a number of cases, to verify my findings by consulting the Spanish Archives.

A major primary source on Nationalist policy during the Civil War, and extensively used in Part IV, is the *Noticiero de España*, a weekly news bulletin produced by Franco's Press Office in Burgos from the beginning of September 1937. Intended both for his own information at a desperately busy time, and for the edification of leading members of his 'Movement', it was a curious mixture of factual information and propaganda of the kind that emanates from all governments of countries at war. Its special interest lies in the fact that it was produced for internal consumption by a small, selected readership. In its original form, only half a dozen copies or so of each issue were produced. Until towards the end of the Civil War, each number consisted of typewritten sheets or carbon copies, with photographs pasted down on separate pages, the whole held together in office files. Later, the *Noticiero* was duplicated in slightly larger numbers; it ran well into the Second World War, the last issue, No. 204, being dated 6 September 1941. Issues often reached a hundred pages and more. Its coverage was surprisingly wide, ranging over international affairs as well as Spanish developments, and including book reviews. Particularly valuable were the economic analyses of M. Sebastián, and the military ones by L. M. Lojendio.

The other major primary source has been the Spanish Foreign Ministry Archives. It is, by definition, difficult to gain access to Spanish State papers; for where the British have – or had – a fifty-year rule (lately shortened to thirty years), the Spaniards have a '1900 rule'. Anything that happened this century is out of bounds. This is hard on historians, since the banned period lengthens every year. One day, perhaps, the starting year will be advanced; until it is, scholarly requests are perforce circumscribed. (A further obstacle lies in the amiable chaos that reigns over Spanish archives and libraries in general.)

The Spanish authorities, however, kindly made much hitherto inaccessible material available to me, especially the dispatches of Franco's envoy to London, the duke of Alba, from 1938 to 1945. During this entire period, Franco conducted his own foreign policy. His instructions to the duke, and the duke's responses, are of the highest interest. Lively in style, always perceptive – although clearly owing more to the British right-wing politicians among whom he naturally moved, than to the Labour politicians among whom he was *persona non grata* – invariably accurate and fearless, the duke's dispatches were a vital factor in Franco's determination to keep out of the World War in the face of Hitler's threats and blandishments. My selection from this rich and fascinating collection has, of course, been confined to material of direct relevance to Franco's conduct of affairs. It includes accounts, hitherto unpublished, of conversations about Spain with Winston Churchill, Anthony Eden and other British statesmen and politicians.

Yet another important source has consisted of written answers, often copious and detailed, to questions of fact and chronology which I addressed at intervals to General Franco's Civil and Military Households, and which were invaluable to me in settling disputed dates, in explaining, sometimes in the General's own words, his attitude at various critical times, and generally in supplementing disclosures in my direct exchanges with Franco.

Specific references to books and documents are tabulated in the next section of this book. The notes that follow draw attention to sources, both primary and secondary, which I found useful, and introduce them approximately in the order of their appearance. The more important books are given brief descriptive notes; others are simply listed. This is therefore a selected bibliography; although the list includes some of the books that do not bear specific source references, it is by no means an exhaustive one.

Part I: Man, Myth and History

The opening chapter was written in Madrid in November 1965, immediately after my first audience with Franco, and remains substantially untouched. Though mainly impressionistic, it does draw on:

Luis de Galinsoga, in collaboration with General Franco Salgado, *Centinela de Occidente* (Barcelona, 1956). By a time-serving journalist who was later forced out of the editorship of the *Vanguardia Española* in a storm of Catalan indignation against him as a Castilian appointee and who died in 1967. Though sycophantic, the most important single source on Franco's life. Most of the material was provided by Franco's cousin, admirer, constant companion and aspiring Boswell, General Franco Salgado. (Henceforth, *Centinela.*)

Joaquín Arrarás, *Francisco Franco* (Burgos, 1938). First of the 'approved' biographies. Adulatory but fresh; valuable for Moroccan period and initial phase of Nationalist rising. (Henceforth, *Arrarás, Franco.*)

Captain B. H. Liddell Hart, *The Other Side of the Hill* (London, 1948.) Valuable insights on Nazi attitudes towards Spain. (Henceforth, *Liddell Hart.*)

Count Galeazzo Ciano, *Diplomatic Papers, 1936–42*, ed. Malcolm Muggeridge (London, 1948). A rich source. (Henceforth, *Ciano, Papers.*)

'Luis Ramírez', *Francisco Franco: Historia de un Mesianismo* (Paris, 1964); French translation (Paris, 1965). Name hides identity of an unknown enemy of Franco's. A Nationalist critic, J.-M. Garate Cordoba (in a useful essay on Franco's biographers, in the literary review *Punta Europa*, Madrid, February 1966) describes the author as a Spanish Communist exiled in France, but Ramirez claims to be a Christian Democrat living in Spain. In fact, he often writes from the Marxist standpoint. Sourly hostile, but factual and interesting on Franco's early life, though he never mentions sources. From the Civil War on, a polemic of little value. (Henceforth, *Ramírez.*)

Claude Martin, *Franco, Soldado y Estadista* (Madrid, 1965). By a long way, the best 'approved' biography, consistently accurate, chronologically sound and historically in perspective. Sycophantic, nevertheless, because it omits or elides anything that might damage Franco's reputation. Able Spanish translation by José Patricio Montojo is more up to date than the original French (Paris, 1959), and translator's notes are original and informative. (Henceforth, *Martin*.)

Hugh Thomas, *The Spanish Civil War* (London, 1961). Brilliant and comprehensive study, unfortunately marred by many inaccuracies, even in revised Penguin edition (London, 1965) to which my source references apply. Though misleading in details, and basically pro-Republican, broadly speaking presents true and objective picture. (Henceforth, *Thomas.*)

Gabriel Jackson, *The Spanish Republic and the Civil War, 1931–39* (Princeton, N.J., 1965). Painstaking and usually accurate, but inconsistent and partisan (Republican bias). (Henceforth, *Jackson.*)

Part I, 2, is an interpretative synthesis. I acknowledge, as others have, a debt to:

Gerald Brenan, *The Spanish Labyrinth* (Cambridge, 1962, 2nd edition). The most profound inquiry into social background to Spanish Civil War. Decreasingly reliable and intellectually honest as it approaches 1936; evidence assembled does not bear out conclusions drawn. (Henceforth, *Brenan.*)

Also useful:

C. A. M. Hennessy, *Modern Spain* (London, 1965). A brilliantly succinct introduction.

Encyclopædia Britannica (1955 ed.), vol. 21, pp. 131–41, article by Professor William Christopher Atkinson.

H. Livermore, *A History of Spain* (London, 1958). Clear and readable.

Raymond Carr's massive *Spain 1808–1939* (Oxford, 1966), which appeared after this chapter was finished, reaches conclusions very similar to mine about the breakdown of liberalism in Spain. (Henceforth, *Carr.*)

Part II: War

Consistently useful: *Arrarás, Franco, Martin* and *Centinela*. Some useful material in:

S. F. A. Coles, *Franco of Spain* (London, 1955). Patchy and padded with frivolous digressions. (Henceforth, *Coles.*)

Francisco Salva Miquel and Juan Vicente, *Francisco Franco* (Barcelona, 1959). Anecdotal hagiography.

For general background:
Brenan; and Salvador de Madariaga, *Spain* (London, 1961): readable, generous, liberal and illuminating, especially on failure of Spanish Republic; view of Franco obscured by blind spot. (Henceforth, *Madariaga*.)

For Moroccan background:
Above all, Franco's 1922 journal, *Diario de una Bandera* (reprinted, Madrid, 1956). Also:
General Goded, *Marruecos, las Etapas de la Pacificación* (Madrid, 1932). Standard military history. (Henceforth, *Marruecos*.)
Enciclopedia Universal Illustrada (Bilbao). Together with *Marruecos*, early volumes (published long before Franco was in power), authenticate Franco's precocious feats of arms.

Viscount de Eza, *Mi Responsabilidad en el Desastre como Ministro de la Guerra* (Madrid, 1923). A former War Minister's apologia for the Anual disaster.

Some factual material in a long string of apologias of the general by other generals (though facts are not their strong point), notably:
General Carlos de Silva, *General Millán Astray* (Barcelona, 1956).
General Jorge Vigón, *General Mola, el Conspirador* (Barcelona, 1957).
General Esteban Infantes, *General Sanjurjo* (Barcelona, 1957).
General F. Javier Marinas, *General Varela* (Barcelona, 1957).

Part III: Peace

This part deals with the dying phase of the monarchy, and with the Republic until the outbreak of the Civil War. *For biographical detail, Martin, Centinela* and *Arrarás, Franco,* remain indispensable.
For historical background:
Madariaga, Carr, Thomas and *Jackson*, all useful in apposition, and sometimes opposition, to each other; the most objective, though not always the most readable, is *Carr*.

Henry Buckley, *The Life and Death of the Spanish Republic* (London, 1939). Engaging eye-witness account by a British journalist with strong Republican sympathies. Still resident in Madrid, Mr Buckley has shed earlier hostility towards Franco; but his book remains fresh and essential.

Joaquín Arrarás, *Historia de la Segunda República Española*, vols I and II (Madrid, 1964); Vol. III in preparation. This major work by a

Nationalist, though partisan, is objectively factual, generally accurate and lively in style. Far more substantial than the same author's biography of Franco. Overwhelming indictment of the Republic. The final volume not having appeared when this book was being written, source references to latter period are to author's own one-volume abridgment of entire work (Madrid, 1965).

Historia de la Cruzada Española, ed. Arrarás, 44 vols (Madrid, 1940–3). Officially sponsored, and propagandist, but enormously informative.

On the fall of Primo de Rivera's Dictatorship and of Alfonso XIII, the works of two distinguished brothers, sons of a statesman:

Gabriel Maura y Gamazo, *Bosquejo Histórico de la Dictadura* (Madrid, 1930). Intellectually rigorous; severe on Primo de Rivera.

Miguel Maura, *Así Cayó Alfonso XIII* (4th ed., Barcelona, 1966). Leading memoir by a former Republican Minister; shows Manuel Azaña's indifference to order as a major cause of the Spanish conflict.

Other memoirs and chronicles:

Emilio Mola Vidal, *Obras Completas* (Valladolid, 1940). Provides insight into bitterness and frustration of a literary general who was the leading Nationalist conspirator.

Manuel Azaña y Díaz, *Memorias Íntimas* (ed. Arrarás, Madrid, 1939); and *Mi Rebelión en Barcelona* (Bilbao, 1935). A considerable writer who failed as a statesman.

Gonzalo Queipo de Llano, *El General Queipo de Llano* (1930); and *El Movimiento Reivindicativo de Cuatro Vientos* (Madrid, 1931). A swashbuckler reminisces.

Diego Hidalgo, *¿ Por qué fui Lanzado del Ministerio de la Guerra?* (Madrid, 1934). Republican Minister who admired Franco.

Alejandro Lerroux, *La Pequeña Historia* (Buenos Aires, 1945). A shady but flamboyant politician's memoirs.

Indalecio Prieto, *Discursos en America* (Mexico, 1944). A relatively moderate Socialist leader looks back.

E. López de Ochoa, *De la Dictadura a la República* (Madrid, 1930); and *Campaña Militar de Asturias en Octubre de 1934* (Madrid, 1936). A Republican general executed by the Republicans.

On the rise of Spanish fascism:

Stanley G. Payne, *Falange* (London, 1962). One of the best books on contemporary Spain, by an American scholar. (Henceforth, *Payne.*)

Felipe Ximénez de Sandoval, *José Antonio* (*Biografía Apasionada*) (Barcelona, 1941).

On the rise of Communism in Spain:

José Manuel Martínez Bande, *La Intervención Comunista en la Guerra de España* (Madrid, 1965). An official publication; factual and accurate. English translation now available (1967).

Leonard Schapiro, *The Communist Party of the Soviet Union* (London, 1960). Most authoritative treatment of subject.

On the origins and development of religious persecution by the Republic:

Antonio Montero Moreno, *Historia de la Persecución Religiosa en España, 1936–1939* (Madrid, 1961). Exhaustive treatment.

Part IV: Civil War

Among the biographies, *Martin* and *Centinela* remain indispensable. Also:

Fernando de Valdesoto, *Francisco Franco* (Madrid, 1945). Anecdotal hagiography; occasionally useful.

General Millán Astray, *Franco el Caudillo* (Salamanca, 1939). Adulatory speeches and articles by Franco's former chief in the Spanish Foreign Legion.

Among the general works, *Thomas, Jackson, Madariaga, Carr* and *Cruzada*. An outstanding new documentary source is the serialized *Crónica de la Guerra Española* (Buenos Aires, 1966–7); rich in contemporary photographs and Press coverage, and evidently written with unstated cooperation of Spanish authorities. If a definitive history of the Civil War is ever written, it will need to cover the same ground as *Crónica* and take account of two outstanding first productions of the official *Sección de Estudios Sobre la Guerra de Liberación de España*: *Cien Libros Básicos Sobre la Guerra de España*, and *Los Documentos de la Primavera Trágica*, both edited by Ricardo de la Cierva y Hoces (Madrid, 1966). From 1937 on, a major primary source is *Noticiero de España*, published in Burgos, then in Madrid (see introduction to these Notes).

On the Nationalist military conspiracy:

Cruzada and *Arrarás, Historia.*

Félix Maíz, *Alzamiento en España* (Pamplona, 1952). Carlist account.

Manuel Goded, *Un Faccioso Cien por Cien* (Saragossa, 1938). Son vindicates father's memory.

José María Iribarren, *Con el General Mola* (Aragon, 1937).

Felipe Bertrán Guëll, *Momentos Interesantes de la Historia de España en este Siglo: Preparación y Desarrollo del Alzamiento Nacional* (Valladolid, 1939).

Antonio Lizarza Iribarren, *Memorias de la Conspiración: Cómo se Preparó en Navarra la Conspiración* (Pamplona, 1953). Carlist account.

José Antonio Primo de Rivera, *Obras Completas* (Madrid, 1952). By the founder of the *Falange*.

Juan Antonio Ansaldo, *¿Para qué?* (Buenos Aires, 1951). A disgruntled monarchist who piloted the plane in which Sanjurjo met his death.

On Franco's role and involvement with Axis Powers:

Cruzada, Centinela.

Luis Bolín, *Spain: the Vital Years* (London, 1967). Interesting memoirs of journalist who organized Franco's flight from Canaries to Morocco and later became his Press chief in Salamanca.

Charles Foltz, Jr, *The Masquerade in Spain* (Boston, 1948).

Roberto Cantalupo, *Fu la Spagna* (Milan, 1948). A self-pitying memoir by Mussolini's first envoy to Franco's régime. Of outstanding interest and value.

Count Galeazzo Ciano, *Ciano's Diary, 1937–38*, intr. Malcolm Muggeridge (London, 1947). Yields interesting details.

Dr Karl Abshagen, *Canaris* (London, 1956).

Documents on German Foreign Policy, Series D (1937–45), vol. III, *Germany and the Spanish Civil War, 1936–39.* A mine of information. (Henceforth, *Documents.*)

Dante A. Puzzo, *Spain and the Great Powers, 1936–41* (New York, 1962). Competent synthesis, marred by Republican bias.

On Franco's rise to supreme power:

General Alfredo Kindelán, *Mis Cuadernos de Guerra* (Madrid, 1955). A kingmaker's recollections, important though wildly inaccurate.

Jean Créac'h, *Le Coeur et l'Epée* (Paris, 1958). By a French journalist, long resident in Spain. Inaccurate, but not without insight.

On the international Communist conspiracy:

Jesús Hernández Tomás, *Yo, Ministro de Stalin en España* (2nd ed., Madrid, 1954).

General Walter Krivitsky, *Yo, Jefe del Servicio Secreto Militar Soviético* (Guadalajara, 1945). Of great interest. Available in English: *In Stalin's Secret Service* (New York, 1939).

Luigi Longo, *Le Brigate Internazionali in Spagna* (Rome, 1956). By the present head of Italian Communist Party. Louis Fischer, *Men and Politics* (London, 1941). Burnett Bolloten, *The Grand Camouflage* (London, 1961). Not the most readable account, but perhaps of no other book on contemporary Spain can it be said that it defies fault-finding.

David T. Cattell, *Communism and the Spanish Civil War* (Berkeley, 1955).

On military matters:

Manuel Aznar, *Historia Militar de la Guerra de España* (Madrid, 1961 ed.). A Nationalist account.

Noticiero:

Robert G. Colodny, *The Struggle for Madrid* (New York, 1958). Outstanding.

A leading contemporary social account: Franz Borkenau, *The Spanish Cockpit* (London, 1937).

On the Burgos period:

Payne, Documents, Centinela, Martin. Ramón Serrano Súñer, *Entre Hendaya y Gibraltar* (Madrid, 1947). The liveliest Spanish memoir of the period, by a man who became second only to Franco in power. (Henceforth, *Entre Hendaya*).

Sir Robert Hodgson, *Spain Resurgent* (London, 1953). By Britain's semi-official envoy to Burgos.

Duke of Alba's Dispatches (Spanish Foreign Ministry Archives). (Henceforth, *Alba.*) See introduction to these Notes.

On reprisals after the Civil War:

Spain and the Rule of Law (International Commission of Jurists, Geneva, 1962). A hostile pamphlet with useful factual and documentary material. (Henceforth, *Jurists.*)

Foltz, Jackson, Thomas and *Payne* all contribute something; so, among the favourable accounts, do *Hodgson* and Sir Arthur F. Loveday, *Spain 1923–48* (London, 1949) – a plodding work with many useful facts. (Henceforth, *Loveday.*) One anecdote (favourable) comes from: José María Doussinague, *España Tenía Razón* (Madrid, 1949) – a first-rate memoir, despite its petulant, defiant tone, rich in quotations from documents to which the author had access as permanent head of the Spanish Foreign Ministry, some of which appear to be still in his possession.

Part V: World War

On Franco Spain's relations with Axis Powers:

Documents are the major published source. In this section I have drawn heavily from Vols III, VIII, XI and XII. Last volume ends series so far published, but merely takes the story to end of 1941. For major developments after that date, one must turn to documents still unpublished, which, *inter alia*, provide details of Hitler's later plans to invade Spain. These include many documents available in microfilm and still untranslated; and Walter Warlimont: *Die Strategie der Deutschen Obersten Führung im zweiten Vierteljahr 1943* (in typescript, 1950), or 'Strategy of the German Armed Forces High Command April–June 1943' (Historical division, European Command, Operational History Branch; Office of the Chief of Military History, Washington). Captain Sir Basil Liddell Hart's *Private Archives*, especially the original records of his post-war interrogations of German generals, and certain letters, provided interesting material (see introduction to these Notes). Also available, in mimeograph, are:

Fuehrer Conferences on Naval Affairs, 1940 (London, Admiralty, 1947), and *Fuehrer Naval Conferences, 1939–41, 1942* and *1943* (Washington, 1946–7). In sum, these typewritten, microfilmed or mimeographed documents correct distorted impressions aroused by:

The Spanish Government and the Axis (Washington, United States Government Printing Office, 1946, European Series 8, Official German Documents) – a deliberately misleading selection; and *Report of the Sub-Committee on the Spanish Question* (United Nations Security Council, New York, 1946).

Other important published sources include:

Kriegstagebuch des Oberkommandos der Wehrmacht, 1940–45 (Frankfurt-am-Main). Diary of the German High Command.

Hugh Trevor-Roper, ed., *Hitler's War Directives, 1939–45* (London, 1964) – texts from Walter Hubatsch, *Hitlers Weisungen für die Kriegführung, 1939–45*; and *Hitler's Table Talk, 1941–44* (London, 1953).

Walter Schellenberg, *The Schellenberg Memoirs: A record of the Nazi Secret Service*, with introduction by Allan Bullock (London, 1956).

Documents Secrets du Ministère des Affaires Etrangères d'Allemagne: Espagne. (French translation of a Soviet selection, Paris, 1946).

Ciano, Papers, and *Ciano's Diary, 1939–43*, ed. Malcolm Muggeridge (London, 1947). Both are important sources. In contrast, *I Documenti Diplomatici Italiani* (Rome, 1962), Ottava Serie, vol. XIII, yields only minor pickings.

Liddell Hart, Entre Hendaya and *Doussinague.*

Dr Paul Schmidt, *Hitler's Interpreter* (London, 1951).

Among *articles*, the following were specially useful:

Der Spiegel (Hamburg), No. 18 for 1963. Hitler's plans to unseat Franco. Introduction to article runs: '*Im Frühjar 1943 versuchten die*

Führer des Drittens Reiches, Spaniens kriegsunwilligen Diktator Francisco Franco durch eine Revolte in der Spanischen Einheitpartei, der Falange, zu stürzen und damit den Einmarsch deutscher Truppen ins neutrale Spanien zu ermöglichen' ('Early in 1943, the Führer of the Third Reich was seeking to overthrow the Spanish dictator, Francisco Franco, who was reluctant to enter the war, through a revolt in the single Spanish party, the Falange, and thereby make possible the entry of German troops into neutral Spain').

Military Review (Fort Leavenworth, Kansas), June 1964: *Hitler's Military Plans and Spain 1942–43*. By Charles B. Burdick. A scholarly piece of research, condensed from the same writer's longer article in *Wehrwissenschlaftliche Rundschau* for March 1963.

Revue de Défense Nationale (Paris), December 1964. *Hitler et l'Espagne*. By Henry Marchat.

La Vanguardia Española (Barcelona), 8, 15, 22 and 29 December 1963; and 8, 19 January and 2, 9, 16 and 23 February 1964. *La Estrategia de las Victorias Incruentas* ('The Strategy of Bloodless Victories'). By José Díaz de Villegas. An authoritative Spanish account.

On Franco Spain's relations with the Allied Powers, the most important published sources are:

Sir Samuel Hoare (Lord Templewood), *Ambassador on Special Mission* (London, 1946). Elegantly written, but petty and dishonest.

Carlton J. H. Hayes, *Wartime Mission in Spain* (New York, 1945). The American Ambassador is fairer and more objective than the British. A Spanish view of both books is in José María de Areílza, *Embajadores sobre España* (Madrid, 1947). See also *Doussinague, Loveday, Madariaga, Martin* and *Centinela*, and:

Eduardo Comín Colomer, *La República en el Exilio* (Madrid, 1957). (Henceforth, *Colomer.*)

Sir Winston Churchill, *Step by Step* (London, 1939) and *War Memoirs* (London, 1952), especially vols 5 (*Closing the Ring*) and 6 (*Triumph and Tragedy*).

K. W. Watkins, *Britain Divided: The Effect of the Spanish Civil War on British Political Opinion* (London, 1963). This calm and reasonably impartial study is worth reading.

A major unpublished source is *Alba* (see introduction to these Notes).

On Spanish domestic developments:

Payne (especially) and *Martin* are best; but *Doussinague, Loveday, Documents, Ciano, Diary, Hoare* and *Hayes* all yield useful material.

Part VI: 'Spanish Peace'

To a large extent, this section is based on my own material, including notes of interviews, BBC talks and articles, together with cuttings from the British, French, American and Spanish Press, especially *The Times*, *Daily Telegraph* and *The Economist* (London); *Le Monde* and *Le Figaro* (Paris); the *New York Times* and *Time* magazine (New York); and *ABC* and *Arriba* (Madrid). For convenience sake, most of my references are to:

Martin, Payne, and Benjamin Welles, *Spain: the Gentle Anarchy* (London, 1965). Mr Welles, a former *New York Times* correspondent in Spain, has packed much information into his readable but sometimes superficial book. Specially valuable on Spanish–American relations.

Madariaga and *Colomer* also yield some material.

Various official publications have been consulted.

These include:

25 Años de Paz Española (1964), in four volumes; and its small companion, *Viva la Paz: España Hoy*. Useful for statistics.

España en su Prensa, 1964, 1965 and 1966.

Crónica de un Año de España, 1963–4, 1964–5 and 1965–6.

Alianza Dinámica (1964). Official account of Spanish–United States treaties.

La España que no Perteneca a la OTAN. NATO without Spain.

The Spanish Red Book on Gibraltar (1965) and *The Spanish Proposals on Gibraltar* (1966).

Economic and Social Development Program for Spain, 1964–67, (Baltimore, 1965). English translation of key first volume of Spain's first development plan.

Leyes Fundamentales del Reino (Madrid, 1967). The redrafted texts of the Fundamental Laws, amounting to a new Constitution.

There is nothing of bibliographical interest in Part VII: '*Before God and History*'. Parts IV, V and VI have involved frequent references to Franco's interviews in many Spanish and foreign newspapers and to the official collections of his speeches:

Colección de Proclamas y Arengas del Excmo Sr General Don Francisco Franco (Seville, 1937).

Franco ha dicho, 1936–42 (Madrid, 1947).

Palabras del Caudillo (Madrid, 1943).

Discursos y Mensajes del Jefe del Estado, 1951–4.

Source References

Part 1: Man Myth and History

1. Man and Myth (pp. 3–13)

1. Luis de Galinsoga and Franco Salgado: *Centinela de Occidente*, p. 293. (Henceforth, *Centinela*.)
2. Joaquín Arrarás: *Franco*, p. 29. (Henceforth, *Arrarás, Franco*.)
3. *Ciano's Diplomatic Papers*, p. 402. (Henceforth, *Ciano, Papers*.)
4. Luis Ramírez: *Francisco Franco*, p. 61. (Henceforth, *Ramírez*.)
5. Claude Martin: *Franco, Soldado y Estadista*, p. 122. (Henceforth, *Martin*.)
6. Hugh Tomas: *The Spanish Civil War*, Appendix Two, pp. 789 *et seq*. (Henceforth, *Thomas*.)
7. Gabriel Jackson: *The Spanish Republic and the Civil War, 1931–39*, Appendix D, pp. 526 *et seq*. (Henceforth, *Jackson*.)

2. The Social and Historical Background (pp. 13–28)

1. H. Livermore: *A History of Spain*, p. 361. (Henceforth, *Livermore*.)
2. G. Brenan: *The Spanish Labyrinth*, p. 209. (Henceforth, *Brenan*.)
3. *Brenan*, p. 9.

Part II: War

1. Early Days (pp. 29–37)

1. *Arrarás, Franco*, p. 14.
2. S. F. A. Coles: *Franco of Spain*, p. 60, (Henceforth, *Coles*.)
3. *Ramírez*, p. 36.
4. Francisco Salva Miquel and Juan Vicente: *Francisco Franco*, p. 33.
5. *Martin*, p. 18.
6. Salvador de Madariaga: *Spain*, p. 79. (Henceforth, *Madariaga*.)

2. Moroccan Days (pp. 37–44)

1. General Goded: *Marruecos; las Etapas de la Pacificación*, pp. 29 and 33. (Henceforth, *Marruecos*.)
2. This account of Franco's first stay in Morocco is largely based on the biographies of Arrarás and Martin.
3. Jorge Vigón: *General Mola*, p. 25.

4. General Esteban Infantes: *General Sanjurjo*, p. 42. (Henceforth, *Sanjurjo*.)

3. Garrison Duty (pp. 44–53)

1. Private Information.
2. *Ramírez*, p. 67.
3. I am indebted to Joaquín Arrarás for this information.
4. *Coles*, p. 77.
5. *Martin*, p. 34, and translator's note.
6. *Brenan*, p. 64.
7. *Ramírez*, p. 70.
8. *Sanjurjo*, p. 63.
9. *Centinela*, p. 35.
10. General Carlos de Silva: *General Millán Astray*, p. 120. (Henceforth, *de Silva*.)

4. The Spanish Foreign Legion (pp. 53–69)

1. *De Silva*, pp. 128–9.
2. *Martin*, p. 55.

5. Enter a Dictator (pp. 69–79)

1. *Brenan*, p. 75.
2. *Martin*, pp. 62–3.
3. *Centinela*, pp. 83–4.
4. *Brenan*, p. 74.
5. *Martin*, pp. 68–9.
6. *Arrarás, Franco*, p. 100.
7. *Centinela*, p. 89.

6. The Alhucemas Landing (pp. 79–85)

1. *Arrarás, Franco*, p. 108.
2. *Centinela*, p. 97.
3. *Arrarás, Franco*, pp. 113–14.
4. *Marruecos*, p. 199.
5. *Ibid.*, p. 213.

Part III: Peace

1. The King's Favourite General (pp. 87–107)

1. *Martin*, p. 90.
2. *Ibid.*, pp. 91–92.
3. *Ibid.*, p. 92.

T

4. *Arrarás, Franco*, pp. 150–1.
5. Raymond Carr: *Spain 1808–1939*, p. 588. (Henceforth, *Carr*.) Also, E. López de Ochoa: *De la Dictadura a la República*, pp. 155–68.
6. *Madariaga*, p. 360.
7. *Martin*, p. 98.
8. *Arrarás, Franco*, pp. 156–7.
9. Henry Buckley: *The Life and Death of the Spanish Republic*, pp. 22–3. (Henceforth, *Buckley*.)
10. *Carr*, p. 592.
11. *Ibid.*, p. 595; Also, Alejandro Lerroux: *La Pequeña Historia*, pp. 53–8. (Henceforth, *Lerroux*.)
12. Gonzalo Queipo de Llano: *El General Queipo de Llano*, pp. 214–23.
13. *Martin*, pp. 99 (n.) and 100.
14. *Carr*, p. 594.
15. Emilio Mola Vidal: *Obras Completas*, p. 408. (Henceforth, *Mola*.)
16. *Mola*, pp. 410–12.
17. Gonzalo Queipo de Llano: *El Movimiento Reinvindicativo de Cuatro Vientos*, esp. p. 92 *et seq.*
18. *Martin*, p. 101.
19. *Carr*, p. 597.
20. *Madariaga*, p. 369.
21. *Carr*, p. 601.
22. Joaquín Arrarás: *Historia de la Segunda República Española*, vol. I, p. 8. (Henceforth, *Arrarás, Historia*.)
23. Full text, *Arrarás, Historia*, vol. I, pp. 14–15.
24. *Ibid.*, vol. I, p. 18.
25. *Martin*, pp. 104–5.
26. *Lerroux*, pp. 568–9.

2. The Second Republic (pp. 107–27)

1. *Buckley*, pp. 83–4.
2. *Arrarás, Historia*, vol. I, p. 29. Both he and Buckley give valuable thumbnail sketches of the most important politicians of the Republic.
3. *Buckley*, pp. 84–7.
4. Juan Ventosa y Calvell: *La Situación Política y Los Problemas Económicos de España*, pp. 10–15 and 148.
5. *Arrarás, Historia*, vol. I, p. 35.
6. *Ibid.*, p. 33.

7. *Ibid.*, vol. II, p. 39.
8. *Ibid.*, vol. I, pp. 49–50.
9. *Martin*, p. 113. See *Centinela*, p. 151, for a slightly different version.
10. *Arrarás, Historia*, vol. I, p. 48.
11. *Ibid.*, pp. 73–100.
12. Antonio Montero Moreno: *Historia de la Persecución Religiosa en Epaña*, p. 25.
13. *Jackson*, pp. 32–5.
14. Miguel Maura: *Así cayó Alfonso XIII*, p. 251.
15. *Jackson*, p. 37.
16. Cf. *Carr*, pp. 594–5, and 616.
17. *Mola*, p. 950. (From *El Pasado, Azaña y el Porvenir*.)
18. *Ibid.*, p. 1187 (from a 1937 speech, quoting himself in retrospect).
19. *Martin*, p. 114; *Centinela*, pp. 152–4.
20. *Arrarás, Franco*, p. 166.
21. *Martin*, p. 115, quoting Franco's Service Record (*Hoja de Servicios*).
22. *Ibid.*, p. 116.
23. *Arrarás, Historia*, vol. I, p. 116.
24. *Ibid.*, pp. 120–2.
25. *Brenan*, p. 239.
26. *Ibid.*, p. 238.
27. *Centinela*, p. 168.
28. *Ibid.*, p. 158.
29. *Madariaga*, pp. 415–16; *Carr*, pp. 61–9; *Arrarás, Historia*, vol. I, chaps XVIII–XXII.
30. *Martin*, p. 118.
31. *Centinela*, pp. 158–9.
32. *Ibid.*, p. 159.

3. Defender of the Republic (pp. 127–49)

1. *Arrarás, Historia*, vol. II, pp. 72–4.
2. *Ibid.*, p. 81.
3. *Brenan*, p. 259.
4. *Arrarás, Franco*, p. 168.
5. *Ibid.*, p. 169.
6. *Ibid.*, pp. 170–1.
7. *Brenan*, p. 267.
8. *Ibid.*, p. 269.
9. *Arrarás, Historia*, vol. II, pp. 296–7.

T*

10. Diego Hidalgo; ¿ *Por qué fui lanzado del Ministerio de la Guerra?* pp. 77–9. (Henceforth, *Hidalgo.*)

11. *Arrarás, Historia,* vol. II, pp. 312 *et seq.*

12. *Ibid.,* p. 228.

13. For a terse account of the origins of Spanish Fascism, see *Thomas* pp. 97–101. For a fuller account, see Stanley G. Payne: *Falange.* (Henceforth, *Payne.*)

14. *Payne,* pp. 52–8.

15. *Thomas,* p. 110; José Manuel Martínez Bande: *La Intervención Comunista en la Guerra de España,* pp. 13–14. (Henceforth, *Intervención.*)

16. *Thomas,* p. 109.

17. *Thomas,* p. 102, quoting article by 'A. Brons' in *International Communism,* 15 December 1933.

18. *Intervención,* pp. 16–17.

19. Felipe Ximénez de Sandoval: *José Antonio,* pp. 323 *et seq.* See also *Payne,* pp. 86–7 and notes.

20. Quoted in *Madariaga,* p. 459 (n.6).

21. *Brenan,* p. 281.

22. *Jackson,* pp. 145–6; *Thomas,* p. 116 and n.

23. *Arrarás, Franco,* p. 184.

24. *Hidalgo,* pp. 83–4.

25. *Brenan,* pp. 287–8.

26. *Arrarás, Historia,* vol. II, pp. 466–7.

27. *Ibid.,* p. 466.

28. *Arrarás, Franco,* p. 186.

29. The best account of these events is in *Centinela,* one of whose authors, Franco Salgado, was a participant in them.

30. *Martin,* p. 127.

31. *Centinela,* pp. 169–70.

32. *Ibid.,* p. 169; *Arrarás, Historia,* vol. II, pp. 611–12.

33. *Arrarás, Historia,* vol. II, p. 612.

34. *Centinela,* p. 174.

35. *Arrarás, Historia,* vol. II, p. 614. E. López de Ochoa, in *Campaña Militar de Asturias en octubre de 1.934,* is remarkably discreet about his relations with Yagüe. See also *Historia de la Cruzada Española,* Tomo VII, pp. 247–8. (Henceforth, *Cruzada.*)

36. *Brenan,* p. 297 (n.).

37. *Arrarás, Historia,* vol. II, p. 633.

38. *Ibid.,* p. 638.

39. *Brenan,* p. 288.

40. *Cruzada*, vol. VII, pp. 258–9.
41. *Arrarás, Historia (abr.)*, p. 295.
42. *Martin*, pp. 129–30.
43. Indalecio Prieto: *Discursos en America*, pp. 102–4.
44. *Madariaga*, pp. 434–5.
45. *Hidalgo*, p. 81.
46. *Lerroux*, p. 354.

4. Mortal Sickness of the Republic (pp. 149–65)

1. *Jackson*, pp. 165–7, usefully summarizes the Azaña story, which is recounted at length in Azaña's own book *Mi Rebelión en Barcelona* (Madrid, 1935), and Frank Sedgwick, *The Tragedy of Manuel Azaña*, (Columbus, Ohio, 1963).
2. *Martin*, p. 131; *Arrarás, Franco*, pp. 192 and 196.
3. *Arrarás, Franco*, p. 194.
4. *Ibid.*, p. 198; *Arrarás, Historia (abr.)*, p. 358; *Martin*, p. 134.
5. *Martin*, p. 135.
6. *Thomas*, p. 135 (n.).
7. *Ibid.*, p. 130; *Arrarás, Historia (abr.)*, pp. 369–70; *Intervención*, pp. 18–20; Leonard Schapiro, *The Communist Party of the Soviet Union*, pp. 482 *et seq.*
8. *Arrarás, Historia (abr.)*, p. 370; *Thomas*, p. 140 (n.).
9. *Arrarás, Historia (abr.)*, p. 376.
10. *Thomas*, p. 135 (n.)
11. *Martin*, p. 138.
12. *Arrarás, Franco*, pp. 223–4.
13. *Arrarás, Historia (abr.)*, pp. 380–4.
14. *Arrarás, Franco*, pp. 225–7.

Part IV : Civil War

1. The Conspirators (pp. 167–86)

1. *Cruzada*, vol. IX, p. 467.
2. Manuel Goded: *Un Faccioso Cien por Cien*, pp. 25–7. (Henceforth, *Faccioso*.)
3. Félix Maíz: *Alzamiento en España*, pp. 50–1. (Henceforth, *Maíz*.)
4. *Martin*, p. 144.
5. *Payne*, p. 104.
6. *Arrarás, Franco*, p. 230.
7. *Centinela*, p. 188.

8. *Arrarás, Franco*, p. 231.

9. *Payne*, p. 106. My own inquiries confirm Payne's version of the facts.

10. José Antonio Primo de Rivera: *Obras Completas*, pp. 891 *et seq.*

11. Juan Antonio Ansaldo; *¿Para qué?*, p. 121. (Henceforth, *Ansaldo.*)

12. *Maíz*, p. 82.

13. *Arrarás, Historia (abr.)*, pp. 425–6.

14. *Centinela*, pp. 195–6.

15. *Arrarás, Historia (abr.)*, p. 475.

16. *Ibid.*, p. 476.

17. *Centinela*, p. 196; *Martin*, p. 154.

18. *Martin*, p. 153.

19. *Ibid.*, translator's note.

20. *Centinela*, p. 198.

21. *Arrarás, Historia (abr.)*, p. 497.

22. *Centinela*, p. 197.

23. *Jackson*, p. 228.

24. *Arrarás, Historia (abr.)*, p. 498.

25. *Ibid.*, pp. 496–7.

26. Full texts in: *Crónica de la Guerra Española* (Buenos Aires, 1966), No. 6, (Henceforth, *Crónica.*)

27. *Carlist Archives*, Seville: quoted in *Thomas*, p. 167.

28. *Arrarás, Historia (abr.)*, p. 500.

29. *Ibid.*, p. 501.

30. *Jackson*, p. 226.

31. *Centinela*, p. 222.

2. Franco's 'Original Sin' (pp. 186–200)

1. *Thomas*, pp. 186–8; *Jackson*, pp. 286–7.

2. *Faccioso*, p. 59.

3. *Ansaldo*, Book II, pp. 135–45.

4. *Thomas*, p. 194; Felipe Bertrán Güell: *Preparación y desarollo del Alzamiento Nacional*, pp. 77 *et seq.*; José María Iribarren: *Con el General Mola*, pp. 64–6; *Maíz*, p. 304; *Cruzada*, XIII, p. 472; *Crónica*, No. 6.

5. *Thomas*, p. 192.

6. *Centinela*, p. 243.

7. *Martin*, p. 172 and translator's note.

8. *Ibid.*, p. 184 and translator's note.

9. General Millán Astray: *Franco el Caudillo*, p. 27. (Henceforth, *Millán Astray*.)

10. Antonio Lizarza Iribarren: *Memorias de la Conspiración*, pp. 24–6, and 33.

11. Luis Bolín: *Spain: the Vital Years*, p. 162; *Thomas*, p. 282.

12. Roberto Cantalupo: *Fu la Spagna*, p. 63. (Henceforth, *Cantalupo*.)

13. *Cruzada*, X, p. 126.

14. Dante A. Puzzo: *Spain and the Great Powers, 1936–1941*, p. 67. (Henceforth, *Puzzo*.)

15. *Mola*, p. 1167.

16. *Documents on German Foreign Policy, Series D*, vol. III, No. 2, p. 4. (Henceforth, *Documents*.)

17. Charles Foltz, Jr.: *The Masquerade in Spain*, pp. 46–7. (Henceforth, *Foltz*.)

18. *Documents*, vol. III, p. 1; *Cruzada*, X, p. 127.

19. *Puzzo*, p. 61.

20. Dr Karl Abshagen: *Canaris*, pp. 108–15. (Henceforth, *Canaris*.)

21. *Martin*, pp. 191–2.

22. *Documents*, vol. III, No. 16, p. 16.

23. *Centinela*, p. 251.

24. *Millán Astray*, p. 29.

25. *Martin*, pp. 192–3, translator's note.

26. *Centinela*, pp. 255–6.

3. Franco's Apotheosis (pp. 200–15)

1. General Kindelán: *Mis Cuadernos de Guerra*, p. 21. (Henceforth, *Kindelán*.)

2. *Martin*, p. 200.

3. *Puzzo*, pp. 69–73.

4. *Martin*, p. 202.

5. *Intervención*, p. 25.

6. *Thomas*, pp. 302–3.

7. *Martin*, p. 203.

8. J. del Río Sáinz: *La Defensa del Alcázar de Toledo*, in 'Noticiero de España', No. 4, 25 February 1937, Hemeroteca Nacional, Madrid. (Henceforth, *Noticiero*.)

9. *Centinela*, pp. 258–9.

10. *Kindelán*, p. 23.

11. *Ibid.*, pp. 51–6; Joaquín Arrarás, *article in* 'ABC', Madrid, 1 October 1966; *Martin*, pp. 212–19.

12. *Thomas*, p. 365.

4. Franco in Salamanca (pp. 216–25)

1. *Centinela*, pp. 279–80.
2. *Ramírez*, p. 231.
3. *Ibid.*, p. 224.
4. *Ibid.*, p. 228.
5. *Documents*, vol. III, No. 586, p. 661.
6. *Martin*, p. 251 and translator's note.
7. *Ibid.*, p. 221.
8. *Centinela*, p. 269.
9. *Martin*, p. 223.
10. *Documents*, vol. III, No. 92, p. 103, and No. 96, pp. 105–7.
11. Jesús de Galíndez: *Los Vascos en el Madrid sitiado*, p. 66.
12. *Thomas*, p. 403; Fernando de Valdesoto: *Francisco Franco*, p. 180.
13. *Documents*, vol. III, Nos. 109, 110, 111, pp. 121–2.
14. *Ibid.*, No. 113, pp. 123–5.
15. *Ciano, Papers*.
16. *Documents*, vol. III, No. 148, p. 159.

5. Franco's difficult Allies (pp. 225–34)

1. *Documents*, vol. III, No. 113, pp. 124–5, and No. 214, p. 236.
2. *Jackson*, pp. 335–6.
3. *Cantalupo*, p. 65.
4. *Ibid.*, pp. 131–7.
5. *Centinela*, pp. 284–5.
6. There are many conflicting accounts of Kleber's story; the only authentic one is probably that of Walter G. Krivitsky, *Yo, Jefe del Servicio Secreto Militar Soviético* pp. 142–3. (Henceforth, *Krivitsky*.)
7. *Cantalupo*, pp. 109–12.
8. Luigi Longo: *Le Brigate Internazionali in Spagna*, pp. 285 *et seq.*
9. *Cantalupo*, p. 207; *Jackson*, p. 352.
10. *Centinela*, p. 288.
11. *Cantalupo*, pp. 204–5.
12. *Ibid.*, p. 210.

6. Franco imposes Unity (pp. 234–43)

1. Franz Borkenau: *The Spanish Cockpit*, p. 279.
2. *Thomas*, p. 449.
3. *Documents*, vol. III, No. 243, p. 268.
4. *Payne*, Chapter XI.

5. Ramon Serrano Suñér: *Entre Hendaya y Gibraltar*, pp. 29–32. (Henceforth, *Entre Hendaya*.)
6. *Documents*, vol. III, No. 248, pp. 277–9.
7. *Ibid.*, No. 243, p. 269.
8. *Ibid.*, No. 252, p. 281.
9. *Payne*, pp. 170–2.

7. The Conquest of the North (pp. 243–59)

1. *Cantalupo*, pp. 230–4.
2. *Jackson*, pp. 358–9.
3. *Martin*, pp. 271–2.
4. *Documents*, vol. III, No. 249, p. 279, and No. 251, p. 281.
5. *Ibid.* No. 247, p. 276.
6. *Ibid.*, No. 390, p. 410.
7. *Ibid.*, No. 390, pp. 408–12.
8. *Martin*, p. 276.
9. Private information.
10. Manuel Aznar: *Historia Militar de la Guerra de España*, vol. II, p. 237; *Kindelán*, p. 100.
11. *Martin*, pp. 277–8.
12. *Ibid.*, p. 280.
13. *Noticiero*, No. 1, 4 September 1937.
14. *Ibid.*, No. 39, 11 June 1938.
15. *Ibid.*, No. 4, 25 September 1937: M. Sebastián: *Peseta blanca y peseta roja.*
16. *Ibid.*, No. 5, 2 October 1937.
17. *Documents*, vol. III, No. 234, p. 256.
18. *Ibid.*, Nos. 391, 392, 394 and 397.
19. *Noticiero*, No. 7, 16 October 1937.
20. *Ibid.*, No. 8, 23 October 1937.
21. *Ibid.*, No. 9, 30 October 1937.
22. *Documents*, vol. III, No. 454, pp. 478–9.
23. *Ibid.*, No. 469, p. 508.
24. *Ibid.*, No. 470, pp. 508–10.
25. Sir Robert Hodgson: *Spain Resurgent*, pp. 81 and 84. (Henceforth, *Hodgson*.)
26. *Documents*, vol. III, No. 475, pp. 518–19.
27. *Ibid.*, No. 484, pp. 527–9.
28. *Jackson*, p. 415.
29. *Documents*, vol. III, No. 477, p. 521.

8. Franco 'blends' a Government (pp. 259–71)

1. Burnett Bolloten: *The Grand Camouflage*, pp. 301–6.
2. *Krivitsky*, p. 146.
3. *Madariaga*, p. 522.
4. *Documents*, vol. III, No. 502, p. 556.
5. *Martin*, p. 293.
6. *Noticiero*, No. 18, 1 January 1938; No. 26, 26 February 1938.
7. *Ibid.*, No. 18, 1 January 1938.
8. *ABC*, 1 October 1961: Interview with Lt-Gen. Antonio Barroso.
9. *Noticiero*, No. 26, 26 February 1938.
10. *Ibid.*
11. *Payne*, p. 192.
12. *Entre Hendaya*, pp. 64–5.
13. *Noticiero*, No. 23, 5 February 1938.
14. *Thomas*, pp. 229–32, for a general picture. *The General Cause*, and *Moreno, op. cit.*, for details.
15. *Noticiero*, No. 34, 7 May 1938, quoting a public tribute to Franco by General Jouart, a former French military attaché in Madrid, in a Paris speech on 27 April 1938.
16. *Payne*, pp. 15 and 79.
17. *Noticiero*, No. 27, 19 March 1938.

9. Franco's most difficult Year (pp. 271–84)

1. *Noticiero*, No. 31, 16 April 1938.
2. *Documents*, vol. III, No. 564, p. 640.
3. *Ciano's Diary*, 1932–8, entry for 19 April 1938, p. 104.
4. *Documents*, vol. III, No. 550, pp. 624–6.
5. *Ibid.*, No. 551, p. 626.
6. *Ciano's Diary*, 1937–8, pp. 91–2.
7. *Hodgson*, pp. 126–7.
8. *Duke of Alba*, report of 28 March 1938, Spanish Foreign Ministry Archives, Madrid. (Henceforth, *Alba*.)
9. *Foreign Ministry Archives*, Madrid.
10. Jesús Hernández Tomás: *Yo, Ministro de Stalin en España*, pp. 201 et seq.
11. *Thomas*, pp. 666–7; *Madariaga*, pp. 528–9.
12. *Centinela*, p. 306.
13. *Martin*, p. 316.
14. *Documents*, vol. III, No. 660, pp. 742–5.
15. *Thomas*, p. 675.

16. *Documents*, vol. III, No. 658, p. 741.
17. *Ibid.*, No. 659, pp. 741–2.
18. *Martin*, p. 320.
19. *Centinela*, pp. 309–10.
20. *Foreign Ministry Archives*, Madrid.
21. *Alba*, 5 October 1938.
22. *Documents*, vol. III, No. 664, p. 747.
23. *Ibid.*, No. 669, p. 752.
24. *Ibid.*, No. 673, p. 757.
25. *Ibid.*, No. 672, p. 756.
26. *Ibid.*, p. 754.
27. Sir Basil Liddell Hart: *The Other Side of the Hill*, p. 123. (Henceforth, *Liddell Hart*.)
28. *Ciano's Diary*, 1937–8, entry for 29 August 1938, p. 148.
29. *Documents*, vol III., No. 660, pp. 742–5; and *Payne*, p. 185.
30. *Documents*, vol. III, No. 586, p. 658; *Thomas*, p. 673.
31. *Documents*, vol. III, No. 660, p. 743.
32. *Documents*, vol. III, No. 586, pp. 657–8.
33. *Noticiero*, No. 34, 7 May 1938.
34. *Documents*, vol. III, No. 601, pp. 684–5.
35. *Ibid.*, No. 626, pp. 710–11.
36. *Ibid.*, No. 660, p. 745.
37. *Ibid.*, No. 675, p. 761.
38. *Ibid.*, No. 699, pp. 797 and 801.
39. *Ibid.*, No. 740, pp. 848–9.

10. Franco's Crushing Victory (pp. 285–91)

1. *Martin*, p. 323; and *Documents*, vol. III, No. 699, p. 796.
2. *Documents*, vol. III, No. 596, pp. 675–81.
3. *Ibid.*, No. 686, p. 788.
4. *Ibid.*, No. 691, p. 785.
5. *Ibid.*, No. 703, pp. 808–9.
6. *Ibid.*, No. 685, p. 776.
7. *Ibid.*, No. 687, pp. 779–80.
8. *Martin*, p. 326.
9. *Madariaga*, p. 531.
10. *Martin*, p. 350.

11. Triumph and Retribution (pp. 292–8)

1. *Noticiero*, No. 88, 20 May 1938.
2. *Martin*, p. 338.

3. *Spain and the Rule of Law* (International Commission of Jurists, Geneva, 1962), p. 65. (Henceforth, *Jurists*.)
4. Sir Arthur Loveday: *Spain 1923–48*, pp. 162–3. (Henceforth, *Loveday*.)
5. *Jackson*, pp. 538–9.
6. *Foltz*, p. 97.
7. *Payne*, pp. 242, and 296 (n. 6).
8. Information given to me by the late Bernard Malley in a conversation in November 1965.
9. *Hodgson*, p. 102.
10. *Jurists*, p. 65.
11. José María Doussinague: *España Tenia Razón*, pp. 277–8. (Henceforth, *Doussinague*.)

Part V: World War

1. Neutrality (pp. 299–313)

1. *Documents*, vol. III, No. 757, p. 867; *Ciano, Papers*, p. 291.
2. *Documents*, vol. III, No. 733, p. 884; *Ciano, Papers*, p. 291. (Ciano talk with Franco, 19 July 1939.)
3. *Alba*, No. 326, 9 March 1939.
4. *Ibid.*, 27 April 1939.
5. *Madariaga*, p. 570.
6. *Ciano, Papers*, pp. 290–5.
7. For instance, *Puzzo*, pp. 222–3.
8. Sir Samuel Hoare: *Ambassador on Special Mission*, p. 51. (Henceforth, *Hoare*.)
9. *I Documenti Diplomatici Italiani*, vol. XIII, No. 641, p. 388.
10. *Ibid.*, No. 642, p. 388; *Doussinague*, pp. 12–13.
11. Interview in the Madrid Press, 3 October 1939.
12. *Documents*, vol. VIII, No. 242, p. 268.
13. *Puzzo*, p. 214.
14. Hugh Seton-Watson: *Fascism, Right and Left*, in '*Journal of Contemporary History*' (London), No. 1, 1966.
15. *Doussinague*, p. 22.
16. *Documents*, vol. VIII, No. 663, p. 879.
17. *Ibid.*, No. 284, pp. 324–5.
18. *Ciano's Diary*, 1939–43, pp. 99–100.
19. *Hoare*, p. 58.
20. *Entre Hendaya*, pp. 108–9.
21. *Ibid.*, p. 138.

22. *Doussinague*, p. 23 *et seq.*
23. *Ibid.*, pp. 35–6.
24. Interview in *Arriba*, 25 February 1951.

2. Non-Belligerency (pp. 313–26)

1. *Ciano's Diary*, 1939–43, p. 249, 13 May 1940.
2. *Alba*, No. 545, 20 May 1940.
3. *Hoare*, p. 48.
4. *Ibid.*, p. 48.
5. *Ibid.*, p. 49.
6. *Martin*, p. 374.
7. *Hoare*, p. 66.
8. Sr Serrano Súñer himself, in conversation in Madrid, November 1965.
9. *Entre Hendaya*, p. 152.
10. *Ibid.*, p. 159.
11. *Hoare*, p. 48.
12. *Ibid.*, pp. 58–9.
13. *Ibid.*, p. 63.
14. *Loveday*, p. 172.
15. *Spanish Government and the Axis*, No. 2, pp. 6–7.
16. *Ibid.*, No. 3, p. 8.
17. *Fuehrer Conferences on Naval Affairs*, 1940 (Admiralty, 1947) (Henceforth, *Naval Affairs*), vol. II, pp. 17–21.
18. *Entre Hendaya*, p. 160.
19. *Ibid.*, pp. 165–83.
20. *Ciano, Papers*, p. 388.
21. *Ibid.*
22. *Entre Hendaya*, p. 181.
23. *Ibid.*, p. 183.
24. *Ciano, Papers*, p. 389.
25. *Documents*, vol. XI, No. 70, pp. 106–8.
26. *Ibid.*, No. 88, pp. 153–5.
27. Dr Paul Schmidt: *Hitler's Interpreter*, p. 190. (Henceforth, *Schimdt*.)
28. *Ibid.*, p. 191.
29. *Entre Hendaya*, p. 183.
30. *Ciano's Diary*, 1939–43, p. 294.
31. *Ibid.*, p. 295.
32. *Ciano, Papers*, p. 394.
33. *Ibid.*, p. 396.

3. Franco v. Hitler, Game One (pp. 326–33)

1. *Ciano's Diary*, 1939–43, p. 297.
2. *Hoare*, p. 68.
3. *Doussinague*, p. 41.
4. *Hoare*, p. 72.
5. *Ciano, Papers*, p. 402.
6. *Ibid.*, p. 399. (Von Bismarck to Ciano, 20 November 1942.)
7. *Ibid.*, p. 401. (Florence, 28 November 1940.)
8. *Schmidt*, p. 194.
9. *Ibid.*, p. 195.
10. *Centinela*, p. 358, quoting *Neue Frankfurter Illustrierte*.
11. *Centinela*, p. 354.
12. *Ibid.*, p. 359.
13. *Naval Affairs*, 1940, pp. 78 and 103.
14. *Alba*, No. 1126, 9 December 1940.

4. Franco v. Hitler, Game Two (pp. 333–41)

1. Such as *Puzzo*, p. 236.
2. *Schmidt*, pp. 197–9.
3. *Documents*, vol. XI, No. 235, p. 402.
4. *Ibid.*, No. 335, p. 574.
5. *Entre Hendaya*, p. 238.
6. *Documents*, vol. XI, No. 352, p. 601.
7. *Ibid.*, No. 414, p. 725.
8. *Ibid.*, No. 420, p. 739.
9. *Ibid.*, No. 448, p. 782.
10. *Ibid.*, No. 268, p. 445.
11. *Ibid.*, No. 500, pp. 852–3.
12. *Canaris*, p. 112; *Thomas*, p. 298.
13. *Documents*, vol. XI, No. 473, p. 812.
14. *Ibid.*, No. 476, pp. 816–17.
15. *Ibid.*, No. 323, pp. 527–31.
16. *Ibid.*, No. 479, p. 824.
17. *Ibid.*, No. 629, p. 1056.
18. *Ibid.*, No. 677, p. 1140.
19. *Ibid.*, No. 682, pp. 1157–8.
20. *Ibid.*, No. 695, pp. 1173–5.
21. *Ibid.*, No. 702, pp. 1183–4.
22. *Ibid.*, No. 718, pp. 1208–10.
23. *Ibid.*, No. 725, pp. 1217–18.
24. *Ibid.*, No. 728, pp. 1222–3.

25. *Naval Affairs*, 1941, p. 13.
26. *Puzzo*, p. 232.
27. *Documents*, vol. XII, No. 22, p. 37.
28. *Ibid.*, No. 95, pp. 176–8.
29. *Ibid.*, No. 73, pp. 131–2.

5. Franco v. Hitler, Game and Match (pp. 341–352)

1. *Liddell Hart*, p. 237.
2. *Documents*, vol. XII, No. 469, p. 731.
3. *Ibid.*, No. 453, p. 711.
4. *Ibid.*, No. 574, pp. 928–30.
5. *Entre Hendaya*, pp. 204–11.
6. *Ibid.*, p. 208 quoting *Daily Telegraph* of 28 November 1945.
7. *Documents*, vol. XII, No. 671, p. 1080.
8. *Ibid.*, No. 70, p. 81.
9. *Ibid.*, No. 273, p. 441.
10. *Ibid.*, No. 314, pp. 498–9.
11. *Ibid.*, No. 467, p. 774.
12. *Ibid.*, No. 555, pp. 971–2.
13. *Kriegstagebuch des Oberkommandos der Wehrmacht, 1940–1945*, 1942, pp. 135–6.
14. Hugh Trevor-Roper: *Hitler's War Directives*, p. 121. (Words quoted, however, are from American translation of this directive.)
15. Weidenfeld and Nicolson: *Hitler's Table Talk* (intr. Trevor-Roper) p. 519.
16. *Ibid.*, pp. 267–70.
17. For instance, Georges Roux: *Hitler contre Franco*, in *Miroir de l'Histoire* (Paris), July 1965.
18. *Der Spiegel* (Hamburg), No. 18, 1963.
19. Walter Schellenberg: *Memoirs*, p. 133.
20. *La Vanguardia Española* (Barcelona), 9 February 1964.
21. *Fuehrer Naval Conferences* (Washington), 1942, pp. 126–7. (Henceforth, *Conferences*.)
22. *Ibid.*, pp. 142–6.
23. *Ibid.*, p. 146.
24. Walter Warlimont: *Report, 1950, Strategy of the German Armed Forces High Command, April-June 1943*, Historical Division European Command, Operational History Branch, *Washington* (typewritten), pp. 87 *et seq.*
25. *Conferences*, 1943, pp. 25–9.

26. Sir Basil Liddell Hart: *Private Archives*. (Third talk with Blumentritt, 3 December 1945.)
27. *Conferences*, 1943 (Annexe to Conference 12–15 May), pp. 66–7.

6. Allied Pressures (pp. 352–8)

1. *Hoare*, p. 273.
2. *Doussinague*, p. 271.
3. Carlton J. H. Hayes; *Wartime Mission in Spain*, pp. 243–4. (Henceforth, *Hayes*.)
4. *Alba*, No. 19, 6 January 1941.
5. *Ibid.*, No. 326, 12 May 1941.
6. *Ibid.*, No. 446, 30 June 1941.
7. *Ibid.*, No. 616, 20 September 1941.
8. *Ibid.*, No. 504, 30 July 1941.
9. *Doussinague*, pp. 66 *et seq.*
10. *Hayes*, p. 87.
11. *Entre Hendaya*, p. 210.
12. *Doussinague*, p. 234.

7. Competing Fears (pp. 359–69)

1. *Martin*, p. 392.
2. With Serge Groussard, *Le Figaro*, 20 June 1958.
3. *Documents Secrets du Ministère des Affaires Etrangères d'Allemagne*, p. 86, 19 February 1942. (Henceforth, *Documents Secrets*.)
4. *Alba*, No. 87, 20 February 1942.
5. *Ibid.*, No. 55, 10 February 1942.
6. *Ibid.*, No. 414, 20 July 1942.
7. *Ibid.*, No. 261, 10 May 1942.
8. *Ibid.*, No. 389 10 July 1942.
9. *Ibid.*, No. 414, 20 July 1942.
10. *Ibid.*, No. 439 30 July 1942.
11. *Martin*, pp. 398–9.
12. *Ibid.*, p. 398.
13. *Doussinague*, p. 207.
14. *Martin*, p. 390.
15. *Hayes*, p. 71.
16. *Ibid.*, p. 72.
17. *Ibid.*, p. 73.
18. *Alba*, No. 632, 25 October 1942.
19. *Doussinague*, p. 82.
20. *Hayes*, p. 87.

21. *Ibid.*, pp. 89–90.
22. *Ibid.*, p. 91.
23. *Hoare*, pp. 177–8.
24. *Hayes*, p. 92.
25. *Ibid.*, p. 93.
26. *Ibid.*, p. 96.
27. *Doussinague*, p. 206.

8. One War, or Three? (pp. 369–75)

1. *Hayes*, pp. 30–1.
2. *Ibid.*, p. 161.
3. *Ibid.*, p. 159.
4. *Alba*, No. 368, 11 August 1943.
5. *Ibid.*, 15 September 1944.
6. *Doussinague*, p. 143. (*Hoare*, p. 185, says *he* sought out Franco.)
7. *Hoare*, p. 185.
8. *Ibid.*, p. 190.
9. *Ibid.*, p. 195.
10. *Documents Secrets*, pp. 143–52. (24 February, 3 and 8 March 1943.)
11. *Doussinague*, p. 215.
12. *Ibid.*, pp. 215–23.
13. *Ibid.*, pp. 294–300.

9. The Screw Tightens (pp. 375–88)

1. *Hayes*, p. 166.
2. *Hoare*, pp. 197–204.
3. *Ibid.*, p. 204.
4. *Hayes*, p. 166.
5. *Hoare*, p. 219.
6. *Ibid.*, p. 222.
7. *Hayes*, p. 166.
8. *Ibid.*, p. 163.
9. *Alba*, No. 502, 30 October 1943.
10. *Hoare*, p. 170.
11. *Hayes*, p. 196.
12. *Ibid.*, pp. 185–6.
13. *Ibid.*, p. 200.
14. *Hoare*, p. 249.
15. *Ibid.*, p. 230.
16. *Ibid.*, p. 233.
17. *Hayes*, pp. 112–19.

18. *Ibid.*, p. 119.
19. *Ibid.*, p. 113.
20. *Hoare*, p. 234; *Loveday*, p. 231.
21. *Hoare*, p. 237.

10. Spain Ostracized (pp. 388–413)

1. *Alba*, No. 245, 31 May 1944.
2. *Hayes*, p. 240.
3. *Doussinague*, pp. 318–24. (My account supplements Doussinague's.)
4. *Hayes*, p. 241.
5. *Ibid.*, p. 242.
6. *Alba*, No. 297, 31 July 1944.
7. *Hoare*, p. 273.
8. *Loveday*, p. 211.
9. *Alba*, No. 375, 1 October 1944.
10. *Hayes*, p. 258.
11. *Ibid.*, p. 258.
12. Eduardo Comín Colomer: *La República en el exilio*, p. 384. (Henceforth, *Colomer.*)
13. Sir Winston Churchill: *Step by Step* (1939), p. 88. (Henceforth, *Step by Step.*)
14. Sir Winston Churchill: *War Memoirs*, vol. V, pp. 553–4. (Henceforth, *Churchill.*)
15. *Hoare*, p. 283.
16. *Ibid.*, p. 283.
17. *Alba*, No. 504, 30 December 1944.
18. *Churchill*, vol. VI, pp. 616–17.
19. *Hoare*, p. 267.
20. *Churchill*, vol. VI, p. 400.
21. *Ibid.*, pp. 498–9.
22. *Ibid.*, p. 582.
23. *Ibid.*, p. 566.
24. *Madariaga*, p. 595.
25. *Martin*, p. 439.
26. *Centinela*, p. 387.
27. *Madariaga*, p. 598.
28. *Loveday*, p. 224.

11. Divide and Rule (pp. 413–34)

1. *Martin*, p. 353.

2. *Payne*, p. 205.
3. *Martin*, pp. 353–5.
4. *Ibid.*, p. 352.
5. *Ciano's Diary*, 1939–43, entry for 23 July 1939, p. 117.
6. *Payne*, pp. 207–8.
7. *Ibid.*, pp. 208–11.
8. *Ibid.*, pp. 216–20.
9. *Ibid.*, pp. 221–4.
10. *Ibid.*, p. 213.
11. *Doussinague*, p. 130.
12. *Payne*, pp. 234–5.
13. *Doussinague*, pp. 131–2.
14. *Payne*, pp. 225 *et seq.*
15. *Ibid.*, pp. 232–3.
16. *Ibid.*, p. 235. (*Hoare*, p. 165, turns the facts upside down when he claims that Serrano defended Domínguez against Franco.)
17. *Martin*, p. 411.
18. *Documents*, vol. III, No. 740, pp. 849–50.
19. *Loveday*, p. 195.
20. *Ibid.*, p. 194.
21. *Ibid.*, p. 196.
22. *Hayes*, p. 131.
23. *Ibid.*, p. 135.
24. *Ibid.*, p. 131.
25. *Alba*, No. 159, 9 April 1943.
26. *Hayes*, p. 132.
27. *Loveday*, p. 179.
28. *Ibid.*, p. 179.
29. *Ibid.*, p. 197.
30. *Ibid.*, pp. 198–200.
31. *Ibid.*, p. 203.

Part VI: 'Spanish Peace'

1. Franco Consolidates (pp. 435–40)

1. Benjamin Welles: *Spain: The Gentle Anarchy*, pp. 345–6. (Henceforth, *Welles*.)
2. *Madariaga*, p. 599.
3. *Ibid.*, p. 599; *Colomer*, pp. 255 *et seq.*

2. Franco almost Clubbable – I (pp. 441–6)

1. *Madariaga*, p. 601.
2. *Martin*, p. 458.
3. *Welles*, p. 268.
4. Interview with *Hearst Press* correspondent, Karl von Wilgand, 13 February 1951.
5. *Welles*, p. 287.

3. Franco's Masterly Inertia (pp. 446–56)

1. *Welles*, pp. 352–4.
2. *Ibid.*, pp. 357–9.
3. *Ibid.*, pp. 359–64.
4. *Ibid.*, pp. 365–6.
5. *Arriba*, 27 February 1955.
6. *Martin*, p. 549.
7. *Welles*, p. 125.
8. *Ibid.*, pp. 125–8; *Payne*, pp. 251–62.

4. Towards Affluence (pp. 456–72)

1. *Welles*, p. 319.
2. Private Information.
3. Private Information.
4. *Welles*, pp. 128–30.
5. *Martin*, p. 560.

5. Franco almost Clubbable – II (pp. 472–85)

1. See: *Concordato entre la Santa Sede y España*, Ministerio de Asuntos Exteriores, Madrid, 1953.
2. E.g., *Alianza Dinámica*, p. 15, Servicio Informativo Español, Madrid, 1964.
3. See *Martin*, p. 472.
4. *Crónica de un Año de España*, 1963–4, Madrid, p. 285.
5. *Welles*, pp. 250–1.
6. *Cantalupo*, p. 233.

Part VII: 'Before God and History'

2. The World (pp. 506–12)

1. *Step by Step*, p. 88.
2. *Ibid.*, p. 305.

Index

U